SPURGEON'S
SERMONS
ON JESUS AND THE
HOLY SPIRIT

SPURGEON'S
❧ SERMONS ❧
ON JESUS AND THE
HOLY SPIRIT

Charles H. Spurgeon

HENDRICKSON
PUBLISHERS

Spurgeon's Sermons on Jesus and the Holy Spirit

© 2006 Hendrickson Publishers Marketing, LLC
P. O. Box 3473
Peabody, Massachusetts 01961–3473

ISBN: 978-1-59856-054-1

Printed in the United States of America

Third Printing—April 2013

Cover Art: "The Baptism of Jesus," from Julius Schnorr von Carolsfeld's Die Bibel in Bildern (Leipzig, Georg Wigand, 1853). Courtesy of the Pitts Theology Library, Candler School of Theology, Emory University. Used with permission.

Table of Contents

Sermons on the Second Coming of Christ

Sermons on the Holy Spirit

receive: for the Holy Ghost was not yet given; because that Jesus was not yet glorified.)—John 7:38–39

Nevertheless I tell you the truth; it is expedient for you that I go away: for if I go not away, the Comforter will not come unto you; but if I depart, I will send him unto you.—John 16:7

Delivered on Lord's Day morning, September 5, 1886, at the Metropolitan Tabernacle, Newington. No. 1918.

"Yet now be strong, O Zerubbabel," saith the Lord; "and be strong, Joshua, son of Josedech, the high priest, and be strong, all ye people of the land," saith the Lord, "and work: for I am with you," saith the Lord of hosts: "according to the word that I covenanted with you when ye came out of Egypt, so my spirit remaineth among you: fear ye not."—Haggai 2:4–5

Delivered on Lord's Day morning, April 10, 1891, at the Metropolitan Tabernacle, Newington. No. 2200.

And I will put my spirit within you.—Ezekiel 36:27

A sermon intended for reading on Lord's Day, July 19, 1891, at the conference of the Pastors' College Evangelical Association. No. 2213.

He shall glorify me: for he shall receive of mine, and shall shew it unto you. All things that the Father hath are mine: therefore said I, that he shall take of mine, and shall shew it unto you.—John 16:14–15

Indexes

Preface

CHARLES HADDON SPURGEON, 1834–1892

Ask most people today who Charles Haddon Spurgeon was, and you might be surprised at the answers. Most know he was a preacher, others remember that he was Baptist, and others go so far as to remember that he lived in England during the nineteenth century. All true, yet Charles Haddon Spurgeon was so much more.

Born into a family of Congregationalists in 1834, Spurgeon's father and grandfather were both Independent preachers. This designation seems benign today, but in the mid-nineteenth century, they describe a family committed to a Nonconformist path—meaning they did not conform to the established Church of England. Spurgeon grew up in a rural village, virtually cut off from the Industrial Revolution rolling over most of England.

Spurgeon was born again at a Primitive Methodist meeting in 1850, at age sixteen. He soon became a Baptist (to the sorrow of his mother) and almost immediately began to preach. Considered a preaching prodigy—"a boy wonder of the fens"—Spurgeon attracted huge audiences and garnered a reputation that reached throughout the countryside and into London. As a result of his great success, Spurgeon was invited to preach at the New Park Street Chapel in London in 1854, when he was just nineteen. When he first preached at the church, they were unable to fill even two hundred seats.

Within the year, Spurgeon filled the twelve-hundred-seat church to over-flowing; he soon began preaching in larger and larger venues, outgrowing each, until finally in 1861, the Metropolitan Tabernacle was completed, which held six thousand people. This would be Spurgeon's home base for the rest of his career, until his death in 1892 at age fifty-seven.

Spurgeon married Susannah Thompson in 1856 and soon they had twin sons, Charles and Thomas, who would both later follow him in his work. Spurgeon opened Pastors' College, a training school for preachers, and it trained over nine hundred preachers during his lifetime. He also opened orphanages for underprivileged children, providing educations to each of the orphans. And with Susannah, he developed a program to publish and distribute Christian literature. He is said to have preached to over ten million people in his forty years of ministry. His sermons sold over twenty-five thousand copies each week, and were translated into twenty languages. He was utterly committed to spreading the Gospel, through preaching and through the written word.

During Spurgeon's lifetime, the Industrial Revolution transformed England from a rural, agricultural society to an urban, industrial society, with all the attendant difficulties and horrors of a society in major transition. The people displaced by these sweeping changes—the factory workers, the shop-keepers—became Spurgeon's congregation. Since he was from a small village himself and then transplanted to a large and inhospitable city, Spurgeon was a common man, and he understood innately the spiritual needs of the common people. He was a communicator who made the Gospel so relevant, who spoke so brilliantly to people's deepest needs, that listeners welcomed his message.

Keep in mind that Spurgeon preached in the days before microphones or speakers; in other words, he preached without benefit of amplifier systems. Once he preached to a crowd of over twenty-three thousand people without mechanical amplification. He himself was the electrifying presence on the platform: he did not stand and simply read a stilted sermon. Spurgeon used an outline, developing his themes extemporaneously, and speaking "in common language to common people." His sermons were filled with stories and poetry, drama and emotion. He was larger than life, always in motion, striding back and forth across the stage. He gestured broadly, acted out stories, used humor, and painted word pictures. For Spurgeon, preaching was about communicating the truth of God, and he would use any gift at his disposal to accomplish this.

Spurgeon's preaching was anchored in his spiritual life, a life rich in prayer and the study of Scripture. He was not tempted by fashion, be it theological, social, or political. Scripture was the cornerstone of Spurgeon's life and his preaching. He was mostly an expositional preacher, exploring a passage of Scripture for its meanings both within the text itself as well as in the lives of each member of his congregation. To Spurgeon, scripture is alive and specifically relevant to people's lives, regardless of their social status, economic situation, or the time in which they live.

One has a sense that Spurgeon embraced God's revelation completely: God's revelation through Jesus Christ, through Scripture, and through his own prayer and study. For him, revelation was not a finished act: God still reveals himself, if one makes oneself available. Some recognize Spurgeon for the mystic he was, one who was willing and eager to explore the mysteries of God, able to live with those bits of truth that do not conform to a particular system of theology, and perfectly comfortable with saying "This I know, and this I don't know—yet will I trust."

This treasury of sermons includes many of Spurgeon's about various aspects of Jesus Christ and about the Holy Spirit. These sermons are not a series: they were not created or intended to be sequential. Rather, they are representative of Spurgeon's finest teaching and thinking, culled from an entire lifetime of preaching. These are stand-alone sermons, meant to explore specific aspects in the life and teaching of Jesus Christ and the Person and work of the Holy Spirit.

Each of these sermons was preached at different times in Spurgeon's career, and each has distinct characteristics. They have not been homogenized or edited to sound as though they are all of a kind. Instead, they reflect the preacher himself, allowing the voice of this remarkable man to ring clearly as he guides the reader into a particular account, a particular event—to experience, with Spurgeon, God's particular revelation.

And as you read, *listen*. These are words meant to be heard, not merely read. Listen carefully and you will hear the cadences of Spurgeon's remarkable preaching, the echoes of God's timeless truth traveling across the years. And above all, enjoy Spurgeon's enthusiasm, his fire, his devotion, and his zeal for God revealed in Jesus Christ and the Holy Spirit.

Sermons on Christmas

The First Christmas Carol

Delivered on Sabbath morning, December 20, 1857 at the Music Hall, Royal Surrey Gardens. No. 168.

Glory to God in the highest, and on earth peace, good will toward men.—Luke 2:14

It is superstitious to worship angels; it is but proper to love them. Although it would be a high sin, and an act of misdemeanor against the Sovereign Court of Heaven to pay the slightest adoration to the mightiest angel, yet it would be unkind and unseemly, if we did not give to holy angels a place in our heart's warmest love. In fact, he that contemplates the character of angels, and marks their many deeds of sympathy with men, and kindness towards them, cannot resist the impulse of his nature—the impulse of love towards them.

The one incident in angelic history to which our text refers, is enough to weld our hearts to them forever. How free from envy the angels were! Christ did not come from Heaven to save their compeers [companions] when they fell. When Satan, the mighty angel, dragged with him a third part of the stars of Heaven, Christ did not stoop from his throne to die for them; but he left them to be reserved in chains and darkness until the last great day. Yet angels did not envy men. Though they remembered that he took not up angels, yet they did not murmur when he took up the seed of Abraham; and though the blessed Master had never condescended to take the angel's form, they did not think it beneath them to express their joy when they found him arrayed in the body of an infant.

How free, too, they were from pride! They were not ashamed to come and tell the news to humble shepherds. Methinks, they had as much joy in pouring out their songs that night before the shepherds, who were watching with their flocks, as they would have had if they had been commanded by their Master to sing their hymn in the halls of Caesar. Mere men —men possessed with pride, think it a fine thing to preach before kings and princes; and think it great condescension now and then to have to minister to the humble crowd. Not so the angels. They stretched their willing wings, and gladly sped from their bright seats above, to tell the shepherds on the plain by night, the marvelous story of an Incarnate God.

And mark how well they told the story, and surely you will love them! Not with the stammering tongue of him that tells a tale in which he hath no interest; nor even with the feigned interest of a man that would move the passions of others, when he feeleth no emotion himself; but with joy and gladness, such as angels only can know. They sang the story out, for they could not stay to tell it in heavy prose. They sang, "Glory to God on high, and on earth peace, good will towards men." Methinks, they sang it with gladness in their eyes; with their hearts burning with love, and with breasts as full of joy as if the good news to man had been good news to themselves. And, verily, it was good news to them, for the heart of sympathy makes good news to others, good news to itself.

Do you not love the angels? Ye will not bow before them, and there ye are right; but will ye not love them? Doth it not make one part of your anticipation of Heaven, that in Heaven you shall dwell with the holy angels, as well as with the spirits of the just made perfect? Oh, how sweet to think that these holy and lovely beings are our guardians every hour! They keep watch and ward about us, both in the burning noon-tide, and in the darkness of the night. They keep us in all our ways; they bear us up in their hands, lest at any time we dash our feet against stones. They unceasingly minister unto us who are the heirs of salvation; both by day and night they are our watchers and our guardians, for know ye not, that "the angel of the Lord encampeth round about them that fear him."

Let us turn aside, having just thought of angels for a moment, to think rather of this song, than of the angels themselves. Their song was brief, but as Kitto[1] excellently remarks, it was

> well worthy of angels expressing the greatest and most blessed truths, in words so few, that they become, to an acute apprehension, almost oppressive by the pregnant fullness of their meaning—"Glory to God in the highest on earth peace, good will toward men."

We shall, hoping to be assisted by the Holy Spirit, look at these words of the angels in a fourfold manner. I shall just suggest some instructive thoughts arising from these words, then some emotional thoughts; then a few prophetical thoughts; and afterwards, one or two preceptive [instructive] thoughts.

---

[1] Kitto: apparently John Kitto (1804–1854), deaf English biblical scholar.

I. First then, in the words of our text, there are many *instructive thoughts.*

The angels sang something which men could understand—something which men ought to understand—something which will make men much better if they will understand it. The angels were singing about Jesus who was born in the manger. We must look upon their song as being built upon this foundation. They sang of Christ, and the salvation which he came into this world to work out. And what they said of this salvation was this: they said, first, that it gave glory to God; secondly, that it gave peace to man; and, thirdly, that it was a token of God's good will towards the human race.

1. First, they said that this salvation gave glory to God. They had been present on many august occasions, and they had joined in many a solemn chorus to the praise of their Almighty Creator. They were present at the creation: "The morning stars sang together, and all the sons of God shouted for joy." They had seen many a planet fashioned between the palms of Jehovah, and wheeled by his eternal hands through the infinitude of space. They had sung solemn songs over many a world which the Great One had created. We doubt not, they had often chanted "Blessing and honor, and glory, and majesty, and power, and dominion, and might, be unto him that sitteth on the throne," manifesting himself in the work of creation. I doubt not, too, that their songs had gathered force through ages. As when first created, their first breath was song, so when they saw God create new worlds then their song received another note; they rose a little higher in the gamut of adoration. But this time, when they saw God stoop from his throne and become a babe, hanging upon a woman's breast, they lifted their notes higher still, and reaching to the uttermost stretch of angelic music, they gained the highest notes of the divine scale of praise, and they sang, "Glory to God in the highest," for higher in goodness they felt God could not go. Thus their highest praise they gave to him in the highest act of his godhead. If it be true that there is a hierarchy of angels, rising tier upon tier in magnificence and dignity—if the apostle teaches us that there be "angels, and principalities, and powers, and thrones, and dominions," amongst these blest inhabitants of the upper world—I can suppose that when the intelligence was first communicated to those angels that are to be found upon the outskirts of the heavenly world, when they looked down from Heaven and saw the new-born babe, they sent the news backward to the place whence the miracle first proceeded, singing,

> *Angels, from the realms of glory,*
> *Wing your downward flight to earth,*
> *Ye who sing creation's story,*
> *Now proclaim Messiah's birth;*
> *Come and worship,*
> *Worship Christ, the new-born King.*

And as the message ran from rank to rank, at last, the presence angels, those four cherubim that perpetually watch around the throne of God—those wheels with eyes—took up the strain, and, gathering up the song of all the inferior grades of angels, surmounted the divine pinnacle of harmony with their own solemn chant of adoration, upon which the entire host shouted, "The highest angels praise thee."—"Glory to God in the highest." Ay, there is no mortal that can ever dream how magnificent was that song. Then, note, if angels shouted before and when the world was made, their hallelujahs were more full, more strong, more magnificent, if not more hearty when they saw Jesus Christ born of the Virgin Mary to be man's redeemer—"Glory to God in the highest."

What is the instructive lesson to be learned from this first syllable of the angels' song? Why this, that salvation is God's highest glory. He is glorified in every dew-drop that twinkles to the morning sun. He is magnified in every wood flower that blossoms in the copse, although it live to blush unseen, and waste its sweetness in the forest air. God is glorified in every bird that warbles on the spray; in every lamb that skips the mead. Do not the fishes in the sea praise him? From the tiny minnow to the huge Leviathan, do not all creatures that swim the water bless and praise his name? Do not all created things extol him? Is there aught beneath the sky, save man, that doth not glorify God? Do not the stars exalt him, when they write his name upon the azure of Heaven in their golden letters? Do not the lightnings adore him when they flash his brightness in arrows of light piercing the midnight darkness? Do not thunders extol him when they roll like drums in the march of the God of armies? Do not all things exalt him, from the least even to the greatest? But sing, sing, oh universe, till thou hast exhausted thyself, thou canst not afford a song so sweet as the song of Incarnation. Though creation may be a majestic organ of praise, it cannot reach the compass of the golden canticle—Incarnation! There is more in that than in creation, more melody in Jesus in the manger, than there is in worlds on worlds rolling their grandeur round the throne of the Most High. Pause, Christian, and consider this a minute. See how every attribute is here magnified. Lo! what wisdom is here. God becomes man that God may be just, and the justifier of the ungodly. Lo! what power, for where is power so great as when it concealeth power? What power, that Godhead should unrobe itself and become man! Behold, what love is thus revealed to us when Jesus becomes a man. Behold, ye what faithfulness! How many promises are this day kept? How many solemn obligations are this hour discharged? Tell me one attribute of God that is not manifest in Jesus. and your ignorance shall be the reason why you have not seen it so. The whole of God is glorified in Christ; and though some part of the name of God is written in the universe, it is here best read—in him who was the Son of Man, and, yet, the Son of God.

But, let me say one word here before I go away from this point. We must learn from this, that if salvation glorifies God, glorifies him in the highest degree, and makes the highest creatures praise him, this one reflection may be added—then, that doctrine which glorifies man in salvation, cannot be the gospel. For salvation glorifies God. The angels were no Arminians: they sang, "Glory to God in the highest." They believe in no doctrine which uncrowns Christ, and puts the crown upon the head of mortals. They believe in no system of faith which makes salvation dependent upon the creature, and which really gives the creature the praise, for what is it less than for a man to save himself—if the whole dependence of salvation rests upon his own free will? No, my brethren; there may be some preachers, that delight to preach a doctrine that magnifies man; but in their gospel angels have no delight. The only glad tidings that made the angels sing, are those that put God first, God last, God midst, and God without end, in the salvation of his creatures, and put the crown wholly and alone upon the head of him that saves without a helper. "Glory to God in the highest," is the angels' song.

2. When they had sung this, they sang what they had never sung before. "Glory to God in the highest" was an old, old song; they had sung that from before the foundations of the world. But, now, they sang as it were a new song before the throne of God: for they added this stanza—"on earth, peace." They did not sing that in the garden. There was peace there, but it seemed a thing of course, and scarce worth singing of. There was more than peace there; for there was glory to God there. But, now, man had fallen, and since the day when cherubim with fiery swords drove out the man, there had been no peace on earth, save in the breast of some believers, who had obtained peace from the living fountain of this incarnation of Christ. Wars had raged from the ends of the world; men had slaughtered one another, heaps on heaps. There had been wars within as well as wars without. Conscience had fought with man, Satan had tormented man with thoughts of sin. There had been no peace on earth since Adam fell. But, now, when the new-born King made his appearance, the swaddling band with which he was wrapped up was the white flag of peace. That manger was the place where the treaty was signed, whereby warfare should be stopped between man's conscience and himself, man's conscience and his God. It was then, that day, the trumpet blew—"Sheathe the sword, oh man, sheathe the sword, oh conscience, for God is now at peace with man, and man at peace with God." Do you not feel, my brethren, that the gospel of God is peace to man? Where else can peace be found but in the message of Jesus? Go, legalist, work for peace with toil and pain, and thou shalt never find it. Go, thou, that trustest in the law: go thou, to Sinai: look to the flames that Moses saw, and shrink, and tremble, and despair: for peace is nowhere to be found, but in him, of whom it is said, "This man shall be peace." And what a peace it is, beloved! It is peace like a river, and righteousness like the waves of the sea. It is the peace of God that passeth all understanding, which keeps our hearts and minds through Jesus Christ our Lord. This sacred peace between the pardoned soul and God the pardoner; this marvelous "at-one-ment" between the sinner and his judge, this was it that the angels sung when they said, "peace on earth."

3. And, then, they wisely ended their song with a third note. They said, "Good will to man." Philosophers have said that God has a good will toward man; but I never knew any man who derived much comfort from their philosophical assertion. Wise men have thought from what we have seen in creation that God had much good will toward man, or else his works would never have been so constructed for their comfort; but I never heard of any man who could risk his soul's peace upon such a faint hope as that. But I have not only heard of thousands, but I know them—who are quite sure that God has a good will towards men; and if you ask their reason, they will give a full and perfect answer. They say, "He has good will toward man, for he gave his Son." No greater proof of kindness between the Creator and his subjects possibly be afforded than when the Creator gives his only begotten and well beloved Son to die. Though the first note is God-like, and though the second note is peaceful, this third note melts my heart the most. Some think of God as if he were a morose being who hated all mankind. Some picture him as if he were some abstract subsistence [basic life-form] taking no interest in our affairs. Hark ye: God has "good will toward men." You know what good will means. Well: all that it means, and more, God has to you, ye sons and daughters of Adam. Swearer, you have cursed God; he has not fulfilled his curse on you; he has good will towards you, though you have no good will towards him. Infidel, you have sinned high and hard against the Most High; he has said no hard things against you, for he has good will towards men. Poor sinner, thou hast broken his laws; thou art half afraid to come to the throne of his mercy lest he should spurn thee; hear thou this, and be comforted—God has good will towards men, so good a will that he has said, and said it with an oath too, "As I live, saith the Lord, I have no pleasure in the death of him that dieth, but had rather that he should turn unto me and live;" so good a will moreover that he has even condescended to say, "Come, now, let us reason together, though your sins be as scarlet, they shall be as wool; though they be red like crimson, they shall be whiter than snow." And if you say, "Lord, how shall I know that thou hast this good will towards me," he points to yonder manger, and says,

> Sinner, if I had not a good will towards thee, would I have parted with my Son? if I had not good will towards the human race, would I have given up my Son to become one of that race, that he might, by so doing, redeem them from death?

Ye that doubt the Master's love, look ye to that circle of angels; see their blaze of glory; hear their song, and let your doubts die away in that sweet music and be buried in a shroud of harmony. He has good will to men; he is willing to pardon; he passes by iniquity, transgression, and sin. And mark thee, if Satan shall then add, "But though God hath good will, yet he cannot violate his justice, therefore his mercy may be ineffective, and you may die;" then listen to that first note of the song, "Glory to God in the highest," and reply to Satan and all his temptations, that when God shows good will to a penitent sinner, there is not only peace in the sinner's heart, but it brings glory to every attribute of God, and so he can be just, and yet justify the sinner, and glorify himself.

I do not pretend to say that I have opened all the instructions contained in these three sentences, but I may perhaps direct you into a train of thought that may serve you for the week. I hope that all through the week you will have a truly merry Christmas by feeling the power of these words, and knowing the unction of them. "Glory to God in the highest, on earth peace, good will toward men."

II. Next, I have to present to you some *emotional thoughts.*

Friends, doth not this verse, this song of angels, stir your heart with happiness? When I read that, and found the angels singing it, I thought to myself,

> Then, if the angels ushered in the gospel's great Head with singing, ought I not to preach with singing? And ought not my hearers to live with singing? Ought not their hearts to be glad and their spirits to rejoice?

Well, thought I there be some somber religionists ,who were born in a dark night in December, that think a smile upon the face is wicked, and believe that for a Christian to be glad and rejoice is to be inconsistent. Ah! I wish these gentlemen had seen the angels when they sang about Christ, for if angels sang about his birth, though it was no concern of theirs, certainly men might to sing about it as long as they live, sing about it when they die, and sing about it when they live in Heaven forever. I do long to see in the midst of the church more of a singing Christianity. The last few years have been breeding in our midst a groaning and unbelieving Christianity. Now, I doubt not its sincerity, but I do doubt its healthy character. I say it may be true and real enough, God forbid I should say a word against the sincerity of those who practice it, but it is a sickly religion.

Watts hit the mark when he said,

> *Religion never was designed*
> *To make our pleasures less.*

It is designed to do away with some of our pleasures, but it gives us many more, to make up for what it takes away, so it does not make them less. O ye, that see in Christ nothing but a subject to stimulate your doubts and make the tears run down your cheeks; O ye that always say,

> *Lord, what a wretched land is this,*
> *That yields us no supplies,*

…Come ye hither and see the angels. Do they tell their story with groans, and sobs, and sighs? Ah, no; they shout aloud, "Glory to God in the highest." Now, imitate them, my dear brethren. If you are professors of religion, try always to have a cheerful carriage. Let others mourn; but

> Why should the children of a king
> Go mourning all their days?

Anoint your head and wash your face: appear not unto men to fast. Rejoice in the Lord always, and again I say unto you, rejoice. Specially this week be not ashamed to be glad. You need not think it a wicked thing to be happy. Penance and whipping and misery are no such very virtuous things, after all. The damned are miserable; let the saved be happy. Why should you hold fellowship with the lost by feelings of perpetual mourning? Why not rather anticipate the joys of Heaven, and begin to sing on earth that song which you will never need to end? The first emotion, then, that we ought to cherish in our hearts, is the emotion of joy and gladness.

Well, what next? Another emotion is that of confidence. I am not sure that I am right in calling that an emotion, but still in me it is so much akin to it, that I will venture to be wrong if I be so.

Now, if when Christ came on this earth, God had sent some black creature down from Heaven, (if there be such creatures there) to tell us, "Glory to God in the highest, and on earth peace, good will toward men," and if with a frowning brow and a stammering tongue he delivered his message, if I had been there and heard it, I should have scrupled to believe him, for I should have said, "You don't look like the messenger that God would send—stammering fellow as you are— with such glad news as this." But when the angels came, there was no doubting the truth of what they said, because it was quite certain that the angels believed it; they told it as if they did, for they told it with singing, with joy and gladness. If some friend, having heard that a legacy was left you, and should come to you with a solemn countenance, and a tongue like a funeral bell, saying, "Do you know so-and-so has left you £10,000?" Why, you would say, "Ah! I dare say," and laugh in his face. But if your brother should suddenly burst into your room and exclaim, "I say, what do you think? You are a rich man, So-and-so has left you £10,000!" Why, you would say, "I think it is very likely to be true, for he looks so happy over it."

Well, when these angels came from Heaven, they told the news just as if they believed it; and though I have often wickedly doubted my Lord's good will, I think I never could have doubted it while I heard those angels singing. No, I should say, "The messengers themselves are proof of the truth, for it seems they have heard it from God's lips; they have no doubt about it, for see how joyously they tell the news." Now, poor soul, thou that art afraid lest God should destroy thee, and thou thinkest that God will never have mercy upon thee, look at the singing angels and doubt if thou darest. Do not go to the synagogue of long-faced hypocrites to hear the minister who preaches with a nasal twang, with misery in his face, whilst he tells you that God has goodwill towards men. I know you won't believe what he says, for he does not preach with joy in his countenance, he is telling you good news with a grunt, and you are not likely to receive it. But go straightway to the plain where Bethlehem shepherds sat by night, and when you hear the angels singing out the gospel, by the grace of God upon you, you cannot help believing that they manifestly feel the preciousness of telling. Blessed Christmas, that brings such creatures as angels to confirm our faith in God's goodwill to men!

III. I must now bring before you the third point. There are some *prophetic utterances* contained in these words.

The angels sang "Glory to God in the highest, on earth peace, good will toward men." But I look around, and what see I in the wide, wide world? I do not see God honored. I see the heathen bowing down before their idols, I mark the Romanist casting himself before the rotten rags of his relics, and the ugly figures of his images. I look about me, and I see tyranny lording it over the bodies and souls of men; I see God forgotten; I see a worldly race pursuing mammon; I see a bloody race pursuing Moloch; I see ambition riding like Nimrod over the land, God forgotten, his name dishonored. And was this all the angels sang about? Is this all that made them sing "Glory to God in the highest?" Ah! no. There are brighter days approaching. They sang "Peace on earth." But I hear still the clarion of war; and the cannon's horrid roar; not yet have they turned the sword into a ploughshare, and the spear into a pruning hook! War still reigns.

Is this all that the angels sang about? And whilst I see wars to the ends of the earth, am I to believe that this was all the angels expected? Ah! no, brethren; the angels' song is big with prophecy; it travaileth in birth with glories. A few more years, and he that lives them out shall see why angels sang; a few more years, and he that will come, shall come, and will not tarry. Christ the Lord will come again, and when he cometh he shall cast the idols from their thrones; he shall dash down every fashion of heresy and every shape of idolatry; he shall reign from pole to pole with illimitable sway: he shall reign, when like a scroll, yon blue heavens have passed away. No strife shall vex Messiah's reign, no blood shall then be shed; they'll hang the useless helmet high, and study war no more. The hour is approaching when the temple of Janus shall be shut forever, and when cruel Mars shall be hooted from the earth. The day is coming when the lion shall eat straw like the ox, when the leopard shall lie down with the kid; when the weaned child shall put his hand upon the cockatrice[2] den and play with the asp. The hour approacheth; the first streaks of the sunlight bare made glad the age in which we live. Lo, he comes with trumpets and with clouds of glory; he shall come for whom we look with joyous expectation, whose coming shall be glory to his redeemed, and confusion to his enemies. Ah! brethren, when the angels sang this there was an echo through the long aisles of a glorious future. That echo was—

> *Hallelujah! Christ the Lord*
> *God Omnipotent shall reign.*

Ay, and doubtless the angels heard by faith the fullness of the Song,

> *Hark! the song of jubilee*
> *Loud as mighty thunders' roar,*
> *Or the fullness of the sea,*
> *When it breaks upon the shore.*

"Christ the Lord Omnipotent reigneth."

IV. Now, I have one more lesson for you, and I have done. That lesson is *preceptive [instructive]*.

I wish everybody that keeps Christmas this year, would keep it as the angels kept it. There are many persons who, when they talk about keeping Christmas, mean by that, the cutting of the bands of their religion for one day in the year, as if Christ were the Lord of misrule, as if the birth of Christ should be celebrated like the orgies of Bacchus. There are some very religious people, that on Christmas would never forget to go to church in the morning. They believe Christmas to be nearly as holy as Sunday, for they reverence the tradition of the elders. Yet their way of spending the rest of the day is very remarkable; for if they see their way straight up stairs to their bed at night, it must be by accident. They would not consider they had kept Christmas in a proper manner, if they did not verge on gluttony and drunkenness. They are many who think Christmas cannot possibly be kept, except there be a great shout of merriment and mirth in the house, and added to that the boisterousness of sin. Now, my brethren, although we, as successors of the Puritans, will not keep the day in any religious sense whatever, attaching nothing more to it than to any other day: believing that every day may be a Christmas for ought we know, and wishing to make every day Christmas, if we can, yet we must try to set an example to others how to behave on that day; and especially since the angels gave glory to God: let us do the same.

Once more the angels said, "Peace to men:" let us labor, if we can, to make peace next Christmas day. Now, old gentleman, you won't take your

---

2   Cockatrice: a mythical monster: a serpent hatched from a cock's egg. Could kill by a glance.

son in: he has offended you. Fetch him at Christmas. "Peace on earth;" you know: that is a Christmas Carol. Make peace in your family. Now, brother, you have made a vow that you will never speak to your brother again. Go after him and say, "Oh, my dear fellow, let not this day's sun go down upon our wrath." Fetch him in, and give him your hand. Now, Mr. Tradesman, you have an opponent in trade, and you have said some very hard words about him lately. If you do not make the matter up today, or tomorrow, or as soon as you can, yet do it on that day. That is the way to keep Christmas peace on earth and glory to God.

And oh, if thou hast anything on thy conscience, anything that prevents thy having peace of mind, keep thy Christmas in thy chamber, praying to God to give thee peace; for it is peace on earth, mind, peace in thyself, peace with thyself, peace with thy fellow men, peace with thy God. And do not think thou hast well celebrated that day till thou canst say, "O God,

> With the world, myself, and thee
> I ere I sleep at peace will be."

And when the Lord Jesus has become your peace, remember, there is another thing: good will towards men. Do not try to keep Christmas without keeping good will towards men. You are a gentleman, and have servants. Well, try and set their chimneys on fire with a large piece of good, substantial beef for them. If you are men of wealth, you have poor in your neighborhood. Find something wherewith to clothe the naked, and feed the hungry, and make glad the mourner. Remember, it is good will towards men. Try, if you can, to show them goodwill at this special season; and if you will do that, the poor will say—with me—that indeed they wish there were *six* Christmases in the year.

Let each one of us go from this place determined, that if we are angry all the year round, this next week shall be an exception; that if we have snarled at everybody last year, this Christmas time we will strive to be kindly affectionate to others; and if we have lived all this year at enmity with God, I pray that by his Spirit he may this week give us peace with him; and then, indeed, my brother, it will be the merriest Christmas we ever had in all our lives. You are going home to your father and mother, young men; many of you are going from your shops to your homes. You remember what I preached on last Christmas time. Go home to thy friends, and tell them what the Lord hath done for thy soul, and that will make a blessed round of stories at the Christmas fire. If you will each of you tell your parents how the Lord met with you in the house of prayer; how, when you left home, you were a gay, wild blade, but have now come back to love your mother's God, and read your father's Bible. Oh, what a happy Christmas that will make! What more shall I say?

May God give you peace with yourselves; may he give you good will towards all your friends, your enemies, and your neighbors; and may he give you grace to give glory to God in the highest. I will say no more, except at the close of this sermon to wish everyone of you, when the day shall come, the happiest Christmas you ever had in your lives.

> *Now with angels round the throne,*
> *Cherubim and seraphim,*
> *And the church, which still is one,*
> *Let us swell the solemn hymn;*
> *Glory to the great I AM!*
> *Glory to the Victim Lamb.*
>
> *Blessing, honor, glory, might,*
> *And dominion infinite,*
> *To the Father of our Lord,*
> *To the Spirit and the Word;*
> *As it was all worlds before,*
> *Is, and shall be evermore.*

A Christmas Question

Delivered on Sabbath morning, December 25, 1859, at Exeter Hall, Strand. No. 291.

For unto us a child is born, unto us a son is given.—Isaiah 9:6

Upon other occasions I have explained the main part of this verse—"the government shall be upon his shoulders, his name shall be called Wonderful, Counselor, the Mighty God." If God shall spare me, on some future occasion I hope to take the other titles, "The Everlasting Father, the Prince of Peace." But now this morning the portion which will engage our attention is this, "Unto us a child is born, unto us a Son is given." The sentence is a double one, but it has in it no tautology [redundancy]. The careful reader will soon discover a distinction; and it is not a distinction without a difference. "Unto us a *child* is born, unto us a *Son* is *given*." As Jesus Christ is a child in his human nature, he is born, begotten of the Holy Ghost, born of the Virgin Mary. He is as truly-born, as certainly a child, as any other man that ever lived upon the face of the earth. He is thus in his humanity a child born. But as Jesus Christ is God's Son, he is not born; but given, begotten of his Father from before all worlds, begotten—not made, being of the same substance with the Father. The doctrine of the eternal affiliation of Christ is to be received as an undoubted truth of our holy religion. But as to any explanation of it, no man should venture thereon, for it remaineth among the deep things of God—one of those solemn mysteries indeed, into which the angels dare not look, nor do they desire to pry into it—a mystery which we must not attempt to fathom, for it is utterly beyond the grasp of any finite being. As well might a gnat seek to drink in the ocean, as a finite creature to comprehend the Eternal God. A God whom we could understand would be no God. If we could grasp him he could not be infinite: if we could understand him, then were he not divine. Jesus Christ then, I say, as a Son, is not born to us, but given. He is a boon bestowed on us, "For God so loved the world, that he *sent* his only begotten *Son* into the world." He was not born in this world as God's Son, but he was *sent*, or was given, so that you clearly perceive that the distinction is a suggestive one, and conveys much good truth to us. "Unto us a *child* is *born*, unto us a *Son* is *given*."

This morning, however, the principal object of my discourse, and, indeed, the sole one, is to bring out the force of those two little words, *"unto us."* For you will perceive that here the full force of the passage lies. "For *unto* us a child is born, *unto* us a Son is given." The divisions of my discourse are very simple ones. First, *is it so?* Secondly, *if it is so, what then?* Thirdly, *if it is not so, what then?*

I. In the first place, *is it so?*

Is it true that *unto us* a child is born, *unto us* a Son is given? It is a fact that a child is born. Upon that I use no argument. We receive it as a fact, more fully established than any other fact in history, that the Son of God became man, was born at Bethlehem, wrapped in swaddling clothes, and laid in a manger. It is a fact, too, that a Son is given. About that we have no question. The infidel may dispute, but we, professing to be believers in Scripture, receive it as an undeniable truth, that God has given his only begotten Son to be the Savior of men. But the matter of question is this: Is this child born *to us*? Is he given *to us*? This is the matter of anxious enquiry. Have we a personal interest in the child that was born at Bethlehem? Do we know that he is our Savior?—that he has brought glad tidings to us?—that to us he belongs? and that we belong to him? I say this is matter of very grave and solemn investigation. It is a very observable fact, that the very best of men are sometimes troubled with questions with regard to their own interest in Christ, while men who never are troubled at all about the matter are very frequently presumptuous deceivers, who have no part in this matter. I have often observed that some of the people about whom I felt most sure, were the very persons who were the least sure of themselves. It reminds me of the history of a godly man named Simon Brown, a minister in the olden times in the City of London. He became so extremely sad in heart, so depressed in spirit, that at last he conceived the idea that his soul was annihilated. It was all in vain to talk to the good man, you could not persuade him that he had a soul; but all the time he was preaching, and praying, and working, more like a man that had two souls than none. When he preached, his eyes poured forth plenteous floods of tears, and when he prayed, there was a divine fervor and heavenly prevalence in every petition. Now so it is with many Christians. They seem to be the very picture of godliness; their life is admirable, and their conversation heavenly, but yet they are always crying,—

> *'Tis a point I long to know,*
> *Oft it causes anxious thought,*
> *Do I love the Lord or no?*
> *Am I his or am I not?*

So does it happen, that the best of men will question while the worst of men will presume. Ay, I have seen the men about whose eternal destiny I had serious questioning, whose inconsistencies in life were palpable and glaring, who have prated [chattered] concerning their sure portion in Israel, and their infallible hope, as though they believed others to be as easily duped as themselves. Now, what reason shall we give for this foolhardiness? Learn it from this illustration: you see a number of men riding along a narrow road upon the edge of the sea. It is a very perilous path, for the way is rugged and a tremendous precipice bounds the pathway on the left. Let but the horse's foot slip once, and they [the horse and rider] dash downwards to destruction. See how cautiously the riders journey, how carefully the horses place their feet. But do you observe yon rider, at what a rate he dashes along, as if he were riding a steeple-chase with Satan? You hold up your hands in an agony of fear, trembling lest every moment his horse's foot should slip, and he should be dashed down; and you say, why so careless a rider? The man is a blind rider on a blind horse. They cannot see where they are. He thinks he is on a sure road, and therefore it is that he rides so fast. Or to vary the picture; sometimes when persons are asleep, they take to walking and they will climb where others will not think of venturing. Giddy heights that would turn our brain seem safe enough to them. So there be many spiritual sleep-walkers in our midst, who think that they are awake. But they are not. Their very presumption in venturing to the high places of self-confidence, proves that they are somnambulists; not awake, but men who walk and talk in their sleep. It is, then, I say, really a matter of serious questioning with all men, who would be right at last, as to whether this child is born to us, and this Son given to us?

I shall now help you to answer the question.

1. If this child who now lies before the eyes of your faith, wrapped in swaddling clothes in Bethlehem's manger, is born to *you*, my hearer, then *you are born again!* For this child is not born to you unless you are born to this child. All who have an interest in Christ are, in the fullness of time, by grace, converted, quickened, and renewed. All the redeemed are not yet converted, but they will be. Before the hour of death arrives, their nature shall be changed, their sins shall be washed away, they shall pass from death unto life. If any man tells me that Christ is his Redeemer, although he has never experienced regeneration, that man utters what he does not know; his religion is vain, and his hope is a delusion. Only men who are born again

can claim the babe in Bethlehem as being theirs. "But" saith one, "how am I to know whether I am born again or not?" Answer this question also by another: has there been a change effected by divine grace *within you*? Are your loves the very opposite of what they were? Do you now hate the vain things you once admired, and do you seek after that precious pearl which you at one time despised? Is your heart thoroughly renewed in its object? Can you say that the bent of your desire is changed? That your face is Zionward, and your feet set upon the path of grace? That whereas your heart once longed for deep draughts of sin, it now longs to be holy? And whereas you once loved the pleasures of the world, they have now become as draff [dregs] and dross [scum] to you, for you only love the pleasures of heavenly things, and are longing to enjoy more of them on earth, that you may be prepared to enjoy a fullness of them hereafter? Are you renewed within? For mark, my hearer, the new birth does not consist in washing the outside of the cup and platter, but in cleansing the inner man. It is all in vain to put up the stone upon the sepulcher, wash it extremely white, and garnish it with the flowers of the season; the sepulcher itself must be cleansed. The dead man's bones that lie in that charnel-house of the human heart must be cleansed away. Nay, they must be made to live. The heart must no longer be a tomb of death, but a temple of life. Is it so with you, my hearer? For recollect, you may be very different in the outward, but if you are not changed in the inward, this child is not born to you.

But I put another question. Although the main matter of regeneration lies within, yet it manifests itself without. Say, then, has there been a change in you in the exterior? Do you think that others who look at you would be compelled to say, "this man is not what he used to be?" Do not your companions observe a change? Have they not laughed at you for what they think to be your hypocrisy, your puritanism, your sternness? Do you think now that if an angel should follow you into your secret life, should track you to your closet and see you on your knees, that he would detect something in you which he could never have seen before? For, mark, my dear hearer, there must be a change in the outward life, or else there is no change within. In vain you bring me to the tree, and say that the tree's nature is changed. If I still see it bringing forth wild grapes, it is a wild vine still. And if I mark upon you the apples of Sodom and the grapes of Gomorrah, you are still a tree accursed and doomed, notwithstanding all your fancied experience. The proof of the Christian is in the living. To other men, the proof of our conversion is not what you *feel*, but what you *do*. To yourself, your feelings may be good enough evidence, but to the minister and others who judge of you, the outward walk is the main guide. At the same time, let me observe that a man's outward life may be very much like that of a Christian, and yet there may be no religion in him at all. Have you ever seen two jugglers in the street with swords, pretending to fight with one another? See how they cut, and slash, and hack at one another, till you are half afraid there will soon be murder done. They seem to be so very much in earnest that you are half in the mind to call in the police to part them. See with what violence that one has aimed a terrific blow at the other one's head, which his comrade dexterously warded off by keeping a well-timed guard. Just watch them a minute, and you will see that all these cuts and thrusts come in a prearranged order. There is no heart in the fighting after all. They do not fight so roughly as they would if they were real enemies. So, sometimes I have seen a man pretending to be very angry against sin. But watch him a little while, and you will see it is only a fencer's trick. He does not give his cuts out of order, there is no earnestness in his blows, it is all pretense, it is only mimic stage-play. The fencers, after they have ended their performance, shake hands with one another, and divide the coppers which the gaping throng have given them; and so does this man do: he shakes hands with the devil in private, and the two deceivers share the spoil. The hypocrite and the devil are very good friends after all, and they mutually rejoice over their profits: the devil leering because he has won the soul of the professor, and the hypocrite laughing because he has won his pelf [money]. Take care, then, that your outward life is not a mere stage-play, but that your antagonism to sin is real and intense; and that you strike right and left, as though you meant to slay the monster, and cast its limbs to the winds of Heaven.

I will put another question. If thou hast been born again, there is another matter by which to try thee. Not only is thy inward self altered, and thy outward self too, but the very root and principle of thy life must become totally new. When we are in sin, we live to self, but when we are renewed, we live to God. While we are unregenerate, our principle is to seek our own pleasure, our own advancement; but that man is not truly born again who does not live with a far different aim from this. Change a man's principles, and you change his feelings, you change his actions. Now, grace changes the principles of man. It lays the axe at the root of the tree. It does not saw away at some big limb, it does not try to alter the sap; but it gives a new root, and plants us in fresh soil. The man's inmost self, the deep rocks of his principles, upon which the topsoil of his actions rest, the soul of his manhood, is thoroughly changed, and he is a new creature in Christ. "But," says one, "I see no reason why I should be born again." Ah, poor creature, it is because thou hast never seen thyself. Didst thou ever see a man in the looking-glass of the Word of God? What a strange monster he is! Do you know, a man by nature has his heart where his feet ought to be—that is to say, his heart is set upon the earth, whereas he ought to be treading it beneath his feet; and stranger mystery still, his heels are where his heart should be:—that is to say, he is kicking against the God of Heaven when he ought to be setting his affections on things above. Man by nature when he sees clearest, only looks down, can only see that which is beneath him, he cannot see the things which are above; and strange to say, the sunlight of Heaven blinds him; light from Heaven he looks not for. He asks for his light in darkness. The earth is to him his Heaven, and he sees suns in its muddy pools and stars in its filth. He is, in fact, a man turned upside down. The fall has so ruined our nature, that the most monstrous thing on the face of the earth is a fallen man. The ancients used to paint griffins, gryphons, dragons, chimeras, and all kinds of hideous things; but if a skillful hand could paint man accurately, none of us would look at the picture, for it is a sight that none ever saw except the lost in Hell; and that is one part of their intolerable pain, that they are compelled always to look upon themselves. Now, then, see you not that ye must be born again, and unless ye are so, this child is not born to you.

2. But I go forward. If this child is born to you, you are a *child,* and the question arises, are you so? Man grows from childhood up to manhood naturally; in grace men grow from manhood down to childhood; and the nearer we come to true childhood, the nearer welcome to the image of Christ. For was not Christ called "a child," even after he had ascended up to Heaven? "Thy holy child Jesus." Brethren and sisters, can you say that you have been made into children? Do you take God's Word just as it stands, simply because your heavenly Father says so? Are you content to believe mysteries without demanding to have them explained? Are you ready to sit in the infant class, and be a little one? Are you willing to hang upon the breast of the church, and suck in the unadulterated milk of the Word—never questioning for a moment what your divine Lord reveals, but believing it on his own authority, whether it seemed to be above reason, or beneath reason, or even contrary to reason? Now, "except ye be converted and become as little children," this child is not born to you; except like a child you are humble, teachable, obedient, pleased with your Father's will and willing to assign all to him, there is grave matter of question whether this child is born *to you.* But what a pleasing sight it is to see a man converted and made into a little child. Many times has my heart leaped for joy, when I have seen a giant infidel who used to reason against Christ, who had not a word in his dictionary bad enough for Christ's people, come by divine grace to believe the gospel. That man sits down and weeps, feels the full power of salvation, and from that time drops all his questionings becomes the very reverse of what he was. He thinks himself meaner than the meanest believer. He is content to do the meanest work for the church of Christ, and takes his station—not with Locke or Newton, as a mighty Christian philosopher—but with Mary as a simple learner, sitting at Jesus' feet, to hear and learn of him. If ye are not children, then this child is not born to you.

3. And now let us take the second sentence and put a question or two upon that. Is this son given to us? I pause a minute to beg your personal attention. I am trying, if I may, so to preach that I may make you all question yourselves. I pray you, let not one of you exempt himself from the ordeal, but let each one ask

himself, if it true that unto me a Son is given? Now, if this Son is given *to you, you are a son yourself.* "For unto as many as received him, to them gave he power to become the sons of God." "Christ became a Son that in all things he might be made like unto his brethren." The Son of God is not mine to enjoy, to love, to delight in, unless I am a son of God too. Now, my hearer, have you a *fear* of God before your eyes—a filial fear, a fear which a child has lest it should grieve its parent? Say have you a child's *love* to God? Do you trust to him as your father, your provider, and your friend? Have you in your breast "The spirit of adoption whereby we cry, Abba, Father?" Are there times with you when on your knees you can say, "My Father and my God?" Does the Spirit bear witness with your spirit that you are born of God? and while this witness is born, does your heart fly up to your Father and to your God, in ecstasy of delight, to clasp him who long ago hath clasped you in the covenant of his love, in the arms of his effectual grace? Now, mark my hearer, if thou dost not sometimes enjoy the spirit of adoption, if thou art not a son or daughter of Zion, then deceive not thyself: this Son is not given to thee.

4. And, then, to put it in another shape: if unto us a Son is given, then *we are given to the Son.* Now, what say you to this question also? Are you given up to Christ? Do you feel that you have nothing on earth to live for but to glorify him? Can you say in your heart, "Great God, if I be not deceived, I am wholly thine?" Are you ready today to write over again your consecration vow? Canst thou say,

> Take me! All that I am and all I have, shall be forever thine. I would give up all my goods, all my powers, all my time, and all my hours, and thine I would be—wholly thine.

"Ye are not your own: ye are bought with a price." And if this Son of God be given to you, you will have consecrated yourself wholly to him; and you will feel that his honor is your life's object, that his glory is the one great desire of your panting spirit. Now is it so, my hearer? Ask thyself the question. I pray thee, and do not deceive thyself in the answer.

I will just repeat the four different proofs again. If unto me a child is born, then I have been born again; and, moreover, I am now in consequence of that new birth, a child. If, again, a Son has been given to me, then I am a son; and again I am given to that Son who is given to me. I have tried to put these tests in the way that the text would suggest them. I pray you carry them home with you. If you do not recollect the words, yet do recollect to search yourselves, and see, my hearers, whether you can say, "Unto me this Son is given." For, indeed, if Christ is not *my* Christ, he is of little worth to me. If I cannot say he loved me and gave himself for me, of what avail is all the merit of his righteousness, or all the plenitude of his atonement? Bread in the shop is well enough, but if I am hungry and cannot get it, I starve although granaries be full. Water in the river is well enough, but if I am in a desert and cannot reach the stream, if I can hear it in the distance and am yet lying down to die of thirst, the murmuring of the rill, or the flowing of the river, helps to tantalize me, while I die in dark despair. Better for you, my hearers to have perished as Hottentots [African Bushmen], to have gone down to your graves as dwellers in some benighted land, than to live where the name of Christ is continually hymned and where his glory is extolled, and yet to go down to your tombs without an interest in him, unblessed by his gospel, unwashed in his blood, unclothed of his robe of righteousness. God help you, that you may be blessed in him, and may sing sweetly "Unto us a child is born, unto us a Son is given."

II. This brings me to my second head, upon which I shall be brief. *Is it so? If it is so, what then?*

If it is so, why am I doubtful today? Why is my spirit questioning? Why do I not realize the fact? My hearer, if the Son is given to thee, how is it that thou art this day asking whether thou art Christ's, or not? Why dost thou not labor to make thy calling and election sure? Why tarriest thou in the plains of doubt? Get thee up, get thee up to the high mountains of confidence, and never rest till thou canst say, without a fear that thou art mistaken, "I know that my Redeemer liveth. I am persuaded that he is able to keep that which I have committed to him." I may have a large number of persons here to whom it is a matter of uncertainty as to whether Christ is theirs or not. Oh, my dear hearers, rest not content unless you know assuredly that Christ is yours, and that you are Christ's. Suppose you should see in tomorrow's newspaper, (although, by the way, if you believed anything you saw there you would probably be mistaken) but suppose you should see a notification that some rich man had left you an immense estate. Suppose, as you read it, you were well aware that the person mentioned was a relative of yours, and that it was likely to be true. It may be you have prepared tomorrow for a family meeting, and you are expecting brother John and sister Mary and their little ones to dine with you. But I very much question whether you would not be away from the head of the table to go and ascertain whether the fact were really so. "Oh," you could say, "I am sure I should enjoy my Christmas dinner all the better if I were quite sure about this matter;" and all day, if you did not go, you would be on the tip-toe of expectation; you would be, as it were, sitting upon pins and needles until you knew whether it were the fact or not. Now there is a proclamation gone forth today, and it is a true one, too, that Jesus Christ has come into the world to save sinners. The question with you is whether he has saved you, and whether you have an interest in him. I beseech you, give no sleep to your eyes, and no slumber to your eyelids, till you have read your "title clear to mansions in the skies." What, man! shall your eternal destiny be a matter of uncertainty to you? What! is Heaven or Hell involved in this matter, and will you rest until you know which of these shall be your everlasting portion? Are you content while it is a question whether God loves you, or whether he is angry with you? Can you be easy while you remain in doubt as to whether you are condemned in sin, or justified by faith which is in Christ Jesus? Get thee up, man. I beseech thee by the living God, and by thine own soul's safety, get thee up and read the records. Search and look, and try and test thyself, to see whether it be so or not. For if it be so, why should not we know it? If the Son is given to me, why should not I be sure of it? If the child is born to me, why should I not know it for a certainty, that I may even now live in the enjoyment of my privilege—a privilege, the value of which I shall never know to the full, till I arrive in glory?

Again, if it be so, another question. *Why are we sad?* I am looking upon faces just now that appear the very reverse of gloomy, but mayhap the smile covers an aching heart. Brother and sister, why are we sad this morning, if unto us a child is born, if unto us a Son is given? Hark, hark to the cry! It is "Harvest home! Harvest home!" See the maidens as they dance, and the young men as they make merry. And why is this mirth? Because they are storing the precious fruits of the earth, they are gathering together unto their barns wheat which will soon be consumed. And what, brothers and sisters—have we the bread which endureth to eternal life, and are we unhappy? Does the worldling rejoice when his corn is increased, and do we not rejoice when, "Unto us a child is born, and unto us a Son is given?" Hark, yonder! What means the firing of the Tower [Tower of London—Royal residence] guns? Why all this ringing of bells in the church steeples, as if all London were mad with joy? There is a prince born; therefore there is this salute, and therefore are the bells ringing. Ah, Christians, ring the bells of your hearts, tire the salute of your most joyous songs, "For unto us a child is born, unto us a Son is given." Dance, O my heart, and ring out peals of gladness! Ye drops of blood within my veins, dance everyone of you! Oh! all my nerves become harp strings, and let gratitude touch you with angelic fingers! And thou, my tongue, shout—shout to his praise who hath said to thee—"Unto thee a child is born, unto thee a Son is given." Wipe that tear away! Come, stop that sighing! Hush yon murmuring. What matters your poverty? "Unto you a child is born." What matters your sickness? "Unto you a Son is given." What matters your sin? For this child shall take the sin away, and this Son shall wash and make you fit for Heaven. I say, if it be so,

> Lift up the heart, lift up the voice,
> Rejoice aloud! ye saints, rejoice!

But, once more, if it be so, what then? *Why are our hearts so cold?* and why is it that we do so little for him who has done so much for us? Jesus, art thou mine? Am I saved? How is it that I love thee so little? Why is it that when I preach I am not more in earnest, and when I pray I am not more intensely fervent? How is it that we give so little to Christ, who gave himself for us? How is it that we serve him so

23

sadly who served us so perfectly? He consecrated himself wholly; how is it that our consecration is marred and partial? [How is it that] we are continually sacrificing to self and not to him?

O beloved brethren, yield yourselves up this morning. What have you got in the world? "Oh," saith one, "I have nothing; I am poor and penniless, and all but homeless." Give thyself to Christ. You have heard the story of the pupils to a Greek philosopher. On a certain day it was the custom to give to the philosopher a present. One came and gave him gold. Another could not bring him gold but brought him silver. One brought him a robe, and another some delicacy for food. But one of them came up, and said, "Oh, Solon, I am poor, I have nothing to give to thee, but yet I will give thee something better than all these have given; I give thee myself." Now, if you have gold and silver, if you have aught of this world's goods, give in your measure to Christ; but take care, above all, that you give yourself to him, and let your cry be from this day forth,

> *Do not I love thee, dearest Lord?*
> *Oh search my heart and see,*
> *And turn each cursed idol out*
> *That dares to rival thee.*

> *Do not I love thee from my soul?*
> *Then let me nothing love:*
> *Dead be my heart to every joy,*
> *When Jesus cannot move.*

III. Well, now I have all but done, but give your solemn, very solemn attention, while I come to my last head:—*if it is not so, what then?*

Dear hearer, I cannot tell where thou art—but wherever thou mayst be in this hall, the eyes of my heart are looking for thee, that when they have seen thee, they may weep over thee. Ah! miserable wretch, without a hope, without Christ, without God. Unto thee there is no Christmas mirth, for thee no child is born; to thee no Son is given. Sad is the story of the poor men and women, who during the week before last fell down dead in our streets through cruel hunger and bitter cold. But far more pitiable is thy lot, far more terrible shall be thy condition in the day when thou shalt cry for a drop of water to cool thy burning tongue, and it shall be denied thee; when thou shalt seek for death, for grim cold death—seek for him as for a friend, and yet thou shalt not find him. For the fire of Hell shall not consume thee, nor its terrors devour thee. Thou shalt long to die, yet shalt thou linger in eternal death—dying every hour, yet never receiving the much coveted boon of death. What shall I say to thee this morning? Oh! Master, help me to speak a word in season, now. I beseech thee, my hearer, if Christ is not thine this morning, may God the Spirit help thee to do what I now command thee to do. First of all, confess thy sins; not into my ear, nor into the ear of any living man. Go to thy chamber and confess that thou art vile. Tell him thou art a wretch undone without his sovereign grace. But do not think there is any merit in confession. There is none. All your confession cannot merit forgiveness, though God has promised to pardon the man who confesses his sin and forsakes it. Imagine that some creditor had a debtor who owed him a thousand pounds. He calls upon him and says, "I demand my money." But, says the other, "I owe you nothing." That man will be arrested and thrown into prison. However, his creditor says, "I wish to deal mercifully with you, make a frank confession, and I will forgive you all the debt." "Well," says the man, "I do acknowledge that I owe you two hundred pounds." "No," says he, "that will not do." "Well, sir, I confess I owe you five hundred pounds," and by degrees he comes to confess that he owes the thousand. Is there any merit in that confession? No; but yet you could see that no creditor would think of forgiving a debt which was not acknowledged. It is the least that you can do, to acknowledge your sin; and though there be no merit in the confession, yet true to his promise, God will give you pardon through Christ. That is one piece of advice. I pray you take it. Do not throw it to the winds; do not leave it as soon as you get out of Exeter Hall [this building]. Take it with you, and may this day become a confession-day with many of you. But next, when you have made a confession, I beseech you renounce yourself.

You have been resting perhaps in some hope that you would make yourself better, and so save yourself. Give up that delusive fancy. You have seen the silkworm: it will spin, and spin, and spin, and then it will die where it has spun itself a shroud. And your good works are but a spinning for yourself a robe for your dead soul. You can do nothing by your best prayers, your best tears, or your best works, to merit eternal life. Why, the Christian who is converted to God, will tell you that he cannot live a holy life by himself. If the ship in the sea cannot steer itself aright, do you think the wood that lies in the carpenter's yard can put itself together, and make itself into a ship, and then go out to sea and sail to America? Yet, this is just what you imagine. The Christian who is God's workmanship can do nothing, and yet you think you can do something. Now, give up self. God help you to strike a black mark through every idea of what you can do.

Then, lastly, and I pray God help you here, my dear hearers, when thou hast confessed thy sin and given up all hope of self-salvation, go to the place where Jesus died in agony. Go then in meditation to Calvary. There he hangs. It is the middle cross of these three. Methinks I see him now. I see his poor face emaciated, and his visage more marred than that of any man. I see the beady drops of blood still standing round his pierced temples—marks of that rugged thorn-crown. Ah, I see his body naked—naked to his shame. We may tell all his bones. See there his hands rent with the rough iron, and his feet torn with the nails. The nails have rent through his flesh. There is now not only the hole through which the nail was driven, but the weight of his body has sunken upon his feet, and see the iron is tearing through his flesh. And now the weight of his body hangs upon his arms, and the nails there are rending through the tender nerves. Hark! earth is startled! He cries, *"Eli, Eli, lama sabachthani?"* Oh, sinner, was ever shriek like that? God hath forsaken him. His God has ceased to be gracious to him. His soul is exceedingly sorrowful, even unto death. But hark, again, he cries, "I thirst!" Give him water! Give him water! Ye holy women let him drink. But no, his murderers torture him. They thrust into his mouth the vinegar mingled with gall—the bitter with the sharp, the vinegar and the gall. At last, hear him, sinner, for here is your hope. I see him bow his awful head. The King of Heaven dies. The God who made the earth has become a man, and the man is about to expire. Hear him! He cries, "It is finished!" And he gives up the ghost. The atonement is finished, the price is paid, the bloody ransom counted down, the sacrifice is accepted. "It is finished!" Sinner, believe in Christ. Cast thyself on him. Sink or swim, take him to be thy all in all. Throw now thy trembling arms around that bleeding body. Sit now at the feet of that cross, and feel the dropping of the precious blood. And as you go out, each one of you say in your hearts,

> *A guilty, weak, and helpless worm,*
> *On Christ's kind arms I fall,*
> *He is my strength and righteousness,*
> *My Jesus, and my all.*

God grant you grace to do so for Jesus Christ's sake. May the grace of our Lord Jesus Christ, and the love of God, and the fellowship of the Holy Ghost, be with you all, forever and ever. Amen and Amen.

No Room for Christ in the Inn

Delivered on Sunday morning, December 21, 1862, at the Metropolitan Tabernacle, Newington. No. 485.

And she brought forth her firstborn son, and wrapped him in swaddling clothes, and laid him in a manger; because there was no room for them in the inn.—Luke 2:7

It was needful that it should be distinctly proven, beyond all dispute, that our Lord sprang out of Judah. It was necessary, also, that he should be born in Bethlehem-Ephratah, according to the word of the Lord which he spake by his servant Micah. But how could a public recognition of the lineage of an obscure carpenter and an unknown maiden be procured? What interest could the keepers of registers be supposed to take in two such humble persons? As for the second matter, Mary lived at Nazareth in Galilee, and there seemed every probability that the birth would take place there; indeed, the period of her delivery was so near that, unless absolutely compelled, she would not be likely to undertake a long and tedious journey to the southern province of Judea. How are these two matters to be arranged? Can one turn of the wheel effect two purposes? It can be done! It shall be done! The official stamp of the Roman empire shall be affixed to the pedigree of the coming Son of David, and Bethlehem shall behold his nativity. A little tyrant, Herod, by some show of independent spirit, offends the greater tyrant, Augustus. Augustus informs him that he shall no longer treat him as a friend, but as a vassal; and albeit Herod makes the most abject submission, and his friends at the Roman court intercede for him, yet Augustus, to show his displeasure, orders a census to be taken of all the Jewish people, in readiness for a contemplated taxation, which, however, was not carried out till some ten years after. Even the winds and waves are not more fickle than a tyrant's will; but the Ruler of tempests knoweth how to rule the perverse spirits of princes. The Lord our God has a bit for the wildest war horse, and a hook for the most terrible leviathan. Autocratical Caesars are but puppets moved with invisible strings, mere drudges to the King of kings. Augustus must be made offended with Herod; he is constrained to tax the people; it is imperative that a census be taken; nay, it is of necessity that inconvenient, harsh, and tyrannical regulations should be published, and every person must repair to the town to which he was reputed to belong; thus, Mary is brought to Bethlehem, Jesus Christ is born as appointed, and, moreover, he is recognized officially as being descended from David by the fact that his mother came to Bethlehem as being of that lineage, remained there, and returned to Galilee without having her claims questioned, although the jealousy of all the women of the clan would have been aroused had an intruder ventured to claim a place among the few females to whom the birth of Messias was now by express prophecies confined. Remark here the wisdom of a God of providence, and believe that all things are ordered well.

When all persons of the house of David were thus driven to Bethlehem, the scanty accommodation of the little town would soon be exhausted. Doubtless friends entertained their friends till their houses were all full, but Joseph had no such willing kinsmen in the town. There was the caravanserai, which was provided in every village, where free accommodation was given to travelers; this, too, was full, for coming from a distance, and compelled to travel slowly, the humble couple had arrived late in the day. The rooms within the great brick square were already occupied with families; there remained no better lodging, even for a woman in travail, than one of the meaner spaces appropriated to beasts of burden. The stall of the ass was the only place where the child could be born. By hanging a curtain at its front, and perhaps tethering the animal on the outer side to block the passage, the needed seclusion could be obtained, and here, in the stable, was the King of Glory born, and in the manger was he laid.

My business this morning is to lead your meditations to the stable at Bethlehem, that you may see this great sight—the Savior in the manger, and think over the reason for this lowly couch—"because there was no room for them in the inn."

I. I shall commence by remarking that *there were other reasons why Christ should be laid in the manger.*

1. I think it was intended thus *to show forth his humiliation.* He came, according to prophecy, to be "despised and rejected of men, a man of sorrows and acquainted with grief;" he was to be "without form or comeliness," "a root out of a dry ground." Would it have been fitting that the man who was to die naked on the cross should be robed in

purple at his birth? Would it not have been inappropriate that the Redeemer who was to be buried in a borrowed tomb, should be born anywhere but in the humblest shed, and housed anywhere but in the most ignoble manner? The manger and the cross, standing at the two extremities of the Savior's earthly life, seem most fit and congruous the one to the other. He is to wear through life a peasant's garb; he is to associate with fishermen; the lowly are to be his disciples; the cold mountains are often to be his only bed; he is to say, "Foxes have holes, and the birds of the air have nests, but the Son of Man hath not where to lay his head;" nothing, therefore, could be more fitting than that in his season of humiliation, when he laid aside all his glory, and took upon himself the form of a servant, and condescended even to the meanest estate, he should be laid in a manger.

2. By being in a manger, *he was declared to be the king of the poor.* They, doubtless, were at once able to recognize his relationship to them, from the position in which they found him. I believe it excited feelings of the tenderest brotherly kindness in the minds of the shepherds, when the angel said—"This shall be a sign unto you; you shall find the child wrapped in swaddling-clothes and lying in a manger." In the eyes of the poor, imperial robes excite no affection: a man in their own garb attracts their confidence. With what pertinacity will workingmen cleave to a leader of their own order, believing in him because he knows their toils, sympathizes in their sorrows, and feels an interest in all their concerns! Great commanders have readily won the hearts of their soldiers by sharing their hardships and roughing it as if they belonged to the ranks. The King of Men, who was born in Bethlehem, was not exempted in his infancy from the common calamities of the poor—nay, his lot was even worse than theirs. I think I hear the shepherds comment on the manger-birth, "Ah!" said one to his fellow,

> then he will not be like Herod the tyrant; he will remember the manger and feel for the poor; poor helpless infant, I feel a love for him even now. What miserable accommodation this cold world yields its Savior; it is not a Caesar that is born today; he will never trample down our fields with his armies, or slaughter our flocks for his courtiers. He will be the poor man's friend, the people's monarch; according to the words of our shepherd-king, he shall judge the poor of the people; he shall save the children of the needy.

Surely the shepherds, and such as they—the poor of the earth—perceived at once that here was the plebeian king; noble in descent, but still, as the Lord hath called him, "one chosen out of the people." Great Prince of Peace! The manger was thy royal cradle! Therein wast thou presented to all nations as Prince of our race, before whose presence there is neither barbarian, Scythian, bond nor free; but thou art Lord of all. Kings, your gold and silver would have been lavished on him if ye had known the Lord of Glory, but inasmuch as ye knew him not, he was declared with demonstration to be a leader and a witness to the people. The things which *are not,* under him shall bring to nought the things that are, and the things that *are despised which God hath chosen,* shall under his leadership break in pieces the might, and pride, and majesty of human grandeur.

3. Further, in thus being laid in a manger, he did, as it were, *give an invitation to the most humble to come to him.* We might tremble to approach a throne, but we cannot fear to approach a manger. Had we seen the Master at first riding in state through the streets of Jerusalem with garments laid in the way, and the palm-branches strewed, and the people crying, "Hosanna!" we might have thought, though even the thought would have been wrong, that he was not approachable. Even there, riding upon a colt, the foal of an ass, he was so meek and lowly, that the young children clustered about him with their boyish "Hosanna!" Never could there be a being more approachable than Christ. No rough guards pushed poor petitioners away; no array of officious friends were allowed to keep off the importunate widow or the man who clamored that his son might be made whole; the hem of his garment was always trailing where sick folk could reach it, and he himself had a hand always ready to touch the disease, an ear to catch the faintest accents of misery, a soul going forth everywhere in rays of mercy, even as the light of the sun streams on every side beyond that orb itself. By being laid in a manger he proved himself a priest taken from among men, one who has suffered like his brethren, and therefore can be touched with a feeling of our infirmities. Of him it was said "He doth eat and drink with publicans and sinners;" "this man receiveth sinners and eateth with them." Even as an infant, by being laid in a manger, he was set forth as the sinner's friend. Come to him, ye that are weary and heavy-laden! Come to him, ye that are broken in spirit, ye who are bowed down in soul! Come to him, ye that despise yourselves and are despised of others! Come to him, publican and harlot! Come to him, thief and drunkard! In the manger there he lies, unguarded from your touch and unshielded from your gaze. Bow the knee, and kiss the Son of God; accept him as your Savior, for he puts himself into that manger that you may approach him. The throne of Solomon might awe you, but the manger of the Son of David must invite you.

4. Methinks there was yet another mystery. You remember, brethren, that this place was *free to all;* it was an inn—and please to remember the inn in this case was not like our hotels, where accommodation and provision must be paid for. In the early and simple ages of the world, every man considered it an honor to entertain a stranger; afterwards, as traveling became more common, many desired to shift the honor and pleasure upon their neighbors; wherefore should they engross all the dignity of hospitality? Further on still, some one person was appointed in each town and village, and was expected to entertain strangers in the name of the rest; but, as the ages grew less simple, and the pristine glow of brotherly love cooled down, the only provision made was the erection of a huge square block, arranged in rooms for the travelers, and with lower stages for the beasts, and here, with a

certain provision of water and in some cases chopped straw for the cattle, the traveler must make himself as comfortable as he could. He had not to purchase admittance to the caravanserai, for it was free to all, and the stable especially so. Now, beloved, our Lord Jesus Christ was born in the stable of the inn to show how free he is to all comers. The Gospel is preached to every creature and shuts out none. We may say of the invitations of Holy Scripture,

> *None are excluded hence but those*
> *Who do themselves exclude;*
> *Welcome the learned and polite,*
> *The ignorant and rude.*

> *Though Jesus' grace can save the prince,*
> *The poor may take their share;*
> *No mortal has a just pretense*
> *To perish in despairs.*

Class exclusions are unknown here, and the prerogatives of caste are not acknowledged. No forms of etiquette are required in entering a stable; it cannot be an offense to enter the stable of a public caravanserai. So, if you desire to come to Christ, you may come to him just as you are; you may come *now*. Whosoever among you hath the desire in his heart to trust Christ is free to do it. Jesus is free to you; he will receive you; he will welcome you with gladness, and to show this, I think, the young child was cradled in a manger. We know that sinners often imagine that they are shut out. Oftentimes the convicted conscience will write bitter things against itself and deny its part and lot in mercy's stores. Brother, if *God* hath not shut thee out, do not shut thyself out. Until thou canst find it written in the Book that thou mayest not trust Christ; till thou canst quote a positive passage in which it is written that he is not able to save thee, I pray thee take that other word wherein it is written—"He is able to save unto the uttermost them that come unto God by him." Venture on that promise; come to Christ in the strength and faith of it, and thou shalt find him free to all comers.

5. We have not yet exhausted the reasons why the Son of Man was laid in a manger. It was at the manger that *the beasts were fed*; and does the Savior lie where weary beasts receive their provender, and shall there not be a mystery here? Alas, there are some men who have become so brutal through sin, so utterly depraved by their lusts, that to their own consciences, everything manlike has departed—but even to such, the remedies of Jesus, the Great Physician, will apply.

We are constantly reading in our papers of men who are called incorrigible, and it is fashionable just now to demand ferociously that these men should be treated with unmingled severity. Some few years ago all the world went mad with a spurious humanity, crying out that gentleness would reform the brutal thief whom harsh punishments would harden hopelessly; now the current has turned, and everybody is demanding the abandonment of the present system. I am no advocate for treating crimi-nals daintily; let their sin bring them a fair share of smart; but if by any means they can be reformed, pray let the means be tried. The day will come when the paroxysm of this gar-roting fever is over, we shall blush to think that we were frightened by silly fears into a dangerous interference with a great and good work which hitherto has been successfully carried on. It is a fact that under the present system, which (abating some faults that it may be well to cure) is an admirable one, crime is growing less frequent, and the class of gross offenders has been materially lessened. Whereas in 1844, 18,490 convicts were transported,[1] in 1860 the corresponding number was 11,533, and that notwithstanding the increase of the population. The ticket-of-leave system, when the public would em-ploy the convicts and so give them a chance of gaining a new character,[2] —worked so well that little more than one percent in a year were re-convicted, and even now only five per cent, per annum are found returning to crime and to prison. Well, now, if the five percent receive no good, or even become worse, ought we not to consider the other ninety-five, and pause awhile before we give loose to our vengeance and exchange a Christian system of hopeful mercy for the old barbarous rule of unmitigated severity. Beware, fellow citizens, beware of restoring the old idea that men can sin beyond hope of reformation, or you will generate criminals worse than those which now trouble us. The laws of Draco must ever be failures, but fear not for the ultimate triumph of plans which a Christian spirit has suggested.

I have wandered from the subject —I thought I might save some from the crime of opposing true philanthropy on account of a sudden panic; but I will return at once to the manger and the babe. I believe our Lord was laid in the manger where the beasts were fed, to show *that even beast-like men may come to him and live.* No creature can be so degraded that Christ cannot lift it up. Fall it may, and seem to fall most certainly to Hell, but the long and strong arm of Christ can reach it even in its most desperate degradation; he can bring it up from apparently hopeless ruin. If there be one who has strolled in here this morning whom society abhors, and who abhors himself, my Master in the stable with the beasts presents himself as able to save the vilest of the vile, and to accept the worst of the worst even now. Be-lieve on him and he will make thee a new creature.

6. But as Christ was laid where beasts were fed, you will please to recollect that after he was gone, *beasts fed there again.* It was only his presence which could glorify the manger, and here we learn that if Christ were taken away, *the world would go back to its former heathen darkness.* Civilization itself would die out, at least that part of it which really civilizes man, if the religion of Jesus could be extinguished. If Christ were taken away from the human heart, the most holy would become de-based again, and those who claim kinship with angels would soon prove that they

---

[1] Transported: shipped overseas to colonies as punishment, just short of hanging.

[2] Character: getting a good work reference.

have relationship to devils. The manger, I say, would be a manger for beasts still, if the Lord of Glory were withdrawn, and we should go back to our sins and our lusts if Christ should once take away his grace and leave us to ourselves. For these reasons which I have mentioned, methinks, Christ was laid in a manger.

II. But still the text says that he was laid in a manger because there was no room for him in the inn, and this leads us to the second remark, *that there were other places besides the inn which had no room for Christ.*

The palaces of emperors and the halls of kings afforded the royal stranger no refuge? Alas! My brethren, seldom is there room for Christ in palaces! How could the kings of earth receive the Lord? He is the Prince of Peace, and they delight in war! He breaks their bows and cuts their spears in sunder; he burneth their war-chariots in the fire. How could kings accept the humble Savior? They love grandeur and pomp, and he is all simplicity and meekness. He is a carpenter's son, and the fisherman's companion. How can princes find room for the new-born monarch? Why, he teaches us to do to others as we would that they should do to us, and this is a thing which kings would find very hard to reconcile with the knavish tricks of politics and the grasping designs of ambition. O great ones of the earth, I am but little astonished that amid your glories, and pleasures, and wars, and councils, ye forget the Anointed, and cast out the Lord of All. There is no room for Christ with the kings. Look throughout the kingdoms of the earth now, and with here and there an exception, it is still true—"The kings of the earth stand up, and the rulers take counsel together, against the Lord and against his Anointed." In Heaven we shall see here and there a monarch; but ah! how few; indeed a child might write them.

"Not many great men after the flesh, not many mighty are chosen." State-chambers, cabinets, throne-rooms, and royal palaces, are about as little frequented by Christ as the jungles and swamps of India by the cautious traveler. He frequents cottages far more often than regal residences, for there is no room for Jesus Christ in regal halls.

> When the Eternal bows the skies
> To visit earthly things,
> With scorn divine he turns his eyes
> From towers of haughty kings.
>
> He bids his awful chariot roll
> Far downward from the skies,
> To visit every humble soul
> With pleasure in his eyes.

But there were *senators, there were forums of political discussion, there were the places where the representatives of the people make the laws*—was there no room for Christ there? Alas! My brethren, none, and to this day there is very little room for

Christ in parliaments. How seldom is religion recognized by politicians! Of course a state-religion, if it will consent to be a poor, tame, powerless thing, a lion with its teeth all drawn, its mane all shaven off, and its claws all trimmed—yes, that may be recognized; but the true Christ and they that follow him and dare to obey his laws in an evil generation, what room is there for such? Christ and his gospel—Oh! This is sectarianism, and is scarcely worthy of the notice of contempt. Who pleads for Jesus in the senate? Is not his religion, under the name of sectarianism, the great terror of all parties? Who quotes his golden rule as a direction for prime ministers, or preaches Christ-like forgiveness as a rule for national policy? One or two will give him a good word, but if it be put to the vote whether the Lord Jesus should be obeyed or no, it will be many a day before the *ayes* have it. Parties, policies, place-hunters, and pleasure-seekers exclude the Representative of Heaven from a place among representatives of Earth.

Might there not be found some room for Christ *in what is called good society*? Were there not in Bethlehem some people that were very respectable, who kept themselves aloof from the common multitude; persons of reputation and standing—could not they find room for Christ? Ah! Dear friends, it is too much the case that there is no room for him in what is called good society. There is room for all the silly little forms by which men choose to trammel themselves; room for the vain niceties of etiquette; room for frivolous conversation; room for the adoration of the body, there is room for the setting up of this and that as the idol of the hour, but there is too little room for Christ, and it is far from fashionable to follow the Lord fully. The advent of Christ would be the last thing which gay society would desire; the very mention of his name by the lips of love would cause a strange sensation. Should you begin to talk about the things of Christ in many a circle, you would be tabooed at once. "I will never ask that man to my house again," so-and-so would say—"if he must bring his religion with him." Folly and finery, rank and honor, jewels and glitter, frivolity and fashion, all report that there is no room for Jesus in their abodes.

But is there not room for him *on the Exchange*? Cannot he be taken to the marts of commerce? Here are the shop-keepers of a shop-keeping nation—is there not room for Christ here? Ah! Dear friends, how little of the spirit, and life, and doctrine of Christ can be found here! The trader finds it inconvenient to be too scrupulous; the merchant often discovers that if he is to make a fortune he must break his conscience. How many there are—well, I will not say they tell lies directly, but still, still, still—I had better say it plainly—they do lie indirectly with a vengeance. Who does not know as he rides along that there must be many liars abroad? For almost every house you see is "The cheapest house in London," which can hardly be; full sure they cannot all be cheapest! What sharp practice some indulge in! What puffery and falsehood! What cunning and sleight of hand! What woes would my Master pronounce on some of you if he looked into your shop windows, or stood behind your counters. Bankruptcies, swindlings, and frauds are so abundant that in hosts of cases there is no room for Jesus in the mart or the shop.

Then there are *the schools of the philosophers*—surely they will entertain him. The wise men will find in him incarnate wisdom; he, who as a youth is to become the teacher of doctors, who will sit down and ask them questions and receive their answers, surely he will find room at once among the Grecian sages, and men of sense and wit will honor him.

> Room for him, Socrates and Plato! Stoics and Epicurians, give ye way; and you, ye teachers of Israel, vacate your seats; if there is no room for this child without your going, go; we must have him in the schools of philosophy if we put you all forth.

No, dear friends, but it is not so; there is very little room for Christ in colleges and universities, very little room for him in the seats of learning. How often learning helps men to raise objections to Christ! Too often learning is the forge where the nails are made for Christ's crucifixion; too often human wit has become the artificer who has pointed the spear and made the shaft with which his heart should be pierced. We must say it, that philosophy, falsely so called—for true philosophy, if it were handled aright, must ever be Christ's friend—philosophy, falsely so called, hath done mischief to Christ, but seldom hath it served his cause. A few with splendid talents, a few of the erudite and profound have bowed like children at the feet of the Babe of Bethlehem, and have been honored in bowing there, but too many, conscious of their knowledge, stiff and stern in their conceit of wisdom, have said—"Who is Christ, that we should acknowledge him?" They found no room for him in the schools.

But there was surely one place where he could go—it was *the Sanhedrim*, where the elders sit. Or could he not be housed in the priestly chamber where the priests assemble with the Levites? Was there not room for him in the temple or the synagogue? No, he found no shelter there; it was there, his whole life long, that he found his most ferocious enemies. Not the common multitude, but the priests, were the instigators of his death, the priests moved the people to say "Not this man, but Barabbas." The priests paid out their shekels to bribe the popular voice, and then Christ was hounded to his death. Surely there ought to have been room for him in the Church of his own people; but there was not. Too often in the priestly church, when once it becomes recognized and mounts to dignity, there is no room for Christ. I allude not now to any one denomination, but take the whole sweep of Christendom, and it is strange that when the Lord comes to his own, his own receives him not. The most accursed enemies of true religion have been the men who pretended to be its advocates. It is little marvel when bishops undermine the popular faith in revelation; this is neither their first nor last offense. Who burned the martyrs, and made Smithfield a field of blood, a burning fiery furnace, a great altar for the Most High God? Why, those who professed to be anointed of the Lord, whose shaven crowns had received episcopal benediction. Who put John Bunyan in prison? Who chased such men as Owen and the Puritans from their pulpits? Who harried the Covenanters upon the mountains? Who, sirs, but the professed messengers of Heaven and priests of God? Who have hunted the baptized saints in every land, and hunt them still in many a Continental state? The priests ever; the priests ever; there is no room for Christ with the prophets of Baal, the servants of Babylon. The false hirelings that are not Christ's shepherds, and love not his sheep, have ever been the most ferocious enemies of our God and of his Christ. There is no room for him where his name is chanted in solemn hymns and his image lifted up amid smoke of incense. Go where ye will, and there is no space for the Prince of peace but with the humble and contrite spirits, which by grace he prepares to yield him shelter.

III. But now for our third remark, *the inn itself had no room for him; and this was the main reason why he must be laid in a manger.*

What can we find in modern times which stands in the place of the inn? Well, there is *public sentiment free to all.* In this free land, men speak of what they like, and there is a public opinion upon every subject; and you know there is free toleration in this country to everything—permit me to say, toleration to everything but Christ. You will discover that the persecuting-spirit is now as much abroad as ever. There are still men at whom it is most fashionable to sneer. We never scoff at Christians now-a-days; we do not sneer at that respectable title, lest we should lose our own honor; we do not now-a-days, talk against the followers of Jesus under that name. No; but we have found out a way of doing it more safely. There is a pretty word of modern invention—a very pretty word—the word *"Sectarian."* Do you know what it means? A sectarian means a true Christian; a man who can afford to keep a conscience, and does not mind suffering for it; a man who, whatever he finds to be in that old Book, believes it, and acts upon it, and is zealous for it.

I believe that the men aimed at under the term, "sectarians," are the true followers of Christ, and that the sneers and jeers, and all the nonsense that you are always reading and hearing, is really aimed at the Christian, the true Christian, only he is disguised and nicknamed by the word sectarian. I would give not a farthing for your religion, nay, not even the turn of a rusty nail, unless you will sometimes win that title. If God's Word be true, every atom of it, then we should act upon it; and whatsoever the Lord commandeth, we should diligently keep and obey, remembering that our Master tells us if we break one of the least of his commandments, and teach men so, we shall be least in his kingdom. We ought to be very jealous, very precise, very anxious, that even in the minutiae of our Savior's laws, we may obey, having our eyes up to him as the eyes of servants are to their mistresses. But if you do this, you will find you are not tolerated, and you will get the cold shoulder in society. A zealous Christian will find as truly a cross to carry now-a-days, as in the days of Simon the Cyrenian. If you will hold your tongue, if you will leave sinners to perish, if you will never endeavor to propagate your faith, if you will silence all witnessing for truth, if, in fact, you will renounce all the attributes of a Christian, if you will cease to be what a Christian must be, then the world will say, "Ah! That is right; this is the religion we like." But if you will believe, believe firmly, and if you let your belief actuate your life, and if your belief is so precious that you feel compelled to spread it, then at once you will find that there is no room for Christ even in the inn of public sentiment, where everything else is received. Be an infidel, and none will therefore treat you contemptuously; but be a Christian, and many will despise you. "There was no room for him in the inn."

How little room is there for Christ, too, *in general conversation*, which is also like an inn. We talk about many things; a man may now-a-days talk of any subject he pleases; no one can stop him and say, "There is a spy catching your words; he will report you to some central authority." Speech is very free in this land; but, ah! how little room is there for Christ in general talk! Even on Sunday afternoon how little room there is for Christ in some professed Christian's houses. They will talk about ministers, tell queer anecdotes about them—perhaps invent a few, or, at least, garnish the old ones, and add to them, and make them a little more brilliant; they will talk about the Sunday school, or the various agencies in connection with the Church, but how little they say about Christ! And if someone should in conversation make this remark, "Could we not speak upon the Godhead and manhood, the finished work and righteousness, the ascension, or the second advent of our Lord Jesus Christ," why we should see many, who even profess to be followers of Christ, who would hold up their heads and say, "Why, dear, that man is quite a fanatic, or else he would not think of introducing such a subject as that into general conversation." No, there is no room for him in the inn; to this day he can find but little access there.

I address many who are working-men. You are employed among a great many artisans day after day; do you not find, brethren—I know you do—that there is very little room for Christ *in the workshop*. There is room there for everything else; there is room for swearing; there is room for drunkenness; there is room for lewd conversation; there is room for politics, slanders, or infidelities, but there is no room for Christ. Too many of our working men think religion would be an encumbrance, a chain, a miserable prison to them. They can frequent the theater, or listen in a lecture-hall, but the house of God is too dreary for them. I wish I were not compelled to say so, but truly in our factories, workshops, and foundries, there is no room for Christ. The world is elbowing and pushing for more room, till there is scarce a corner left where the Babe of Bethlehem can be laid.

As for the inns of modern times—who would think of finding Christ there? Putting out of our catalogue those hotels and roadside houses which are needed for the accommodation of travelers, what greater curse have we than our taverns and pothouses? What wider gates of Hell? Who would ever resort to such places as we have flaring with gas light at the corners of all our streets to find Christ there? As well might we expect to find him in the bottomless pit! We should be just as likely to look for angels in Hell, as to look for Christ in a gin palace! He who is separate from sinners, finds no fit society in the reeking temple of Bacchus. There is no room for Jesus in the inn. I think I would rather rot or feed the crows, than earn my daily bread by the pence of fools, the hard-earnings of the poor man, stolen from his ragged children, and his emaciated wife. What do many publicans fatten upon but the flesh, and bones, and blood, and souls of men. He who grows rich on the fruits of vice is a beast preparing for the slaughter. Truly, there is no room for Christ among the drunkards of Ephraim. They who have anything to do with Christ should hear him say,

> Come ye out from among them, and be ye separate; touch not the unclean thing, and I will receive you, and be a father unto you, and ye shall be my sons and daughters.

There is no room for Christ now-a-days even in the places of public resort.

IV. This brings me to my fourth head, which is the most pertinent, and the most necessary to dwell upon for a moment. *Have you room for Christ? Have you room for Christ?*

As the palace, and the forum, and the inn, have no room for Christ, and as the places of public resort have none, have *you* room for Christ?

"Well," says one, "I have room for him, but I am not worthy that he should come to me." Ah! I did not ask about worthiness; have you room for him? "Oh," says one, "I have an empty void the world can never fill!" Ah! I see you have room for him. "Oh! But the room I have in my heart is so base!" So was the manger. "But it is so despicable!" So was the manger a thing to be despised. "Ah! But my heart is so foul!" So, perhaps, the manger may have been. "Oh! But I feel it is a place not at all fit for Christ!" Nor was the manger a place fit for him, and yet there was he laid." "Oh! But I have been such a sinner; I feel as if my heart had been a den of beasts and devils!" Well, the manger had been a place where beasts had fed. Have you room for him? Never mind what the past has been; he can forget and forgive. It mattereth not what even the present state may be, if thou mournest it. If thou hast but room for Christ he will come and be thy guest. Do not say, I pray you, "I hope *I shall have* room for him;" the time *is come* that he shall be born; Mary cannot wait months and years. Oh! Sinner, if thou hast room for him, let him be born in thy soul today. "Today if ye will hear his voice, harden not your hearts as in the provocation." "Today is the accepted time; today is the day of salvation." Room for Jesus! Room for Jesus now! "Oh!" saith one, "I have room for him, but will he come?" Will he come indeed! Do you but set the door of your heart open, do but say, "Jesus, Master, all unworthy and unclean I look to thee; come, lodge within my heart," and he will come to thee, and he will cleanse the manger of thy heart, nay, will transform it into a golden throne, and there he will sit and reign forever and forever. Oh! I have such a free Christ to preach this morning! I would I could preach him better. I have such a precious loving, Jesus to preach, he is willing to find a home in humble hearts. What! Are there no hearts here this morning that will take him in? Must my eye glance round these galleries and look at many of you who are still without him, and are there none who will say, "Come in, come in?" Oh! It shall be a happy day for you if you shall be enabled to take him in your arms and receive him as the consolation of Israel! You may then look forward even to death with joy, and say with Simeon—"Lord, now lettest thou thy servant depart in peace, according to thy word, for mine eyes have seen thy salvation." My Master wants room! Room for him! Room for him! I, his herald, cry aloud,

> Room for the Savior! Room! Here is my royal Master—have you room for him? Here is the Son of God made flesh—have you room for him? Here is he who can forgive all sin—have you room for him? Here is he who can take you up out of the horrible pit and out of the miry clay—have you room for him? Here is he who when he cometh in will never go out again, but abide with you forever to make your heart a Heaven of joy and bliss for you—have you room for him?

'Tis all I ask. Your emptiness, your nothingness, your want of feeling, your want of goodness, your want of grace—all these will be but room for him. Have you room for him? Oh! Spirit of God, lead many to say, "Yes, my heart is ready." Ah! Then he will come and dwell with you.

> *Joy to the world, the Savior comes,*
> *The Savior promised long;*
> *Let every heart prepare a throne*
> *And every voice a song.*

V. I conclude with the remark, that if you have room for Christ, then from this day forth remember, *the world has no room for you.*

For the text says not only that there was no room for him, but look—"There was no room *for them*"—no room for Joseph, nor for Mary, any more than for the babe.

Who are his father, and mother, and sister, and brother, but those that receive his word and keep it? So, as there was no room for the blessed Virgin, nor for the reputed father, remember henceforth there is no room in this world for any true follower of Christ. There is no room for you to take your *ease*; no, you are to be a soldier of the cross, and you will find no ease in all your life-warfare. There is no room for you to sit down *contented with your own attainments*, for you are a traveler, and you are to forget the things that are behind, and press forward to that which is before; no room for you *to hide your treasure* in, for here the moth and rust doth corrupt; no room for you *to put your confidence*, for "Cursed is he that trusteth in man, and maketh flesh his arm." From this day there will be no room for you *in the world's good opinion*—they will count you to be an offscouring; no room for you in the world's *polite society*—you must go without [outside] the camp, bearing his reproach. From this time forth, I say, if you have room for Christ, the world will hardly find room of sufferance for you; you must expect now to be laughed at; now you must wear the fool's cap in men's esteem; and your song must be at the very beginning of your pilgrimage.

> *Jesus, I thy cross have taken,*
> *All to leave and follow thee;*
>
> *Naked, poor, despised, forsaken,*
> *Thou from hence my all shall be.*

There is no room for you in the worldling's love. If you expect that everybody will praise you, and that your good actions will all be applauded, you will quite be mistaken. The world, I say, has no room for the man who has room for Christ. If any man love the world, the love of the Father is not in him. "Woe unto you when all men speak well of you." "Ye are not of the world, even as Christ is not of the world." Thank God, you need not ask the world's hospitality. If it will give you but a stage for action, and lend you for an hour a grave to sleep in, 'tis all you need; you will require no permanent dwelling place here, since you seek a city that is to come, which hath foundations; whose builder and maker is God. You are hurrying through this world as a stranger through a foreign land, and you rejoice to know that though you are an alien and a foreigner here, yet you are a fellow citizen with the saints, and of the household to God. What say you, young soldier, will you enlist on such terms as these? Will you give room for Christ when there is to be henceforth no room for you—when you are to be separated forever, cut off from among the world's kith and kin mayhap—cut off from carnal confidence forever? Are you willing, notwithstanding all this, to receive the traveler in? The Lord help you to do so, and to him shall be glory forever and ever. Amen.

Holy Work for Christmas

Delivered on Sunday morning, December 24, 1863, at the Metropolitan Tabernacle, Newington. No. 666.[1]

And when they had seen it, they made known abroad the saying which was told them concerning this child. And all they that heard it wondered at those things which were told them by the shepherds. But Mary kept all these things, and pondered them in her heart. And the shepherds returned, glorifying and praising God for all the things that they had heard and seen, as it was told unto them.—Luke 2:17–20

Every season has its own proper fruit: apples for autumn, holly berries for Christmas. The earth brings forth according to the period of the year, and with man there is a time for every purpose under Heaven. At this season, the world is engaged in congratulating itself and in expressing its complimentary wishes for the good of its citizens; let me suggest extra and more solid work for Christians. As we think today of the birth of the Savior, let us aspire after a fresh birth of the Savior in our hearts; that as he is already "formed in us the hope of glory," we may be "renewed in the spirit of our minds;" that we may go again to the Bethlehem of our spiritual nativity and do our first works, enjoy our first loves, and feast with Jesus as we did in the holy, happy, heavenly days of our espousals. Let us go to Jesus with something of that youthful freshness and excessive delight which was so manifest in us when we looked to him at the first; let him be crowned anew by us, for he is still adorned with the dew of his youth, and remains "the same

---

[1] Spurgeon preached a brief, summary version of this sermon at the end of the "TheGreat Birthday," page 83 of this volume, which was preached on Christmas Eve 1876, 13 years later.

yesterday, today, and forever." The citizens of Durham, though they dwell not far from the Scotch border, and consequently in the olden times were frequently liable to be attacked, were exempted from the toils of war because there was a cathedral within their walls, and they were set aside to the bishop's service, being called in the olden times by the name of "holy work-folk." Now, we citizens of the New Jerusalem, having the Lord Jesus in our midst, may well excuse ourselves from the ordinary ways of celebrating this season; and considering ourselves to be "holy work-folk," we may keep it after a different sort from other men, in holy contemplation and in blessed service of that gracious God, whose unspeakable gift the newborn King is to us.

I selected this text this morning because it seemed to indicate to me four ways of serving God, four methods of executing holy work and exercising Christian thought. Each of the verses sets before us a different way of sacred service. Some, it appears, published abroad the news, told to others what they had seen and heard; some wondered with a holy marveling and astonishment; one, at least, according to the third of the verses, pondered, meditated, thought upon these things; and others, in the fourth place, glorified God and gave him praise. I know not which of these four did God best service, but I think if we could combine all these mental emotions and outward exercises, we should be sure to praise God after a most godly and acceptable fashion.

I. To begin then, in the first place, we find that some celebrated the Savior's birth by *publishing abroad* what they had heard and seen; and truly we may say of them *that they had something* to rehearse in men's ears well worth the telling.

That for which prophets and kings had waited long, had at last arrived, and arrived to them. They had found out the answer to the perpetual riddle. They might have run through the streets with the ancient philosopher, crying, "Eureka! Eureka!" for their discovery was far superior to his. They had found out no solution to a mechanical problem or metaphysical dilemma, but their discovery was second to none ever made by men in real value, since it has been like the leaves of the tree of life to heal the nations, and a river of water of life to make glad the city of God. They had seen angels; they had heard them sing a song all strange and new. They had seen more than angels—they had beheld the angel's King, the Angel of the Covenant whom we delight in. They had heard the music of Heaven, and when near that manger, the ear of their faith had heard the music of earth's hope, a mystic harmony which should ring all down the ages—the grave sweet melody of hearts attuned to praise the Lord, and the glorious swell of the holy joy of God and man rejoicing in glad accord. They had seen God incarnate—such a sight that he who gazeth on it must feel his tongue unloosed, unless indeed an unspeakable astonishment should make him dumb. Be silent when their eyes had seen such a vision? Impossible! To the first person they met outside that lowly stable door they began to tell their matchless tale, and they wearied not till nightfall, crying, "Come and worship! Come and worship Christ, the new-born King!" As for us, beloved, have we also not something to relate which demands utterance? If we talk of Jesus, who can blame us? This, indeed, might make the tongue of him that sleeps to move—the mystery of God incarnate for our sake, bleeding and dying that we might neither bleed nor die, descending that we might ascend, and wrapped in swaddling bands that we might be unwrapped of the grave-clothes of corruption. Here is such a story, so profitable to all hearers that he who repeats it the most often does best, and he who speaks the least hath most reason to accuse himself for sinful silence.

They had something to tell, *and that something had in it the inimitable blending which is the secret sign and royal mark of Divine authorship; a peerless marrying of sublimity and simplicity;* angels singing!—Singing to shepherds! Heaven bright with glory! Bright at midnight! God! A Babe!! The Infinite! An Infant of a span long!! The Ancient of Days! Born of a woman!! What more simple than the inn, the manger, a carpenter, a carpenter's wife, a child? What more sublime than a "multitude of the heavenly host" waking the midnight with their joyous chorales, and God himself in human flesh made manifest? A child is but an ordinary sight; but what a marvel to see that Word which was,

> in the beginning with God, tabernacling among us that we might behold his glory—the glory as of the only begotten of the Father, full of grace and truth?

Brethren, we have a tale to tell, as simple as sublime. What simpler?—"Believe and live." What more sublime?—"God was in Christ reconciling the world unto himself!" A system of salvation so wonderful that angelic minds cannot but adore as they meditate upon it; and yet so simple that the children in the temple may fitly hymn its virtues as they sing. "Hosanna! Blessed is he that cometh in the name of the Lord." What a splendid combining of the sublime and the simple have we in the great atonement offered by the incarnate Savior! Oh make known to all men this saving truth!

The shepherds need no excuse for making everywhere the announcement of the Savior's birth, *for what they told, they first received from Heaven.* Their news was not muttered in their ears by Sybilline oracles,[2] not brought to light by philosophic search, not conceived in poetry nor found as treasure trove among the volumes of the ancient; but it was revealed to them by that notable gospel preacher who led the angelic host, and testified, "Unto you is born this day, in the city of David, a Savior, which is Christ the Lord." When Heaven entrusts a man with a merciful revelation, he is bound to deliver the good tidings to others. What, keep that a

---

[2] Sibylline Oracles: certain collections of supposed prophecies, emanating from the sibyls or divinely inspired seeresses, which were widely circulated in antiquity. (Catholic Encyclopedia)

secret whose utterance eternal mercy makes to charm the midnight air? To what purpose were angels sent, if the message were not to be spread abroad? According to the teaching of our own beloved Lord, we must not be silent, for he bids us "What ye hear in secret, that reveal ye in public; and what I tell you in the ear in closets, that proclaim ye upon the house-tops." Beloved, you have heard a voice from Heaven—you twice-born men, begotten again unto a lively hope, you have heard the Spirit of God bearing witness of God's truth with you, and teaching you of heavenly things. You then must keep this Christmas by telling to your fellow-men what God's own Holy Spirit has seen fit to reveal to you.

But though the shepherds told what they heard from Heaven, remember that *they spoke of what they had seen below.* They had, by observation, made those truths most surely their own which had first been spoken to them by revelation. No man can speak of the things of God with any success until the doctrine which he finds in the book, he finds also in his heart. We must bring down the mystery and make it plain, by knowing, by the teaching of the Holy Ghost, its practical power on the heart and conscience. My brethren, the gospel which we preach is most surely revealed to us by the Lord; but, moreover, our hearts have tried and proved, have grasped, have felt, have realized its truth and power. If we have not been able to understand its heights and depths, yet we have felt its mystic power upon our heart and spirit. It has revealed sin to us better; it has revealed to us our pardon. It has killed the reigning power of sin, it has given us Christ to reign over us, the Holy Spirit to dwell within our bodies as in a temple. Now we *must speak.* I do not urge any of you to speak of Jesus who merely know the Word as you find it in the Bible—your teaching can have but little power; but I do speak earnestly to you who know its mighty influence upon the heart, who have not only heard of the babe but have seen him in the manger, taken him up in your own arms and received him as being born to you, a Savior to you, *Christos,* the anointed for you, Jesus, the Savior from sin for you. Beloved, can you do otherwise than speak of the things which you have seen and heard? God has made you to taste and to handle of this good word of life, and you must not, you dare not hold your peace, but you *must* tell to friends and neighbors what you have felt within.

These were shepherds, *unlettered men.* I will warrant you they could not read in a book; there is no probability that they even knew a single letter. They were shepherds, but they preached right well; and, my brethren, whatever some may think, preaching is not to be confined to those learned gentlemen who have taken their degrees at Oxford or at Cambridge, or at any college or university. It is true that learning need not be an impediment to grace, and may be a fitting weapon in a gracious hand, but often the grace of God has glorified itself by the plain clear way in which unlettered men have understood the gospel and have proclaimed it. I would not mind asking the whole world to find a master of arts now living who has brought more souls to Christ Jesus than Richard Weaver.[3] If the whole bench of bishops have done a tenth as much in the way of soul-winning as that one man, it is more than most of us give them credit for. Let us give to our God all the glory, but still let us not deny the fact that this sinner saved, with the brogue of the collier still about him, fresh from the coal pit, tells the story of the cross by God's grace in such a way that right reverend fathers in God might humbly sit at his feet to learn the way to reach the heart and melt the stubborn soul. It is true an uneducated brother is not fitted for all work—he has his own sphere—but he is quite able to tell of what he has seen and heard, and so it strikes me is every man in a measure. If you have seen Jesus and heard his saving voice, if you have received truth as from the Lord, felt its tremendous power as coming from God to you, and if you have experienced its might upon your own spirit, why you can surely tell out what God has written within. If you cannot get beyond that into the deeper mysteries, into the more knotty points, well, well, there are some who can, and so you need not be uneasy; but you can at least reveal the first and foundation truths, and they are by far the most important. If you cannot speak in the pulpit, if as yet your cheek would mantle with a blush, and your tongue would refuse to do her office in the presence of many, there are your children, you are not ashamed to speak before them; there is the little cluster round the hearth on Christmas night, there is the little congregation in the workshop, there is a little audience somewhere to whom you might tell out of Jesu's love to lost ones. Do not get beyond what you know; do not plunge into what you have not experienced, for if you do you will be out of your depth, and then very soon you will be floundering and making confusion worse confounded. Go as far as you know; and since you do know yourself a sinner and Jesus a Savior, and a great one too, talk about those two matters, and good will come of it. Beloved, each one in his own position, tell what you have heard and seen; publish that abroad among the sons of men.

But *were they authorized?* It is a great thing to be authorized! Unauthorized ministers are most shameful intruders! Unordained men entering the pulpit, who are not in the apostolical succession—very horrible! Very horrible indeed! The Puseyite mind utterly fails to fathom the depth of horror which is contained in the idea of an unauthorized man preaching, and a man out of the apostolical succession daring to teach the way of salvation. To me this horror seems very like a schoolboy's fright at a hobgoblin which his fears had conjured up. I think if I saw a man slip through the ice into a cold grave, and I could rescue him from drowning, it would not be so very horrible to me to be the means of saving him, though I may not be employed by the Royal Humane Society. I imagine if I saw a fire, and heard a poor woman scream at an upper window, and likely to be burned alive, if I should wheel the fire-escape up to the window, and preserve her life, it would not

---

[3] Richard Weaver: former coal miner and semi-pro boxer turned Methodist evangelist.

be so very dreadful a matter, though I might not belong to the regular Fire Brigade. If a company of brave volunteers should chase an enemy out of their own county, I do not know that it would be anything so shocking, although a whole army of mercenaries might be neglecting their work in obedience to some venerable military rubric which rendered them incapable of effective service. But mark you, the shepherds and others like them are in the apostolical succession, and they are authorized by divine ordinance, for every man who hears the gospel is authorized to tell it to others. Do you want authority? Here it is in confirmation strong from Holy Writ: "Let him that heareth say, Come"—that is, let every man who truly hears the gospel bid others come to drink of the water of life. This is all the warrant you require for preaching the gospel according to your ability. It is not every man who has ability to preach the Word; and it is not every man that we should like to hear preach it in the great congregation, for if all were mouth, what a great vacuum the church would be; yet every Christian in some method should deliver the glad tidings. Our wise God takes care that liberty of prophesying shall not run to riot, for he does not give efficient pastoral and ministerial gifts to very many; yet every man according to his gifts, let him minister. Everyone of you, though not in the pulpit, yet in the pew, in the workshop, somewhere, anywhere, everywhere, do make known the savor of the Lord Jesus. Be this your authority: "Let him that heareth say, Come." I never thought of asking any authority for crying "Fire," when I saw a house burning; I never dreamed of seeking any authority for doing my best to rescue a poor perishing fellow-man, nor do I mean to seek it now! All the authority you want, any of you, is not the authority which can stream from prelates decorated with lawn sleeves, but the authority which comes direct from the great Head of the Church, who gives authority to everyone of those who hear the gospel, to teach every man his fellow, saying, "Know the Lord."

Here, dear brethren, is one way for you to keep a right holy, and in some sense a right merry, Christmas. Imitate these humble men, of whom it is said, "When they had seen it they made known abroad the saying which was told them concerning the child."

II. We set before you, now, another mode of keeping Christmas, by *holy wonder, admiration, and adoration.*

"And all they that heard it wondered at those things which were told them by the shepherds." We shall have little to say of those persons who merely wondered, and did nothing more. Many are set a wondering by the Gospel. They are content to hear it, pleased to hear it; if not in itself something new, yet there are new ways of putting it, and they are glad to be refreshed with the variety. The preacher's voice is unto them as the sound of one that giveth a goodly tune upon an instrument. They are glad to listen. They are not skeptics, they do not cavil, they raise no difficulties; they just say to themselves, "It is an excellent gospel, it is a wonderful plan of salvation. Here is most astonishing love, most extraordinary condescension." Sometimes they marvel that these things should be told them by shepherds; they can hardly understand how unlearned and ignorant men should speak of these things, and how such things should ever get into these shepherds' heads, where they can have learned them, how it is that they seem so earnest about them, what kind of operation they must have passed through to be able to speak as they do. But after holding up their hands and opening their mouths for about nine days, the wonder subsides, and they go their way and think no more about it. There are many of you who are set a-wondering whenever you see a work of God in your district. You hear of somebody converted who was a very extraordinary sinner, and you say, "It is very wonderful!" There is a revival; you happen to be present at one of the meetings when the Spirit of God is working gloriously: you say, "Well, this is a singular thing! very astonishing!" Even the newspapers can afford a corner at times for very great and extraordinary works of God the Holy Spirit; but there all emotion ends; it is all wondering, and nothing more. Now, I trust it will not be so with any of us; that we shall not think of the Savior and of the doctrines of the gospel which he came to preach simply with amazement and astonishment, for this will work us but little good.

On the other hand, there is another mode of wondering which is akin to adoration, if it be not adoration. I think it would be very difficult to draw a line between holy wonder and real worship, for when the soul is overwhelmed with the majesty of God's glory, though it may not express itself in song, or even utter its voice with bowed head in humble prayer, yet it silently adores. I am inclined to think that the astonishment which sometimes seizes upon the human intellect at the remembrance of God's greatness and goodness is, perhaps, the purest form of adoration which ever rises from mortal men to the throne of the Most High. This kind of wonder I recommend to those of you who, from the quietness and solitariness of your lives, are scarcely able to imitate the shepherds in telling out the tale to others: you can at least fill up the circle of the worshippers before the throne by wondering at what God has done.

Let me suggest to you that holy wonder at what God has done should be very natural to you. That God should consider his fallen creature, man, and instead of sweeping him away with the besom [twig broom] of destruction, should devise a wonderful scheme for his redemption, and that he should himself undertake to be man's Redeemer, and to pay his ransom price, is, indeed, marvelous! Probably it is most marvelous to you in its relation to yourself, that you should be redeemed by blood; that God should forsake the thrones and royalties above to suffer ignominiously below for you. If you know yourself, you can never see any adequate motive or reason in your own flesh for such a deed as this. "Why such love to me?" you will say. If David, sitting in his house, could only say, "Who am I, O Lord God, and what is mine house, that thou hast brought me hitherto?" what should you and I say? Had we been the most meritorious of individuals, and had unceasingly kept the Lord's commands, we could not have deserved such a priceless boon as incarnation; but [as] sinners, offenders, who revolted and went from God, further and further, what shall we say of this incarnate God dying for us, but "Herein is love, not that we loved God but that God loved us." Let your soul lose itself in wonder, for wonder, dear friends, is in this way a very practical emotion. Holy wonder will lead you to grateful worship; being astonished at what God has done, you will pour out your soul with astonishment at the foot of the golden throne with the song,

> Blessing, and honor, and glory, and majesty, and power, and dominion, and might be unto Him who sitteth on the throne and doeth these great things to me.

Filled with this wonder it will cause you a godly watchfulness; you will be afraid to sin against such love as this. Feeling the presence of the mighty God in the gift of his dear Son, you will put off your shoes from off your feet, because the place whereon you stand is holy ground. You will be moved at the same time to a glorious hope. If Jesus has given himself to you, if he has done this marvelous thing on your behalf, you will feel that Heaven itself is not too great for your expectation, and that the rivers of pleasure at God's right hand are not too sweet or too deep for you to drink thereof. Who can be astonished at anything when he has once been astonished at the manger and the cross? What is there wonderful left, after one has seen the Savior? The nine wonders of the world! Why, you may put them all into a nutshell—machinery and modern art can excel them all; but this one wonder is not the wonder of earth only, but of Heaven and earth, and even Hell itself. It is not the wonder of the olden time, but the wonder of all time and the wonder of eternity. They who see human wonders a few times, at last cease to be astonished; the noblest pile that architect ever raised, at last fails to impress the onlooker; but not so this marvellous temple of incarnate Deity; the more we look the more we are astonished, the more we become accustomed to it, the more have we a sense of its surpassing splendor of love and grace. There is more of God, let us say, to be seen in the manger and the cross, than in the sparkling stars above, the rolling deep below, the towering mountain, the teeming valleys, the abodes of life, or the abyss of death. Let us then spend some choice hours of this festive season in holy wonder, such as will produce gratitude, worship, love, and confidence.

III. A third manner of holy work, namely, *her sacred heart pondering and preserving,* you will find in the next verse.

One at least, and let us hope there were others, or at any rate, let us ourselves be others—one kept all these things and pondered them in her heart. She wondered: she did more—she pondered. You will observe there was an exercise on the part of this blessed woman of the three great parts of her being; her memory—she kept all these things; her affections—she kept them in her heart; her intellect—she pondered them, considered them, weighed them, turned them over; so that memory, affection, and understanding, were all exercised about these things. We delight to see this in Mary, but we are not at all surprised when we recollect that she was in some sense the most concerned of all on earth, for it was of her that Jesus Christ had been born. Those who come nearest to Jesus and enter the most closely into fellowship with him, will be sure to be the most engrossed with him. Certain persons are best esteemed at a distance, but not the Savior; when you shall have known him to the very full, then shall you love him with the love which passeth knowledge; you shall comprehend the heights, and depths, and lengths, and breadths of his love; and when you shall do so, then your own love shall swell beyond all length and breadth, all height and depth. The birth most concerned Mary, and therefore she was the most impressed with it. Note the way in which her concern was shown; she was a woman, and the grace which shines best in the female is not boldness—that belongs to the masculine mind; but affectionate modesty is a feminine beauty, and hence we do not read so much of her telling abroad as pondering within. No doubt she had her circle, and her word to speak in it; but for the most part she, like another Mary, sat still in the house. She worked, but her work was most directly for him, her heart's joy and delight. Like other children, the holy child needed care, which only a mother's hand and heart could exercise; she was therefore engrossed with him. O blessed engrossment! Sweet engagement!

Count not that to be unacceptable service which occupies itself rather with Jesus than with his disciples or his wandering sheep. That woman who broke the alabaster box and poured the ointment upon our Jesus himself was blamed by Judas, and even the rest of the disciples thought that the poor had lost a benefit, but "she hath wrought a good work on me" was the Savior's answer. I desire to bring you to this thought, that if during this season you retiring quiet ones cannot speak to others, or have no desirable opportunity or suitable gift for that work, you may sit still with Jesus and honor him in peace. Mary took the Lord in her arms; oh that you may bear him in yours! She executed works for his person directly; do you imitate her. You can love him, bless him, praise him, study him, ponder him, comprehend his character, study the types that set him forth, and imitate his life; and in this way, though your worship will not blaze forth among the sons of men, and scarcely benefit them as some other forms of work, yet it will both benefit you and be acceptable to your Lord. Beloved, remember what you have heard of Christ, and what he has done for you; make your heart the golden cup to hold the rich recollections of his past loving-kindness; make it a pot of manna to preserve the heavenly bread whereon saints have fed in days gone by. Let your memory treasure up everything about Christ which you have either heard, or felt, or known, and then let your fond affections hold him fast evermore. Love him! Pour out that alabaster box of your heart, and let all the precious ointment of your affection come streaming on his feet. If you cannot do it with joy, do it sorrowfully: wash his feet with tears, wipe them with the hairs of your head; but do love him, love the blessed Son of God, your ever tender Friend. Let your intellect be exercised concerning the Lord Jesus. Turn over and over by meditation what you read. Do not be lettermen—do not stop at the surface; dive into the depths. Be not as the swallow, which toucheth the brook with her wing, but as the fish which penetrates the lowest wave. Drink deep draughts of love; do not sip and away, but dwell at the well as Isaac did at the well Lahai-roi. [4] Abide with your Lord: let him not be to you as a wayfaring man that tarrieth for a night, but constrain him, saying, "Abide with us, for the day is far spent." hold him, and do not let him go. The word "ponder," as you know, means to weigh. Make ready the scales of judgment. Oh, but where are the scales that can weigh the Lord Christ? "He taketh up the isles as a very little thing"—who shall take him up? "He weigheth the mountains in scales." In what scales shall we weigh him? Be it so, if your understanding cannot comprehend, let your affections apprehend; and if your spirit cannot compass the Lord Jesus in the arms of its understanding, let it embrace him in the arms of your affection. Oh, beloved, here is blessed Christmas work for you, if, like Mary, you lay up all these things in your heart and ponder upon them.

IV. The last piece of holy Christmas work is to come. "The shepherds returned," we read in the twentieth verse, *"glorifying and praising God* for all the things that they had heard and seen, as it was told unto them."

Returned to what? *Returned to business* to look after the lambs and sheep again. Then if we desire to glorify God we need not give up our business.

Some people get the notion into their heads that the only way in which they can live for God is by becoming ministers, missionaries, or Bible women. Alas! how many of us would be shut out from any opportunity of magnifying the Most High if this were the case. The shepherds went back to the sheep-pens glorifying and praising God. Beloved, it is not office, it is earnestness; it is not position, it is grace which will enable us to glorify God. God is most surely glorified in that cobbler's stall where the godly worker, as he plies the awl sings of the Savior's love, ay, glorified far more than in many a prebendal[5] stall where official religiousness performs its scanty duties. The name of Jesus is glorified by yonder carter as he drives his horse and blesses his God, or speaks to his fellow laborer by the roadside, as much as by yonder divine who, throughout the country like Boanerges[6], is thundering out the gospel. God is glorified by our abiding in our vocation. Take care you do not fall out of the path of duty by leaving your calling, and take care you do not dishonor your profession while in it; think not much of yourselves, but do

---

[4] After Abraham's death, Isaac lived at the well Lahai-roi.

[5] Property endowment that provides the stipend for clergy.

[6] Mark 3:17 James and John, sons of Thunder.

not think too little of your callings. There is no trade which is not sanctified by the gospel. If you turn to the Bible, you will find the most menial forms of labor have been in some way or other connected either with the most daring deeds of faith, or else with persons whose lives have been otherwise illustrious; keep to your calling, brother, keep to your calling! Whatever God has made thee, when he calls thee abide in that, unless thou art quite sure, mind that calling, unless thou art quite sure that he calls thee to something else. The shepherds glorified God though they went to their trade.

They glorified God though they were shepherds. As we remarked, they were not men of learning. So far from having an extensive library full of books, it is probable they could not read a word; yet they glorified God. This takes away all excuse for you good people who say, "I am no scholar; I never had any education, I never went even to a Sunday-school." Ah, but if your heart is right, you can glorify God. Never mind, Sarah, do not be cast down because you know so little; learn more if you can, but make good use of what you do know. Never mind, John; it is indeed a pity that you should have had to toil so early, as not to have acquired even the rudiments of knowledge; but do not think that you cannot glorify God. If you would praise God, live a holy life; you can do that by his grace, at any rate, without scholarship. If thou wouldst do good to others, be good thyself; and that is a way which is as open to the most illiterate as it is to the best taught. Be of good courage! Shepherds glorified God, and so may you. Remember there is one thing in which they had a preference over the wise men. The wise men wanted a star to lead them; the shepherds did not. The wise men went wrong even with a star, stumbled into Jerusalem; the shepherds went straight away to Bethlehem. Simple minds sometimes find a glorified Christ where learned heads, much puzzled with their lore, miss him. A good doctor used to say, "Lo, these simpletons have entered into the kingdom, while we learned men have been fumbling for the latch." It is often so; and so, ye simple minds, be ye comforted and glad.

The *way* in which these shepherds honored God is worth noticing. They did it by praising him. Let us think more of sacred song than we sometimes do. When the song is bursting in full chorus from the thousands in this house, it is but a noise in the ear of some men; but inasmuch as many true hearts, touched with the love of Jesus, are keeping pace with their tongues, it is not a mere noise in God's esteem, there is a sweet music in it that makes glad his ear. What is the great ultimatum of all Christian effort? When I stood here the other morning preaching the gospel, my mind was fully exercised with the winning of souls, but I seemed while preaching to get beyond that. I thought,

> Well, that is not the chief end after all—the chief end is to glorify God, and even the saving of sinners is sought by the right-minded as the means to that end.

Then it struck me all of a sudden,

> If in psalm singing and hymn singing we do really glorify God, we are doing more than in the preaching; because we are not then in the means, we are close upon the great end itself.

If we praise God with heart and tongue we glorify him in the surest possible manner, we are really glorifying him then. "Whoso offereth praise, glorifieth me," saith the Lord. Sing then, my brethren! Sing not only when you are together but sing alone. Cheer your labor with psalms, and hymns, and spiritual songs. Make glad the family with sacred music. We sing too little, I am sure, yet the revival of religion has always been attended with the revival of Christian psalmody. Luther's translations of the psalms were of as much service as Luther's discussions and controversies; and the hymns of Charles Wesley, and Cennick and Toplady, and Newton, and Cowper, aided as much in the quickening of spiritual life in England as the preaching of John Wesley and George Whitefield. We want more singing. Sing more and murmur less, sing more and slander less, sing more and cavil less, sing more and mourn less. God grant us today, as these shepherds did, to glorify God by praising him.

I have not quite done with them. What was the subject of their praise? It appears that *they praised God for what they had heard*. If we think of it, there is good reason for blessing God every time we hear a gospel sermon. What would souls in Hell give if they could hear the gospel once more, and be on terms in which salvation grace might come to them? What would dying men give whose tune is all but over, if they could once more come to the house of God, and have another warning and another invitation? My brethren, what would you give sometimes when you are shut up by sickness and cannot meet with the great congregation, when your heart and your flesh cry out for the living God? Well, praise God for what you have heard. You have heard the faults of the preacher; let him mourn them. You have heard his Master's message: do you bless God for that? Scarcely will you ever hear a sermon which may not make you sing if you are in a right mind. George Herbert says, "Praying is the end of preaching." So it is, but praising is its end too. Praise God that you hear there is a Savior! Praise God that you hear that the plain of salvation is very simple! Praise God that you have a Savior for your own soul! Praise God that you are pardoned, that you are saved!

Praise him for what you have heard, but observe, *they also praised God for what they had seen*. Look at the twentieth verse—"heard and seen." There is the sweetest music—what we have experienced, what we have felt within, what we have made our own—the things that we have made touching the King. Mere hearing may make some music, but the soul of song must come from seeing with the eye of faith. And, dear friends, you who have seen with that God-given eyesight, I pray you, let not your tongues be steeped in sinful silence, but loud to the praise of sovereign grace: wake up your glory and awake psaltery and harp.

One point for which they praised God was *the agreement between what they had heard and what they had seen*. Observe the last sentence. "As it was told them." Have you not found the gospel to be in yourselves just what the Bible said it would be? Jesus said he would give you grace—have you not had it? He promised you rest—have you not received it? He said that you should have joy, and comfort, and life through believing in him—have you not had all these? Are not his ways ways of pleasantness, and his paths paths of peace? Surely you can say with the queen of Sheba, "The half has not been told me." I have found Christ more sweet than his servants could set him forth as being. I looked upon the likeness as they painted it, but it was a mere daub as compared with himself—the King in his beauty. I have heard of the goodly land, but oh! it floweth with milk and honey more richly and sweetly than men were ever able to tell me when in their best trim for speech. Surely, what we have seen keeps pace with what we have heard. Let us then glorify and praise God for what he has done.

This word to those who are not yet converted, and I have done [finished]. I do not think you can begin at the seventeenth verse, but I wish you would begin at the eighteenth. You cannot begin at the seventeenth—you cannot tell to others what you have not felt; do not try it. Neither teach in the Sunday-school, nor attempt to preach if you are not converted. Unto the wicked, God saith, "What hast thou to do to declare my statutes?" But I would to God you would begin with the eighteenth verse—wondering! Wondering that you are spared—wondering that you are out of Hell—wondering that still doth his good Spirit strive with the chief of sinners. Wonder that this morning the gospel should have a word for you after all your rejections of it and sins against God. I should like you to begin there, because then I should have good hope that you would go on to the next verse and change the first letter, and so go from wondering to pondering. Oh sinner, I wish you would ponder the doctrines of the cross. Think of thy sin, God's wrath, judgment, Hell, thy Savior's blood, God's love, forgiveness, acceptance, Heaven—think on these things. Go from wondering to pondering. And then I would to God thou couldst go on to the next verse, from pondering to glorifying. Take Christ, look to him, trust him. Then sing "I am forgiven," and go thy way a believing sinner, and therefore a sinner saved, washed in the blood, and clean. Then go back after that to the seventeenth verse, and begin to tell to others.

But as for you Christians who are saved, I want you to begin this very afternoon at the seventeenth.

> Then will I tell to sinners round
> What a dear Savior I have found:
> I'll point to thy redeeming blood,
> And say—"Behold the way to God!"

Then when the day is over, get up to your chambers and wonder, admire and adore; spend half an hour also like Mary in pondering and treasuring up the day's work and the day's hearing in your hearts, and then close all with that which never must close—go on tonight, tomorrow, and all the days of your life, glorifying and praising God for all the things that you have seen and heard. May the Master bless you for Jesus Christ's sake. Amen.

God Incarnate, the End of Fear

Delivered on Sunday morning, December 23, 1866, at the
Metropolitan Tabernacle, Newington. No. 727.

"And the angel said unto them, 'Fear not.'"—Luke 2:10

No sooner did the angel of the Lord appear to the shepherds, and the glory of the Lord shine round about them, than they were sore afraid. It had come to this, that man was afraid of his God, and when God seat down his loving messengers with tidings of great joy, men were filled with as much fright as though the angel of death had appeared with uplifted sword. The silence of night and its dreary gloom caused no fear in the shepherds' hearts, but the joyful herald of the skies, robed in mildest glories of grace, made them sore afraid. We must not condemn the shepherds on this account as though they were peculiarly timid or ignorant, for they were only acting as every other person in that age would have done under the same circumstances. Not because they were simple shepherds were they amazed with fear, but it is probable that if they had been well-instructed prophets they would have displayed the same feeling; for there are many instances recorded in Scripture, in which the foremost men of their time trembled and felt a horror of great darkness when special manifestations of God were vouchsafed to them.

In fact, a slavish fear of God was so common, that a *tradition* had grown out of it, which was all but universally received as nothing less than truth. It was generally believed that every supernatural manifestation was to be regarded as a token of speedy death. "We shall surely die because we have seen God" was not only Manoah's

55

conclusion, but that of most men of his period. Few indeed were those happy minds who, like Manoah's wife, could reason in a more cheerful style, "If the Lord had meant to destroy us, he would not have shewed us such things as these." It became the *settled conviction* of all men, whether wise or simple, whether good or bad, that a manifestation of God was not so much to be rejoiced in as to be dreaded; even as Jacob said, "How dreadful is this place! it is none other but the house of God."

Doubtless the spirit which originated this tradition was much fostered by the *legal dispensation,* which is better fitted for trembling servants than for rejoicing sons. It was of the bond woman, and it gendered into bondage. The solemn night in which its greatest institution was ordained was a night of trembling: death was there in the slaughter of the lamb; blood was there sprinkled on a conspicuous part of the house; fire was there to roast the lamb, all the emblems of judgment were there to strike the mind with awe. It was at the dread hour of midnight when the solemn family conclave was assembled, the door being shut; the guests themselves standing in an uneasy attitude, and awestricken, for their hearts could hear the wings of the destroying angel as he passed by the house. Afterwards, when Israel came into the wilderness, and the law was proclaimed, do we not read that the people stood afar off and that bounds were set about the mount, and if so much as a beast touched the mountain, it must be stoned, or thrust through with a dart? It was a day of fear and trembling when God spake unto them out of the fire. Not with the melting notes of harp, psaltery, or dulcimer, did God's law come to his people's ears; no soft wings of angels brought the message, and no sunny smiles of Heaven sweetened it to the mind; but with sound of trumpet and thunder, out of the midst of blazing lightnings, with Sinai altogether on a smoke, the law was given. The law's voice was, "Come not nigh hither!" The spirit of Sinai is fear and trembling. The legal ceremonies were such as rather to inspire fear than to beget trust. The worshipper at the temple saw bloodshed from the first of the year to the end of the year; the morning was ushered in with the blood-shedding of the lamb, and the evening shades could not gather without blood again being spilt upon the altar. God was in the midst of the camp, but the pillar of cloud and fire was his unapproachable pavilion. The emblem of his glory was concealed behind the curtain of blue and scarlet and fine twined linen; behind which only one foot might pass, and that but once in the year. Men spake of the God of Israel with bated breath, and with voices hushed and solemn. They had not learned to say, "Our Father which art in Heaven." They had not received the spirit of adoption, and were not able to say "Abba"; they smarted under the spirit of bondage, which made them sore afraid when by any peculiar glory the Lord displayed his presence among them.

At the bottom of all this slavish dread lay *sin.* We never find Adam afraid of God, nor of any manifestation of Deity while he was in Paradise an obedient creature, but no sooner had he touched the fatal fruit than he found that he was naked, and hid himself. When he heard the voice of the Lord God walking in the garden in the cool of the day,

Adam was afraid and hid himself from the presence of the Lord God amongst the trees of the garden. Sin makes miserable cowards of us all. See the man who once could hold delightful converse with his Maker, now dreading to hear his Maker's voice and skulking in the grove like a felon who knows his guilt, and is afraid to meet the officers of justice.

Beloved, in order to remove this dread nightmare of slavish fear from the breast of humanity, where its horrible influence represses all the noblest aspirations of the soul, our Lord Jesus Christ came in the flesh. This is one of the works of the devil which he was manifested to destroy. Angels came to proclaim the good news of the advent of the incarnate God, and the very first note of their song was a foretaste of the sweet result of his coming to all those who shall receive him. The angel said, "Fear not," as though the times of fear were over, and the days of hope and joy had arrived. "Fear not." These words were not meant for those trembling shepherds only, but were intended for you and for me, yea all nations to whom the glad tidings shall come. "Fear not." Let God no longer be the object of your slavish dread! Stand not at a distance from him any more. The Word is made flesh. God has descended to tabernacle among men, that there may be no hedge of fire, no yawning gulf between God and man.

Into this subject I wish to go this morning as God may help me. I am sensible of the value of the theme, and am very conscious that I cannot do it justice. I would earnestly ask God the Holy Spirit to make you drink of the golden cup of the incarnation of Christ such draughts as I have enjoyed in my quiet meditations. I can scarce desire more delight for my dearest friends. There is no antidote for fear more excellent than the subject of that midnight song, the first and best of Christmas chorales, which from its first word to its last note chimes out the sweet message, which begins with, "Fear not;"

> *It is my sweetest comfort, Lord,*
> *And will forever be,*
> *To muse upon the gracious truth*
> *Of thy humanity.*
>
> *Oh joy! there sitteth in our flesh,*
> *Upon a throne of light,*
> *One of a human mother born,*
> *In perfect Godhead bright!*
>
> *Though earth's foundations should be moved,*
> *Down to their lowest deep;*
> *Though all the trembling universe*
> *Into destruction sweep;*
>
> *Forever God, forever man,*
> *My Jesus shall endure;*
> *And fix'd on him, my hope remains*
> *Eternally secure.*

Dear friends, I shall first detain your attention with a few remarks upon *the fear* of which I have already spoken; then, secondly, we shall invite your earnest attention to *the remedy* which the angels came to proclaim; and then, thirdly, as we may have time, we shall endeavor to *make an application of this remedy* to various cases.

I. Turning to *the fear* of the text, it may be well to discriminate.

There is a kind of fear towards God from which we must not wish to be free. There is that lawful, necessary, admirable, excellent fear which is always due from the creature to the Creator, from the subject to the king, ay, and from the child toward the parent. That holy, filial fear of God, which makes us dread sin, and constrains us to be obedient to his command, is to be cultivated: "we had fathers of our flesh, and we gave them reverence, shall we not be in subjection to the Father of spirits and live?" This is the "fear of the Lord which is the beginning of wisdom." To have a holy awe of our most holy, just, righteous, and tender Parent is a privilege, not a bondage. Godly fear is not the "fear which hath torment;" perfect love doth not cast out, but dwells with it in joyful harmony. The angels perfectly love God, and yet with holy fear they veil their faces with their wings as they approach him; and when we shall in glory behold the face of God, and shall be filled with all his fullness, we shall not cease humbly and reverently to adore the Infinite Majesty. Holy fear is a work of the Holy Ghost, and woe unto the man who does not possess it; let him boast as he may, his "feeling himself without fear" is a mark of his hypocrisy.

The fear which is to be avoided is *slavish fear;* the fear which perfect love casts out, as Sarah cast out the bondwoman and her son. That trembling which keeps us at a distance from God, which makes us think of him as a Spirit with whom we can have no communion; as a being who has no care for us except to punish us, and for whom consequently we have no care, except to escape if possible from his terrible presence. This fear sometimes arises in men's hearts from their *thoughts dwelling exclusively upon the divine greatness.* Is it possible to peer long into the vast abyss of Infinity and not to fear? Can the mind yield itself up to the thought of the Eternal, Self-existent, Infinite One without being filled, first with awe and then with dread? What am I? An aphis [aphid] creeping upon a rosebud is a more considerable creature in relation to the universe of beings than I can be in comparison with God. What am I? A grain of dust that does not turn the scale of the most delicate balance, is a greater thing to man than a man is to Jehovah. At best we are less than nothing and vanity. But there is more to abase us than this. We have had the impertinence to be disobedient to the will of this great One; and now the goodness and greatness of his nature are as a current against which sinful humanity struggles in vain, for the irresistible torrent must run its course, and overwhelm every opponent. What does the great God seem to us out of Christ but a stupendous rock, threatening to crush us, or a fathomless sea, hastening to swallow us up? The contemplation of the divine greatness may of itself fill man with horror, and cast him into unutterable misery! Dwell long upon such themes, and like Job, you will tremble before Jehovah, who shaketh the earth out of her place, and the pillars thereof tremble.

Each one of the sterner attributes of God will cause the like fear. Think of his power by which he rolls the stars along, and lay thine hand upon thy mouth. Think of his wisdom by which he numbers the clouds, and settles the ordinances of Heaven. Meditate upon any one of these attributes, but especially upon his justice, and upon that devouring fire which burns unceasingly against sin, and it is no wonder if the soul becomes full of fear. Meanwhile, let a *sense of sin* with its great whip of wire, flagellate the conscience, and man will dread the bare idea of God. For this is the burden of the voice of conscience to guilty man,

> If thou wert an obedient creature, this God were still terrible to thee, for the heavens are not pure in his sight, and he charged his angels with folly. What art thou that thou shouldst be just with God, or have any claims upon him; for thou hast offended, thou hast lifted the hand of thy rebellion against the infinite majesty of omnipotence—what can become of thee? What can be thy portion but to be set up forever as a monument of his righteous wrath?

Now such a fear as that being very easily created in the thoughtful mind, and being indeed, as it seems to me, the natural heritage of man as the result of sin, is most doleful and injurious. For wherever there is a slavish dread of the Divine Being, it *alienates man most thoroughly from his God.* We are by our evil nature enemies to God, and the imagination that God is cruel, harsh, and terrible, adds fuel to the fire of our enmity. Those whom we slavishly dread, we cannot love. You could not make your child show forth love to you if its little heart was full of fear; if it dreaded to hear your footstep, and was alarmed at the sound of your voice, it could not love you. You might *obey* some huge ogre because you were afraid of him, but to *love* him would be impossible. It is one of the master-pieces of Satan to deceive man by presenting to his mind a hateful picture of God. He knows that men cannot love that which terrifies them, and therefore he paints the God of grace as a hard, unforgiving being who will not receive the penitent and have pity upon the sorrowful. God is love! Surely if men had but grace enough to see the beauty of that portrait of God—that miniature sketched with a single line, "God is love!" they would willingly serve such a God. When the Holy Ghost enables the mind to perceive the character of God, the heart cannot refuse to love him. Base, fallen, depraved as men are, when they are illuminated from on high so as to judge rightly of God, their hearts melt under the genial beams of divine love, and they love God because he has first loved them. But here is the master-piece of Satan, that he will not let the understanding perceive the excellence of God's character, and then the heart cannot love that which the understanding does not perceive to be loveable.

In addition to alienating the heart from God, this fear *creates a prejudice against God's gospel of grace*. There are persons in this place this morning who believe that if they were religious, they would be miserable. It is the settled conviction of half [of] London that to trust in Jesus and to be obedient to God, which is the essence of all true religion, would be wretchedness itself. "Oh," says the worldly man, "I should have to give up my pleasure if I were to become a Christian." Now, this is one of the most wicked slanders that ever was invented, and yet it has current belief everywhere. It is the popular theology that to be an enemy to God is happiness, but to be the friend of God is misery. What an opinion men must have of God, when they believe that to love him is to be wretched! Oh, could they comprehend, could they but know how good God is, instead of imagining that his service would be slavery, they would understand that to be his friends is to occupy the highest and happiest position which created beings can occupy.

This fear in some men puts them out of all heart of ever being saved. Thinking God to be an ungenerous being, they keep at a distance from him, and if there be some sweet attractions now and then in a sermon, some gentle meltings of conscience, the good desire never matures into the practical resolve. They do not say, "I will arise and go unto my Father," because they do not know him as a Father, they only know him as a consuming fire. A man does not say, "I will arise and go unto a consuming fire." Nay, but, like Jonah, he would fain pay his fare, regardless of the expense, and go to Tarshish to flee from the presence of the Lord. This it is that makes calamity of being a man at all to most men, that they cannot get away from God, since they imagine that if they could but escape from his presence they would then wander into bliss; but being doomed to be where God is, then they conceive that, for them, wretchedness and misery alone remain. The soft warnings of mercy and the thunderings of justice are alike powerless upon men so long as their hearts are seared and rendered callous by an unholy dread of God.

This wicked dread of God frequently *drives men to extremities of sin*. The man says,

> There is no hope for me; I have made one fatal mistake in being God's enemy, and I am irretrievably ruined. There is no hope that I shall ever be restored to happiness or peace. Then what will I do? I will cast the reins upon the neck of my passions, I will defy fate and take my chance. I will get such happiness as may be found in sin. If I cannot be reconciled to Heaven, I will be a good servant of Hell.

Hence men have been known to hasten from one crime to another with a malicious inventiveness of rebellion against God, as if they could never be satisfied nor contented till they had heaped up more and more rebellions against the majesty of God, whom in their hearts they dreaded with a burning Satanic dread mingled with hate. If they could but comprehend that he is still willing to receive the rebellious, that his bowels yearn towards sinners; if they could but once believe that he is love, and willeth not the death of a sinner but had rather that he should turn unto him and live, surely the course of their lives must be changed—but the god of this world blindeth them, and maligns the Lord until they count it folly to submit to him.

Dear friends, this evil which works a thousand ills, operates in ways of evil quite innumerable. *It dishonors God.* Oh, it is infamous, it is villainous to make out our God, who is light and in whom is no darkness at all, to be an object of horrible fear. It is infernal; I may say no less; it is devilish to the highest degree to paint him as a demon, who is Jehovah, the God of Love. Oh, the impertinence of the prince of darkness, and the madness of man to consent thereunto, that God should be depicted as being unwilling to forgive, unkind, untender, hard, cruel; whereas he is love; supremely and above all things, love. He is just, but all the more truly loving because he is just. He is true, and therefore sure to punish sin, yet even punishing sin because it were not good to let sin go unpunished. This is base ingratitude on the part of a much-receiving creature, that he should malign his benefactor.

The evil which is thus done to God, recoils upon man, for this *fear hath torment.* [There is] no more tormenting misery in the world than to think of God as being our implacable foe. You Christians who have lost for a while the spirit of adoption, you who have wandered to a distance from God, nothing can be more tormenting to you than the fear that the Lord has cast you away and will not again receive you. You backsliders, nothing can hold you back from your heavenly Father like a dread of him. If you can but really know that he is not to be dreaded with slavish fear, you will come to him as your child does to you, and you will say,

> My Father, I have offended—pity me! My Father, I am vexed and grieved for my sin—forgive me, receive me again to thine arms, and help me by thy mighty grace that henceforth I may walk in thy commandments, and be obedient to thy will.

My dear friends, you who know anything about spiritual life, do not you feel, that when you have sweet thoughts of God breathed into you from above, and have his special love to you shed abroad in your hearts, it is then that you are holiest! Have you not perceived that the only way in which you can grow in that which is morally and spiritually lovely, is by having your gracious God high in your esteem, and feeling his precious love firing your hearts?

That they may be like little children is the very thing which God desires for his elect ones. It is this, which his Spirit works in his chosen; it is to this that we must come if we are to be meet [qualified] to be partakers of the inheritance of the saints in light. Slavish fear is so opposed to the child-like spirit that it is as the poison of asps to it. Dread and fear bring out everything in us that is of the man rather than of the child, for it stirs us up to resist the object of our fear. An assured confidence in the goodness of God casts out fear and brings forth everything that is child-like in us. Have you never seen a child trust to some big rough man, and melt him down by its trustfulness? It trusted where there was no ground for trust, apparently, and made ground for itself. That same child simply and implicitly trusting in a good and generous father is a noble picture, and if I, a poor, weak, feeble child, conscious that I am such, knowing that I am all folly and weakness, can just believe in my good, great God, through Jesus Christ, and come and trust myself with him, and leave him to do as he likes with me, believing that he will not be unkind, and cannot be unwise; if I can wholly repose in his love and be obedient to his will, why then I shall have reached the highest point that the creature can reach; the Holy Ghost will then have wrought his finished work in me, and I shall be fit for Heaven. Beloved, it is because fear opposes this, and prevents this, that I would say with the angel, "Fear not."

II. I fear I weary you while I speak upon this somewhat dolorous theme, and therefore with as much brevity as the abundance of the matter may permit, let us notice in the second place, *the cure for this fear,* which the angel came to proclaim.

It lies in this: "Unto you is born this day in the city of David, a Savior, which is Christ the Lord."

> *'Till God in human flesh I see,*
> *My thoughts no comfort find;*
> *The holy, just and sacred Three,*
> *Are terrors to my mind.*
>
> *But if Immanuel's face appear,*
> *My hope, my joy begins;*
> *His name forbids my slavish fear,*
> *His grace removes my sins.*

That is the remedy—God with us—God made flesh. Let us try and show this from the angel's song.

According to the text, they were not to fear, first of all, because *the angel had come to bring them good news.* How does it run? It says, "I bring you good tidings of great joy." But what was this gospel? Further on we are told that the gospel was the fact that Christ was born. So, then, it is good news to men that Christ is born, that God has come down and taken manhood into union with himself. Verily this is glad tidings. He who made the heavens slumbers in a manger. What then? Why then, God is not of necessity an enemy to man, because here is God actually taking manhood into alliance with Deity.

There cannot be permanent, inveterate, rooted enmity between the two natures, or otherwise the divine nature could not have taken the human into hypostatical union with itself. Is there not comfort in that? Thou art a poor, erring, feeble man, and that which makes thee afraid of the Lord is this fear that there is an enmity between God and man; but there need not be such enmity, for thy Maker has actually taken manhood into union with himself.

Dost thou not see another thought? The Eternal seems to be so far away from us. He is infinite, and we are such little creatures. There appears to be a great gulf fixed between man and God, even on the ground of creatureship. But observe, he who is God has also become man. We never heard that God took the nature of angels into union with himself; we may therefore say that between Godhead and angelhood there must be an infinite distance still; but here the Lord has actually taken manhood into union with himself; there is therefore no longer a great gulf fixed: on the contrary, here is a marvellous union; Godhead has entered into marriage bonds with manhood. O my soul, thou dost not stand now like a poor lone orphan wailing across the deep sea after thy Father, who has gone far away and cannot hear thee; thou dost not now sob and sigh like an infant left naked and helpless, its Maker having gone too far away to regard its wants or listen to its cries. No, thy Maker has become like thyself. Is that too strong a word to use? He without whom was not anything made that was made, is that same Word who tabernacled among us and was made flesh—made flesh in such a way that he was tempted in all points like as we are, yet without sin. O manhood, was there ever such news as this for thee! Poor manhood, thou weak worm of the dust, far lower than the angels, lift up thy head, and be not afraid! Poor manhood, born in weakness, living in toil, covered with sweat, and dying at last to be eaten by the worms, be not thou abashed even in the presence of seraphs, for next to God is man, and not even an archangel can come in between; nay, not next to God, there is scarcely that to be said, for Jesus, who is God, is man also; Jesus Christ, eternally God, was born, and lived and died as we also do. That is the first word of comfort to expel our fear.

The second point that takes away fear is that this man who was also God was *actually born*. Observe the angel's word, "Unto you is *born*."

Our Lord Jesus Christ is, in some senses, more man than Adam. Adam was not born; Adam never had to struggle through the risks and weaknesses of infancy; he knew not the littlenesses of childhood—he was full grown at once. Father Adam could not sympathize with me as a babe and a child. But how man-like is Jesus! He is cradled with us in the manger; he does not begin with us in mid-life, as Adam, but he accompanies us in the pains and feebleness and infirmities of infancy, and he continues with us even to the grave. Beloved, this is such sweet comfort. He that is God this day was once an infant: so that if my cares are little and even trivial and comparatively infantile, I may go to him, for he was once a child. Though the great ones of the earth may sneer at the child of poverty, and say, "You are too mean, and your trouble is too slight for pity;" I recollect with humble joy, that the King of Heaven did hang upon a woman's breast, and was wrapped in swaddling bands, and therefore I tell him all my griefs.

How wonderful that he should have been an infant, and yet should be God over all, blessed forever! I am not afraid of God now; this blessed link between me and God, the holy child Jesus, has taken all fear away.

Observe, the angel told them somewhat of his *office*, as well as of his birth. "Unto you is born this day a *Savior*." The very object for which he was born and came into this world was that he might deliver us from sin. What, then, was it that made us afraid? Were we not afraid of God because we felt that we were lost through sin? Well then, here is joy upon joy. Here is not only the Lord come among us as a man, but made man in order to save man from that which separated him from God. I feel as if I could burst out into a weeping for some here, who have been spending their living riotously and gone far away from God their Father by their evil ways. I know they are afraid to come back. They think that the Lord will not receive them, that there is no mercy for such sinners as they have been. Oh, but think of it—Jesus Christ has come to seek and to save that which was lost. He was born to save. If he does not save, he was born in vain, for the object of his birth was salvation. If he shall not be a Savior, then the mission of God to earth has missed its end, for its design was that lost sinners might be saved. Lost one, lost one, if there were news that an angel had come to save thee, there might be some cheer in it; but there are better tidings still. *God* has come; the Infinite, the Almighty, has stooped from the highest Heaven that he may pick thee up, a poor undone and worthless worm. Is there not comfort here? Does not the incarnate Savior take away the horrible dread which hangs over men like a black pall?

Note that the angel did not forget to describe *the person* of this Savior—"A Savior which is *Christ*." There is his manhood. As man he was anointed. *"The Lord."* There is his Godhead. Yes, this is the solid truth upon which we plant our foot. Jesus of Nazareth is God; he who was conceived in the womb of the virgin and born in Bethlehem's manger, is now, and always was, God over all, blessed forever. There is no gospel if he be not God. It is no news to me to tell me that a great prophet is born. There have been great prophets before; but the world has never been redeemed from evil by mere testimony to the truth, and never will be. Tell me that God is born, that God himself has espoused our nature, and taken it into union with himself, then the bells of my heart ring merry peals, for now may I come to God, since God has come to me.

You will observe, dear friends, however, that the pith of what the angel said lay in this. *"Unto you."* You will never get true comfort from the incarnate Savior till you perceive your personal interest in him. Christ as man was a representative man. There never were but two thoroughly representative men; the first is Adam: Adam obedient, the whole race stands, Adam disobedient, the whole race falls. "In Adam all die." Now, the man Jesus is the second great representative man. He does not represent the whole human race, he represents as many as his Father gave him; he represents a chosen company. Now, whatever Christ did, if you belong to those who are in him, he did for *you*. So that Christ circumcised or Christ crucified, Christ dead or Christ living, Christ buried or Christ risen, you are a partaker of all that he did and all that he is, for you are reckoned as one with him. See then, the joy and comfort of the incarnation of Christ. Does Jesus, as man, take manhood up to Heaven? He has taken me up there. Father Adam fell, and I fell, for I was in him. The Lord Jesus Christ rises, and I rise, if I am in him. See, beloved, when Jesus Christ was nailed to the cross, all his elect were nailed there, and they suffered and died in him. When he was put into the grave, the whole of his people lay slumbering there in him, for they were in the loins of Jesus as Levi was in the loins of Abraham; and when he rose, they rose and received the foretaste of their own future resurrection, because he lives, they shall live also; and now that he has gone up on high to claim the throne, he has claimed the throne for every soul that is in him. Oh, this is joy indeed! Then how can I be afraid of God, for this day, by faith, I, a poor undeserving sinner, having put my trust in Jesus, am bold to say that I sit upon the throne of God. Think not that we have said too much, for in the person of Christ every believer is raised up together, and made to sit together in heavenly places in Christ Jesus. Because as Jesus is there, representatively, we are each one of us there in him.

I wish that I had power to bring out this precious doctrine of the incarnation as I could desire, but the more one muses upon it, the more happy one becomes. Let us view it as an all-important truth, that Jesus, the Son of God, has really come in the flesh. It is so important a truth, that we have three witnesses appointed to keep it before us upon earth. We have been insisting many times in this place upon the spirituality of Christian worship. We have shown that the outward in religion, by itself, availeth nothing; it is the inward spirit that is the great thing. I must confess that I have sometimes said in myself, I hope not rebelliously, "What is this Baptism for, and what is this Communion of the Lord's Supper for?" These two outward ordinances, whatever may be their excellent uses, have been the two things around which more errors have clustered than around anything else; and I have heard it said by friends inclined to follow more fully the teachings of the Quakers,

> Why not put aside the outward and visible altogether? Let it be the Spirit Baptism, and not the water; let there be no bread and wine, but let there be fellowship with Christ without the outward sign.

I must confess, though I dare not go with it, because I hope to be held fast by the plain testimony of Scripture, yet my heart has somewhat gone with the temptation, and I have half said, "Men always will pervert these two ordinances, would not it be as well to have done with them?" While I have been exercised upon the point, conscious that the ordinances must be right, and must be held, I have rested upon that text, "There are three that bear witness in earth: the Spirit, the water, and the blood." And what do they bear witness to? They bear witness to the mission of Jesus as the Christ: in other words, to the real incarnation of God. They bear witness to the materialism of Christ. Have you ever noticed that when people have given up the two outward ordinances, they have usually betrayed a tendency to give up the literal fact that "God was made flesh"? The literal fact that Christ was really a man has generally been doubted or thrown into the background when the two outward ordinances have been given up, and I believe that these two symbolical ordinances, which are a link between the spiritual and the material, are set up on purpose to show that Christ Jesus, though most gloriously a spirit, was also a man clothed in a body of real flesh and blood like our own; so that he could be touched and handled even as he said, "Handle me and see; a spirit hath not flesh and bones as ye see me have." When I think of the Holy Spirit who bears witness that Christ was really a man, I thank him for that witness; then I turn to the water, and when I read that Christ was publicly baptized in Jordan, I perceive that he could not have been a phantom; he could not have been a mere spectral appearance, for he was immersed in water; he must have been a solid substantial man. The preservation of the ordinance of baptism is a witness to the reality of the incarnate God. Then comes the blood, he could not have shed blood on Calvary if he had been a spectre. There could have been no blood streaming down from his side when the spear pierced him if he had been only a ghostly apparition; he must have been solid flesh and blood like ourselves; and as often as we come to his table, and we take the cup and hear it said, "This cup is the new covenant in my blood," there is a third witness on earth to the fact that Jesus did appear in very flesh and blood among men. So that the Spirit, the water, and the blood, are the three standing testimonies in the church of God, that Christ was God, and that he was also really, solidly, and substantially man. I shall delight in the ordinances all the more because of this. Those two ordinances serve to make us recollect that Christ was really flesh and blood, and that religion has something to do with this flesh and blood of ours. This very body is to rise again from the tomb; Jesus came to deliver this poor flesh from corruption; and so, while we must ever keep the spiritual uppermost, we are prevented from casting away the material body as though that were of the devil. Christ purified as well the realm of matter as the realm of spirit; and in both he reigns triumphant. There is much comfort here.

III. Lastly, we can only occupy a few seconds in *applying the cure to various cases.*

Child of God, you say, "I dare not come to God today, I feel so weak." Fear not, for he that is born in Bethlehem said, "A bruised reed I will not break, and the smoking flax I will not quench." "I shall never get to Heaven," says another; "I shall never see God's face with acceptance; I am so tempted." "Fear not," for ye have not an high priest which cannot be touched with a feeling of your infirmities, for he was tempted in all points like as ye are. "But I am so lonely in the world," says another, "no man cares for me." There is one man at any rate who does so care; a true man like yourself. He is your brother still, and does not forget the lonely spirit.

But I hear a sinner say, "I am afraid to go to God this morning and confess that I am a sinner." Well, do not go to God but go to Christ. Surely you would not be afraid of him. Think of God in Christ, not out of Christ. If you could but know Jesus, you would go to him at once; you would not be afraid to tell him your sins, for you would know that he would say, "Go, and sin no more." "I cannot pray," says one, "I feel afraid to pray." What, afraid to pray when it is a man who listens to you? You might dread the face of God, but when God in human flesh you see, why be alarmed? Go, poor sinner, go to Jesus. "I feel," says one, "unfit to come." You may be unfit to come to God, but you cannot be unfit to come to Jesus. There is a fitness necessary to stand in the holy hill of the Lord, but there is no fitness needed in coming to the Lord Jesus. Come as you are, guilty, and lost, and ruined. Come just as you are, and he will receive you. "Oh," says another, "I cannot trust." I can understand your not being able to trust the great invisible God, but cannot you trust that dying, bleeding Son of Man who is also the Son of God?" "But I cannot hope," says another, "that he would even look on me:" and yet he used to look on such as you are. He received publicans and sinners and ate with them, and even harlots were not driven from his presence. Oh, since God has thus taken man into union with himself, be not afraid! If I speak to one who by reason of sin has wandered so far away from God that he is even afraid to think of God's name, yet inasmuch as Jesus Christ is called "the sinner's Friend," I pray thee think of him, poor soul, as *thy* friend. And, oh! may the Spirit of God open thy blind eyes to see that there is no cause for thy keeping away from God, except thine own mistaken thoughts of him!

May you believe that he is able and willing to save to the uttermost! May you understand his good and gracious character, his readiness to pass by transgression, iniquity, and sin! And may the sweet influences of grace constrain you to come to him this very morning! God grant that Jesus Christ may be formed in you, the hope of glory; and then you may well sing, "Glory to God in the highest; on earth peace, and goodwill toward men." Amen.

"God with Us"

Delivered on Lord's Day morning, December 26, 1875, at the Metropolitan Tabernacle, Newington. No. 1270.

They shall call his name Emmanuel, which being interpreted is, "God with us."—Matthew 1:23

Those words, "being interpreted," salute my ear with much sweetness. Why should the word "Emmanuel" in the Hebrew, be interpreted at all? Was it not to show that it has reference to us Gentiles, and therefore it must needs be interpreted into one of the chief languages of the then existing Gentile world, namely, the Greek? This "being interpreted" at Christ's birth, and the three languages employed in the inscription upon the cross at his death, show that he is not the Savior of the Jews only, but also of the Gentiles. As I walked along the quay at Marseilles, and marked the ships of all nations gathered in the port, I was very much interested by the inscriptions upon the shops and stores. The announcements of refreshments or of goods to be had within were not only printed in the French language, but in English, in Italian, in German, in Greek, sometimes in Russian and Swedish. Upon the shops of the sail-makers, the boat-builders, the ironmongers, or the dealers in ship stores, you read a polyglot announcement, setting forth the information to men of many lands. This was a clear indication that persons of all nations were invited to come and purchase, that they were expected to come, and that provision was made for their peculiar wants. "Being interpreted" must mean that different nations are addressed. We have the text put first in the Hebrew "Emmanuel," and afterwards it is translated into the Gentile tongue, "God with us;" "being interpreted," that we may know that we are invited, that we are welcome, that God has seen our necessities and has provided for us, and that now we may freely come, even we who were sinners of the Gentiles, and far off from God. Let us preserve with reverent love both forms of the precious name, and wait the happy day when our Hebrew brethren shall unite their "Emmanuel" with our "God with us."

Our text speaks of a *name* of our Lord Jesus. It is said, "They shall call his name Emmanuel." In these days we call children by names which have no particular meaning. They are the names, perhaps, of father or mother or some respected relative, but there is no special meaning as a general rule in our children's names. It was not so in the olden times. Then names meant something. Scriptural names, as a general rule, contain teaching, and especially is this the case in every name ascribed to the Lord Jesus. With him names indicate things. "His name shall be called Wonderful, Counselor, the Mighty God, the everlasting Father, the Prince of Peace," because he really is all these. His name is called Jesus, but not without a reason. By any other name Jesus would not be so sweet, because no other name could fairly describe his great work of saving his people from their sins. When he is said to be called this or that, it means that he really is so. I am not aware that anywhere in the New Testament our Lord is afterwards called Emmanuel. I do not find his apostles, or any of his disciples, calling him by that name literally; but we find them all doing so in effect, for they speak of him as "God manifest in the flesh," and they say, "The word was made flesh and dwelt among us, and we beheld his glory, the glory as of the only-begotten of the Father, full of grace and truth." They do not use the actual word, but they again interpret and give us free and instructive renderings, while they proclaim the sense of the august title and inform us in diverse ways what is meant by God being with us in the person of the Lord Jesus Christ. It is a glorious fact, of the highest importance, that since Christ was born into the world, God is with us.

You may divide the text, if you please, into two portions: *"God,"* and then *"God with us."* We must dwell with equal emphasis upon each word. Never let us for a moment hesitate as to the Godhead of our Lord Jesus Christ, for his Deity is a fundamental doctrine of the Christian faith. It may be we shall never understand fully how God and man could finite in one person, for who can, by searching, find out God. These great mysteries of godliness, these "deep things of God," are beyond our measurement: our little skiff might be lost if we ventured so far out upon this vast, this infinite ocean, as to lose sight of the shore of plainly revealed truth. But let it remain as a matter of faith that Jesus Christ, even he who lay in Bethlehem's manger, and was carried in a woman's arms, and lived a suffering life, and died on a malefactor's cross, was, nevertheless, "God over all, blessed forever," "upholding all things by the word of his power." He was not an angel—that the apostle has abundantly disproved in the first and second chapters of the epistle to the Hebrews: he could not have been an angel, for honors are ascribed to him which were never bestowed on angels. He was no subordinate deity or being elevated to the Godhead, as some have absurdly said—all these things are dreams and falsehoods;

he was as surely God as God can be, one with the Father and the ever-blessed Spirit. If it were not so, not only would the great strength of our hope be gone, but as to this text, the sweetness had evaporated altogether. The very essence and glory of the incarnation is that he was God who was veiled in human flesh: if it was any other being who thus came to us in human flesh, I see nothing very remarkable in it, nothing comforting, certainly. That an angel should become a man is a matter of no great consequence to me: that some other superior being should assume the nature of man brings no joy to my heart, and opens no well of consolation to me. But "God with us" is exquisite delight. "*God* with us": all that "God" means—the Deity, the infinite Jehovah—with us; this, this is worthy of the burst of midnight song, when angels startled the shepherds with their carols, singing "Glory to God in the highest, and on earth peace, good will to men." This was worthy of the foresight of seers and prophets, worthy of a new star in the heavens, worthy of the care which inspiration has manifested to preserve the record. This, too, was worthy of the martyr deaths of apostles and confessors, who counted not their lives dear unto them for the sake of the incarnate God; and this, my brethren, is worthy at this day of your most earnest endeavors to spread the glad tidings, worthy of a holy life to illustrate its blessed influences, and worthy of a joyful death to prove its consoling power. Here is the first truth of our holy faith—"Without controversy, great is the mystery of godliness, God was manifest in the flesh." He who was born at Bethlehem is God, and "God with us." God—there lies the majesty; "God with us," there lies the mercy. God—therein is glory; "God *with us*," therein is grace. God alone might well strike us with terror; but "God with us" inspires us with hope and confidence. Take my text as a whole, and carry it in your bosoms as a bundle of sweet spices to perfume your hearts with peace and joy. May the Holy Spirit open to you the truth, and the truth to you. I would joyfully say to you in the words of one of our poets—

> Veil'd in flesh the Godhead see;
> Hail the incarnate Deity!
> Pleased as man with men to appear,
> Jesus our Immanuel here.

First, *let us admire this truth; then let us consider it more at length*; and after that *let us endeavor personally to appropriate it.*

I. Let us admire this truth.

"God with us." Let us stand set a reverent distance from it, as Moses, when he saw God in the bush, stood a little back, and put his shoes from off his feet, feeling that the place whereon he stood was holy ground. This is a wonderful fact, God the Infinite once dwelt in the frail body of a child, and tabernacled in the suffering form of a lowly man. "God was in Christ." "He made himself of no reputation, and took upon him the form of a servant, and was made in the likeness of men."

Observe first, the wonder of *condescension* contained in this fact, that God who made all things should assume the nature of one of his own creatures, that the self-existent should be united with the dependent and derived, and the Almighty linked with the feeble and mortal. In the case before us, the Lord descended to the very depth of humiliation, and entered into alliance with a nature which did not occupy the chief place in the scale of existence. It would have been great condescension for the infinite and incomprehensible Jehovah to have taken upon himself the nature of some noble spiritual being, such as a seraph or a cherub; the union of the divine with a created *spirit* would have been an unmeasurable stoop—for God to be one with *man* is far more. Remember that in the person of Christ, manhood was not merely quickening spirit, but also suffering, hungering, dying, flesh and blood. There was taken to himself by our Lord all that materialism which makes up a body, and a body is, after all, but the dust of the earth, a structure fashioned from the materials around us. There is nothing in our bodily frame but what is to be found in the substance of the earth on which we live. We feed upon that which groweth out of the earth, and when we die we go back to the dust from whence we were taken. Is not this a strange thing, that this grosser part of creation, this meaner part, this dust of it, should, nevertheless, be taken into union, with that pure, marvelous, incomprehensible, divine being of whom we know so little, and can comprehend nothing at all? Oh, the condescension of it! I leave it to the meditations of your quiet moments. Dwell on it with awe. I am persuaded that no man has any idea how wonderful a stoop it was for God thus to dwell in human flesh, and to be "God with us."

Yet, to make it appear still more remarkable, remember that the creature whore nature Christ took, was a being that had sinned. I can more readily conceive the Lord's taking upon himself the nature of a race which had never fallen; but, lo, the race of man stood in rebellion against God, and yet a man did Christ become, that he might deliver us from the consequences of our rebellion, and lift us up to something higher than our pristine purity. "God sending his own Son in the likeness of sinful flesh, has condemned sin in the flesh." "Oh, the depths," is all that we can say, as we look on and marvel at this stoop of divine love.

Note, next, as you view this marvel at a distance, what a *miracle of power* is before us. Have you ever thought of the power displayed in the Lord's fashioning a body capable of union with Godhead? Our Lord was incarnate in a body, which was truly a human body, but yet in some wondrous way was prepared to sustain the indwelling of Deity. Contact with God is terrible; "He looketh on the earth and it trembleth; he toucheth the hills and they smoke." He puts his feet on Paran, and it melts, and Sinai dissolves in flames of fire. So strongly was this truth inwrought into the minds of the early saints, that they said, "No man can see God's face and live;" and yet here was a manhood which did not merely see the face of God, but which was inhabited by Deity. What a human frame was this, which could abide the presence of Jehovah! "A body hast thou prepared me." This was indeed a body curiously wrought, a holy thing, a special product of the Holy Spirit's power. It was a body like our own, with nerves as sensitive, and muscles as readily strained, with every organization as delicately fashioned as, our own, and yet God was in it. It was a frail barque to bear such a freight. Oh, man Christ, how couldst thou bear the Deity within thee! We know not how it was, but God knoweth. Let us adore this hiding of the Almighty in human weakness, this comprehending of the Incomprehensible, this revealing of the Invisible, this localization of the Omnipresent. Alas, I do but babble! What are words, when we deal with such an unutterable truth? Suffice it to say, that the divine power was wonderfully seen in the continued existence of the materialism of Christ's body, which else had been consumed by each a wondrous contact with divinity. Admire the power which dwelt in "God with us."

Again, as you gaze upon the mystery, consider what *an ensign of good will* this must be to the sons of men. When the Lord takes manhood into union with himself in this matchless way, it must mean good to man. God cannot mean to destroy that race which he thus weds unto himself. Such a marriage as this, between man and God, must mean peace; war and destruction are never thus predicted. God incarnate in Bethlehem, to be adored by shepherds, augurs nothing but "peace on earth and mercy mild." O ye sinners, who tremble at the thought of the divine wrath, as well you may, lift up your heads with joyful hope of mercy and favor, for God must be full of grace and mercy to that race which he so distinguishes above all others by taking it into union with himself. Be of good cheer, O men of women born, and expect untold blessings, for "unto us a child is born, unto us a Son is given." If you look at rivers, you can often tell whence they come, and the soil over which they have flowed, by their color: those which flow from melting glaciers are known at once. There is a text concerning a heavenly river which you will understand if you look at it in this light: "He showed me a pure river of the water of life, clear as crystal, proceeding out of the throne of God, and *of the Lamb*." Where the throne is occupied by Godhead and the appointed Mediator—the incarnate God, the once bleeding Lamb—then the river must be pure as crystal, and be a river, not of molten lava of devouring wrath, but a river of the water of life. Look you to "God with us" and you will see that the consequences of incarnation must be pleasant, profitable, saving, and ennobling to the sons of men.

I pray you to continue your admiring glance, and look upon "God with us" once more *as a pledge of our deliverance*. We are a fallen race, we are sunken in the mire, we are sold under sin, in bondage and in slavery to Satan; but if God comes to our race, and espouses its nature, why then, we must retrieve our fall, it cannot be possible for the gates of Hell to keep those down who have God with them. Slaves under sin and bondsmen beneath the law, hearken to the trump of jubilee, for one has come among you, born of a woman, made under the law, who is also mighty God, pledged to set you free. He is a Savior, and a great one: able to save, for he is Almighty, and pledged to do it, for he has entered the lists and put on the harness for the battle. The champion of his people is one who will not fail nor be discouraged, till the battle is fully fought and won. Jesus coming down from Heaven is the pledge that he will take his people up to Heaven, his taking our nature is the seal of our being lifted up to his throne. Were it an angel that had interposed, we might have some fears; were it a mere man, we might go beyond fear, and sit down in despair; but if it be "God with us," and God has actually taken manhood into union with himself, then let us "ring the bells of Heaven" and be glad; there must be brighter and happier days, there must be salvation to man, there must be glory to God. Let us bask in the beams of the Sun of Righteousness, who now has risen upon us, a light to lighten the Gentiles, and to be the glory of his people Israel.

Thus we have admired at a distance.

II. And, now, in the second place, let us come nearer and *consider the subject more closely.*

What is this? What means this, "God with us"? I do not expect this morning to be able to set forth all the meaning of this short text, "God with us," for indeed, it seems to me to contain the whole history of redemption. It hints at man's being without God, and God's having removed from man on account of sin. It seems to tell me of man's spiritual life, by Christ's coming to him, and being formed in him the hope of glory. God communes with man, and man returns to God, and receives again the divine image as at the first. Yea, Heaven itself is "God with us." This text might serve for a hundred sermons without any wire drawing; yea, one might continue to expatiate upon its manifold meanings forever. I can only at this time give mere hints of lines of thought which you can pursue at your leisure, the Holy Spirit enabling you.

This glorious word Emmanuel means, first, that God in Christ is *with us in very near association.* The Greek particle here used is very forcible, and expresses the strongest form of *"with."* It is not merely "in company with us" as another Greek word would signify, but "with," "together with," and "sharing with." This preposition is a close rivet, a firm bond, implying, if not declaring, close fellowship. God is peculiarly and closely "with us." Now, think for a while, and you will see that God has in very deed come near to us in very close association. He must have done so, for he has taken upon himself our nature, literally our nature—flesh, blood, bone, everything that made a body; mind, heart, soul, memory, imagination, judgment, everything that makes a rational man. Christ Jesus was the man of men, the second Adam, the model representative man. Think not of him as a deified man, any more than you would dare to regard him as a humanized God, or demigod. Do not confound the natures nor divide the Person: he is but one person, yet very man as he is also very God. Think of this truth then, and say, "He who sits on the throne is such as I am, sin alone excepted." No, 'tis too much for speech, I will not speak of it; it is a theme which masters me, and I fear to utter rash expressions. Turn the truth over and over, and see if it be not sweeter than honey and the honeycomb.

> *Oh joy! there sitteth in our flesh,*
> *Upon a throne of light,*
> *One of a human mother born,*
> *In perfect Godhead bright!*

Being with us in our nature, God was with us in *all our life's pilgrimage*. Scarcely can you find a halting-place in the march of life at which Jesus has not paused, or a weary league which he has not traversed. From the gate of entrance, even to the door which closes life's way, the footprints of Jesus may be traced. Were you in the cradle? He was there. Were you a child under parental authority? Christ was also a boy in the home at Nazareth. Have you entered upon life's battle? Your Lord and Master did the same; and though he lived not to old age, yet through incessant toil and suffering he bore the marred visage which attends a battered old age. Are you alone? So was he, in the wilderness, and on the mountain's side, and in the garden's gloom. Do you mix in public society? So did he labor in the thickest press. Where can you find yourself, on the hilltop, or in the valley, on the land or on the sea, in the daylight or in darkness—where, I say, can you be, without discovering that Jesus has been there before you? What the world has said of her great poet, we might with far more truth say of our Redeemer—

> *A man so various that he seemed to be*
> *Not one, but all mankind's epitome.*

One harmonious man he was, and yet all saintly lives seem to be condensed in his. Two believers may be very unlike each other, and yet both will find that Christ's life has in it points of likeness to their own. One shall be rich and another shall be poor, one actively laborious and another patiently suffering, and yet each man in studying the history of the Savior shall be able to say—"his pathway ran hard by my own." He was made in all points like unto his brethren. How charming is the fact that our Lord is "God with us," not here and there, and now and then, but evermore.

Especially does this come out with sweetness in his being "God with us" *in our sorrows*. There is no pang that rends the heart, I might almost say not one which disturbs the body, but what Jesus Christ has been with us in it all. Feel you the sorrows of poverty? He "had nowhere to lay his head." Do you endure the griefs of bereavement? Jesus "wept" at the tomb of Lazarus. Have you been slandered for righteousness' sake, and has it vexed your spirit? He said "Reproach hath broken mine heart." Have you been betrayed? Do not forget that he too had his familiar friend, who sold him for the price of a slave. On what stormy seas have you been tossed which have not also roared around his boat? Never glen of adversity so dark, so deep, apparently so pathless, but what in stooping down you may discover the footprints of the Crucified One. In the fires and in the rivers, in the cold night and under the burning sun, he cries, "I am with thee. Be not dismayed, for I am both thy companion and thy God."

Mysteriously true is it that, when you and I shall come to *the last, the closing scene*, we shall find that Emmanuel has been there. He felt the pangs and throes of death, he endured the bloody sweat of agony and the parching thirst of fever. He knew the separation of the tortured spirit from the poor fainting flesh, and cried, as we shall, "Father, into thy hands I commend my spirit." Ay, and the grave he knew, for there he slept, and left the sepulcher perfumed and furnished to be a couch of rest, and not a charnel-house of corruption. That new tomb in the garden makes him God with us till the resurrection shall call us from our beds of clay, to find him God with us in newness of life. We shall be raised up in his likeness, and the first sight our opening eyes shall see shall be the incarnate God. "I know that my Redeemer liveth, and though, after my skin, worms devour this body, yet in my flesh shall I see God." "God with us." I in my flesh shall see him as the man, the God. *And so to all eternity* he will maintain the most intimate association with us. As long as ages roll he shall be "God with us." Has he not said, "Because I live, ye shall live also"? Both his human and divine life will last on forever, and so shall our life endure. He shall dwell among and lead us to living fountains of waters, and so shall we be forever with the Lord.

Now, my brethren, if you will review these thoughts, you shall find good store of food; in fact, a feast even under that one head. God, in Christ, is with us in the nearest possible association.

But, secondly, *God in Christ is with us in the fullest reconciliation*. This, of course, is true, if the former be true. There was a time when we were parted from God; we were without God, being alienated from him by wicked works, and God also was removed from us by reason of the natural rectitude of character which thrusts iniquity far from him. He is of purer eyes than to behold iniquity, neither can evil dwell with him. That strict justice with which he rules the world requires that he should hide his face from a sinful generation. God who looks with complacency upon guilty men is not the God of the Bible, who is in multitudes of places set forth as burning with indignation against the wicked. "The wicked and him that loveth violence, his soul hateth." But, now the sin which separated us from God has been put away by the blessed sacrifice of Christ upon the tree, and the righteousness, the absence of which must have caused a gulf between unrighteous man and righteous God, that righteousness, I say, has been found, for Jesus has brought in everlasting righteousness. So that now, in Jesus, God is with us, reconciled to us—the sin which caused his wrath being forever put away from his people. There are some who object to this view of the case, and I, for one, wilt not yield one jot to their objections. I do not wonder that they cavil at certain unwise statements, which I like no better than they do; but, nevertheless, if they oppose the atonement as making a recompense to injured justice, their objections shall have no force with me. It is most true that God is always love, but his stern justice is not opposed thereto. It is also most certainly true that towards his people he always was, in the highest sense, love, and the atonement is the *result* and not the *cause* of divine love; yet, still viewed in his rectoral character, as a judge and lawgiver, God is "angry with the wicked every day," and apart from the reconciling sacrifice of Christ, his own people were "heirs of wrath even as others." There was anger in the heart of God, as a righteous judge, against those who have broken his holy law, and the reconciliation has a bearing upon the position of the judge of all the earth as well as upon man. I for one shall never cease to say, "O Lord, I will praise thee, for though thou wast angry with me, thine anger is tamed away, and thou comfortest me." God can now be with man, and embrace sinners as his children, as he could not have righteously done had not Jesus died. In this sense, and in this sense only, did Dr. Watts write some of his hymns which have been so fiercely condemned. I take leave to quote two verses, and to commend them as setting forth a great truth if the Lord be viewed as a judge, and represented as the awakened conscience of man rightly perceives him. Our poet says of the throne of God:

> Once 'twas the seat of dreadful wrath,
> And shot devouring flame;
> Our God appeared, consuming fire,
> And vengeance was his name.

> Rich were the drops of Jesus' blood,
> Which calmed his frowning face,
> Which sprinkled o'er the burning throne,
> And turn'd the wrath to grace.

So that now Jehovah is not God against us, but "God with us," he has "reconciled us to himself by the death of his Son."

A third meaning of the text "God with us" is this, *God in Christ is with us in blessed communication.* That is to say, now he has come so near to us as to enter into commerce with us, and this he does in part by hallowed conversation. Now he speaks *to* us and *in* us. He has in these last days spoken to us by his Son and by the Divine Spirit with the still small voice of warning, consolation, instruction, and direction. Are you not conscious of this? Since your souls have come to know Christ, have you not also enjoyed intercourse with the Most High? Now, like Enoch, you "walk with God," and, like Abraham, you talk with him as a man talketh with his friend. What are those prayers and praises of yours but the speech which you are permitted to have with the Most High; and he replies to you when his Spirit seals home the promise or applies the precept, when with fresh light he leads you into the doctrine or bestows brighter confidence as to good things to come. Oh yes, God is with us now, so that when he cries, "Seek ye my face" our heart says to him, "Thy face, Lord, will I seek." These Sabbath gatherings, what mean they to many of us but "God with us." That communion table, what means it but "God with us"? Oh, how often in the breaking of bread and the pouring forth of the wine in the memory of his atoning death, have we enjoyed his real presence, not in a superstitious, but in a spiritual sense, and found the Lord Jesus to be "God with us." Yes, in every holy ordinance, in every sacred act of worship, we now find that there is a door opened in Heaven and a new and living way by which we may come to the throne of grace. Is not this a joy better than all the riches of earth could buy?

And it is not merely in speech that the Lord is with us, but God is with us now by powerful *acts* as well as words. "God with us"—why it is the inscription upon our royal standard, which strikes terror to the heart of the foe, and cheers the sacramental host of God's elect. Is not this our war cry, "The Lord of hosts is with us, the God of Jacob is our refuge." As to our foes within, God is with us to overcome our corruptions and frailties; and as to the adversaries of truth without, God is with his church, and Christ has promised that he ever will be with her "even to the end of the world." We have not merely God's word and promises, but we have seen his acts of grace on our behalf, both in Providence and in the working of his blessed Spirit.

The Lord hath made bare his holy arm in the eyes of all the people.

> In Judah is God known: his name is great in Israel. In Salem also is his tabernacle, and his dwelling place in Zion. There brake he the arrows of the bow, the shield, and the sword, and the battle.

"God with us"—oh, my brethren, it makes our hearts leap for joy, it fills us with dauntless courage. How can we be dismayed when the Lord of hosts is on our side?

Nor is it merely that God is with us in acts of power on our behalf, but in emanations of his own life into our nature by which we are at first new born, and afterwards sustained in spiritual life. This is more wonderful still. By the Holy Spirit, the divine seed which "liveth and abideth forever" is sown in our souls, and from day to day we are strengthened with might by his Spirit in the inner man.

Nor is this all, for as the masterpiece of grace, the Lord, by his Spirit, even dwells in his people. God is not incarnate in us as in Christ Jesus, but only second in wonder to the incarnation is the indwelling of the Holy Spirit in believers. Now is it "God with us" indeed, for God dwelleth in us. "Know ye not," says the apostle, "that your bodies are the temples of the Holy Ghost." "As it is written, I will dwell in them, and I will walk in them." Oh, the heights and depths then comprehended in those few words, "God with us."

I had many more things to say unto you, but time compels me to sum them up in brief. The Lord becomes "God with us" *by the restoration of his image in us.* "God with us" was seen in Adam when he was perfectly pure, but Adam died when he sinned, and God is not the God of the dead but of the living. Now we, in receiving back the new life and being reconciled to God in Christ Jesus, receive also the restored image of God, and are renewed in knowledge and true holiness. "God with us" means sanctification, the image of Jesus Christ imprinted upon all his brethren.

God is with us, too, let us remember, and leave the point, *in deepest sympathy.* Brethren, are you in sorrow? God is in Christ sympathetic to your grief. Brethren, have you a grand object? I know what it is, it is God's glory; therein also you are sympathetic with God, and God with you. What, let me inquire, is your greatest joy? Have you not learned to rejoice in the Lord? Do you not joy in God by Jesus Christ? Then God also joyeth in you. He rests in his love, and rejoices over you with singing, so that there is God with us in a very wonderful respect, inasmuch as through Christ our aims and desires are like those of God. We desire the same thing, press forward with the same aim, and rejoice in the same objects of delight. When the Lord says, "This is my beloved Son, in whom I am well pleased," our heart answers, "Ay, and in him we are well pleased too." The pleasure of the Father is the pleasure of his own chosen children, for we also joy in Christ; our very soul exults at the sound of his name.

III. I must leave this delightful theme when I have said two or three things about *our personal appropriation* of the truth before us.

"God with us." Then, if Jesus Christ be "God with us," let us come to God without any question or hesitancy. Whoever you may be, you need no priest or intercessor to introduce you to God, for God has introduced himself to you. Are you children? Then come to God in the child Jesus, who slept in Bethlehem's manger. Oh, ye greyheads, ye need not keep back, but like Simeon come and take him in your arms, and say, "Lord, now lettest thou thy servant depart in peace, according to thy word, for mine eyes have seen thy salvation." God sends an ambassador who inspires no fear: not with helmet and coat of mail, bearing lance, does Heaven's herald approach us, but the white flag is held in the hand of a child, in the hand of one chosen out of the people, in the hand of one who died, in the hand of one who, though he sits in glory, wears the nail-print still. O man, God comes to you as one like yourself. Do not be afraid to come to the gentle Jesus. Do not imagine that you need to be prepared for an audience with him, or that you want the intercession of a saint, or the intervention of priest or minister. Anyone could have come to the babe in Bethlehem. The horned oxen, methinks, ate of the hay on which he slept, and feared not. Jesus is the friend of each one of us, sinful and unworthy though we be. You, poor ones, you need not fear to come, for see, in a stable he is born, and in a manger he is cradled. You have not worse accommodation than his, you are not poorer than he. Come and welcome to the poor man's Prince, to the peasants' Savior. Stay not back through fear of your unfitness; the shepherds came to him in all their deshabille. I read not that they tarried to put on their best garments, but in the clothes in which they wrapped themselves that cold midnight they hastened just as they were to the young child's presence. God looks not at garments, but at hearts, and accepts men when they come to him with willing spirits, whether they be rich or poor. Come, then; come, and welcome, for God indeed is "God with us."

But, oh, let there be no delay about it. It did seem to me, as I turned this subject over, yesterday, that for any man to say, "I will not come to God," after God has come to man in such a form as this, were an unpardonable act of treason. Peradventure, you knew not God's love when you sinned, as you did; peradventure, though you persecuted his saints, you did it ignorantly in unbelief; but, behold your God extends the olive branch of peace to you, extends it in a wondrous way for he himself comes here to be born of a woman, that he may meet with you who were born of women too, and save you from your sin. Will you not hearken now that he speaks by his Son? I can understand that you ask to hear no more of his words when he speaks with the sound of a trumpet, waxing exceeding loud and long, from amidst the flaming crags of Sinai; I do not wonder that you are afraid to draw near when the earth rocks and reels before his awful presence; but now he restrains himself and veils the splendor of his face, and comes to you as a child of humble mien, a carpenter's son. Oh, if he comes so, will you turn your backs upon him? Can ye spurn him? What better ambassador could you desire? This embassage of peace is so tenderly, so gently, so kindly, so touchingly put, that surely you cannot have the heart to resist it. Nay, do not turn away, let not your ears refuse the language of his grace, but say, "If God is with us, we will be with him." Say it, sinner, say, "I will arise and go to my Father and will say unto him, 'Father, I have sinned.'"

And as for you who have given up all hope, you that think yourselves so degraded and fallen that there can be no future for you—there is hope for you yet, for you are a man, and the next being to God is a man. He that is God is also man, and there is something about that fact which ought to make you say,

> Yes, I may yet discover, mayhap, brotherhood to the Son of man who is the Son of God—I, even I, may yet be lifted up to be set among princes, even the princes of his people, by virtue of my regenerated manhood which brings me into relation with the manhood of Christ—and so into relation with the Godhead.

Fling not yourself away, oh man, you are something too hopeful after all to be meat for the worm that never dies, and fuel for the fire that never can be quenched. Turn you to your God with full purpose of heart, and you shall find a grand destiny in store for you.

And now, my brethren, to you the last word is, "let us be with God, since God is with us." I give you for a watchword through the year to come, "Emmanuel, God with us." You, the saints redeemed by blood, have a right to all this in its fullest sense—drink into it and be filled with courage. Do not say, "We can do nothing." Who are ye that can do nothing? God is with you. Do not say "The church is feeble and fallen upon evil times"—nay, "God is with us." We need the courage of those ancient soldiers, who were wont to regard difficulties only as whetstones upon which to sharpen their swords. I like Alexander's talk—when they said there were so many thousands, so many millions perhaps of Persians. "Very well," says he, "it is good reaping where the corn is thick. One butcher is not afraid of a thousand sheep." I like even the talk of the old Gascon, who said when they asked him, "Can you and your troops get into that fortress? It is impregnable?" "Can the sun enter it?" said he. "Yes." "Well, where the sun can go, we can enter." Whatever is possible or whatever is impossible, Christians can do at God's command, for God is with us. Do you not see that the word, "God with us," puts impossibility out of all existence? Hearts that never could else be broken will be broken if God be with us. Errors which never else could be confuted can be overthrown by "God with us." Things impossible with men are possible with God. John Wesley died with that upon his tongue, and let us live with it upon our hearts. "The best of all is God with us." Blessed Son of God, we thank thee that thou hast brought us that word. Amen.

The Great Birthday

Delivered on Lord's Day morning, December 24, 1876, at the Metropolitan Tabernacle, Newington. No. 1330.

The angel said unto them, "Fear not: for, behold, I bring you good tidings of great joy, which shall be to all people."—Luke 2:10

There is no reason upon earth beyond that of ecclesiastical custom why the 25th of December should be regarded as the birthday of our Lord and Savior Jesus Christ any more than any other day from the first of January to the last day of the year; and yet some persons regard Christmas with far deeper reverence than the Lord's-day. You will often hear it asserted that "The Bible and the Bible alone is the religion of Protestants," but it is not so. There are Protestants who have absorbed a great deal beside the Bible into their religion, and among other things they have accepted the authority of what they call "the Church," and by that door all sorts of superstitions have entered. There is no authority whatever in the word of God for the keeping of Christmas at all, and no reason for keeping it just now except that the most superstitious section of Christendom has made a rule that December 25th shall be observed as the birthday of the Lord, and the church by law established in this land has agreed to follow in the same track. You are under no bondage whatever to regard the regulation. We owe no allegiance to the ecclesiastical powers which have made a decree on this matter, for we belong to an old-fashioned church which does not dare to make laws, but is content to obey them. At the same time, the day is no worse than another, and if you choose to observe it, and observe it unto the Lord, I doubt not he will accept your devotion: while if you do not observe it, but unto the Lord observe it not, for fear of encouraging superstition and will-worship, I doubt not but what you shall be as accepted in the non-observance as you could have been in the observance of it. Still, as the thoughts of a great many Christian people will run at this time towards the birth of Christ, and as this cannot be wrong, I judged it meet to avail ourselves of the prevailing current, and float down the stream of thought. Our minds will run that way, because so many around us are following customs suggestive of it—therefore let us get what good we can out of the occasion. There can be no reason why we should not, and it may be helpful that we should, now consider the birth of our Lord Jesus. We will do that voluntarily which we would refuse to do as a matter of obligation: we will do that simply for convenience sake which we should not think of doing because enjoined by authority or demanded by superstition.

The shepherds were keeping their flocks by night; probably a calm, peaceful night, wherein they felt the usual difficulty of keeping their weary eyelids still uplifted as sleep demanded its due of them. On a sudden, to their amazement, a mighty blaze lit up the heavens, and turned midnight into midday. The glory of the Lord, by which, according to the idiom of the language, is meant the greatest conceivable glory, as well as a divine glory, surrounded and alarmed them, and in the midst of it they saw a shining spirit, a form the like of which they had never beheld before, but of which they had heard their fathers speak, and of which they had read in the books of the prophets, so that they knew it to be an angel. It was indeed no common messenger from heaven, but "the angel of the Lord," that choice presence angel, whose privilege it is to stand nearest the heavenly majesty, "'mid the bright ones doubly bright," and to be employed on weightiest errands from the eternal throne. "The angel of the Lord came upon them." Are you astonished that at first they were afraid? Would not you be alarmed if such a thing should happen to you? The stillness of the night, the suddenness of the apparition, the extraordinary splendor of the light, the supernatural appearance of the angel—all would tend to astound them, and to put them into a quiver of reverential alarm; for I doubt not there was a mixture both of reverence and of fear in that feeling which is described as being "sore afraid." They would have fallen on their faces to the ground in fright, had there not dropped out of that "glory of the Lord" a gentle voice, which said, "Fear not." They were calmed by that sweet comfort, and enabled to listen to the announcement which followed. Then that voice, in accents sweet as the notes of a silver bell, proceeded to say,

> Behold, I bring you good tidings of great joy, which shall be to all people. For unto you is born this day in the city of David a Savior, which is Christ the Lord.

They were bidden to shake off all thoughts of fear, and to give themselves up to joy. Doubtless they did so, and amongst all mankind there were none so happy at that dead of night as were these shepherds, who had seen an amazing sight, which they would never forget, and now were consulting whether they should not haste away to gaze upon a sight which would be more delightful still, namely, the Babe whereof the angel spoke.

May great joy be upon us also, while our thought shall be that *the birth of Christ is the cause of supreme joy*. When we have spoken upon this we shall have to enquire, *to whom does that joy belong;* and thirdly, we shall consider, *how they shall express that joy* while they possess it. May the Holy Spirit now reveal the Lord Jesus to us, and prepare us to rejoice in him.

I. The birth of Christ should be the subject of supreme joy.

Rightly so. We have the angelic warrant for rejoicing because Christ is born. It is a truth so full of joy that it caused the angel who came to announce it to be filled with gladness. He had little to do with the fact, for Christ took not up angels, but he took up the seed of Abraham; but I suppose that the very thought that the Creator should be linked with the creature, that the great Invisible and Omnipotent should come into alliance with that which he himself had made, caused the angel as a creature to feel that all creatureship was elevated, and this made him glad. Beside, there was a sweet benevolence of spirit in the angel's bosom which made him happy because he had such gladsome tidings to bring to the fallen sons of men. Albeit they are not our brethren, yet do angels take a loving concern in all our affairs. They rejoice over us when we repent, they are ministering spirits when we are saved, and they bear us aloft when we depart; and sure we are that they can never be unwilling servants to their Lord, or tardy helpers of his beloved ones. They are friends of the Bridegroom and rejoice in his joy, they are household servants of the family of love, and they wait upon us with an eager diligence, which betokens the tenderness of feeling which they have towards the King's sons. Therefore the angel delivered his message cheerfully, as became the place from which he came, the theme which brought him down, and his own interest therein. He said, "I bring you good tidings of great joy," and we are sure he spake in accents of delight. Yea, so glad were angels at this gospel, that when the discourse was over, one angel having evangelized and given out the gospel for the day, suddenly a band of choristers appeared and sang an anthem loud and sweet that there might be a full service at the first propounding of the glad tidings of great joy. A multitude of the heavenly host had heard that a chosen messenger had been sent to proclaim the new-born King, and, filled with holy joy and adoration, they gathered up their strength to pursue him, for they could not let him go to earth alone on such an errand. They overtook him just as he had reached the last word of his discourse, and then they broke forth in that famous chorale, the only one sung of angels that was ever heard by human ears here below, "Glory to God in the highest, and on earth peace, good will toward men." Thus, I say, they had full service; there was gospel ministry in rich discourse concerning Christ, and there was hearty and devout praise from a multitude all filled with heavenly joy. It was so glad a message that they could not let it be simply spoken by a solitary voice, though that were an angel's, but they must needs pour forth a glad chorus of praise, singing unto the Lord a new song. Brothers, if the birth of Jesus was so gladsome to our cousins the angels, what should it be to us? If it made our neighbors sing who had comparatively so small a share in it, how should it make us leap for joy? Oh, if it brought Heaven down to earth, should not our songs go up to Heaven? If Heaven's gate of pearl was set open at its widest, and a stream of shining ones came running downward to the lower skies, to anticipate the time when they shall all descend in solemn pomp at the glorious advent of the great King; if it emptied Heaven for a while to make earth so glad, ought not our thoughts and praises and all our loves to go pouring up to the eternal gate, leaving earth a while that we may crowd Heaven with the songs of mortal men? Yea, verily, so let it be.

> Glory to the new-born King!
> Let us all the anthem sing
> "Peace on earth, and mercy mild;
> God and sinners reconciled."

For, first, *the birth of Christ was the incarnation of God*: it was God taking upon himself human nature—a mystery, a wondrous mystery, to be believed in rather than to be defined. Yet so it was that in the manger lay an infant, who was also infinite, a feeble child who was also the Creator of Heaven and earth. How this could be, we do not know but that it was so, we assuredly believe, and therein do we rejoice: for if God thus take upon himself human nature, then manhood is not abandoned nor given up as hopeless. When manhood had broken the bonds of the covenant, and snatched from the one reserved tree the fruit forbidden, God might have said,

> I give thee up, O Adam, and cast off thy race. Even as I gave up Lucifer and all his host, so I abandon thee to follow thine own chosen course of rebellion!

But we have now no fear that the Lord has done this, for God has espoused manhood and taken it into union with himself. Now manhood is not put aside by the Lord as an utterly accursed thing, to be an abomination unto him for ever, for Jesus, the Well-beloved, is born of a virgin. God would not so have taken manhood into union with himself if he had not said, "Destroy it not, for a blessing is in it." I know the curse has fallen upon men because they have sinned, but evidently not on manhood in the abstract, for else had not Christ come to take upon himself the form of man and to be born of woman. The word made flesh means hope for manhood, notwithstanding its fall. The race is not to be outlawed, and marked with the brand of death and Hell, and to be utterly abandoned to destruction, for, lo, the Lord hath married into the race, and the Son of God has become the Son of man. This is enough to make all that is within us sing for joy.

Then, too, if God has taken manhood into union with himself, he loves man and means man's good. Behold what manner of love God hath bestowed upon us, that he should espouse our nature! For God had never so united himself with any creature before. His tender mercy had ever been over all his works, but they were still so distinct from himself that a great gulf was fixed between the Creator and the created, so far as existence and relationship are concerned. The Lord had made many noble intelligences, principalities, and powers of whom we know little; we do not even know what those four living creatures may be who are nearest the eternal presence; but God had never taken up the nature of any of them, nor allied himself with them by any actual union with his person. But, lo, he has allied himself with man, that creature a little lower than the angels, that creature who is made to suffer death by reason of his sin; God has come into union with man, and therefore full sure he loves him unutterably well, and has great thoughts of good towards him. If a king's son doth marry a rebel, then for that rebel race there are prospects of reconciliation, pardon, and restoration. There must be in the great heart of the Divine One wondrous thoughts of pity and condescending love, if He deigns to take human nature into union with himself. Joy, joy forever, let us sound the loud cymbals of delight, for the incarnation bodes good to our race.

If God has taken manhood into union with himself then God will feel for man, he will have pity upon him, he will remember that he is dust, he will have compassion upon his infirmities and sicknesses. You know, beloved, how graciously it is so, for that same Jesus who was born of a woman at Bethlehem is touched with the feelings of our infirmities, having been tempted in all points like as we are. Such intimate practical sympathy would not have belonged to our great High Priest if he had not become man. Not even though he be divine, could he have been perfect in sympathy with us if he had not also become bone of our bone and flesh of our flesh. The Captain of our salvation could only be made perfect through suffering; it must needs be that, since the children were partakers of flesh and blood, he himself also should take part of the same. For this again we may ring the silver bells, since the Son of God now intimately sympathizes with man because he is made in all points like unto his brethren.

Further, it is clear that if God condescends to be so intimately allied with manhood, he intends to deliver man, and to bless him. Incarnation prophesies salvation. Oh, believing soul, thy God cannot mean to curse thee. Look at God incarnate! What readest thou there but salvation? God in human flesh must mean that God intends to set man above all the works of his hands, and to give him dominion, according to his first intent, over all sheep and oxen and all that pass through the paths of the sea and the air; yea it must mean that there is to be a man beneath whose feet all things shall be placed, so that even death itself shall be subject unto him. When God stoops down to man, it must mean that man is to be lifted up to God. What joy there is in this! Oh that our hearts were but half alive to the incarnation! Oh that we did but know a thousandth part of the unutterable delight which is hidden in this thought, that the Son of God was born a man at Bethlehem! Thus you see that there is overflowing cause for joy in the birth of Christ, because it was the incarnation of the Deity.

But further, the angel explained our cause for joy by saying that *he who was born, was unto us a Savior.* "Unto you is born this day a Savior." Brothers and sisters, I know who will be gladdest today to think that Christ was born a Savior. It will be those who are most conscious of their sinnership. If you would draw music out of that ten-stringed harp, the word "Savior," pass it over to a sinner. "Savior" is the harp, but "sinner" is the finger that must touch the strings and bring forth the melody. If thou knowest thyself lost by nature and lost by practice, if thou feelest sin like a plague at thy heart, if evil wearies and worries thee, if thou hast known of iniquity the burden and the shame, then will it be bliss to thee even to hear of that Savior whom the Lord has provided. Even as a babe, Jesus the Savior will be precious to thee, but most of all because he has now finished all the work of thy salvation. Thou wilt look to the commencement of that work, and then survey it even to its close, and bless and magnify the name of the Lord. Unto you, O ye who are of sinners the chief, even unto you, ye consciously guilty ones, is born a Savior. He is a Savior by birth: for this purpose is he born. To save sinners is his birthright and office. It is henceforth an institution of the divine dominion, and an office of the divine nature to save the lost. Henceforth God has laid help upon One that is mighty, and exalted One chosen out of the people, that he may seek and save that which was lost. Is there not joy in this? Where else is there joy if not here?

Next the angel tells us that *this Savior is Christ the Lord,* and there is much gladness in that fact. "Christ" signified *anointed.* Now when we know that the Lord Jesus Christ came to save, it is most pleasant to perceive in addition that the Father does not let him enter upon his mission without the necessary qualification. He is anointed of the Highest that he may carry out the offices which he has undertaken: the Spirit of the Lord rested upon him without measure. Our Lord is anointed in a threefold sense, as prophet, priest, and king. It has been well observed that this anointing, in its threefold power, never rested upon any other man. There have been kingly prophets, David to wit; there was one kingly priest, even Melchizedek; and there have also been priestly prophets, such as Samuel. Thus it has come to pass that two of the offices have been united in one man, but the whole three—prophet, priest, and king, never met in one thrice-anointed being, until Jesus came. We have the fullest anointing conceivable in Christ, who is anointed with the oil of gladness above his fellows, and as the Messiah, the sent One of God, is completely prepared and qualified for all the work of our salvation. Let our hearts be glad. We have not a nominal Savior, but a Savior fully equipped; one who in all points is like ourselves, for he is man, but in all points fit to help the feebleness which he has espoused, for he is the anointed man. See what an intimate mingling of the divine and human is found in the angel's song. They sing of him as "a Savior," and a Savior must of necessity be divine, in order to save from death and Hell; and yet the title is drawn from his dealings with humanity. Then they sing of him as "Christ," and that must be human, for only man can be anointed, yet that unction comes from the Godhead. Sound forth the jubilee trumpets for this marvelously Anointed One, and rejoice in him who is your priest to cleanse you, your prophet to instruct you, and your king to deliver you. The angels sang of him as Lord, and yet as born; so here again the godlike in dominion is joined with the human in birth. How well did the words and the sense agree.

The angel further went on to give these shepherds cause for joy by telling them that while their Savior was born to be the Lord, yet he was so *born in lowliness* that they would find him a babe, wrapped in swaddling clothes, lying in a manger. Is there cause of joy there? I say, ay, indeed there is, for it is the terror of the Godhead which keeps the sinner oftentimes away from reconciliation; but see how the Godhead hath graciously concealed itself in a babe, a little babe—a babe that needed to be wrapped in swaddling bands like any other new-born child. Who feareth to approach him? Who ever heard of trembling in the presence of a babe? Yet is the Godhead there. My soul, when thou canst not for very amazement stand on the sea of glass mingled with fire, when the divine glory is like a consuming fire to thy spirit, and the sacred majesty of Heaven is altogether overpowering to thee, then come thou to this babe, and say,

> Yet God is here, and here can I meet him in the person of his dear Son, in whom dwelleth all the fullness of the Godhead bodily.

Oh, what bliss there is in incarnation if we remember that herein God's omnipotence cometh down to man's feebleness, and infinite majesty stoops to man's infirmity.

Now mark, the shepherds were not to find this babe wrapped in Tyrian purple nor swathed in choicest fabrics fetched from afar.

> *No crown bedecks his forehead fair,*
> *No pearl, nor gem, nor silk is there.*

Nor would they discover him in the marble halls of princes, nor guarded by praetorian legionaries, nor lackied by vassal sovereigns, but they would find him the babe of a peasant woman—of princely lineage it is true—but of a family whose stock was dry and forgotten in Israel. The child was reputed to be the son of a carpenter. If you looked on the humble father and mother, and at the poor bed they had made up, where aforetime oxen had come to feed, you would say "This is condescension indeed." O ye poor, be glad, for Jesus is born in poverty, and cradled in a manger. O ye sons of toil rejoice, for the Savior is born of a lowly virgin, and a carpenter is his foster father. O ye people, oftentimes despised and downtrodden, the Prince of the Democracy is born, one chosen out of the people is exalted to the throne. O ye who call yourselves the aristocracy, behold the Prince of the kings of the earth, whose lineage is divine, and yet there is no room for him in the inn. Behold, O men, the Son of God, who is bone of your bone, intimate with all your griefs, who in his after life hungered as ye hunger, was weary as ye are weary, and wore humble garments like your own; yea, suffered worse poverty than you, for he was without a place whereon to lay his head. Let the heavens and the earth be glad, since God hath so fully, so truly come down to man.

Nor is this all. The angel called for joy, and I ask for it too, on this ground, that *the birth of this child was to bring glory to God in the highest, on earth peace, good will toward men.* The birth of Christ has given such glory to God as I know not that he could ever have had here by any other means. We must always speak in accents soft and low when we talk of God's glory; in itself it must always be infinite and not to be conceived by us, and yet may we not venture to say that all the works of God's hands do not glorify him so much as the gift of his dear Son, that all creation and all providence do not so well display the heart of Deity as when he gives his Only Begotten and sends him into the world that men may live through him? What wisdom is manifested in the plan of redemption of which the incarnate God is the center! What love is there revealed! What power is that which brought the Divine One down from glory to the manger; only omnipotence could have worked so great a marvel! What faithfulness to ancient promises! What truthfulness in keeping covenant! What grace, and yet what justice! For it was in the person of that newborn child that the law must be fulfilled, and in his precious body must vengeance find recompense for injuries done to divine righteousness. All the attributes of God were in that little child most marvelously displayed and veiled. Conceive the whole sun to be focused to a single point and yet so softly revealed as to be endurable by the tenderest eye—even thus the glorious God is brought down for man to see him, born of a woman. Think of it. The express image of God in mortal flesh! The heir of all things cradled in a manger! Marvelous is this! Glory to God in the highest! He has never revealed himself before as he now manifests himself in Jesus.

It is through our Lord Jesus being born that there is already a measure of peace on earth and boundless peace yet to come. Already the teeth of war have been somewhat broken, and a testimony is borne by the faithful against this great crime. The religion of Christ holds up its shield over the oppressed, and declares tyranny and cruelty to be loathsome before God. Whatever abuse and scorn may be heaped upon Christ's true minister, he will never be silent while there are downtrodden nationalities and races needing his advocacy, nor will God's servants anywhere, if faithful to the Prince of Peace, ever cease to maintain peace among men to the utmost of their power. The day cometh when this growing testimony shall prevail, and nations shall learn war no more. The Prince of Peace shall snap the spear of war across his knee. He, the Lord of all, shall break the arrows of the bow, the sword and the shield and the battle, and he shall do it in his own dwelling-place even in Zion, which is more glorious and excellent than all the mountains of prey. As surely as Christ was born at Bethlehem, he will yet make all men brothers, and establish a universal monarchy of peace, of which there shall be no end. So let us sing if we value the glory of God, for the new-born child reveals it; and let us sing if we value peace on earth, for he is come to bring it. Yea, and if we love the link which binds glorified Heaven with pacified earth—the good will towards men which the Eternal herein manifests, let us give a third note to our hallelujah and bless and magnify Immanuel, God with us, who has accomplished all this by his birth among us. "Glory to God in the highest, and on earth peace, good will toward men."

I think I have shown you that there was room enough for joy to the shepherds, but you and I, who live in later days, when we understand the whole business of salvation, ought to be even more glad than they were, though they glorified and praised God for all the things that they had heard and seen. Come, my brethren, let us at least do as much as these simple shepherds, and exult with our whole souls.

II. Secondly, let us consider *to whom this joy belongs.*

I was very heavy yesterday in spirit, for this dreary weather tends greatly to depress the mind.

> *No lark could pipe to skies so dull and gray.*

But a thought struck me and filled me with intense joy. I tell it out to you, not because it will seem anything to you, but as having gladdened myself. It is a bit all for myself to be placed in a parenthesis; it is this, that the joy of the birth of Christ in part *belongs to those who tell it*, for the angels who proclaimed it were exceedingly glad, as glad as glad could be. I thought of this and whispered to my heart, "As I shall tell of Jesus born on earth for men, I will take license to be glad also, glad if for nothing else that I have such a message to bring to them." The tears stood in my eyes, and stand there even now, to think that I should be privileged to say to my fellow men, "God has condescended to assume your nature that he might save you." These are as glad and as grand words as he of the golden mouth could have spoken. As for Cicero and Demosthenes, those eloquent orators had no such theme to dwell upon. Oh, joy, joy, joy! There was born into this world a man who is also God. My heart dances as David danced before the ark of God.

This joy was meant, not for the tellers of the news alone, *but for all who heard it.* The glad tidings "shall be unto all people." Read "all the people," if you like, for so, perhaps, the letter of the original might demand. Well, then, it meant that it was joy to all the nation of the Jews—but assuredly our version is truer to the inner spirit of the text; it is joy to all people upon the face of the earth that Christ is born. There is not a nation under Heaven but what has a right to be glad because God has come down among men. Sing together, ye waste places of Jerusalem. Take up the strain, O ye dwellers in the wilderness, and let the multitude of the isles be glad thereof! Ye who beneath the frigid zone feel in your very marrow all the force of God's north wind, let your hearts burn within you at this happy truth. And ye whose faces are scorched by the heat of the torrid sun, let this be as a well of water unto you. Exult and magnify Jehovah that his Son, his Only Begotten, is also brother to mankind.

> *O wake our hearts, in gladness sing!*
> *And hail each one the newborn King,*
> *Till living song from loving souls*
> *Like sound of mighty waters rolls.*

But brethren, they do not all rejoice, not even all of those who know this glorious truth, nor does it stir the hearts of half mankind. To whom, then, is it a joy? I answer, to all who believe it, and especially to all who believe it as the shepherds did, with that faith which staggers not through unbelief. The shepherds never had a doubt: the light, the angels, and the song were enough for them; they accepted the glad tidings without a single question. In this the shepherds were both happy and wise, ay, wiser than the would-be wise whose wisdom can only manifest itself in caviling [quibbling]. This present age despises the simplicity of a childlike faith, but how wonderfully God is rebuking its self conceit. He is taking the wise in their own craftiness. I could not but notice in the late discovery of the famous Greek cities and the sepulchers of the heroes, the powerful rebuke which the spirit of skepticism has received. These wise doubters have been taken on their own ground and put to confusion. Of course they told us that old Homer was himself a myth, and the poem called by his name was a mere collection of unfounded legends and mere tales. Some ancient songster did but weave his dreams into poetry and foist them upon us as the blind minstrel's song: there was no fact in it, they said, nor indeed in any current history; everything was mere legend. Long ago these gentlemen told us that there was no King Arthur, no William Tell, no anybody indeed. Even as they questioned all sacred records, so have they cast suspicion upon all else that common men believe. But lo, the ancient cities speak, the heroes are found in their tombs; the child's faith is vindicated. They have disinterred the king of men, and this and other matters speak in tones of thunder to the unbelieving ear, and say,

"Ye fools, the simpletons believed and were wiser than your 'culture' made you. Your endless doubts have led you into falsehood and not into truth."

The shepherds believed and were glad as glad could be, but if Professor—— (never mind his name) had been there on that memorable night, he would certainly have debated with the angel, and denied that a Savior was needed at all. He would coolly have taken notes for a lecture upon the nature of light, and have commenced a disquisition upon the cause of certain remarkable nocturnal phenomena which had been seen in the fields near Bethlehem. Above all he would have assured the shepherds of the absolute non-existence of anything superhuman. Have not the learned men of our age proved that impossibility scores of times with argument sufficient to convince a wooden post? They have made it as plain as that three times two are eighteen, that there is no God, nor angel, nor spirit. They have proved beyond all doubt, as far as their own dogmatism is concerned, that everything is to be doubted which is most sure, and that nothing is to be believed at all except the infallibility of pretenders to science. But these men find no comfort, neither are they so weak as to need any, so they say. Their teaching is not glad tidings but a wretched negation, a killing frost which nips all noble hopes in the bud, and in the name of reason steals away from man his truest bliss. Be it ours to be as philosophical as the shepherds, for they did not believe too much, but simply believed what was well attested, and this they found to be true upon personal investigation. In faith lies joy. If our faith can realize [make real], we shall be happy now. I want this morning to feel as if I saw the glory of the Lord still shining in the heavens, for it was there, though I did not see it. I wish I could see that angel, and hear him speak; but, failing this, I know he did speak, though I did not hear him. I am certain that those shepherds told no lies, nor did the Holy Ghost deceive us when he bade his servant Luke write this record. Let us forget the long interval between and only recollect that it was really so. Realize that which was indeed matter of fact, and you may almost hear the angelic choir up in yonder sky singing still, "Glory to God in the highest, and on earth peace, good will toward men." At any rate, our hearts rehearse the anthem and we feel the joy of it, by simply believing, even as the shepherds did.

Mark well, that believing what they did, these simple-minded shepherds *desired to approach nearer* the marvelous babe. What did they do but consult together and say, "Let us now go even unto Bethlehem and see this thing which has come to pass"? O beloved, if you want to get the joy of Christ, come near to him. Whatever you hear about him from his own book, believe it; but then say, "I will go and find him." When you hear the voice of the Lord from Sinai, draw not nigh unto the flaming mountain—the law condemns you, the justice of God overwhelms you. Bow at a humble distance and adore with solemn awe. But when you hear of God in Christ, hasten hither. Hasten hither with all confidence, for you are not come unto the mount that might be touched, and that burned with fire, but ye are come unto the blood of sprinkling, which speaketh better things than that of Abel. Come near, come nearer, nearer still. "Come," is his own word to those who labor and are heavy laden, and that selfsame word he will address to you at the last—"Come, ye blessed of my Father, inherit the kingdom prepared for you from before the foundation of the world." If you want joy in Christ, come and find it in his bosom, or at his feet; there John and Mary found it long ago.

And then, my brethren, do what the shepherds did when they came near. They rejoiced to see the babe of whom they had been told. You cannot see with the physical eye, but you must meditate, and so see with the mental eye this great, and grand, and glorious truth that the Word was made flesh and dwelt among us. This is the way to have joy today, joy such as fitly descends from Heaven with the descent of heaven's King. Believe, draw near, and then fixedly gaze upon him, and so be blest.

> Hark how all the welkin rings
> Glory to the King of kings!
> Peace on earth and mercy mild,
> God and sinners reconciled.
>
> Veil'd in flesh the Godhead see;
> Hail the incarnate Deity,
> Pleased as man with men to appear,
> Jesus our Immanuel here.

III. My time has fled, else I desired to have shown, in the third place, *how that joy should be manifested.*[1]

I will only give a hint or two. The way in which many believers in Christmas keep the feast we know too well. This is a Christian country, is it not? I have been told so so often that I suppose it must be true. It is a Christian country! But the Christianity is of a remarkable kind! It is not only that in the olden time "Christmas broached the mightiest ale," but nowadays Christmas keepers must needs get drunk upon it. I slander not our countrymen when I say that drunkenness seems to be one of the principal items of their Christmastide delight. If Bacchus were born at this time I do think England keeps the birthday of that detestable deity most appropriately, but tell me not that it is the birth of the holy child Jesus that they thus celebrate. Is he not crucified afresh by such blasphemy? Surely to the wicked, Jesus saith, "What hast thou to do to keep my birthday and mention my name in connection with thy gluttony and drunkenness?" Shame that there should be any cause for such words. Tenfold shame that there should be so much.

---

[1] This is a brief summary of "Holy Work for Christmas" (see page of this volume), which was preached on Christmas Eve 1863, thirteen years earlier.

You may keep his birthday all the year round, for it were better to say he was born every day of the year than on any one, for truly in a spiritual sense he is born every day of every year in some men's hearts, and that to us is a far weightier point than the observation of holy days. Express your joy, first, as the angels did, by public ministry. Some of us are called to speak to the many. Let us in the clearest and most earnest tones proclaim the Savior and his power to rescue man. Others of you cannot *preach*, but you can *sing*. Sing then your anthems, and praise God with all your hearts. Do not be slack in the devout use of your tongue, which are the glory of your frames, but again and again and again lift up your joyful hymns unto the new-born King. Others of you can neither preach nor sing. Well, then, you must do what the shepherds did, and what did they? You are told twice that they *spread the news*. As soon as they had seen the babe, they made known abroad the saying that was told them, and as they went home they glorified God. This is one of the most practical ways of showing your joy. Holy conversation is as acceptable as sermons and anthems. There was also one who said little, but thought the more: "Mary pondered all these things in her heart." Quiet, happy spirit, weigh in thy heart the grand truth that Jesus was born at Bethlehem. Immanuel, God with us;—weigh it if you can; look at it again and again, examine the varied facets of this priceless brilliant, and bless, and adore, and love, and wonder, and yet adore again this matchless miracle of love.

Lastly, *go and do good to others*. Like the wise men, bring your offerings, and offer to the new-born King your heart's best gold of love, and frankincense of praise, and myrrh of penitence. Bring everything of your heart's best, and somewhat of your substance also, for this is a day of good tidings, and it were unseemly to appear before the Lord empty. Come and worship God manifest in the flesh, and be filled with his light and sweetness by the power of the Holy Spirit. Amen.

Out of Egypt

Delivered on Lord's Day morning, August 20, 1882, at the Metropolitan Tabernacle, Newington. No. 1675.

When he arose, he took the young child and his mother by night, and departed into Egypt: and was there until the death of Herod: that it might be fulfilled which was spoken of the Lord by the prophet, saying, "Out of Egypt have I called my son."—Matthew 2:14–15

When Israel was a child, then I loved him, and called my son out of Egypt.—Hosea 11:1

Egypt occupies a very singular position towards Israel. It was often the shelter of the seed of Abraham. Abraham himself went there when there was a famine in the land of his sojourn. To Egypt, Joseph was taken that he might escape from the death intended for him by his envious brethren, and become the foster-father of the house of Israel. Into Egypt, as we all right well know, went the whole family of Jacob, and there they sojourned in a strange land. There Moses acquired the learning which was so useful to him. It was out of the spoils of Egypt that the furniture of the Tabernacle was made, as if to show that God intended to take out of heathen hands an offering to his own glory, just as afterwards the timber of the Temple was hewn by Hiram the Phoenician, that the Gentiles might have a share in building the Temple, in token that they would one day be made fellow heirs with Israel. But while Egypt was for awhile the shelter of the house of Israel, it became afterwards the house of bondage, and a country fraught with danger to the very existence of the elect nation. There was a very useful purpose to be served by their going down into Egypt for a while, that they might be consolidated into a nation, and might acquire many useful arts which they could not have learned while they were wandering about in Palestine. The lesson was valuable, but it was learned in much misery. They had to smart beneath tile lash, and faint beneath their labor: the iron bondage entered into Israel's soul, so that an exceeding great and bitter cry went up unto Heaven. Yet, when the heaviest burdens were laid on their shoulders, the day of liberty was dawning: when the tally of bricks was doubled, Moses was born. When man had come to his extremity of persecution, then God took his opportunity of salvation, and led his Israel out of Egypt in the teeth of their tyrant master. It had been at first a Goshen to them, a place of great abundance in the Delta of the Nile; but afterwards it became a Mizriam to them, for that is the Hebrew word for Egypt, and it means a place of straits and tribulations. The point that is meant to be brought forward by the prophet is that they were called out of Egypt, for it was not possible for them to mingle with the sons of Ham and lose their separate existence. They were on the banks of the Nile, and at first dwelt there in much comfort, but this seductive ease was not allowed to hold them: full soon they were heavily oppressed, and their existence was threatened; yet both from the comfort of Egypt and from the captivity of Egypt they were called, and at the call of God, they came forth. The living seed may go into strange places, but it can never be destroyed. The host of God may walk through fire, but it shall not be burned. God has made the living seed immortal, and it cannot die, for it is born of God. Out of deadly lands, where every breath is disease, they shall be called by the eternal voice. Those whom God has chosen may be cast far, but they shall never be cast away; they may dwell among a people like the Egyptians, most superstitious and debased, a nation of whom even the heathen, Juvenal, made sport when he said, "Oh, happy people, who grow their gods in their kitchen gardens," for they worshipped leeks and onions, and all kinds of beasts and fowls, and creeping things; but the children of the Lord cannot be suffered to remain among such a people, for the Lord desires to make of Israel, and of all believers, a people separated unto himself. Out of the midst of guilty Egypt the Lord called his people, whom he had formed for himself, to show forth his praise. The abundance of superstition, though it be like the sea, shall not quench the spark of the divine life in the living family of God: it shall burn on amidst the waves until the God who first enkindled it shall, by his own right hand, pluck it from among the billows, and set it as a light upon a candlestick that it may give light to all that are in the house. Neither Egypt of old, nor Babylon, nor Rome can destroy the seed royal; out of all dangers the church must emerge the better for her affliction. "Out of Egypt have I called my son," is a text worthy to be made a proverb, for it is true all through the history of the chosen seed. They are called out from amongst the surrounding race of rebels, and when the call comes, none can hold them back. It were easier to restrain the sun from rising than to hold the redeemed of the Lord in perpetual servitude. "The Breaker has gone up before them, and their King at the head of them": who shall block up their road? God is still calling them out, and until the very last of his elect shall be ingathered, it shall still stand true, "Out of Egypt"—and out of anywhere else that is like to Egypt, out of the worst and vilest places, out of the places where they are held fast in bitter bondage, out of these—"have I called my son."

At this time I shall first call your attention to the text in Hosea according to the sense in which the prophet first uttered it. He speaks of the *natural seed called out from the sheltering world,* for Egypt was a sheltering world to Israel, the natural seed, and they were called out of it by the omnipotent power of God. Secondly, we shall notice *the divine seed called out literally from a sheltering Egypt,* and brought up from it into the land of Judea, that he might be the glory of his people Israel. Thirdly, we shall spend a little time in considering *the chosen seed,* those who are given unto Christ of the Father: these also must come out from the world, whether it be friendly or hostile. The Lord hath said to them, "This is not your rest, for it is polluted": he is saying the same today. [However,] still is it true of the spiritual seed as of our Lord Jesus and of the natural seed, "Out of Egypt have I called my son." May the Holy Spirit be our teacher while we handle this great subject.

I. Let us think of *the natural seed* of Israel, as called out of Egypt, for with them this wonderful text began to be expounded.

It is well worth considering, for this constituted one of the loftiest lyrics of Hebrew poetry. The deliverance of the people of God out of Egypt "with a high hand and with an outstretched arm" is a song which the nation never wearied of singing, and which we ought never to weary of singing either, for at the close of all things we and all the spirits redeemed shall sing the song of Moses, the servant of God and of the Lamb. The great redemption of the Exodus shall always be so eminent a type of the greater redemption upon the cross that the two may be blended together, and words that were sung concerning the first deliverance may be readily enough used as expressions of our joy in our salvation from death and Hell.

> *From Egypt lately come,*
> *Where death and darkness reign,*
> *Seek our new, our better home,*
> *Where we our rest shall gain.*
> *Hallelujah!*
> *We are on our way to God.*

While speaking upon this natural seed I want you to notice, first, that if they are to be called out of Egypt, *they must first go down into Egypt.* They cannot come out of it if they have not first gone into it. I do not know of anything that could have tempted them down into Egypt, for it had nothing to offer which was better than Canaan; but the fathers of the tribes were driven there by a famine which troubled the whole world. The Lord sent a man before them, even Joseph, who laid up in store food for the seven years of famine, and Israel went down into Egypt that they might not die, but might be cherished by Joseph, who had become lord of the land.

The Lord may, in order to prevent his people falling into a worse evil, permit them to go into that which seems hopeful, but ultimately turns out to be a great trial to them. Suffering is infinitely preferable to sinning; the Lord may therefore send us sorrow to keep us from iniquity. Dear friend, the Lord who reads your heart may know that it is absolutely necessary for you to be tried, and so spiritually to go down into Egypt. He may send a famine to drive you there; he may place you under great tribulations, and so he may bring you down both mentally and spiritually into a sad condition, where you shall sigh and cry by reason of bondage. Do not look upon this as a strange thing, for all God's gold must pass through the fire. It is one of the marks of God's elect that they are afflicted. The Lord Jesus saith. "As many as I love, I rebuke and chasten." Depend upon it that if you are one of the true seed you must go down into Egypt: for the Lord said to Abraham, "Know of a surety that thy seed shall be a stranger in a land that is not theirs." The escutcheon [shield] of the chosen bears the emblem of a smoking furnace and a burning lamp. Even if the world shelters you, it will sooner or later become to you the house of bondage: yet into that house of bondage you must go, for there is a great educational process going on in affliction to prepare us for the land which floweth with milk and honey. Egypt is one of the early lessons; strangely early with some; their religious life begins with a cloudy morning and threatening of storm. This will work them lasting good. "It is good for a man that he bear the yoke in his youth;" hence we have "When Israel was a child, then I loved him and called my son out of Egypt." The earliest days of Israel were in Egypt, the nation in its infancy was called from thence. While the divine life has not yet attained to maturity, we meet with straits and troubles, and have to go down into Egypt and feel the weight of the yoke upon our shoulders. This is one of God's ways of preparing us for freedom, for he that has never tasted of the bitterness of bondage will never be able to appreciate the sweets of the liberty wherewith Christ makes men free. So Israel must first go down into Egypt; he descends that he may rise to greater heights.

Note next, that *it was while in Egypt, and at the worst time of their bondage in Egypt, that they received the first notification that the nation was to be called the son of God.* Israel is not called a son until Moses comes to Pharaoh and says, "Israel is my son, even my firstborn: and I say unto thee, 'Let my son go, that he may serve me.'" God had been with Abraham, and called him his friend, but I do not perceive that he called him his son, or that Abraham addressed the Lord as "Our Father which art in Heaven." Neither do I find similar sweet words flowing from the lips of Isaac or of Jacob; but when Israel was in bondage, then it was that the Lord revealed Israel's adoption, and openly declared, "Israel is my son, even my firstborn." He scourgeth every son whom he receiveth, and he receives them even while the scourge is sorely bruising them. They were a poor downtrodden nation—a nation of slaves, begrimed with brick-earth, and bleeding beneath the lash of their taskmasters! The Egyptians must have utterly despised a people who yielded so readily to all their exactions: they looked upon them as a herd of slaves, who had not the spirit to rebel, whatever cruelties they might endure. But now it is, while they are lying among the pots, and their faces are stained with tears, that the Lord, openly before proud Pharaoh, owns the nation as his son, saying, "Israel is my son, even my firstborn." I think I see Pharaoh's grim, sardonic smile as he seems to say, "Those slaves, those wretched brickmakers, whom the lowest of my people despise—if these are Jehovah's firstborn, what care I for him or them?" Learn hence, dear brothers and sisters, that God is not ashamed of his children when they are in their worst estate. We are told concerning our Lord Jesus, "For which cause he is not ashamed to call them brethren." Ay, and not when they put on their beautiful array, and when the jewels are in their ears, and when they are led forth with music and dancing, and when they shout over Egyptian chivalry drowned in the Red Sea, will they be more the Lord's children than they are in the house of bondage. The Lord God speaks of their adoption for the first time when they are still under the oppressor, and when it seems impossible that they can be rescued. The Lord speaks very plainly to the haughty Pharaoh, "Let my son go that he may serve me; and if thou refuse to let him go, behold I will slay thy son, even thy firstborn." Oh, but is it not a blessed thing to go down into the Egypt of tribulation, if there, for the first time, we learn our adoption of the Lord? Is it not a sweet thing even to be under the heaviest bondage if you are by such means made to understand better than ever you did before what it is to be a son and a heir, a joint heir with Jesus Christ? The firstborn of every creature is he, and we are the church of the firstborn whose names are written in Heaven. The heritage of the firstborn belongs to Jesus, and to us in him; and we often know this best when our heart is broken for sin, and when our troubles are overwhelming our spirit. "Fear not," saith he, "I will help thee." "'Fear not, thou worm Jacob, and ye men of Israel; I will help thee,' saith the Lord, and thy Redeemer, the Holy One of Israel." Yes, it was in Egyptian bondage that they received the first witness of the Spirit that they were, as a people, the sons of God.

When it became clear that they were really the sons of God, then *they suffered persecution for it*. A place which, as I have said, was at first their shelter, now became the iron furnace of oppression. Their hard labors are doubled, their male children were ordered to be cast into the river, and edicts of the most intolerable kind were fulminated against them. Now, brethren, Satan soon knows the man that God has owned to be his son, and he seeks to slay him even as Herod sought to kill Jesus. When the man-child was born, the Dragon knew who that man-child was, and sought to destroy him, and vomited forth floods to sweep him away, until we read that the earth helped the woman, and there were given to her wings of a great eagle that she might fly into the wilderness, into her place, where she is nourished from the face of the serpent. No sooner is the child of God really acknowledged to be such, than at once the seed of the serpent will hiss about him, and if they can, will cast their venom upon him: at any rate, they will bite at his heel, till God has taught him in the name of Jesus to break the serpent's head. Rest assured that this is another mark of the election of grace. All that will live godly in Christ Jesus must suffer persecution. In Ishmael's case it was seen that, he that is born after the flesh, persecuteth him that is born after the Spirit, and so it is now. You cannot expect to pass through this Vanity Fair without exciting the jeers and sneers of the ungodly; for the Lord's inheritance is unto him as a speckled bird: the birds round about her are against her. Every David has his Saul, every Nehemiah his Sanballat, and every Mordecai his Haman.

But now comes the crown of the text, that is, "I have called my son out of Egypt," and *out of Egypt, Israel must come.* For Egypt was not Israel's portion: it was "a land that was not theirs." My brethren, we are not citizens of "the great city which spiritually is called Sodom and Egypt, where also our Lord was crucified"; and the best thing in this present evil world is not your portion nor mine. Friendly Egypt, sheltering Egypt, was not Israel's inheritance. He gave them no portion even in the land of Goshen by a covenant of salt. They might tarry there for awhile, but out of it they must come, as it is written "thou hast brought a vine out of Egypt." The best side of the world, when it seems warmest and tenderest to us, is not the place whereon we may lie down with comfort. The bosom of our God—that is the true shelter of his people, and there we must find rest. If we are dwelling in the world, and are tempted to be of the world, and to take up with the riches of Egypt, we must by grace be taught to cast all this behind our back, for we have not our portion in this life, neither can we have our inheritance until we enter upon the life that is to come. Jacob said on his death-bed, "Bury me not, I pray thee, in Egypt," and Joseph gave commandment concerning his bones that they should not remain in Pharaoh's land. Even so, the saints of God are weary of the world's dominions; they tremble like a bird out of Egypt.

Not in Egypt would God reveal himself to his people. What saith he? "Come ye out from among them: be ye separate, and I will be a Father unto you, and ye shall be my sons and daughters." When he called Israel his son it is in connection with this coming out. "Out of Egypt have I called my son." And you and I must be fetched out from the world and all its associations, and truly severed from it, if we are ever to come to know the Lord our God. In Egypt, God was not known, but "in Judah is God known: his name is great in Israel." His people must not permanently reside in a strange country. The land of tombs was no fit home for a living people whose God was the living God: therefore it is written, "Out of Egypt have I called my son"; and the heathen knew it, for they said one to another, "Behold, there is a people come out of Egypt."

There were many difficulties in connection with this calling of Israel out of Egypt. Perhaps one of the chief obstacles was their own wish to stop there; for, strange as it may seem, though it was a house of bondage to them, they did not wish to stir from it at the first. Their spirit was broken by their sore bondage, so that they did not receive Moses and Aaron as they ought to have done, but they even chided with them. Ah, brethren, the chief work of God with us is to make us willing to go out, willing by faith to follow Jesus, willing to count the reproach of Christ greater riches than all the treasures of Egypt. He did make them willing, and they went out at last right joyfully, marching in rank, like a trained army; not needing to be driven, but hasting to escape out of the enemy's country. Moreover, the Lord made them able to go, as well as willing, for it is very beautiful to think that there were no sick people in the whole nation of Israel at that time of the going out. We read—"There was not one feeble person in all their tribes." What a splendid thing for a whole nation to have no weaklings! There was no need to carry any in the ambulance, but they all went marching forth with steady foot out of the dominions of Pharaoh. O child of God, has God given you the will to get out of the bondage of the sin and the corruption of this crooked generation? He that gives you the will, will give you the power. Perhaps you are crying, "Who shall deliver me? To will is present with me, but how to perform that which I would, I find not." Rest assured that God the Holy Spirit, who has given you the will, will also give you the strength, and you shall come marching out of Egypt, having eaten of the Paschal Lamb. The Lord stunned their enemies, so that they begged them to be gone, and bribed them to make haste. With blow upon blow he smote the Egyptians, till on that dreadful night, when shrieks of pain went up from every house in Egypt, the Egyptians hastened them to go. "We be all dead men," said they, "unless you go"; and even their taskmasters urged them to immediate flight. Our God knows how to make even the wicked men of the world cast out the Christian: they cannot endure him when once his adoption is made known; they grow tired of his melancholy presence, tired of his convictions of sin, and of that gloomy face which he carries about with him, and they say, "Go out, go out, we cannot endure you." They perceive something in him which is foreign to themselves, and so they thrust him out. Egypt was glad when they departed, and so even the world itself seems glad to be rid of the Lord's elect when God's time is come to set a difference between Israel and Egypt.

The spiritual meaning of all this is that from under the power of sin, of Satan, and of the world, God will certainly call his own redeemed. They shall not abide in the land of Egypt; sin shall not be pleasant to them; they shall not continue under Satan's power, but they shall break his yoke from off their neck. The Lord will help them, and strengthen them, so that they shall clean escape from their former slavery. With a high hand and an outstretched arm, brought he up Israel out of the land of Egypt, and with that same high hand and outstretched arm will he save his own elect, whom he has loved from before the foundations of the world, and whom he has purchased with his most precious blood. They, too, shall sing as Israel did, "Sing unto the Lord, for he hath triumphed gloriously," in the day when God shall deliver them. So far we have spoken of the natural seed.

II. Now we turn with pleasure to *the divine seed,* the man Christ Jesus.

He had to be called out by an angel from the sheltering Egypt into which Joseph and his mother had fled with him. I dare say when you have read that passage in Hosea, you have said, "I cannot see that it has anything to do with Christ." The passage in Hosea is about Israel evidently, for God is speaking of Israel both before and after the verse; but look ye: the natural seed of Israel is the shell of the egg of which the divine seed is the life. God calls Israel his son. What for? Because within that nation lay that seed which afterwards was known as the Well-beloved, the Son of the Highest. They were the shell, and therefore to be preserved for the sake of the Blessed One who, according to the flesh, lay within the race. I do not think the Lord would have cared about the Jews more than for any other nation, if it had not been that in due time He was to be born of them, even he in whom is his delight, that choice one of the Father, the Son whom he loveth. So when he brought his son out of Egypt, it means first that he rescued the external, nominal, outward sonship; but the core, the living core within, is this Son, this true Son, of whom the Lord said, putting all others aside, "This is my beloved Son, in whom I am well pleased." And the passage, if 1 had time to show you, could not be limited to Israel, for if it had been it would lose much of its accuracy. Why, think you, was the passage made so obscure? For it is obscure confessedly, and anyone reading it without the spiritual teaching which Matthew received would never have perceived that Christ was going down into Egypt to fulfill that word. I take it, the reason of the obscurity was this—that its fulfillment might be of the Lord alone. Suppose his father and mother had known these prophecies, and had purposely set themselves to fulfill them, there would have existed a kind of collusion which would have beclouded the wonderful wisdom of God in bearing testimony to his Son. Mary and Joseph may have known of this prophecy, but I greatly question whether they perceived that it referred to their son at all, or to the Son of the Highest: but now they must do the very thing that God says shall be done, without knowing that they are fulfilling a Scripture. One of the worst things you and I can ever attempt is to try and fulfill a prophecy. Good mistress Rebecca [Isaac's wife] wanted to fulfill a prophecy, and what a mess she made of it! She endeavored to make her second son the heir, and in the attempt she brought upon him and herself a world of sorrow. Had she not better have let the prophecy alone? Surely, if a prophecy is made of God, God will see that it comes to pass. If it is a Chaldaic prophecy, a prophecy of soothsayers and magi, no doubt they will try to make their own oracle true; but the Lord, who seeth the end from the beginning and ordaineth all things, can speak positively of the future. If any of you set up as prophets, beware of prophesying till you know that you can make it good. God doth not need such petty provision: he wants no help from us: his word will surely be established. Mary and Joseph did not try to fulfill the prophecy, for they could not have understood it to mean what it did mean. It was purposely put in a dark and cloudy form, but still the Lord knew what he was doing: "That it might be fulfilled, which was spoken of the Lord by the prophet, saying, 'Out of Egypt have I called my Son.'"

Remember one thing, that all the words of God in the Old Testament and the New refer to Christ; and what is more, that all the works of God have an opened window towards Christ. Yes, I say that in the creation of the world, the central thought of God was his Son Jesus, and he made the world with a view to his death, resurrection, and glorious reign. From every midge that dances in the summer sunbeam up to the great leviathan in the sea, the whole design of the world worketh toward the seed in whom the earth is blessed. In providence it is just the same: every event, from the fall of a leaf to the rise of a monarchy, is linked with the kingdom of Jesus. I have not time to show this, but it is so; and if you choose to think it over, you will clearly perceive it. He set the bounds of the nations according to the number of the children of Israel, and everything that has happened or ever shall happen in the outside world, all has a look towards the Christ and that which comes of the Christ. I love to find Jesus everywhere—not by twisting the Psalms and other Scriptures to make them speak of Christ when they do nothing of the kind, but by seeing him where he truly is. I would not err as Cocceius did, of whom they said his greatest fault was that he found Christ everywhere; but I would far rather err in his direction than have it said of me, as of another divine of the same period, that I found Christ nowhere. Would it not be better to see him where he is not, than to miss him where he is? The pattern of the things on earth is in Heaven; is, in fact, in Jesus, the Son of God. He is the pattern according to which the Tabernacle and the Temple were builded; ay, and the pattern according to which this brave world was made, and worlds which are yet to be revealed. All the treasures of the wisdom of God are hidden in Christ, and in Christ they are made manifest. I do not wonder therefore that this passage in Hosea should point to him.

It is certain that our blessed Lord is in the highest sense the Son of God. "Out of Egypt have I called my son," Write the word SON in capitals—and it must mean him: it cannot with emphasis mean anyone else. I would rather give up the idea that Hosea even thought of Israel, than think that the Holy Spirit did not intend that we should see Jesus in those memorable words, "My son." It came to pass that our Lord must find no room in Israel, and so must go down into Egypt. There was no room for the young child in the inn; and now the Edomite, the child-devouring Herod, has risen, and there is no room for the new-born King anywhere in Palestine. Alas, how sad a picture of the visible church—where Christ, at times, can find no room! What with contending sects, Pharisees and Sadducees, there would seem to be no more room for Christ in the church today than there used to be. By fear of Herod, his parents are made anxious, and by angelic direction they must go down into Egypt, where Herod's warrant would not run. Heathen Egypt will shield, while hypocritical Judea will slay. Jesus, like another Joseph, must be carried down into Egypt, that the young child's life may be preserved. Here he has a foretaste of his life-trials, and early begins his life of affliction. The King of the Jews flees from his own dominions, the Lord of all must know the heart of a stranger in the land of Egypt. The poet represents his mother as saying—

> *Through the desert wild and dreary,*
> *Following tracts explored by few,*
> *Sad at heart, and worn, and weary,*
> *We our toilsome march pursue.*
> *Israel's homes lie far behind us,*
> *Yet we pause not to look back,*
> *Lest the keen pursuer find us,*
> *Lest grim murder scent our track.*
>
> *Eagles o'er our heads are whirling,*
> *Each careering towards her nest;*
> *E'en the wolf and fox are stealing*
> *To the covert of their rest;*
> *Every fowl and noxious creature*
> *Finds on earth its lair and bed*
> *But the infant Lord of Nature*
> *Hath not where to lay his head.*
>
> *Yes, my babe, sweet sleep enfolds thee*
> *On thy fainting mother's arm;*
> *God in his great love beholds thee,*
> *Angels guard thy rest from harm.*
> *Earth and Hell in vain beset thee,*
> *Kings against thy life conspire;*
> *But our God can ne'er forget thee,*
> *Nor his arm that shields thee, tire.*

Mark well, that, if the Lord Jesus Christ had willed it, even though but a babe, he might have blasted Herod, as he did another Herod in after days, and he might have made him to be eaten of worms. The glorious Jehovah could have sent a legion of angels, and have driven the Idumaean dynasty from off the throne, if so it had pleased him; but no violence was used—a gentler course was chosen. When Jesus stands up to fight, he wars by nonresistance. He says, "My kingdom is not of this world, else would my servants fight." He conquers by flight rather than by fight. He taught his people when persecuted in one city to flee to another; and never did he bid them form bands, and battle with their persecutors. That is not according to Christ's law or example. A fighting church is the devil's church, but a hearing and enduring church—that is Christ's church. His parents fled with him by night, and took him down into Egypt, that he might be sheltered there. Traditions tell us wonderful stories about what happened when Jesus went into Egypt, but as none of them are inspired, I need not waste your time with them. The only one that might look like fact, is that his parents sheltered themselves in a temple wherein idol gods were ranged, and when the child entered, all the images fell down. Certainly, if not actually true, it is a poetical description of that which happens wherever the holy child puts in an appearance. Every idol god falls before him. Down he must go, whether it be Dagon, or Baal, or Ashtaroth, or whatever the god may be called; ay, and he that wears the triple tiara on the seven hills, and calls himself the vicar of God on earth, must come down, and all his empire must sink like a millstone in the flood. We do not know how the young child and Joseph and Mary lived in Egypt, except that they had received gold from the Magi, and that being a carpenter, not a hedge carpenter, but one skilled in joinery and wheelwrighting, Joseph could find plenty of work in Egypt, where vast multitudes of Jews were already settled. Whether our Lord was carried to Alexandria or not we cannot tell. The probability is that there he was housed, for it was the great rendezvous of his nation and the center of their learning: there had the Bible been translated into the Greek tongue by the seventy, and there flourished schools of Jews much more liberal than those in Judea. It is, therefore, not unlikely that the Prince of Peace went to that region where we have most unhappily illustrated Christianity with cuts—not all of wood, nor all innocent of blood. But Jesus could not stop in Egypt. "Out of Egypt have I called my son." His parents by a brave act of faith went back at the command of the angel to the Holy Land: thy land, O Immanuel! Jesus could not stay in Egypt, for he was no Egyptian. He did not come to exercise a ministry among the Egyptians. He was sent only to the lost sheep of the house of Israel, in his public working. Being called out of Egypt, the heavenly vision was not disobeyed. His foster-parent Joseph took him back, and they settled in Nazareth. Yet remember he had been in Egypt, and this was a prophecy of blessing to that land; for wherever Jesus goes the air is sweetened. Every plot of land that his foot hath ever trodden on shall be his forever. What said God to Jacob? "The land whereon thou liest will I give thee." And the same is true to Jacob's great descendant. Jesus has slept in Egypt, and Egypt is his own. God has given it to him, and his it shall be; glory be to his blessed name.

III. Let us turn to think of *the chosen seed* that shall be brought out of Egypt.

Here I would remark that this passage may be taken, and should be taken, literally. God has a chosen people who shall assuredly come out of the very Egypt which now exists. It is remarkable that early in the gospel day the truth was gladly received in Egypt. Egypt became the land of saints and divines, and as it had once been the source and home of civilization, so it became an active camp for the soldiers of the cross. Under the successors of Mahomet all this was swept away, and now the Crescent's baneful beam falls where once the heavenly sun shed out its infinite glory, and scattered health among the sons of men. Egypt did turn to God, and it will turn again. Let me read you this passage from Isaiah 19:

> In that day shall five cities in the land of Egypt speak the language of Canaan, and swear to the Lord of hosts; one shall be called, the city of destruction. In that day shall there be an altar to the Lord in the midst of the land of Egypt, and a pillar at the border thereof to the Lord. And it shall be for a sign and for a witness unto the Lord of hosts in the land of Egypt: for they shall cry unto the Lord because of the oppressors, and he shall send them a savior, and a great one, and he shall deliver them, And the Lord shall be known to Egypt, and the Egyptians shall know the Lord in that day, and shall do sacrifice and oblation; yea, they shall vow a vow unto the Lord, and perform it. And the Lord shalt smite Egypt: he shall smite and heal it: and they shall return even to the Lord, and he shall be entreated of them, and shall heal them. In that day shall there be a highway out of Egypt to Assyria, and the Assyrian shall come into Egypt, and the Egyptian into Assyria, and the Egyptians shall serve with the Assyrians. In that day shall Israel be the third with Egypt and with Assyria, even a blessing in the midst of the land: whom the Lord of hosts shall bless, saying, Blessed be Egypt my people, and Assyria the work of my hands, and Israel mine inheritance.

So that we feel clear that our God has yet a son to call out of Egypt, and he will call him. There shall be a seed to serve him even in the midst of the down-trodden people who live by the Nile-floods, for God hath said it. There is one passage to which I should like to refer you, because it is so full of comfort. (Jeremiah 43:12) "And he shall array himself with the land of Egypt,"—think of that—putting it on as Joseph put on his coat of many colors—"as a shepherd putteth on his garment; and he shall go forth from thence in peace." Yet shall Christ wear as a robe of honor this land of Egypt, and again shall it be true, "Out of Egypt have I called my son."

Let us learn from this, that out of the strangest and oddest places God will call his son. Certain brethren among us go the lodging-houses in Mint-street, Kent-street, and other places. Can any good thing come out of them? Assuredly, it can, for "Out of Egypt have I called my son." Out of Thieves' Acre and Ketch's Warren, saints shall come. Some of you perhaps know of holes and corners in London where a decent person scarcely dares to be seen: do not pass by these abominable haunts, for out of such Egypts will the Lord call his sons. The worst field is often the most hopeful. Here is virgin soil, unploughed, untilled. What harvests may be won by willing workers! Oh ye brave hands, thrust in the ploughshare and break up this neglected soil, for thus saith the Lord, "Out of Egypt have I called my son." Many of you who live in the midst of Israel, and hear the gospel every day, remain disobedient; but some from the lowest and vilest parts of the earth shall yet be called with an effectual calling, and they shall obey, for it is written, "Out of Egypt have I called my son."

But we will take the text, and conclude with it, in a spiritual sense. All men are in Egypt spiritually, but God calls out his own sons. Sin is like Pharaoh, a tyrant that will not yield: he will not let men go; but he *shall* let them go, for God saith, "Out of Egypt have I called my son." We are in a world which is the destroyer of grace as Pharaoh was the destroyer of Israel's little ones. You do not think a good thought but what it is laughed out of you: you scarcely catch a word of Scripture, but as soon as you get home you are compelled to forget it. Nevertheless out of that—"Out of Egypt have I called my son." You shall be delivered yet. Put you your trust in Jesus Christ, for "to as many as received him, to them gave he power to become the sons of God," and out of Egypt will he call every son of his.

Perhaps you are in the dark, as the Egyptians were during the plague, or as when God turned the dark side of the pillar to Egypt. Ah, but if you are one of his, if you will but trust Jesus, which is the mark of being God's elect, out of darkness will God call you; out of thick Egyptian night will he fetch you, and your eyes shall be made glad with the light of the gospel of Christ.

Perhaps you dwell in the midst of superstition, for the Egyptians were horribly given to superstition, but yet out of that, will God call his people. I look to see priests converted. I hope yet to see leaders of the gospel found among men that were once steeped to the throat in superstition. Why not? "Out of Egypt have I called my son." Where did Luther come from but from the monastery, and he preached the word with thunder and lightning from Heaven, and God blessed it to the emancipation of nations. He will bring others of that kind; out of all sorts of ignorance and superstition he will fetch them, to the praise of the glory of his grace. I feel encouraged to pray for those who appear to be hopeless: I feel as if I must cry to God, "Bring them out of Egypt, Lord, the worst, the vilest." You here that know what Egypt is, and are in it, and know you are in it, oh, believe that the Emancipator has come, the Redeemer has appeared; with an offering of blood has he stood before God, and given Egypt for a ransom, Ethiopia and Seba for you. Oh, that he might win those with power whom he has bought with price, and to him be glory, world without end. Amen.

He Shall Be Great

Delivered on Lord's Day evening, December 2, 1883, at the Metropolitan Tabernacle, Newington. No. 1760. *Being his last sermon before his journey to the South of France.*

He shall be great.—Luke 1:32

S trictly speaking, I suppose these words refer to the human nature of our Lord Jesus Christ, for it is as to his humanity that Christ was born of Mary. The context runs thus—

> Behold, thou shalt conceive in thy womb, and bring forth a son, and shalt call his name *Jesus*. He shall be great, and shall be called the Son of the Highest: and the Lord God shall give unto him the throne of his father David. And he shall reign over the house of Jacob forever; and of his kingdom there shall be no end.

The angel of the Lord thus spake concerning the manhood of "that holy thing" that should be born of the favored virgin by the overshadowing of the power of the Highest. As to his divinity, we must speak concerning him in another style than this: but, as a man, he was born of the virgin, and it was said to her before his birth, "He shall be great."

The man Christ Jesus stooped very low. In his first estate he was not great; he was very little when he hung upon his mother's breast. In his after estate he was not great; but despised, rejected, and crucified. Indeed, he was so poor that he had nowhere to lay his head; and he was so cast out by the tongues of men that they called him a "fellow," mentioned him among drunken men and wine-bibbers, and even accused him of having a devil, and being mad. In the esteem of the great ones of the earth, he was an ignorant Galilean of whom they said, "We know not whence he is." His life binds up more fitly with the lowly annals of the poor than with the [royal] court-circular or whatever stood for that in Caesar's day. In his own time his enemies could not find a word base enough to express their contempt of him. He was brought very low in his trial, condemnation, and suffering. Who thought him great when he was covered with bloody sweat, or when he was sold at the price of a slave, or when a guard came out against him with swords, and with lanterns, and with torches, as if he had been a thief? Who thought him great when they bound him and led him to the judgment-seat as a malefactor? or when the abjects smote him, blindfolded him, and spat in his face? or when he was scourged, led through the streets bearing his cross, and afterwards hung up between two thieves to die? Truly he was brought very low, and a sword pierced through his mother's heart as she saw the sufferings of her holy Son. When she knew that he was dead, and buried in a borrowed tomb, she must have painfully pondered in her heart the words from Heaven concerning him, and thought within herself,

> The angel said he should be great, but who is made so vile as he? He said that he should be called the "Son of the Highest," but, lo! he is brought into the dust of death; and men seal his sepulcher, and cast out his name as evil.

Still, while I think that our text most fitly applies to the manhood of Christ in the first place, I rejoice to think that—

> He who on earth as man was known,
> And bore our sins and pains,
> Now, seated on the eternal throne,
> The God of glory reigns.

The very man who was despised and spat upon, sits glorious on his Father's throne. As man he is anointed "King of kings, and Lord of lords." As man he has been lifted up from the lowest depths, and set in the greatest heights to reign forever and ever. Peter and the apostles testified, "This Jesus hath God raised up, whereof we all are witnesses, he being by the right hand of God exalted." Stephen also said, "Behold, I see the heavens opened, and the Son of man standing on the right hand of God." While we believe that, and rejoice in it, we shall be wise never to dissociate the deity of Christ from his humanity, for they make up one person. I cannot help remarking that in the New Testament you find a disregard of all rigid distinction of the two natures in the person of our Lord when the Spirit speaks concerning him. The two natures are so thoroughly united in the person of Christ that the Holy Ghost does not speak of the Lord Jesus with theological exactness, like one who writes a creed, but he speaks as to men of understanding, who know and rejoice in the truth of the one indivisible person of the Mediator. For instance, we read in Scripture of "the blood of God": Paul saith in Acts 20:28, "Feed the church of God, which he hath purchased with his own blood." Now, strictly speaking, there can be no blood of God, and the expression looks like a confusion of the two natures; but this is intentional, that we may clearly see that the two natures are so joined together that the Holy Ghost does not stop to dissect and set out differences; but he says of the united person of our blessed Lord, that which is strictly true either of his humanity or of his deity. He is called both "God, our Savior," and "the man Christ Jesus." The combined natures of the man, the God, Christ Jesus our Lord, are one person; and all the acts of either nature may be ascribed to that one person. Hence I, for one, do not hesitate to sing such verses as these—

> *He that distributes crowns and thrones,*
> *Hangs on a tree, and bleeds and groans:*
> *The Prince of Life resigns his breath;*
> *The king of Glory bows to death.*
>
> *Well might the sun in darkness hide,*
> *And shut his glories in,*
> *When God, the mighty Maker, died*
> *For man, the creature's sin.*
>
> *See how the patient Jesus stands,*
> *Insulted in his lowest case!*
> *Sinners have bound the Almighty hands,*
> *And spit in their Creator's face.*

We shall not labor, therefore, to preserve the niceties of theology, but we shall at this time freely speak of our Lord as he is in his Godhead and in his manhood, and apply our text to the whole Christ, declaring the divine promise that "He shall be great."

While my brother was praying for me [before the sermon,] I was wishing that I had the tongues of men and of angels with which to set forth my theme tonight; and yet I shall retract my wish, for the subject is such, that if my words were the commonest that could be found—yea, if they were ungrammatical, and if they were put together most uncouthly, it would little matter; for a failure awaits me in any case: the subject far transcends all utterance. Jesus is such a one that no oratory can ever reach the height of his glory, and the simplest words are best suited to a subject so sublime. Fine words would be but tawdry things to hang beside the unspeakably glorious Lord. I can say no more than that *he is great.* If I could tell forth his greatness with choral symphonies of cherubim, yet should I fail to reach the height of this great argument. I will be content if I can touch the hem of the garment of his greatness. If the Lord will but set us in a cleft of the rock, and only make us see the back parts of his character, we shall be overcome by the vision. As yet, even of Jesus, the face of his full glory cannot be seen, or if seen, it cannot be described. Were we caught up to the third Heaven we should have little to say on coming back, for we should have seen things which it were not lawful for us to utter. I shall not therefore fail with loss of honor if I tell you that my utmost success at this time will but touch the fringe of the splendor of the Son of man. This is not the time of his clearest revealing. The day is coming for the manifestation of the Lord; as yet he shineth not forth among men in his noontide. His second advent shall more fully reveal him. Then shall his people "shine forth as the sun in the kingdom of their Father," because he also shall rise in the clear face of Heaven as the Sun of Righteousness, greatly blessing the sons of men.

I. Let me touch my theme as best I can by, first of all, saying of our adorable Lord Jesus that *he is great from many points of view.*

I might have said from *every* point of view; but that is too large a truth to be surveyed at one sitting. Mind would fail us, life would fail us, time would fail us: eternity and perfection will alone suffice for that boundless meditation. But from the points of view to which I would conduct you for a moment, the Lord Jesus Christ is emphatically great.

First, *in the perfection of his nature.* Think, my brethren. There was never such a being as our Well-Beloved. He is peerless and incomparable. He is divine, and therefore unique. He is "Light of light, very God of very God." Jesus is truly equal with God, one with the Father. Oh, the greatness of Godhead! Jehovah is a being infinite, immeasurable, incomprehensible, inconceivable! He filleth all things, and yet is not contained by all things. He is indeed great beyond any idea of greatness that has ever dawned upon us. All this is true of the Only-Begotten.

In the beginning was the Word, and the Word was with God, and the Word was God. The same was in the beginning with were made by him; and without him was not anything made that was made.

For of him, and through him, and to him, are all things: to whom be glory forever, amen.

He is before all things, and by him all things consist.

But our Lord Jesus is also man, and this makes the singularity of his person, that he should be perfectly and purely God, and as truly and really man. He is not humanity deified: he is not Godhead humanized. I have admitted latitude of expression; but there is, in fact, no confusion of the substance. He *is* God. He *is* man. He is all that God is, and all that man is, as God created him. He is as truly God as if he were not man, and yet as completely and perfectly man as if he were not God. Think of this wondrous combination! *a* perfect manhood without spot or stain of original or actual sin, and then the glorious Godhead combined with it! Said I not truly that Jesus stands alone? He is not greatest of the great; but great where all else are little. He is not something among all; but all where all else are nothing. Who shall be compared with him? He counts it not robbery to be equal with God, and among men he is the Firstborn of every creature; among the risen ones, he is the Firstborn by his resurrection from the dead; among the glorified, he is the source and object of glory. I cannot compass his nature: who shall declare his generation? He is one with us, and yet inconceivably beyond us. Our nature is limited, sinful, fallen; but his nature is unbounded, holy, divine. When Jehovah looks on us we ask, "What is man, that thou art mindful of him? and the son of man, that thou visitest him?" But "when he bringeth in the first-begotten into the world, he saith, 'And let all the angels of God worship him.'" Shall it not truly be said as to his nature, "He is great"?

He is great also *in the grandeur of his offices*. Remember that he has for our sakes undertaken to be our Redeemer. You see your bondage, brethren. You know it, for some of you have worn the fetters till they have entered into your soul: from such slavery he came to redeem us. Behold his Zion in ruins, heaps on heaps, smoking, consumed! He comes to rebuild and to restore. This is his office—to build up the old wastes, and to restore the temple of the living God, which had been cast down by the foe. To accomplish this he came to be our Priest, our Prophet, and our King; in each office glorious beyond compare. He came to be our Savior, our Sacrifice, our Substitute, our Surety, our Head, our Friend, our Lord, our Life, our All. Pile up the offices, and remember that each one is worthy of a God. Mention them as you may, and truly you shall never remember them all; for he, the express image of his Father's glory, has undertaken every kind of office, that he might perfectly redeem his people, and make them to be his own for ever. In each office he has gained the summit of glory, and therein he is and shall be great.

Have you ever stood in Westminster Abbey when some great warrior was being buried, and when the herald pronounced his various titles? He has been greatly honored of his queen, and of the nation, for which he has fought so valiantly, and he is prince of this, and duke of that, and count of the other, and earl of something else: and the titles are many and brilliant. What a parade it is! "Vanity of vanities! All is vanity!" What boots [use is] it to the senseless clay that it is buried with pomp of heraldry? But I stand at the tomb of Christ, and I say of his offices, that they are superlatively grand; and, moreover, that they are not buried, neither is he among the dead. He lives and bears his honors still in the fullness of their splendor. He is all to his people still; every office he still carries on, and will carry on till he shall deliver up the kingdom to God, even the Father, and God shall be all in all. Oh, the splendor of this Christ of God in the mighty offices which he sustains! He is the Standard-bearer among ten thousand. Who is like unto him in all eternity?

The government shall be upon his shoulder: and his name shall be called Wonderful, Counselor, the Mighty God, the Everlasting Father, the Prince of Peace.

Hosanna to the son of David: blessed is he that cometh in the name of the Lord!

Let our hearts give him our adoring praise tonight, for he is great in the glorious offices which God has heaped upon him.

His nature and his offices would alone furnish us with a lengthened theme; but oh! my brethren, the Lord Jesus is great *in the splendor of his achievements*. He does not wear an office whose duty is neglected; but his name is faithful and true. He is no holder of a sinecure; he claims to have finished the work which his Father gave him to do. He has undertaken great things, and, glory be to his name, he has achieved them. His people's sins were laid upon him, and he bore them up to the cross, and on the cross he made an end of them, so that they will never be mentioned against them anymore forever. Then he went down into the grave, and slept there for a little season; but he tore away the bars of the sepulcher and left death dead at his feet, bringing life and immortality to light by his resurrection. This was his high calling, and he has fulfilled it. His victory is complete, the defeat of the foe is perfect. "O death, where is thy sting? O grave, where is thy victory?" Springing upward from the tomb when the appointed days were come, he opened Heaven's gates to all believers, according to the word, "The breaker is come up before them, and their king shall pass before them, and the Lord on the head of them." As he opened the golden gates, he led captivity captive; and, receiving gifts for men, he cast down a royal largess among the poorest of his people, that they might be enriched thereby. This was his object, and the design has been carried out without flaw or failure. Within the veil he went, our Representative, to take possession of our crowns and thrones, which he holds for us to this day by the tenure of his own cross. Having purchased the inheritance, and paid off the heavy mortgage that lay upon it, he has taken possession of the Canaan wherein our souls shall dwell at the end of the days when we shall stand in our lot. Is it not proven that he is great? Conquerors are great, and he is the greatest of them. Deliverers are great, and he is the greatest of them. Liberators are great, and he is the greatest of them. Saviors are great, and he is the greatest of them. They that multiply the joys of men are truly great, and what shall I say of him who has bestowed everlasting joy upon his people, and entailed it upon them by a covenant of salt for ever and ever? Well didst thou say, O Gabriel, "He shall be great," for great indeed he is!

He shall be great, again, *in the prevalence of his merits*. Never being had such merit as Christ. His life and death cover all believers from head to foot with a perfect obedience to the law. With royal Gesture are they clad: Solomon in all his glory was not arrayed like one of those. His blood has washed believers white as the driven snow, and his righteousness has made them to be "accepted in the Beloved." He has such merit with God that he deserves of the Most High whatsoever he wills to ask; and he asks for his people that they shall have every blessing needful for eternal life and perfection. He is great, indeed, my brethren, when we think that he has clothed us all in his righteousness, and washed us all in his blood. Nor us alone, but ten thousand times ten thousand of his redeemed stand today in the wedding-dress of his eternal merit, and plead before God a claim that never can be denied—the claim of a perfect obedience which must always please the Father's heart.

Oh, what mercy is that which has turned our Hell to Heaven, transformed our disease into health, and lifted us from the dunghill, and set us among the princes of his people! In infinite power to remove sin, to perfume with acceptance, to clothe with righteousness, to win blessings, to preserve saints, and to save to the uttermost, the Lord Jesus is great beyond all greatness.

My theme will never be exhausted, though I may be. Let me not delay to add that our Lord Jesus Christ is great *in the number of his saved ones*. I do not believe in a little Christ, or a little Heaven, or a little company before the throne, or a few that shall be saved. Hear you this, for I would fain reply to a lie that is often stated, and is the last resort of those who assail the doctrines of grace. They say that we believe that God has left the great mass of his creatures to perish, and has arbitrarily chosen an elect few. We have never thought such a thing. We believe that the Lord has an elect many; and it is our joy and delight to think of them as a number that no man can number. "Oh," they say, "you think that the few who go to your little Bethel or Salem are the elect of God." That, sirs, is what you invent for your own purposes, but we have never said anything of the sort. We rejoice to believe that as many as the stars of Heaven shall the redeemed of Christ be—that as many as the sands that are upon the sea-shore, even an innumerable company, are those for whom Christ has shed his precious blood that he might effectually redeem them. As I look up to the Heaven of the sanctified, my mind's eye does not see a few dozen saints met together in select circles of exclusiveness; but my eyes are dazzled with the countless lights which shine each one from the illustrious brows of the redeemed; lustrous I say, for each glorified one wears upon his forehead the name of the Most High. My heart is glad to turn away from the multitude that throng the broad way, and to see a greater multitude that throng the heavenly fields, and, day without night, celebrate redemption by the blood of the Lamb. Have they not washed their robes, and made them white in his blood? In all things our Lord will have the pre-eminence, and this shall be the case in the number of his followers: he shall therein vanquish his great enemy. His redeemed shall fly as a cloud, as doves to their windows. Countless as the drops of morning dew shall his people be in the day of his power. He shall be great in the host of his adherents in glory.

Multitudes upon earth are even now pursuing their road to Heaven, and greater hosts are yet to follow them. A day shall be when the people of God shall be increased exceedingly, above anything that we see at this present; they shall spring up as the grass and as willows by the watercourses, as if every stone that heard the ripple of the brook had been turned into a man. The seed of the Lord Jesus Christ shall multiply till arithmetic shall be utterly baffled, and numeration shall fail. He is great—a great Savior of a great mass of great sinners, who shall by his redeeming arm be brought safely, without fail, to his right hand in the endless glory. As the tribes of the natural Israel increased exceedingly, so also shall the spiritual Israel. The Lord shall multiply his Zion with men as with a flock, and thus shall the King of Israel be great.

Brethren and sisters, the Lord Jesus Christ shall be great *in the estimation of his people*. If I were to try tonight to praise my Lord to the highest heavens, my brother might well follow me, and extol our Lord much more. Then I would get up from my seat again, and I would not rest until I found yet loftier praises for my Lord and God. Then might nay dear brother return to the happy task, and excel me yet again, and then, for sure, I would be on my feet a third time, and keep up the hallowed rivalry, lauding and magnifying Jesus to my mind's utmost, and, if the Lord permitted, we would never leave off, for I would give in to no man in my desire to extol my Lord Jesus. I am sure that none of his people would give way to others in a humble sense of supreme indebtedness; but each one would say, "There is something which he has done for me which he never did for you. There is some point of view in which he is greater to me than he is to you." Brothers, I admit that there are many points in which he is greater to you than he is to me; but yet to me he is higher than Heaven, vaster than eternity, more delightful than Paradise, more blessed than blessedness itself. If I could speak of him according to my soul's desire, I would speak in great capital letters, and not in the small italics which I am compelled to use. If I could speak as I would, I would make winds and waves my orators, and cause the whole universe to become one open mouth with which to tell out the praises of Emmanuel. If all eternity would speak, as though it, too, were but one tongue, yet it could not tell out all the charms of his love and the sureness of his faithfulness and his truth. We must leave off somewhere, but, truly, if it be the point of our estimation of him, we never can express our overwhelming sense of his honor, his excellence, his sweetness. Oh, that he were praised by every creature that has breath! Oh, that every minute placed another gem in his crown! Oh, that every soul that breathes did continue to breathe out nothing but hosannas and hallelujahs unto him, for he deserves all possible praises! Do you hear the crash of the multitudinous music of heaven? It is like many waters, and like the mighty waves of the sea, but it is all for him. Can you catch the charming notes of "harpers harping with their harps"? Their harpings are all for him. Can you conceive the unutterable joys of the glorified? Every felicity of eternity is a song to his honor. Heaven and earth shall yet be full of the out-shinings of his glory. Who can look the sun in the face in the height of his noontide? Who can tell the illimitable greatnesses of the Son of God? To him, even to him, let all praises be, for he has redeemed our souls with blood, and set the captives free: he has made us unto our God both kings and priests, and we shall reign with him forever and forever. Truly, he is great, and shall be great eternally.

But, oh, brethren, how great must Christ be *in the glory of Heaven!* We have never seen that. Some of us shall see it full soon.

> *For we are in the border-land,*
> *The heavenly country's near at hand:*
> *A step is all 'twixt us and rest,*
> *E'en now we converse with the blest.*

But the greatness of Christ in Heaven—surely this is the grand sight for which we long to go to Heaven—that we may behold his glory, "the glory which he had with the Father before the world was," and the glory which he has gained by his service of the Father here below. Has he not said, "Father, I will that they also, whom thou hast given me, be with me where I am; that they may behold my glory"? What honor and majesty surround our Prince in the metropolis of his empire! What is this city? Whence comes its brightness? The sun is dim, the moon no more displays herself. "The glory of God did lighten it, and the Lamb is the light thereof": the whole city shines in the Redeemer's glory. And who are these that come trooping down the golden streets?—these shining ones, each one comparable to a living, moving sun? each one as bright as the star of the morning? Ask them whence comes their brightness, and they tell you that the glory of Christ has risen upon them, and they are reflecting his brightness as the moon reflects the effulgence of the sun. If you sit down with one of these shining ones, and hear him tell his story, the sum of the matter will be, "Not unto us; but unto him that loved us, be honor and glory." This will be the substance of every testimony—"He loved me, and gave himself for me;" only they will put it something like this—"HE loved *me*. He, that great HE." How they will pronounce it as they point to his glory—"HE loved me—that little *me*." They will sink their voices, oh, so low, as with wonder and surprise they express their admiration that ever he could have loved such unworthy ones as they were.

But I must not—dare not—try to touch upon the *glory of Christ upon the throne of the Father*. Certain great divines have written upon the glory of Christ, but I will warrant you that, when they died and went to Heaven, they half wished that they could come back again to amend their most glowing pages. Ah me, what can ignorance say of the All-wise? What do blinking owls know of high noon? What do we poor limited creatures, babes of yesterday, know of the Infinite, the Ancient of Days, and of the splendor that comes from the Firstborn at the right hand of the Most High? It would need an angel to tell us that; but, peradventure, if he did, either we should not understand, or else what we did understand would overpower us, and we should fall before our Lord as dead. The heavens are now telling the glory of our Lord, but the half of it will never be told throughout ages of ages. Assuredly, concerning our adorable Lord Jesus it is true—"He shall be great."

II. Now, by your leave, I want to turn the subject a little round, and look at it in another light. "He shall be great," and he is so, for *he deals with great things*.

He is a Savior, and a great one. As I have already said, it was a *great ruin* which he came to restore. The wind came from the abyss and smote the four corners of the house of manhood, and it fell and lay along. Devils laughed and triumphed as they saw God's handiwork despoiled. Human nature sank in shame, Paradise was blasted, sin was triumphant, and the fiery sword was set at Eden's gate to exclude us. It was a hideous ruin. But, oh! when Christ came, he brought a great salvation. He came to prepare a better Paradise, and to plant in it a better tree of life, and to give us possession of it upon a better tenure than before. Oh, he is a great Savior; he wrought amid the chaos of the fall, and restored what Adam had destroyed!

And, beloved, we were covered with *great sin*—some of us especially so. But "he shall be great," and therefore he makes short work of great sin. Great sinners, what a joy it ought to be to you to think that he is great, and, therefore, has come to rescue such as you are, and deal with such difficulties as beset and surround *you*; for what if sin be great? His arrangement for its removal is great too. Look there at Calvary, and, if you can see it through your blinding tears, behold the sacrifice he offered once for all to put away sin. Regard the old Tabernacle and its faulty types—Aaron has offered his bullock which has smoked to Heaven, but no result has followed. Aaron has brought his lambs, and goats, and rams, and their blood in basins is thrown at the altar foot: the whole soil of the Tabernacle is saturated with the blood of bullocks and of goats: but no result has come of it. These can never take away sin. See now the greater sacrifice which Jesus brings. That great High Priest of ours is great indeed, for he has offered up *himself,* without spot, unto God! Lo, on his great altar there smokes to Heaven no longer clouding incense or burning flesh, but the body and soul of the appointed Substitute are offered up in sacrifice for men. We have none of us a due conception of the grandeur of that vicarious offering, which at once and forever made an end of sin. Think of it carefully and in detail. Count it no light thing that he who was the Father's equal, that he who was pure and perfect in both natures, became a curse for us, and was made sin for us, and presented himself as a victim to justice on our behalf. This is a wonder among wonders, as much exceeding miracle as miracle exceeds the most common-place fact. It overtops the highest Alps of thought, that he who was offended should expiate the offense, he who was perfect should suffer punishment, he who was all goodness should be made sin, and he who was all love should be forsaken of the God of love. What merit and majesty are found in his glorious oblation! Great is the sin, but greater is the sacrifice. The atonement has covered the guilt, and left a margin of abounding righteousness.

Beloved, what a mercy it is for us that we have such a High-Priest, for if you and I are burdened tonight with great transgression, there is *great pardons* to be had—pardon so great that it actually annihilates the sin—pardon so great that the sin is cast behind Jehovah's back, while the pardon rings out perpetual notes of joy and peace in the soul.

> *His the pardon, ours the sin,—*
> *Great the sin, the pardon great,*
> *Great his good which healed our ill,*
> *Great his love which killed our hate.*

He shall be great indeed who has wrought us so great salvation.

And now, dear friends, you and I, being greatly pardoned through the great sacrifice, are journeying through the wilderness toward Canaan, and we have *great wants* and many, pressing upon us every day. We are poverty itself, and only All-sufficiency can supply us, but that is found in Jesus. We need great abundance of food: the heavenly bread lies around about the camp, and each may fill his omer. We require rivers of living water: the smitten rock yields us a ceaseless flood; the out-flow never ceases. We have great demands, but Christ has *great supplies*. Between here and Heaven we shall have, perhaps, greater wants than we have yet known; but, all along, every halting-place is ready, provender is laid up, good cheer is stored, nothing has been overlooked. The commissariat of the Eternal is absolutely perfect. Do you feel sometimes so thirsty for grace that, like Behemoth, you could drink up Jordan at a draught? More than that river could hold is given you. Drink abundantly, for Christ has prepared you a bottomless sea of grace to fill you with all the fullness of God. Stint not yourselves, and doubt not your Savior: wherefore should you limit the Holy One of Israel? Be great in your experience of his all-sufficiency, and great in your praises of his bounty, and then in Heaven you shall pour at his feet great treasures of gratitude for ever and ever.

Yes, and he is a Christ of *great preparations*. He is engaged before the throne today in preparing a *great Heaven* for his people; it will be made up of great deliverance, great peace, great rest, great joy, great victory, great discovery, great fellowship, great rapture, great glory. He is preparing for his redeemed no little Heaven, no starveling banquet, no narrow delight. He is a great Creator, and he is creating a great Paradise wherein a great multitude shall be greatly happy forever and ever. "He shall be great"—great in the bliss of his innumerable elect. If we once get within the pearly gates, and walk those golden streets, we are not ashamed tonight to vow that he shall be great; we will make him glorious before his holy angels. If praises can make him great, our praises shall ring out day and night at the very loudest, and ten thousand times ten thousand of the glorified shall join with us in perpetual hallelujahs to him who loved us before all worlds, and will love us when all worlds shall cease to be. "He shall be great." He must be great. If we live, it shall be our business to sing, like the Virgin, "My soul doth magnify the Lord, and my spirit hath rejoiced in God my Savior."

III. I have come to a close when I have said a few words upon the last point, which is this: *his greatness will soon appear.*

It now lies under a cloud to men's blear[y] eyes. They still belittle him with their vague and vain thoughts; but it shall not always be so. It is midnight with his honor here just now; or if it be not midnight, it is much the same, for men are stone blind. But it will not be darkness long, nor shall human minds be blinded for ever. My eyes foresee the dawning. Did you hear the clarion just now? I dream not that ears of flesh can catch the sound as yet; but the ears of faith can hear it. The trumpet rings out exceeding loud and long, and after the trumpet there is heard this voice: "Behold, the Bridegroom cometh! Go ye forth to meet him." Hear ye not the shouts of armies—"Lo, he cometh! Lo, he cometh! Lo, he cometh!" Right gladly I hear the cry. Let the world ring with the joy-note. He comes. That trumpet proclaims him. I shall propound no order now as to how predicted events shall happen; but I know this, that the Lord shall reign forever and ever, King of kings, and Lord of lords. Hallelujah! "He shall be great." The nations shall bow at his feet. Rebellious enemies shall own him as their King. The whole universe shall be filled with the glory of God. There shall be left no space where this light shall not shine. "He shall be great." To him "every knee shall bow, and every tongue confess that Jesus Christ is Lord, to the glory of God the Father."

Fret not yourselves, brethren, because of the false doctrine which roams through the world today. Worry not your hearts as though the Christ were defeated. He is clad in shining armor, through which no dart of error can ever pierce. He lingers for a little while upon the hills, surveying the battlefield with eagle-eye. He leaves his poor servants to prove how weak they are, as they almost turn their backs in the day of battle. He lets Heaven and earth see the weakness of an arm of flesh. But courage, brethren! The Prince Emmanuel hastens! You may hear his horse hoofs on the road. He is near to come. On white horses shall his chosen follow him, going forth "conquering and to conquer," for the battle is the Lord's, and he will deliver the enemy into our hands. The Lord shall reign for ever and ever; king of kings! Hallelujah! "He must reign, till he hath put all enemies under his feet."

The day is coming when the mighty progress of the gospel shall make Christ to be great among men, and then you need not listen long to hear that other trumpet which shall wake the sleeping dead. The Risen One descends. *Resurrection* is at hand! Oh, what greatness will be upon Christ in that hour when all shall leave their graves, even the whole multitude of the slain of death! He shall be glorious among them, the Firstfruits of the resurrection, illustrious in those who rise by virtue of his rising. Oh, what honor will he have that day! Jesus, thou art he whom thy brethren shall praise as they see thee victorious over death in all those quickened myriads.

Then shall come the *Judgment*; and oh, how great will Christ be in men's eyes in that day when he sits upon the throne and holds the scales of justice, and judges men for the deeds done in the body! I warrant you that none will deny his Godhead in that day. None will proclaim themselves his adversaries in that dread hour. The earth is reeling! The sky is crumbling! The stars are falling! The sun is quenched! The moon is black as sackcloth of hair! and Jesus is sitting on the throne! A cry is heard from all his enemies. "Hide us, mountains. Rocks fall upon us. Hide us from his face." That face of his—calm, quiet, and triumphant, shall be terrible to them. They will cry in horror, "Hide us from the face of him that sitteth on the throne, and from the wrath of the Lamb." But they cannot be hidden. Fly whither they may, those eyes pursue them—those eyes of love more terrible than flames of wrath. Oil, though it be soft, yet burns full furiously; and love on fire is Hell. Fiercer than a lion on his prey is love when once it groweth angry for holiness' sake and truth's sake. In that day those who know his love shall admire him beyond measure; but those who know his wrath shall equally feel that "he is great." Though it be their Hell to feel it, yet shall they know that there is none so great as he, when he shall take the iron rod, and dash them in pieces like a potter's vessel. Their cries of remorse and despair, as they rise up to the throne of his awful majesty, shall proclaim to an awe-struck universe that Jesus is great.

Kiss the Son, lest he be angry, and ye perish from the way, when his wrath is kindled but a little. Blessed are all they that put their trust in him.

He shall be great, finally, *when he shall gather all his elect about him*—when all the souls redeemed by blood shall assemble within his palace-gate to worship him. Oh, what a sight it will be when he is seen as the center, while, far away from north, south, east, and west, a blazing host of shining ones, all glorious in his glory, shall in ever-widening circles surround his person and his throne, all bowing down before the Son of God, and crying, "Hallelujah!" as they adore him! Not one will doubt him there, nor oppose him there. Oh, what a sight it shall be when every one shall praise him to the uttermost; when from every heart shall leap up reverent love, when every tongue shall sound forth his honors, when there shall be no division, no discord, no jarring notes; but countless armies shall as one man adore the Lord whom they love! Again they say, "Hallelujah!" and the incense of their adoration goeth up for ever and ever. Oh, for that grandest of cries, "Hallelujah! Hallelujah!

the Lord God omnipotent reigneth, and his Son is exalted to sit with him upon the throne of his glory for ever and ever." Truly, he shall be great.

Oh, make him great tonight, poor sinner, by trusting him! Make him great tonight, dear child of God, by longing for him. Make him great as you come to the table by hungering after him. Count it a great privilege to eat and drink with him with overflowing delight. Come with a great hunger and a great thirst after him, and take him into your very self, and say, "He is my bread: he is my drink: he is my life: he is my all." All the while let your spirit live by adoring, and let every pulse of your body beat to his honor. Tune your hand, your heart, your tongue to this one song, "Hallelujah, hallelujah, hallelujah! Unto him that loved us and died for us, and rose again, be glory for ever and ever!"

> To the Lamb that was slain, all honor be paid,
> Let crowns without number encircle his head:
> Let blessing, and glory, and riches, and might,
> Be ascribed evermore by angels of light.

The Great Birthday and Our Coming of Age

Delivered on Lord's Day morning, December 21, 1884, at the Metropolitan Tabernacle, Newington. No. 1815.

Even so we, when we were children, were in bondage under the elements of the world: but when the fullness of the time was come, God sent forth his Son, made of a woman, made under the law, to redeem them that were under the law, that we might receive the adoption of sons. And because ye are sons, God hath sent forth the Spirit of his Son into your hearts, crying, "Abba, Father."—Galatians 4:3–6

The birth of our Lord Jesus Christ into this world is a wellspring of pure, unmingled joy. We associate with his crucifixion much of sorrowful regret, but we derive from his birth at Bethlehem nothing but delight. The angelic song was a fit accompaniment to the joyful event, and the filling of the whole earth with peace and good will is a suitable consequence of the condescending fact. The stars of Bethlehem cast no baleful light: we may sing with undivided joy, "Unto us a child is born, unto us a son is given." When the Eternal God stooped from Heaven and assumed the nature of his own creature who had rebelled against him, the deed could mean no harm to man. God in our nature is not God against us, but God with us. We may take up the young child in our arms and feel that we have seen the Lord's salvation; it cannot mean destruction to men. I do not wonder that the men of the world celebrate the supposed anniversary of the great birthday as a high festival with carols and banquets. Knowing nothing of the spiritual meaning of the mystery, they yet perceive that it means man's good, and so in their own rough way they respond to it. We who observe no days which are not appointed of the Lord, rejoice continually in our Prince of Peace, and find in our Lord's manhood, a fountain of consolation.

To those who are truly the people of God, the incarnation is the subject of a thoughtful joy, which ever increases with our knowledge of its meaning, even as rivers are enlarged by many trickling brooks. The Birth of Jesus not only brings us hope, but the certainty of good things. We do not merely speak of Christ's coming into relation with our nature, but of his entering into union with ourselves, for he has become one flesh with us for purposes as great as his love. He is one with all of us who have believed in his name.

Let us consider by the light of our text the special effect produced upon the church of God by the coming of the Lord Jesus Christ in human flesh. You know, beloved, that his coming a second time will produce a wonderful change upon the church. "Then shall the righteous shine forth as the sun." We are looking forward to his second advent for the uplifting of the church to a higher platform than that upon which it now stands. Then shall the militant become triumphant, and laboring become exultant. Now is the time of battle, but the second advent shall bring both victory and rest. Today our King commands us to conflict, but soon he shall reign upon Mount Zion, with his ancients gloriously. When he shall appear we shall be like him, for we shall see him as he is. Then shall the bride adorn herself with her jewels, and stand ready for her Husband. The whole waiting creation which now groaneth and travaileth together in harmony with the birthpangs of the church shall then come to her time of deliverance, and enter into the glorious liberty of the children of God.

This is the promise of the second advent; but what was the result of the first advent? Did that make any difference in the dispensation of the church of God? Beyond all doubt it did. Paul here tells us that we were minors, in bondage under the elements of the world, until the fullness of time was come, when "God sent forth his Son, made of a woman, made under the law." Some will say, "He is speaking here of the Jews"; but he expressly guards us in the previous chapter against dividing the church into Jews and Gentiles. To him it is only one church, and when he says we were in bondage he is talking to the Galatian Christians, who were many of them Gentiles; but in truth he regards them neither as Jews nor Gentiles, but as part of the one and indivisible church of God. In those ages in which election mainly embraced the tribes of Israel, there were always some chosen ones beyond that visible line, and in the mind of God the chosen people were always regarded as neither Jews nor Gentiles, but as one in Christ Jesus. So Paul lets us know that the church up to the time of the coming of Christ was like a child at school under tutors and governors; or like a young man not yet arrived at years of discretion, and therefore most fitly kept under restraint. When Jesus came, his great birthday was the day of the coming of age of the church: then believers remained no more children but became men in Christ Jesus. Our Lord by his first advent brought the church up out of her nonage and her pupilage into a condition of maturity, in which it was able to take possession of the inheritance, and claim and enjoy its rights and liberties. It was a wonderful step from being under the law as a schoolmaster, to come from under its rod and rule into the freedom and power of a full-grown heir, but such was the change for believers of the old time, and in consequence there was a wonderful difference between the highest under the Old Testament and the lowest under the New. Of them that are born of woman there was not born a greater than John the Baptist, and yet the least in the kingdom of Heaven was greater than he. John the Baptist may be compared to a youth of nineteen, still an infant in law, still under his guardian, still unable to touch his estate, but the least believer in Jesus has passed his minority, and is "no more a servant, but a son; and if a son, then an heir of God through Christ."

May the Holy Spirit bless the text to us while we use it thus. First, let us *consider in itself the joyful mission of the Son of God*, and then let us consider the *joyful result which has come of that mission*, as it is expressed in our text.

I. I invite you to *consider the joyful mission of the son of God.*

The Lord of Heaven has come to earth; God has taken upon himself human nature. Hallelujah!

This great transaction was accomplished at the right time: "When the fullness of the time was come, God sent forth his Son, made of a woman." The reservoir of time had to be filled by age after age, and when it was full to the brim the Son of God appeared. Why the world should have remained in darkness for four thousand years, why it should have taken that length of time for the church to attain her full age, we cannot tell, but this we are told, that Jesus was sent forth when the fullness of time was come. Our Lord did not come before his time nor behind his time: he was punctual to his hour, and cried to the moment—"Lo, I come." We may not curiously pry into the reasons why Christ came when he did; but we may reverently muse thereon. The birth of Jesus is the grandest light of history, the sun in the seasons of all time. It is the pole-star of human destiny, the hinge of chronology, the meeting-place of the waters of the past and the future. Why happened it just at that moment? Assuredly it was so predicted. There were prophecies many which pointed exactly to that hour. I will not detain you just now with them; but those of you who are familiar with the Old Testament scriptures well know that, as with so many fingers, they pointed to the time when the Shiloh should come, and the great sacrifice should be offered. He came at the hour which God had determined. The infinite Lord appoints the date of every event; all times are in his hand. There are no loose threads in the providence of God, no stitches are dropped, no events are left to chance. The great clock of the universe keeps good time, and the whole machinery of providence moves with unerring punctuality. It was to be expected that the greatest of all events should be most accurately and wisely timed, and so it was. God willed it to be when and where it was, and that will is to us the ultimate reason.

If we might suggest any reasons which can be appreciated by ourselves, we should view the date in reference to the church itself as to the time of her coming of age. There is a measure of reason in appointing the age of twenty-one as the period of a man's majority, for he is then mature, and full grown. It would be unwise to make a person to be of age while only ten, eleven, or twelve; everybody would see that such boyish years would be unsuitable. On the other hand, if we were detained from being of age till we were thirty, everyone would see that it was a needless and arbitrary postponement. Now, if we were wise enough, we should see that the church of God could not have endured gospel light earlier than the day of Christ's coming: neither would it have been well to keep her in gloom beyond that time. There was a fitness about the date which we cannot fully understand, because we have not the means of forming so decided an estimate of the life of a church as of the life of a man. God alone knows the times and seasons for a church, and no doubt to him the four thousand years of the old dispensation male up a fit period for the church to abide at school, and bear the yoke in her youth.

The time of coming of age of a man has been settled by law with reference to those that are round about him. It were not meet for servants that the child of five or six should be master: it were not meet in the world of commerce that an ordinary boy of ten or twelve should be a trader on his own account. There is a fitness with reference to relatives, neighbors, and dependents. So was there a fitness in the time when the church should come to her age with regard to the rest of mankind. The world must know its darkness that it might value the light when it should shine forth, the world must grow weary of its bondage that it might welcome the great Emancipator. It was God's plan that the world's wisdom should prove itself to be folly; he meant to permit intellect and skill to play themselves out, and then he would send his Son. He would allow man to prove his strength to be perfect weakness, and then he would become his righteousness and strength. Then, when one monarch governed all lands, and when the temple of war was shut after ages of bloodshed, the Lord whom the faithful sought suddenly appeared. Our Lord and Savior came when time was full, and like a harvest ready for his reaping, and so will he come again when once more the age is ripe and ready for his presence.

Observe, concerning the first advent, that *the Lord was moving in it towards man.* "When the fullness of the time was come, God sent forth his Son." We moved not towards the Lord, but the Lord towards us. I do not find that the world in repentance sought after its Maker. No; but the offended God himself in infinite compassion broke the silence, and came forth to bless his enemies. See how spontaneous is the grace of God. All good things begin with him.

It is very delightful that God should take an interest in every stage of the growth of his people from their spiritual infancy to their spiritual manhood. As Abraham made a great feast when Isaac was weaned, so doth the Lord make a feast at the coming of age of his people. While they were as minors under the law of ceremonial observances, he led them about and instructed them. He knew that the yoke of the law was for their good, and be comforted them in the bearing of it; but he was glad when the hour came for their fuller joy. Oh, how truly did the Psalmist say, "How precious are thy thoughts unto me, O God! how great is the sum of them!" Tell it out with joy and gladness, that the blessings of the new dispensation under which we dwell are the spontaneous gifts of God, thoughtfully bestowed in great love, wherein he hath abounded towards us in all wisdom and prudence. When the fullness of time was come, God himself interposed to give his people their privileges; for it is not his will that any one of his people should miss a single point of blessedness. If we are babes, it is not his wish; he would have us men. If we are famished, it is not by his desire, he would fill us with the bread of Heaven.

Mark the divine interposition—"God sent forth his Son." I hope it may not seem wearisome to you if I dwell upon that word "sent,"—"God sent forth his Son." I take great pleasure in that expression, for it seals the whole work of Jesus. Everything that Christ did was done by commission and authority of his Father. The great Lord, when he was born at Bethlehem, and assumed our nature, did it under divine authorization; and when he came and scattered gifts with both his hands among the sons of men he was the messenger and ambassador of God. He was the Plenipotentiary of the Court of Heaven. At the back of every word of Christ there is the warrant of the Eternal; at the back of every promise of Christ there is the oath of God. The Son doeth nothing of himself, but the Father worketh with him and in him. O soul, when thou dost lean on Christ, thou dost rely upon no amateur Savior, no uncommissioned Redeemer; but upon One who is sent of the Most High, and therefore is authorized in everything that he does. The Father saith, "This is my beloved Son; hear ye him:" For in hearing him you are hearing the Most High. Let us find joy, then, in the coming of our Lord to Bethlehem, because he was sent.

Now run your eye to the next word: "When the fullness of time was come, God sent forth *his Son.*" *Observe the Divine person who was sent.* God sent not an angel, nor any exalted creature, but "his Son." How there can be a Son of God we know not. The eternal filiation of the Son must for ever remain one of those mysteries into which we must not pry. It were something like the sin of the men of Beth-shemesh if we were to open the ark of God to gaze upon the deep things of God. It is quite certain that Christ is God; for here he is called "his Son." He existed before he was born into this world; for God "sent" his Son. He was already in being or he could not have been "sent." And while he is one with the Father, yet he must be distinct from the Father and have a personality separate from that of the Father, otherwise it could not be said that God sent his Son. God the Father was not made of a woman, nor made under the law, but only God the Son, therefore, while we know and are assured that Christ is one with the Father, yet is his distinctness of personality most clearly to be observed.

Admire that God should have only one begotten Son, and should have sent him to uplift us. The messenger to man must be none other than God's own Son. What dignity is here! It is the Lord of angels that is born of Mary; it is he without whom was not anything made, who deigns to hang at a woman's breast and to be wrapped in swaddling bands. Oh, the dignity of this, and consequently, oh, the efficiency of it! He that has come to save us is no weak creature like ourselves, he that has taken upon himself our nature is no being of limited strength, such as an angel or a seraph might have been; but he is the Son of the Highest. Glory be to his Blessed name! Let us dwell on this with delight.

> *If some prophet had been sent*
> *With salvation's joyful news,*
> *Who that heard the blest event*
> *Could their warmest love refuse?*
>
> *But 'twas he to whom in Heaven*
> *Hallelujahs never cease;*
> *He, the mighty God, was given—*
> *Given to us—a Prince of Peace.*
>
> *None but he who did create us*
> *Could redeem from sin and Hell;*
> *None but he could reinstate us*
> *In the rank from which we fell.*

Press on, still keeping to the very words of the text, for they are very sweet. *God sent his Son in real humanity*—"made of a woman." The Revised Version properly hath it, "born of a woman." Perhaps you may get nearer to it if you say, "Made to be born of a woman," for both ideas are present, the *factum* and the *natum*, the "being made" and the "being born." Christ was really and truly of the substance of his mother, as certainly as any other infant that is born into the world is so. God did not create the human nature of Christ apart, and then transmit it into mortal existence by some special means; but his Son was made and born of a woman. He is, therefore, of our race, a man like ourselves, and not man of another stock. You are to make no mistake about it; he is not only of humanity, but of your humanity; for that which is born of a woman is brother to us, be it born when it may. Yet there is an omission, I doubt not intentional, to show how holy was that human nature, for he is born of a woman, not of a man. The Holy Spirit overshadowed the Virgin, and "that holy thing" was born of her without the original sin which pertains to our race by natural descent. Here is a pure humanity though a true humanity; a true humanity though free from sin. Born of a woman, he was of few days and full of trouble; born of a woman, he was compassed with our physical infirmities; but as he was not born of man, he was altogether without tendency to evil or delight therein. I beg you to rejoice in this near approach of Christ to us. Ring out the glad bells, if not in the spires and steeples, yet within your own hearts; for gladder news did never greet your ear than this, that he that is the Son of God was also "made of a woman."

Still further it is added, that God sent his Son *"made under the law,"* or born under the law; for the word is the same in both cases; and by the same means by which he came to be of a woman, he came under the law. And now admire and wonder! The Son of God has come under the law. He was the Law-maker and the Law-giver, and he is both the Judge of the law and the Executioner of the law, and yet he himself came under the law. No sooner was he born of a woman than he came under the law: this voluntarily and yet necessarily. He willed to be a man, and being a man he accepted the position, and stood in the place of man as subject to the law of the race. When they took him and circumcised him according to the law, it was publicly declared that he was under the law. During the rest of his life you will observe how reverently he observed the commands of God. Even to the ceremonial law as it was given by Moses he had scrupulous regard. He despised the traditions and superstitions of men, but for the rule of the dispensation he had a high respect.

By way of rendering service unto God on our behalf, he came under the moral law. He kept his Father's commandments. He obeyed to the full both the first and the second tables; for he loved God with all his heart, and his neighbor as himself. "I delight to do thy will, O my God," saith he, "yea, thy law is within my heart." He could truly say of the Father, "I do always those things that please him." Yet it was a marvelous thing that the King of kings should be under the law, and especially that he should come under the penalty of the law as well as the service of it. "Being found in fashion as a man, he humbled himself, and became obedient unto death, even the death of the cross." As our Surety and Substitute he came under the curse of the law; being made a curse for us. Having taken our place and espoused our nature, though without sin himself, he came under the rigorous demands of justice, and in due time he bowed his head to the sentence of death. "He laid down his life for us." He died the just for the unjust, to bring us to God. In this mystery of his incarnation, in this wonderful substitution of himself in the place of sinful men, lies the ground of that wonderful advance which believers made when Jesus came in the flesh. His advent in human form commenced the era of spiritual maturity and freedom.

II. I ask you now, therefore, in the second place, to *contemplate the joyous result which has come of our Lord's incarnation.*

I must return to what I have said before—*this coming of Christ has ended the minority of believers.* The people of God among the Jews were, before Christ came, the children of God, but they were mere babes or little children. They were instructed in the elements of divine knowledge by types, emblems, shadows, symbols: when Jesus was come there was an end of that infantile teaching. The shadows disappear when the substance is revealed; the symbols are not wanted when the person symbolized is himself present. What a difference between the teaching of our Lord Jesus Christ when he shows them plainly of the Father and the teaching of the priests when they taught by scarlet wool and hyssop and blood! How different the teaching of the Holy Ghost by the apostles of our Lord, and the instruction by meats and drinks and holy days. The old economy is dim with smoke, concealed with curtains, guarded from too familiar an approach; but now we come boldly to the throne, and all with unveiled face behold as in a glass the glory of God.

The Christ has come, and now the kindergarten school is quitted for the college of the Spirit, by whom we are taught of the Lord to know even as we are known. The hard governorship of the law is over. Among the Greeks, boys and youths were thought to need a cruel discipline: while they went to school they were treated very roughly by their pedagogues and tutors. It was supposed that a boy could only imbibe instruction through his skin, and that the tree of knowledge was originally a birch; and therefore there was no sparing the rod, and no mitigation of self-denials and hardships. This fitly pictures the work of the law upon those early believers. Peter speaks of it as a yoke, which neither they nor their fathers were able to bear (Acts 15:10). The law was given amid thunder and flaming fire, and it was more fitted to inspire a wholesome dread than a loving confidence. Those sweeter truths, which are our daily consolation, were hardly known, or but seldom spoken. Prophets did speak of Christ, but they were more frequently employed in pouring out lamentations and denunciations against children that were corrupters. Methinks, one day with Christ was worth a half century with Moses.

When Jesus came, believers began to hear of the Father and his love, of his abounding grace, and the kingdom which he had prepared for them. Then the doctrines of eternal love, and redeeming grace, and covenant faithfulness were unveiled, and they heard of the tenderness of the Elder Brother, the grace of the great

Father, and the indwelling of the ever-blessed Spirit. It was as if they had risen from servitude to freedom, from infancy to manhood. Blessed were they who in their day shared the privilege of the old economy, for it was wonderful light as compared with heathen darkness; yet, for all that, compared with the noontide that Christ brought, it was mere candle-light. The ceremonial law held a man in stern bondage: "You must not eat this, and you must not go there, and you must not wear this, and you must not gather that." Everywhere you were under restraint, and walked between hedges of thorn. The Israelite was reminded of sin at every turn, and warned of his perpetual tendency to fall into one transgression or another. It was quite right that it should be so, for it is good for a man that, while he is yet a youth, he should bear the yoke, and learn obedience; yet it must have been irksome. When Jesus came, what a joyful difference was made. It seemed like a dream of joy, too glad to be true. Peter could not at first believe in it, and needed a vision to make him sure that it was even so. When he saw that great sheet let down, full of all manner of living creatures and four-footed things, and was bidden to kill and eat, he said, "Not so, Lord; for I have never eaten anything that is common or unclean." He was startled indeed when the Lord said, "What God hath cleansed, that call not thou common." That first order of things "stood only in meats and drinks, and diverse washings, and carnal ordinances, imposed on them until the time of reformation;" but Paul saith, "I know, and am persuaded by the Lord Jesus, that there is nothing unclean of itself." Prohibition upon mere ceremonial points, and commands upon carnal matters are now abolished, and great is our liberty: we shall be foolish indeed if we suffer ourselves to be again entangled with the yoke of bondage. Our minority was ended when the Lord, who had aforetime spoken to us by his prophets, at last sent his Son to lead us up to the highest form of spiritual manhood.

Christ came, we are told next, *to redeem those who are under the law:* that is to say, the birth of Jesus, and his coming under the law, and his fulfilling the law, have set all believers free from it as a yoke of bondage. None of us wish to be free from the law as a rule of life, we delight in the commands of God, which are holy, and just, and good. We wish that we could keep every precept of the law, without a single omission or transgression. Our earnest desire is for perfect holiness; but we do not look in that direction for our justification before God. If we be asked today, "Are we hoping to be saved by ceremonies?" we answer, "God forbid." Some seem to fancy that baptism and the Lord's Supper have taken the place of circumcision and the Passover, and that while Jews were saved by one form of ceremonial, we are to be saved by another. Let us never give place to this idea; no, not for an hour. God's people are saved, not by outward rites, nor forms, nor priestcraft, but because "God sent forth his Son, made of a woman, made under the law," and he has so kept the law that by faith his righteousness covers all believers, and we are not condemned by the law. As to the moral law, which is the standard of equity for all time, it is no way of salvation for us. Once we were under it, and strove to keep it in order to earn the divine favor; but we have now no such motive. The word was, "This do and thou shalt live," and we therefore strove like slaves to escape the lash, and earn our wage; but it is so no longer. Then we strove to do the Lord's will that he might love us, and that we might be rewarded for what we did; but we have no design of purchasing that favor now, since we freely and securely enjoy it on a very different ground. God loves us out of pure grace, and he has freely forgiven us our iniquities, and this out of gratuitous goodness. We are already saved, and that not by works of righteousness which we have done, or by holy acts which we hope to perform, but wholly of free grace. If it be of grace, it is no more of works, and that it is all of grace from first to last is our joy and glory. The righteousness that covers us was wrought out by him that was born of a woman, and the merit by which we enter Heaven is the merit, not of our own hands or hearts, but of him that loved us, and gave himself for us. Thus are we redeemed from the law by our Lord's being made under the law; and we become sons and no more servants, because the great Son of God became a servant in our stead.

"What!" saith one; "then do you not seek to do good works?" Indeed we do. We have talked of them before, but we actually perform them now. Sin shall not have dominion over us, for we are not under law, but under grace. By God's grace we desire to abound in works of holiness, and the more we can serve our God, the happier we are. But this is not to save ourselves, for we are already saved. O sons of Hagar, ye cannot understand the freedom of the true heir, the child born according to promise! Ye that are in bondage, and feel the force of legal motives, ye cannot understand how we should serve our Father who is in Heaven with all our heart and all our soul, not for what we get by it, but because he has loved us, and saved us, irrespective of our works. Yet it is even so; we would abound in holiness to his honor, and praise, and glory, because the love of Christ constraineth us. What a privilege it is to cease from the spirit of bondage by being redeemed from the law! Let us praise our Redeemer with all our hearts.

We are redeemed from the law in its operation upon our mind: it breeds no fear within us now. I have heard children of God say sometimes, "Well, but don't you think if we fall into sin we shall cease to be in God's love, and so shall perish?" This is to cast a slur upon the unchangeable love of God. I see that you make a mistake, and think a child is a servant. Now, if you have a servant, and he misbehaves himself, you say, "I give you notice to quit. There is your wage; you must mind another master." Can you do that to your son? Can you do that to your daughter? "I never thought of such a thing," say you. Your child is yours for life. Your boy behaved very badly to you: why did you not give him his wages and start him [on his way]? You answer, that he does not serve you for wages, and that he is your son, and cannot be otherwise. Just so. Then always know the difference between a servant and a son, and the difference between the covenant of works and the covenant of grace.

I know how a base heart can make mischief out of this, but I cannot help it: the truth is the truth. Will a child rebel because he will always be a child? Far from it; it is this which makes him feel love in return. The true child of God is kept from sin by other and better forces than a slavish fear of being turned out of doors by his Father. If you are under the covenant of works, then, mind you, if you do not fulfill all righteousness you will perish: if you are under that covenant, unless you are perfect you are lost; one sin will destroy you, one sinful thought will ruin you. If you have not been perfect in your obedience, you must take your wages and be gone. If God deals with you according to your works, there will be nothing for you but, "Cast out this bondwoman and her son." But if you are God's child, that is a different matter; you will still be his child even when he corrects you for your disobedience.

"Ah," saith one, "then I may live as I like." Listen! If you are God's child, I will tell you how you will like to live. You will desire to live in perfect obedience to your Father, and it will be your passionate longing from day to day to be perfect even as your Father which is in Heaven is perfect. The nature of sons which grace imparts is a law unto itself: the Lord puts his fear into the hearts of the regenerate so that they do not depart from him. Being born again and introduced into the family of God, you will render to the Lord an obedience which you would not have thought of rendering to him if you had only been compelled by the idea of law and penalty. Love is a master force, and he that feels its power will hate all evil. The more salvation is seen to be of grace, the deeper and more mighty is our love, and the more does it work towards that which is pure and holy. Do not quote Moses for motives of Christian obedience. Do not say, "The Lord will cast me away unless I do this and that." Such talk is of the bondswoman and her son; but it is very unseemly in the mouth of a true-born heir of Heaven. Get it out of your mouth. If you are a son, you disgrace your father when you think that he will repudiate his own; you forget your spiritual heirship and liberty when you dread a change in Jehovah's love. It is all very well for a mere babe to talk in that ignorant fashion, and I don't wonder that many professors know no better, for many ministers are only half-evangelical; but you that have become men in Christ, and know that he has redeemed you from the law, ought not to go back to such bondage. "God sent forth his Son, made of a woman, made under the law, to redeem them that were under the law."

What else has he come for? Notice further, *"That we might receive the adoption of sons."* The Lord Jesus Christ has come in human flesh that his people might, to the full, realize, grasp, and enjoy, "the adoption of sons." I want you this morning to see if you can do that. May the Holy Spirit enable you. What is it to receive the adoption of sons? Why to feel,

> Now I am under the mastery of love, as a dear child, who is both loved and loving. I go in and out of my Father's house not as a casual servant, called in by the day or the

week, but as a child at home. I am not looking for hire as a servant, for I am ever with my Father, and all that he has is mine. My God is my Father, and his countenance makes me glad. I am not afraid of him, but I delight in him, for nothing can separate me from him. I feel a perfect love that casteth out fear, and I delight myself in him.

Try now and enter into that spirit this morning. That is why Christ has come in the flesh—on purpose that you, his people, may be, to the full, the adopted children of the Lord, acting out and enjoying all the privileges which sonship secures to you.

And then, next, exercise your heirship. One who is a son, and knows he is an heir of all his father's estates, does not pine in poverty, nor act like a beggar. He looks upon everything as his own; he regards his father's wealth as making him rich. He does not feel that he is stealing if he takes what his father has made to be his own, but he makes free with it. I wish believers would make free with the promises and blessings of their God.

Help yourselves, for no good thing will the Lord withhold from you. All things are yours: you only need to use the hand of faith. Ask what thou wilt. If you appropriate a promise it will not be pilfering: you may take it boldly and say, "This is mine." Your adoption brings with it large rights: be not slow to use them. "If children, then heirs; heirs of God, and joint heirs with Christ." Among men, sons are only heirs, heirs in possession, when the father is dead; but our Father in Heaven lives, and yet we have full heirship in him. The Lord Jesus Christ was made of a woman on purpose that his dear people might at once enter into their heirship.

You ought to feel a sweet joy in the perpetual relationship which is now established between you and God, for Jesus is still your brother. You have been adopted, and God has never cancelled adoption yet. There is such a thing as regeneration, but there is not such a thing as the life then received dying out. If you are born unto God, you are born unto God. The stars may turn to coals, and the sun and moon may become clots of blood, but he that is born of God has a life within him which can never end: he is God's child, and God's child he shall be. Therefore let him walk at large like a child, an heir, a prince of the blood royal, who bears a relationship to the Lord which neither time nor eternity can ever destroy. This is why Jesus was made of a woman and made under the law, that he might give us to enjoy the fullness of the privilege of adopted sons.

Follow me a minute a little further. The next thing that Christ has brought us by being made of a woman is, "Because ye are sons, God *hath sent forth the Spirit of his Son into your hearts.*" Here are two sendings. God sent his Son, and now he sends his Spirit. Because Christ has been sent, therefore the Spirit is sent, and now you shall know the Holy Ghost's indwelling because of Christ's incarnation. The Spirit of light, the Spirit of life, the Spirit of love, the Spirit of liberty, the same Spirit that was in Christ Jesus is in you. That same Spirit which descended upon Jesus in the waters of baptism also descended upon you. You, O child of God, have the Spirit of

God as your present guide and Comforter; and he shall be with you forever. The life of Christ is your life, and the Spirit of Christ is your Spirit; wherefore, this day be exceeding glad, for you have not received the spirit of bondage again to fear, but ye have received the Spirit of adoption.

There we finish, for Jesus has come *to give us the cry* as well as the spirit of adoption, "whereby we cry, Abba, Father." According to ancient traditions no slave might say, "Abba, Father," and according to the truth as it is in Jesus none but a man who is really a child of God, and has received the adoption, can truly say, "Abba, Father." This day my heart desires for everyone of you, my brethren, that because Christ has been born into the world, you may at once come of age, and may at this hour confidently say, "Abba, Father." The great God, the Maker of Heaven and earth, is my Father, and I dare avow it without fear that he will disown the kindred. The Thunderer, the ruler of the stormy sea, is my Father, and notwithstanding the terror of his power, I draw near to him in love. He who is the Destroyer, who says, "Return, ye children of men," is my Father, and I am not alarmed at the thought that he will call me to himself in due time. My God, thou who shalt call the multitudes of the slain from their graves to fire, I look forward with joy to the hour when thou shalt call and I shall answer thee. Do what thou wilt with me, thou art my Father. Smile on me: I will smile back and say "My Father." Chasten me, and as I weep I will cry, "My Father." This shall make everything work good to me, be it never so hard to bear. If thou art my Father, all is well to all eternity. Bitterness is sweet, and death itself is life, since thou art my Father. Oh, trip ye merrily home, ye children of the living God, saying each one within himself,

> I have it, I have it. I have that which cherubim before the throne have never gained; I have relationship with God of the nearest and the dearest kind, and my spirit for her music hath this word, "Abba, Father; Abba, Father."

Now, dear children of God, if any of you are in bondage under the law, why do you remain so? Let the redeemed go free. Are you fond of wearing chains? Are you like Chinese women that delight to wear little shoes which crush their feet? Do you delight in slavery? Do you wish to be captives? You are not under the law, but under grace; will you allow your unbelief to put you under the law? You are not a slave. Why tremble like a slave? You are a child; you are a son; you are an heir; live up to your privileges. Oh, ye banished seed, be glad! You are adopted into the household of God; then be not as a stranger. I hear Ismael laughing at you: let him laugh. Tell your Father of him, and he will soon say, "Cast out this bondwoman and her son." Free grace is not to be mocked by human merit; neither are we to be made sad by the forebodings of the legal spirit. Our soul rejoices, and, like Isaac, is filled with holy laughter; for the Lord Jesus has done great things for us whereof we are glad. To him be glory for ever and ever. Amen.

Sermons on
the Love of Christ

Love's Birth and Parentage

Delivered on Lord's Day morning, June 11, 1876, at the Metropolitan Tabernacle, Newington. No. 1299.

We love him, because he first loved us.—1 John 4:19

Very simple words, but very full of meaning. I think I might say of this sentence what the poet says of prayer: it is "the simplest form of speech that infant lips can try," and yet it is one of the "sublimest strains that reach the majesty on high." Take a little believing child and ask her why she loves the Savior, and she will reply at once, "Because he loved me and died for me:" then ascend to Heaven where the saints are perfect in Christ Jesus and put the same question, and with united breath the whole choir of the redeemed will reply, "He hath loved us and washed us from our sins in his own blood." When we begin to love Christ, we love him because he first loved us; and when we grow in grace till we are capable of the very highest degree of spiritual understanding and affection, we still have no better reason for loving him than this, "Because he first loved us."

This morning, in trying to preach from the text, I would pray the Holy Spirit that every person here may first *feel* it. It is wonderful the difference between a text read and heard and a text *felt* within the soul. Oh, that you this morning may be able to say from your hearts because you cannot help saying it, *"We love him."* If I were to say no more, but sit down in silence, and if you were all to spend the next three quarters of an hour in exercising the emotion of love to God, it would be time most profitably spent. It is beyond measure beneficial to the soul to take her fill of love with the Lord Jesus; it is the sweet cure for all her ailments for her to have leisure to delight herself in the Lord, and faith enough to dwell at ease in his perfections. Be sure, then, to let your hearts have room, and scope, and opportunity for indulging and inflaming the sacred passion of love to God. If the second part of the text shall also be made equally vivid to you by the power of faith—*"He first loved us"*—your hearts will be satisfied as with marrow and fatness. If the exceeding love of God in Christ Jesus shall be shed abroad in your hearts by the Holy Spirit, you will want no sermon from me: your inward experience will be better than any discourse. May your love, like a drop of dew, be exhaled and carried up into the boundless Heaven of God's love; may your heart ascend to the place where your treasure is, and rest itself upon the heart of God. Blessed shall you be if in your hearts Christ's love and yours shall both be fully known and felt at this moment. O, blessed Spirit, cause it to be so. Thus should we have the text in action, and that is a thousand times better than the mere quiet letter. If you have visited the picture galleries at Versailles, where you see the wars of France from the earliest ages set forth in glowing colors upon the canvas, you cannot but have been struck with the pictures, and interested in the terrible scenes. Upstairs in the same palace there is a vast collection of portraits. I have traversed those galleries of portraits without much interest, only here and there pausing to notice a remarkable countenance. Very few persons linger there, everybody seems to walk on as quickly as the polished floors allow. Now, why is it that you are interested by the portraits downstairs and not by those upstairs? They are the same people; very many of them in the same dress; why do you not gaze upon them with interest? The reason lies here: the portrait in still life, as a rule, can never have the attraction which surrounds a scene of stirring action. There you see the warrior dealing a terrible blow with his battle axe, or the senator delivering himself of an oration in the assembly, and you think more of them than of the same bodies and faces in repose. Life is impressive; action awakens thought. It is just so with the text. Look at it as a matter of doctrinal statement; "We love him, because he first loved us," and if you are a thoughtful person you will consider it well; but feel the fact itself, feel the love of God, know it within our own souls, and manifest it in our lives, and how engrossing it becomes. May it be so by the power of the Holy Spirit this morning; may you be loving God while you are hearing, and may I be loving him intensely while I am preaching.

With this as an introduction, I shall use the text for four purposes; first, *for doctrinal instruction*; then, *for experimental information*; thirdly, *for practical direction*; and fourthly, *for argumentative defense.*

I. We shall use the text briefly for *doctrinal instruction;* and one point of doctrinal instruction is very clear, namely, that *God's love to his people is first.*

"He first loved us." Now, make sure of this point of doctrine, because forgetfulness about it is connected with much error, and with more ignorance. The love of God to us precedes our love to God. According to Scripture it must be first in the most eminent sense, because it is eternal. The Lord chose his people in Christ Jesus from before the foundations of the world, and to each one of his people that text may be applied—"Yea, I have loved thee with an everlasting love." His mercy is from everlasting to them that fear him. From all eternity the Lord looked upon his people with an eye of love, and as nothing can be before eternity, his love was *first*. Certainly he loved us before we had a being, for did he not give his Son to die for us nearly nineteen hundred years ago, long before our infant cries had saluted our mother's ear? He loved us before we had any desire to be loved by him, yea when we were provoking him to his face, and displaying the fierce enmity of our unrenewed hearts. Remember "his great love wherewith he loved us even when we were dead in sin." "God commendeth his love toward us, in that, while we were yet sinners, Christ died for us." When we had not as yet one throb of spiritual feeling, one pulse of hope, or one breathing of desire, the Lord loved us even then.

The love of God is before our seeking; he draws us before we run after him. We do not seek that love; that love seeks us. We wander further and further from it, resist it, and prove ourselves unworthy of it: such are our nature and our practice, that they offer nothing congenial to divine love, but the love of God arises in its freeness and stays our mad career by its power over the conscience and the will. "Ye have not chosen me, but I have chosen you," is the voice of sovereign grace; let our response be, "By the grace of God, we are what we are."

The Lord's love is before any repentance on our part. Impenitent sinners never would repent if God did not love them first. The Lord hates sin, but yet he loves sinners; he compassionately loved us when sin was pleasant to us, when we rolled it under our tongue as a sweet morsel, when neither the thunders of his law nor the wooings of his gospel could persuade us to turn from it. When in our bosoms there were no convictions of sin, when there were no evangelical lamentations because of offenses against a gracious God, he loved us then. Today, brethren, we are possessors of faith in Jesus Christ, but our faith in Jesus Christ did not come before his love; on the contrary, our faith rests in what that love has done for us of old. When we were unbelieving and hard of heart, and resisted the testimony of the Holy Spirit, and put from us the word of eternal life, even then the Lord pitied us, and had mercy upon us; and continued still to invite, still to entreat, still to persuade, till at last the happy hour came when we believed and entered into a sense of his love. There are many things about you now, beloved of the Lord, which are the objects of divine approbation, but they were not there at first; they did not precede divine love, but are the fruits of it. To use an old English word which has somewhat lost its meaning, the love of God is *preventing* love—it goes before any right motions of the soul, and in order of time it is *first*, before any desires, wishes, aspirations, or prayers on our part. Are you this day devout? Yet he loved you not at the first because you were devout, for originally you were not so: his love was first before your devotion. Are you this day holy? Blessed be his name for it; but he loved you when you were unholy; your holiness follows upon his love, he chose you that you might be holy. You are becoming like him by the sanctifying influences of his blessed Spirit, and he loves his image in you, but he loved you when that image was not there: yea he looked on you with infinite compassion when you were heirs of wrath even as others, and the image of the devil was conspicuous both upon your character and your nature. However early in life you began to love the Lord, his love was first. This is very wonderful, but blessed be his name, we know that it is true, and we rejoice in it.

The fact is that the love of God, as far as we know anything about it, had no reason derived from us upon which to ground itself. He loved us because he would love us, or, as our Lord put it, "Even so, Father; for so it seemed good in thy sight." He had reasons in his own nature, good reasons, fetched from the best conceivable place, namely from his own perfections; but those reasons he has not been pleased to communicate to us. He bids us know that he will have mercy on whom he will have mercy, and will have compassion on whom he will have compassion. Thus he tries the loyal submissiveness of our hearts, and I trust we are able to bow in reverent silence to his righteous will.

Divine love is its own cause, and does not derive its streams from anything in us whatsoever. It flows spontaneously from the heart of God, finding its deep wellsprings within his own bosom. This is a great comfort to us, because, being uncreated, it is unchangeable. If it had been set upon us because of some goodness in us, then when the goodness was diminished, the love would diminish too. If God had loved us second and not first, or had the cause of the love been in us, that cause might have altered, and the supposed effect, namely, his love, would have altered too; but now, whatever may be the believer's condition today, however he may have wandered, and however much he may be groaning under a sense of sin, the Lord declares, "I do earnestly remember him still." The Lord did not love you at first because you had no sin; he foreknew all the sin you ever would have, it was all present before his sacred mind, and yet he loved you, and he loves you still. "I am God; I change not; therefore ye sons of Jacob are not consumed." O blessed love of God, since thou art first, we will give thee the first place in our thoughts, the highest throne in our hearts, the royal position in our souls; glorifying thee, for thou art first!

Another part of the doctrine of the text is this, that *the love of God is the cause of our love to God*. A thing may be first and another second, and yet the first may not be the cause of the second, there may be no actual link between the two: but here we have it unmistakably, "We love him *because* he first loved us"; which signifies not merely that this is the motive of which we are conscious in our love, but that this is the force—the divine power—which created love in us. I put it to you, should we have loved God had he not first given his Son to die for us? Had there been no redeeming sacrifice, should we have had any love to God? Unredeemed men, left to go on like fallen angels in their sin, would have had no more love to God than fallen angels have. How could they? But the Son given to redeem is the great foundation of love. God gives his Son, and so reveals his own love, and creates ours. Is not his love seen to be the cause of ours when we remember Calvary?

But he might have given his Son to die for men, beloved, and yet you and I might not have loved him, because we might not have been aware of the great fact. It is no small grace on God's part that "to you is the word of this salvation sent." While the heathen have never heard it, by the arrangement of his gracious providence, you have been favored with the good news. You have it in your homes in the form of the Holy Scriptures, you hear it every Sabbath day from the pulpit. How would you have ever come to love him if he had not sent his gospel to you? The gift of his Son Jesus, and the providence which leads the herald of mercy to the saved one's door, are evident causes of man's love to God. But more than this, Christ died and the gospel is preached, and yet some men do not love him. Why not? Because of the hardness of their hearts. But others do love him: shall I trace this to the natural betterness of their hearts? I dare not, and much less do they. There is no believer who would ask me to do so in his own case; but I must trace it to the influence of the Holy Spirit, going with the revelation of the love of God in Christ Jesus, affecting the heart, and creating faith and love and every grace in the soul. Beloved, if you love God, it is with no love of yours, but with the love which he has planted in your bosoms. Unrenewed human nature is a soil in which love to God will not grow. There must be a taking away of the rock, and a supernatural change of the barren ground into good soil, and then, as a rare plant from another land, love must be planted in our hearts and sustained by power divine, or else it never will be found there. There is no love to God in this world that is of the right kind except that which was created and formed by the love of God in the soul.

Put the two truths together, that the love of God is first, and that the love of God is the cause of our love, and I think you will be inclined henceforth to be believers in what are commonly called the doctrines of grace. To me it is very wonderful that they are not received by all churches, because they are practically acknowledged by all Christians on their knees. They may preach as they like, but they all pray according to the doctrines of grace; and those doctrines are so consistent with the Christian's experience, that it is notable that the older a believer becomes, and the more deeply he searches into divine truth, the more inclined he is to give the whole of the praise of his salvation to the grace of God, and to believe in those precious truths which magnify, not the free will of man, but the free grace of the Ever Blessed. I want no better statement of my own doctrinal belief than this, "We love him, because he first loved us." I know it has been said that he loved us on the foresight of our faith and love and holiness. Of course the Lord had a clear foresight of all these, but remember that he had also the foresight of our want of love, and our want of faith, and our wanderings, and our sins, and surely his foresight in one direction must be supposed to operate as well as his foresight in the other direction. Recollect also that God himself did not foresee that there would be any love to him in us arising out of ourselves, for there never has been any, and there never will be; he only foresaw that we should believe because he gave us faith, he foresaw that we should repent because his Spirit would work repentance in us, he foresaw that we should love, because he wrought that love within us; and is there anything in the foresight that he means to give us such things, that can account for his giving us such things? The case is self-evident—his foresight of what he means to do cannot be his reason for doing it. His own eternal purpose has made the gracious difference between the saved and those who willfully perish in sin. Let us give all the glory to his holy name, for to him all the glory belongs. His preventing grace must have all the honor.

II. Secondly, we shall use the text *for experimental information;* **and here, first, we learn that** *all true believers love God.*

"We love him," and we all love him for one reason, "because he first loved us." All the children of God love their Father. I do not say that they all feel an equal love, or that they all feel as much love as they should: who among us does? I will not say that they do not sometimes give cause to doubt their love; nay, I will urge that it is well for them to examine, even as Christ examined Peter, and said, "Simon, son of Jonas, lovest thou me?" But there is love in the heart of every true-born child of God; it is as needful to spiritual life as blood is to natural life. Rest assured there has never been born into the kingdom of God one solitary individual destitute of love to God. You may be deficient in some virtues (you should not be), but yet the root of the matter may be in you; but if you be without love you are as a sounding brass and as a tinkling cymbal, and whatever your outer works, though you give your body to be burned, and all your goods to feed the poor, yet, if there be no love to God in your soul, the mark of God's sheep is not upon you, and your spot is not the spot of his children. Rest assured that whosoever is born of God loveth God.

Observe carefully the kind of love which is essential to every Christian—"We love him, because he first loved us." Much has been said about disinterested love to God; there may be such a thing, and it may be very admirable, but it is not mentioned here. I trust, beloved, we know what it is to love God because of his superlative excellence and goodness, and surely the more we know him, the more we shall love him for what he is, but yet unless we love him because he first loved us, whatever other sort of love we may have or think we have, it does not prove us to be children of God. This is the love we must have; the other form of love, if it be true, will grow up in us afterwards; that however, is not essential, nor need we exalt it unduly: loving God because he first loved us is a sufficient evidence of grace in the soul. Gratitude has been vilified as a mean virtue, but indeed it is a noble emotion, and is one of the most forcible of spiritual motives. Let a man love God admiringly because of what he is, but yet there must run side by side with it this grateful love of God, because he first loved him, or else he lacks that which John says is to be found in all the saints. Beloved, do not vex yourselves about any supposed higher degrees, but see to it that you love him because he first loved you. You may not be able to rise into those heights into which others of your brethren have ascended, because you are as yet only a babe in grace; but you are safe enough, if your love be of this simple character, that it loves because it is loved.

Within this humble form of love which is so essential, there dwells a gracious sense of unworthiness, so needful to a true Christian. We feel that we did not deserve the love which God sheds upon us, and this humility we must have, or we lack one mark of a child of God. There is also in this lowly form of gracious affection a clear recognition of the fact that the Lord's love is graciously bestowed, and this also is essential to a Christian, and becomes, to him, the main source of his obedience and affection. If a man only loves me as much as I deserve to be loved, I do not feel under any very strong obligations, and consequently do not feel any very intense gratitude, but because the Lord's love is all of pure grace and comes to us as utterly undeserving ones, therefore we love him in return. See whether such a humble, grateful love towards God dwells in your hearts, for it is a vital point.

Love to God wherever it is found is a sure evidence of the salvation of its possessor. If you love the Lord in the sense described, then he loved you first, and loves you now. You want no other evidence but this to assure yourself that you abide in the love of God—that you love him. I was told by a venerable brother some little time ago a story of our famous preacher, Robert Hall. He charmed the most learned by the majesty of his eloquence, but he was as simple as he was great, and he was never happier than when conversing with poor believers upon experimental godliness. He was accustomed to make his journeys on horseback, and having been preaching at Clipstone, he was on his way home, when he was stopped by a heavy fall of snow at the little village of Sibbertoft. The good man who kept the "Black Swan," a little village hostelry, came to his door and besought the preacher to take refuge beneath his roof, assuring him that it would give him great joy to welcome him. Mr. Hall knew him to be one of the most sincere Christians in the neighborhood, and therefore got off his horse and went into the little inn. The good man was delighted to provide for him a bed, and a stool, and a candlestick in the prophet's chamber, for that rustic inn contained such an apartment. After Mr. Hall had rested awhile by the fire the landlord said. "You must needs stop here all night, sir; and if you do not mind I will call in a few of my neighbors, and if you feel that you could give us a sermon in my taproom they will all be glad to hear you." "So let it be, sir," said Mr. Hall, and so it was: the taproom became his cathedral, and the "Black Swan" the sign of the gospel banner. The peasants came together, and the man of God poured out his soul before them wondrously. They would never forget it, for to hear Mr. Hall was an event in any man's life. After all were gone, Mr. Hall sat down, and there came over him a fit of depression: out of which he strove to rise by conversation with his host.

"Ah, sir," said the great preacher, "I am much burdened, and am led to question my own condition before God. Tell me now what you think is a sure evidence that a man is a child of God."

"Well, Mr. Hall," said the plain man, "I am sorry to see you so tried; you doubt yourself, but nobody else has any doubt about you. I hope the Lord will cheer and comfort you, but I am afraid I am not qualified to do it."

"Never mind, friend, never mind, tell me what you think the best evidence of a child of God?"

"Well, I should say, sir," said he, "if a man loves God, he must be one of God's children."

"Say you so," said the mighty preacher, "then it is well with me," and at that signal he began to magnify the Lord at such a rate that his hearer afterwards said that it was wonderful to hear him, as for about an hour he went on with glowing earnestness, declaring, the loveliness of God. "O sir," said he who told the tale,

> you should have heard him. He said, "Love God, sir? Why I cannot help loving him, how could I do otherwise?" And then he went on to speak about the Almighty and his love and grace, extolling the Lord's greatness, and goodness, and glory in redemption, and all that he did for his people, till he said, "Thank you, thank you, my friend—if love to him is an evidence of being God's child, I know I have it, for I cannot help loving him. I take no credit to myself; he is such a lovely being, and has done so much for us, that I should be more brutish than any man if I did not love and adore him."

That which cheered that good and great man's heart may, perhaps, cheer yours. If you are loving God you must have been loved of God: true love could not have come into your heart in any other conceivable way; and you may rest assured that you are the object of his eternal choice.

But oh, *if you do not love God, dear hearer, I invite you to think for a minute upon your state!* Hear of God and not love him? You must be blind. Know anything about his character and not adore him? Your heart must be like the heart of Nabal when it was turned into stone. See God in Christ bleeding on the cross for his enemies and not love him! O Hell, thou canst not be guilty of a worst offense than this! Herein is love, shall it have no acknowledgment? It is said that a man cannot feel that he is loved without in some measure returning the flame: but what shall I say of a mind which beholds Christ's love but feels no love in return? It is brutish, it is devilish. God have mercy upon it. Breathe you the same prayer, O unloving heart, and say, "Lord, forgive me, and by thy Holy Spirit renew me, and give me henceforth to be able to say, 'I also in my humble fashion love God because he first loved me.'"

III. Thirdly, we shall use the text as a matter *of practical detection.*

I earnestly trust that there are some here who, although they do not love God at present, yet desire to do so. Well, dear friend, *the text tells you how to love God.* You say, perhaps, "Oh, I shall love God when I have improved my character, and when I have attended to the external duties of religion." But are you going to get love to God out of yourself? Is it there, then? "No," say you. How, then, will you get it from where it is not? You may go often to an empty iron safe before you will bring a thousand pound note out of it, and you may look a long time to your own heart before you will bring out of it a love to God which is not there. What is the way by which a heart may be made to love God? The text shows us the method of the Holy Spirit. He reveals the love of God to the heart, and then the heart loves God in return. If, then, you are aroused this morning to desire to love God, use the method which the text suggests—meditate upon the great love of God to man, especially upon this, "God so loved the world that he gave his only begotten Son, that whosoever believeth in him should not perish, but have everlasting life." See clearly that you have by faith to trust your soul with Christ, and perceive that it is vast love which sets before you such a way of salvation in which the only thing required of you is that you *be nothing,* and trust Christ to be everything, and even that faith he gives you as a gift of his Spirit, so that the plan of salvation is all of love. If you want to repent, do not so much consider your sin as the love of Jesus in suffering for your sin; if you desire to believe, do not so much study the doctrine as study the person of Jesus Christ upon the cross, and if you desire to love, think over perpetually, till it breaks your heart, the great love of Jesus Christ in laying down his life for his worthless foes. The love of God is the birthplace of holy love. Not there in your hearts where you are attempting an absurdly impossible feat, namely, to create love in the carnal mind which cannot be reconciled to God; but there in the heart of Jesus, must love be born, and then it shall come down to you. You cannot force your mind into the condition of believing even a common thing, nor can you sit there and say, "I will love so and so," of whom you know nothing. Faith and love are second steps arising out of former steps. "Faith cometh by hearing," and love comes by contemplation; it flows out of a sense of the love of Christ in the soul even as wine flows from the clusters in the wine-press. Go thou to the fragrant mystery of redeeming love, and tarry with it till in those beds of spices thine own garments shall be made to smell of myrrh and aloes and cassia. There is no way of sweetening thyself but by tasting the sweetness of Jesus Christ; the honey of his love will make thy whole nature to be as a honeycomb, every cell of thy manhood shall drop sweetness.

Brethren, if we wish to sustain the love we have received, we must do the same thing. At the present moment you are loving God, and desire still to love him; be wise, then, and feed love on love, it is its best food. This is the honey which will keep your sweetness sweet; this is the fire which will keep your flame flaming. Could we be separated from the love of Christ, our love would die out like a lamp in yonder streets when cut off from the main. He who quickened us into the life of love must keep us alive, or we shall become loveless and lifeless.

And if, perchance, your love has grown somewhat cold; if you long to revive it, do not begin by doubting God's love to you; that is not the way of reviving but of weakening love. Believe in divine love, my brother, over the head of the coldness of your heart; trust in Jesus Christ as a sinner if you cannot rejoice in him as a saint, and you will get your love back again. You see the flowing fountain, how it gushes with a constant stream; and here I bring a pitcher and set it down, so that the stream rushes into it and fills it till it overflows. In this manner our souls ought to be filled with the love of Christ. But you have taken away your pitcher, and it has become empty, and now you say to yourself, "Alas, alas, there is nothing here! What shall I do? This pitcher is empty." Do? Why do what you did at first; go and set it under the flowing stream, and it will soon be full again; but it will never get full by your removing it into a dry place. Doubting is the death of love; only by the hand of faith can love be fed with the bread of heaven.

Your tears will not fill it; you may groan into it, but sighs and moans will not fill it; only the flowing fountain can fill the vacuum. Believe thou that God loves thee still: even if thou be not a saint, believe thou in the mighty love of Christ towards sinners, and trust thyself with him, and then his love will come pouring in till thy heart is full again to overflowing. If you want to rise to the very highest state of love to Christ, if you desire to enjoy ecstatic, or to be perfectly consecrated, if you aim at an apostle's self-denial, or at a martyr's heroism, or if you would be as like to Christ as the spirits are in heaven, no tool can grave you to this image but love, no force can fashion you to the model of Christ Jesus but the love of Jesus Christ shed abroad in your soul by the Holy Ghost. Keep to this, then, as a matter of practical direction. Dwell in the love of God to you that you may feel intense love to God.

Once more, as a practical direction, *if you love God, show it as God showed his love to you.* You cannot do so in the same degree, but you may in the same manner. God loved the worthless; love ye the worthless. God loved his enemies; love ye your enemies. The Lord loved them practically: love not in word only, but in deed and in truth. He loved them to self-sacrifice, so that Jesus gave himself for us: love ye to self-sacrifice also. Love God so that you could die a thousand deaths for him: love him till you make no provision for the flesh, but live alone for his glory; let your heart burn with a flame that shall consume you till the zeal of God's house shall have eaten you up. "We love him, *because* he first loved us," therefore let us love him as he loved us; let his love be both motive and model to us.

> Lov'd of my God, for him again,
> With love intense I burn;
> Chosen of him ere time began
> I choose him in return.

IV. Our text suggests to us *an argumentative defence.*

You will see what I mean when I observe first, that our love to God seems to want an apology. We have heard of an emperor casting eyes of love upon a peasant girl. It would have been monstrous for her to have first looked up to him as likely to be her husband; everybody would have thought her to be bereft of her senses had she done so; but when the monarch looked down upon her and asked her to be his queen, that was another thing. She might take leave to love from his love. Often does my soul say,

> O God, I cannot help loving thee, but *may* I? Can this poor heart of mine be suffered to send up its love to thee? I, polluted and defiled, nothingness and emptiness and sinfulness, may I say, "Yet do I love thee, O my God, almighty as thou art"? "Holy, holy, holy," is the salutation of the seraphim, but may I say "I love thee, O my God"?

Yes, I may, because he first loved me. *There* is love's license to soar so high.

> Yet I may love thee too, O Lord,
> Almighty as thou art,
> For thou hast stoop'd to ask of me
> The love of my poor heart

Then, again, if any should enquire of us, as they did of the spouse . . .

> What is thy beloved more than another beloved, O thou fairest among women? What is thy beloved more than another beloved, that thou dost so charge us? What is this passion that you have for God, this love you bear to his incarnate Son?

. . . we have a conclusive argument as against them, even as we had a quietus for our own fears. We reply,

> We love him, because he first loved us, and if you did but know that he loved you, if you did but know that he has done for you what he has done for us, you would love him too. You would not want to ask us why, you would wonder why you do not love him too.

> His love if all the nations knew,
> Sure the whole world will love him too.

We shall not want to all eternity any other defense for loving God than this, "Because he first loved us."

Here is also an argument for the lover of the old orthodox faith. It has been said by some that the doctrines of grace lead to licentiousness, but our text is a most excellent shield against that attack. Brethren, we believe that the Lord loved us, first, and most freely, not because of our tears or prayers, nor because of our foreseen faith, nor because of anything in us, but first. Well, what comes out of that? Do we therefore say, "If he loved us when we were in sin, let us continue in sin, that grace may abound," as some have wickedly said? God forbid. The inference we draw is, "We love him, because he first loved us." Some can be swayed to morality by fear, but the Christian is sweetly drawn to holiness by love. We love him, not because we are afraid of being cast into Hell if we do not—that fear is gone, we who are justified by God can never be condemned; nor because we are afraid of missing Heaven, for the inheritance is entailed upon as many of us as are joint heirs with Jesus Christ. Does this blessed security lead us to carelessness? No, but in proportion as we see the greatness and the infinity of the love of God, we love him in return, and that love is the basis of all holiness, and the groundwork of a godly character. The doctrine of grace, though often maligned, has proved in the hearts of those who have believed it to be the grandest stimulus to heroic virtue, and he who affirms otherwise knows not what he says.

Last of all, here is a noble argument to silence a gainsaying world. Do you see what a wonderful text we have here? It is a description of Christianity. Men say they are weary of the old faith, and beg us to advance with the times—how shall we reply to them? They want something better, do they? The philosophers who pander to the age are going to give it a better religion than Christianity! Are they? Let us see. We shall, however, wait very long before their false promises will approximate to fulfillment. Let us rather look at what we really have already. Our text is a circle. Here is love descending from Heaven down to man, and here is love ascending from man to God, and so the circle is completed. The text treats alone of love. We love the Lord, and he loves us. The text resembles Anacreon's harp,[1] which resounded love alone. Here is no word of strife, selfishness, anger, or envy; all is love, and love alone. Now, it comes to pass that out of this love between God and his people there grows (see the context of my text) love to men, for "he that loveth God loveth his brother also." The ethical essence of Christianity is love, and the great master doctrine that we preach when we preach Jesus Christ is this—"God has loved us, we love God, and now we must love one another." O ye nations, what gospel do you desire better than this? This it is that will put aside your drums, your cannons, and your swords. When men love God and love each other, what need for all the bloodstained pageantry of war? And this will end your slavery, for who will call his brother his slave when he has learned to love the image of God in every man?

[1] Anacreon was a notable Greek lyrical poet, best known for writing hyms to wine.

Who is he that will oppress and domineer when he has learned to love his God and love the creatures God has made? Behold, Christianity is the Magna Charta of the universe. Here is the true "Liberty, Equality, and Fraternity," which men will seek for in vain in politics; here is the sacred Communism which will injure no man's rights, but will respect every man's griefs, and succor every man's needs; here is, indeed, the birth principle of the golden age of peace and joy, when the lion shall eat straw like the ox, and the weaned child shall play on the cockatrice's den.[2] Spread it, then, and let it circulate throughout the whole earth—God's love first, our love to him next, and then the universal love which shuts not out a man of any color, of any class, or of any name, but calls upon itself to love both God and man, because God is loved.

The Lord bless this meditation to you, by his Spirit, for Christ's sake. Amen.

---

[2] Cockatrice: a mythcal serpent hatched from a cock's egg, which could kill with a glace.

Life's Need and Maintenance

Delivered on Lord's Day morning, June 18, 1876, at the Metropolitan Tabernacle, Newington. No. 1300.

None can keep alive his own soul.—Psalm 22:29

We must commence by noticing the connection, that we may arrive at the first meaning of the words. There is a day coming when the true God will be acknowledged as Lord and God by all mankind, for the twenty-seventh verse tells us—"All the ends of the world shall remember and turn unto the Lord: and all the kindreds of the nations shall worship before thee." In that day the greatest of men will bow before him. The verse from which we cull our text says: "All they that be fat upon earth shall eat and worship." The prosperous ones, those who have grown rich and great, shall receive good at the hands of the Savior, and shall rejoice to adore him as the author of their fatness. Kings shall own him as their King, and lords accept him as their Lord. Then shall not only the riches of life, but the poverty of death also, render him homage, for as men shall go down to the dust of the grave, in their feebleness and weakness they shall look up to him for strength and solace, and shall find it sweet to worship him in death. Men shall know that the keys of death are in his hands. "All they that go down to the dust shall bow before him," and it shall be known all the world over that the issues of life are in the hands of Jesus Christ; they shall understand that he is appointed as Mediator to rule over all mortal things, for the government shall be upon his shoulder; he shall open and no man shall shut, and shut and no man shall open, for it is his sovereign prerogative to kill and to make alive, and "none can keep alive his own soul." I pass on from this meaning with the hopeful belief that this dispensation is not to end, as some suppose, without the conquest of the world to Christ. Surely "all kings shall bow before him, all nations shall serve him." The shame of the cross shall be followed by honor and glory, "men shall be blessed in him, all nations shall call him blessed." The conviction grows with me every day, the more I read the Scriptures, that the disheartening views of some interpreters are not true, but that ere the whole of prophecy shall be wrought into history, the kingdoms of this world shall become the kingdoms of our Lord and of his Christ.

Leaving this, we come to consider a more spiritual meaning, which we believe to be as truly the sense of the passage as the other. You will notice, if you read the psalm carefully, when you come to its close, that our Savior seems to delight himself in being made food for the saved ones among the sons of men. In the 26th verse he says, "The meek shall eat and be satisfied." Here he is thinking of the poor among men, to whom he has ever been the source of abounding comfort: to them his gospel has been preached, and thousands of them have found in him food for their souls, which has satisfied them, filled their mouths with praise, and made their hearts live for ever. The poor from the highways and hedges feast to the full at his royal table, yea, the blind, and the halt, and the lame, the very beggars of the streets are among his household guests. Christ is very mindful of the poor and needy, he redeems their soul from deceit and violence, and their blood is precious in his sight. Especially do the poor in spirit feed on Jesus; over them he pronounced the first benediction of the sermon on the mount, and of them he declares, "theirs is the kingdom of heaven." What a feast do poor perishing spirits enjoy in Jesus when his flesh becomes to them meat indeed, and his blood is drink indeed.

Nor is this all the feeding upon Christ, for in the 29th verse, we hear of it again. Not only the poor feed upon the bread of heaven, but the great, the rich, and the strong live upon him too: "all they that be fat upon earth shall eat and worship," there is no other way of life for them, for "none can keep alive his own soul." The saints, too, when they have grown in grace, when they have supplied their hunger, and are fat and flourishing in the courts of the Lord's house, must still eat of the same heavenly food; the fat need Jesus as much as the lean, the strong as much as the feeble, for none can do without him, "none can keep alive his own soul." Thus the rich and the poor meet together, and Jesus is the food of them all. The empty and the full alike draw near to the Redeemer's fullness and receive grace for grace.

Among those who feel their need of Jesus, there are some of a mournful type of character, who count themselves ready to perish. They dare not number themselves among the meek who shall eat and be satisfied, much less could they think of themselves as the fat upon earth who shall eat and worship, but they stand back from the feast as utterly unworthy to draw near. They dare not believe themselves to be spiritually alive unto God, they reckon themselves among those that go down into the pit, they bear the sentence of death in themselves and are prisoners under bondage through fear. Their sense of sin and personal unworthiness is so conspicuous, and so painful, that they are afraid to claim the privileges of the living in Zion. They fear that their faith is expiring, their love is dying out, their hope is withered, and their joy clean departed. They compare themselves to the smoking flax, and think themselves to be even more offensive than the nauseous smell given forth by the smoking wick. To such comes the word which precedes my text: "They that go down to the dust shall bow before him." Christ shall be worshipped even by them; their last moments shall be cheered by his presence. When through depression of spirit, through the assaults of Satan, and through inability to see the work of the Spirit in their souls, they shall be brought so low as to be down to the dust, they shall be lifted up from their misery and made to rejoice in the Lord their Redeemer, who will say unto them—"Shake thyself from the dust; arise and sit down: loose thyself from the bands of thy neck, O captive daughter of Zion." When souls are thus brought down, they begin to learn for themselves that "none can keep alive his own soul." A poor broken-hearted spirit knows this, for he fears that the inner life within his soul is at its last gasp, and he is afraid that his faith and love, and all his graces will be as bones scattered at the grave's mouth, and then he learns what I trust we shall believe at this time without such a painful experience to teach it to us, namely, that none of us can keep our own soul alive, but that we must have food continually from above, and visitations of the Lord to preserve our spirits. Our life is not in ourselves, but in our Lord. Apart from him, we could not exist spiritually, even for a moment. We cannot keep our own soul alive as to grace. That is to be the subject of this morning's meditation, and may the Holy Spirit render it profitable to us!

I. The first point of consideration out of which the rest will come is this— *the inner life must be sustained by God.*

We are absolutely dependent upon God for the preservation of our spiritual life. We all of us know that none of us can *make* his own soul live. Thou hast destroyed thyself, but thou canst not make thyself to live again. Spiritual life must always be the gift of God; it must come from without, it cannot arise from within. Between the ribs of death, life never takes its birth; how could it? Shall the ocean beget fire, or darkness create light? You shall go to the charnel house as long as you please, but, unless the trump of the resurrection shall sound there, the dry bones will remain in their corruption. The sinner is "dead in trespasses and sins," and he never will have even so much as a right desire towards God, nor a pulse of spiritual life, until Jesus Christ, who is "the resurrection and the life," shall quicken him. Now, it is important for us to remember that we are as much dependent upon the Lord Jesus and the power of his Spirit for being kept alive as we were for being made alive at the first. "None can keep alive his own soul." Do you remember when first you hung upon Christ for everything? That same entire dependence must be exercised every day of your life, for there is need of it. You remember your former nakedness, your poverty, your emptiness, your misery, your death apart from Christ; remember that the case is not one whit better if you could now be separated from sin. If now you have any grace, or any holiness, or any love, you derive it entirely from him, and from moment to moment his grace must be continued to you; for if connection between you and Christ should by any possibility be severed, you would cease spiritually to live. That is the truth we want to bring forward.

Here let us remark that this is not at all inconsistent with the undying nature of the spiritual life. When we were born again there was imparted to us a new and higher nature called the Spirit. This is a fruit of the Spirit of God, and it can never die; it is an "incorruptible seed which liveth and abideth for ever." When it is imparted to the soul, it makes us partakers of the divine nature, and it keeps us so that the evil one toucheth us not so as utterly to destroy us. Yet this fact is quite consistent with the assertion that we cannot keep our own soul alive, for though we live, it is because the Lord keeps us alive. The newborn nature is safe because the Lord protects it; it survives the deadly influences of the world because the Lord continues to quicken it. Our new nature is united to the person of Christ, and we live because he lives. We are not kept alive by independent power, but by perpetual renewal from the Lord.

This is true of every man living. "None can keep alive his own soul"—no, not one. You young people think, perhaps, that old Christians get on better than you do; you imagine that their experience preserves them, but indeed they cannot keep their own souls alive any more than you can. You tried and tempted ones sometimes look with envy upon those who dwell at ease, as though their spirituality was self-supporting, but no, they cannot keep their own souls alive any more than you can. You know your own difficulties, but you do not know those of others; rest assured, however, that to all men there are these difficulties, and that no man can keep his own soul alive.

This is the truth at all times: at no one moment can we keep ourselves alive. While sitting in this house of prayer, you may dream that assuredly you can keep yourself here, but it is not so. You might sin the foulest of sins in your heart while sitting here, and you might grieve the Holy Spirit, and cloud your life for years while worshipping among the people of God. You are not able to keep your own soul alive in your happiest and holiest moments. From your knees you might rise to blaspheme, and from the communion table you might go to the seat of the scorner if you were left to yourself.

> All our strength at once would fail us,
> If deserted, Lord, by thee
> Nothing then could aught avail us,
> Certain our defeat would be:
> Those who hate us
> Thenceforth their desire would see.

I seldom find myself so much in danger as when I have been in close communion with God. After the most ecstatic devotion, one is hardly prepared for the coarse temptations of this wicked world. When we come down, like Moses from the mount, if we encounter open sin, we are apt to grow indignant and break all the commandments in the vehemence of our wrath. The sudden change from the highest and holiest contemplations to the trifles and vexations of earth subjects the soul to so severe a trial that the poet did well to say—

> *We should suspect some danger nigh*
> *When we perceive too much delight.*

Even when our delight is of a spiritual kind we are apt to be off our guard after having been filled with it, and then Satan avails himself of the opportunity. We are never safe unless the Lord keeps us. If we could take you, my brethren, place you in the society of saints, give you to keep perpetual Sabbath-day, make every meal a sacrament, and set you nothing to say or do but what should he directly calculated to promote the glory of God, yet even there you could not keep your own soul alive. Adam in perfection could not keep himself in Paradise—how can his imperfect children be so proud as to rely upon their own steadfastness? Among angels there were those who kept not their first estate—how shall man then hope to stand, except he be upheld.

Why is this? How know we that our text is true? We gather arguments from the analogies of nature. We do not find that we can keep our own bodies alive. We need divine preservation, or disease and death deftly will soon make us their prey. We are not self-contained as to this mortal existence, any one of us, nay, not for five minutes can we live upon ourselves. Take away the atmospheric air, and who could keep himself alive? The heaving lungs need their portion of air, and if they cannot be satisfied, the man soon becomes a corpse. Deprive us of food, leave us for a week without meat or drink, and see if we can keep our natural soul alive. Take away from us the means of warmth in the time when God's cold rules the year, and death would soon ensue. Now, if the physical life is not to be sustained by itself, much less can the higher and spiritual life; it must have food, it must have the Spirit to sustain it. The Scriptures present to us the figure of a member of the body which dies if severed from the vital organs, and of the branch which is dried up if cut off from the stem. Toplady versifies the thought and sings—

> *Quicken'd by thee, and kept alive,*
> *I flourish and bear fruit;*
> *My life I from thy sap derive,*
> *My vigor from thy root.*
>
> *I can do nothing without thee;*
> *My strength is wholly thine:*
> *Wither'd and barren should I be*
> *If sever'd from the vine.*

Yonder lamp burns well, but its future shining is dependent upon a fresh supply of oil; the ship in rapid motion borrows force from the continuance of the wind, and the sails hang idle if the gale ceases; the river is full to the bank, but if the clouds should never again pour out their floods, it would become a dry trackway. All things depend on others, and the whole upon the Great Supreme: nothing is self-sustained; save God himself, no being necessarily exists, and even immortal souls are only so because he has set his seal upon them, and declared that they shall inherit life eternal, or in consequence of sin shall sink into everlasting punishment. Hence we are sure that "none can keep alive his own soul."

But we need not rely upon analogy—we can put the matter to the test. Could any believer among us keep any one of his graces alive? You, perhaps, are a sufferer, and hitherto you have been enabled to be patient: but suppose the Lord Jesus should withdraw his presence from you, and your pains should return again, ah, where will your patience be? Or, I will suppose you are a worker, and you have done great things for the Lord: like Samson you have been exceeding strong; but let the Lord be once withdrawn, and leave you to attempt his work alone, you will soon discover that you are as weak as other men, and will utterly fail. Holy joy, for instance, take that as a specimen: did you rejoice in Lord this morning when you woke? It is very sweet to wake up and hear the birds singing within your heart, but you cannot maintain that joy, nay, not even for an hour, do what you will. "All my fresh springs are in thee," my God, and if I am to joy and rejoice, thou must anoint me continually with the oil of gladness. Have you not sometimes thought in the morning, "I feel so peaceful and calm, so resigned to the divine will, I think I shall be able to keep up this placid spirit all day long." Perhaps you have done so, and if so, I know you have praised God for it; but if you have become perturbed, you have learned again that *to will* is present with you, but how *to perform* that which you would, you find not. Well, if for any one fruit of the Spirit we are dependent upon the Lord, how much more will this be true as to the essential life from which each of these graces springs?

This truth is equally illustrated by our need of help in every *act* of the divine life. Dear friends, have you ever tried what it is to perform any spiritual act apart from the divine power? What a dull, dead affair it becomes! What a mechanical thing prayer is without the Spirit of God. It is a parrot's noise, and nothing more; a weariness, a slavish drudgery. How sweet it is to pray when the Spirit gives us feeling, unction, access with boldness, pleading power, faith, expectancy, and full fellowship; but if the Spirit of God be absent from us in prayer, our infirmities prevail against us, and our supplication loses all prevalence. Did you ever resolve to praise God, and come into the congregation where the sweetest psalms were being sent to heaven, but could you praise God till the Holy Spirit came like a divine wind and loosed the fragrance of the flowers of your soul? You know you could not; you used the sacred words of the sweet singers of Israel, but hosannas languished on your tongue and your devotion died. I know that it is dreadful work to be bound to preach when one is not conscious of the aid of the Spirit of God! It is like pouring water out of bottomless buckets, or feeding hungry souls out of empty baskets. A true sermon—such as God will bless—no man can preach of himself; he might as well try to sound the archangel's trumpet. We must have thee, O blessed Spirit, or we fail! O God, we must have thy power, or every action that we perform is but the movement of an automaton, and not the acceptable act of a living, spiritual man.

Have you never, dear friends, had to know that you cannot keep alive your own soul by your own blunderings and failings, when you have resolved to be very wise and correct? Did you ever get into a self-sufficient state and say, "Now, I shall never fall into that temptation again, for I am the burnt child that dreads the fire," and yet into that very sin you have fallen? Have you not said, "Well, I understand that business; there is no need to wait upon God for direction in so simple a matter, for I am well up in every particular relating to it, and I can manage the affair very well"? And have you not acted as foolishly in the whole concern, as the Israelites did in the affair of the Gibeonites, when they were deceived by the old shoes and clouted, and the moldy bread, and asked no counsel of the Lord? I tell you our strength, whenever we have any, is our greatest weakness, and our fancied wisdom is our real folly. When we are weak, we are strong. When in a sense of entire dependence upon God, we dare not trust ourselves, we are both wise and safe. Go, young man, even you who are a zealous Christian, go without your morning prayer into the house of business, and see what will befall you. Venture, my sister, down into your little family without having called upon God for guidance, and see what you will do. Go with a strong resolve that you will never be guilty of the weakness which dishonored you a few days ago, and depend upon the strength of your own will, and the firmness of your own purpose, and see if you do not ere long discover to your shame how great your weakness is. Nay, try none of these experiments, but listen to the word which tells you, "none can keep alive his own soul."

And now, should any think that he can keep his own soul alive, let me ask him to look at the enemies which surround him. A sheep in the midst of wolves is safe compared with the Christian in the midst of ungodly men. The world waylays us, the devil assaults us, behind every bush there lurks a foe. A spark in mid-ocean is not more beset, a worm is not more defenseless. If the sight of foes without be not enough to make us confess our danger, look at the foes within. There is enough within thy soul, O Christian, though thou be one of the best of saints, to destroy thee in an hour unless the grace of God guard thee and keep thy passions in check, and prevent thy stubborn will from asserting its own rebellious determinations. Oh, what a powder magazine the human heart is, even at the best; if some of us have not been blown up it has been rather because Providence has kept away the sparks than because of there being any lack of powder within. Oh, may God keep us, for if he leaves us, we want no devil to destroy us—we shall prove devils to ourselves; we shall need no tempters except the dire lusting after evil which now conceals itself so craftily within our own bosom.

Certainly, dear brethren, we may be quite sure that "none can keep alive his own soul;" when we remember that in the gospel, provision is made for keeping our soul alive. The Holy Spirit is given that he may continually quicken and preserve us, and Jesus Christ himself lives that we may live also. To what purpose would be all the splendid provisions and the special safeguards of the covenant of grace for the preservation of the spiritual life, if that spiritual life could preserve itself? Why doth the Lord declare, "I the Lord do keep it," if it can keep itself? The granaries of Egypt, so full of corn, remind us that there is a famine in the land of Canaan: the treasures laid up in Christ Jesus assure us that we are in need of them. God's supplies are never superfluous, but are meant to meet real wants. Let us, then, all acknowledge that no man among us can keep alive his own soul.

II. This brings me, secondly and briefly, to notice that *this truth brings glory to Christ.*

"None can keep alive his own soul." Weak-minded professors are prone to trust in man, but they have here an evident warning against such folly. How can they trust in a man who cannot keep alive his own soul? Shall I crouch at the feet of my fellow man and ask him to hear my confession and absolve me, when I know that he cannot keep alive his own soul? Shall I look up to him and call him "father in God," and expect to receive grace from the laying on of his hand, when I learn that he is a weak, sinful being like myself? He cannot keep alive his own soul—what can he do for me? If he lives before God, he has to live upon the daily charity of the Most High: what can he have to give to me? Oh, look not to your fellow virgins for the oil of grace, for they have not enough for themselves and you, and whatever name a man may dare to take, whether he be priest, Father, or Pope, look not to him, but look to Jesus, in whom all fullness dwells.

The glory which redounds [reflects back] to Christ from our daily dependence is seen in his becoming to us our daily bread, his flesh is meat indeed, and his blood is drink indeed, and we must feed upon these continually, or die. Eating is not an operation to be performed once only, but throughout life, and so we have to go to Jesus again and again and find sustenance in him as long as life lasts. Beloved, we honored our Lord at first when he saved us, and through being daily dependent upon him, we are led to honor him every day; and if we are right-hearted, we shall honor him more and more every day, as we more and more perceive our indebtedness to him. He is our daily bread whereon we feed continually, and the living water whereof we continually drink; he is the light which everlastingly shines upon us, he is in fact daily to us, our all in all, and all this prevents our forgetting him. As at the first he saved us, so he saves us still; and as at the first we prized him, we prize him still.

More than that, as our life is maintained, not only by him, but by our abiding in union with him, this leads us to abide in love towards him. Union is the source of communion and love. The wife remains a happy wife by loving fellowship with her husband. When the betrothed one is married to her beloved, the wedding day is not the end of it all; the putting on of the ring is the beginning, not the end. And so, when we believe in Jesus, we are saved, but we must not idly feel "it is all done now." No, it is only begun. Now is the life of dependence, the life of faith, the life of obedience, the life of love, the life of union commenced, and it is to be continued for ever. This makes us love, honor, and adore our Lord Jesus, since we only live by being one with him.

We have also to remember that our life is daily supported by virtue of what the living Redeemer is still doing for us, as well as by receiving the fruit of his death, and of our spiritual union with him. He ever liveth to make intercession for us, and therefore he is "able to save to the uttermost them that come unto God by him." The life of the ascended Redeemer is intimately bound up with our life—"Because I live ye shall live also." How this honors Christ, for we are thus led to realize a living Savior, and to love him as a living, breathing, acting person. It is a pity when men only think of a dead Savior, or of a baby Savior, carried in the Virgin's arms, as the church of Rome does; it is our joy to have a living Christ, for while he lives, we cannot die; and while he pleads, we cannot be condemned. Thus we are led to remember him as a living Savior, and to give him honor.

But oh, my brethren, what must be the fullness of Christ, when all the grace which the saints have must come out of him, and not merely all they have had, but all they obtain every day comes from him. If there be any virtue, if there be any praise, if there be anything heavenly, if there be anything divine, of his fullness have we received it, and grace for grace. What must be that power which protects and preserves myriads of saints from temptation, and keeps them amid perils as many as the sands of the sea! What must be that patience which watches over the frail children of God in all their weaknesses and wanderings, in all their sufferings, in all their infirmities! What must be his grace which covers all their sin, and what his strength, which supports them under all their trials! What must the fountainhead be, when the streams which flow to any one of us are so deep that we cannot fathom them, so broad that I cannot measure them! Yet millions of happy spirits are each one receiving as much as any one of us may be, and still there is a fullness abiding in Christ the same as before, for it has pleased the Father that in him should all fullness dwell. Not a saint lives a moment apart from him, for "none can keep alive his own soul." The cries of babes in grace and the shouts of strong men who divide the spoil, all come from the life which he lends and the strength which he gives. Between the fates of Hell and the gates of Heaven in all those pilgrims whose faces are towards the royal city, all the Life is Christ's life, and all the strength is Christ's strength, and he is in them, working in them to will and to do of his own good pleasure. Blessed be the name of the Lord Jesus, who thus supplies all his people. Does not this display the exceeding riches of his grace?

III. Thirdly and practically, *this subject suggests the path of wisdom for ourselves.*

"None can keep alive his own soul," then, my dear brothers and sisters, what manner of persons ought we to be?

Let me have your earnest thoughts on this point for a minute. Do not let any one among us look back to a certain day and say, "On that occasion I was regenerated and converted, and that is enough." I fear that some of you get into a very bad condition by saying, "If I can prove that I was converted on such a day that will do." This is altogether unjustifiable talk.

Conversion is a turning into the right road; the next thing is to walk in it. The daily going on in that road is as essential as the first starting, if you would reach the desired end. To strike the first blow is not all the battle; to him that overcometh the crown is promised. To start in the race is nothing, many have done that who have failed; but to hold out till you reach the winning post is the great point of the matter. Perseverance is as necessary to a man's salvation as conversion. Do remember this: you not only want grace to begin with, but grace with which to abide in Christ Jesus.

Learn, also, that we should diligently use all those means whereby the Lord communicates fresh support to our life. A man does not say, "Well, I was born on such and such a day, that is enough for me." No, the good man needs his daily meals to maintain him in existence. Being alive, his next consideration is to *keep* alive, and therefore he does not neglect eating, nor any operation which is essential to life. So you, dear friends, must labor for the meat which endureth to life eternal, you must feed on the bread of heaven. Study the Scriptures daily—I hope you do not neglect that. Be much in private prayer, your life cannot be healthy if the mercy seat be neglected. Do not forsake the assembling of yourselves together, as the manner of some is. Be eager to hear the word, and endeavor both to understand and practice it. Gather with God's people in their more spiritual meetings, when they join in prayer and praise, for these are healthful means of sustaining the inner life. If you neglect these you cannot expect that grace will be strong within you, you may even question if there be any life at all. Still, remember that even if a man should eat and drink, that would not keep him alive without the power of God, and many die with whom there is no lack either of air or food. You must, therefore, look beyond the outward means, to God himself to preserve your soul, and be it your daily prayer, "Oh Savior, by whom I began to live, daily enable me to look to thee that I may draw continuous life from thy wounds, and live because thou livest." Take these things home and practice them.

Keep, dear friends, also clear of everything which has a tendency to destroy life. A sane man does not willingly take poison: if he knew it, he would not touch the cup in which it had been contained. We are careful to avoid any adulteration in our food which might be injurious to life and health: we have our chemists busily at work to analyze liquids, lest haply inadvertently we should imbibe death in the water which we drink. Brethren, now let us be equally careful as to our souls. Keep your chemist at work analyzing the things of this life. Let conscience and understanding fit up their laboratory and prove all things. Analyze the sermon of the eloquent preacher, lest you drink in novelties of doctrine and arrant falsehoods, because he happens to put them prettily before you. Analyze each book you read, lest you should become tainted with error, while you are interested with the style and manner, smartness and elegance of your author. Analyze the company you keep; test and try everything, lest haply you should be committing spiritual suicide, or carelessly squandering life away. Ask the Lord, the preserver of men, above all things, to keep you beneath the shadow of his wings, that you may not be afraid for the pestilence that walketh in darkness, nor for the destruction which wasteth at noonday, because his truth has become your shield and buckler, and you are safe.

Watch your life carefully, but look to Jesus Christ from day to day for everything. Do not become self-satisfied, so as to say, "Now I am rich and increased in goods." If ever a child of God imitates the rich man in the parable, and says, "Soul, take thine ease, thou hast much goods laid up for many years," he is a fool as much as the rich man was. I have known some become very exalted in spiritual things, the conflict is almost over with them, temptation has no power, they are masters of the situation, and their condition is of the most elevated kind. Well, ballooning is very pleasant to those who like it, but I think he is safest who keeps on the ground: I fear that spiritual ballooning has been very mischievous to a great many, and has turned their heads altogether. Their high conceit is falsehood. After all, my friend, to tell you the truth very plainly, you are no better than other people, though you think you are, and in one point I am sure you miserably fail, and that is in humility. When we hear you declare what a fine fellow you are, we suspect that you wear borrowed plumes, and are not what you seem. A peacock is a beautiful bird, what can be more brilliant? But I am not enraptured with his voice, nor are you; and so there may be fine feathers about certain people, perhaps a little too fine, but while they are showing themselves off, we know that there is a weak point about them, and we pray that it may not cause dishonor to the cause of Christ. It is not our part to be hunting about for the failings of our fellow

Christians, yet boasting has a tendency to make us examine the boaster. The practical thing is to believe that when we are proud ourselves there is something wrong about us. Whenever we stand before the looking-glass and think what fine fellows we are, we had better go at once to the great Physician and beseech him to give us medicine for our vanity. Mr. Peacock, you are certainly very handsome, but you should hear yourself croak. Professor, there are fine points about you, but there are sorry ones too: be humble and so be wise. Brother, if you get an inch above the ground you are just that inch too high. If you have anything apart from Christ, if you can live five minutes on past experience, if you think that you can live on yesterday's grace, you make a mistake. You put the manna by so very cannily, you stored it up in the cupboard with such self-content. Go to it tomorrow morning instead of joining the rest of your brethren in gathering the fresh manna which will fall all around the camp. Go to the cupboard where you stored up yesterday's manna! Ah, as soon as you open the door, you close it again. Why did you shut that door so speedily? Well, we need not look inside the cupboard, the smell is enough; it has happened as Moses foretold it; it has bred worms and it stinks, as he said it would. Cover it up as quickly as you can. Dig a deep hole and throw it all in and bury it, that is the only thing to do with such rottenness. Day by day go to Christ and you will get your manna sweet, but begin to live on past or present attainments and they will breed worms and stink as sure as you are a man. Do not try it, for "none can keep alive his own soul."

IV. Last of all, *this subject indicates a way of usefulness* for everyone here present who is a child of God.

I think the great business of the Christian's life is to serve God, and that he can do mainly by aiming at the conversion of sinners. It is a grand thing to be blessed of God to turn sinners from the error of their ways; but listen, brethren, there is equally good work to be done by helping struggling saints. The old Roman said he thought it as much an honor to preserve a Roman citizen as to slay an enemy of his country, and he was right. There is as much acceptance before God in the work of instrumentally preserving souls alive as in being made the means of making souls to live at the first; the upholding of believers is as needful an exercise for Christian workers as the ingathering of unbelievers. I want you to think of this. If there is a person nearly drowned, a man will leap into the water to bring him out, and he gets great credit for it, and deserves it, and so when a man saves a soul from death by earnest ministry, let him be glad and thank God. But if a man be starving, and ready to die, and you give him bread; or if he be not reduced to that point, but would have been so had you not interfered, you have done as good an action in preserving life as the other friend who snatched life from between the jaws of death. You must never think little of the work which instructs the ignorant Christian, which clears the stumbling-blocks out of the way of the perplexed believer, which comforts the feeble-minded and supports the weak. These needful works must be done, while soul-saving must not be left undone. Perhaps some of you never will be the means of the conversion of many; then try to be the means of comfort to as many as you can. To be the means, in the hand of the Holy Ghost, of nurturing the life which God has given is a worthy service, and very acceptable with God. I would urge the members of this church to watch over one another. Be pastors to each other. Be very careful over the many young people that are come among us, and, if you see any backslide, in a gentle and affectionate manner endeavor to bring them back. Do you know any despondent ones? Lay yourselves out to comfort them. Do you see faults in any? Do not tell them of them hastily, but labor as God shall help you to teach them a better way. As the Lord often preserves you by the help of others, so in return seek to be in God's hands the means by which he shall keep your brethren from going astray, from sinking in despair, or from falling into error. I hold it out to you as a good and blessed work to do—will you try to accomplish it?

Now, if you say "Yes," and I think every Christian here says "Yes," then I am going to speak to you "concerning the collection, brethren." This is Hospital Sunday, and we must contribute our full share. Do you see any connection between this subject and the collection? I think I do. Here are these poor sick folk, who will die unless they be carefully looked to, unless medicine and a physician's skill be provided for them. I know you are ready enough to look after sick souls; the point to which I have brought you is one which involves such readiness. Well, now, he who would look after a sick soul, will be sure to care for a sick body. I hope you are not of the same class as the priest in the fable who was entreated by a beggar to give him a crown. "By no means," said the reverend father, "why should I give you a crown? "Will you give me a shilling, holy father?" No, he would not give him a shilling, nor even a penny. "Then," said he, "holy father, will you of your charity give me a farthing?" No, he would not do anything of the sort. At last the beggar said, "Would not your reverence be kind enough to give me your blessing?" "Oh yes, my son, you shall have it at once; kneel down and receive it." But the man did not kneel down to receive it, for he reasoned that if it had been worth a farthing the holy father would not have given it to him, and so he went his way.

Men have enough practical sense always to judge that if professed Christians do not care for their bodily wants, there cannot be much sincerity in their zeal for men's souls. If a man will give me spiritual bread in the form of a tract, but would not give me a piece of bread for my body, how can I think much of him? Let practical help to the poor go with the spiritual help which you render to them. If you would help to keep a brother's soul alive in the higher sense, be not backward to do it in the more ordinary way. You have an opportunity of proving your sincerity, and gratifying your charity, for the boxes will go round at once.

"Marvelous Lovingkindness"

Delivered at the Metropolitan Tabernacle, Newington, on Thursday evening, October 20, 1881. Intended for reading on Lord's Day, November 25, 1900. Published in 1900. No. 2702.

Shew thy marvelous lovingkindness.—Psalm 17:7

The Lord's people, in the time of their trouble, know where to go for comfort and relief. Being taught of God, they do not hew out to themselves broken cisterns, which can hold no water; but they turn to the ever-flowing fountain, they go to the well-head—even to God himself; and there they cast themselves down, and drink to the full. David, when he wrote this Psalm, was evidently in very great distress; and, therefore, he says, "I have called upon thee, for thou wilt hear me, O God: incline thine ear unto me, and hear my speech." What he wanted was his God; as Dr. [Isaac] Watts expresses it—

> In darkest shades, if He appear,
> My dawning is begun;
> He is my soul's sweet morning star,
> And he my rising sun.

Believers draw comfort both from God's ordinary and extraordinary dealings with them, for they regard God's lovingkindness as being both an ordinary and an extraordinary thing. I have heard of a good sister who, when a friend narrated to her some very gracious dealing of God, was asked the question, "Is it not very wonderful?" and she replied, "No; it is not wonderful, for it is just like him." Begging her pardon, and admitting the great truth that she meant to convey, I think it is still more wonderful that it should be "just like him." The wonder of extraordinary love is that God should make it such an ordinary thing, that he should give to us "marvelous lovingkindness," and yet should give it so often that it becomes a daily blessing, and yet remains marvelous still. The marvels of men, after you have seen them a few times, cease to excite any wonder. I suppose there is scarcely a building, however costly its materials, and however rare its architecture, as to which, sooner or later, you will not feel that you have seen enough of it. But God's wonderful works never pall upon you. You could gaze upon Mont Blanc, or you could stand and watch Niagara, yet never feel that you had exhausted all its marvels. And everyone knows how the ocean is never twice alike. They who live close to it, and look upon it every hour of the day, still see God's wonders in the deep.

That God should bless us every day, is a theme for our comfort. God's ordinary ways charm us. The verse before our text says, "I have called upon thee, for thou wilt hear me, O God." [That is,]

> I know thou wilt, for the blessing that I am about to ask from thee is a thing that I have been accustomed to receive from thee. I know thou wilt hear me, for thou hast heard me in the past; it is a habit of thine to listen to my supplications, and to grant my requests.

I hope we can argue in a similar fashion; yet, at the same time, God's people draw equal comfort from the extraordinary character of the mercies he bestows upon them. They appeal to him to show them his "marvelous lovingkindness," to let them see the wonderful side of it as well as the common side of it, to let them behold his miracles of mercy, his extravagances of love, his superfluities of kindness—I scarcely know what words to use when talking of what the apostle Paul calls "the riches of his grace, wherein he hath abounded toward us in all wisdom and prudence," "the exceeding riches of his grace in his kindness toward us through Christ Jesus."

I want, on this occasion, to dwell upon the extraordinary side of God's lovingkindness; and, using our text as a prayer, to say to the Lord in the language of David, "Shew thy marvelous lovingkindness." Sometimes, a man is brought into such a condition that he feels that, if God does not do something quite out of the common order of things, he will assuredly perish. He has now come to such a pass that, if some extraordinary grace is not displayed towards him, all is over with him. Well, now, such a brother may think that God will not give this extraordinary grace to him; he may be troubled at the idea that some marvelous thing is needed. It is to meet that suggestion of unbelief that I am going to address you now.

I. And my first remark is, that *all the lovingkindness of God is marvelous.*

The least mercy from God is a miracle. That God does not crush our sinful race, is a surprising mercy. That you and I should have been spared to live—even though it were only to exist in direst poverty, or in sorest sickness—that we should have been spared at all, after what we have been, and after what we have done, is a very marvelous thing. The explanation of the marvel is given in the Book of Malachi: "I am the Lord, I change not; therefore ye sons of Jacob are not consumed." If God had possessed such a short temper as men often have, he would have made short work with us all; but he is gracious and longsuffering, and therefore he is very patient with us. The very least mercy that we ever receive from God is a very wonderful thing; but when we think of all that is meant by this blessed word "lovingkindness"—which is a compound of all sorts of sweetnesses, a mixture of fragrances to make up one absolutely perfect perfume—when we take that word "lovingkindness," and think over its meaning, we shall see that it is a marvelous thing indeed that it describes.

For, first, it is *marvelous for its antiquity.* To think that God should have had lovingkindness towards men or [before] ever the earth was, that there should have been a covenant of election—a plan of redemption—a scheme of atonement—that there should have been eternal thoughts of love in the mind of God towards such a strange being as man, is indeed marvelous. "What is man, that thou art mindful of him? and the son of man, that thou visitest him?" Read these words now with the tears in your eyes: "I have loved thee with an everlasting love: therefore with lovingkindness have I drawn thee;" and when you know that this passage refers to you, tell me if it is not "marvelous lovingkindness." God's mind is occupied with thoughts concerning things that are infinitely greater than the destiny of any one of us, or of all of us put together; yet he was pleased to think of us in love from all eternity, and to write our names upon his hands and upon his heart, and to keep the remembrance of us perpetually before him, for his "delights were with the sons of men." This antiquity makes it to be indeed "marvelous lovingkindness."

Next, think of *its discriminating character,* that God's lovingkindness should have come to the poorest, to the most illiterate, the most obscure, and often to the most guilty of our race. Remember what Paul wrote about this matter:

> not many wise men after the flesh:, not many mighty, not many noble, are called: but God hath chosen the foolish things of the world to confound the wise; and God hath chosen the weak things of the world to confound the things which are mighty; and base things of the world, and things which are despised, hath God chosen, yea, and things which are not, to bring to naught things that are: that no flesh should glory in his presence.

Dr. Watts expresses the same thought in his verses—

> *When the Eternal bows the skies*
> *To visit earthly things,*
> *With scorn divine he turns his eyes*
> *From towers of haughty kings.*

> *He bids his awful chariot roll*
> *Far downward from the skies,*
> *To visit every humble soul,*
> *With pleasure in his eyes.*

God's choice is marvelous. I know of no better word to apply to his lovingkindness to his chosen than that which is applied in the text: "thy marvelous lovingkindness."

> *What was there in you that could merit esteem,*
> *Or give the Creator delight?*
> *"Twas even so, Father," you ever must sing,*
> *"Because it seem'd good in thy sight."*

There is no other explanation of this wondrous mercy, this "marvelous lovingkindness," than the poet gives—

> *His love, from eternity fix'd upon you,*
> *Broke forth, and discover'd its flame,*
> *When each with the cords of his kindness he drew,*
> *And brought you to love his great name.*

So, beloved, think over the antiquity of God's lovingkindness, and then of the discriminating character of it, and surely you will be full of adoring wonder.

After that, think also of *the self-sacrificing nature of his lovingkindness*—that, when God had set his heart on man, and had chosen his people before the foundation of the world, then he should give—what? Himself. Ay, nothing short of that—that he should not only give us this world, and his providence, and all its blessings, and the world to come, and all its glories; but that, in order to [secure] our possession of these things, he should give his own Son to die for us. Well might the apostle John write, "Herein is love, not that we loved God, but that he loved us, and sent his Son to be the propitiation for our sins." It was not that Christ died for us when we were righteous, "for scarcely for a righteous man, will one die—but God commendeth his love toward us, in that, while we were yet sinners, Christ died for us." "When we were yet without strength, in due time Christ died for the ungodly." Isaiah had long before explained the mystery: "It pleased the Lord to bruise him: he hath put him to grief." You who love your children—to lose one of whom would be worse than to die—can realize a little of what must have been the Father's love to you in giving up his only-begotten Son that you might live through him. Dwell on this great truth, dear friends, meditate on it, and ask the Holy Spirit to lead you into its heights, and depths, and lengths, and breadths, for these lips cannot fully speak of its wonders. As you think over the Lord's ancient lovingkindnesses which were ever of old, his distinguishing love towards his redeemed, and his self-sacrificing love in giving up his Only-begotten, you will be obliged to say, "It is marvelous lovingkindness; it is marvelous lovingkindness indeed."

Then go on to think of *the marvelous constancy of it*. That one should begin to love another, is not so very wonderful; but that love, after it has been despised and ill-requited, should still continue—that the sweet love of Christ should not long ago have curdled into jealousy, and from jealousy have soured into indignation, is an extraordinary thing. He loved us, brothers and sisters, when we did not even know him., and yet hated the Unknown; when we did. not even dimly understand his love to us, and peradventure even ridiculed it, or at least neglected it. Yet he kept on loving us until he loved us into loving him. But even since then, what has been our character? Are you satisfied with what you have been towards the Well-beloved? Are you content with your conduct towards the Bridegroom of your souls? I trow that you are not; and yet, notwithstanding your lukewarmness, your backsliding, your dishonoring of his name, your unbelief, your pride, your love of others, he still loves you; and even now, if you are not enjoying fellowship with him, he has not gone away from you, for his word still is, "Behold, I stand at the door, and knock." He loves, he loves on, and he loves still. Many waters cannot quench his love, neither can the floods drown it. It is indeed "marvelous loving kindness." Can you think of a better adjective than that? I cannot, yet I am conscious that *even it* does not fully express the miraculous character of this all-enduring love which will not take our "No" for an answer, but still says,

> Yes—"yea, I will betroth thee unto me in righteousness, and in judgment, and in lovingkindness, and in mercies. I will even betroth thee unto me in faithfulness, and thou shalt know the Lord."

Oh, this wonderful, this matchless, this unparalleled, this inconceivable, this infinite love! No human language can adequately describe it, so let us sit still, and marvel at that which we cannot even understand.

There is much in God's lovingkindness to be marveled at *in its strange ingenuity*. I might keep on with this topic for ever, applying one word and another to it; yet I should never have shown you even the tithe of its wonders, for it is an altogether inexhaustible theme. But it is wonderful how God deals with us with such a sacred ingenuity of tenderness. He seems to be always thinking of something for our good; while we, on our part, appear to be always testing his love in one way or another. Some fresh want is discovered, only to receive a new supply of grace. Some fresh sin breaks out, only to be blotted out with the ever-pardoning blood of Jesus. We get into fresh difficulties only to receive fresh aid. The further I go on my way to heaven, the more I do admire the road, as well as wonder at the goal to which that road shall bring me. "O world of wonders!" said John Bunyan; "I can say no less." They tell us, nowadays, that the world is worn-out, and that there is no joy in life, and nothing fresh to afford delight. Ah, me! they talk of the attractions of fiction and of the playwright's art, and I know not what besides. They must needs travel all round the world to get a new sensation; and many a man today is like the

Emperor Tiberius, who offered large sums of money to anyone who could invent a new pleasure, meaning, alas! too often, a new vice, or a new way of practicing it. But staying at home with Christ has more wonders in it than gadding abroad with all the wisest of the world. There is more to marvel at in half an inch of the way to Heaven than there is in a thousand leagues of the ordinary pathway of unbelieving men. They call their joys by the name of "life," and say that they must "see life;" but the apostle John tells us that "he that hath the Son hath life; and he that hath not the Son of God hath not life;" that is to say, he is dead. Death has its varieties of worms and rottenness; there are charnel-houses *and* charnel-houses, various processes and methods of corruption, and no doubt there is a science that men may learn in the cemetery, and call it life, if they like; but, oh! if they did but once see Christ upon the cross, they would learn that they had been blind till then. If they did but know his lovingkindness, they would rejoice in it in the sick-chamber, in the long weary night watches, when every bone prevented sleep; they would even recognize it in the arrows of death that smote wife, and child, and brother. They would see it, not only in the table loaded for the supply of hunger, and in the garments furnished against the cold, and in every common blessing of providence; but they would also see it in every despondency, in every deficiency, in every cross, and every loss; and, seeing it, they would keep on saying, "It is all for the best; it is far better than the best could have been if it had been left to me. It is marvelous; it is marvelous lovingkindness." I do believe that, when we get to Heaven, one of the wonders of the glory-land will be to look back upon the road over which we have traveled. It will be marvelous to note the way in which God has led us; and we shall, as our hymn puts it—

> Sing with rapture and surprise,
> His lovingkindness in the skies.

I must now leave this part of my subject with you, only again urging you to think over the truth of which I have been speaking, that all God's lovingkindness to his people is marvelous.

II. Now, secondly, *this lovingkindness, we should desire to see.*

The psalmist says, "Shew thy marvelous lovingkindness;" and we ought to ask God to let us see it; and that, I think, in four ways.

First, *"Let me see it with my intellect, that I may adore."* Help me, O blessed Spirit, to see and understand what is the lovingkindness of God to my soul! I know that it is written of some that "they shall understand the lovingkindness of the Lord." Let me be among the number of those truly wise ones. O Lord, make me wise to see the end and design of thy providence, as well as the providence itself! Make me wise to perceive how thou hast prepared thy grace to meet my depravity, how thou dost adapt thine upholdings to the slipperiness of the way, and to the feebleness of my feet. Often shed a ray of light upon some passage in my life which otherwise I could not comprehend; and let the light stay there till I begin to see and to knew why thou didst this and why thou didst that. "Shew thy marvelous lovingkindness." I am sure, dear friends, that the lessons of a man's own life are too often neglected; but there is in the life of any ordinary child of God—let me pick you out wherever you may be, John, Mary, Thomas—enough to fill you with wonder and admiration of the lovingkindness of the Lord, if your mind be but sufficiently illuminated to perceive the hand of God in it, and to see what God purposed by it. He sometimes uses strange means for producing blessed results. With his sharp axe, he will cut down all our choice trees; as by a whirlwind or a tornado, he will devastate our gardens, and make our fields a desolation; and he will do it all in order that he may drive us away from the City of Destruction, and make us go on pilgrimage to the Celestial City, where the axe can never come, and the leaves will never fade. In his mysterious dealings with us, the Lord often seems to push us backward that we may go forward, and to deluge us with sorrow that he may immerse us into blessing. That is his way of working wondrously; and if we did but understand it, according to the prayer of the text, "Shew thy marvelous lovingkindness," we should be full of adoring wonder.

The next meaning I would give to this prayer would be, *"Lord, show thy lovingkindness to my heart, that I may give thee thanks."* Lord, I know that thou hast been very good to me; but I pray thee to show my heart how good thou hast been, by letting me see how unworthy I have been of this, thy kindness. It is very profitable, sometimes, to sit down, and rehearse the lovingkindness of God, mingling with it penitential reflections upon your own shortcoming. If you do this, you will at last break out with some such cry as this, "Why is all this mercy shown *to me?*" I know a dear brother in Christ, a clergyman, whose name is Curme; he divides it into two syllables, *"Cur me,"* so as to make it mean, "Why me? Why is all this goodness given to me, Lord?" And that is a question which I, too, would fain ask, "Why me, Lord?"

> Why was I made to hear thy voice,
> And enter while there's room;
> When thousands make a wretched choice,
> And rather starve than come?

Is *this* kindness, and *this*, and *this*, all meant for me? Can it really be intended for me? Such reflections as these will make me realize more than ever, how "marvelous" is God's "lovingkindness" to me, and will fill my soul with adoring gratitude and thanksgiving.

Then, next, we ought to pray the Lord to *show his "marvelous lovingkindness" to our faith, that we may again confide in him.* If he will cause the eye of our faith to see that he has this "marvelous lovingkindness" toward us, we shall be the more ready to rely upon him in all the straits into which we may yet be brought. Dost thou believe it, my dear friend? Brother in Christ, dost thou believe that God loves thee? Thou knowest how sweet it is to be sure that thy child loves thee. Though it may well do so, because of its many obligations to thee, yet is it sweet for its warm cheek to touch thine, and to hear it say, "Father, I love you." But, oh! it is sweeter far for God to say, "I love you." Read the Song of Solomon through, and be not afraid to appropriate the message of that sweet and matchless Canticle. Hear in it the voice of Jesus saying to thee," Thou art all fair, my love; there is no spot in thee." "Thou hast ravished my heart, my sister, my spouse; thou hast ravished my heart with one of thine eyes, with one chain of thy neck." Such words as those may be sensuous to those who are sensuous, but they are deeply spiritual to those who are spiritual; and, oh, the bliss of having such words as those to come from the Christ of God *to us!* Why, sometimes, when our Lord thus speaks to us, we hardly know how to hear our excess of joy. I would not ask for a better holiday than to have one hour alone with Jesus; to be undisturbed by any earthly care, and just to think of nothing else but the love of God—the love of God to me. Oh, that it now were shed abroad, in all its fullness, in this poor heart of mine! O love divine, what is there that can ever match thine inexpressible sweetness? Truly it is "marvelous lovingkindness." Again I ask you—"Do you believe this? Are you sure you do?" Pray God to show it to your faith distinctly and clearly, so that you shall be absolutely sure of it, and practically depend upon it whenever you need it.

One other meaning of the text may be, *"Show thy 'marvelous lovingkindness' to me now in my experience, that I may rest in thee."* Let me now, at this present moment, O my God, experience something of that lovingkindness in my soul, in whatever condition I may happen to be, that I may be so flooded with the consciousness of it that I may do nothing else but sit in solemn silence before thee, and adore thee, while beholding the blazing splendor of thy love!

I cannot say any more about this part of my theme, but must leave you to fill up the gaps in the sermon. This is not a topic upon which one should venture to speak if he wants to say all that should or could be said upon it.

III. So, thirdly, dear friends, I remark that *it should be our desire*—**and there are times when it should** *especially* **be our desire**—*to see this "marvelous lovingkindness" of God displayed to us in its marvellousness.*

I will make plain to you what I mean directly; and, first, we would see it as *pardoning great sin.* I expect we have here, in this assembly, at least one whose sin lies very heavy on his conscience. We do not find many such people come out to week-evening services, but yet I thank God that they do come here. Your sin is very great, dear friend. I cannot exaggerate it, because your own sense of its greatness far surpasses any descriptions I could give. You feel that, if God were to pardon you, it would be a marvelous thing. If he were, in one moment, to take all your guilt away, and to send you home completely forgiven, it would be a marvelous thing. Yes, it would—it would; but I beg you to pray this prayer, "Lord, show forth thy marvelous lovingkindness in me." God is constantly doing wonders; then, glorify his name by believing that he can work this miracle of mercy for you. Do not be afraid even to sing—

> Great God of wonders! all thy ways
> Are matchless, God-like, and divine;
> But the fair glories of thy grace
> More God-like and unrivall'd shine:
> Who is a pardoning God like thee?
> Or who has grace so rich and free?

Believe on the Lord Jesus Christ, and thou shalt be saved, and saved immediately. Trust him now; and marvelous though it will be to you, I have shown you that God's lovingkindness is *all* marvelous, and that the extraordinary is ordinary with God, and that the marvelous is but an everyday thing with him. Pray for this "marvelous lovingkindness" to be manifested to you, and you shall have it. One said, "If God ever saves me, he shall never hear the last of it." You may say the same, and resolve that, henceforth, having had much forgiven, you will love much; having been saved from great sin, you will tell it on earth, and tell it in Heaven; and, if you could, you would even wish to make Hell itself resound with the wondrous story—

> Tell it unto sinners tell,
> I am, I am out of Hell—

—"and what is more, I am on the road to Heaven, for God's 'marvelous lovingkindness' has been shown to me."

So God's lovingkindness may be seen as pardoning great sin; and next, it may be seen *as delivering from deep trouble*. I may be addressing some poor child of God who is sorely perplexed. These are very trying times, and we constantly meet with godly people who have a sincere desire to provide things honest in the sight of all men, but who do not find it easy to do so. Some very gracious people have got into a cleft stick; and however they will get out, they cannot imagine. If this is your case, dear friend, I expect you feel very much as John Fawcett's hymn puts it—

> My soul, with various tempests test'd,
> Her hopes o'erturn'd, her projects cross'd,
> Sees every day new straits attend,
> And wonders where the scene will end.

Well, now, if you are ever brought through all your troubles, it will be "marvelous lovingkindness" to yea, will it not? Then, go to God with the prayer, "Show me thy marvelous lovingkindness," and he will do it. He will bring you up, and out, and *through*—not, perhaps, in the way you would like to come, but he will bring you out in the *best* way.

> Trust in the Lord, and do good; so shalt thou dwell in the land, and verily thou shalt be fed. Delight thyself also in the Lord; and he shall give thee the desires of thine heart. Commit thy way unto the Lord; trust also in him; and he shall bring it to pass.

Always expect the unexpected when you are dealing with God. Look to see, *in* God, and *from* God, what you never saw before; for the very things which will seem to unbelief to be utterly impossible, will be those which are most likely to happen when you are dealing with him whose arm is omnipotent, and whose heart is faithful and true. God grant you grace, dear friend, thus to use the prayer of our text as the means of delivering you from deep trouble!

Here is another way to use it. I think you may pray it thus—at all events, I mean to do so, whether you will or not—"Lord, reveal thy marvelous lovingkindness to me, *so as to give me high joys and ecstasies of delight.*" I sometimes envy those good people who never go up and never go down, always keeping at one level; theirs must be a very pleasant experience indeed. Still, if ever I do get on the high horse, then I go up far beyond anything I can describe; if ever I do ride upon the clouds, then I do not envy the people who keep along the smooth road. Oh, what deep depressions some of us have had! We have gone down to the very bottoms of the mountains, and the earth with her bars has seemed to be about us for ever; but, after just one glimpse of God's everlasting love, we have been up there where the callow lightnings flash, resting and trusting among the tempests, near to God's right hand. I think—nay, I am sure—we may pray for this experience. Should not the preacher of the Word wish to know the fullness of love divine? Should not the teacher of the young long to learn all that he can concerning God's infinite love? Though this is the love that passeth knowledge, should not every Christian wish to know all that is knowable of this great love of God? Then let us pray: "Shew thy marvelous lovingkindness." It was truly said, "Thou canst not see God's face, and live;" but I have been inclined to say, "Then, let me see God's face, and die." John Welsh said, when God was flooding his soul with a sense of his wondrous love, "Hold, Lord, hold! I am but an earthen vessel, and thou wilt break me." If I had been there, and I could have borne no more, I would have said, "Do not hold, Lord; break the poor earthen vessel, let it go all to pieces; but anyhow, let thy love be revealed in me!" Oh, that I might even die of this pleasurable pain of knowing too much of God, too much of the ineffable delight of fellowship with him! Let us be very venturesome, beloved, and pray, "Shew thy marvelous lovingkindness."

And, when we have done that, I think we may put up this prayer for ourselves, *as to our own usefulness.* You want to do good, dear brother—dear sister. Well, then, pray to God,

> Show me thy marvelous lovingkindness, O Lord! Use even such a feeble creature as I am. Let Heaven, and earth, and Hell itself, see that thou canst save souls by poor ignorant

men as well as by inspired apostles and learned doctors. Lord, in my chapel, show thy marvelous lovingkindness. Crowd it with people, and bring many of them to Christ. In my class, Lord, show thy marvelous lovingkindness. If there never was a Sunday-school class in which all were saved, Lord, let it be done in mine. Make it a marvelous thing.

A dear brother, who prayed at the prayer-meeting before this service, kept on pleading that God would bless me again, as he had done before. I liked that prayer; it was as if the friend meant to say to the Lord,

> Whatever thou didst in years gone by, do the like over again. If ever it was a marvelous thing to see how the people thronged to hear the Word, Lord, make it more marvelous still.

I recollect when some people called our early success "a nine days' wonder." Well, well, well—it has been a good long nine days, anyhow. But, oh, that we might have another nine days like it—just such another nine days! May God be pleased to send us as many conversions as we had at the first—ay, and I shall add, "and ten times as many!" And if ever there have been revivals in the Church of God that have been really marvelous, brothers and sisters, let us take up the cry,

> Lord, show thy marvelous lovingkindness again. Send us another Whitefield, and another Wesley, if such will be the kind of men that will bless the world. Send us another Luther, another Calvin, another Zwingle, if such be the men that will bless the world. Lord, send us another Augustine, or another Jerome, if such be the men by whom thou wilt bless the world. But, in some way or other, Lord, show us thy marvelous lovingkindness.

"Oh, but!" some would say, "we do not want any excitement. That is an awful thing, you know—anything like excitement." And, then, perhaps, they add, "We have heard so much of what has been done in previous revivals. It has all ended in smoke, and therefore we really dread the repetition of such an experience." Well, then, brother, you go home, and pray, "Lord, shew me thy moderate lovingkindness." When you are on your knees, tonight, pray, "Lord, save half-a-dozen souls here and there."

> *We are a garden wall'd around,*
> *Chosen and made peculiar ground;*
> *A little spot, enclosed by grace*
> *Out of the world's wide wilderness—*

"Lord, make it yet smaller, screw us up tighter still, to the glory of thy blessed name!" I don't think any of you can pray that prayer; you shall if you like; but, for my part, I mean to pray, and I hope many of you will join me in it, and may God hear us! "Show us thy marvelous lovingkindness." Oh, for some new miracle of mercy to be wrought in the earth! Oh, for some great thing to be done, such as was done of old! Shall it be so, or not? On this promise it shall depend: "Open thy mouth wide, and I will fill it." But if our mouths be not open, we cannot expect to get the blessing: "According to your faith, be it unto you." The Lord grant that our faith may expect to see his "marvelous lovingkindness" displayed yet more and more! Amen and Amen.

A Blessed Gospel Chain

Published on Thursday, August 4, 1904. Delivered at the Metropolitan Tabernacle, Newington on Lord's Day evening, July 2, 1876. No. 2895.

Jesus answered and said unto him, "If a man love me, he will keep my words: and my Father will love him, and we will come unto him, and make our abode with him."—John 14:23

This is a blessed chain of gospel experience. Our text is not meant for the men of the world, who have their portion in this life, but for the chosen, and called, and faithful, who are brought into the inner circle of Christ's disciples, and taught to understand the mysteries of his kingdom. It was in answer to the question of Jude as to how Christ would manifest himself to his own, and not to the world, that these words were spoken—and Christ explained that it would be manifest who were his own people, by certain marks and signs. They would be those who love him, and keep his commandments, and so win the complacency of the Father; and the Father and the Son would come to these loving and obedient disciples, and make their abode with them. God grant that all of us may be able to take each of the steps here mentioned, so that our Lord may manifest himself to us as he does not unto the world!

The subject upon which I am about to speak to you is one which the preacher cannot handle without the people. I must have God's people with me in spirit to help me while I am dealing with such a topic as this. You know that, in the Church of England service, there are certain places where the clergyman says, "saying after me," so that it is not simply the minister alone uttering the prayer or the confession, but he is a sort of preceptor leading the rest of the congregation. In a similar style, I want you people of God, as the Holy Spirit shall enable you, to bend all your thoughts and energies in this direction, and step by step to climb with me to these distinct spiritual platforms—ascending from the one to the other by the Spirit's gracious aid, that your fellowship may be with the Father, and with his Son, Jesus Christ.

I. Our text begins with the first link in this golden chain, namely, *love to Christ*: "If a man love me."

This "if" seems to me to stand at the portals of our text, like a sentinel at the gate of a palace, to prevent anybody from entering who ought not to enter. It is an "if" that may be passed round the present assembly, for I fear that all in this house do not love the Lord Jesus Christ. If you cannot answer in the affirmative the question asked by the lips of Jesus himself, "Lovest thou me?"—you have nothing to do with the rest of this verse. Indeed, what have you to do with any of the privileges revealed in the Bible, or with any of the blessings promised there, so long as you are without love to Christ? Let that "if" stand, then, as with a drawn sword, like the cherubim at the gate of the garden of Eden, to keep you from venturing to intrude where you have no right to go if you do not love the Lord Jesus Christ: "If a man love me."

Art thou a lover of the Lord, dear hearer? Put not that question aside, but answer it honestly, in his sight, for *there are some who only pretend to love him*, but really do not—some who make a loud profession, but their language is hypocritical, for their conduct is not consistent therewith. Do you love the Lord Jesus with your whole heart? He is well worthy of your love, so let the question go round the whole assembly, and not miss any one of us, "Lovest thou me?"

For there are some, too, who are *Christ's disciples only by profession*. All they give him is a cold-hearted assent to his teaching. Their head is convinced, and, in a measure, their life is not altogether inconsistent with their profession; but their heart is dead; or, if it be at all alive, it is like that of the church of Laodicea, neither cold nor hot, but lukewarm; and that is a state which Christ abhors. He must occupy the throne of our hearts, and be the best loved of all, or else we lack that which is essential to true Christianity.

"If a man love me," says Christ; so, do you love him? I do not ask whether you love his offices, though I hope you do. You love the Prophet, the Priest, the King, the Shepherd, the Savior, and whatsoever other title he assumes; each of these names is music to your ear—but do you love Christ himself? I will not ask whether you love his work, especially the great redemption which comprehends such innumerable blessings. I hope you do; but it is a personal love to Christ that is spoken of here. Jesus says, "If any man love *me*." Have you realized Christ, personally, as still alive, and gone into Heaven, and soon to come again in all the glory of his Father and of the holy angels! Say, brother, sister, dost thou love him? "If," says Christ, "If a man love me," so it is right and wise for each one of us to put that question to ourselves, even though we know that we can answer it satisfactorily, and say—

> *Yes, I love thee, and adore;*
> *Oh, for grace to love thee more!*

And if there should be any doubt about the matter, we ought to put the question, pointedly, again, and again, and again, and let not ourselves escape till there is a definite answer given one way or another. Heart of mine, dost thou really love the Savior? Brothers and sisters, put this question to yourselves; and if you do love him, let your love well up like a mighty geyser—the hot spring that leaps up to a great height. So let the hot spring of your love to Jesus leap up now, and let each one of you say to him,

> *My Jesus, I love thee, I know thou art mine,*
> *For thee all the follies of sin I resign;*
> *My gracious Redeemer, my Savior art thou,*
> *If ever I loved thee, my Jesus 'tis now.*

If you can do so, then you may add—

> *I will love thee in life, I will love thee in death,*
> *And praise thee all long as thou lendest me breath;*
> *And say when the death-dew lies cold on my brow,*
> *If ever I loved thee, my Jesus, 'tis now.*

Remember that, *if you do love him, he must have loved you first.* Think of his ancient love—the love that was fixed upon you or [before] ever the earth was, when he saw you in the glass of futurity, and beheld all that you would be in the ruinous fall of Adam, and by your own personal transgression, and yet loved you, notwithstanding all. Think of him, when the fullness of time was come, stripping himself of all his glory, and descending from the throne of infinite majesty to the manger of humiliation, and being there, as a babe, swaddled in his weakness. Will you not love him who became God incarnate for you? Think of him all through his life—a life of poverty, for he had not where to lay his head;—a life of rejection, for "he came unto his own, and his own received him not";—a life of pain, for he bare our sicknesses;—a life of dishonor, for he was despised and rejected of men. Will you further think of him in the garden of Gethsemane? Will not your love be stirred as you watch the bloody sweat, and hear his groans and mark his tears, as he pleads with God until he prevails? Follow him to the judgment-seat, and hear him there charged with sedition and with blasphemy, if you can bear it. Then see the soldiers, as they spit in his face and mock him, while they thrust a reed into his hand for a scepter, and put on his brow a crown of thorns as his only diadem. See him tied up to be scourged, till the cruel thongs lacerate and tear his precious flesh, and he suffers agonies indescribable. And when you have followed him as far, go further still, and stand at the cross-foot, and mark the crimson stream that flows from his hands, and feet, and side. Stand and watch him when the soldier's spear has pierced his heart, and made the blood and water flow forth for your pardon and cleansing. Did he suffer all this for you, and do you not love him in return? May I not tell that "*if*" to get out of the way, and let you pass in, that you may take the next step? Track him as he rises from the grave for you, as he ascends to Heaven for you, and obtains great gifts for you; and as yonder, before his Father's face, he pleads for you; and as there he governs all things, as King of kings, and Lord of lords, and governs all for you; as there he prepares many mansions for his own people; and as there he gets ready to come to earth the second time, that he may receive his people unto himself, that where he is, they may be also forever and for evermore. As you think of all this, love the Lord, ye who are his saints, ye who have been washed in his blood, love him! Ye who are wearing the spotless robe of his righteousness—love him. Ye who call him "Husband," love him—ye who are married to him—united in bonds that can never be severed.

II. If this be true of you, let us pass on to the next point, that of *keeping Christ's words.*

"If any man love me, says Christ, "he will keep my words. "Let us see how far we have kept his words.

I trust that, first, we keep his words *by treasuring them, and prizing them.* Brothers and sisters, I hope that we venerate every word that Christ has ever uttered. I trust that we desire to treasure up every syllable that he has ever spoken. There is not a word of his recorded in the Gospels, or in any other of the inspired pages of revelation, by which we do not set more store than by much fine gold.

I trust that we keep Christ's words, next, by *trying to know them.* Are you all diligent students of the Word? Do you search the Scriptures? Do you live upon the truth that the Lord hath spoken? You should do so, for every word that cometh out of his mouth is the true food of your souls. I must ask you whether you are doing these two things. Are you keeping Christ's words by prizing them, and by seeking to be so familiar with them that you know what his words are?

Then, next, do you endeavor to lift the latch, and *to find your way into the inner meaning of his words?* Do you pierce the shell to get at the kernel? Does the Spirit of God lead you into all truth, or are you content with the rudiments of the faith? This is the way to keep Christ's words, namely, by endeavoring, to your very utmost, to understand what the meaning of those words may be.

Then, when you know the meaning of them, do you seek to keep them in your hearts? Do you love what Christ has spoken, so that you delight to know what it is, and love it because it is his doctrine? Will you sit at his feet, and receive the instruction that he is willing to impart? Have you attained to that stage that you even love his rebukes? If his words come home to you, and sharply reprove you, do you love them even then, and lay bare your heart before him, that you may feel more and more the faithful wounds of this your beloved Friend? Do you also love his precepts? Are they as sweet to you as his promises; or, if you could do as you wish, would you cut them out of the Bible, and get rid of them? O brothers and sisters, it is a blessed proof that grace has been largely given to us when even the smallest word uttered by Jesus Christ is more precious to us than all the diamonds in the world, and we feel that we only want to know what he has said, and to love whatever he has spoken.

"If a man love me, he will keep my words." This declaration of our Lord suggests this question—*"Do we keep his words practically?"* That is a most important point, for you will not be able to get any further if you stumble here. Do you endeavor, in a practical way, to keep all his moral precepts? Are you trying to be, in your lives, as far as you can, like him; or are you selfish, unkind, worldly? Are you endeavoring to be like him who hath left you an example that you should follow in his steps? Come, answer honestly. Is this the object of your being? Are you seeking to be molded by the Holy Spirit in that way? And are you practically keeping Christ's words as to the precepts of the gospel? Have you believed on him? Believing on him, have you been baptized according to his command? Being baptized, do you come to his table, according to his bidding, "This do in remembrance of me"? Or do you turn on your heel, and say that these are nonessential things?

Beloved, if your heart is right with God, you will want to know all his words, and to put them into practice. What care I about the words of any earthly church? They are only the words of men; but search ye, and find the words of Christ; and wherever they lead you, even though you are the only one who has ever been led in that way, follow wherever he leads. You cannot take the next step mentioned in my text unless you can deliberately say,

> Yes, Lord, "thy words were found, and I did eat them; and thy word was unto me the joy and rejoicing of mine heart; for I am called by thy name, O Lord God of hosts;" and I long to walk in all thy statutes and ordinances, blamelessly, even to the end of my days.

You may err, you may make mistakes; you may commit sin; but the intent of your heart must be that, having loved the Lord, you will keep his words in those various senses that I have mentioned.

III. If you have been enabled to pass through these two gates, you may now come to the next one, which tells us of *a high privilege and great joy:* **"He will keep my words,** *and my Father will love him."*

What wonderful words these are—"My Father will love him"! It is quite certain that he will do so; for, when a man loves Jesus, he is in sympathy with the Eternal Father himself. You know, my brethren, that the Father's love is fixed upon his only-begotten Son. One with himself in his essential Deity, he has loved him from eternity; but since Jesus has been obedient unto death, "even the death of the cross," we cannot imagine what must be the Father's complacency in the blessed person of our risen and ascended Lord. This is a deep subject, and there is no human mind that can ever fathom the depths of it, and tell how truly and how wonderfully the Father loves his everlasting Son. So, you see, brethren, that, if we love Jesus Christ, our heart meets the heart of God, for the Father also loves him. Have you never felt, when you have been trying to praise Jesus, that you are doing, in your feeble way, just what God has always been doing in his own infinite way? The ever-blessed Spirit is continually glorifying Jesus; and when you are doing the same, God and you—though with very unequal footsteps—are treading the same path, and are in sympathy the one with the other.

Then, besides the fact that you are in sympathy with the Father in having one object of love, you are also in sympathy with him as to character. Jesus said, "If a man love me, he will keep my words." Well, when you are keeping Christ's words—when the divine Spirit is making you obedient to Jesus, and like to Jesus—you are treading the path where your heavenly Father would have you walk, and therefore he loves you.

Let me make a clear distinction here. I am not now speaking about the general love of God towards all mankind—that love of benevolence and beneficence which is displayed even towards the thankless and the evil. Neither am I speaking, just now, concerning the essential love of God towards his own elect, whom he loves, irrespectively of their character, because of his own sovereign choice of them from eternity; but I am speaking of that complacent love which God, as a Father, has towards his own children. You know that you often say to your child, "If you do this or that, your father will love you;" yet you know that a father will love his child, as his child, and always must do so—even if his character is not all that the father desires it to be. But what a love that is which a father has to a good, dutiful, obedient child! It is a love of which he talks to him again and again, a love which he manifests to him in many sweet and kindly words, a love which he displays to him in many actions which he would not otherwise have done, bestowing upon him many favors which it would not have been safe to bestow upon him if he had been a naughty, disobedient child. Never forget that our heavenly Father exercises wise discipline in his house. He has rods for his children who disobey him, and he has smiles for his children who keep his commands. If we walk contrary to him, he has told us that he will walk contrary to us; but if our ways please him, there are many choice favors which he bestows upon us. This teaching is not suggestive of legal bondage, for we are not under law, but under grace; but this is the law of God's house under the rule of grace—for instance, if a man keeps the Lord's commandments, he will have power with God in prayer; but when a man lives habitually in sin, or even occasionally falls into sin, he cannot pray so as to prevail, he cannot win the ear of God as he used to do. You know right well that, if you have offended the Lord in any way, you cannot enjoy the gospel as you did before you so sinned. The Bible, instead of smiling upon you, seems to threaten you, in every text and every line; it seems to rise up, as in letters of fire, and burn its way into your conscience.

It is certainly true that the Lord deals differently with his own children according to their condition and character. So, when a man is brought into such a state of heart that he keeps Christ's words, then his character is of such a kind that God can take a complacent delight in him, and in this sense can love him. It is in such a case as this that the Father will let us know that he loves us, that he will assure us of that love, and shed it abroad in our hearts by the Holy Ghost. He will give us special blessings, perhaps in providence, but certainly in grace. He will give us special joy and rejoicing; our horn shall be exalted, and our feet shall stand upon the high places of the earth. All things—even his trials—shall be blessed to the man who walks aright, with God; and the way to do that is to love Christ, and to keep his words. Of such a man, Jesus says, "My Father will love him."

IV. If you have passed through these three gates, you come to another which bears this inscription, *"We will come unto him."*

This is a singular use of the plural pronoun: *"We* will come unto him." It is a proof of the distinct personality of the Father and of the Son. Jesus says, "If a man love me," (do not forget the previous links in this blessed gospel chain,) "he will keep my words: and *my Father will love him;*" and then follows this gracious assurance: "We will come unto him." Does not this mean, first, *distance removed?* There is no longer a gap between such a man's soul and his God. He feels heavy in heart, perhaps, and thinks, "I cannot get near to God;" but he hears this comforting message, "We will come unto him;" and, soon, over all the mountains of division that there may have been in the past, like a roe, or a young hart, the Well-beloved comes; and the great Father, when he sees, in the distance his child returning to him, runs to meet him, and folds him to his heart. What a wondrous divine coming this is! Christ and his Father, by the Holy Spirit, come to pay the believer a most gracious visit. Yes, beloved, if you are living in love to Christ, and keeping his words, there will not be any distance separating you from the Father and the Son, but the text will be blessedly fulfilled in your experience, "We will come unto him."

And, while it means distance removed, it also means *honor conferred.* Many a great nobleman has beggared himself that he might receive a prince or a king into his house; the entertainment of royalty has meant the mortgaging of his estates; that is, a poor return for the honor of receiving a visit from his sovereign. But, behold, my brothers and sisters, how different it is with us. The obedient lover of the

Lord Jesus Christ has the Father and the Son to visit him, and he is greatly enriched by their coming. He may be very poor, but Jesus says, "We will come unto him." He may be obscure and illiterate, but Jesus says, "We will come unto him. "Do you all, dear friends, know what this coming means? Did you ever know the Son to come to you with his precious blood applied to your conscience, till you realized that every one of your sins was forgiven? Have you taken Jesus up in your arms, spiritually, as old Simeon did literally, and said, with him, "Lord, now lettest thou thy servant depart in peace, according to thy word, for mine eyes have seen thy salvation"? Has Jesus seemed, to your faith, to be as near to you as one who sat on the same chair with you, and talked with you in most familiar conversation? It has been so with some of us, and it has often been so.

This also has meant *knowledge increased*. Jesus has revealed himself to us by coming to us, even as he came to the two disciples on the way to Emmaus. Then, in addition, have you not known the Father come to you, in his divine relationship, yet making you feel yourself his child, and causing you to realize that he loved you as truly as you love your own children, only much more deeply and fervently than human love can ever be? Have you not received, at his hands, such tokens for good, and such benedictions as only he could give, so that you felt the divine Fatherhood to be something coming very near to you, and the Spirit of God, operating within you, has made you cry, "Abba, Father," with an unstammering tongue? "We will come unto him." The Savior will come, and the Father will come, and the blessed Spirit will represent them both in the believer's heart.

So, "We will come unto him," means distance removed, honor conferred, and knowledge increased; and it also means *assistance brought*; for, if the Father and the Son come to us, what more can we need? With their gracious presence in our souls, we have omnipotence and omniscience, infinity and all sufficiency, on our side, and grace to help us in every time of need.

V. The last clause of the text, and the sweetest of all, is, *"and make our abode with him."*

Can you catch the full meaning of that phrase? Jesus says that the Father and the Son will visit us; they will come to us, as the three blessed ones came to Abraham when he was at the tent door, and he entertained the Lord and his attendant angels; but they did not make their abode with him. They went on their way, and Abraham was left in the plains of Mamre. God often visited Abraham, and spake familiarly with him, but our Savior's promise goes beyond that; he says, "We will come unto him, and make our *abode* with him." To make your abode with a person, is for that person and yourself to have the same house and home, and to live together. In this case, it means that the Lord will make his people to be his temple, wherein he will dwell continually. "We will come unto him, and make our abode with him." I have turned that thought over and over again until I have got the sweetness of it into my own heart; but I cannot communicate it to your minds and hearts; only the Holy Spirit can do that.

See what this expression means. *What knowledge of one another is implied here!* Do you want to know a person? You must live with him; you do not really know anybody, however much you may think you know, until you have done so. But, oh, if the Father and the Son come and live with us, we shall know them—know the Father and the Son! This is not the portion of carnal minds; neither is it for professing Christians who have not fulfilled the conditions laid down by our Lord; but it is for those who love Christ, and keep his words, those who consciously live in the enjoyment of the Father's complacency, and who have fellowship with the Father and with the Son by the Spirit. To these privileged individuals, God reveals himself in his triune personality, and to them he will make known all that is in his covenant of love and mercy.

This expression also implies *a sacred friendship*; for, when God comes to dwell with men, he does not thus dwell with his enemies, but only with those who love him, and between whom and himself there is mutual sympathy. O beloved, if God the Father and God the Son shall indeed come to dwell with us, it will be to us a proof of wondrous love, and dear familiarity, and intense friendship! If you go to live with an earthly friend, it is quite possible for you to stay too long, and to outstay your welcome. But God knows all about the man with whom he comes to live, and Jesus says, "We will make our abode with him," because he knows that his Spirit has purified and sanctified that heart, and made it ready to receive himself, and his Father, too. You remember how Jeremiah pleaded with the Lord not merely to be as a sojourner: "O the hope of Israel, the Savior thereof in time of trouble, why shouldest thou be as a stranger in the land, and as a wayfaring man that turneth aside to tarry for a night?" But this is not the way that the Father and the Son deal with us, for Jesus says that they will make their abode with us. Does not this imply a very sacred friendship indeed between God and our soul?

It also reveals *the complete acceptance of the man before God;* for, when anyone comes to stay with you, it is taken for granted that you exercise hospitality towards him; he eats and drinks in your house; and, for the time, he makes himself at home with you. "But," you ask, "is it possible that God should accept the hospitality of man?" Yes, it is; listen to the words of Christ himself: "Behold, I stand at the door, and knock: if any man hear my voice, and open the door, I will come in to him, and will sup with him, and he with me." Oh, the blessedness of thus entertaining the King of kings! Then will he drink of my milk and my wine, and eat the pleasant fruits that are grown in the garden of my soul. Will that which I present to him be acceptable to him? It must be, or else he would not live in my house! And when the Father and the Son come to dwell in the soul of the believer, then all that he does will be accepted; if he is himself accepted, his thoughts and his words, his prayers and his praises, his almsgiving and his labors for Christ will be accepted by both the Father and the Son.

What a blessed state for anyone to reach! For then it shall come to pass that this reception, on God's part, from us, shall be followed by a sevenfold reception, on our part, from him. You do not imagine, I hope, that, when God the Father and God the Son make their abode in a man, that the man will continue to be just as he was when they came to him. No, my brethren; the Lord pays well for his lodging; where he stays, he turns everything that he touches into gold. When he comes into a human heart, it may be dark, but he floods it with the light of heaven. It may have been cold before, but he warms it with the glow of his almighty love. A man without the indwelling of God is like the bush in Horeb when it was only a bush; but when the Father and the Son come to him, then it is with him as when the bush burned with fire, yet was not consumed. The Lord brings Heaven to you when he comes to you, and you are rich beyond the intents of bliss. All things are yours, for you are Christ's, and Christ is God's, and Christ and God have come to make their abode with you.

Now, according to our Lord's promise, "We will come to him, and will make our abode with him," it is implied that *there they mean to stop.* Let me take your thoughts back, for a minute, to the earlier links in this blessed gospel chain, and remind you that it is only *"if a man love me,"* and it is only *"if he keep my words,"* that the Savior's promise applies: "We will come unto him, and make our abode with him." Have the Father and the Son come to your heart? Then, I charge you, do nothing that might cause them to depart from you even for a moment. If you ever get into conscious enjoyment of the divine indwelling, be jealous of your heart lest it should ever from your Lord depart, or drive him from you. Say, with the spouse, "I charge you, O daughters of Jerusalem, that ye stir not up, nor awake my love, until he please."

"But," perhaps you ask, "can we keep him? Can we keep him always?" I believe you can. By the blessed help of the Divine Spirit, who has taught you to love him, and to keep his words, you may have near and dear fellowship with your Lord by the month and by the year together. I am sure that we have too low a standard of the possibilities of Christian fellowship, and Christian enjoyment, and Christian living. Aim at the highest conceivable degree of holiness; and, though you will not be perfect, never excuse yourselves because you are not. Always aim at something higher and yet higher still than you have already reached; ask the Lord to come and abide with you forever. You will be happy Christians if you attain to this privilege, and keep in that condition; and we shall be a blessed church if the most or all of us should attain to it. I mean to go in for this blessing, by God's gracious help; will not you, my brother, my sister? Can any of you be content to live a lower life than is possible to you? I hope you will not be; but that you will reach all of these steps that I have pointed out to you, and ask God in prayer to help you to surmount them.

> Lord, help me to love Jesus. Set my soul on fire with love to him. Lord, enable me to keep all his words, and never to trifle with his truth in anything. And then, Father, look upon me with complacency. Make me such that thou canst take delight in me. See the resemblance to thy Son in me, because thou hast made me to be like him; and then, Father, and Savior, come and abide with me forever and ever. Amen.

Such a prayer as that, truly presented, will be answered, and the Lord shall get glory from it.

But, alas! many of you have nothing to do with this text because you do not love Christ; and the first thing you have to do is not to think about loving him, but about trusting him, for you know that the only way of salvation is by trusting Christ; so, if you do not trust him, you are not in the way of salvation. Have you ever thought of what is involved in being an unbeliever? The apostle John says, "He that believeth not, God hath made him a liar; because he believeth not the record that God gave of his Son." Do you really mean to make God out to be a liar? Surely, you cannot; the very thought is too horrible to be entertained for a moment. Well, then, believe his record concerning his Son. That record declares that he is the propitiation for our sins; then, if you rely upon that propitiation, and trust to him who made it, you are saved.

I often have the remark made to me, by an anxious soul, "But, sir, I cannot believe; I wish I could." This is the answer which I generally give to the person who says that: "What! you cannot believe? Come, now, let us have that matter out. You cannot believe God? Could you believe me?" Of course, the answer is, "Oh, yes, sir; I can believe you!" I reply—

> Yes, I suppose that is because you have confidence in my character, and believe that I would not tell you a lie. Then, in the name of everything that is good and reasonable, how is it that you dare say that you cannot believe God? Is he a liar? Has he ever given you any cause to say to him, "I cannot believe you"? What do you mean? Give me some reason why you cannot believe God? What has he done that you cannot believe him?

Well, they do not quite see it in that light; but, still, they return to that sentence, "I cannot believe." Well now, sinner, if Jesus Christ were present, and he were to say to you, "Trust me, and I will save you; believe my promise, and you shall enter into eternal life;" would you look him in the face, and say, "I cannot believe thee"? And if he asked you the question, "Why canst thou not believe me?" what would be your reply? Surely, a man can believe what is true. There have been times with me, since I have known the Savior, when it seemed to me as if I could not doubt my Lord—as if I could not find a reason, even if I ransacked Heaven, and earth, and

Hell, why I should doubt him. I protest that I do not know any reason why I should not trust Christ; I cannot conceive of any. Well, will men continue this monstrous, unjust, ungenerous conduct? Alas, they will.

"But," says someone, "if I do trust my soul to Christ, will he save me?" Try him, and see; you have his own promise that he will cast out none who come unto him. So, if thou believest in the Lord Jesus Christ this very moment—this very moment thou art saved. What more need I say? May the Blessed Spirit cause you to cease, by your unbelief, from practically making God a liar, and may you now come and trust in Jesus, the Substitute and Surety for his people! So shall you rest your weary hearts upon his loving bosom, and it shall be well with you forever and ever. May God bless you all, for Jesus Christ's sake! Amen.

Love at Leisure

Published on Thursday, March 16, 1905. Delivered at the Metropolitan Tabernacle, Newington on Sunday evening, December 3, 1876. No. 2927.

Mary, which also sat at Jesus' feet, and heard his word.—Luke 10:39

Mary was full of a love to Christ which could be very active and self-sacrificing. I have read to you of her pouring the precious box of spikenard upon our Lord for his anointing. She was therefore one who not only waited and listened, but she served the Lord after her sort and fashion. If she had been simply contemplative and nothing more, we might, perhaps, have considered her somewhat of a one-sided character, and while pointing to that which was good in her as an example, we might have had to comment on her deficiencies, but she did more than sit at the Master's feet. Beloved, if we ever serve the Lord as Mary did, we shall do well.

Now, since she was able thus to serve, she becomes a safe example for us in this other matter of restful faith. The portion of her life occupied in sitting at her Master's feet may instruct and help us. I feel I can safely hold her up to you as an example in all respect, and the more so because, for the particular incident just now before us, she received the Master's express commendation. He praised her also for bringing the box of ointment, but, on this occasion, he praised her too, saying that she had chosen the good part which should not be taken from her. He could not have more conspicuously set his seal of approbation on her conduct than he did. I am not going to say much about her, but I want to speak to those of you who love the Lord as Mary did, to try if I cannot entice you for your own rest and for your own encouragement into following her example in this particular incident, namely, that of sitting at the feet of the Lord Jesus Christ. I have already said you can see that the example is only part of her life—one side of it; at another time I may take the other side, and exhort you to follow her also in that; but for this next hour or so, I want you to leave out the other side of her character and stick only to this. Consider it well, for I am persuaded that this is the true preparation for the other—that contemplation and rest at the Savior's feet will give you strength which will enable you afterwards to anoint his feet according as your heart's love shall dictate.

On this occasion, then, we have only to do with Mary sitting at our Savior's feet. There shall be four heads which you will not forget: *love at leisure*—sitting down; *love in lowliness*—sitting at Jesus' feet; *love listening*—she heard his words; *love learning*—she heard his words to most blessed purpose: all the while, she chose the good part.

I. First, then, *love at leisure.*

That is a point which I want you specially to notice. You that have families to feed and clothe, know how, all day long, you are busy—very busy, perhaps; the husband is away from early morning till the evening comes; the children have gone to school, and the wife is occupied in a hundred household things. But now the evening meal is over, and there is a warm fire burning on the hearth. Is it not one of the most pleasant sights of English interiors to see the family gathered around the fire, just to sit still for a little while to talk, and to indulge in those domestic loves which are the charm of that sweet English word "home"? May an Englishman never cease to think of the word "home" as the most musical word that ever dropped from mortal lips! Now love is quiet and still, and, I was about to say, care-less. Outside it has to watch its words, but inside it is playful, it is at ease, it disports itself, fearless of all adversaries. It takes its rest. The armor is put off, and the soldier feels the day's battle is done. He stands not on his guard any longer. He is amongst those that love him, and he feels that he is free. I do not know what life would be if there were not some of those sweet leisure moments when love has nothing else to do except to love—those intervals, these oases[1] in the desert of life, wherein to love is to be happy, and to be loved, is to be doubly blest.

Now, Christian people ought to have such times. *Let us put aside our service for awhile.* I am afraid that even those who are busy in the Master's work and are not occupied much with lower things, yet overlook the necessity for love to be at leisure. Now tonight, at any rate, you that work longest and toil most, and have to

---

[1] Oases: plural of oasis.

think the hardest, can ask the Lord to make this a leisure time between you and Jesus. You are not called upon to help Martha to prepare the banquet. Just sit still now—sit still and rest at Jesus' feet, and let nothing else occupy the next hour, but sitting still and loving and being loved by him.

Can we not get rid of worldly cares? We have had enough of them during the six days: let us cast the whole burden of them upon our Lord. Let us roll them up and leave them all at the throne of grace. They will keep till tomorrow, and there is no doubt whatever that they will plague us enough then, unless we have faith enough to master them. But now put them on the shelf. Say, "I have nothing to do with you now—any one of you. You may just be quiet. My soul has gone away from you, up to the Savior's bosom, there to rest and to delight herself in him."

And then *let us try to banish all church cares also.* Holy cares should not always trouble us. As I came here just now, I said to myself,

I will try tonight not to think about how I shall preach, or how this part of the sermon may suit one class of my hearers or that part another. I will just be like Lazarus was, of whom it is written that "Lazarus was one of them that sat at the table with him."

You know that the preacher to such a congregation as this may often find himself like Martha, combined with much serving if he forgets that he is but a servant of the Master, and has only to do his bidding. You may well excuse us. But it must not be so tonight. Whether you are deacon or elder, or preacher, or hearer, you must have nothing to do tonight with anything, outside of our blessed Lord and our own hearts. Our love shall claim this time for her own rest. No, Martha, even though you are getting ready to feast Christ, we will not hear the clatter of dishes or the preparation of the festival. We must now sit just there at his feet, and look up, and have no eyes except for him, no ears except for him, no heart except for him. It shall be love's leisure night tonight.

And, in truth, beloved, we have plenty of reason for resting. *Let us sit at Jesus' feet because our salvation is complete.* He said, "It is finished," and he knew that he had wrought it all. The random-price is paid for thee, O my soul; not one drop has been withheld of the blood that is thy purchase. The robe of righteousness is woven from top to bottom; there is not one thread for thee to add. It is written, "Ye are complete in him," and however frail we be, yet are we "perfect in Christ Jesus," and in spite of all our sin we are "accepted in the beloved." If it be so, O love, hast thou not room for leisure; is not this thought a divan upon which thou mayest stretch thyself, and find that there is space enough for thee to take thy fullest ease? Thy rest is not like the peace of the ungodly of whom it is said, "The bed is shorter than that a man may stretch himself upon it." Here is perfect rest for thee; a couch long enough and broad enough for all thy need. And if, perchance, thou shouldest remember, O my heart, that thou hast sin yet to overcome, and corruption within thee yet to combat, bethink thee this night that Christ has put away all thy sin, for he is "the end of the law for righteousness to everyone that believeth," and that he has overcome the world on thy behalf, and said to thee, "Be of good cheer." Thou hast to fight, but thy foe is a routed foe. It is a broken-headed dragon that thou hast to go to battle with, and the victory is sure, for thy Savior has pledged himself to it. Thou mayest well take thy leisure, for the past is blotted out and the future is secure. Thou art a member of Christ's body, and as such thou canst not die. Thou art a sheep of his pasture, and as such, he will never lose thee. Thou art a jewel of his crown, and as such, he will never take his eye or his heart off from thee. Surely then thou mayest take thy leisure.

Let us rest also because we have received so much from our Master. Be sure to remember, O heart that wouldest have leisure for love, that though thou hast many mercies to receive, there are not many to come as thou hast had already. Thou hast great things yet to learn, but not such great things as thou hast been taught already. He that has found Christ Jesus to be his Savior has found more than he will ever find again, even though he find a Heaven, since even Heaven itself is in the loins of Christ, and he that getteth Jesus hath got an eternity of bliss in him. If God gave thee Christ, all else is small compared with the gift thou already hast. Take thy leisure, then, and rejoice in thy Lord himself and in his infinite perfections.

As to the Lord's work, we may well take leisure for love, because it is his work. It will go on rightly enough. It is his work, the saving of those souls. It is well that we are so eager, it were better if we were more eager. But just now we may lay even our eagerness aside, for it is not ours to save: it is his, and he will do it. He will give you soon to see of the travail of his soul. Christ will not die in vain. Election's decree shall not be frustrated, and redemption's purpose shall not be turned aside. Therefore rest.

Besides, my heart, *what canst thou do, after all?* Thou art so little and so altogether insignificant; if thou dost worry thyself into thy grave, what canst thou accomplish? God did well enough before thou wert born, and he will do well enough when thou art gone home. Therefore fret not thyself. I have sometimes heard of ministers that have been quite exhausted by the preparation of a single sermon for the Sunday. I am told, indeed, that one sermon on a Sunday is as much as any man can possibly prepare. It is such laborious work to elaborate a sermon. And then I say to myself, "Did my Lord and Master require his servants to preach such sermons as that?" Is it not probable that they would do a great deal more good, if they never tried to do any such fine things, but just talked out of their hearts of the simplest truths of his blessed gospel?[2] I turn to the Old Testament, and I find that he told his priests to wear white linen, but he also told them never to wear anything that caused sweat, from which I gather that he did not want his priests in the temple to be puffing and blowing and sweating and boiling like a set of slaves. He meant that his service, although they threw their strength into it, should never be

---

[2] Spurgeon, an incredibly prolific writer, generally preached three times a week from about age 20. He left a legacy of 3561 sermons (which were taken down in shorthand as he preached) when he died at the age of 57 — and wrote many other pieces, as well.

wearisome to them. He is not a taskmaster like Pharaoh, exacting his tale of bricks, and then again a double tale, giving his servants no straw wherewith to make them. No, but he says, "Take my yoke upon you, and learn of me, for I am meek and lowly in heart and ye shall find rest unto your souls. For my yoke is easy and my burden is light." Therefore it seems to me that, with all the work his people do—and they ought to do it so as to pour their whole life on his head like a box of precious spikenard, yet he did not mean them to go up and down about his service, stewing and worrying and killing their very lives out of them about this and that and the other. They will do his service a great deal better if they will very often come and sit down at his feet, and say, "Now I have nothing to do but to love him—nothing to do but to receive his love into my soul." Oh, if you will seek after such quiet communion you will be sure to work with a holy might that shall consume you. First take in the strength by having these blessed leisures at the Savior's feet. "He that believeth shall not make haste." He shall have such peace and restfulness, such quiet and calm, that he shall be in no hurry of fear or fright, but he shall be like the great Eternal who, with all that he doeth—and he worketh hitherto, and guideth the whole universe which is full of stupendous wonders—yet never breaks the eternal leisure in which his supreme mind for over dwells.

Well, if we cannot keep up such leisure as that, at least let us have it tonight. I invite you, persuade you, and entreat you, beloved Mary and others like you, to do nothing but just enjoy the leisure of love, and sit at Jesus' feet.

II. The second thing is *love in its lowliness.*

Love wants to spend her time with Christ: she picks her place, and her place is down at his feet. She doth not come to sit at the table with him, like Lazarus, but she sitteth down on the ground at his feet.

Observe that *love in this case does not take the position of honor.* She is not a busy housewife, managing affairs, but a lowly worshipper who can only love. Some of us have to be managers for Christ; managing this and managing that; but perhaps love is most at home when she forgets that she has anything to manage. She leaves it to manage itself, or better still, she trusts the Lord to manage it all, and just subsides from a manager into a disciple, from a worker into a penitent, from a giver-forth into a receiver, from a somebody, which grace has made her, to a nobody, glad to be nothing, content to be at his feet, just to let him be everything, while self sinks and sinks away. Do not let me only *talk* about this, beloved, but let it be done. Love your Lord now. Let your hearts remember him. Behold his robes of love, all crimsoned with his heart's blood. You shall take your choice whether you look up to him on the cross, or on the throne. Let it be as suits your mind best tonight; but in any case say unto him, "Lord, what am I, and what is my father's house, that thou hast loved me so?"

Sit near thy Lord, but sit at his feet. Let such words as these be upon thy lip,

Lord, I am not worthy to be called by thy grace. I am not worthy to be written in thy book of life. I am not worthy that thou shouldest waste a thought on me, much less that thou shouldest shed thy blood for me. I do remember now what I was when thou didst first deal with me. I was cold, careless and hard towards thee, but very wanton and eager towards the world, giving my heart away to a thousand lovers, and seeking comfort anywhere except in thee. And when thou didst come to me, I did not receive thee. When thou didst knock at my door, I did not open to thee, though thy head was wet with dew and thy locks with the drops of the night. And, oh! since through thy grace I have admitted thee, and thou and I have been joined together in bonds of blessed union, yet how ill have I treated thee! O my Lord! how little have I done for thee! How little have I loved thee! I could faint in thy presence to think that if thou didst examine me and question me, I could not answer thee one of a thousand of the questions thou mightest ask of me. Thy book accuses me of negligence in reading it. Thy throne of grace accuses me of slackness in prayer. The assemblies of thy people accuse me that I have not been hearty in worshipping. There is nothing, either in providence or in nature, or in grace, but what might bring some accusation against me. The world itself might blame me that my example so little rebukes it; and my very family might charge that I do not bless my household as I should.

That is right, dear brother, or sister. Sink; go on sinking; be little; be less; be less still; be still less; be least of all; be nothing.

Lift up thine eyes from thy lowly place to him who merits all thy praise. Say to him,

But what art thou, beloved, that thou shouldest have thought of me, before ever the earth was, that thou shouldest take me to thyself to be thine, and then for me shouldest leave the royalties of Heaven for the poverties of earth, and shouldest even go down to the grave, that thou mightest lift me up and make me to sit with thee at thy right hand? Oh! what wonders thou hast wrought on me; and I am not worthy of the least of thy mercies; and yet thou hast given me great and unspeakable blessings. If thou hadst only let me be a doorkeeper in thy house, I had been happy; but thou hast set me among princes. If thou hadst given me the crumbs from thy table, as dogs are fed, I had been satisfied; but thou hast put me among the children. If thou hadst said that I might just stand outside the gates of Heaven now and then, on gala days, to hear thy voice, it would have been bliss for me; but now thou hast promised me that I shall be with thee where thou art, to behold thy glory and to be a partake of it, world without end.

Do not such thoughts as these make you sink? I do not know how it is with you, but, the more I think of the Lord's mercies, the more I grow downward. I could weep to think that he should lavish so much on one that gives him no return at all, for so it seems to my heart, that it is with me. What do you think of yourself? What are your faith, your love, your liberality, your prayers, your works? Dare you call them anything? Do you imagine that the Lord is pleased with your past? Would he not rather say to you, "Thou haste bought me no sweet cane with money, neither hast thou filled me with the fat of thy sacrifices; but thou hast made me to serve with thy sins and wearied me with thy iniquities." So we sit down again at his feet, and from that place we would not wish to rise. Love's leisure shall be spent in acts of humiliation. We will bow at the feet that were pierced for our redemption.

III. But now, in the third place, here is *love listening*.

She is down there in the place of humility, but she is where she can catch each word as it falls, and she is there with that object. She wishes to hear all that Christ has to say, and she wishes to hear it close at hand. She wants to hear the very tones in which he speaks and the accents with which he delivers each precept. She loves to look up and see that eye which has such meaning in it, and that blessed countenance which speaks as much as the lips themselves; and so she sits there, and she looks with her eyes toward him as a handmaid's eyes are to her mistress; and then, with her ears and her eyes, she drinks in what he has to say.

Now, beloved, I want you just to do that. Say in prayer now, "Speak, Lord, for thy servant heareth;" and then with your ear open, *hear what he says by his word*. Perhaps there is some text that has come home to your soul today. Hear it. Hear it well. It would not be much use for anyone to try to preach a sermon in the center of the city in the middle of the day. If you stood near St. Paul's Cathedral, with all that traffic going by, and all that rumbling, roaring, and shouting, why, the big bell itself might speak, and you would hardly hear it. But when it is night, and all is still, then you can hear the city clocks strike; and you might hear a man's voice even though it was not a very strong one, if he went through the streets, and delivered a message with which he had been entrusted. Well, our blessed Lord often takes advantage of those quiet times when the man has a broken leg, and cannot get to work, but must be still in the hospital, or when the woman is unable to get about the house, to attend to her ordinary duties, but is so helpless that she cannot do anything else but think. Then comes the Lord, and he begins to bring to our remembrance what we have done in days past, and to talk with us as he never has the opportunity of doing at any other time. But it is far more blessed to find time ourselves, so that the Lord will not need to afflict us in order to get us quickly at his feet. Oftentimes the God Shepherd in caring for the sheep *"maketh* us lie down," but he is glad when we come of our own accord, that we may rest and listen to his word.

Listen to what he is saying to you by providence. Perhaps a dear child is sick at home, or you have losses and crosses in business. It may not seem to you as if these things come from your loving Lord, but they are perhaps the pressure of his hand to draw you to his side that he may tell you his secret. Perhaps it has been mercy that has come to you in another way. You have been prospered, you have been converted, you have had much joy in your family. Well, the Lord has a voice in all that he does to his people; so listen tonight. If you listen you will be obliged to say, "What shall I render to the Lord for his benefits to me?"

Listen also to what the Spirit says in your soul. Listen, for it is not till you get your soul quiet that you can hear what the Spirit of God is saying. I have known such a clatter of worldliness or pride, or some other noise, in the soul of man, that the still small voice of the Holy Spirit has been drowned, to the serious detriment of the disciple. Now, I hope you have really done with all your cares and left them outside the Tabernacle[3] tonight, that even the cares about your class in the Sunday-school and about your preaching engagement tomorrow, and everything else, have been put aside, and that now you are just sitting down at Jesus' feet, and listening. While you listen in that fashion, in lowly spirit at his feet, you are likely to hear him say some word to you which, perhaps, may change the whole tenor of your life. I do not know what God the Lord will speak, but "he will speak peace to his people." Sometimes he speaketh in such a way that a turbid life has become clear; a life of perplexity has become decided and distinctly happy; and a life of weakness has become a career of strengths; and a life that seemed wasted for a while has suddenly sprung up into eminent usefulness.

Keep thine ear open, Mary. Keep thy ear open, brother, and thou wilt hear what Jesus Christ has to speak.

But now let me say, while you are sitting and listening, *you will do well to listen as much to him as to what he has to say,* for Christ himself is the Word, and his whole life is a voice. Oh, sit you down, sit down and listen. I wish I had not to talk tonight, and could sit down and do it for myself, and just look up at him, God over all, blessed for ever, and yet brother to my soul, a partaker of flesh and blood! This very fact, that he is incarnate, speaks to me, that God is in human flesh speaks comfort to my soul, such as no words could ever convey. God in my nature, God become my brother, my helper, my head, my all! Could not my soul leap out of the body for joy at the incarnation, if there were nothing else but that revealed to us?

Now let me look up again, and see my Lord with the wounds, as Mary did not see him, but as we now may, with hands and feet pierced, with scarred side and marred visage, tokens of the ransom price paid in his pangs and griefs and death. Is it not wonderful to see thy sin forever blotted out, and blotted out so fully, and blotted out by such means as this! Why, if there were not an audible word, those wounds are mouths which speak his love. The most eloquent mouths that ever spoke are the wounds of Christ. Listen! listen! Every drop of blood says, "Peace"; every wound says, "Pardon; life, eternal life."

---

[3] Spurgeon's church, the Metropolitan Tabernacle, which held up to 6000 people.

And now see thy beloved once again. He is risen from the dead, and his wounds bleed no more; yea, he has gone into the glory, and he sits at the right hand of God, even of the Father. It is well for thee, dear brother or sister, that thou canst not literally sit at his feet in that guise, for if thou couldest only see him as he is, I know what would happen unto thee—even that which happened unto John when he saw him with his head and his hair white like wool, as white as snow, and his eyes as a flame of fire, and his feet as if they burned in a furnace. Thou wouldest swoon away. John says, "When I saw him, I fell at his feet as dead." You cannot sit at those feet of glory till you have left this mortal clay, or until it has been made like unto his glorious body; but you may in faith do so, and what will his glory say to you? It will say, "This is what you shall receive; this is what you shall share; this is what you shall see for ever and ever." He will say to you—even to you who mourn your insignificance and in lowliness sit at his feet—"Beloved, thou shalt partake of the glory which the Father gave me, even that which I had with him before the world was. Soon, when a few more moons have waxed and waned, soon thou shalt be with me where I am." Oh, what bliss is this! Never mind Martha's frowns; forget her for the moment and keep on sitting at Jesus' feet. She may come in and grumble, and say that something is neglected; tell her she should not neglect it then; but now your business is not with plates or pots, but to do as your Master has permitted you to do, namely, to sit at his feet and listen to him.

IV. So I close by saying, in the fourth place, that here is *love learning*.

Whilst she listened, she was being taught, because she sat at Jesus' feet with her heart all warm—sitting in the posture of lowliness—she was, as few could hear them, *hearing words so as to spy out their secret meaning*. You know the difference between a man's voice at a distance, saying something, and his being very near you. You know how much the face can say, and the eyes can say, and the lips can say; and there is many a deaf man that has heard another speak though he has never heard a sound—he has known the meaning by the very motion of the lips and the gleams of the countenance. Ah, and if you get into such near fellowship with Christ as to sit at his feet, you will get his meaning. When the letter kills others, you will see the secret meaning that is hidden within, and you will rejoice.

She got at his meaning, and then she was *hearing the words so as to drink in the meaning*. "They sit down at thy feet," says the old Scripture, "everyone shall receive of thy words." Beloved, that is a great promise—to receive of his words. Some people hear the words, but do not receive them, but there sat Mary where, as the words fell, they dropped upon her as snowflakes drop into the sea and are absorbed. So each word of Jesus dropped into her soul, and became part and parcel of her nature, they fired and filled her very being.

What she learnt, she remembered. *We see love learning what she will treasure up.* Mary never forgot what she heard that day. It remained with her forever; it seasoned her whole life. The words of her Master were with her all the days she was watching, all the days she was waiting, she was waiting after they had been spoken. They kept her watching and waiting, till at last love's instinct told her that the time was come, and then she went upstairs where she had put away the choice ointment for which she spent her money. She had laid it up and kept it till the time should come, and just before the Savior's death and burial she fetched it down, the gift which she had hoarded up for him, and she poured it out in adoration.

As she sat at his feet, she resolved to love him more and more. *Love was learning to love better.* As she had listened and learnt, the learning had crystallized itself into resolves to be, among women, the most devoted to him. Perhaps, little by little, she had laid by this great price which she had paid for the spikenard. Be it as it may, it was dear to her, and she brought it down when the time was come, and put it all on him with a joyous liberality and love. Well, now, I want you just to learn of Jesus after that fashion, and, by-and-by, when the time comes, you, too, may do some deed for Christ that shall fill the house in which you dwell with sweet perfume; yea, shall fill the earth with it, so that, if man scents it not, yet God himself shall be delighted with the fragrance you pour, out of love, upon his Son.

We are going to have the communion, here are the emblems of his blessed body and blood; and I hope they will help us to have nothing to do but to think of him; nothing to do but to be lowly in his presence; nothing to do but to listen to his words and to drink in his teaching.

But there are some here that do not love him. It may be that God will lay you low by affliction in order to bring you to the feet of Jesus. Perhaps he will allow disaster and disappointment to overtake you in the world, to win you to himself. If any of you have had this experience, or are passing through it just now, do not trifle with it, I pray you; for, while we are in this life, if the Lord comes to us to remind us of our sin, he does it in the greatness of his mercy, and in order that he may bring salvation to us. It will be quite another thing in the next life, if you die unrepentant and unforgiven. Then you may indeed dread the coming of God to bring your sin to remembrance; but while you are here, if the Lord is so speaking to you, incline your ear, and hearken to his voice, however harshly it may seem to sound in your ears. Even if he should strip thee, be glad to be stripped by him. If he should wound thee, and bruise thee, willingly give thyself up to be wounded and bruised by him; yea, even if he should slay thee, rejoice to be slain by him, for remember that he clothes those whom he strips, he heals those whom he wounds, and he makes alive those whom he kills. So it is a blessed thing to undergo all those terrible operations of law-work at the hands of the Most High, for it is in that way that he comes to those whom he means to bless.

I cannot preach to you, for the time has gone; but, do you know, I think one of the most dreadful things that can ever be said of man is that he does not love Christ. I should be sorry to enter on my list of friends the man that did not love his mother; yea, I would not call him a man. Dead is that heart to every noble sentiment that loves not her that bare him; and yet there might be some justifiable cause to excuse even that. But not to love the Christ, the God that stooped to bleed for man—this is inexcusable. I dare not to-night utter, as my own, what Paul said, but, very pointedly and solemnly, I would remind you, who love not Christ, of it. Paul says, "If any man love not the Lord Jesus Christ, let him be *anathema maran-atha*,"—cursed at the coming. Sometimes when I think of my Lord, and my heart grows hot with admiration of his self-denying love, I think I could almost invoke the imprecation on the head of him that does not, would not, could not love the Christ of God. But better than that, I will ask his blessing for you, and I say, "Father, forgive them, for they know not what they do!"

Here our sermon closes, and may God's blessing rest on it.

The Poor Man's Friend

Published on Thursday, September 26, 1907. Delivered at the Metropolitan Tabernacle, Newington, on Lord's Day evening, June 8, 1873. No. 3059.

The poor committeth himself unto thee.—Psalm 10:14

God is the poor man's friend. The poor man, in his helplessness and despair, leaves his case in the hands of God, and God undertakes to care for him. In the days of David—and I suppose, in this respect, the world has but little improved—the poor man was the victim of almost everybody's cruelty, and sometimes he was very shamefully oppressed. If he sought redress for his wrongs, he generally only increased them, for he was regarded as a rebel against the existing order of things; and when he asked for even a part of what was his by right, the very magistrates and rulers of the land became the instruments of his oppressors, and made the yoke of his bondage to be yet heavier than it was before. Tens of thousands of eyes, full of tears, have been turned to Jehovah, and he has been invoked to interpose between the oppressor and the oppressed; for God is the ultimate resort of the helpless. The Lord executeth righteousness and judgment for all that are oppressed; he undertakes the cause of all those that are downtrodden.

If the history of the world be rightly read, it will be found that no case of oppression has suffered to go long unpunished. The Assyrian empire was a very cruel one, but what is now left of Nineveh and Babylon? Go to the heaps of ruins by the banks of the Tigris and the Euphrates, and see what will become of an empire which is made to be only an instrument of oppression in the hands of an emperor and the great men under him. It has ceased to be more than a name; its power has vanished, and its palaces have been destroyed. In later times, there sprang up the mighty empire of Rome; and even now, wherever we wander, we see traces of its greatness and splendor. How came it to fall? Many reasons have been assigned, but you may rest assured that at the bottom of them all was the cruelty practiced towards the slaves and other poor people, who were absolutely in the power of the aristocracy and oligarchy who formed the dominant party in the empire. There is a fatal flaw in the foundations of any throne that executes not justice; and it matters not though the empire seems to stand high as heaven, and to raise its pinnacles to the skies, down it must come if it be not founded upon right. When ten thousand slaves have cried to God apparently in vain, it has not really been in vain, for he has registered their cries, and in due season has avenged their wrongs; and when the poor toilers, who have reaped the rich man's fields, have been deprived of their hardly-earned wages, and have cast their plaints into the court of heaven, they have been registered there, and God has, at the right time, taken up their cause, and punished their oppressors.

For many years the Black slaves cried to God to deliver them, and at last deliverance came, to the joy of the emancipated multitudes, yet not without suffering to all the nations that had been concerned in that great wrong. And here, too, if the employers of labor refuse to give to the agricultural laborer his just wage, God will surely visit them in his wrath. At this very day, we have serfs in England who, with sternest toil, cannot earn enough to keep body and soul together, and to maintain their families as they ought to be maintained; and where masters are thus refusing to their laborers a fair remuneration for their work. Let them know that, whoever may excuse them, and whatever may be said of the laws of political economy, God does not judge the world by political economy. He judges the world by this rule, that men are bound to do that which is just and right to their fellowmen; and it can never be right that a man should work like a slave, be housed worse than a horse, and have food scarcely fit for a dog. But if the poor commit their case to God, he will undertake it; and I, as one of God's ministers, will never cease to speak on behalf of the rights of the poor. The whole question has two sides—the rights of the masters, and the rights of the men. Let not the men do as some workmen do, ask more than they ought; yet, on the other hand, let not the masters domineer over their men, but remember that God is the Master of us all, and he will see that right is done to all. Let us all act rightly towards one another, or we shall feel the weight of his hand, and the force of his anger.

Now, having thus given the literal meaning of my text, I am going to spiritualize it, which I should have no right to do if I had not first explained the primary reference of David's words, "The poor committeth himself unto thee."

I. *There are spiritually poor men.*

These do what other poor men have done in temporal things, they commit their case into the hands of God.

Let me try to find out the spiritually poor. They are, first, *those who have no merits of their own.* There are some people, in the world, who are, according to their own estimate, very rich in good works. They think that they began well, and that they have gone on well, and they hope to continue to do well right to the end of their lives. They do confess, sometimes, that they are miserable sinners, but that is merely because that expression is in the *Prayer Book.* They are half sorry it is there, but they suppose that it must have been meant for other people, not for themselves. So far as they know, they have kept all the commandments from their youth up, they have been just in their dealings with their fellowmen, and they do not feel that they are under any very serious obligations even to God himself. I have nothing to say to such people except to remind them that the Lord Jesus Christ said, "They that are whole have no need of the physician, but they that are sick: I came not to call the righteous, but sinners to repentance." Christ came to bring healing to those who are spiritually sick; you say that you are perfectly well, so you must go your own way, and Christ will go in another direction—towards sinners.

Further, the poor people of whom I am speaking, are not only totally without anything like merit, absolutely bankrupt of any goodness, and devoid of anything of which they could boast, but they are also *without strength to perform any such good works in the future.* They are so poor, spiritually, that they cannot even pray as they would, and they do not even feel their poverty as they would like to feel it. After having read this Bible, they wish they could re-read it with greater profit; and when they weep oven sin, they feel their own sin in their very tears, and want to weep in penitence over their tears. They are such poor people that they can do absolutely nothing without Christ, and so poor that, in them, that is, in their flesh, there dwelleth no good thing. They did think once that there might be something good in them; but they have searched their nature through most painfully, and they have discovered that, unless grace shall do everything for them, where God is they can never come.

Perhaps some of you say, "These must be very bad people." Well, they are no better that they should be, yet I may tell you another thing concerning them, they are no worse than many of those who think themselves a great deal better. They have this lowly opinion of themselves because the grace of God has taught them to think rightly and truthfully about themselves in relation to God. They are, in outward appearance, and as far as we can judge, quite as good as others, and better than some. In certain respects, they might be held up as examples to others. This is what we say of them, but they have not a good word to say of themselves; rather, do they put their finger upon their lips, and blush at the remembrance of what they feel themselves to be; or if they must speak of themselves at all, they say, "All we like sheep have gone astray, we have turned everyone to his own way."

II. That brings me to notice, secondly, *what these poor people do.*

They commit themselves unto God. This is a very blessed description of what true faith does. The poor in spirit feel that their case is so desperate that they cannot kept it in their own charge, and therefore they commit it to God. I will try to show you how they do that.

First, *they commit their case to God as a debtor commits his case to a surety.* The man is so deeply in debt that he cannot pay his creditors even a farthing in the pound; but here is someone who can pay everything that the debtor owes, and he says to him, "I will stand as security for you; I will be bondsman for you; I will give full satisfaction to all your creditors, and discharge all your debts." There is no person who is thus deeply in debt, who would not be glad to know of such a surety, both able and willing to stand in his stead, and to discharge all his responsibilities. If the surety said to this poor debtor, "Will you make over all your liabilities to me? Will you sign this document, empowering me to take all your debts upon myself, and to be responsible for you? Will you let me be your bondsman and surety?" "Ah!" the poor man would reply, "that I will, most gladly." That is just what spiritually poor men have done to the Lord Jesus Christ—committed their case, with all their debts and liabilities, into the hands of the Lord Jesus Christ, and he has undertaken all the responsibility for them.

I think I hear someone say, "But will Christ really stand in the sinner's place in such a way as that?" Oh, yes! for he did stand, in anticipation, in the sinner's place before the foundation of the world, and he actually stood there when he died upon the accursed tree, by his death obtaining a full discharge of the debts of all those whose Surety he had become. Dear soul, wilt thou not commit all thy affairs into his hands? Art thou not willing to let him stand as thy Surety, to clear thee of all thy liabilities? "Willing?" say you; "ah! that I am; and not only willing, but right glad shall I be for him to take my place, and relieve me of the burden that is crushing me to the dust." Then it is done for you, and so done that it can never be undone. Suppose that one of you had taken all my debts upon you, and that you were quite able and willing to pay them, I should not go home, and fret myself about my debts. I should rejoice to think that, you had taken them upon yourself, and that therefore they would no longer be mine. If Christ has taken your sins upon himself—and he has done so if you have truly trusted him, your sins have ceased to be; they are blotted out forever. Christ nailed to his cross the record of everything that was against us; and, now, every poor sinner, who is indebted to God's law, and who trusteth in

Christ, may know that his debt is cancelled, and that he is clear of all liability for it forever.

Next, *we commit our case to Christ as a client does to a solicitor and advocate.* You know that, when a man has a suit at law (I hope that none of you may ever have such a suit), if he has an advocate to plead his cause, he does not plead for himself. He will probably get into trouble if he does. It is said that, when Erskine was pleading for a man who was being tried for murder, his client, being dissatisfied with the way in which his defense was being conducted, wrote on a slip of paper, "I'll be hanged if I don't plead for myself." Erskine wrote in reply, "You'll be hanged if you do!" It is very much like that with us; if we attempt to plead for ourselves, we shall be sure to go wrong. We must have the Divine Advocate who alone can defend us against the suits of Satan, and speak with authority on our behalf even before the bar of God. We must commit our case to him, that he may plead for us, and then it will go rightly enough.

Remember also that any man who has committed his case to an advocate, must not interfere with it himself. If anybody from the other side should wait upon him, and say, "I wish to speak to you about that suit," he must reply, "I cannot go into the matter with you; I must refer you to my solicitor." "But I want to reason about it; I want to ask you a few questions about the case." "No," says he, "I cannot listen to what you have to say, you must go to my solicitor." How much trouble Christians would save themselves if, when they have committed their case into the hands of Jesus, they would leave it there, and not attempt to deal with it on their own account! I say to the Devil, when he comes to tempt me to doubt and fear,

> I have committed my soul to Jesus Christ, and he will keep it in safety. You must bring your accusations to him, not to me. I am his client, and he is my Counselor. Why should I have such an Advocate as he is, and then plead for myself?

John does not say, "If any man sin, let him be his own advocate;" but he says, "If any man sin, we have an Advocate with the Father, Jesus Christ the righteous." Dear brother, leave your case with Christ; he can handle it wisely, you cannot. Remember that, if the Devil and you get into an argument, he is much older than you are, and far more clever than you are, and he knows a great many points of law that you do not know. You should always refer him to the Savior, who is older than he is, and knows much more about law and everything else than he does, and who will answer him so effectually as to silence him forever. So, poor tried and tempted soul, commit your case to the great Advocate, and he will plead for you before the Court of King's Bench in heaven, and your suit will be sure to succeed through his advocacy.

Further, *sinners commit their case to Christ as a patient commits his case to the physician.* We, poor sin-sick sinners, put our case into the hands of Jesus, that he may heal us of all our depravities, and evil tendencies, and infirmities. If anyone asks,

"Will he undertake my case if I come to him?" I answer—"Yes, he came to be the Physician of souls, to heal all who trust him." There never was a case in which he could not heal, for he has a wonderful remedy, a catholicon [universal remedy], a cure for all diseases. If you put your case into his hands, the Holy Spirit will shed abroad his love in your heart, and there is no spiritual disease that can withstand that wondrous remedy. Are you predisposed to quickness of temper? He can cure that. Are you inclined to be indolent? Is there a sluggish spirit within you? He can cure that. Are you proud, or are your tendencies towards covetousness, worldliness, lust, or ambition? Christ can cure all these evils. When he was on this earth, he had all manner of patients brought to him, yet he never was baffled by one case, and your case, whatever it may be, will be quite an easy one to him if you only go and commit it into his hands. This building seems to me like a great hospital full of sin-sick souls, and I pray the great Physician to come here, and heal them. Nay, I must correct myself, for he is here; and, as he walks through these aisles, and round these galleries, I beseech you to say to him, "Good Master, I commit myself to thee. I take thee to be my Savior. O save me from my constitutional temperament, and my besetting sins, and everything else that is contrary to thy holy will!" He will hear you, for he never yet refused to heed the cry of a poor sin-sick soul. Do not let him go by you without praying to him, "Son of David, have mercy on me!" Come, Lord, and lay thy hands upon each one of us and we shall be made perfectly whole!

As to the future, the spiritually poor commit themselves to Christ in the same way in which the pilgrims described in *The Pilgrim's Progress* committeth themselves to the charge of Mr. Greatheart, that he might fight all their battles for them, and conduct them safely to the Celestial City. In the old war times, when the captains of merchant vessels wanted to go to foreign countries, and they were afraid of being captured by the privateers of other nations, they generally went in company under the convoy of a man-of-war to protect them, and that is the way you and I must go to heaven. Satan's privateers will try to capture us, but we commit ourselves to the protection of Jesus, the Lord High Admiral of all the seas, and we poor little vessels sail safely under his convoy. When any enemy seeks to attack us, we need not be afraid. He can blow them all out of the water if he pleased, but he will never suffer one of them to injure a solitary vessel that is entrusted to his charge. Sinner, give thyself up to the charge of Jesus, to be convoyed to heaven; and thou over-anxious child of God, lay down all thine anxieties at the feet of Jesus, and rest in his infinite power and love, which will never let thee be lost.

I might thus multiply figures and illustrations of how we commit ourselves to Christ. We do it very much in the way in which our blind friends, sitting under the pulpit, got here this evening—*they came by committing themselves to the care of guides.* Some of them can walk a good long way without a guide, but others could not have found their way here tonight without some friend upon whose arm they could lean. That is the way to get to Heaven, by leaning upon Jesus. Do not expect to see him, but trust yourself to him, and lean hard upon him. He loves to be trusted, and faith has a wonderful charm for him. I was once near the Mansion House, and as I stood there, a poor blind man, who wished to cross over to the Bank, said to me, "Please, sir, lead me across; I know you will, for I am blind." I was not sure that I could do so, for it is not an easy task to lead a blind man across that part where so many cabs and omnibuses are constantly passing, but I managed it as best I could. I do not think I could have done it if the poor man had not said to me, "I know you will;" for then I thought that I must. And if you come to Christ, and say, "Lord Jesus, wilt thou lead me to heaven?" and tell him that you are sure that he will never let a poor blind soul miss its way, that you are sure you can trust him, that he is such a kind-hearted Savior that he will never thrust away a guilty sinner who thus commits himself into his hands, and I am sure that he will be glad to save you, and that he will rejoice over you as he leads you safely home to heaven. If any of you can see with your natural eyes, and yet are blind spiritually, be glad that there is a blessed Guide to whom you can commit yourself, and do commit yourself to him. Christ leads the blind by a way that they know not, and he will continue to lead them until he brings them to the land where they will open their eyes, and see with rapture and surprise the splendors of paradise, and rejoice that they are all their own forever.

Is not this work of the poor committing themselves to Christ a very easy task? It is a very easy thing for a debtor to commit his debts to his surety, for anyone to commit his case to his advocate, for a patient to trust himself to his physician, for a pilgrim to feel safe under a powerful convoy, and for a blind man to trust in his guide—all this is very simple and easy. It does not need much explanation, and faith in Jesus is just as simple and just as easy as that. Why is it that we sometimes find that faith is difficult? It is because we are too proud to believe in Jesus. If we did but see ourselves as we really are, we should be willing enough to trust the Savior; but we do not like going to Heaven like blind people who need a guide, or like debtors who cannot pay a farthing in the pound. We want to have a finger in the pie, we want to do something towards our own salvation, we want to have some of the praise and glory of it. God save us from this evil spirit!

While it is a very simple thing for the spiritually poor to commit themselves to Christ, let me also say that it is an act which greatly glorifies God. Christ is honored when any soul trusts in him; it is a joy to his heart to be trusted. When the feeble cling to him, he feels such joy as mothers feel when their little ones cling to them. Christ is glad when poor sin-sick souls come and trust him. It was for this very purpose that he came into the world, to meet the needs of guilty sinners. So this plan, while it is easy for us, is glorifying to him.

And I will add that it is a plan that never fails any who trust to it. There never was a single soul that committed its case to Christ, and then found him fail, and there never shall be such a soul so long as the earth endureth. He that believeth in Christ shall not be ashamed or confounded, world without end. "He that believeth on the Son hath everlasting life," and everlasting life can never be taken away from one who has received it.

I close by asking a question—"If the spiritually poor commit themselves unto God, what comes of it?" Why, it makes them very happy. But are they not sinful? Oh, yes; but they commit themselves to God's grace, and his grace blots out all their sins forever. Are they not feeble? Oh, yes; but their feebleness leads them to commit themselves to his omnipotence; and his strength is made perfect in their weakness. Are they not needy? Oh, yes; but then they bring their needs to him, and they receive out of his fullness "grace for grace." But are they not often in danger? Oh, yes, in a thousand dangers; but they come, and hide beneath the shadow of God's wings, and he covers them with his feathers, and there they rest in perfect security. His truth becomes their shield and buckler, so that they need not fear any foe. But are they not apt to slip? Oh, yes; but they commit themselves to him who gives his angels charge over them, to keep them in all their ways, and to bear them up in their hands, lest they should dash their feet against a stone. But are they not very fickle and changeable? Oh, yes; but they commit themselves to him who says, "I am Jehovah; I change not." But are they not unworthy? Oh, yes, in themselves they are utterly unworthy; but they commit themselves to him who is called the Lord their righteousness; and when they are clothed in his righteousness, they are looked upon by God as being "without spot or wrinkle, or any such thing." But have they no sickness? Yes, but they commit themselves to Jehovah-Rophi, the Lord the Healer, and he either heals their sickness, or gives them the grace to endure it. Are they not poor? Yes, many of them are extremely so; but they commit themselves to the faithful Promiser, and so bread is given them, and their water is sure. But don't they expect to die? Oh, yes, unless the Lord should first come; but they are not afraid to die. This is the point, above all others, in which the spiritually poor commit themselves unto God. They have learnt that sweet prayer of David so well that it is often on their tongues, "Into thine hand I commit my spirit: thou hast redeemed me, O Lord God of truth." They did commit their spirit into God's hands years ago, and he has kept them until now, and they know that he will not fail them in their dying hour.

In conclusion, I pray every spiritually poor heart to commit itself to God. I like to do this every morning. Satan often comes and says, "You are no Christian; all your supposed Christian experience is false." Very well, suppose it has been false; then I will start afresh; saint or no saint, I will begin over again by trusting Christ to be my Savior. When you, dear friend, wake tomorrow morning, let this be the first thing that you do—commit yourself to Jesus Christ for the whole of the day. Say,

> My Lord, here is my heart, which I commit to thee. While I am away from home, may my heart be full of fragrance of thy blessed presence; and when I return at night, may I still find my heart in thy kind keeping!

And every night, ere we go to sleep, let us pray—

> *Should swift death this night o'ertake us,*
> *And our couch become our tomb;*
> *May the morn in Heaven awake us,*
> *Clad in light and deathless bloom.*

Are you going to a foreign land? Then, renew the committal of your life to God. Are you going to change your state, and enter upon the joys and responsibilities of married life? Then commit yourself to God. Are you going to a new situation, or opening a new business? Is any change coming over you? Then, make a new committal, or a re-committal of your soul to the Lord Jesus—only take care that you do it heartily and thoroughly, and make no reserve. I rejoice to feel that I have committed myself to Christ, as the slave of old committed himself to his master. When the time came for him to be set free under the Jewish law, he said to his master, "No, I do not want to go. I love you, I love your children, I love your household, I love your service; I do not want to be free." Then you know that the master was to take an awl, and fasten him by the ear to the doorpost. I suppose this was done to see whether the man really wanted to remain with his master, or not. Ah, beloved! some of us have had our ears bored long ago; we have given ourselves up to Christ, and we have a mark upon us which we can never lose. Were we not buried with him by baptism unto death—a symbol that we are dead to the world, and buried to the world, for his dear sake? Well, in that same way, give yourself wholly up to Jesus; commit yourself to him. As that young bride, commits all her life's joys and hopes to that dear bridegroom into whose face she looks so lovingly, so, O souls, commit yourselves to that dearest Bridegroom in earth or heaven—the Lord Jesus Christ. Commit yourselves to him, to love and to be loved—his to obey, his to serve, and his to be kept—his in life—and you need not add "till death us do part," but you may say "till death shall wed us more completely, and we shall sit together at the marriage banquet above; and be forever and forever one before the throne of God." Thus the poor soul commits itself unto Christ, is married unto Christ, gets the portion which Christ possesses, becomes Christ's own, and then lives with Christ forever. Oh, that this might be the time in which many a man and many a woman would commit themselves unto Christ! I do not merely mean you who are poor in pocket, but you who are poor in spirit, I am asking you to commit yourselves unto Christ. Do not put it off, but may this be the very hour in which you shall be committed to Christ, and he shall take possession of you to be his forever and forever! Amen and Amen.

"Oh, How He Loves!"

Published on Thursday, December 15, 1910. Delivered at the Metropolitan Tabernacle, Newington, on Lord's Day evening, July 7, 1872. No. 3228.

Then said the Jews, "Behold how he loved him!"—John 11:36

It was at the grave of Lazarus that Jesus wept, and his grief was so manifest to the onlookers that they said, "Behold how he loved him!" Most of us here, I trust, are not mere onlookers, but we have a share in the special love of Jesus. We see evidences of that love, not in his tears, but in the precious blood that he so freely shed for us; so we ought to see further into his heart than they did, and to know more of him than they could in the brief interval in which they had become acquainted with him. When we think of his love to us, we may well cry, "Behold how he has loved us!"

These Jews expressed their wonder at the love that Jesus had for his friend Lazarus; they did not keep that wonder to themselves, but they said "Behold how he loved him!" In these days, we are too apt to repress our emotions. I cannot say that I greatly admire the way in which some enthusiastic folk shout "Glory!" "Hallelujah!" "Amen," and so on, in the midst of sermons and prayers; yet I would sooner have a measure of that enthusiastic noise than have you constantly stifling your natural emotions, and checking yourself from giving utterance to your heart's truer feelings. If we were in a right state mind and heart, we should often say to one another, "How wondrous has the love of Jesus been to us!" Our conversation with one another as brethren and sisters in Christ, would often be upon this blessed subject. We waste far too much of our time upon trifles; it would be well if the love of Jesus so engrossed our thoughts that it engrossed our conversation too. I fear that many who profess to be Christians, go for a whole year, or even longer, without telling out to others what they are supposed to have experienced of the love of Jesus; yet this ought not to be the case. If we were as we should be, one would frequently say to another, "How great is Christ's love to me, my brother! Dost thou also say that it is great to thee?" Such talk as that between the saints on earth would help us to anticipate the time when we shall want no other theme for conversation in the land beyond the river.

I am going just to remind you of some very simple truths in order to excite the hearts of those of you who are coming to the communion to increased love to the dear Lord and Savior who has loved you so intensely as to die for you. And first, beloved, let us think of *what the love of Christ has done FOR us*; secondly, of *what his love has done TO us*; and then, thirdly, I want to say that I am afraid *our love to Christ will never cause any wonder except on account of the littleness of it.*

I. So, first, let us quietly think over *what the love of Christ has done* for us.

When did Christ's love begin to work for us? It was long before we were born, long before the world was created; far, far back, *in eternity, our Savior gave the first proof of his love to us, espousing our cause.* By his divine foresight, he looked upon human nature as a palace that had been plundered, and broken down, and in its ruins he perceived the owl, the bittern [a wading bird], the dragon, and all manner of unclean things. Who was there to undertake the great work of restoring that ruined palace? No one but the Word, who was with God, and who was God. "He saw that there was no man, and wondered that there was no intercessor: therefore his own arm brought salvation unto him; and his righteousness, it sustained him." Ere the angels began to sing, or the sun, and moon, and stars threw their first beams athwart primeval darkness, Christ espoused the cause of his people, and resolved not only to restore to them all the blessings that he foresaw that they would lose, but also to add to them richer favors than could ever have been theirs except through him. Even from eternity his delights were with the sons of men; and when I think of him, in that far-distant past of which we can form so slight a conception, becoming "the head over all things to the church" which then existed only in the mind of God, my very soul cries out in a rapture of delight, "Behold how he loved us!"

Remember, too, that in that eternal secret council, *the Lord Jesus Christ became the Representative and Surety of his chosen people.* There was to be, in what was then the far remote future, a covenant between God and man; but who was there who was both able and willing to sign that covenant on man's behalf, and to give a guarantee that men's part of that covenant should be fulfilled? Then it was that the Son of God, well knowing all that such a suretyship would involve, undertook to be the Surety for his people, to fulfill the covenant, on their behalf, and to meet all its demands which he foresaw that they would be unable to meet. Then the eternal Father gave into Christ's charge the souls that he had chosen unto eternal life— though ages, of which we can have so faint an idea, were to elapse before those souls were to be created; and the eternal Son covenanted to redeem all those souls after they had fallen through sin, to keep them by his grace, and to present them "faultless" before the presence of his Father with exceeding joy. Thus, as Jacob became accountable to Laban for the whole flock committed to his charge, Jesus Christ, "that great Shepherd of the sheep, through the blood of the "everlasting covenant," undertook to redeem and guard the whole flock entrusted to his care, so that when, at the last great muster, they should pass under the hand of him that telleth them, not one of them should be missing, and the blessed Shepherd-Son should be able to say to his Father, "Those that thou gavest me I have kept, and not one of them is lost." It was in the everlasting covenant that our Lord Jesus Christ became our Representative and Surety, and engaged on our behalf to fulfill all his Father's will; and as we think of this great mystery of mercy, surely all of us who are truly his must exclaim with grateful adoration, "Behold how he loved us!"

I have been speaking of very ancient tidings, but let us now come to matters that we can more clearly comprehend. In the fullness of time, our Lord Jesus Christ left the glories of heaven, and took upon him our nature. We know so little of what the word "Heaven" means that we cannot adequately appreciate the tremendous sacrifice that the Son of God must have made in order to become the Son of Mary. The holy angels could understand far better than we can what their Lord and ours gave up when he renounced the royalties of Heaven, and all the honor and glory which rightly belonged to him as the Son of the Highest, and left his throne and crown above to be born as the Babe of an earthly mother, yet even to them there were mysteries about his incarnation which they could not fathom; and as they followed the footprints of the Son of man on his wondrous way from the manger to the cross and to the tomb, they must often have been in that most suggestive attitude of which Peter wrote, "which things the angels desire to look into." To us, the incarnation of Christ is one of the greatest marvels in the history of the universe, and we say with Paul, "Without controversy, great is the mystery of godliness: God was manifest in the flesh." The omnipotent Creator took the nature of a creature into indissoluble union with his divine nature, and marvel of marvels, that creature was man. "He took not on him the nature of angels, but he took on him the seed of Abraham." For an angel to become an emmet [ant], if that were possible, would be nothing at all in comparison with the condescension of Christ in becoming the Babe of Bethlehem; for, after all, angels and emmets are only creatures formed by Christ, working as one of the persons of the ever-blessed Trinity—for John, writing under the inspiration of the Holy Spirit, expressly saith, "All things were made by him; and without him was not anything made that was made." O glorious bridegroom of our hearts, there never was any other love like thine! That the eternal Son of God should leave his Father's side, and stoop so low as to become one with his chosen people, so that Paul could truly write, "We are members of his body, of his flesh, and of his bones," is such a wonder of condescending grace and mercy that we can only exclaim again and again, "Behold how he loved us!"

Then, "being found in fashion as a man," *he took upon himself human sickness and suffering.* All our infirmities that were not sinful Jesus Christ endured—the weary feet, the aching head, and the palpitating heart, "that it might be fulfilled which was spoken by Esaias the prophet, saying, 'Himself took our infirmities, and bare our sicknesses.'" This was a wondrous proof of love, that the ever-blessed Son of God, who needed not to suffer, should have been willing to be compassed with infirmity just like any other man is. "We have not a high priest who cannot be touched with the feeling of our infirmities; but was in all points tempted like as we are, yet without sin."

But if you want to see the love of Jesus at the highest point it ever reached, you must, by faith, gaze upon him when *he took upon himself the sins of all his people,* as Peter writes, "who his own self bare our sins, in his own body on the tree. "Oh, how could one who was so pure, so absolutely perfect, ever bear so foul a load? Yet he did bear it, and the transfer of his people's sin from them to him was so complete that the inspired prophet wrote, "The Lord hath laid on him the iniquity of us all," and the inspired apostle wrote, "He hath made him to be sin for us, who knew no sin, that we might be made the righteousness of God in him." When a man marries a woman who is deeply in debt, well knowing the burden that he is taking upon himself even though it is enough to crush him all his life, we may well say, "Behold how he loves her!" That was what Christ did for his church when he took her into an eternal marriage union with himself. Although she had incurred such liabilities as could not have been discharged if she had spent all eternity in Hell, he took all her debts upon himself and then paid then unto the utter most farthing; for we must never forget that, when Christ bore his people's sins, he also bore the full punishment of them. In fulfillment of the great eternal covenant, and in prospect of all the glory and blessings that would follow from Christ's atoning sacrifice, "it pleased the Lord to bruise him; he hath put him to grief." We cannot have the slightest conception of what that bruising and that grief must have been. We do not know what our Lord's physical and mental agonies must have been, yet they were only the shell of his sufferings; his soul-agony was the kernel, and it was that which made him cry, "My God, my God, why hast, thou forsaken me?" Then it was that the precious "corn of wheat" fell into the ground and died; and dying, brought forth "much fruit" of which Heaven and eternity alone can tell the full tale. I cannot speak of this wondrous mystery as I fain would do, but, you who know even in part what it means, must join me in saying, "Behold how he loved us!"

Further than that, *Christ has so completely given himself to us that all that he has is ours.* He is the glorious Husband, and his Church is his bride, the Lamb's wife; and there is nothing that he has which is not also hers even now, and which he will not share with her forever. By a marriage bond which cannot be broken, for he hateth putting away, he hath espoused her unto himself in righteousness and truth, and she shall be one with him throughout eternity. He has gone up to his Father's house to take possession of the many mansions there, not for himself, but for his people; and his constant prayer is,

> Father, I will that they also, whom thou hast given me, be with me where I am; that they may behold my glory, which thou hast given me: for thou lovest me before the foundation of the world.

Jesus has an ever-flowing fountain of joy in his heart, but he desires that his joy may be in you if you belong to him, and that your joy may be full; and everything else that he has is yours as much as it is his, so entirely you will again join with me in saying, "Behold how he loved us!"

II. Now, secondly, let us consider *what Christ has done to us,* for each of his acts of love should cause us to exclaim, "Behold how he loved us!"

Think, dear brethren and sisters in, Christ, *how the Lord dealt with us in the days of our unregenracy.* He called us again and again, but we would not go to him; and the more lovingly he called us, the more resolutely we hardened our hearts, and refused to accept his gracious invitation. With some of us, this refusal lasted for years; and we wonder now that the Lord waited for us so long. If a rich man invites a pauper to a feast, and the poor man is indifferent to the invitation, or positively refuses to accept it, he gets no second invitation, for man does not press his charity upon the needy; but when we even scoffed at our Lord's call, and made all manner of excuses for not coming to the gospel banquet, he would not take our "No" for an answer, but called, and called, again and again, until at last we could hold out no longer, and had to yield to the sweet compulsion of his grace. Do you not remember, beloved, how you received pardon, and justification, and adoption, and the indwelling of the Spirit, and how the many "exceeding great and precious promises" were brought to you, like the various courses at a royal festival served upon golden dishes adorned with priceless gems? Oh, that blessed, blessed day in which you first came and sat among the guests at the great King's table! As you look back upon it, your heart glows in grateful remembrance of Christ's mercy to you, and you cannot help saying, "Behold how he loved us!"

Many days have passed since then, and I ask you now to recollect *what Christ has done to us since we first trusted in him.* Has his love for you cooled in the slightest degree? We have all of us tried that love by our wandering and waywardness, but we have not quenched it, and its fire still burns just as vehemently as at the first. We have sometimes fallen so low that our hearts have been like adamant, incapable of emotion; yet Jesus has loved us all the while, and softened our hard hearts as the glorious sun melts the icebergs of the sea. We were like the insensible grass which calls not for the dew, yet the dew of his love gently fell upon us; and though we had not sought it, our heart was refreshed by it. Our Lord has indeed proved how he loved us by the gracious way in which he has borne with our many provocations, and think too, beloved, with what gifts he has enriched us, with what comforts he has sustained us, with what divine energy he has renewed our failing strength, and with what blessed guidance he has led and is still leading us! Take thy pencil and paper, and try to set down in figures or in words thy total indebtedness to his love; where wilt thou begin, and when thou hast begun, where wilt thou finish? If thou wert to record only one out of a million of his love-gifts to thee, would the whole world be able to contain the books that might be written concerning them? No; all thou canst say is, "Behold *how* he has loved us!"

There have been time of which I will not say much just now, for some here would not understand what I mean—when we have seemed to stand in the very suburbs of Heaven, where we could hear the bells pealing forth celestial music from the invisible belfries, and our hearts were ravished with the sound of the heavenly harpers harping with their harps, and the ten thousand times ten thousand white-robed choristers singing the song of Moses and of the Lamb. Nay, note then that the King himself hath brought us into his banqueting house, and his banner over us has been love. He has not only permitted us to sit at his feet, as Mary did, but he has allowed us to pillow our head on his bosom, as John did, and even condescended to let us put our finger into the print of the nails in our rapturous familiar fellowship with him who is not ashamed to call us his brethren. I must not continue in this strain—not for lack of matter, but for lack of time in which to speak concerning him, so must [I] again say, "Behold *how* he loved us!"

I must, however, mention one more proof of Christ's love, and that is this: *he has made us long for Heaven, and given us at least a measure of preparation for it.* We are expecting that one of these days, if the chariot and horses of fire do not stop at our door, our dear Lord and Savior will fulfill to us his promise, "If I go and prepare a place for you, I will come again, and receive you unto myself; that where I am, there ye may be also." To a true believer in Jesus, the thought of departing from this world and going to be "forever with the

Lord," has nothing of gloom associated with it. This earth is the place of our banishment and exile; Heaven is our home. We are like the loving wife who is sundered by thousands of miles of sea and land from her dear husband, and we are longing for the great reunion with our beloved Lord, from whom we shall then never again be separated. I cannot hope to depict the scene when he shall introduce us to the principalities and powers in heavenly places, and bid us sit with him in his throne, even as he sits with his Father in his throne. Surely then the holy angels, who have never sinned, will unite in exclaiming, "Behold, how he loved them!" It is a most blessed thought, to my mind, that we may be up there before the hands of that clock complete another round; and if not so soon as that, it will not be long before all of us who love the Lord will be with him where he is, and then the least among us shall know more of his love than the greatest of us can ever know while here below. Meanwhile, we have much of the joy of Heaven even while we are upon this earth; for, as Paul wrote to the Ephesians,

> God, who is rich in mercy, for his great love wherewith he loved us, even when we were dead in sins, hath quickened us together with Christ, (by grace ye are saved;) and hath raised us up, together, and made us sit together in heavenly places in Christ Jesus.

III. The closing portion of my sermon is to be very practical. Did anybody ever say of any one of us here, *"Behold, how he loves Christ"*?

If someone did say that of *you*, my brother or sister, was it true? I think I hear your answer "Oh, I do love him! He knows all things, and he knows that I love him." But do you love him so fervently that strangers or even your more intimate acquaintances would say of your love to Jesus, what the Jews said of his love to Lazarus, "Behold how he loved him!" "I wish," says one, "I could do so." Then listen for a minute or two while I tell you of *what some saints have done to show how they loved their Lord.*

There have been *those who have suffered for Christ's sake*. They have lain in damp dungeons, and have refused to accept liberty at the price of treachery to their Lord and his truth. They have been stretched upon the rack, yet no torture could make them yield up their fidelity to God. If you have read *Foxe's Book of Martyrs*, you know how hundreds of brave men, and women, and children too, stood at the stake, gloriously calm, and often triumphantly happy, and were burnt to death for Christ's sake, while many of those who looked on learnt to imitate their noble example, and others who heard their dying testimonies, and their expiring songs, (not groans) could not help exclaiming, "Behold how these martyrs love their Master!"

There have been others *who have shown their love to their Lord by untiring and self-sacrificing service.* They have labored for him, at times, under great privations and amid many perils, some as missionaries in foreign lands, and others with equal zeal in this country. Their hearts were all aglow with love for their dear Lord and Savior, and they spent their whole time and strength in seeking to win souls for him, so that those who knew them could not help saying, "Behold how they love their Lord!" Some of us can never hope to wear the ruby crown of martyrdom, yet we may be honored by receiving the richly-jeweled crown from the hand of Christ as he says to each of his true laborers, "Well done, thou good and faithful servant . . . enter thou into the joy of thy Lord."

Then we have known *some saints who showed their love to their Lord by weeping over sinners and praying for their conversion.* There have been gracious men and women, who could not sleep at night because of their anxiety about the eternal welfare of their relatives and friends, or even of lost ones who were personally unknown to them; and they have risen from their beds to agonize in prayer for sinners who were either calmly sleeping, and not even dreaming of their doom, or else at that very hour were adding to their many previous transgressions. There have been others who could not hear a blasphemous word as they passed along the street, without feeling a holy indignation at the injury that was being done to their best Friend, and at the same time their eyes filled with tears of pity for the poor blasphemers and their hearts poured out a stream of supplication for those who were thus ignorantly or wantonly sinning against the Most High. They have been like Jeremiah weeping over the lost, and like Moses and Paul ready to sacrifice their own souls for the sake of others, until men have been compelled to say, "Behold how these weeping and pleading saints love their Lord, and love lost sinners for his sake!"

Others have proven their love to their Lord by the way in which they have given of their substance to his cause. They have not only given a tithe of all they had to the great Melchizedek, but they have counted it a high privilege to lay all that they had upon his altar, counting that their gold was never so golden as when it was all Christ's, and that their lands were never so valuable as them as when they were gladly surrendered to him. Alas, that there should be so few, even in the Church of Christ, who thus imitate their Lord who freely gave himself and all he had that he might save his people! Blessed will the Church be when she gets back to the Pentecostal consecration which was the fitting culmination of the Pentecostal blessing: "All that believed were together, and had all things common; and sold their possessions and goods, and parted them to all men, as every man had need."

Another most admirable way of proving our love to Christ is by being scrupulously careful to please him in little things as well as in the more important matters.

One of the worst signs of this present evil age is that so little is thought of even the *great* things of Christ—his atoning sacrifice, his high priestly character and work, his kingly rule, and so on; while the *little* things of Christ, those that are less by comparison with these, are often utterly despised. There was a time in Scotland, when men of God signed the Solemn League and Covenant[1] with their blood; how many would do that today? One jewel in Christ's crown, that priceless Koh-i-noor of the crown rights of the King of kings, was sufficient to call into the battlefield the noblest of Scotland's sons; but, today, the very crown of Christ itself is kicked about, like a football, by some of his professed servants, for they set up their own fallible judgments against his infallible revelation, and so practically say, "We will not have this Man to reign over us!" In this land, in the most glorious days that England has ever seen, our Puritan forefathers were so scrupulous that men called them strait-laced, sour-faced, bigoted, and I know not what; but, nowadays, many of the truths for which they contended, and for which many of them resisted even unto blood, are said to be unimportant or of no account whatever. The special truth which distinguishes us as a denomination is regarded by many with supreme contempt.

Not long ago, a professedly Christian minister said that he did not care a penny about baptism! If he belongs to Christ he will have to answer to his Master for that saying; but I could not utter such sentence as that without putting my very soul in peril. He who really loves his Lord will not trifle with the least jot or tittle of his Lord's will. Love is one of the most jealous things in the universe. "God is a jealous God" because "God is love." The wife who truly loves her husband will not harbor even a wanton imagination; her fidelity to him must not be stained even by an unchaste thought. So must it be with every true lover of the Lord Jesus Christ. God grant that we, beloved brethren and sisters in Christ, may do our Lord's will so scrupulously, in great things and little things, and in all things alike, that those who see us in our daily life may be compelled to say, "Behold how these Christians love Jesus Christ, their Lord and Savior!"

Yet, beloved, remember that when our love has reached its climax, it can only be like a solitary dewdrop trembling on a leaf compared with the copious showers of love that pour continually from the heart of our dear Lord and Master. Put all our loves together, and they will not fill a tiny cup—and there before us flows the fathomless, limitless, shoreless ocean of the love of Jesus; yet let us have all the love for him that we can. May the Holy Spirit fill our souls to the brim with love to Jesus, for his dear name's sake! Amen.

---

[1] 1643: "The Solemn League and Covenant for Reformation and Defence of Religion, the honour and happiness of the King, and the peace and safety of the three kingdoms of Scotland, England, and Ireland."

Unparalleled Lovingkindnesses

Published on Thursday, March 23, 1911. Delivered at New Park Street Chapel, Southwark, on Tuesday evening, Nov. 17, 1863. No. 3242.

Lord, where are thy former lovingkindnesses,
which thou swarest unto David in thy truth?—Psalm 89:49

T he Lord had made an everlasting covenant with David, ordered in all things and sure, yet that covenant was not intended to preserve him from trouble. When this Psalm was written, he had been brought very low. His crown had been cast down to the ground, his enemies had rejoiced over him, and he had become a reproach to his neighbors. Then his thoughts flew back to the happier days of the pact, and the covenant which the Lord had made with him, and either David himself, or Ethan writing of his behalf enquired, in the words of our text, "Lord, where are thy former lovingkindnesses, which thou swarest unto David in thy truth?"

I. Applying this passage to the people of God, I remark, first, that *we have received have mercies in the past.*

Is that too common a matter for you to think and talk about? If you know it so well, why do you forget it so often? The mercies of God wake us every morning, so that we are as used to them as we are to the sunlight, yet some of us think but little of them. They follow us till the night, and we get as accustomed to them as we do to our beds, yet perhaps some of us think less of them than we do of our beds. We have providential mercies every moment of the day, and every day of our lives; we can never tell the number of them, for they are more than the sands upon the sea-shore. I am going, however, to speak of the spiritual mercies with which God has enriched us—the blessings of the upper springs; and it will help you to recall them if I take the list of them that is given at the beginning of the 103rd Psalm.

Turn to it, and read, first, *"who forgiveth all thine iniquities."* All of us to whom these words belong should constantly remember that we are pardoned souls. We were not so once; oh, what would we not have given then to know what we do know now? At that time, our iniquities possessed upon us as a burden that we could not bear, the stings of conscience gave us no rest, and the terrors of Hell got hold upon us. When I was under conviction of sin, I felt that I would willingly have given my eyes, my hands, my all, if I might but be able to say, "I am a forgiven soul." So, now that we *are* pardoned, let us not forget the Lord's lovingkindness in forgiving all our iniquities. If thou, my hearer, canst forget it, I may well question whether thine iniquities have ever been forgiven, for the pardon of sin is so great a mercy that the song which it evokes from the heart must last forever.

The next mercy in the psalmist's list is, *"who healeth all thy diseases."* Bethink thee again, my brother or my sister, what the Lord hath done for thee in this respect. Once, pride possessed thee like a burning fever, and long prevented thee from submitting to God's simple plan of salvation, but thou hast been cured of that terrible malady, and now thou art sitting humbly at the feet of Jesus rejoicing in being saved by grace. Perhaps thou wast once like the demoniac of old; the chains of morality could not bind thee, and the fetters of human law could not restrain thee; thou didst cut and wound thyself, and thou wast a terror unto others; but, now, thanks be unto God, thou art so completely healed that there is not even a scar left to show where thou wast wounded. Wilt thou not praise the Lord for this unspeakable mercy? What wouldst thou not have given for it once, when thy many diseases held thee in their cruel grip? Then cease not to praise Jehovah-Rophi, "the Lord that healeth thee."

The next mercy also demands a song of grateful praise: *"who redeemeth thy life from destruction."* Thou hast been saved from going down into the pit, the ransom price has been paid for thee, and thou hast been redeemed, not with silver and gold, "but with the precious blood of Christ, as of a lamb without blemish and without spot." Remember that now there is no wrath against thee in the heart of God, for his righteous anger on account of thy sin was all poured out upon the head of his dear Son, thy Surety and Substitute. The Devil has no claim upon thee now, for thou hast been redeemed by Christ unto the last farthing. Then canst thou forget to praise him who has done such great things for thee? What wouldst thou not have given, at one time, to have had half a hope that thou wert a redeemed soul, when thy poor knees were sore through thy long praying, and thy voice was hoarse with crying unto God? Thou wouldst gladly have bartered the light of day, and the comforts of life, and the joys of friendship for the assurance of thy redemption. Well, then, since thou hast now obtained that priceless boon, forget not to praise the Lord for all his lovingkindness towards thee.

For the next clause in the Psalm is this, *"who crowneth thee with lovingkindness and tender mercies."* Think, brother or sister in Christ, what the Lord hath done for thee. Not content with saving thee from Hell, he hath adopted thee into his own family, made thee a son or a daughter of the King of kings, and set a royal crown upon thy head, a crown of "lovingkindness and tender mercies." Thou art made an heir of God, and a joint-heir with Jesus Christ, is not this unparalleled lovingkindness? Is not this indeed the tender mercy of our God towards thee? Then canst thou ever forget such lovingkindness and tender mercy? There have been times in the past history of some of us, when that ancient prophecy has been most graciously fulfilled in our experience, "Ye shall go out with joy, and be led forth with peace: the mountains and the hills shall break forth before you into singing, and all the trees of the field shall clap their hands." So, as we remember the former lovingkindnesses of the Lord, we rejoice that he still crowneth us with lovingkindnesses and tender mercies.

We must not forget the next verse: *"who satisfieth thy mouth with good things; so that thy youth is renewed like the eagle's."* If we are in Christ Jesus, we have all that we want, we are perfectly satisfied. We do not want a better Savior, we do not want a better hope, we do not want a better Bible, we do not want better promises. We *do* want more faith, but we do not want a better ground of faith. We do desire to have more love to our Lord, but we do not desire a better object for our love. We desire ever to dive deeper and deeper, but only in the fathomless sea of Jesus' love. Others are roaming hither and thither, vainly seeking satisfaction, but our mouth is so filled with good things that we are satisfied. We asked, and the Lord gave unto us. We prayed for pardon, and the Lord fully forgave us for Jesus' sake. We have received so much mercy from him that our soul is satisfied, and soars aloft as on eagle's wings, leaving all terrestrial cares, and sorrows, and doubts far below us amid the earth-born clouds above which we have mounted by God's grace.

II. Now, having thus briefly recalled the Lord's former lovingkindnesses, I have to remind you, in the second place, that *we are not always conscious of the same flow of mercy toward us.*

The psalmist asks, "Lord, where are thy former lovingkindnesses?" Well, where are they? Why, they are where they used to be, though we do not always realize them. The Lord's mercies have not changed, but our perception of them is not always as vivid as it ought to be. Let us again consider the mercies of which I have already spoken to you.

"Who forgiveth all thine iniquities." There are times when a Christian fears whether his sins are really forgiven. He is saved, yet he has a doubt whether he is saved or not. All his past sins seem to rise up before him, and the foul suggestion of unbelief is, "Can it be possible that all those sins have been put away? Have all those mountains of iniquity been cast into the Red Sea of the Savior's atoning blood?" Many young believers who judge themselves too much by their feelings, are apt to imagine that they have been deceived, and that they are still under condemnation. If I have any brethren or sisters like that here, let me assure them that there are times when the very best of the saints have to cry out in the bitterness of their soul, "Lord, where are thy former lovingkindnesses?" The believer in Christ is always justified so far as the law of God is concerned, but he does not always hear the proclamation of pardon in the court of conscience. God's sun is always shining, but there are clouds that obscure its beams—yet it is only hidden for a while. So is it with the lovingkindness of the Lord with regard to the forgiveness of sin; whether we always realize it or not, the forgiveness that has once been bestowed upon us will never be withdrawn from us, world without end.

It is the same with the next mercy: *"who healeth all thy diseases."* It may be that there are some of us here who know that the great Physician has healed our soul maladies, yet at times unbelief and other evil diseases cause us sore pain and agony of spirit. It is with us as it was in the days of Noah, when the fountains of the great deep were broken up, and happy are we if we can now float in the ark of our faith above the awful sea of our depravity which threatens to drown every spiritual comfort and cover every hope. If I were to look within my own heart for comfort and hope, I should often be in despair; but when I look away to my Lord alone, then I realize what he has done and is still doing for me, for he still "healeth" all my diseases. Marvel not, dear friends, if you cannot see yourselves growing in grace as you would like to do. When a farmer goes to look at his root-crops, he is not so much concerned as to the appearance of the part that is above, ground, he wants to know how that part is flourishing that is out of sight. So, very often, a Christian is growing under ground, as it were—growing in grace, and knowledge, and love, and humility, though he may not have so many virtues and graces that are visible to other people, or even to himself. Sanctification is being wrought in the saints according to the will of God, but it is a secret work. Yet, in due time, the fruit of it will be manifest, even ass the farmer at the proper season digs up his roots, and rejoices that his labor has not been expended upon them in vain.

Notice too that next mercy: *"who redeemeth thy life from destruction."* Now mark this, those who are once redeemed are always redeemed. The price of their redemption was paid upon Calvary, and that great transaction can never be reversed. I dare to put it very strongly, and to say that they were as fully redeemed when they were dead in trespasses and sins as they will be when they stand in the full blaze of Jehovah's presence before the eternal throne. They were not then conscious of their redemption, but their unconsciousness did not alter the fact of their redemption.

So is it with the believer; there are dark days and cloudy days in his experience, but he is just as truly saved in the dark and cloudy day as when the sun is shining brightly, and the clouds have all been blown away. In the old days of slavery, when a slave's freedom had been purchased, there may have been times when he had not much to eat, or when he had many aches and pains, but such things did not affect the fact that he was a free man. Suppose someone had said to him, "My poor fellow, you have nothing in the cupboard, you are very sick and ill, you are still a slave." He would have replied, "That is not good reasoning. I know that I was redeemed, for I saw the price paid for my ransom. I have my free papers, and I shall never again be a slave." So is it with believers. The Son of God hath made them free by giving himself as a ransom for them, so they shall be "free indeed." Their redemption does not depend upon their realization of it, but upon their Redeemer who has made it effective for them.

The same principle applies to the next mercy: *"who crowneth thee with lovingkindness and tender mercies."* There may be some Christians here who need to learn a lesson that one good Methodist tried to teach another whom he meet at the [church] class meeting. It grieved him as he heard over and over again the story of his brother's trials and troubles, but nothing about the multitudes of mercies with which he was continually being crowned; so one day he said to him, "My brother, I wish you would change your residence; you do not live in the right part of the town." "How is that?" enquired the other.

> Why, you live where I used to live, down in Murmuring Street. It is very dark and narrow, the chimneys always smoke, the lamps never burn brightly there, and all sorts of diseases abound in that unhealthy quarter. I got tired of living in Murmuring Street, so I took a new house in Content Street. It is a fine, wide, open street, where the breezes of Heaven can freely blow, so the people who dwell there are healthy and happy; and though all the houses in the street are of different sizes, it is a very remarkable thing that, they are all of them just the right size for the people, who live in them. The apostle Paul used to live in that street, for he said, "I have learned, in whatsoever state I am, therewith to be content"; so I would advise you, my brother, to move into Content Street as soon as you can.

That was very good advice, and we may pass it on to any murmurers or grumblers whom we know. Think, beloved, how the Lord is still crowning you with lovingkindness and tender mercies. I know you are not strong, but then you have not that acute pain you used to have. I know that you are growing old, but that only means that you are getting so much nearer Heaven. I know your friends are fewer than they used to be, but then those who are left are true friends. So you see that you are still crowned with lovingkindness and tender mercies.

So is it with the last mercy in the list: *"who satisfieth thy mouth with good things."* I will venture to say that the Christian has not one real want that is not satisfied with the good things that God has provided for him. If he has any other want, or thinks he has, it is better for him not to have that want supplied. If we want the pleasures of sin, it is a great mercy that God will not give them to us, for the supply of such a want would be our soul's damnation. If we could gather any comfort through following that which is evil, it is of the Lord's mercy that such comfort is not our portion.

> *This world is ours and worlds to come;*
> *Earth is our lodge, and Heaven our home. . .*

. . . so what can we want beside?

III. Now, thirdly, *why are we not always conscious of the same flow of mercy toward us?*

Sometimes we miss our former comforts as the result of sin. Sin indulged is a certain barrier to happiness. No one can enjoy communion with Christ while turning aside to crooked ways. To the extent to which a believer is inconsistent with his profession, to that extent will he be unhappy; and it will be no cause for surprise if he has to cry, "Lord, where are thy former lovingkindnesses?" We must always distinguish between the punishment of sin which Christ endured on his people's behalf, and the fatherly chastisement with which God visits upon them their wrong-doing. Though he will not condemn them as a Judge, he will chastise them as a Father; and they cannot expect to enjoy the loving-kindness of the Lord while they are enduring the strokes of his rod because of their transgressions.

We may also lose a comfortable sense of God's mercy *through neglecting to use the means of grace.* Leave off the regular reading of your Bible, and then you will be like the man who misses his meals, and so grows weak and languid. Neglect private prayer, and then see whether you will not have to cry, with Job, "Oh that I were as in months past, as in the days when God preserved me, when his candle shined upon my head, and when by his light I walked through darkness." Stop [stay] away from the prayer-meeting, and then, if your soul is not sad, it ought to be. If a man will not come where there is a fire, is it surprising that he cries that he cannot get warm? The neglect of the means of grace causes many to enquire, "Lord, where are thy former lovingkindnesses?"

The same result follows *when any idol is set up in our heart.* While we worship the Lord alone, the temple of our heart will be filled with his glory; but if we set up an idol upon his throne, we shall soon hear the rushing of wings, and the divine voice saying, "Let us go hence." God and mammon cannot abide in the same house. Remember that you serve a jealous God, and be very careful not to provoke him to jealousy. Every idol must be cast down, or his comfortable presence cannot be enjoyed.

Coldness of heart towards God is another cause of the loss of enjoyment of his favor. When the heart grows spiritually cold, the whole being soon gets out of order. If the heart be warm and vigorous, the pulsations throughout the entire frame will be kept strong and healthy; but when the heart is cold, the blood will be chilled in the veins, and all the powers will be benumbed and paralyzed. So, beloved, see to it that, in the power of the Holy Spirit, you maintain the love of your espousals, that pristine warmth of holy affection which you delighted to manifest when first you knew the Lord; or else you will soon have to cry, "Lord, where are thy former lovingkindnesses?" Live near to God, and this shall not often be your cry; but if you backslide from him, this shall soon be your sorrowful enquiry. If you have to mourn an absent God, seek to know the reason why he has withdrawn himself from you, and repent of the sin that has separated you from him.

IV. Now, lastly, *let us remember that the divine covenant remains firm and steadfast under all changing circumstances.*

The covenant made with David was established by the oath of God, and Paul, writing to the Hebrews, says that

> God, willing more abundantly to show unto the heirs of promise the immutability of his counsel, confirmed it by an oath, that by two immutable things, in which it was impossible for God to lie, we might have a strong consolation, who have fled for refuge to lay hold upon the hope set before us.

For our consolation, let us remember, first, that the *parties to the covenant are always the same*. God has not one set of chosen ones today, and another set tomorrow. In the Lamb's book of life, there are not erasures of certain names, and the insertion of others in their place. No, beloved, that is not the way in which the Lord deals with his elect; he does not play fast and loose with them like that. He does not love them one day, and hate them the next. Oh, no!

> *Whom once he loves, he never leaves,*
> *But loves them to the end.*

And, next, *the seal of the covenant is always the same*. It is sealed with the precious blood of Jesus; his one great sacrifice on Calvary made the covenant forever sure.

> *'Tis signed, and sealed, and ratified,*
> *In all things ordered well.*

We do not seal the covenant, Christ himself has done that; it is his blood that makes the covenant sure to all for whom he stood as Surety and Substitute. This is our consolation even when we have no present enjoyment of the blessings that are secured to us by the covenant. Even the sealing of the Spirit is not the seal of the covenant, though it is to us the certain evidence of our interest in the covenant; it is like a seal to our copy of the covenant. The great deed itself, sealed with the blood of Jesus, is safely preserved in the archives of Heaven where none can mutilate or steal or destroy it.

Further, *the efficacy of the covenant is always the same.* It is not like human covenants, which may or may not be fulfilled, or which may become void through lapse of time. This covenant is eternal, covering past, present, and future, and it shall be fulfilled to the last jot and tittle, for he who sware unto David will certainly perform all that he has promised to his own chosen people.

> The voice that rolls the stars along
> Speaks all the promises.

When God said, "Let there be light," there was light; and when that same God says, "Let there be light in that dark soul," the light at once enters the heart, and it is divinely illuminated. Thus it has come to pass that we, who were sometimes darkness, now are light in the Lord; and to us comes the apostolic injunction, "Walk as children of light." The efficacy of the covenant does not depend upon us; if it did, it would be a poor, feeble, fickle thing that would fail us just when we needed it most. There would be no hope of our ever getting to Heaven if we had to depend upon our own efforts, or our own merits, or anything of our own; our comfort arises from the fact that the covenant is made on our behalf by our great Representative and Redeemer, who will himself see that all that is guaranteed to us in the covenant is fulfilled in due season. There rolls the glorious chariot of salvation, in which all believers are riding to Heaven. Death and Hell cannot stop it, all the fears of any who are in it will not affect their eternal safety, and not one of them shall be found to be missing in the day when the roll of the redeemed is called in glory. Be of good courage, believer, for thou art saved in the Lord with an everlasting salvation. Even though thou hast for a while to mourn the loss of the Lord's former lovingkindnesses, search thine heart to see how far that loss has been caused by thine own sin, and then return unto the Lord with all thine heart, and he will renew to thee his former favors, and give to thee new mercies of which thou hast not as yet even dreamed.

As for those here who have no former lovingkindnesses of the Lord to which they can look back, I pray that this may be the beginning of better days to them. May they think of the mercies which the Lord has bestowed upon others, and may they cry unto him, "Lord, do to us as thou hast done, to them; adopt us also into thy family as thy sons and thy daughters, and let us share in all the blessings that thou givest unto thy children!" Remember, dear friends, that it is by simple and sincere faith in the crucified Christ of Calvary that sinners are eternally saved; it is by his blood that we, who once were afar off, are now made nigh. Whosoever believeth in him shall not be ashamed or confounded; therefore, my hearer, believe thou on the Lord Jesus Christ, and thou shalt be saved, and God shall be glorified. So may it be, for Jesus' sake! Amen.

Christ, the Tree of Life

Published on Thursday, May 25, 1911. Delivered at the Metropolitan Tabernacle, Newington. No. 3251.

In the midst of the street of it, and on either side of the river, was there the tree of life, which bare twelve manner of fruits, and yielded her fruit every month: and the leaves of the tree were for the healing of the nations.—Revelation 22:2

You will remember that, in the first paradise, there was a tree of life in the midst of the garden. When Adam had offended, and was driven out, God said, "Lest he put forth his hand, and take of the tree of life, and eat, and live forever, therefore the Lord God drove out the man." It has been supposed by some, that this tree of life in the garden of Eden was intended to be the means of continuing man in immortality, that his feeding upon it would have supported him in the vigor of unfailing youth, preserved him from exposure to decay, and imparted, by a spiritual regeneration, the seal of perpetuity to his constitution. I do not know about that. If it were so, I can understand the reason why God would not have the first man, Adam, become immortal in the lapsed state he was then in, but ordained that the old nature should die, and that the immortality should be given to a new nature, which should be formed under another leadership, and quickened by another Spirit.

The text tells us that, in the center of the new paradise, the perfect paradise of God—from which the saints shall never be driven, seeing it is to be our perpetual heritage—there is also a tree of life. But here we translate the metaphor; we do not understand that tree to be literal. We believe our Lord Jesus Christ to be none other than that tree of life, whose leaves are for the healing of the nations. We can scarcely conceive of any other interpretation, as this seems to us to be so full of meaning, and to afford us such unspeakable satisfaction.

At any rate, beloved, if this be not the absolute purpose of the sublime vision that John saw, it is most certainly true that our Lord Jesus Christ is life from the dead, and life to his own living people. He is all in all to them; and by him, and by him alone, must their spiritual life be maintained. We are right enough, then, in saying that Jesus Christ is a tree of life, and we shall so speak of him in the hope that some may come and pluck of the fruit, and eat and live forever. Our desire shall be so to use the sacred allegory that some poor dying soul may be encouraged to lay hold on eternal life by laying hold on Jesus Christ.

First, *we shall take the tree of life in the winter with no fruit on it;* secondly, *we shall try to show you the tree of life budding and blossoming;* and, thirdly, *we shall endeavor to show you the way to partake of its fruits.*

I. And first, my brethren, I have to speak to you of *Jesus Christ, the tree of life, in the winter.*

You will at once anticipate that I mean by this figure, to describe *Jesus in his sufferings,* in his dark winter days, when he did hang upon the cross, and bleed, and die; when he had no honor from men and no respect from any; when even God the Father hid his face from him for a season, and he was made sin for us, that we might be made the righteousness of God in him. My dear friends, you will never see the tree of life aright unless you first look at the cross. It was there that this tree gathered strength to bring forth its after-fruit. It was there, we say, that Jesus Christ, by his glorious merits and his wondrous work achieved upon the cross, obtained power to become the Redeemer of our souls, and the Captain of our salvation.

Come with me, then, by faith, to the foot of the little mound of Calvary, and let us look up and see this thing that came to pass. Let us turn aside as Moses did when the bush burned, and see this great sight. It is the greatest marvel that ever earth, or Hell, or Heaven beheld, and we may well spend a few minutes in beholding it.

Our Lord Jesus, the ever-living, the immortal, the eternal, became man, and, being found in fashion as a man, he humbled himself, and died the death of the cross. That death was not on his own account. His humanity had no need to die. He might have lived on, and have seen no death if so he had willed. He had committed no offense, no sin—and therefore no punishment could fall upon him.

> For sins not his own
> He died to atone.

Every pang upon the cross was substitutionary; and for you, ye sons of men, the Prince of glory bled, the Just for the unjust, that he might bring you to God. There was no smart for himself, for his Father loved him with a love ineffable; and he deserved no blows from his Father's hand, but his smarts were for the sins of his enemies, for your sins and mine, that by his stripes we might be healed, and that through his wounds, reconciliation might be made with God.

Think, then, of the Savior's death upon the cross. Mark ye well that *it was an accursed death*. There were many ways by which men might die, but there was only one death which God pronounced to be accursed. He did not say, "Cursed is he that dies by stoning, or by the sword, or by a millstone being fastened about his neck, or by being eaten of worms," but it was written, "Cursed is everyone that hangeth on a tree." By no other death than that one, which God did single out as the death of the accursed, could Jesus Christ die. Admire it, believer, that Jesus Christ should be made a curse for us. Admire, and love; let your faith and your gratitude blend together.

It was a death *of the most ignominious kind*. The Roman law subjected only felons to it and I believe not even felons unless they were slaves. A freed Roman must not so die, nor a subject of any of the kingdoms that Rome had conquered, but only the slave who was bought and sold in the market could be put to this death. The Jews counted Jesus worthy to be sold as a slave, and then they put him to a slave's death for you.

Besides, they added to the natural scorn of the death, *their own ridicule*. Some passed by, and wagged their heads. Some stood still, and thrust out their tongues at him. Others sat down, and watched him there, and satisfied their malice and their scorn. He was made the center of all sorts of ridicule and shame. He was the drunkard's song, and even they that were crucified with him reviled him. And all this he suffered for us. Our sin was shameful, and he was made to be a shame for us. We had disgraced ourselves, and dishonored God, and therefore Jesus was joined with the wicked in his death, and made as vile as they.

Besides, *the death was exceedingly painful*. We must not forget the pangs of the Savior's body, for I believe when we begin to depreciate the corporeal sufferings, we very soon begin to drag down the spiritual sufferings too. It must be a fearful death by which to die, when the tender hands and feet are pierced, and when the bones are dislocated by the jar of erecting the cross, and when the fever sets in, and the mouth becomes hot as an oven, and the tongue is swollen in the mouth, and the only moisture given is vinegar mingled with gall. Ah, beloved! the pangs that Jesus knew, none of us can guess. We believe that Hart has well described it when he says that he bore . . .

> All that incarnate God could bear,
> With strength enough, and none to spare.

You cannot tell the price of griefs, and groans, and sighs, and heart-breakings, and soul-tearings, and rendings of the spirit, which Jesus had to pay, that he might redeem us from our iniquities.

It was a lingering death. However painful a death may be, it is always satisfactory to think that it is soon over. When a man is hanged, after our English custom, or the head is taken from the body, the pain may be great for the instant, but it is soon over and gone. But in crucifixion a man lives so long that, when Pilate heard that the Savior was dead, he marveled that he was dead already. I remember hearing a missionary say that he saw a man in Burma crucified, and that he was alive two days after having been nailed to the cross; and I believe there are authenticated stories of persons who have been taken down from the cross after having hung for forty-eight hours, and after all, have had their wounds healed, and have lived for years. It was a lingering death that the Savior had to die.

O my brethren, if you put these items together, they make up a ghastly total, which ought to press upon our hearts, if we are believers, in the form of grateful affection, or if we are unbelievers, provoking us to shame that we do not love him who loved the sons of men so much.

And *the death of the Lord Jesus Christ for us*, we must also add, *was penal*. He died this death of the condemned. Perhaps most men would feel this to be the worst feature. For if a man shall die by never so painful a death—if it be accidental, it misses the sting which must come into it if it be caused by law, and especially if it be brought by sin, and after sentence has been passed in due form. Now, our Lord Jesus Christ was condemned by the civil and ecclesiastical tribunals of the country to die. And what was more, "It pleased the Lord to bruise him, he hath put him to grief." Jesus Christ died without any sin of his own, yet he died a penal death, because our sins were counted as his. He took upon him our iniquities as though they were his own, and then, being found in the sinner's place, he suffered, as if he had been a sinner, the wrath that was due for sin.

Beloved, I wish it were in my power to set forth Christ crucified, Christ visibly crucified amongst you! Oh, that, I could so paint him that the eyes of your heart could see him! I wish that I could make you feel the dolor of his griefs, and sip that bitter cup which he had to drain to the dregs. But if I cannot do this, it shall suffice me to say that *that death is the only hope for sinners*. Those wounds of his are the gate to Heaven. The smarts and sufferings of Immanuel are the only expiatory sacrifice for human guilt. O ye who would be saved, turn your eyes hither! Look unto him: and be ye saved, all the ends of the earth. There is life in a look at him, but there is life nowhere else. Despise him, and you perish. Accept him, and you shall never perish, neither shall all the powers of Hell prevail against you. Come, guilty souls! Jesus wants not your tears or your blood; his tears can cleanse you; his blood can purify you. If your heart be not as broken as you would have it, it is his broken heart, not yours, that shall merit Heaven for you. If you cannot be what you could, he was for you what God would have him to be. God is contented with him, so be you also contented with him; and come and trust him. Oh, now may delays be over, and difficulties all be solved, and just as you are, without one plea, but that the Savior bled, come to your heavenly Father, and you shall be "accepted in the Beloved."

Thus, then, Jesus Christ hanging on the cross is the tree of life in its winter time.

II. And now let me show you, as I may be enabled, *that self-same tree of life when it had blossomed and brought forth fruit.*

The he stands—Jesus, still the same Jesus—and yet how changed! The same Jesus, but clothed with honor instead of shame, able now to save them to the uttermost that come unto God by him. My text says of this tree that it bears "twelve manner of fruits." I suppose that is intended to signify that a perfect and complete assortment of all supplies for human necessities is to be found in Christ—all sorts of mercies for all sorts of sinners; all kinds of blessings to suit all kinds of necessities. We read of the palm tree—that every bit of it is useful, from its root to its fruit. So is it with the Lord Jesus Christ. There is nothing in him that we could afford to do without. There is nothing about Jesus that is extraneous or superfluous. You can put him to use in every part, in every office, in every relationship.

A tree of life is for food. Some trees yield rich fruit. Adam in the garden lived only on the fruit of the garden. *Jesus Christ is the food of his people,* and what dainties they have! What satisfying food, what plenteous food, what sweet food, what food precisely suitable to all the wants of their souls Jesus is! As for manna, it was angels' food; but what shall I say of Christ? He is more than that, for-

> Never did angels taste above,
> Redeeming grace and dying love.

Oh, how richly you are fed! The flesh of God's own Son is the spiritual meat of every heir of Heaven. Hungry souls, come to Jesus if you would be fed.

Jesus gives his people drink also. There are some tropical trees which, as soon as they are tapped, yield liquids as sweet and rich as milk, and many drink and are refreshed by them. Jesus Christ's heart blood is the wine of his people. The atonement which he has perfected by his sufferings is the golden cup out of which they drink, and drink again, till their mourning souls are made glad, and their fainting hearts are strengthened and refreshed. Jesus gives us the water of life, the wines on the lees well refined, the wine and milk, without money and without price. What a tree of life to yield us both meat and drink!

Jesus is a tree of life yielding clothing too. Adam went to the fig tree for his garments, and the fig leaves yielded him such covering as they could. But we come to

Christ and we find, not fig leaves, but a robe of righteousness that is matchless for its beauty, comely in its proportions, one which will never wear out, which exactly suits to cover our nakedness from head to foot, and when we put it on, makes us fair to look upon, even as Christ himself. O ye who would be rearrayed till ye shall be fit to stand amongst the courtiers of the skies, come ye to Jesus, and find garments such as you need upon this tree of life!

This tree also yields medicine. "The leaves of the tree were for the healing of the nations." Lay a plaster upon any wound, and if it be but the plaster of King Jesus, it will heal it. But one promise from his lips, but one leaf from this tree, but one word from his Spirit but one drop of his blood, and this is heaven's court-plaster indeed. It is true that there was no balm in Gilead, there was no physician there; and, therefore, the hurt of the daughter of Israel's people was not healed. But there *is* balm in Jesus, there is a Physician at Calvary, and the hurt of the daughter of God's people shall be healed if she will but fly to Jesus Christ for healing.

And what shall I more say? Is there anything else your spirits can want? O children of God, Christ is all! O ye ungodly ones, who have been roaming through the world to find the tree that should supply your wants, stop here. This "apple tree among the trees of the wood" is the tree which your souls require. Stay here, and you shall have all that you need. For listen—*this tree yields a shelter from the storm.* Other trees are dangerous when the tempest howls; but he that shelters beneath the tree of the Lord Jesus shall find that all the thunder-bolts of God shall fly by him, and do him no injury. He cannot be hurt who clings to Jesus. Heaven and earth should sooner pass away than a soul be lost that hides beneath the boughs of this tree. And oh, you who have hidden there to shelter from the wrath of God, let me remind you that in every other kind of danger it will also yield you shelter; and if you are not in danger, yet still in the hot days of care you shall find the shade of it to be cool and genial. The spouse in Solomon's Song said, "I sat down under his shadow with great delight, and his fruit was sweet to my taste." Get Christ and you have got comfort, joy, peace, and liberty, and when the trouble comes, you shall find shelter and deliverance by coming near to him.

He is the tree of life, then, yielding twelve manner of fruits, those fruits being always ripe and always ready, for they ripen every month, all being free to all who desire them, for the leaves are not for the healing of *some*, but "for the healing of the nations." What a large word! Then there are *enough* of these leaves for the healing of all the nations that shall ever come into the world. Oh, may God grant that none of you may die from spiritual sickness when these leaves can heal you, and may none of you be filling yourselves with the sour grapes of this world, the poisonous grapes of sin, while the sweet fruits of Christ's love are waiting, which would refresh you and satisfy you.

III. And now I have to show you *how to get at the fruit of this tree of life.*

That is the main matter. Little does it boot [accomplish] to tell that there is fruit, unless we can tell how it can be got at. I wish that all here really wanted to know the way, but I am afraid many care very little about it. Dr. Payson had once been out to tea with one of his people who had been particularly hospitable to him, and when he was going, the doctor said, "Well, now, madam, you have treated me exceedingly well, but how do you treat my Master?" That is a question I should like to put to some of you. How do you treat my Master? Why, you treat him as if he were not Christ, as if you did not want him. But you do need him. May you find him soon, for when you come to die, you will want him then, and perhaps then you may not find him.

Well, *the way to get the fruit from this tree is by faith.* That is the hand that plucks the golden apples. Canst thou believe? That is the thing. Canst thou believe that Jesus is the Son of God, that he died upon the cross? "Yes," sayest thou, "I believe that." Canst thou believe that, in consequence of his sufferings, he is able to save? "Ay," sayest thou. Canst thou believe that he will save thee? Wilt thou trust him, to save thee? If so, thou art saved. If thy soul comes to Jesus, and says, "My Lord, I believe in thee, that thou art able to save to the uttermost, and now I throw myself upon thee," that is faith.

When Mr. Andrew Fuller was going to preach before an Association, he rode to the meeting on his horse. There had been a good deal of rain, and the rivers were very much swollen. He got to one river which he had to cross. He looked at it, and he was half afraid of the strong current, as he did not know the depth. A farmer who happened to be standing by, said, "It is all right, Mr. Fuller, you will get through it all right, sir; the horse will keep its feet." Mr. Fuller went in, and the water got up to the girth, and then up to the saddle, and he began to get uncomfortably wet. Mr. Fuller thought he had better turn round, and he was going to do so when the same farmer shouted, "Go on, Mr. Fuller; go on; I know it is all right;" and Mr. Fuller said, "Then I will go on; I will go by faith." Now, sinner, it is very like that with you. You think that your sins are so deep that Christ will never be able to carry you over them; but I say to you,

It is all right, sinner; trust Jesus, and he will carry you through Hell itself, if that is needful. If you had all the sins of all the man that have ever lived, and they were all yours—if you could trust him, Jesus Christ would carry you through the current of all that sin. It is all right, man! Only trust Christ. The river may be deep, but Christ's love is deeper still. It is all right, man! Do not let the devil make you doubt my Lord and Master. He is a liar from the beginning, and the father of lies, but my Master is faithful and true. Rest on him, and all will be well. The waves may roll, the river may seem to be deeper than you thought it to be—and rest assured it is much deeper than you know it to be—but the almighty arm of Jesus—that strong arm that can shake the heavens and the earth, and move the pillars thereof as Samson moved the pillars of Gaza's gates—that strong arm can hold you up, and bear you safely through, if you do but cling to it, and rest on it. O soul, rest in Jesus, and you are saved!

Once again. *If at the first you do not seem to get the fruit from this tree, shake it by prayer.* "Oh!" say you, "I *have* been praying." Yes, but a tree does not always drop its fruit at the first shake you give it. Shake it again, man; give it another shake! And sometimes, when the tree is loaded, and is pretty firm in the earth, you have to shake it to and fro, and at last you plant your feet, and get a hold of it, and shake it with might and main, till you strain every muscle and sinew to get the fruit down. And that is this way to pray. Shake the tree of life until the mercy drops into your lap. Christ loves for men to beg hard of him. You cannot be too importunate. That which might be disagreeable to your fellow-creatures when you beg of them, will be agreeable to Christ. Oh, get ye to your chambers, get ye to your chambers, ye that have not found Christ; get to your bed-sides, to your little closets, and "seek the Lord while he may be found, call ye upon him while he is near." May the Spirit of God constrain you to pray. May he constrain you to continue in prayer. Jesus must hear you. The gate of Heaven is open to the sturdy knocker that will not take a denial. The Lord enable you so to plead that, at the last, you will be able to say, "Thou hast heard my voice and my supplication; thou hast inclined thine ear unto me; therefore will I pray unto thee as long as I live."

May God add his blessing to these rambling thoughts, for Jesus sake! Amen.

Sermons on the Second Coming of Christ

An Awful Premonition

At the Metropolitan Tabernacle, Newington. Published 1864. No. 594.

Verily I say unto you, there be some standing here, which shall not taste of death, till they see the Son of Man coming in his kingdom.—Matthew 16:28

I must confess that I have frequently read this verse with but a vague sense of its profound impressiveness, and I have passed it over rapidly because I did not understand it clearly. Though well acquainted with the usual interpretations, none of them had ever satisfied my mind. It seemed to me as if the text had awakened surprise without suggesting a simple obvious meaning, and therefore, the good commentators had invented explanations, and offered suggestions, widely different one from another, but all equally obscure and improbable. Lately, however, in reading a volume of sermons by Bishop Horseley, I have met with altogether a new view of the passage, which I firmly believe to be the correct one.

Though I do not suppose I shall carry the judgment of all of you with me, yet I shall do my best to bring out of it that terrible denunciation which I believe the Savior has here left on record. With his own cross and passion in view, he was admonishing his disciples to steadfastness, appealing to them at any sacrifice to take up their cross and follow him. [He is] then portraying the inestimable value of the soul, and reflecting on the horror of the soul being lost—a doom, the full force of which, it would be impossible to comprehend until he should come in the glory of his Father, with all his holy angels. [Then] he stopped short, looked upon some of the company, and said in words like these, "There are certain persons standing here who shall never taste of death till they see the Son of Man coming in his kingdom."

Now what did he mean by this? Obviously, it is either a marvelous promise to some who were his disciples indeed, or else it is a portent of woe to others who should die in their sins. How do the popular interpretations of our learned expositors look at it?

Some say it refers to the transfiguration, and it certainly is remarkable that the account of the transfiguration immediately follows this verse, both in Mark and in Luke, as well as in this record of Matthew. But can you for a moment bring your minds to believe that Christ was describing his transfiguration when he spoke of "the Son of Man coming in his kingdom"? [Determine] whether you can see any connection between the transfiguration and the preceding verse, which says, "For the Son of Man shall come in the glory of his Father with his angels; and then he shall reward every man according to his works"? We grant you that Christ was in his glory upon Mount Tabor, but he did not there "reward every man according to his works," nor is it fair to call that a "coming" of the Son of Man at all. He did not "come" on Mount Tabor, for he was on the earth already; and it is a misuse of language to construe that into an advent. Besides, where would be the occasion for such a solemn prefix—"Verily I say unto you"? Does it not raise expectation merely to cause disappointment, if he intended no more than this—"There be some standing here who shall see me transfigured"? That scene [of transformation] took place six days afterwards. The next verse tells you so, "And after six days Jesus taketh Peter, James, and John his brother, and bringeth them up into an high mountain apart." Why, the majesty of the prediction, which carries our thoughts forward to "the last things" in the world's history, makes us shrink from accepting an immediate fulfillment of it all. I cannot imagine, therefore, that the transfiguration is in the slightest degree referred to here; and I do not think that anyone would have thought of such a thing unless he had been perplexed and utterly nonplussed for an explanation.

And again—though it seems almost incredible—Dr. Gill endorses this view, and moreover says, that it also refers to the descent of the Holy Ghost. At this I am staggered. How any man can find an analogy with Pentecost in the connection here I cannot think. Pentecost took place six months after this event, and why Jesus Christ should say, "Verily I say unto you there be some standing here who will live six months," I really cannot comprehend. It seems to me that my Master did not waste people's time by talking such platitudes. Who that reads this passage can think it has any reference to the descent of the Holy Ghost: "For the Son of Man shall come in the glory of his Father with his angels; and then shall he reward every man according to his works?" Did Christ come at Pentecost in the glory of his Father? Was there then any company of angels? Did he then reward every man according to his works? Scarcely can the descent of the Holy Spirit, or the appearance of cloven tongues [Acts 2:3], like as of fire, be called the "coming of the Son of Man in the glory of his Father with his angels, to give every man according to his works," without a gross misuse of our mother tongue, or a strange violation of symbolic imagery.

Both these constructions, however, which I now mention, have now been given up as unsatisfactory by those modern students who have thought most carefully upon the subject. The third [construction] still holds its ground, and is currently received, though I believe it to be quite as far from the truth as the others. Will you carefully read the chapter through at your leisure, and see if you can find anything about the siege of Jerusalem in it? Yet this is the interpretation that finds favor at the present time: some persons were standing there who would be alive when Jerusalem should be destroyed by the Romans!! Nothing surely could be more foreign to the entire scope of our Lord's discourse, or the narrative of the evangelists. There is not the slightest shadow of a reference to the siege of Jerusalem. It is the coming of the Son of Man which is here spoken of, "in the glory of his Father with his angels, to reward men according to their works." Whenever Jesus spoke of the siege of Jerusalem and of its coming, he was wont to say, "Verily I say unto you, this generation shall not pass till all these things be fulfilled;" but he never singled out some few persons and said to them, "Verily I say unto you, there be some standing here, which shall not taste of death, till the city of Jerusalem is besieged and destroyed."

If a child were to read this passage, I know what he would think it meant: he would suppose Jesus Christ was to come, and there were some standing there who should not taste of death until really and literally he did come. This, I believe, is the plain meaning.

"Well," says one, "I am surprised; do you think, then, that this refers to the apostle John?" No; by no means. The fable passed current [it was rumored], you know, that John was to live till Christ came again. But John himself repudiated it. For at the end of his gospel, he says,

> Then went this saying abroad among the brethren, that that disciple should not die: yet Jesus said not unto him, He shall not die; but, if I will that he tarry till I come, what is that to thee?

This, you see, was putting a suppositions case, and in no sense [uses] the language of prediction.

Now, dear brethren, if you are so far convinced of the unreasonableness of each of these efforts to solve the difficulty by feigning a sense, I shall hope to have your minds in readiness for that explanation which appears to me to harmonize with every requirement. I believe the "coming" here spoken of, is the coming of the Son of God to judgment at the last great and terrible assize[1], when he shall judge the righteous, and separate the wicked from among them.

The next question is—"Of whom were the words spoken?" Are we warranted in supposing that our Lord intended this sentence as a gracious promise, or a kindly expectation that he would kindle in the breast of his disciples? I trow [think] not. To me it appears to have no reference whatever to any man who ever had grace in his soul: such language is far more applicable to the ungodly than the wicked. It may well have been aimed directly at those followers who should apostatize [abandon one's beliefs] from the faith, grasp at the world, shrink at the cross, endeavor to save their lives, but really lose them, and barter their souls. At the glorious appearing of Christ, there are some who will taste death, but will they be the righteous? Surely, my dear friends, when Christ comes, the righteous will not die; they will be caught up with the Lord in the air. His coming will be the signal for the resurrection of all his saints. But mark you, at the time of his coming, the men who have been without God, and without Christ, will begin for the first time to "taste of death." They passed the first stage of dissolution when the soul quitted the body, but they have never known the "taste of death." Till then, they will not have known its tremendous bitterness and its awful horror. They will never drink of the wormwood and the gall, so as really to "taste of death," till the Lord shall come. This tasting of death here may be explained, and I believe it is to be explained, by a reference to the second death, which men will not taste of till the Lord comes. And what a dreadful sentence that was, when the Savior said—perhaps singling out Judas as he spoke—

> Verily I say unto you, there be some standing here, who shall never know what that dreadful word "death" means, till the Lord shall come. You think that if you save your lives, you escape from death. Ah! you do not know what death means. The demise of the body is but a prelude to the perdition of the soul. The grave is but the porch of death; you will never understand the meaning of that terrible word till the Lord comes.

This can have no reference to the saints, because in the eighth chapter of John, and the fifty-first verse, you find this passage—"Verily, verily, I say unto you, 'If a man keep my saying, he shall never see death.'"

Then said the Jews unto him, "Now we know that thou hast a devil. Abraham is dead, and the prophets; and thou sayest, 'If a man keep my saying, he shall never taste of death.'" No righteous man, therefore, can ever "taste of death." He will fall into that deep oblivious sleep in which the body sees corruption; but that is another and a very different thing from the bitter cup referred to as "tasting of death." When the Holy Ghost wanted an expression to set forth that which was the

---

[1]   One of the periodic court sessions formerly held in each of the counties of England and Wales for the trial of civil or criminal cases.

equivalent for the divine wrath, what expression was used?—"Christ, by the grace of God, tasted death for every man." The expression "to taste of death," means the reception of that true and essential death, which kills both the body and the soul, in Hell forever. The Savior said then, (as he might say, I fear, if he stood in this pulpit tonight)—"Verily I say unto you, there be some standing here, which shall not taste of death, till they see the Son of Man coming in his kingdom."

If this be the meaning— and I hold that it is in keeping with the context, it explains the verse, sets forth the reason why Christ bespoke breathless attention with the word "verily," answers both the grammar and the rhetoric, and is not by any argument that I have ever heard of to be moved—if this be so, what thrilling denunciations are contained in my text. O, may the Holy Spirit deeply affect our hearts, and cause our souls to thrill with its solemnity!

What thoughts it stirs up! *Compared with the doom which will be inflicted upon the ungodly at the coming of Christ, the death of nature is nothing.* We go farther: *compared with the doom of the wicked at the coming of Christ, even the torments of souls in a separate state are scarcely anything.* The startling question then comes up: *"are there any sitting or standing here who will have to taste of death when the Lord comes?"*

I. The sinner's death is but a faint presage of the sinner's doom at the coming of the Son of Man in his glory.

Let me endeavor to show the contrast. We can make but little comparison between the two *in point of time.* Many men meet with their death so suddenly that it can scarcely involve any pain to them. They are crushed, perhaps, by machinery; a shot sends them to find a grave upon the battlefield; or they may be speedily poisoned. If they be for hours, or days, or weeks, or months, upon the bed of sickness, yet the real work of dying is but short. It is rather a weary sort of living than an actual sense of dying, while hope lingers, though even in fitful dreams. Dying is but the work of a moment: if it shall be said to last for hours, yet the hours are brief. Misery may count them long, but oh! with what swift wings do they fly! To die, to fall asleep, to suffer, it may be but a pin's prick, and then to have passed away from the land of the living to the realm of shades! But oh! the doom which is to be brought upon the wicked when Christ comes! This is a death which never dies. Here is a heart palpitating with eternal misery. Here is an eye never filmed by the kind finger of generous forgetfulness. Here will be a body never to be stiffened in apathy; never to be laid quietly in the grave, rid of keen pangs, wearing disease, and lingering wretchedness. To die, ye say, is nature's kind release: it bringeth ease. It comes to a man, for this world at least, [as] a farewell to his woes and griefs; but there shall be no ease, no rest, no pause in the destination of impenitent souls. "Depart, ye cursed," shall ever ring along the endless aisles of eternity. The thunderbolt of that tremendous word shall follow the sinner in his perpetual flight from the presence of God; from its baleful influence he shall never be able to escape; no, never. A million years shall make not so much difference to the duration of his agony as a cup of water taken from the sea would to the volume of the ocean. Nay, when millions of years told a million times shall have rolled their fiery orbits over his poor tormented head, he shall be no nearer to the end than he was at first. Talk of *Death!* I might even paint him as an angel when once I think of the terrors of the wrath to come. Soon come, soon gone is Death. That sharp scythe gives but one cut, and down falls the flower and withers in the heat of the sun; but eternity, eternity, eternity, who shall measure its wounds, who shall fathom the depths of the gashes? When eternity wields the whip, how dreadfully will it fall! When eternity grasps the sword, how deep shall be the woundings, how terrible its killing!

> *To linger in eternal pain,*
> *Yet death forever fly.*

You are afraid of death, sinner; you are afraid of death; but were you wise, you would be ten thousand times ten thousand times more afraid of the coming and the judgment of the Son of Man.

In point of loss there is no comparison. When the sinner dies, it is not tasting of death in its true sense, for what does he lose? He loses wife, and children, and friends; he loses all his dainty bits and his sweet draughts. Where now his viol and his lute? Where now the merry dance and the joyful company? For him no more the pleasant landscape nor the gliding stream. For him no more the light of the sun by day, nor the light of moon and stars by night. He has lost at one stroke every comfort and every hope. But then the loss, as far as death is concerned, is but a loss of earthly things, the loss of temporal and temporary comforts, and he might put up with that. It is wretched enough to lose these, but let your imagination follow me, faint as is my power to describe the everlasting and infinite loss of the man who is found impenitent at the last great judgment day. What loses he then? The harps of Heaven and the songs thereof; the joys of God's presence and the light thereof; the jasper sea and the gates of pearl. He has lost peace and immortality, and the crown of life; nay, he has lost all hope, and when a man has lost that, what remaineth to him? His spirit sinks with a terrible depression, more frightful than maniac [manic depressive] ever knew in his wildest moods of grief. His soul sinks never to recover itself into the depths of dark despair, where not a ray of hope can ever reach him. Lost to God; lost to Heaven; lost to time; lost to the preaching of the gospel; lost to the invitation of mercy; lost to the prayers of the gracious; lost to the mercy-seat; lost to the blood of sprinkling; lost to all hope of every sort; lost, lost, forever! Compared with this loss, the losses of death are nothing, and well might the Savior say, that lost spirits shall not even "taste of death" until he shall come, and they shall receive their sentence.

Neither does death bear any comparison with the last judgment *in point of terror*. I do not like to paint the terrors of the dying-bed of unawakened men. Some you know, glide gently into their graves. It is, in fact, the mark of the wicked that they have no bands in their death: but their strength is firm; they are not troubled like other men are. Like the sheep they are laid in the grave. A peaceful death is no sign of grace. Some of the worst of men have died with a smile upon their countenance to have it changed for one eternal weeping. But there are more men of other exquisite sensibility, instructed men, who cannot die like brutes, and they have alarms, and fears, and terrors, when they are on their dying beds. Many an atheist has cried to God under dying pangs, and many an infidel who heretofore could brag and speak high things against God, has found his cheek turn pale and his throat grow hoarse when he has come there. Like the mariner, the boldest man in that great storm reels to and fro, and staggers like a drunken man, and is at his wits' ends; for he finds that it is no child's play to die. I try sometimes to picture that hour, when we shall perhaps be propped up in the bed, or lying down with pillows round about us, be diligently watched; and as they hush their footfalls and gaze anxiously on, there is a whisper that the solemn time has come, and then there is a grappling of the strong man with the stronger than he. Oh! what must it be to die without a Savior—to die in the dark without a light except the lurid glare of the wrath to come! Horrors there are, indeed, around the deathbed of the wicked, but these are hardly anything compared with the terrors of the day of judgment. When the sinner wakes from his bed of dust, the first object he will see will be the great white throne and the Judge seated upon it: the first sound that will greet his ears will be the trumpet sounding—

> *Come to judgment, come to judgment,*
> *Come to judgment, sinner, come.*

He will look up, and there will be the Son of Man on his judgment-throne, the king's officers arranged on either side, the saints on his right hand, and angels round about; then the books will be opened. What creeping horror will come upon the flesh of the wicked man! He knows his turn will arrive in a moment; he stands expecting it; fear takes hold upon him, while the eyes of the Judge look him through and through, and he cries to the rocks to hide him, and the mountains to fall upon him. Happy would he be now to find a friendly shelter in the grave, but the grave has burst its doors, and can never be closed upon him again. He would even be glad to rush back to his former state in Hell, but he must not. The judgment has come, the assize is set; again the trumpet rings—

> *Come to judgment, come to judgment,*
> *Come to judgment, come away.*

And then the book is opened, and the dread sentence is pronounced; and, to use the words of Scripture,

> Death and Hell are cast into the lake of fire. This is the second death. And whosoever was not found written in the book of life was cast into the lake of fire.

The man never knew what death was before. The first death was but a flea-bite: this is death indeed. The first death he might have looked back upon as a dream, compared with this tasting of death now that the Lord has come.

From what we can gleam darkly from hints of Scripture, *the pains of death* are not at all comparable to the pains of the judgment at the second advent. Who will speak in a depreciating manner of the pains of death? If we should attempt to do so, we know that our hearts would contradict us, In the shades of night, when deep sleep falleth upon men, you sometimes suddenly awake. You are alarmed. The terror by night has come upon you.

You expect—you hardly know what it is, but you are half afraid that you are about to die. You know how the cold sweat comes upon the brow. You may have a good hope through grace, but the very thought of death brings a peculiar pang. Or, when death has really come in view, some of us have marked with terrible grief the sufferings of our dearest friends. We have heard the eye-strings break; we have seen the face all pallid, and the cheek all hollow and sunken. We have sometimes seen how every nerve has become a road for the hot feet of pain to travel on, and how every vein has been a canal of grief. We have marked the pains, and moans, and groans, and dying strife that fright the soul away. These, however, are common to man. Not so the pangs which are to be inflicted both on body and on soul at the coming of the Son of God; they are such that I cast a veil over them, fearful of the very thought. Let the Master's words suffice—"Fear him who is able to cast both body and soul into Hell; yea, I say unto you, fear him." Then the body in all the parts shall suffer; the members which were once instruments of unrighteousness shall now be instruments of suffering, And the mind, the major sinner, shall be also the greater sufferer. The memory, the judgment, the understanding, the will, the imagination, and every power and passion of the soul become a deep lake of anguish.

But I spare you these things; oh! spare yourselves! God alone knows with what pain I discourse upon these horrors. Were it not that they must be spoken of, or else I must give my account at the day of judgment as a faithless servant; were it not that I speak of them in mercy to your souls, poor sinners, I would fain forget them altogether, seeing that my own soul has a hope in him who saveth from the wrath to come. But as long as you will not have mercy upon yourselves, we must lay this axe at your root; so long as you will make a mock of sin, and set at nought the terrors of the world to come, we must warn you of Hell. If it be hard to *talk* of these things, what must it be to *endure* them? If a dream makes you quiver from head to foot, what must it be to endure really, and in person, the wrath to come? O souls, were I to speak as I ought, my knees would knock together with trembling now; were you to feel as you should, there would not be an unconverted man among you who would not cry, "Sirs, what must I do to be saved?" I do conjure you to remember that death, with all its pangs, is but a drop of a bucket compared with the deep, mysterious, fathomless, shoreless sea of grief you must endure forever at the coming of the Lord Jesus, except you repent.

Death makes great discoveries. The man thought himself wise, but Death draws the curtain, and he sees written up in large letters—"Thou fool!" He said he was prudent, for he hoarded up his gold and silver, and kept the wages of the laborer; but now he finds that he has made a bad bargain, while the question is propounded to him—"What doth it profit thee, to have gained the world, and to have lost thy soul?" Death is a great revealer of secrets. Many men are not believers at all until they die; but Death comes, and makes short work with their skepticism. It gives but one blow upon the head of doubt, and all is done; the man believes then, only he believes too late. Death gives to the sinner the discovery that there is a God, an angry God, and punishment is wrapped up in the wrath to come.

But how much greater the discoveries that await the day of judgment! What will the sinner see then? He will see the Man who was crucified sitting upon the throne. He will hear how Satan has been defeated in all his craftiest undertakings. Read from those mysterious books, the secrets of all hearts shall then be revealed. Then men shall understand how the Lord reigned supremely even when Satan roared most loudly; how the mischief and the folly of man did, but after all, bring forth the great purposes of God. All this shall be in the books, and the sinner shall stand there defeated, terribly defeated, worsted at every point, baffled, foiled, stultified in every act and every purpose by which he thought to do well for himself; yea, and utterly confounded in all the hostility and all the negligence of his heart towards the living and true God who would and who did rule over him. Too late, he will discover the preciousness of the blood he despised, the value of the Savior he rejected, the glory of the Heaven which he lost, the terror of the Hell to which he is sentenced. How wise, how dreadfully wise will he be when fully aware of his terrible and eternal destruction! Thus sinners shall not taste of death in the real meaning of the term, until the Lord shall come.

II. Still further: in the state of separate spirits, they have not fully tasted of death, nor will they do so until Christ comes.

The moment that a man dies his spirit goes before God. If without Christ, that spirit then begins to feel the anger and the wrath of God. It is as when a man is taken before a magistrate. He is known to be guilty, and therefore he is remanded and put in prison till his trial shall come. Such is the state of souls apart from the body: they are spirits in prison, waiting for the time of their trial. There is not, in the sense in which the Romanist teaches it, any purgatory; yet there is a place of waiting for lost spirits which is in Scripture called "Hell," because it is one room in that awful prison-house in which must dwell forever spirits that die finally impenitent and without faith in Christ. But those of our departed countrymen and fellow citizens of earth who die without Christ, have not yet fully tasted of death, nor can they until the advent of the Lord.

Just consider why not. *Their bodies do not suffer.* The bodies of the wicked are still the prey of the worm; still the atoms are the sport of the winds, and are traversing their boundless cycles, and must do so until they are gathered up into the body again, at the trump of the archangel—at the voice of God.

The ungodly know that their present state is to have an end at the judgment, but after the judgment their state will have no end; it is then to go on, and on, and on, forever and forever, unchanged and unchangeable. Now there may be half a hope, an anticipation of some change, for change brings some relief; but to the finally damned, upon whom the sentence has been pronounced, there is no hope even of a change. Forever and forever shall there be the same ceaseless wheel of misery.

The ungodly, too, in their present state, have not as yet been put to the shame of a public sentence. They have, as it were, merely been cast into prison, the facts being too clear to admit of any doubt as to the sentence, and they are their own tormentors, vexing and paining themselves with the fear of what is yet to come. They have never yet heard that dreadful sentence—"Depart, ye cursed, into everlasting fire, prepared for the devil and his angels."

I was struck, whilst studying this subject, to find how little is said about the pains of the lost while they are merely souls, and how much is said concerning this when the Lord comes. You have that one parable of the rich man and Lazarus, and there it speaks of the soul being already tormented in the flame; but if you turn to the thirteenth chapter of Matthew, and read the parable of the tares, you will find it is at the end of the world that the tares are to be cast into the fire. Then comes the parable of the drag-net. It is when the dispensation comes to an end that the net is to be dragged to shore, and then the good are to be put in vessels, and the bad cast away; and then the Lord says,

> The Son of Man shall send forth his angels, and they shall gather out of his kingdom all things that offend, and them which do iniquity; and shall cast them into a furnace of fire: there shall be wailing and gnashing of teeth.

That memorable description in Matthew of those of whom he said, "I was an hungered, and ye gave me no meat; I was thirsty, and ye gave me no drink," is described as happening when the "Son of Man shall come in his glory, and all his holy angels with him." The apostle Paul, too, tells us plainly in the Epistle to the Thessalonians, that the wicked are to be destroyed at his coming by the brightness of his power. The recompense of the ungodly, like the reward of the righteous, is anticipated now: but the full reward of the righteous is to be at his coming; they are to reign with Christ; their fullness of bliss is to be given them when the King himself in his glory shall sit upon his throne. So, too, the wicked have the beginning of their heritage at death, but the dreadfulness of it is to be hereafter.

At the present moment, death and Hell are not yet cast into the lake of fire. Death is still abroad in the world slaying men; Hell is yet loose; the devil is not yet chained, but still does he go about the "dry places, seeking rest, and finding none." At the last day, at the coming of Christ, "death and Hell shall be cast into the lake of fire." We do not understand the symbol; but if it means anything, one would think it must mean this, that at that day the scattered powers of evil, which are to be the tormentors of the wicked, but which have hitherto been wandering up and down throughout the world, shall all be collected together, and then, indeed, shall it be that the wicked shall begin to "taste of death" as they have never tasted of it before!

My soul is bowed down with terror while I speak these words to you. I scarcely know how to find suitable words to express the weight of thought which is upon me. My dear hearers, instead of speculating upon these matters, let us try to shun the wrath to come; and what can help us to do that better than to weigh the warning words of a dear and loving Savior, when he tells us that at his coming such a doom shall pass upon impenitent souls, that compared with it, even death itself shall be as nothing? Christians, by the faith of their risen Lord, swallow death in victory; but if you die impenitent, you swallow death in ignorance. You do not feel its bitterness now. But, oh! that bitter pill has yet to work its way, and that fierce draught has yet to be drained even to the dregs, unless you repent.

And now, does not the meditation of these terrors prompt *a question?* Jesus said—

> Verily I say unto you, "There be some standing here, which shall not taste of death, till they see the Son of Man coming in his kingdom."

Are there any standing or sitting here who shall not taste of death till then? In that little group addressed by the Savior, stood Judas. He had been trusted by his Master and he was an apostle, but after all, he was a thief and a hypocrite. He, the son of perdition, would not taste of death till Christ should come in his kingdom. Is there a Judas here? I look into your faces, and many of you are members of this church, and others of you I doubt not are members of other Christian churches, but are you sure that you have made sound work of it? Is your religion genuine? Do you wear a mask, or are you an honest man? O sirs, try your own hearts, and since you may fail in the trial, ask the Lord to search you; for as the Lord my God liveth, unless ye thus search yourselves and find that you are in the right, you may come presumptuously to sit at the Lord's table. Though, with a name to live, you may be among his people here, you will have to taste of death when the Lord comes. You may deceive *us*, but you cannot deceive *him*. The preacher reflects that he himself may be mistaken, that he himself may be self-deceived. If it be so, may the Lord open his eyes to know the worst of his own state. Will you put up this prayer for yourselves, professors? Do not be too bold, you who say you are Christ's; never be satisfied till you are quite sure of it; and the best way to be sure is to go again, just as you went at first, and lay hold on eternal life through the power of the blessed Spirit, and not by any strength of your own.

No doubt, however, there stood in that little throng around the Savior some who were careless sinners. He knew that they had been so during the whole of his teaching, and that they would be so still, and therefore they would taste of death at his coming. Are there not some careless persons come in here tonight? I mean you who never think about religion, who generally look upon the Sunday as a day of pleasure, or who loll about in your shirt-sleeves nearly all the day; you who look upon the very name of religion as a bugbear to frighten children with; who mock at God's servants, and contemn [hold in contempt] the very thought of earnestly seeking after the Most High. Oh! will you, will you be among the number of those who taste of death when the Son of Man shall come in his kingdom? Oh! must I ring your death-knell to night? Must my warning voice be lost upon you? I beseech you to recollect that you must either *turn* or *burn*. I beseech you to remember this—

> Let the wicked forsake his way and the unrighteous man his thoughts; and let him turn unto the Lord, and he will have mercy upon him; and to our God, for he will abundantly pardon.

By the wounds of Jesus, sinner, stop and think. If God's dear Son was slain for human sin, how terrible must that sin be! And if Jesus died, how base are you, if you are disobedient to the doctrine of faith! I pray you if you think of your body, give [also] some thought to your soul. "Wherefore do ye spend money for that which is not bread? And your labor for that which satisfieth not?" Hearken diligently unto Jehovah's Word, and eat of that which is good, real, and substantial food. Come to Jesus, and your soul shall live.

And there are some here of another class, Bethsaida sinners, Capernaum sinners. I mean some of you who constantly occupy these pews, and stand in yonder area, and sit in yonder gallery Sunday after Sunday. The same eyes look down on me week after week; the same faces salute me often with a smile when the Sabbath comes, and I pass you journeying to this the Tabernacle of your worship, and yet how many of you are still without God and without Christ! Have I been unfaithful to you? If I have, forgive me, and pray to God both for me and for yourselves that we may mend our ways. But if I have warned you of the wrath to come, why will you choose to walk in the path which leads to it? If I have preached to you Christ Jesus, how is it that his charms move you not, and that the story of his great love doth not bring you to repentance? O that the Spirit of God would come and deal with you, for I cannot. My hammer breaks not your flinty hearts, but God's arm can do it, and O may he turn you yet. Of all sinners over whom a minister ought to weep, you are the worst; for while the careless perish, you perish doubly. You know your Master's will, and yet you do it not. You see heaven's gate set open, and yet you will not enter. Your vicious free-will ruins you; your base and wicked love of self and sin destroys you. "Ye will not come unto me that ye might have life," said Christ. You are so vile that you will not turn even though Jesus should woo you. I do pray you, let the menace of judgment to come, contained in my text, stir you now if you have never been stirred before. May God have pity on you even if you will have no pity upon yourselves.

Peradventure among that company there were some who held the truth, but who held it in licentiousness—and there may be such here present. You believe in the doctrine of election, so do I; but then you make it a cloak for your sin. You hold the doctrine of the perseverance of the saints, but you still persevere in your iniquity. Oh! there is no way of perishing that I know of worse than perishing by making the doctrines of grace an excuse for one's sins. The apostle has well said of such that their damnation is just: it is just to any man, but to a seven-fold degree is it just to such as you are. I would not have you forget the doctrine, nor neglect it, nor despise it, but I do beseech you do not prostitute it, do not turn it to the vile purposes of making it pander to your own carnal ease. Remember, you have no evidence of election except you are holy, and that you have no right to expect you will be saved at the last unless you are saved now. A present faith in a present Savior is the test. O that my Master would bring some of you to trust him tonight. The plan of salvation is simple. Trust Christ, and you are saved; rely upon him and you shall live. This faith is the gift of God, but remember that though God gives it, he works in you to will and to do of his own good pleasure. God does not believe for you; the Holy Spirit does not believe for you; you must believe, or else you will be lost: and it is quite consistent with the fact that it is *the gift of God,* to say that it is also *the act of man.* You must, poor soul, be led to trust the Savior, or into Heaven you can never enter. Is there one here who saith, "I would find the Savior tonight?" Go not to thy bed until thou hast sought him, and seek thou him with sighs and with tears.

Methinks this is a night of grace. I have preached the law and the terrors of the Lord to you, but it will be a night of grace to the souls of some of you. My Master doth but kill you that he may make you alive; he does but wound you that he may make you whole. I feel a sort of inward whisper in my heart that there are some of you who even now have begun your flight from the wrath to come. Whither do ye flee? Fly to Jesus. Haste, sinner, haste. I trust you will find him before you retire to your beds, or if you lie tossing there in doubt and fear, then may he manifest himself unto you before the morning light. Methinks I would freely give my eyes if you might but see Christ, and that I would willingly give my hands if you might but lay hold on him. Do, I conjure you, put not from you this warning, but let it have its proper work upon you and lead you to repentance. May God save you, and may the prayer we have already offered this evening be answered, that the company of you may be found among his elect at his right-hand. To that end let us pray.

Our Father, save us with thy great salvation. We will say unto God, do not condemn us; deliver us from going down to the pit, for thou hast found the ransom; may we not be among the company that shall taste of death when the Son of Man shall come. Hear us, Jesus, through thy blood. God be merciful to us sinners. Amen.

The Reward of the Righteous

Delivered on Sunday morning, January 21, 1866, at the Metropolitan Tabernacle, Newington. No. 671.

When the Son of man shall come in his glory, and all the holy angels with him, then shall he sit upon the throne of his glory: and before him shall be gathered all nations: and he shall separate them one from another, as a shepherd divideth his sheep from the goats: and he shall set the sheep on his right hand, but the goats on the left. Then shall the King say unto them on his right hand, "Come, ye blessed of my Father, inherit the kingdom prepared for you from the foundation of the world: for I was an hungred, and ye gave me meat: I was thirsty, and ye gave me drink: I was a stranger, and ye took me in: naked, and ye clothed me: I was sick, and ye visited me: I was in prison, and ye came unto me."—Matthew 25:31–36

It is exceedingly beneficial to our souls to mount above this present evil world to something nobler and better. The cares of this world and the deceitfulness of riches are apt to choke everything good within us, and we grow fretful, desponding, perhaps proud, carnal. It is well for us to cut down these thorns and briars, for heavenly seed sown among them is not likely to yield a harvest, and I do not know a better sickle with which to cut them down than thoughts of the kingdom to come. In the valleys in Switzerland many of the inhabitants are deformed and dwarfish, and the whole of them wear a sickly appearance, for the atmosphere is charged with miasma, and is close and stagnant; you traverse them as rapidly as you can, and are glad to escape from them. Up yonder on the mountain you will find a hardy race, who breathe the clear fresh air as it blows from the virgin snows of the Alpine summits. It would be well for their frames if the dwellers in the valley could frequently leave their abodes among the marshes and the fever mists, and get themselves up into the clear atmosphere above. It is to such an exploit of climbing that I invite you this morning. May the Spirit of God bear us as upon eagles' wings, that we may leave the mists of fear and the fevers of anxiety, and all the ills which gather in this valley of earth, and get ourselves up to the mountains of future joy and blessedness where it is to be our delight to dwell, world without end! Oh may God disentangle us now for a little while, cut the cords that keep us here below, and permit us to mount! We sit, some of us, like chained eagles fastened to the rock, only that, unlike the eagle, we begin to love our chain, and would, perhaps, if it came really to the test, be loath to have it snapped. May God now grant us grace if we cannot at once escape from the chain of mortal life as to our bodies, yet to do so as to our spirits; and leaving the body like a servant at the foot of the hill, may our soul, like Abraham, go to the top of the mountain, and there may we have communion with the Most High.

While expounding my text, I shall ask your attention this morning, first, *to the circumstances which surround the rewarding of the righteous;* secondly, *to their portion;* and thirdly, *to the persons themselves.*

I. There is *much of teaching in the surrounding circumstances.*

We read, "When *the King shall come in his glory.*" It appears, then, that we must not expect to receive our reward till by-and-by. Like the hireling we must fulfill our day, and then at evening we shall have our penny. Too many Christians look for a present reward for their labors, and if they meet with success, they begin doting upon it as though they had received their recompense. Like the disciples who returned saying, "Lord, even the devils are subject unto us," they rejoice too exclusively in present prosperity; whereas the Master bade them not to look upon miraculous success as being their reward, since that might not always be the case. "Nevertheless," said he, "rejoice not in this, but rather rejoice because your names are written in Heaven." Success in the ministry is not the Christian minister's true reward: it is an earnest, but the wages still wait. The approbation of your fellowmen you must not look upon as being the reward of excellence, for often you will meet with the reverse; you will find your best actions misconstrued, and your motives ill interpreted. If you are looking for your reward here, I may warn you of the apostle's words, "If in this life only we have hope, we are of all men most miserable:" because other men get their reward; even the Pharisee gets his: "Verily, I say unto you, they have their reward;" but we have none here. To be despised and rejected of men is the Christian's lot. [Even] among his fellow Christians he will not always stand in good repute. It is not unmitigated kindness nor unmingled love that we receive even from the saints. I tell you, if you look for your reward to Christ's bride herself you will miss it; if you expect to receive your crown from the hand even of your brethren in the ministry who know your labors, and who ought to sympathize with your trials, you will be mistaken. "When the King shall come in his glory," then is your time of recompense; but not today, nor tomorrow, nor at any time in this world. Reckon nothing which you acquire, no honor which you gain, to be the reward of your service to your Master; that is reserved to the time "when the King shall come in his glory."

Observe with delight the august person by whose hand the reward is given. It is written, "When *the King* shall come." Brethren, we love the King's courtiers; we delight to be numbered with them ourselves. It is no mean thing to do service to him whose head—"Though once 'twas crowned with thorns, is crowned with glory now." But it is a delightful thought that the service of rewarding us will not be left to the courtiers. The angels will be there, and the brethren of the King will be there; but Heaven was not prepared by them, nor can it be given by them. Their hands shall not yield us a coronation; we shall join their songs, but their songs would be no reward for us; we shall bow with them and they with us, but it will not be possible for them to give us the recompense of the reward—that starry crown is all too weighty for an angel's hand to bring, and the benediction all too sweet to be pronounced, even by seraphic lips. The King himself must say, "Well done, good and faithful servant." What say you to this, my dear brother? You have felt a temptation to look to God's servants, to the approbation of the minister, to the kindly look of parents, to the word of commendation from your fellow-worker; all these you value, and I do not blame you; but these may fail you, and therefore never consider them as being the reward. You must wait till the time when the King cometh, and then it will neither be your brethren, your pastors, your parents, nor your helpers, but the King himself who shall say to you, "Come, ye blessed." How this sweetens Heaven! It will be Christ's own gift. How this makes the benediction doubly blessed! It shall come from his lips, which drop like myrrh and flow with honey. Beloved, it is Christ, who became a curse for us, who shall give the blessing to us. Roll ye this as a sweet morsel under your tongues.

The character in which our Lord Jesus shall appear is significant. Jesus will then be revealed as truly *"the King."* "When the *King* shall come." It was to him as King that the service was rendered, and it is from him as King that the reward must therefore come; and so upon the very threshold, a question of self-examination arises:

> The King will not reward the servants of another prince—am I therefore his servant? Is it my joy to wait at the threshold of his gates, and sit like Mordecai at the courts of Ahasnerus—at the entrance of his door? Say, soul, dost thou serve the King?

I mean not the kings and queens of earth; let them have loyal servants for their subjects; but saints are servants of the Lord Jesus Christ, the King of kings—are ye so? If ye be not so, when the King cometh in his glory, there can be no reward for you. I long in my own heart to recognize Christ's kingly office more than ever I have done. It has been my delight to preach to you Christ dying on the cross, and "God forbid that I should glory, save in the cross;" but I want for my own self to realize him on his throne, reigning in my heart, having a right to do as he wills with me, that I may get to the condition of Abraham, who, when God spoke, though it was to tell him to offer up his own Isaac, never asked a question, but simply said, "Here am I." Beloved, seek to know and feel the controlling power of the King, for else when he comes, since you have not known him as King, he cannot know you as servant; and it is only to the servant that the King can give the reward which is spoken of in the text—"When the King shall come."

Now pass on. "When the King shall come in his *glory*." The fullness of that, it is impossible to conceive.

> *Imagination's utmost stretch,*
> *In wonder dies away.*

But this we know—and it is the sweetest thing we can know—that if we have been partakers with Jesus in his shame, we also shall be sharers with him in the luster which shall surround him. Art thou, beloved, one with Christ Jesus? Art thou of his flesh and of his bones? Does a vital union knit thee to him? Then thou art today with him in his shame; thou hast taken up his cross, and gone with him without the camp, bearing his reproach; thou shalt doubtless be with him when the cross is exchanged for the crown. But judge thyself this morning; if thou art not with him in the regeneration, neither shalt thou be with him when he shall come in his glory. If you start back [recoil] from the black side of communion, you shall not understand its bright, its happy period, when the King shall come in his glory and all his holy angels with him. What, are angels with him? And yet he took not up angels, he took up the seed of Abraham. Are the holy angels with him? Come, my soul, then thou canst not be far from him. If his friends and his neighbors are called together to see his glory, what thinkest thou if thou art married to him? Shall thou be distant? Though it be a day of judgment, yet thou canst not be far from that heart, which having admitted angels into intimacy, has admitted thee into union. Has he not said to thee, O my soul, "I have betrothed thee unto me in faithfulness, and in judgment, and in righteousness"? Have not his own lips said it, "I am married unto thee, and my delight is in thee"? Then if the angels, who are but the friends and the neighbors, shall be with him, it is abundantly certain that his own beloved Hephzibah, in whom is all his delight, shall be near to him and shall be a partaker of his splendor. It is when he comes in his glory, and when his communion with angels shall be distinctly recognized—it is then that his unity with his Church shall become apparent. *"Then shall he sit upon the throne of his glory."* Here is a repetition of the same reason why it should be your time and my time to receive the reward from Christ if we be found among his faithful servants. When *he* sits upon his throne, it were not fit that his own beloved ones should be in the mire. When he was in the place of shame, they were with him, and now he is on the throne of gold, they must be with him too. There were no oneness—union with Christ were a mere matter of talk—if it were not certain that when he is on the throne, they shall be upon the throne too.

But I want you to notice one particular circumstance with regard to the time of the reward. It is *when he shall have divided the sheep from the goats.* My reward, if I be a child of God, cannot come to me while I am in union with the wicked. Even on earth you will have the most enjoyment of Christ when you are most separated from this world: rest assured, although the separated path does not seem an easy one, and it will certainly entail upon you persecution and the loss of many friends, yet it is the happiest walking in the world. You conforming Christians, who can enter into the world's mirth to a certain degree, you cannot, you never can know as you now are, the inward joys of those who live in lonely but lovely fellowship with Jesus. The nearer you get to the world, the further you must be from Christ, and I believe the more thoroughly a bill of divorce is given by your spirit to every earthly object upon which your soul can set itself, the more close will be your communion with your Lord. "Forget also thine own country and thy Father's house; so shall the King greatly desire thy beauty, for he is thy Lord, and worship thou him." It is significant that not until the King has separated the sheep from the goats does he say, "Come, ye blessed"; and though the righteous will have enjoyed a felicity as disembodied spirits, yet as risen from the grave in their bodies, their felicity is not fully accomplished till the great Shepherd shall have appeared to separate them once for all, by a great gulf which cannot be passed, from all association with the nations that forget God. Now then, beloved, these circumstances all but together come to this, that the reward of following Christ is not today, is not among the sons of men, is not from men, is not even from the excellent of the earth, is not even bestowed by Jesus while we are here, but the glorious crown of life which the Lord's grace shall give to his people is reserved for the second advent, "when the King shall come in his glory, and all his holy angels with him." Wait with patience, wait with joyful expectation, for he shall come, and blessed be the day of his appearing.

II. We have now to turn to the second point—*the portion itself.*

Every word is suggestive. I shall not attempt to exhaust, but merely to glance at all. The reward of the righteous is set forth by the loving benediction pronounced to them by the Master, but *their very position* gives some foreshadowing of it. He put the sheep on his right hand. Heaven is a position of the most elevated dignity, authoritatively conferred, and of Divine complacency, manifestly enjoyed. God's saints are always at his right hand according to the judgment of faith, but hereafter it shall be more clearly manifested. God is pleased to be close to his people, and to place them near to himself in a place of protection. Sometimes it seems as if they were at the left hand; they certainly have, some of them, less comfort than the worldlings. "I have seen the wicked in great power, and spreading himself like a green bay tree; their eyes stand out with fatness, they have more than heart could wish"; whereas his people are often made to drink waters of a full cup, and their meat and their drink are bittered with wormwood and gall. The world is upside down now; the gospel has begun to turn it the right way uppermost, but when the day of grace is over, and the day of glory comes, then shall it be righted indeed; then those that wandered about in sheep-skins and goat-skins shall be clothed in glittering apparel, being transfigured like the Savior upon [Mt.] Tabor; then those of whom the world was not worthy shall come to a world that shall be worthy of them; then those who were hurried to the stake and to the flames shall triumph with chariots of fire and horses of fire, and swell the splendor of the Master's pompous appearing. Yes, beloved, you shall eternally be the object of Divine complacency, not in secret and unmanifested communion, but your state and glory shall be revealed before the sons of men. Your persecutors shall gnash their teeth when they see you occupying places of honor at his right hand, and themselves, though greater far than you on earth, condemned to take the lowest room. How shall Dives[1] bite his fire-tormented tongue in vain as he sees Lazarus, the beggar on the dunghill, made to sit at the right hand of the King eternal and immortal! Heaven is a place of dignity. "There we shall be as the angels," saith one, but I wot [(archic) I know] we shall be even superior than they. Is it not written of him who in all things is our representative, "Thou hast put all things under his feet"! Even the very seraphs, themselves so richly blessed, what are they but "ministering spirits sent forth to minister to the heirs of salvation?"

But now turning to the welcome uttered by the judge, the first word is "Come." It is the gospel symbol. The law said "Go"; the gospel saith "Come." The Spirit saith it in invitation; the Bride saith it in intercession; "let him that heareth" say it by constantly, laboriously endeavoring to spread abroad the good news. Since Jesus saith "Come," we learn that the very essence of Heaven is communion. "Come!" Ye came near enough to say "Lord, we believe, help thou our unbelief!" [Jesus says:]

> On the cross ye looked to me and were lightened. Ye had fellowship with me in bearing my cross. Ye filled up that which was behind of the sufferings of Christ for his body's sake, which is the Church. Still come! Ever, come! Forever come! Come up from your graves, ye risen ones! Come up from among the ungodly, ye consecrated ones! Come up from where ye cast yourselves down in your humiliation before the great white throne! Come up to wear my crown, and sit with me upon my throne!

Oh, that word has Heaven lurking within it. It shall be to you your joy forever to hear the Savior say to you, "Come." I protest before you, my soul has sometimes been so full of joy that I could hold no more, when my beloved Lord has said

---

[1] *Dives:*—Latin for "rich." Refers to the parable of Lazarus and the rich man, Luke 16:19–30.

"Come" to my soul; for he has taken me into his banqueting house, and his love-banner has waved over my head, and he has taken me away from the world, and its cares and its fears, and its trials and its joys, up to "the top of Amana, from the top of Shenir and Hermon," where he manifested himself to me. When this "Come" shall come into your ear from the Master's lips, there shall not be the flesh to drag you back, there shall be no sluggishness of spirit, no heaviness of heart; you shall come eternally then; you shall not mount to descend again, but mount on and on in one blessed Excelsior forever and forever. The first word indicates that Heaven is a state of communion—"Come."

Then it is *"Come, ye blessed,"* which is a clear declaration that this is a state of happiness. They cannot be more blessed than they are. They have their hearts' desire, and though their hearts have been enlarged and their desires have been expanded by entering into the Infinite, and getting rid of the cramping influences of corruption and of time, yet even when their desire shall know no bounds, they shall have all the happiness that the utmost stretch of their souls can by any possibility conceive. This much, and this is all we know—they are supremely blessed. Their blessedness, you perceive, does not come from any secondary joy, but from the great primary Source of all good. "Come, ye blessed of my Father." They drink the unadulterated wine at the wine-press itself, where it joyously leaps from the bursting clusters; they pluck celestial fruits from the unwithering boughs of the immortal tree; they shall sit at the well-head and drink the waters as they spring with unrivaled freshness from the depths of the heart of Deity; they shall not be basking in the beams of the sun, but they shall be like Uriel, the angel in the sun; they shall dwell in God, and so their souls shall be satisfied with favor, and full and more than full with his presence and benediction.

Notice, once again, that according to the words used, it is a state where they shall recognize their right to be there; a state therefore of perfect freedom, and ease and fearlessness. It is—*"inherit the kingdom."* A man does not fear to lose that which he wins by descent from his parent. If Heaven had been the subject of earning, we might have feared that our merits had not really deserved it, and therefore suspect that one day a Writ of Error would be issued and that we should be ejected; but we *do* know whose sons we are; we know whose love it is that makes glad our spirits, and when we "inherit" the kingdom, we shall enter it not as strangers or as foreigners, but as sons coming to their birthright. Looking over all its streets of gold and surveying all its walls of pearl; we shall feel that we are at home in our own house, and have an actual right, not through merit but through grace, to everything that is there. It will be a state of heavenly bliss; the Christian shall feel that law and justice are on his side, and that those stern attributes have brought him there as well as mercy and loving-kindness. But the word "inherit" here imports full possession and enjoyment. They have inherited in a certain sense before, but now as an heir when he has arrived at full maturity, begins to spend his own money, and to farm his own acres, so do they enter into their heritage. We are not full grown as yet, and therefore are not admitted to full possession. But wait awhile; those grey hairs betoken, my brethren, that you are getting ripe. These, these, these—my still youthful locks[2]— show me, alas, that I may have to tarry for a little longer, and yet I know not, the Lord may soon permit me to sleep with my fathers; but later or earlier, be it as he wills, we shall one day come into possession of the goodly land. Now if it is sweet to be an heir while you are in nonage [not of legal age], what is it to be an heir when arrived at perfect manhood? Was it not delightful to sing that hymn just now, and to behold the land of pure delight, whose everlasting spring and never-withering flowers are just across the narrow stream of death? Oh ye sweet fields! Ye saints immortal who lie down therein! When shall we be with you and be satisfied? If the mere thinking of Heaven ravishes the soul, what must it be to be there, to plunge deep into the stream of blessedness, to dive and find no bottom, to swim and find no shore? To sip of the wine of Heaven as we sometimes do makes our hearts so glad that we know not how to express our joy; but what will it be to drink deep and drink again, and sit forever at the table and know that the feast will never be over and the cups will never be empty, and that there will be no worse wine to be brought out at the last, but if possible better still and better still in infinite progression?

The word *"kingdom,"* which stands next, indicates the richness of the heritage of saints. It is no petty estate, no alms rooms, no happy corner in obscurity. I heard a good man say he should be content to win a corner behind the door. I shall not be. The Lord says we shall inherit a kingdom. We would not be satisfied to inherit less, because less than that would not suit our character. "He hath made us kings and priests unto God," and we must reign forever and ever, or be as wretched as deposed monarchs. A king without a kingdom were an unhappy man. If I were a poor servant, an alms room would be a boon, for it would consort with my condition and degree; but if I am made by grace a king, I must have a kingdom, or I shall not have attained to a position equal to my nature. He who makes us kings will give us a kingdom to fit the nature which he hath bestowed upon us. Beloved, do strive after, more and more, that which the Spirit of God will give you, a kingly heart; do not be among those who are satisfied and contented with the miserable nature of ordinary humanity. A child's glass bead is all the world is, to a truly royal spirit; these glittering diadems are only nursery toys to God's kings; the true jewels are up there; the true treasury wealth looks down upon the stars. Do not stint your soul; be not straitened! Get a kingly heart—ask the King of kings to give it to you, and beg of him a royal spirit. Act royally on earth towards your Lord, and for his sake towards all men. Go about the world not as mean men in spirit and act, but as kings and princes of a race superior to the dirt-scrapers who are on their knees, crawling in the mud after yellow earth. Then, when your soul is royal, remember with joy that your future inheritance shall be all that your kingly soul pants after in its most royal moments. It will be a state of unutterable richness and wealth of soul.

---

[2] Spurgeon (1834–1892) was about 32 years of age when he preached this sermon.

According to the word *"prepared,"* we may conceive it to be a condition of surpassing excellence. It is a kingdom prepared, and it has been so long a time prepared, and he who prepares it is so wondrously rich in resources, that we cannot possibly conceive how excellent it must be. If I might so speak, God's common gifts, which he throws away as though they were but nothing, are priceless; but what will *be* these gifts, upon which the infinite mind of God has been set for ages of ages, in order that they may reach the highest degree of excellence? Long before Christmas chimes were ringing, mother was so glad to think her boy was coming home, after the first quarter he had been out at school, and straightway she began preparing and planning all sorts of joys for him. Well might the holidays be happy when mother had been contriving to make them so. Now in an infinitely nobler manner, the great God has prepared a kingdom for his people; he has thought, "that will please them, and that will bless them, and this other will make them superlatively happy." He prepared the kingdom to perfection; and then, as if that were not enough, the glorious man Christ Jesus went up from earth to Heaven; and you know what he said when he departed,—"I go to prepare a place for you." We know that the infinite God can prepare a place fitting for a finite creature, but the words smile so sweetly at us as we read that Jesus himself, who is a man, and therefore knows our hearts' desires, has had a finger in it; he has prepared it too. It is a kingdom prepared for you, upon which the thoughts of God have been set to make it excellent "from before the foundation of the world."

But we must not pause: it is a *"kingdom prepared for you."* Mark that! I must confess I do not like certain expressions which I hear sometimes, which imply that Heaven is prepared for some who will never reach it; prepared for those who will be driven as accursed ones into the place of torment. I know there is a sacred expression, which says, "let no man take thy crown;" but that refers to the crown of ministerial success, rather than of eternal glory. An expression which grated on my ear the other evening from the lips of a certain good man, ran something in this fashion:

> There is a Heaven prepared for all of you, but if you are not faithful you will not win it. There is a crown in Heaven laid up for you, but if you are not faithful, it will be without wearer.

I do not believe it, I cannot believe it. That the crown of eternal life, which is laid up for the blessed of the Father, will ever be given to anybody else or left without possessor, I do not believe. I dare not conceive of crowns in Heaven and nobody to wear them. Think you that in Heaven, when the whole number of saints is complete, you will find a number of unused crowns? "Ah! what are these for? Where are the heads for these?" "They are in Hell!" Then, brother, I have no particular desire to be in Heaven, for if all the family of Christ are not there, my soul will be wretched and forlorn because of their sad loss, because I am in union with them all.

If one son that believed in Jesus does not get there, I shall lose respect for the promise and respect for the Master too; he must keep his word to every soul that resteth
on him. If your God has gone the length of actually preparing a place for his people
and has made provision for them and been disappointed, he is no God to me, for I
could not adore a disappointed God. I do not believe in such a God. Such a being
would not be God at all. The notion of disappointment in his eternal preparations
is not consistent with Deity. Talk thus of Jupiter and Venus if you please, but the
Infinite Jehovah is, as far as human speech can dishonor him, dishonored by being
mentioned in such a connection. He has prepared a place for you. Here is personal
election. He has made a distinct ordinance for every one of his people that where
he is, there shall they be.

"Prepared from before the foundation of the world." Here is eternal election appearing before men were created, preparing a crown before heads were made to wear
it. And so God had, before the starry skies began to gleam, carried out the decree of
election in a measure which, when Christ shall come, shall be perfected to the
praise of the glory of his grace, "who worketh all things after the counsel of his
will." Our portion then is one prepared from all eternity for us according to the
election of God's grace, one suitable to the loftiest character to which we can ever
attain, which will consist in nearness to Christ, communion with God, and standing forever in a place of dignity and happiness.

**III. And now I have very little time to speak, as I hoped to have spoken this
morning about *the persons who shall come there.***

They are recognizable by a secret and by a public character. Their *name*
is—"blessed of the Father"—the Father chose them, gave his Son for them, justified them through Christ, preserved them in Christ Jesus, adopted them into the
family, and now accepted them into his own house. Their nature you have described in the word "inherit." None can inherit but sons; they have been born
again, and have received the nature of God; having escaped the corruption, which
is in the world through lust, they have become partakers of the Divine nature: they
are sons. Their appointment is mentioned; "inherit the kingdom prepared for you,
from before the foundation of the world." Their name is "blessed," their nature is
that of a child, their appointment is that of God's decree.

Their doings, their outward doings, these we want to speak a minute upon.
They appear to have been distinguished among men for deeds of charity, and these
were not in any way associated with ceremonies or outward observances. It is not
said that they preached—they did so, some of them; it is not said that they
prayed—they must have done so, or they would not have been spiritually alive.
The actions which are selected as their type, are actions of charity to the indigent
and forlorn. Why these? I think, because *the general audience assembled around the*

throne would know how to appreciate this evidence of their newborn nature. The King might think more of their prayers than of their alms, but the multitude would not. He speaks so as to gain the verdict of all assembled. Even their enemies could not object to his calling those blessed who had performed these actions; for if there be an action which wins for men the universal consent to their goodness, it is an action by which men would be served. Against this there is no law. I have never heard of a state in which there was a law against clothing the naked and feeding the hungry. Humanity at once, when its conscience is so seared that it cannot see its own sinfulness, yet detects the virtuousness of feeding the poor. Doubtless this is one reason why these actions were selected. And again, they may have been chosen as evidences of grace, because, as actions, they are a wonderful means of separating between the hypocrite and the true Christian. Dr. Gill has an idea, and perhaps he is right, that this is not a picture of the general judgment, but of the judgment of the professing Church, and if so, it is all the more reasonable to conclude that these works of mercy are selected as the appropriate discerner between the hypocrite and the sincere. I fear that there are some of you high professors who could not stand the test. "Good praying people" they call you, but what do you give to the Lord? Your religion has not touched your pockets. This does not apply to some of you, for there are many here of whom I would venture to speak before the bar of God, that I know their substance to be consecrated to the Lord and his poor, and I have sometimes thought that beyond their means they have given both to the poor and to God's cause. But there are others of a very different disposition. Now here I shall give you a little plain English talk which none can fail to understand. You may talk about your religion till you have worn your tongue out, and you may get others to believe you; and you may remain in the Church twenty years, and nobody ever detect you in anything like an inconsistency; but, if it be in your power, and you do nothing to relieve the necessities of the poor members of Christ's body, you will be damned as surely as if you were drunkards or whoremongers. If you have no care for God's Church, this text applies to you, and will as surely sink you to the lowest Hell as if you had been common blasphemers. That is very plain English, but it is the plain meaning of my text, and it is at my peril that I flinch from telling you of it. "I was an hungred, and ye gave me"—what? good advice; yes, but no meat. "I was thirsty, and ye gave me"—what? a tract, and no drink. "I was naked, and ye gave me"—what? your good wishes, but no clothes. I was a stranger and—ye pitied me, but—ye took me not in. Was sick—you said you could recommend me a doctor, but you did not visit me. I was in prison, I, God's servant, a persecuted one, put in prison for Christ's sake, and you said I should be more cautious; but you did not stand by my side and take a share of the blame, and bear with me reproach for the truth's sake. You see this is a very terrible winnowing fan to some of you niggardly ones whose main object is to get all you can and hold it fast, but it is a fan which frequently must be used. Whoever deceives you or spares you, by the grace of God, I will not, but will labor to be more bold than ever in denouncing sin. "Well," says one, "what are those to do who are so poor that they have nothing to give away?" My dear brother, do you notice how beautifully the text takes care of you? It hints that there are some who cannot give bread to the hungry, and clothes to the naked, but what about them? Why you see they are the persons spoken of as "my brethren," who receive the boon of kindness, so that this passage comforts the poor and by no means condemns them. Certain of us honestly give to the poor all we can spare, and then of course everybody comes to such; and when we say, "Really, I cannot give any more," somebody snarls and says, "Call yourself a Christian?" "Yes, I do: I should not call myself a Christian if I gave away other people's money; I should not call myself a Christian if I gave away what I have not got; I should call myself a thief, pretending to be charitable when I could not pay my debts." I have a very great pity indeed for those people who get into the Bankruptcy Court. I do not mean the debtors, I have seldom much sympathy with them, [but] I have a good deal for the creditors who lose by having trusted dishonest people. If any man should say, "I will live beyond my means in order to get a good character," my dear brother, you begin wrong, that action is in itself wrong. What you have to give, must be that which is your own. "But I shall have to pinch myself," says one, "if I do it." Well, pinch yourself! I do not think there is half the pleasure in doing good till you get to the pinching point. This remark of course applies only to those of us of moderate means, who can soon distribute our alms and get down to the pinch point. When you begin to feel, "Now, I must go without that; now I must curtail these in order to do more good." Oh! you cannot tell; it is then when you really can feel,

> Now I have not given God merely the cheese parings and candle ends that I could not use, but I have really cut out for my Master a good piece of the loaf; I have not given him the old crusts that were getting moldy, but I have given him a piece of my own daily bread, and I am glad to do it, if I can show my love to Jesus Christ by denying myself.

If you are doing this— if you are thus, out of love to Jesus, feeding the hungry, clothing the naked—I believe that these are put down as tests, because they are such blessed detectives between the hypocrites and the really godly people. When you read "for" here, you must not understand it to be that their reward is *because of this,* but that they are *proved to be God's servants* by this; and so, while they do not merit it because of these actions, yet these actions show that they were saved by grace, which is evidenced by the fact that Jesus Christ wrought such and such works in them. If Christ does not work such things in you, you have no part in him; if you have not produced such works as these, you have not believed in Jesus. Now somebody says, "Then I intend to give to the poor in future in order that I may have this reward." Ah, but you are very much mistaken if you do that. The Duke of Burgundy was waited upon by a poor man, a very loyal subject, who brought him a very large root, which he had grown. He was a very poor man indeed, and every root he grew in his garden was of consequence to him; but merely as a loyal offering he brought to his prince the largest his little garden produced. The prince was so pleased with the man's evident loyalty and affection that he gave him a very large sum. The steward thought, "Well, I see this pays; this man has got fifty pounds for his large root, I think I shall make the duke a present." So he bought a horse and he reckoned that he should have in return ten times as much for it as it was worth, and he presented it with that view: the duke, like a wise man, quietly accepted the horse, and gave the greedy steward nothing. That was all. So you say, "Well, here is a Christian man, and he gets rewarded. He has been giving to the poor, helping the Lord's Church, and see he is saved; the thing pays, I shall make a little investment." Yes, but you see the steward did not give the horse out of any idea of loyalty, and kindness, and love to the duke, but out of very great love to himself, and therefore had no return; and if you perform deeds of charity out of the idea of getting to Heaven by them, why it is yourself that you are feeding, it is yourself that you are clothing; all your virtue is not virtue, it is rank selfishness, it smells strong of selfhood, and Christ will never accept it; you will never hear him say, "Thank you" for it. You served yourself, and no reward is due. You must first come to the Lord Jesus Christ, and look to him to save you; you will forever abjure all idea of doing anything to save yourself, and being saved, you will be able to give to the poor and so on without selfishness mixing with your motive, and you will get a reward of grace for the love token which you have given. It is necessary to believe in Christ in order to be capable of true virtue of the highest order. It is necessary to trust Jesus, and to be yourself fully saved, before there is any value in your feeding the hungry or clothing the naked. God give you grace to go to my Master wounded yonder, and to rest in the precious atonement which he has made for human sin; and when you have done that, being loved at such a rate, show that you love in return; being purchased so dearly, live for him that bought you; and among the actions by which you prove it, let these gleam and glisten like God-given jewels—the visiting of the sick, the comforting of the needy, the relieving of the distressed, and the helping of the weak. God accept these offerings as they come from gracious souls, and to him be praise evermore. Amen.

The Great White Throne

Delivered on Sunday evening, August 12, 1866, at the Metropolitan Tabernacle,
Newington. No. 710.

*And I saw a great white throne, and him that sat on it, from whose face the earth and the
Heaven fled away; and there was found no place for them.—Revelation 20:11*

Many of the visions which John saw are very obscure, and although a man
who is assured of his own salvation may possibly be justified in spending his
days in endeavoring to interpret them, yet I am sure of this, that it will not be a
profitable task for unconverted persons. They have no time to spare for specula-
tions, for they have not yet made sure of positive certainties. *They* need not dive
into difficulties, for they have not yet laid a foundation of simplicities by faith in
Christ Jesus. Better far to meditate upon the atonement than to be guessing at the
little horn, and better far to know the Lord Jesus in his power to save, than to fabri-
cate an ingenious theory upon the number of the beast. But this particular vision is
so instructive, so unattended by serious difficulties, that I may invite all here present to consider it, and the more so because it has to do with matters which concern
our own eternal prospects. It may be, if God the Holy Spirit shall illuminate the
eyes of our faith to look and see that "great white throne and him that sat upon it,"
that we may reap so much benefit from the sight as forever to make the arches of
Heaven ring with gratitude that we were brought in this world to look at the "great
white throne," for by so doing we shall not be afraid to look upon it in the day
when the Judge shall sit, and the quick and dead shall stand before him.

I shall, first, endeavor to explain *what John saw;* and then, in the second place, *I shall try to set forth the effect which I think would be produced by this sight if the eyes of our faith should now be fixed thereon.*

I. First, then, I have to call your very earnest attention to *what John saw.*

It was a scene of the last day—that wondrous day whose coming none can tell.

> *For, as a thief unheard, unseen, it steals*
> *Through night's dark shade.*

When the eagle-eyed seer of Patmos, being in the Spirit, looked aloft into the heavens, *he saw a throne,* from which I gather that there is a throne of moral government over the sons of men, and that he who sits upon it presides over all the inhabitants of this world. There is a throne whose dominion reaches from Adam in Paradise down to "the last man," whoever he may be. We are not without a governor, law giver, and judge. This world is not left so that men may do in it as they will, without a legislator, without an avenger, without One to give reward or to inflict punishment. The sinner, in his blindness, looks, but he sees no throne; and therefore he cries, "I will live as I wish—for there is none to call me to account;" but John, with illuminated eye, distinctly saw a throne, and a personal ruler upon it, who sat there to call his subjects to account. When our faith looks through the glass of revelation, it sees a throne too. It were well for us if we felt more fully the influence of that ever-present throne. That "the Lord reigneth" is true, believer, tonight, and true at all times. There is a throne whereon sitteth the King eternal, immortal, invisible; the world is governed by laws made and kept in force by an intelligent lawgiver. There is a moral governor. Men are accountable, and will be brought to account at the last great day, when they shall all be either rewarded or punished. "I saw a great white throne."

How this invests the actions of men with solemnity! If we were left to do exactly as we willed without being called to account for it, it were wise even then to be virtuous, for rest assured it is best for ourselves that we should be good, and it is in itself malady enough to be evil. But we are not so left. There is a law laid down, to break which involves a penalty. There is a lawgiver who looks down and spies every action of man, and who does not suffer one single word or deed to be omitted from his notebook. That governor is armed with power; he is soon coming to hold his assize, and every responsible agent upon the face of the earth must appear at his bar and receive, as we are told, "according to the deeds done in the body, whether they be good or whether they be evil." Let it, then, be gathered from the text that there is, in very deed, a personal and real moral governor of the world, an efficient and suitable ruler, not a mere name, not a myth, not an empty office, but a person who sits on the throne, who judges right, and who will carry out that judgment ere long.

Now, brethren and sisters, we know that this moral governor is God himself, who has an undisputed *right* to reign and rule. Some thrones have no right to be, and to revolt from them is patriotism; but the best lover of his race delights the most in the monarchy of Heaven. Doubtless there are dynasties, which are tyrannies, and governors who are despots; but none may dispute the right of God to sit upon the throne, or wish that another hand held the scepter. He created all, and shall he not judge all? He had a right, as Creator, to lay down his laws, and, as those laws are the very pattern of everything that is good and true: he had, therefore, because of this an eternal right to govern, in addition to the right which belonged to him as Creator. He is the Judge of all, who must do right from a necessity of his nature. Who else, then, should sit upon the throne, and who shall dare to claim to do so? He may cast down the gauntlet to all his creatures, and say, "I am God, and beside me there is none else:" if he reveals the thunder of his power, his creatures must silently own that he is Lord alone. None can venture to say that this throne is not founded upon right.

Moreover, there are some thrones on which the kings, however right, are deficient *in might,* but this is not the case with the King of kings. We constantly see little princes whose crowns fit their heads so ill that they cannot keep them on their brows; but our God has might invincible as well as right infallible. Who shall meet him in the battle? Shall the stubble defy the fire, or shall the wax make war with the flame? Jehovah can easily swallow up his enemies when they set themselves in battle array against him.

> Behold he toucheth the hills, and they smoke; he looketh upon the mountains, and they tremble; he breaketh Leviathan in pieces in the depths of the sea. The winds are his chariots, and the tempests are his messengers. At his bidding there is day, and at his will, night covereth the earth. Who shall stay his band, or say unto him, "What doest thou?"[1]

His throne is founded in right and supported by might. You have justice and truth to settle it, but you have omnipotence and wisdom to be its guards, so that it cannot be moved.

In addition to this, his throne is one from *the power of which none can escape.* The sapphire throne of God, at this moment, is revealed in Heaven, where adoring angels cast their crowns before it; and its power is felt on earth, where the works of creation praise the Lord. Even those who acknowledge not the divine government are compelled to feel it, for he doeth as he wills, not only among the angels in Heaven, but among the inhabitants of this lower world. Hell feels the terror of that throne. Those chains of fire, those pangs unutterable, are the awful shadow of the throne of Deity; as God looks down upon the lost, the torment that flashes through their souls darts from his holiness, which cannot endure their sins. The influence of

---

[1] Portions from Ps. 104.

273

that throne, then, is found in every world where spirits dwell, and in the realms of inanimate nature it bears rule. Every leaf that fades in the trackless forest trembles at the Almighty's bidding, and every coral insect that dwelleth in the unfathomable depths of the sea feels and acknowledges the presence of the all-present King. So, then, my brethren, if such is the throne which John saw, see how impossible it will be for you to escape from its judgment when the great day of assize shall be proclaimed, and the Judge shall issue his summons, bidding you appear. Whither can the enemies of God flee? If up to Heaven their high-flown impudence could carry them, his right hand of holiness would hurl them thence, or, if under Hell's profoundest wave they dive, to seek a sheltering grave, his left hand would pluck them out of the fire, to expose them to the fiercer light of his countenance. Nowhere is there a refuge from the Most High. The morning beams cannot convey the fugitive so swiftly as the almighty Pursuer could follow him; neither can the mysterious lightning flash, which annihilates time and space, journey so rapidly as to escape his far-reaching hand. "If I mount up to Heaven, thou art there; if I make my bed in Hell, thou art there."

It was said of the Roman empire under the Caesars that the whole world was only one great prison for Caesar, for if any man offended the emperor it was impossible for him to escape. If he crossed the Alps, could not Caesar find him out in Gaul? If he sought to hide himself in the Indies, even the swarthy monarchs there knew the power of the Roman arms, so that they would give no shelter to a man who had incurred imperial vengeance. And yet, perhaps, a fugitive from Rome might have prolonged his miserable life by hiding in the dens and caves of the earth. But oh! sinner, there is no hiding from God. The mountains cannot cover you from him, even if they would, neither can the rocks conceal you. See, then, at the very outset how this throne should awe our minds with terror. Founded in right, sustained by might, and universal in its dominion, look ye and see the throne, which John of old beheld.

This, however, is but the beginning of the vision. The text tells us that it was a *"white throne,"* and I would call your attention to that. "I saw a great white throne." Why white? Does not this indicate its immaculate purity? There is no other white throne, I fear, to be found. The throne of our own happy land[2] I believe to be as white and as pure as any throne might well be on earth, but there have been years, even in the annals of that throne, when it was stained with blood, and not many reigns back it was black with debauchery. Not always was it the throne of excellence and purity, and even now, though our throne possesses a lustrous purity, rare enough among earthly thrones, yet in the sight of God there must be in everything that is earthly something that is impure, and therefore the throne is not white to him. As for many other thrones that are still existing, we know that with them

---

[2] England, under Queen Victoria.

all is not white; this is neither the day nor the hour for us to call the princes to the bar of God, but there are some of them who will have much to answer for, because in their schemes of aggrandizement they took no account of the blood which would be shed, or of the rights which would be violated. Principle seldom moves the royal mind, but the knavish law of policy is the basis of king-craft; a policy worthy of highwaymen and burglars, and some kings are little. On the continent of Europe there are not a few thrones, which I might describe as either black, or crimson, as I think of the turpitude [depravity] of the conduct of the monarch, or of the blood through which he has waded his way to dominion.

But this is a great *white* throne, a throne of hallowed monarchy that is not stained with blood nor defiled with injustice. Why, then, is it white for purity? Is it not because *the King who sits on it is pure?* Hark to the thrice sacred hymn of the cherubic band and the seraphic choir, "Holy, holy, holy, Lord God of Sabaoth." Creatures who are perfectly spotless themselves unceasingly reverence and adore the yet superior holiness of the great King. He is too great to need to be unjust, and he is too good to be unkind. This King has done no wrong, and can do no wrong, but he is the only King of whom this can be said without fiction. He who sits on this white throne is himself the essence of holiness, justice, truth, and love. O fairest of all thrones! Who would not be a willing subject of thy peerless government?

Moreover, the throne is pure, because *the law the Judge dispenses—is perfect*. There is no fault in the statute-book of God. When the Lord shall come to judge the earth, there will be found no decree that bears too hardly upon any one of his creatures. "The statutes of the Lord are right;" they are true and righteous altogether. That book of the ten commands in which you find a summary of the divine will, who can improve it? Who can find anything in excess in it, or point out aught that is wanting? "The law of the Lord is perfect, converting the soul," and well may that be a white throne from which there emanates such a law. But you know that with a good law and a good lawgiver, yet sometimes the throne may make mistakes, and it may be stained by ignorance, if not by willful injustice. But the sentence, which shall go forth from this great white throne, shall be so consistent with justice that even the condemned culprit himself must give his unwilling assent to it. "They stood speechless," it is said; speechless because they could neither bear the sentence nor in any way impugn it. It is a white throne, since never was a verdict delivered from it of which the culprit had a right to complain. Perhaps there are some here who view this as a matter of hope, but to ungodly persons it will be the very reverse. Oh! sinner, if you had to be judged before an impure tribunal, you might, perhaps, escape; if the King were not holy, unholiness might, perhaps, go unpunished; if the law were not perfect, offenses might be condoned; or if the sentence were not just, you might through partiality, escape. But where everything is so pure and white,

> *Careless sinner,*
> *What will there become of thee?*

I have thought, too, that perhaps this throne is said to be a white throne to indicate that *it will be eminently conspicuous.* You will have noticed that a white object can be seen from a very great distance. You may have observed, perhaps, on the Welsh mountains, a white cottage far away, standing out conspicuously, for the Welsh like to make their cottages intensely white, so that though you would not have perceived it, had it been left of a stone color, you see it at once, for the bright whitewashed walls catch your eye. I suppose that a marksman would prefer a white object to aim at before almost any other color. And this great white throne will be so conspicuous that all the millions who were dead, but who shall rise at the sound of the last trumpet, shall all see it, nor shall it be possible for a single eye to close itself against the sight. We must see it; it shall be so striking a sight that none of us will be able to prevent its coming before us; "every eye shall see him." Possibly it is called a white throne because of its being such a convincing contrast to all the colors of this sinful human life. There stand the crowd, and there is the great white throne. What can make them see their blackness more thoroughly than to stand there in contrast with the perfections of the law, and the Judge before whom they are standing? Perhaps that throne, all glistening, will reflect each man's character. As each unforgiven man shall look at that white throne, its dazzling whiteness will overcome him, and cover him with confusion and with terror when he sees his own defilement in contrast with it. "O God!" saith he,

> how can I bear to be judged by such a one as thou art? I could face the judgment-seat of my fellows, for I could see imperfections in my judges, but I cannot face thee, thou dread Supreme, for the awful whiteness of thy throne, and the terrible splendor of thy holiness utterly overcome me. Who am I, sinner as I am, that I should dare to stand before that great white throne!

The next word that is used by way of adjective is *"great."* It was a *"great* white throne." You scarcely need me to tell you that it is called a great white throne *because of the greatness of him who sits upon it.* Speak of the greatness of Solomon? He was but a petty prince. Speak of the throne of the Mogul or his Celestial Majesty of China, or of the thrones of Rome and Greece, before which multitudes of beings assembled? They are nothing, mere representatives of associations of the grasshoppers of the world, who are as nothing in the sight of the Lord Jehovah. A throne filled by a mortal is but a shadow of dominion. This will be a great throne, because on it will sit the great God of earth, and Heaven, and Hell, the King eternal, immortal, invisible, who shall judge the world in righteousness, and his people with equity.

Brethren, you will see that this will be a "great white throne" when we remember *the culprits who will be brought before it;* not a handful of criminals, but millions upon millions, "multitudes, multitudes, in the Valley of Decision"; and these not all of the lesser sort, not serfs and slaves alone, whose miserable bodies rested from their oppressors in the silent grave; but the great ones of the earth shall be there; not alone the down-trodden serf who toiled for nought, and felt it sweet to die, but his tyrant master who fattened on his unrewarded toils shall be there; not alone the multitudes who marched to battle at their master's bidding, and who fell beneath the shot and the shell, but the Emperors and Kings who planned the conflict shall be there; crowned heads no greater than heads uncrowned. Men who were demigods among their fellows shall mix with their slaves, and be made as vile as they! What a marvelous procession! With what awe the imagination of it strikes the heart! What a pompous appearing! Aba! Aba! Ye down-trodden multitudes, the great Leveller has put you all upon a footing now! Death laid you in one equal grave, and now judgment finds you standing at one equal bar, to receive the sentence of one who fears no king, and dreads no tyrant, who has no respect of persons, but who deals justice alike to all. Can you picture the sight? Land and sea are covered with the living who once were dead. Hell is empty, and the grave has lost its victims! What a sight will that be! Xerxes on his throne with a million marching before him, must have beheld a grand spectacle, but what will this be? No flaunting banner, but the ensigns of eternal majesty. No gaudy courtiers, but assembled angels! No sound of drum nor roar of culverin [heavy cannon], but the blast of the archangel's trumpet, and the harping of ten thousand times ten thousand holy ones. There will be unrivalled splendor, it is true, but not that of heraldry and war; mere tinsel and gewgaw [cheap showy jewelry] shall have all departed, and in their place there shall be the splendor of the flashing lightning, and the deep bass of the thunder. Jesus the Man of Sorrows, with all his angels with him shall descend, the pomp of Heaven being revealed among the sons of men.

It will be a great white throne, *because of the matters that will be tried there*. It will be no mere quarrel about a suit in Chancery[3], or an estate in jeopardy. Our souls will have to be tried there; our future, not for an age, not for one single century, but forever and forever. Upon those balances shall hang Heaven and Hell; to the right shall be distributed triumph without end, to the left destruction and confusion without a pause, and the destiny of every man and woman shall be positively declared from that tremendous throne! Can you perceive the greatness of it? You must measure Heaven; you must fathom Hell, you must compass eternity, but until you can do this, you cannot know the greatness of this *great* white throne; great, last of all, because throughout eternity there shall always be a looking back to the transactions of that day. That day shall be unto you, ye saints, "the beginning of days," when he shall say, "Come, ye blessed of my Father." And that day shall be to you who perish the beginning of days too; just as that famous night of old in Egypt, when the firstborn were spared in every house where the lamb had shed its blood, was the first of days to Israel, but to Egypt the night when the firstborn felt the

---

[3] A court with jurisdiction in equity.

avenging angel's sword was a dread beginning of nights forever. Many a mother reckoned from that night when the destroyer came, and so shall you reckon throughout a dread eternity from the day when you see this *great* white throne.

Turn not away your eyes from the magnificent spectacle till you have seen the glorious Person mentioned in the words, *"And him that sat on it."* I wonder whether anything I have said has made you solemnly to think of the great day. I am afraid I cannot speak so as to get at your hearts, and if not, I had better be silent; but do now for a moment think upon him who sat upon the great white throne. The most fitting one in all the world will sit upon that throne. It will be God, but hearken, it will also be man. "He shall judge the world by this man. Christ Jesus, according to my gospel," says the apostle. The judge must needs be God. Who but God were fit to judge so many, and to judge so exactly? The throne is too great for any but for him of whom it is written, "Thy throne, O God, is forever and ever; a scepter of righteousness is thy scepter."

Christ Jesus, the Son of God, will judge, and he will judge as man as well as God; and how fitting it is that it should be so! As man he knows our infirmities, he understands our hearts, and we cannot object to this, that our Judge should be himself like unto us. Who better could judge righteous judgment than one who is "bone of our bone and flesh of our flesh"? And then, there is this fitness about it; he is not only God and man, but he is *the* man, the man of men, of all men the most manly, the type and pattern of manhood. He will be the test in his own person, for if a man be like Christ, that man is right, but if a man be otherwise than Christ-like, that man deserves to be condemned. That wondrous Judge needs only look upon his own character to read the law, and to review his own actions to discern whether other men's actions be right or wrong. The thoughts of many hearts were revealed by Christ on earth, and that same Christ shall make an open exhibition of men at the last great day. He shall judge them, he shall discern their spirits, he shall find out the joints and the marrow of their being; the thoughts and intents of the heart he shall lay bare.

Even you, believer, will pass the test before him; let no man deceive you with the delusion that you will not be judged: the sheep appeared before the great dividing Shepherd as well as the goats, those who used their talents were called to account as well as he who buried his pound, and the disciples themselves were warned that their idle words would bring them into judgment. Nor need you fear a public trial. Innocence courts the light. You are not saved by being allowed to be smuggled into Heaven untested and unproved, but you will, in the righteousness of Jesus, pass the solemn test with joy. It may not be at the same moment as the wicked that the righteous shall be judged (I shall not contend for particulars), but I am clear that they will be judged, and that the blood and righteousness of Jesus are provided for this very cause, that they may find mercy of the Lord in *that* day.

O sinner! it is far otherwise with you, for your ruin is sure when the testing time comes. There will be no witnesses needed to convict you, for the Judge knows all. The Christ whom you despised will judge you, the Savior whose mercy you trampled on, in the fountain of whose blood you would not wash, the despised and rejected of men—it is he who shall judge righteous judgment to you, and what will he say but this, "As for these mine enemies, who would not [choose] that I should reign over them, cut them in pieces before my eyes!"

II. I want a few minutes—and I have but too few left—to *draw the inferences which flow from such a sight as this*, and so turn the vision to practical account.

Believer in Christ, a word in thine ear. Canst thou see the great white throne, and him that sits upon it? Methinks I see it now. Then, *let me search myself.* Whatever profession I may make, I shall have to face that great white throne. I have passed the elders; I have been approved by the pastor; I stand accepted by the church; but that great white throne is not passed yet. I have borne a reputable character among my fellow-Christians; I have been asked to pray in public, and my prayers have been much admired, but I have not yet been weighed in the last balances, and what if I should be found wanting! Brother Christian, what about thy private prayers? Canst thou live in neglect of the closet, and yet remember that thy prayers will be tried before the great white throne? Is thy Bible left unread in private? Is thy religion nothing but a public show and sham? Remember the great white throne, for mere pretense will not pass there. Brother Christian, what about thy heart and thy treasure? Art thou a mere money-hunter? Dost thou live as others live? Is thy delight in the fleeting present? Dost thou have dealings with the throne of Heaven? Hast thou a stony heart towards divine things? Hast thou little love to Christ? Dost thou make an empty profession, and nothing more? Oh, think of that great white throne, that great white throne!

Why, there are some of you, who, when I preach a stirring sermon, feel afraid to come again to hear me. Ah! but if you are afraid of my voice, how will you bear his voice who shall speak in tones of thunder? Do searching sermons seem to go through you like a blast of the north wind, chilling your very marrow and curdling your blood? Oh! but what must it be to stand before that dread tribunal? Are you doubting now? What will you be then? Can you not bear a little self-examination? How will you bear that God-examination? If the scales of earth tell you that you are wanting, what message will the scales of Heaven give you? I do conjure you, fellow-professors, speaking to you as I desire to speak now to my own heart, "Examine yourselves, whether ye be in the faith; prove your own selves. Know ye not your own selves, how that Jesus Christ is in you, except ye be reprobates?"

Having spoken a word to the Christian, I should like to say to every one of you, *in remembrance of this great white throne, shun hypocrisy.* Are you tempted to be baptized though you are not a believer, in order to please parents and friends? Beware of that great white throne, and bethink you how your insult to God will look at that great day! Are you persuaded to put on the cloak of religion because it will help your business, or make you seem respectable? Beware, thou hypocrite, beware of that great white throne; for of all the terrors that shall come forth from it, there shall be none more severe than those which shall scathe the mere professor, who made a profession of religion for gain. If you must be damned, be damned anyhow sooner [in any way other] than as a hypocrite; for they deserve the deepest Hell who for gain make a profession of godliness. The ruin of Byends and Hypocrisy[4] will be just indeed. O ye high-flying professors, whose wings are fastened on with wax, beware of the sun which will surely pour its heat upon you, for fearful will be your fall from so great a height!

But there are some of you who say, "I do not make any profession of religion." Still my text has a word to you. Still *I want you to judge your actions by that last great day.* O sir, how about that night of sin? "No," say you, "never mind it; bring it not to my remembrance." It shall be brought to thy remembrance, and that deed of sin shall be published far wider than upon the house-tops, gazetted to all the multitudes who have ever lived since the first man, and thine infamy shall become a byword and a proverb among all created beings. What think you of this, you secret sinners? You lovers of wantonness and chambering? Ah! young man, you have commenced by filching, but you will go on to be a downright thief. It is known, sir, and "be sure your sin will find you out." Young woman, you have begun to dally with sin, and you think none has seen you, but the most Mighty One has seen your acts and heard your words; there is no curtain between him and your sin. He sees you clearly, and what will you do with these sins of yours that you think have been concealed? "It was many years ago," you tell me. Ay, but though buried these many years to you, they are all alive to him, for everything is present to the all-seeing God; and your forgotten deeds shall one day stand out present to you also. My hearers, I conjure you do nothing which you would not do if you thought God saw you, for he *does* see you. Oh! look at your actions in the light of the judgment. Oh! that secret tippling [drinking] of yours, how will that look when God reveals it? That private lust of yours, which nobody knows of; how would you dare to do it if you recollected that God knows it? Young man, it is a secret, a fearful secret, and you would not whisper it in anyone's ear; but it shall be whispered, nay, it shall be thundered out before the world! I pray thee, friend, think of this. There is an observer who takes notes of all that we do, and will publish all to an assembled universe.

---

[4] Reference to John Bunyan's *The Pilgrim's Progress* (1678).

And as for us all, *are we ready to meet that last great day?* I had many things to say unto you, but I cannot keep you to say them now, lest ye grow weary; but if to-night the trumpet should be sounded, what would be your state of mind? Suppose that now every ear in this place should be startled with a blast most loud and dread, and a voice were heard,

> Come to judgment,
> Come to judgment, come away.

Supposing some of you could hide in the vaults and in the foundations, would not many of you rush to the concealment? How few of us might go down these aisles walking steadily into the open air and saying,

> I am not afraid of judgment, for "there is therefore now no condemnation to them that are in Christ Jesus."

Brethren and sisters, I hope there are some of us who could go gladly to that judgment seat, even if we had to traverse the jaws of death to reach it. I hope there are some of us who can sing in our hearts—

> Bold shall I stand in that great day;
> For who aught to my charge shall lay?
> While, through thy blood, absolved I am
> From sin's tremendous curse and blame.

It might put many of us much about, to say that. It is easy to speak of full assurance, but, believe me, it is not quite so easy to have it in right down earnest in trying times. If some of you get the finger-ache, your confidence oozes out at your joints, and if you have but a little sickness, you think, "Ah! it may be cholera, what shall I do?" Can you not bear to die? How then will you bear to live forever? Could you not look death in the face without a shudder? Then how will you endure the judgment? Could you gaze upon death, and feel that he is your friend and not your foe? Could you put a skull upon your dressing-table, and commune with it as your *Memento mori?*[5] Oh! it may well take the bravest of you to do this, and the only sure way is to come as we are to Jesus, with no righteousness of our own to trust to, but finding all in him. When William Carey was about to die, he ordered to have put upon his tombstone this verse:

> A guilty, weak, and helpless worm,
> On Christ's kind arms I fall,
> He is my strength, my righteousness,
> My Jesus, and my all.

---

[5] Latin phrase meaning—"Remember that you are mortal."

I would like to wake up in eternity with such a verse as that in my mind, as I wish to go to sleep in this world with such a hope as that in my heart:

> *Nothing in my hand I bring,*
> *Simply to the cross I cling.*

Ah! I am talking about what some of us will know more of, perhaps, before this week is over. I am speaking now upon themes which you think are a long way off, but a moment may bring them near. A thousand years is a long time, but how soon it flies! One almost seems, in reading English history, to go back and shake hands with William the Conqueror; a few lives soon bring us even to the flood. You who are getting on to be forty years old, and especially you who are sixty or seventy, must feel how fast time flies. I only seem to preach a sermon one Sunday in time to get ready for the next.[6] Time flies with such a whirl that no express train can overtake it, and even the lightning flash seems to lag behind it. We shall soon be at the great white throne; we shall soon be at the judgment bar of God. Oh! let us be making ready for it. Let us not live so much in this present, which is but a dream, an empty show, but let us live in the real, substantial future.

Oh that I could reach some heart here tonight! I have a notion that I am speaking to someone here who will not have another warning. I am sure that with such throngs as crowd here Sabbath after Sabbath, I never preach to the same congregation twice[7]. There are always some here who are dead between one Sunday and another. Out of such masses as these, it must be so, according to the ordinary computation. Who among you will it be who will die this week? Oh! ponder the question well! Who among you will dwell with the devouring flames? Who among you will abide with everlasting burnings? If I knew you I would fain bedew you with tears. If I knew you who are to die this week, I would fain come and kneel down at your side, and conjure you to think of eternal things. But I do not know you, and therefore by the living God I do implore you all to fly to Jesus by faith. These are no trifles, sirs, are they? If they be, I am but a sorry trifler, and you may go your ways and laugh at me; but if they be true and real, it becomes me to be in earnest, and much more does it become *you* to be in earnest. "Prepare to meet thy God!" He cometh! Prepare now! "Now is the accepted time; now is the day of salvation!" The gates of mercy are not closed. Your sin is not unpardonable. You may yet find mercy. Christ invites you. His blood-drops cry to you:

> *Come and welcome,*
> *Come and welcome, sinner come.*

Oh! may the Holy Spirit put life into these poor words of mine, and may the Lord help you to come now. The way to come, you know, is just to trust in Christ. It is all done when you trust in Christ—throw yourselves right on him, having nothing

---

[6] Spurgeon (1834–1892) was about 32 years of age, halfway through his life-span.

[7] The Metropolitan Tabernacle Church seated 6,000 people.

else to trust to. See now, my whole weight leans on the front of this platform. Should this rail give way, I fall. Lean on Christ just in that way.

> *Venture on him, venture wholly,*
> *Let no other trust intrude.*

If you can get a grip of the Cross, and stand there beneath the crimson canopy of the atonement, God himself cannot smite you, and the last tremendous day shall dawn upon you with splendor and delight, and not with gloom and terror.

I must send you away, but not until all believers present have given you an invitation to return to the Lord Jesus. To do this we will sing the following verses:

> *Return, O wanderer, to thy home.*
> *Thy Father calls for thee;*
> *No longer now an exile roam*
> *In guilt and misery;*
> *Return, return.*
>
> *Return, O wanderer, to thy home,*
> *'Tis Jesus calls for thee:*
> *The Spirit and the bride say, Come;*
> *Oh now for refuge flee;*
> *Return, return.*
>
> *Return, O wanderer, to thy home,*
> *'Tis madness to delay;*
> *There are no pardons in the tomb,*
> *And brief is mercy's day.*
> *Return, return.*

Jesus Admired in Them that Believe

Delivered on Lord's Day morning, June 1, 1879, at the Metropolitan Tabernacle, Newington. No. 1477.

When he shall come to be glorified in his saints, and to be admired in all them that believe (because our testimony among you was believed) in that day.—2 Thessalonians 1:10

What a difference between the first and second comings of our Lord! When he shall come a second time, it will be to be glorified and admired, but when he came the first time it was to be despised and rejected of men. He comes a second time to reign with unexampled splendor, but the first time he came to die in circumstances of shame and sorrow. Lift up your eyes, ye sons of light, and anticipate the change, which will be as great for you as for your Lord; for now ye are hidden even as he was hidden, and misunderstood even as he was misunderstood when he walked among the sons of men. "We know that, when he shall appear, we shall be like him; for we shall see him as he is." His manifestation will be our manifestation, and in the day in which he is revealed in glory, then shall his saints be glorified with him.

Observe that our Lord is spoken of as coming in his glory, and as at the same time taking vengeance in flaming fire on them that know not God, and that obey not the gospel. This is a note of great terror to all those who are ignorant of God, and wickedly unbelieving concerning his Christ. Let them take heed, for the Lord will gain glory by the overthrow of his enemies, and those who would not bow before him cheerfully shall be compelled to bow before him abjectly: they shall crouch at his feet, they should lick the dust in terror, and at the glance of his eyes they shall utterly wither away, as it is written, they "shall be punished with everlasting destruction from the presence of the Lord, and from the glory of his power." But this is not the main object for which Christ will come, nor is this the matter in which he findeth his chiefest glory, for, observe, he does this, as it were, by the way, when he comes for another purpose. To destroy the wicked is a matter of necessity in which his spirit takes no delight, for he doth this, according to the text, not so much when he cometh to do it, as when he shall come with another object, namely, "To be glorified in his saints, and to be admired in them that believe."

The crowning honor of Christ will be seen in his people, and this is the design with which he will return to this earth in the latter days, that he may be illustrious in his saints and exceedingly magnified in them. Even now his saints glorify him. When they walk in holiness, they do, as it were, reflect his light; their holy deeds are beams from him who is the Sun of righteousness. When they believe in him they also glorify him, for there is no grace which pays lowlier homage at the throne of Jesus than the grace of faith whereby we trust him, and so confess him to be our all in all. We do glorify our gracious Lord, but, beloved brethren, we must all confess that we do not this as we could desire, for, alas, too often we dishonor him, and grieve his Holy Spirit. By our want of zeal and by our many sins we are guilty of discrediting his gospel and dishonoring his name. Happy, happy, happy day when this shall no more be possible, when we shall be rid of the inward corruption which now worketh itself into outward sin, and shall never dishonor Christ again, but shall shine with a clear, pure radiance, like the moon on the Passover night, when it looketh the sun full in the face, and then shines upon the earth at her best. Today we are like vessels on the wheel, but half fashioned—yet even now somewhat of his divine skill is seen in us as his handiwork. Still the unformed clay is in part seen, and much remains to be done; how much more of the great Potter's creating wisdom and sanctifying power will be displayed when we shall be the perfect products of his hand! In the bud and germ our new nature brings honor to its Author; it will do far more when its perfection manifests the Finisher. Then shall Jesus be glorified and admired in every one of us when the days of the new creation are ended and God shall usher in the eternal Sabbath by pronouncing his grace-work to be very good.

This morning, as God shall help me, I shall speak first of *the special glorification of Christ here intended*: and, secondly, I shall conclude the sermon by calling your attention to *the special considerations which this grand truth suggests*.

I. Let us consider carefully *the special glorification here intended.*

And the first point to note is *the time*. The text saith "When he shall come to be glorified in his saints." The full glorification of Christ in his saints will be when he shall come a second time, according to the sure word of prophecy. He is glorified in them now, for he saith, "All mine are thine, and thine are mine; and I am glorified in them"; but as yet that glory is perceptible to himself rather than to the outer world. The lamps are being trimmed, they will shine ere long. These are the days of preparation before that Sabbath which is in an infinite sense a high day. As it was said of Esther, that for so many months she prepared herself with myrrh and sweet odors before she entered the king's palace, to be espoused of him, even so are we now being purified and made ready for that august day when the perfected church shall be presented unto Christ as a bride unto her husband. John saith of her that she shall be "prepared as a bride adorned for her husband." This is our night, wherein we must watch, but behold the morning cometh, a morning without clouds, and then shall we walk in a seven-fold light because our Well-beloved hath come. That second advent of his will be his revelation: he was under a cloud here, and men perceived him not, save only a few who beheld his glory; but when he comes a second time, all veils will be removed and every eye shall see the glory of his countenance. For this he waits and his church waits with him. We know not when the set time shall arrive, but every hour is bringing it nearer to us, therefore let us stand with loins girt, awaiting it.

Note, secondly, *in whom* this glorification of Christ is to be found. The text does not say he will be glorified "by" his saints, but "*in* his saints." There is a shade of difference, yea, more than a shade, between the two terms. We endeavor to glorify him now by our actions, but then he will be glorified in our own persons, and character, and condition. He is glorified *by what we do,* but he is at the last to be glorified *in what we are.* Who are these in whom Jesus is to be glorified and admired? They are spoken of under two descriptions: "in his saints," and "in all them that believe."

In "his saints," first. All those in whom Christ will be glorified are described as holy ones or saints: men and women who have been sanctified, and made pure, whose gracious lives show that they have been under the teaching of the Holy Spirit, whose obedient actions prove that they are disciples of a Holy Master, even of him who was "holy, harmless, undefiled, and separate from sinners." But, inasmuch as these saints are also said to be believers, I gather that the holiness which will honor Christ at last is a holiness based on faith in him, a holiness of which this was the root—that they first trusted in Christ, and then, being saved, they loved their Lord and obeyed him. Their faith wrought by love and purified their souls, and so cleansed their lives. It is an inner as well as an outer purity, arising out of the living and operative principle of faith. If any think that they can attain to holiness apart from faith in Christ, they are as much mistaken as he who should hope to reap a harvest without casting seed into the farrows. Faith is the bulb, and saintship is the delightfully fragrant flower which cometh of it when planted in the soil of a renewed heart. Beware, I pray you, of any pretense to a holiness arising out of yourselves, and maintained by the energy of your own unaided wills; as well look to gather grapes of thorns or figs of thistles. True saintship must spring from confidence in the Savior of sinners, and if it doth not, it is lacking in the first elements of truth. How can that be a perfect character which finds its basis in self-esteem? How could Christ be glorified by saints who refuse to trust in him?

I would call your attention once again to the second description, "All them that believe." This is enlarged by the hint that they are believers in a certain testimony, according to the bracketed sentence—"because our testimony among you was believed." Now, the testimony of the apostles was concerning Christ. They saw him in the body, and they bore witness that he was "God manifest in the flesh"; they saw his holy life, and they bore witness to it; they saw his death of grief, and they witnessed that "God was in Christ reconciling the world unto himself"; they saw him risen from the dead, and they said, "We are witnesses of his resurrection"; they saw him rise into Heaven, and they bore witness that God had taken him up to his right hand. Now, all that believe this witness are saved. "If thou shalt confess with thy mouth the Lord Jesus, and shalt believe in thine heart that God hath raised him from the dead, thou shalt be saved." All who with a simple faith come and cast themselves upon the incarnate God, living and dying for men, and ever sitting at the right hand of God to make intercession for them—these are the people in whom Christ will be glorified and admired at the last great day. But inasmuch as they are first said to be saints, be it never forgotten that this faith must be a living faith, a faith which produces a hatred of sin, a faith which renews the character and shapes the life after the noble model of Christ, thus turning sinners into saints. The two descriptions must not be violently rent asunder; you must not say that the favored people are sanctified without remembering that they are justified by faith, nor may you say that they are justified by faith without remembering that without holiness no man shall see the Lord, and that at the last the people in whom Christ will be admired will be those holy ones who were saved by faith in him.

So far, then, we see our way, but now a question arises: *by whom* will Christ be thus glorified and admired? He shines *in* his people, but who will see the glory? I answer first, that his people will see it. Every saint will glorify Christ in himself, and admire Christ in himself. He will say, "What a wonder that such a poor creature as I am should be thus perfected! How glorious is my Lord, who has wrought this miracle upon me!" Surely our consciousness of having been cleansed and made holy will cause us to fulfill those words of John Berridge which we sang just now—

> He cheers them with eternal smile,
> They sing hosannas all the while;
> Or, overwhelm'd with rapture sweet,
> Sink down adoring at his feet.

This I know, that when I personally enter Heaven, I shall forever admire and adore the everlasting love which brought me there. Yes, we will all glorify and admire our Savior for what he has wrought in us by his infinite grace.

The saints will also admire Christ in one another. As I shall see you and you shall see your brethren and sisters in Christ all perfect, you will be filled with wonderment, and gratitude, and delight. You will be free from all envy there, and therefore you will rejoice in all the beauty of your fellow saints: their Heaven will be a Heaven to you, and what a multitude of heavens you will have as you will joy in the joy of all the redeemed! We shall as much admire the Lord's handiwork in others as in ourselves, and shall each one praise him for saving all the rest. You will see your Lord in all your brethren, and this will make you praise and adore him world without end with a perpetual amazement of ever-growing delight.

But that will not be all. Besides the blood-bought and ransomed of Christ there will be on that great day of his coming, all the holy angels to stand by and look on and wonder. They marveled much when first he stooped from Heaven to earth, and they desired to look into those things, which then were a mystery to them. But when they shall see their beloved Prince come back with ten thousand times ten thousand of the ransomed at his feet, all of them made perfect by having washed their robes and made them white in his blood, how the principalities and powers will admire him in every one of his redeemed! How they will praise that conquering arm which has brought home all these spoils from the war! How will the hosts of Heaven shout his praises as they see him lead all these captives captive with a new captivity, in chains of love, joyfully gracing his triumph and showing forth the completeness of his victory!

We do not know what other races of innocent creatures there may be, but I think it is no stretch of imagination to believe that, as this world is only one speck in the creation of God, there may be millions of other races in the countless worlds around us, and all these may be invited to behold the wonders of redeeming love as manifested in the saints in the day of the Lord. I seem to see these unfallen intelligences encompassing the saints as a cloud of witnesses, and in rapt vision beholding in them the love and grace of the redeeming Lord. What songs! What shouts shall rise from all these to the praise of the ever blessed God! What an orchestra of praise will the universe become! From star to star the holy hymn shall roll, till all space shall ring out the hosannas of wondering spirits. "The Wonderful, the Counselor, the Mighty God, the Everlasting Father, the Prince of Peace," shall have brought home all the men wondered at, and they with himself shall be the wonder of eternity.

Then shall Satan and his defeated legions, and the lost spirits of ungodly men, bite their lips with envy and rage, and tremble at the majesty of Jesus in that day. By their confessed defeat and manifest despair they shall glorify him in his people, in whom they have been utterly overthrown. They shall see that there is not one lost whom he redeemed by blood, not one snatched away of all the sheep his Father gave him, not one warrior enlisted beneath his banner fallen in the day of battle, but all more than conquerors through him that loved them. What despair shall seize upon diabolic spirits as they discover their entire defeat! Defeated in men who were once their slaves! Poor dupes whom they could so easily beguile by their craftiness—defeated even in these! Jesus triumphant by taking the lambs from between the lion's jaws, and rescuing his feeble sheep from their power, will utterly put them to shame in his redeemed. With what anguish will they sink into the Hell prepared for them, because now they hear with anger all earth and Heaven and every star ringing with the shout, "Hallelujah, Hallelujah, Hallelujah, for the Lord God omnipotent reigneth, and the Lamb hath conquered by his blood."

You see then that there are enough spectators to magnify Christ in his saints; and so, fourthly, let us inquire *in what degree* will the Lord Jesus be glorified? Our answer is, it will be to the very highest degree. He shall come to be glorified in his saints to the utmost, for this is clear from the words, "to be admired." When our translation was made, the word "admired" had to ordinary Englishmen a stronger flavor of wonder than it has to us now. We often speak of admiring a thing in the softer sense of loving it, but the real meaning of the English word, and of the Greek also, is *wonder*: our Lord will be wondered at in all them that believe. Those who look upon the saints will feel a sudden wonderment of sacred delight; they will be startled with the surprising glory of the Lord's work in them; "We thought He would do great things, but this! This surpasseth conception!" Every saint will be a wonder to himself. "I thought my bliss would be great, but not like this!" All his brethren will be a wonder to the perfected believer. He will say,

> I thought the saints would be perfect, but I never imagined such a transfiguration of excessive glory would be put upon each of them. I could not have imagined my Lord to be so good and gracious.

The angels in Heaven will say that they never anticipated such deeds of grace: they did know that he had undertaken a great work, but they did not know that he would do so much *for* his people and *in* his people. The first-born sons of light, used to great marvels from of old, will be entranced with a new wonder as they see the handiwork of Immanuel's free grace and dying love. The men who once despised the saints, who called them canting hypocrites and trampled on them, and perhaps slew them, the kings and princes of the earth who sold the righteous for a pair of shoes, what will they say when they see the least of the Savior's followers become a prince of more illustrious rank than the great ones of the earth, and Christ shining out in everyone of these favored beings? For their uplifting, Jesus will be wondered at by those who once despised both him and them.

My next point leads us into the very bowels of the subject; *in what respects* will Christ be glorified and wondered at? I cannot expect to tell you one tenth part of it. I am only going to give you a little sample of what this must mean; exhaustive exposition were quite impossible to me. I think with regard to his saints, that Jesus will be glorified and wondered at on account of their number—"a number that no man can number." John was a great arithmetician, and he managed to count up to one hundred and forty-four thousand of all the tribes of the children of Israel; but that was only a representative number for the Jewish church: as for the church of God, comprehending the Gentile nations, he gave up all idea of computation, and confessed that it is "a number which no man can number." When he heard them sing he says, "I heard a voice like the voice of many waters and like great thunder." There were so many of them that their song was like the Mediterranean sea lashed to fury by a tempest, nay, not one great sea in uproar, but ocean upon ocean, the Atlantic and the Pacific piled upon each other, and the Arctic upon these, and other oceans upon these, layers of oceans, all thundering out their mightiest roar: and such will be the song of the redeemed, for the crowds which swell the matchless hymn will be beyond all reckoning. Behold, and see, ye who laughed at his kingdom, see how the little one has become a thousand. Now look ye, ye foes of Christ, who saw the handful of corn on the top of the mountains; see how the fruit thereof doth shake like Lebanon, and they of the city do flourish like grass of the earth. Who can reckon the drops of the dew or the sands on the sea shore? When they have counted these then shall they not have guessed at the multitude of the redeemed that Christ shall bring to glory. And all this harvest from one grain of wheat, which, except it had fallen into the ground and died, would have remained alone! What said the Word? "If it die, it shall bring forth much fruit." Is not the prophecy fulfilled? Oh beloved, what a harvest from the lone Man of Nazareth! What fruit from that glorious man—the Branch! Men esteemed him stricken, smitten of God and afflicted; and they made nothing of him, and yet there sprang of him (and he as good as dead) these multitudes which are many as the stars of Heaven. Is he not glorified and wondered at in them? The day shall declare it without fail.

But there is quality as well as quantity. He is admired in his saints because they are, every one of them, proofs of his power to save from evil. My eye can hardly bear, even though it be but in imagination, to gaze upon the glittering ranks of the white-robed ones, where each one outshines the sun, and they are all as if a sevenfold midday had clothed them. Yet all these, as I look at them, tell me, "We have washed our robes—for they were once defiled. We have made them white—but this whiteness is caused by the blood of the Lamb." These were heirs of wrath even as others, these were dead in trespasses and sins; all these like sheep had gone astray and turned everyone to his own way; but look at them and see how he has saved them, washed them, cleansed them, perfected them! His power and grace are seen in all of them. If your eye will pause here and there you will discover some that were supremely stubborn, whose neck was as an iron sinew, and yet he conquered them by love. Some were densely ignorant, but he opened their blind eyes; some grossly infected with the leprosy of lust, but he healed them; some under Satan's most terrible power, but he cast the devil out of them. Oh, how he will be glorified in special cases! In you, drunkard made into a saint, in you, blasphemer turned into a loving disciple, in you, persecutor who breathed out threatening, taught to sing everlastingly a hymn of praise! He will be exceedingly glorified in such. Brethren, beloved in the Lord, in each one of us there was some special difficulty as to our salvation, some impossibility which was possible with God, though it would have been forever impossible with us.

Remember, also, that all those saints made perfect would have been in Hell had it not been for the Son's atoning sacrifice. This they will remember the more vividly, because they will see other men condemned for the sins with which they also were once polluted. The crash of vengeance upon the ungodly will make the saints magnify the Lord the more as they see themselves delivered. They will each feel—

> Oh were it not for grace divine,
> That fate so dreadful had been mine.

In each one, the memory of the horrible pit whence they were drawn and the miry clay out of which they were uplifted shall make their Savior more glorified and wondered at.

Perhaps the chief point in which Christ will be glorified, will be the absolute perfection of all the saints. They shall then be "without spot or wrinkle or any such thing." We have not experienced what perfection is, and therefore we can hardly conceive it; our thoughts themselves are too sinful for us to get a full idea of what absolute perfection must be; but, dear brethren, we shall have no sin left in us, for they are "without fault before the throne of God," and we shall have no remaining propensity to sin. There shall be no bias in the will towards that which is evil, but it shall be fixed forever upon that which is good. The affections will never be wanton again, they will be chaste for Christ. The understanding will never make mistakes. You shall never put bitter for sweet, nor sweet for bitter; you shall be "perfect, even as your Father which is in Heaven is perfect": and truly, brethren, he who worketh this in us will be a wonder. Christ will be admired and adored because of this grand result. O mighty Master, with what strange moral alchemy didst thou work to turn that morose dispositioned man into a mass of love! How didst thou work to lift that selfish Mammonite up from his hoarded gains to make him find his gain in thee? How didst thou overcome that proud spirit, that fickle spirit, that lazy spirit, that lustful spirit—how didst thou contrive to take all these away? How didst thou extirpate [destroy] the very roots of sin, and every little rootlet of sin, out of thy redeemed, so that not a tiny fiber can be found? "The sins of Jacob shall be sought for and they shall not be found, yea, they shall not be, saith the Lord." Neither the guilt of sin nor the propensity to sin—both shall be gone, and Christ shall have done it, and he will be "glorified in his saints, and admired in them that believe."

This is but the beginning, however. There will be seen in every saint, in that last wondrous day, the wisdom and power and love of Christ in having brought them through all the trials of the way. He kept their faith alive when else it would have died out; he sustained them under trials when else they would have fainted; he held them fast in their integrity when temptation solicited them, and they had almost slipped with their feet. Ay, he sustained some of them in prison, and on the rack, and at the stake, and held them faithful still! One might hardly wish to be a martyr, but I reckon that the martyrs will be the admiration of us all, or rather Christ will be admired in them. However they could bear such pain as some of them did endure for Christ's sake, none of us can guess, except that we know that Christ was in them, suffering in his members. Eternally will Jesus be wondered at in them as all intelligent spirits shall see how he upheld them, so that neither tribulation, nor distress, nor nakedness, nor famine, nor sword, could separate them from his love. These are the men that wandered about in sheep-skins and goat-skins, destitute, afflicted, tormented, of whom the world was not worthy, but now they stand arrayed as kings and priests in surpassing glory forever. Verily, their Lord shall be admired in them. Say you not so?

Recollect, dear friends, that we shall see in that day how the blessed Christ, as "Head over all things to his church," has ruled every providence to the sanctification of his people—how the dark days begat showers which made the plants of the Lord to grow, how the fierce sun which threatened to scorch them to the root, filled them with warmth of love divine and ripened their choice fruit. What a tale the saints will have to tell of how that which threatened to damp the fire of grace made it burn more mightily, how the stone which threatened to kill their faith was turned into bread for them, how the rod and staff of the Good Shepherd was ever with them to bring them safely home. I have sometimes thought that if I get into Heaven by the skin of my teeth, I will sit down on the glory-shore and bless forever him who, on a board, or on a broken piece of the ship, brought my soul safe to land; and surely they who obtain an abundant entrance, coming into the fair havens, like a ship in full sail, without danger of shipwreck, will have to praise the Lord that they thus came into the blessed port of peace: in each case the Lord will be specially glorified and admired.

I cannot stop over this, but I must beg you to notice that as a king is glorious in his regalia, so will Christ put on his saints as his personal splendor in that day when he shall make up his jewels. It is with Christ as it was with that noble Roman matron, who, when she called at her friends' houses and saw their trinkets, asked them to come next day to her house, and she would exhibit her jewels. They expected to see ruby, and pearl, and diamond, but she called in her two boys, and said, "These are my jewels." Even so will Jesus, instead of emerald and amethyst, onyx and topaz, exhibit his saints. "These are my choice treasures," saith he, "in whom I will be glorified." Solomon surely was never more full of glory than when he had finished the temple, when all the tribes came together to see the noble structure, and confessed it to be "beautiful for situation, the joy of the whole earth." But what will be the glory of Christ when all the living stones shall be put into their places and his church shall have her windows of agates and her gates of carbuncle, and all her borders of precious stones. Then, indeed, will he be glorified, when the twelve foundations of his new Jerusalem shall be courses of stones most precious, the like of which was never seen.

Now, inasmuch as my text lays special stress upon *believing*, I invite you just for a minute to consider how as believers, as well as saints, the saved ones will glorify their Lord.

First, it will be wonderful that there should be so many brought to faith in him: men with no God, and men with many gods, men steeped in ignorance, and men puffed up with carnal wisdom, great men and poor men, all brought to believe in the one Redeemer and praise him for his great salvation. Will he not be glorified in their common faith? It will magnify him that these will all be saved by faith, and not by their own merits. Not one among them will boast that he was saved by his own good works, but all of them will rejoice to have been saved by that blessedly simple way of "Believe and live," saved by sovereign grace through the atoning blood, looked to by the tearful eye of simple faith. This, too, shall make Jesus glorious, that all of them, weak as they were, were made strong by faith; all of them personally unfit for battle were yet made triumphant in conflict because by faith they overcame through the blood of the Lamb. All of them shall be there to show that their faith was honored, that Christ was faithful to his promise, and never allowed them to believe in vain. All of them standing in heavenly places, saved by faith, will ascribe every particle of the glory to the Lord Jesus only:

> *I ask them whence their victory came?*
> *They, with united breath,*
> *Ascribe their conquest to the Lamb,*
> *Their triumph to his death.*

They believed and were saved, but faith taketh no credit to itself; it is a self-denying grace, and putteth the crown upon the head of Christ, and therefore is it written that he will be glorified in his saints, and he will also be admired in all them that believe.

I have scarcely skirted the subject even now, and time is falling me. I want you to reflect that Jesus will be glorified in the risen bodies of all his saints. Now, in Heaven, they are pure spirits, but when he shall come they shall be clothed again. Poor body, thou must sleep awhile, but what thou shalt be at thine awaking doth not yet appear. Thou art now the shriveled seed, but there is a flower to come of thee which shall be lovely beyond all thought. Though sown in weakness, this body shall be raised in power; though sown in corruption, it shall be raised in incorruption. Weakness, weariness, pain, and death will be banished forever; infirmity and deformity will be all unknown. The Lord will raise up our bodies to be like unto his glorious body. Oh, what a prospect lies before us! Let us remember that this blessed resurrection will come to us because he rose, for there must be a resurrection to the members because the Head has risen. Oh, the charm of being a risen man perfect in body, soul, and spirit! All that charm will be due to Christ, and therefore he will be admired in us.

Then let us think of the absolute perfection of the church as to numbers: all who have believed in him will be with him in glory. The text saith, he will be "admired in *all* them that believe." Now, if some of those who believe perished, he would not be admired in them, but they will all be there, the little ones as well as the great ones. You will be there, you poor feeble folk who when you say "Lord, I believe," are obliged to add "help thou mine unbelief." He shall be admired in all believers without a single exception, and peradventure there shall be more wonder at the going to Heaven of the weak believers than at the stronger ones. Mr. Greatheart, when he comes there, will owe his victories to his Master and lay his laurels at his feet; but fainting Feeblemind, and limping Ready-to-Halt with his crutches, and trembling Little-Faith, when they enter into rest, will make Heaven ring with notes of even greater admiration that such poor creeping worms of the earth should win the day by mighty grace. Suppose that one of them should be missing at last! Stop the harps! Silence the songs! No beginning to be merry while one child is shut out! I am quite certain if as a family we were going to sing our evening hymn of joy and thankfulness, if mother said, "Where is the little mite? Where is the last one of the family?" There would be a pause. If we had to say—she is lost, there would be no singing and no resting till she was found. It is the glory of Jesus that as a shepherd he has lost none of his flock, as the Captain of salvation he has brought many sons to glory, and has lost none, and hence he is admired, not in *some* that believe, nor yet in *all but one*, but he is "admired in *all* them that believe."

Does not this delight you, you who are weak and trembling, that he will be admired in you? There is little to admire in you at present, as you penitently confess; but since Christ is in you now, and will be more fully manifested in you, there will ere long be much to admire. May you partake in the excellence of our divine Lord and be conformed to his likeness, that he may be seen in you and glorified in you.

Another point of admiration will be the eternal safety of all his believing people. There they are safe from fear of harm. Ye dogs of Hell, you howled at their heels and hoped to devour them; but, lo, they are clean escaped from you! What must it be to be lifted above gun-shot of the enemy, where no more watch shall need to be kept, for even the roar of the Satanic artillery cannot be heard? Oh glorious Christ, to bring them all to such a state of safety, thou art indeed to be wondered at forever.

Moreover, all the saints will be so honored, so happy, and so like their Lord, that themselves and everything about them will be themes for never-ending admiration. You may have seen a room hung round with mirrors, and when you stood in the midst you were reflected from every point: you were seen here, and seen there, and there again, and there again, and so every part of you was reflected; just such is Heaven. Jesus is the center, and all his saints like mirrors reflect his glory. Is he human? So are they! Is he the Son of God? So are they sons of God! Is he perfect? So are they! Is he exalted? So are they! Is he a prophet? So are they, making known unto principalities and powers the manifold wisdom of God. Is he a priest? So are they! Is he a King? So are they, for he hath made us priests and kings unto God, and we shall reign forever and ever. Look where you will along the ranks of the redeemed, this one thing shall be seen, the glory of Christ Jesus, even to surprise and wonder.

II. I have no time to make those *suggestions* with which I intended to have finished, and so I will just tell you what they would have been.

First, the text suggests that the principal subject for self-examination with us all should be—"Am I a saint? Am I holy? Am I a believer in Christ?" Yes or no, for on that yes or no must hang your glorification of Christ, or your banishment from his presence.

The next thing is—observe the small value of human opinion. When Christ was here the world reckoned him to be a nobody, and while his people are here they must expect to be judged in the same way. What do worldlings know about it? How soon will their judgment be reversed! When our Lord shall appear, even those who sneered will be compelled to admire. When they shall see the glory of Christ in every one of his people, awe-stricken, they will have nothing to say against us; nay, not even the false tongue of malicious slander shall dare to hiss out a serpent word in that day. Never mind them, then; put up with reproach which shall so soon be silenced.

The next suggestion is a great encouragement to enquirers who are seeking Christ; for I put it to you, you great sinners, if Jesus is to be glorified in saved sinners, would he not be glorified indeed if he saved you? If he were ever to save such a rebel as you have been, would it not be the astonishment of eternity? I mean you who are known in the village as Wicked Jack, or known as a common swearer—what if my Master were to make a saint of you! Bad raw material! Yet suppose he transformed you into a precious jewel, and made you to be as holy as God is holy, what would you say of him? "Say of him?" say you: "I would praise him world without end." Yes, and you shall do so if you will come and trust him. Put your trust in him. The Lord help you to do so at once, and he shall be admired even in you forever and ever.

Our text gives an exhortation to believers also. Will Jesus Christ be honored and glorified in all the saints? Then let us think well of them all, and love them all. Some dear children of God have uncomely bodies, or they are blind or deformed, or maimed; and many of these have scanty purses, and it may be the church knows most of them as coming for alms: moreover, they have little knowledge, little power to please, and they are uncouth in manners, and belong to what are called the lowest ranks of society: do not, therefore, despise them, for one day our Lord will be glorified in them. How he will be admired in yonder poor bedridden woman when she rises from the workhouse to sing "hallelujah" to God and the Lamb among the brightest of the shining ones. Why, methinks the pain, the poverty, the weakness, and the sorrow of saints below will greatly glorify the Captain of their salvation, as they tell how grace helped them to bear their burdens and to rejoice under their afflictions.

Lastly, brethren, this text ought to encourage all of you who love Jesus to go on talking about him to others and bearing your testimony for his name. You see how the apostle Paul has inserted a few words by way of parenthesis. Draw the words out of the brackets, and take them home, "Because our testimony among you was believed." Do you see those crowds of idolatrous heathen, and do you see those hosts of saved ones before the throne? What is the medium which linked the two characters? By what visible means did the sinners become saints? Do you see that insignificant looking man with weak eyes? That man whose bodily presence is weak and whose speech is contemptible? Do you not see his bodkin and needle case? He has been making and mending tents, for he is only a tent-maker. Now, those bright spirits which shine like suns, flashing forth Christ's glory, were made thus bright through the addresses and prayers of that tent-maker. The Thessalonians were heathens plunged in sin, and this poor tent-maker came in among them and told them of Jesus Christ and his gospel; his testimony was believed; that belief changed the lives of his hearers and made them holy, and they, being renewed, came at length to be perfectly holy, and there they are, and Jesus Christ is glorified in them. Beloved, will it not be a delightful thing throughout eternity to contemplate that you went into your Sunday-school class this afternoon, and you were afraid you could not say much, but you talked about Jesus Christ with a tear in your eye, and you brought a dear girl to believe in his saving name through your testimony. In years to come that girl will be among those that shine out to the glory of Christ forever. Or you will get away this evening, perhaps, to talk in a lodging-house to some of those poor, despised tramps; you will go and tell one of those poor vagrants, or one of the fallen women, the story of your Lord's love and blood, and the poor broken heart will catch at the gracious word, and come to Jesus, and then a heavenly character will be begun, and another jewel secured for the Reedemer's diadem. Methinks you will admire his crown all the more because, as you see certain stones sparkling in it, you will say, "Blessed be his name forever: he helped me to dive into the sea and find that pearl for him," and now it adorns his sacred brow. Now, get at it, all of you! You that are doing nothing for Jesus, be ashamed of yourselves, and ask him to work in you that you may begin to work for him, and unto God shall be the glory, forever and ever. Amen and amen.

The Ascension and the Second Advent Practically Considered

Delivered on Lord's Day morning, December 28, 1884, at the Metropolitan Tabernacle, Newington. No. 1817.

And while they looked steadfastly toward Heaven as he went up, behold, two men stood by them in white apparel; which also said, "Ye men of Galilee, why stand ye gazing up into Heaven? This same Jesus, which is taken up from you into Heaven, shall so come in like manner as ye have seen him go into Heaven."—Acts 1:10–11

Four great events shine out brightly in our Savior's story. All Christian minds delight to dwell upon his birth, his death, his resurrection, and his ascension. These make four rounds in that ladder of light, the foot of which is upon the earth, but the top whereof reacheth to Heaven. We could not afford to dispense with any one of those four events, nor would it be profitable for us to forget, or to under-estimate the value of any one of them. That the Son of God was born of a woman creates in us the intense delight of a brotherhood springing out of a common humanity. That Jesus once suffered unto the death for our sins, and thereby made a full atonement for us, is the rest and life of our spirits. The manger and the cross together are divine seals of love. That the Lord Jesus rose again from the dead is the warrant of our justification, and also a transcendently delightful assurance of the resurrection of all his people, and of their eternal life in him. Hath he not said, "Because I live, ye shall live also"? The resurrection of Christ is the morning star of our future glory. Equally delightful is the remembrance of his ascension. No song is sweeter than this—

> Thou hast ascended on high; thou hast led captivity captive, thou hast received gifts for men, yea, for the rebellious also, that the Lord God might dwell among them.

Each one of those four events points to another, and they all lead up to it: the fifth link in the golden chain is our Lord's second and most glorious advent. Nothing is mentioned between his ascent and his descent. True, a rich history comes between; but it lies in a valley between two stupendous mountains: we step from alp to alp as we journey in meditation from the Ascension to the Second Advent. I say that each of the previous four events points to it. Had he not come a first time in humiliation, born under the law, he could not have come a second time in amazing glory "without a sin-offering unto salvation." Because he died once, we rejoice that he dieth no more, death hath no more dominion over him, and therefore he cometh to destroy that last enemy whom he hath already conquered. It is our joy, as we think of our Redeemer as risen, to feel that, in consequence of his rising, the trump of the archangel shall assuredly sound for the awaking of all his slumbering people, when the Lord himself shall descend from Heaven with a shout. As for his ascension, he could not a second time descend if he had not first ascended; but having perfumed Heaven with his presence, and prepared a place for his people, we may fitly expect that he will come again and receive us unto himself, that where he is, there we may be also. I want you, therefore—as in contemplation you pass with joyful footsteps over these four grand events, as your faith leaps from his birth to his death, and from his resurrection to his ascension—to be looking forward, and even hastening unto this crowning fact of our Lord's history; for ere long he shall so come in like manner as he was seen go up into Heaven.

This morning, in our meditation, we will start from the ascension; and if I had sufficient imagination I should like to picture our Lord and the eleven walking up the side of Olivet, communing as they went—a happy company, with a solemn awe upon them, but with an intense joy in having fellowship with each other. Each disciple was glad to think that his dear Lord and Master who had been crucified was now among them, not only alive but surrounded with a mysterious safety and glory which none could disturb. The enemy was as still as a stone: not a dog moved his tongue: his bitterest foes made no sign during the days of our Lord's after-life below. The company moved onward peacefully towards Bethany—Bethany which they all knew and loved. The Savior seemed drawn there at the time of his ascension, even as men's minds return to old and well-loved scenes when they are about to depart out of this world. His happiest moments on earth had been spent beneath the roof where lived Mary and Martha and their brother Lazarus. Perhaps it was best for the disciples that he should leave them at that place where he had been most hospitably entertained, to show that he departed in peace and not in anger. There they had seen Lazarus raised from the dead by him who was now to be taken up from them: the memory of the triumphant past would help the tried faith of the present. There they had heard the voice saying, "Loose him, and let him go," and there they might fitly see their Lord loosed from all bonds of earthly gravitation, that he might go to his Father and their Father. The memories of the place might help to calm their minds and arouse their spirits to that fullness of joy which ought to attend the glorifying of their Lord.

But they have come to a standstill, having reached the brow of the hill. The Savior stands conspicuously in the center of the group, and, following upon most instructive discourse, he pronounces a blessing upon them. He lifts his pierced hands, and while he is lifting them and is pronouncing words of love, he begins to rise from the earth. He has risen above them all, to their astonishment! In a moment he has passed beyond the olives, which seem with their silvery sheen to be lit up by his milder radiance. While the disciples are looking, the Lord has ascended into mid-air, and speedily he has risen to the regions of the clouds. They stand spell-bound with astonishment, and suddenly a bright cloud, like a chariot of God, bears him away. That cloud conceals him from mortal gaze. Though we have known Christ after the flesh, now after the flesh, know we him no more. They are riveted to the spot, very naturally so: they linger long in the place, they stand with streaming eyes, wonder-struck, still looking upward.

It is not the Lord's will that they should long remain inactive; their reverie is interrupted. They might have stood there till wonder saddened into fear. As it was, they remained long enough; for the angel's words may be accurately rendered, "Why have ye stood, gazing up into Heaven?"

Their lengthened gaze needed to be interrupted, and, therefore, two shining ones, such as aforetime met the women at the sepulcher, are sent to them. These messengers of God appear in human form that they may not alarm them, and in white raiment as if to remind them that all was bright and joyous; and these white-robed ministers stood with them as if they would willingly join their company. As no one of the eleven would break silence, the men in white raiment commenced the discourse. Addressing them in the usual celestial style, they asked a question which contained its own answer, and then went on to tell their message. As they had once said to the women, "Why seek ye the living among the dead? He is not here, but is risen;" so did they now say, "Ye men of Galilee, why stand ye gazing up into Heaven? This same Jesus, which is taken up from you into Heaven, shall so come in like manner as ye have seen him go into Heaven." The angels showed their knowledge of them by calling them "men of Galilee," and reminded them that they were yet upon earth by recalling their place of birth. Brought back to their senses, their reverie over, the apostles at once gird up their loins for active service; they do not need twice telling, but hasten to Jerusalem. The vision of angels has, singularly enough, brought them back into the world of actual life again, and they obey the command, "Tarry ye at Jerusalem." They seem to say,

> The taking up of our Master is not a thing to weep about: he has gone to his throne and to his glory, and he said it was expedient for us that he should go away. He will now send us the promise of the Father; we scarcely know what it will be like, but let us, in obedience to his will, make the best of our way to the place where he bade us await the gift of power.

Do you not see them going down the side of Olivet, taking that Sabbath-day's journey into the cruel and wicked city without a thought of fear; having no dread of the bloodthirsty crew who slew their Lord, but happy in the memory of their Lord's exaltation, and in the expectation of a wonderful display of his power. They held fellowship of the most delightful kind with one another, and anon [eventually] entered into the upper room, where, in protracted prayer and communion, they waited for the promise of the Father. You see I have no imagination: I have barely mentioned the incidents in the simplest language. Yet try and realize the scene, for it will be helpful so to do, since our Lord Jesus is to come in like manner as the disciples saw him go up into Heaven.

My first business this morning will be to consider *the gentle chiding* administered by the shining ones—"Ye men of Galilee, why stand ye gazing up unto Heaven?" Secondly, *the cheering description* of our Lord which the white-robed messengers used—"This same Jesus"; and then, thirdly, *the practical truth* which they taught—"This same Jesus, which is taken up from you into Heaven, shall so come in like manner as ye have seen him go into Heaven."

I. First, then, here is *a gentle chiding.*

It is not sharply uttered by men dressed in black, who use harsh speech and upbraid the servants of God severely for what was rather a mistake than a fault. No; the language is strengthening, yet tender: the fashion of a question allows them rather to reprove themselves than to be reproved; and the tone is that of brotherly love, and affectionate concern.

Notice, that *what these saintly men were doing seems, at first sight, to be very right.* Methinks, if Jesus were among us now, we would fix our eyes upon him, and never withdraw them. He is altogether lovely, and it would seem wicked to yield our eyesight to any inferior object so long as he was to be seen. When he ascended up into Heaven it was the duty of his friends to look upon him. It can never be wrong to look up; we are often bidden to do so, and it is even a holy saying of the Psalmist, "I will direct my prayer unto thee, and will look up"; and, again, "I will lift up mine eyes unto the hills, from whence cometh my help." If it be right to look up into Heaven, it must be still more right to look up while Jesus rises to the place of his glory. Surely it had been wrong if they had looked anywhere else—it was due to the Lamb of God that they should behold him as long as eyes could follow him. He is the Sun: where should eyes be turned but to his light? He is the King; and where should courtiers within the palace gate turn their eyes but to their King as he ascends to his throne?

The truth is, there was nothing wrong in their looking up into Heaven; but they went a little further than looking; they stood "gazing." A little excess in right may be faulty. It may be wise to look, but foolish to gaze. There is a very thin partition sometimes between that which is commendable and that which is censurable. There is a golden mean which it is not easy to keep. The exact path of right is often as narrow as a razor's edge, and he must be wise that doth not err either on the right hand or on the left. "Look" is ever the right word. Why, it is "Look unto me, and be saved." Look, aye, look steadfastly and intently: be your posture that of one "looking unto Jesus," always throughout life. But there is a gazing which is not commendable, when the look becomes not that of reverent worship, but of an overweening curiosity; when there mingles with the desire to know what should be known, a prying into that which it is for God's glory to conceal. Brethren, it is of little use to look up into an empty Heaven. If Christ himself be not visible in Heaven, then in vain do we gaze, since there is nothing for a saintly eye to see. When the person of Jesus was gone out of the azure vault above them, and the cloud had effectually concealed him, why should they continue to gaze when God himself had drawn the curtain? If infinite wisdom had withdrawn the object upon which they desired to gaze, what would their gazing be but a sort of reflection upon the wisdom which had removed their Lord? Yet it did seem very right. Thus certain things that you and I may do may appear right, and yet we may need to be chidden out of them into something better: they may be right in themselves, but not appropriate for the occasion, not seasonable, nor expedient. They may be right up to a point, and then may touch the boundary of excess. A steadfast gaze into Heaven may be to a devout soul a high order of worship, but if this filled up much of our working time it might become the idlest form of folly.

Yet I cannot help adding that *it was very natural*. I do not wonder that the whole eleven stood gazing up, for if I had been there, I am sure I should have done the same. How struck they must have been with the ascent of the Master out of their midst! You would be amazed if someone from among our own number now began to ascend into Heaven! Would you not? Our Lord did not gradually melt away from sight as a phantom, or dissolve into thin air as a mere apparition: the Savior did not disappear in that way at all, but he rose, and they saw that it was his very self that was so rising. His own body, the materialism in which he had veiled himself, actually, distinctly, and literally, rose to Heaven before their eyes. I repeat, the Lord did not dissolve, and disappear like a vision of the night, but he evidently rose till the cloud intervened so that they could see him no more. I think I should have stood looking to the very place where his cloudy chariot had been. I know it would be idle to continue so to do, but our hearts often urge us on to acts which we could not justify logically. Hearts are not to be argued with. Sometimes you stand by a grave where one is buried whom you dearly loved: you go there often to weep. You cannot help it, the place is precious to you; yet you could not prove that you do any good by your visits, perhaps you even injure yourself thereby, and deserve to be gently chidden with the question, "why?" It may be the most natural thing in the world, and yet it may not be a wise thing. The Lord allows us to do that which is innocently natural, but he will not have us carry it too far; for then it might foster an evil nature. Hence he sends an interrupting messenger: not an angel with a sword, or even a rod; but he sends some man in white raiment—I mean one who is both cheerful and holy—and he, by his conduct or his words, suggests to us the question, "Why stand ye here gazing?" *Cui bono?* What will be the benefit? What will it avail? Thus our understanding being called into action, and we being men of thought, we answer to ourselves, "This will not do. We must not stand gazing here forever," and therefore we arouse ourselves to get back to the Jerusalem of practical life, where, in the power of God, we hope to do service for our Master.

Notice, then, that the disciples were doing that which seemed to be right and what was evidently very natural, but that it is very easy to carry the apparently right and the absolutely natural too far. Let us take heed to ourselves, and often ask our hearts, "Why?"

For, thirdly, notice that *what they did was not, after all, justifiable upon strict reason*. While Christ was going up it was proper that they should adoringly look at him. He might almost have said, "If ye see me when I am taken up, a double portion of my spirit shall rest upon you." They did well to look where he led the way. But when he was gone, still to remain gazing was an act which they could not exactly explain to themselves, and could not justify to others. Put the question thus:

> What purpose will be fulfilled by your continuing to gaze into the sky? He is gone, it is absolutely certain that he is gone. He is taken up, and God himself has manifestly concealed all trace of him by bidding yonder cloud sail in between him and you. Why gaze ye still? He told you, "I go unto my Father." Why stand and gaze?

We may, under the influence of great love, act unwisely. I remember well seeing the action of a woman whose only son was emigrating to a distant colony. I stood in the station, and I noticed her many tears and her frequent embraces of her boy; but the train came up and he entered the carriage. After the train had passed beyond the station, she was foolish enough to break away from friends who sought to detain her; she ran along the platform, leaped down upon the railroad and pursued the flying train. It was natural, but it had been better left undone. What was the use of it? We had better abstain from acts which serve no practical purpose; for in this life we have neither time nor strength to waste in fruitless action. The disciples would be wise to cease gazing, for nobody would be benefited by it, and they would not themselves be blessed. What is the use of gazing when there is nothing to see? Well, then, did the angels ask, "Why stand ye gazing up into Heaven?"

Again, put another question—what precept were they obeying when they stood gazing up into Heaven? If you have a command from God to do a certain thing, you need not inquire into the reason of the command, it is disobedient to begin to canvas God's will; but when there is no precept whatever, why persevere in an act which evidently does not promise to bring any blessing? Who bade them stand gazing up into Heaven? If Christ had done so, then in Christ's name, let them stand like statues and never turn their heads: but as he had not bidden them, why did they do what he had not commanded, and leave undone what he had commanded? For he had strictly charged them that they should tarry at Jerusalem till they were "endued with power from on high." So what they did was not justifiable.

Here is the practical point for us: *what they did, we are very apt to imitate.* "Oh," say you, "I shall never stand gazing up into Heaven." I am not sure of that. Some Christians are very curious, but not obedient. Plain precepts are neglected, but difficult problems they seek to solve. I remember one who used always to be dwelling upon the vials and seals and trumpets. He was great at apocalyptic symbols; but he had seven children, and he had no family prayer. If he had left the vials and trumpets and minded his boys and girls, it would have been a [good] deal better. I have known men marvelously great upon Daniel, and specially instructed in Ezekiel, but singularly forgetful of the twentieth of Exodus,[1] and not very clear upon Romans the eighth.[2] I do not speak with any blame of such folks for studying Daniel and Ezekiel, but quite the reverse; yet I wish they had been more zealous for the conversion of the sinners in their neighborhoods, and more careful to assist the poor saints. I admit the value of the study of the feet of the image in Nebuchadnezzar's vision, and the importance of knowing the kingdoms which make up the ten toes, but I do not see the propriety of allowing such studies to overlay the common-places of practical godliness. If the time spent over obscure theological propositions were given to a mission in the dim alley near the good man's house, more benefit would come to man and more glory to God.

I would have you understand all mysteries, brethren, if you could; but do not forget that our chief business here below is to cry, "Behold the Lamb!" By all manner of means, read and search till you know all that the Lord has revealed concerning things to come; but first of all, see to it that your children are brought to the Savior's feet, and that you

---

[1] Exd. 20: the 10 Commandments.

[2] Rom. 8: on the law and the Spirit in the life of the Christian.

are workers together with God in the upbuilding of his church. The dense mass of misery and ignorance and sin which is round about us on every side demands all our powers; and if you do not respond to the call, though I am not a man in white apparel, I shall venture to say to you, "Ye men of Christendom, why stand ye gazing up into the mysteries when so much is to be done for Jesus, and you are leaving it undone?" O ye who are curious but not obedient, I fear I speak to you in vain, but I have spoken. May the Holy Spirit also speak.

Others are contemplative but not active—much given to the study of Scripture and to meditation thereon, but not zealous for good works. Contemplation is so scarce in these days that I could wish there were a thousand times as much of it; but in the case to which I refer, everything runs in the one channel of thought, all time is spent in reading, in enjoyment, in rapture, in pious leisure. Religion never ought to become the subject of selfishness, and yet I fear some treat it as if its chief end was spiritual gratification. When a man's religion all lies in his saving his own self, and in enjoying holy things for his own self, there is a disease upon him. When his judgment of a sermon is based upon the one question, "Did it feed *me?*" it is a swinish [pig-like] judgment. There is such a thing as getting a swinish religion in which you are yourself first, yourself second, yourself third, yourself to the utmost end. Did Jesus ever think or speak in that fashion? Contemplation of Christ himself may be so carried out as to lead you away from Christ: the recluse meditates on Jesus, but he is as unlike the busy self-denying Jesus as well can be. Meditation, unattended with active service in the spreading of the gospel among men, well deserves the rebuke of the angel, "Ye men of Galilee, why stand ye gazing up into Heaven?"

Moreover, some are careful and anxious and deliriously impatient for some marvelous interposition. We get at times into a sad state of mind, because we do not see the kingdom of Christ advancing as we desire. I suppose it is with you as it is with me—I begin to fret, and I am deeply troubled, and I feel that there is good reason that I should be, for truth is fallen in the streets, and the days of blasphemy and rebuke are upon us. Then we pine; for the Master is away, and we cry, "When will he be back again? Oh, why are his chariots so long in coming? Why tarries he through the ages?" Our desires sour into impatience, and we commence gazing up into Heaven, looking for his coming with a restlessness which does not allow us to discharge our duty as we should. Whenever anybody gets into that state, this is the word, "Ye men of Galilee, why stand ye gazing up into Heaven?"

In certain cases this uneasiness has drawn to itself a wrong expectation of immediate wonders, and an intense desire for sign-seeing. Ah me, what fanaticisms come of this! In America years ago, one came forward who declared that on such a [particular] day the Lord would come, and he led a great company to believe his crazy predictions. Many took their horses and fodder for two or three days, and went out into the woods, expecting to be all the more likely to see all that was to be seen when once away from the crowded city. All over the States there were people who had made ascension-dresses in which to soar into the air in proper costume. They waited, and they waited, and I am sure that no text could have been more appropriate for them than this, "Ye men of America, why stand ye here gazing up into Heaven?" Nothing came of it; and yet there are thousands in England and America who only need a fanatical leader, and they would run into the like folly.

The desire to know the times and seasons is a craze with many poor bodies whose insanity runs in that particular groove. Every occurrence is a "sign of the times": a sign, I may add, which they do not understand. An earthquake is a special favorite with them. "Now," they cry, "the Lord is coming"; as if there had not been earthquakes of the sort we have heard of lately, hundreds of times since our Lord went up into Heaven. When the prophetic earthquakes occur in diverse places, we shall know of it without the warnings of these brethren. What a number of persons have been infatuated by the number of the beast, and have been ready to leap for joy because they have found the number 666 in some great one's name. Why, everybody's name will yield that number if you treat it judiciously, and use the numerals of Greece, Rome, Egypt, China, or Timbuctoo. I feel weary with the silly way in which some people make toys out of Scripture, and play with texts as with a pack of cards.

Whenever you meet with a man who sets up to be a prophet, keep out of his way in the future; and when you hear of signs and wonders, turn you to your Lord, and in patience possess your souls. "The just shall live by his faith." There is no other way of living among wild enthusiasts. Believe in God, and ask not for miracles and marvels, or the knowledge of times and seasons. To know when the Lord will restore the kingdom is not in your power. Remember that verse which I read just now in your hearing—"It is not for you to know the times or the seasons." If I were introduced into a room where a large number of parcels were stored up, and I was told that there was something good for me, I should begin to look for that which had my name upon it, and when I came upon a parcel and I saw in pretty big letters, *"It is not for you,"* I should leave it alone. Here, then, is a casket of knowledge marked, *"It is not for you* to know the times or the seasons, which the Father hath put in his own power." Cease to meddle with matters which are concealed, and be satisfied to know the things which are clearly revealed.

II. Secondly, I want you to notice *the cheering description* **which these bright spirits give concerning our Lord.**

They describe him thus—"This same Jesus."

I appreciate the description the more because *it came from those who knew him.* "He was seen of angels"; they had watched him all his life long, and they knew him, and when they, having just seen him rise to his Father and his God, said of him,

"This same Jesus," then I know by an infallible testimony that he was the same, and that he is the same.

Jesus is gone, but he still exists. He has left us, but he is not dead; he has not dissolved into nothing like the mist of the morning. "This same Jesus" is gone up unto his Father's throne, and he is there today as certainly as he once stood at Pilate's bar. As surely as he did hang upon the cross, so surely does he, the self-same man, sit upon the throne of God and reign over creation. I like to think of the positive identity of the Christ in the seventh Heaven with the Christ in the lowest deeps of agony. The Christ they spat upon is now the Christ whose name the cherubim and seraphim are hymning day without night. The Christ they scourged is he before whom principalities and powers delight to cast their crowns. Think of it and be glad this morning; and do not stand gazing up into Heaven after a myth or a dream. Jesus lives; mind that you live also. Do not loiter as if you had nothing at all to do, or as if the kingdom of God had come to an end because Jesus is gone from the earth, as to his bodily presence. It is not all over; he still lives, and he has given you a work to do till he comes. Therefore, go and do it.

"This same Jesus"—I love that word, for "Jesus" means *a Savior*. Oh, ye anxious sinners here present, the name of him who has gone up into his glory is full of irritation to you! Will you not come to "this same Jesus"? This is he who opened the eyes of the blind and brought forth the prisoners out of the prison-house. He is doing the same thing today. Oh that your eyes may see his light! He that touched the lepers, and that raised the dead, is the same Jesus still, able to save to the uttermost. Oh that you may look and live! You have only to come to him by faith, as she did who touched the hem of his garment; you have but to cry to him as the blind man did whose sight he restored; for he is the same Jesus, bearing about with him the same tender love for guilty men, and the same readiness to receive and cleanse all that come to him by faith.

"This same Jesus." Why, that must have meant that he who is in Heaven is the same Christ who was on earth, but it must also mean that *he who is to come, will be the same Jesus that went up into Heaven.* There is no change in our blessed Master's nature, nor will there ever be. There is a great change in his condition:

> *The Lord shall come, but not the same*
> *As once in lowliness he came,*
> *A humble man before his foes,*
> *A weary man, and full of woes.*

He will be "the same Jesus" in nature though not in condition: he will possess the same tenderness when he comes to judge, the same gentleness of heart when all the glories of Heaven and earth shall gird his brow. Our eye shall see him in that day, and we shall recognize him not only by the nail-prints, but by the very look of his countenance, by the character that gleams from that marvelous face; and we shall say, "'Tis he! 'Tis he! The self-same Christ that went up from the top of Olivet from the midst of his disciples!" Go to him with your troubles, as you would have done when he was here. Look forward to his second coming without dread. Look for him with that joyous expectancy with which you would welcome Jesus of Bethany, who loved Mary, and Martha, and Lazarus.

On the back of that sweet title came this question, "Why stand ye here gazing into Heaven?" They might have said, "We stay here because we do not know where to go. Our Master is gone." But oh, it is the same Jesus, and he is coming again, so go down to Jerusalem and get to work directly. Do not worry yourselves; no grave accident has occurred; it is not a disaster that Christ has gone, but an advance in his work. Despisers tell us nowadays,

> Your cause is done-for! Christianity is spun out! Your divine Christ is gone; we have not seen a trace of his miracle-working hand, nor of that voice which no man could rival.

Here is our answer: We are not standing gazing up into Heaven—we are not paralyzed because Jesus is away. He lives, the great Redeemer lives; and though it is our delight to lift up our eyes because we expect his coming, it is equally our delight to turn our heavenly gazing into an earthward watching, and to go down into the city, and there to tell that Jesus is risen, that men are to be saved by faith in him, and that whosoever believeth in him shall have everlasting life. We are not defeated, far from it: his ascension is not a retreat, but an advance. His tarrying is not for want of power, but because of the abundance of his long-suffering. The victory is not questionable. All things work for it; all the hosts of God are mustering for the final charge. This same Jesus is mounting his white horse to lead forth the armies of Heaven, conquering and to conquer.

III. Our third point is this: *the great practical truth.*

This truth is not one that is to keep us gazing into Heaven, but one that is to make each of us go to his house to render earnest service. What is it?

Why, first, that *Jesus in gone into Heaven.* Jesus is gone! Jesus is gone! It sounds like a knell. Jesus is taken up from you into Heaven!—that sounds like a marriage peal. He is gone, but he is gone up to the hills whence he can survey the battle; up to the throne, from which he can send us succor. The reserve forces of the omnipotent stood waiting till their Captain came, and now that he is come into the center of the universe, he can send legions of angels, or he can raise up hosts of men for the help of his cause. I see every reason for going down into the world and getting to work, for he is gone up into Heaven and "all power is given unto him in Heaven and in earth." Is not that a good argument—"Go ye *therefore* and teach all nations, baptizing them in the name of the Father, and of the Son, and of the Holy Ghost"?

Jesus will come again. That is another reason for girding our loins, because it is clear that he has not quitted the fight, nor deserted the field of battle. Our great Captain is still heading the conflict; he has ridden into another part of the field, but he will be back again, perhaps in the twinkling of an eye. You do not say that a commander has given up the campaign because it is expedient that he should withdraw from your part of the field. Our Lord is doing the best thing for his kingdom in going away. It was in the highest degree expedient that he should go, and that we should each one receive the Spirit. There is a blessed unity between Christ the King and the commonest soldier in the ranks. He has not taken his heart from us, nor his care from us, nor his interest from us: he is bound up heart and soul with his people, and their holy warfare, and this is the evidence of it, "Behold, I come quickly; and my reward is with me, to give every man according as his work shall be."

Then, moreover, we are told in the text—and this in a reason why we should get to our work—*that he is coming in like manner as he departed*. Certain of the commentators do not seem to understand English at all. "He which is taken up from you into Heaven shall so come in like manner as you have seen him go into Heaven,"—this, they say, relates to his spiritual coming at Pentecost. Give anybody a grain of sense, and do they not see that a spiritual coming is not a coming in the same manner in which he went up into Heaven? There is an analogy, but certainly not a likeness between the two things. Our Lord was taken up; they could see him rise: he will come again, and "every eye shall see him." He went up not in spirit, but *in person*: he will come down *in person*. "This same Jesus shall so come in like manner." He went up as a matter of fact: not in poetic figure and spiritual symbol, but as a matter of fact—"This same Jesus" literally went up. "This same Jesus" will literally come again. He will descend in clouds even as he went up in clouds; and "he shall stand at the latter day upon the earth" even as he stood aforetime. He went up to Heaven unopposed; no high priests, nor scribes, nor Pharisees, nor even one of the rabble opposed his ascension; it were ridiculous to suppose that they could; and when he comes a second time, none will stand against him. His adversaries shall perish; as the fat of rams, shall they melt away in his presence. When he cometh he shall break rebellious nations with a rod of iron, for his force shall be irresistible in that day.

Brethren, do not let anybody spiritualize away all this from you. Jesus is coming as a matter of fact, therefore go down to your sphere of service as a matter of fact. Get to work and teach the ignorant, win the wayward, instruct the children, and everywhere tell out the sweet name of Jesus. As a matter of fact, give of your substance and don't talk about it. As a matter of fact, consecrate your daily life to the glory of God. As a matter of fact, live wholly for your Redeemer. Jesus is not coming in a sort of mythical, misty, hazy way—he is literally and actually coming, and he will literally and actually call upon you to give an account of your stewardship. Therefore—now, today; literally, not symbolically; personally, and not by deputy—go out through that portion of the world which you can reach, and preach the gospel to every creature according as you have opportunity.

For this is what the men in white apparel meant—*be ready to meet your coming Lord.* What is the way to be ready to meet Jesus? If it is the same Jesus that went away from us who is coming, then let us be doing what he was doing before he went away. If it is the same Jesus that is coming, we cannot possibly put ourselves into a posture of which he will better approve than by going about doing good. If you would meet him with joy, serve him with earnestness. If the Lord Jesus Christ were to come today, I should like him to find me at my studying, praying, or preaching. Would you not like him to find you in your Sunday-school, in your class, or out there at the corner of the street preaching, or doing whatever you have the privilege of doing in his name? Would you meet your Lord in idleness? Do not think of it. I called one day on one of our members, and she was whitening the front steps. She got up all in confusion; she said, "Oh dear, sir, I did not know you were coming today, or I would have been ready." I replied, "Dear friend, you could not be in better trim than you are: you are doing your duty like a good housewife, and may God bless you." She had no money to spare for a servant, and she was doing her duty by keeping the home tidy: I thought she looked more beautiful with her pail beside her than if she had been dressed according to the latest fashion. I said to her, "When the Lord Jesus Christ comes suddenly, I hope he will find me doing as you were doing, namely, fulfilling the duty of the hour." I want you all to get to your pails without being ashamed of them. Serve the Lord in some way or other; serve him always; serve him intensely; serve him more and more. Go tomorrow and serve the Lord at the counter, or in the workshop, or in the field. Go and serve the Lord by helping the poor and the needy, the widow and the fatherless; serve him by teaching the children, especially by endeavoring to train your own children. Go and hold a temperance meeting, and show the drunkard that there is hope for him in Christ, or go to the midnight meeting and let the fallen woman know that Jesus can restore her. Do what Jesus has given you the power to do, and then, ye men of Britain, ye will not stand gazing up into Heaven, but you will wait upon the Lord in prayer, and you will receive the Spirit of God, and you will publish to all around the doctrine of "Believe and live." Then when he comes he will say to you, "Well done, good and faithful servant, enter thou into the joy of thy Lord." So may his grace enable us to do. Amen.

Coming Judgment of the Secrets of Men

Delivered on Lord's Day morning, June 12, 1885, at the Metropolitan Tabernacle, Newington. No. 1849.

The day when God shall judge the secrets of men, by Jesus Christ, according to my gospel.—Romans 2:16

It is impossible for any of us to tell what it cost the apostle Paul to write the first chapter of the epistle to the Romans. It is a shame even to speak of the things which are done of the vicious in secret places; but Paul felt that it was necessary to break through his shame, and to speak out concerning the hideous vices of the heathen. He has left on record an exposure of the sins of his day which crimsons the cheek of the modest when they read it, and makes both the ears of him that heareth it to tingle. Paul knew that this chapter would be read, not in his age alone, but in all ages, and that it would go into the households of the most pure and godly as long as the world should stand; and yet he deliberately wrote it, and wrote it under the guidance of the Holy Spirit. He knew that it must be written to put to shame the abominations of an age which was almost past shame. Monsters that revel in darkness must be dragged into the open, that they may be withered up by the light. After Paul has thus written in anguish, he bethought himself of his chief comfort. While his pen was black with the words he had written in the first chapter, he was driven to write of his great delight. He cling to the gospel with a greater tenacity than ever. As in the verse before us, [when] he needed to mention the gospel, he did not speak of it as "the gospel," but as *"my gospel."* "God shall judge the secrets of men by Jesus Christ, according to *my gospel.*" He felt that he could not live in the midst of so depraved a people without holding the gospel with both hands, and grasping it as his very own. *"My gospel,"* saith he. Not that Paul was the author of it, not that Paul had an exclusive monopoly of its blessings, but that he had so received it from Christ himself, and regarded himself as so responsibly put in trust with it, that he could not disown it even for an instant. So fully had he taken it into himself that he could not do less than call it "my gospel." In another place he speaks of "our gospel"; thus using a possessive pronoun, to show how believers identify themselves with the truth which they preach. He had a gospel, a definite form of truth, and he believed in it beyond all doubt; and therefore he spoke of it as "my gospel." Herein we hear the voice of faith, which seems to say,

> Though others reject it, I am sure of it, and allow no shade of mistrust to darken my mind. To me it is glad tidings of great joy: I hail it as "my gospel." If I be called a fool for holding it, I am content to be a fool, and to find all my wisdom in my Lord.
>
> *Should all the forms that men devise*
> *Assault my faith with treacherous art,*
> *I'd call them vanity and lies,*
> *And bind the gospel to my heart.*

Is not this word "my gospel" the voice of love? Does he not by this word embrace the gospel as the only love of his soul—for the sake of which he had suffered the loss of all things, and did count them but dung—for the sake of which he was willing to stand before Nero, and proclaim, even in Caesar's palace, the message from Heaven? Though each word should cost him a life, he was willing to die a thousand deaths for the holy cause. "My gospel," saith he, with a rapture of delight, as he presses to his bosom the sacred deposit of truth.

"My gospel." Does not this show his courage? As much as to say, "I am not ashamed of the gospel of Christ: for it is the power of God onto salvation to everyone that believeth." He says, "my gospel," as a soldier speaks of "my colors," or of "my king." He resolves to bear this banner to victory, and to serve this royal truth even to the death.

"My gospel." There is a touch of discrimination about the expression. Paul perceives that there are other gospels, and he makes short work with them, for he saith, "Though we, or an angel from Heaven, preach any other gospel unto you than that which we have preached unto you, let him be accursed." The apostle was of a gentle spirit; he prayed heartily for the Jews who persecuted him, and yielded his life for the conversion of the Gentiles who maltreated him; but he had no tolerance for false gospellers. He exhibited great breadth of mind, and to save souls he became all things to all men; but when he contemplated any alteration or adulteration of the gospel of Christ, he thundered and lightened without measure. When he feared that something else might spring up among the philosophers, or among the Judaizers, that should hide a single beam of the glorious Sun of Righteousness, he used no measured language; but cried concerning the author of such a darkening influence, "Let him be accursed." Every heart that would see men blessed whispers an "Amen" to the apostolic malediction. No greater curse can come upon mankind than the obscuration of the gospel of Jesus Christ. Paul saith of himself and his true brethren, "We are not as many, which corrupt the word of God"; and he cries to those who turned aside from the one and only gospel, "O foolish Galatians, who hath bewitched you?" Of all new doctrines he speaks as of "another gospel, which is not another; but there be some that trouble you."

As for myself, looking at the matter afresh, amidst all the filthiness which I see in the world at this day, I lay hold upon the pure and blessed Word of God, and call it all the more earnestly, my gospel—mine in life and mine in death, mine against all comers, mine forever, God helping me: with emphasis—"my gospel."

Now let us notice what it was that brought up this expression, "my gospel." What was Paul preaching about? Certainly not upon any of the gentle and tender themes, which we are told nowadays ought to occupy all our time; but he is speaking of the terrors of the law, and in that connection he speaks of "my gospel."

Let us come at once to our text. It will need no dividing, for it divides itself. First, let us consider that *on a certain day God shall judge mankind;* secondly, *on that day God will judge the secrets of men;* thirdly, when he judges the secrets of men, *it will be by Jesus Christ;* and fourthly, *this is according to the gospel.*

I. We begin with the solemn truth, that *on a certain day God will judge men.*

A judgment is going on daily. God is continually holding court, and considering the doings of the sons of men. Every evil deed that they do is recorded in the register of doom, and each good action is remembered and laid up in store by God. That judgment is reflected in a measure in the consciences of men. Those who know the gospel, and those who know it not, alike, have a certain measure of light, by which they know right from wrong; their consciences all the while accusing or else excusing them. This session of the heavenly court continues from day to day, like that of our local magistrates; but this does not prevent but rather necessitates the holding of an ultimate great assize.

As each man passes into another world, there is an immediate judgment passed upon him; but this is only the foreshadowing of that which will take place in the end of the world.

There is a judgment also passing upon nations, for as nations will not exist as nations in another world, they have to be judged and punished in this present state. The thoughtful reader of history will not fail to observe how sternly this justice has dealt with empire after empire, when they have become corrupt. Colossal dominions have withered to the ground, when sentenced by the King of kings. Go ye and ask today,

> Where is the empire of Assyria? Where are the mighty cities of Babylon? Where are the glories of the Medes and Persians? What has become of the Macedonian power? Where are the Caesars and their palaces?

These empires were forces established by cruelty, and used for oppression; they fostered luxury and licentiousness, and when they were no longer tolerable, the earth was purged from their polluting existence. Ah me! what horrors of war, bloodshed, and devastation, have come upon men as the result of their iniquities! The world is full of the monuments, both of the mercy and the justice of God: in fact the monuments of his justice, if rightly viewed, are proofs of his goodness; for it is mercy on the part of God to put an end to evil systems when, like a nightmare, they weigh heavily upon the bosom of mankind. The omnipotent Judge has not ceased from his sovereign rule over kingdoms, and our own country may yet have to feel his chastisements. We have often laughed among ourselves at the ridiculous idea of the New Zealander sitting on the broken arch of London Bridge amid the ruins of this metropolis. But is it quite so ridiculous as it looks? It is more than possible it will be realized if our iniquities continue to abound. What is there about London that it should be more enduring than Rome? Why should the palaces of *our* monarchs be eternal if the palaces of Koyunjik have fallen? The almost boundless power of the Pharaohs has passed away, and Egypt has become the meanest of nations; why should not England come under like condemnation? What are we? What is there about our boastful race, whether on this side of the Atlantic or the other, that we should monopolize the favor of God? If we rebel, and sin against him, he will not hold us guiltless, but will deal out impartial justice to an ungrateful race.

Still, though such judgments proceed every day, yet there is to be a day, a period of time, in which, in a more distinct, formal, public, and final manner, God will judge the sons of men. We might have guessed this by the light of nature and of reason. Even heathen peoples have had a dim notion of a day of doom; but we are not left to guess it, we are solemnly assured of it in Holy Scripture. Accepting this Book as the revelation of God, we know beyond all doubt that a day is appointed in which the Lord will judge the secrets of men.

By judging, is here meant all that concerns the proceedings of trial and award. God will judge the race of men; that is to say, first, there will be a session of majesty, and the appearing of a great white throne, surrounded with pomp of angels and glorified beings. Then a summons will be issued, bidding all men come to judgment, to give in their final account. The heralds will fly through the realms of death, and summon those who sleep in the dust: for the quick and the dead shall all appear before that judgment-seat. John says, "I saw the dead, small and great, stand before God"; and he adds, "The sea gave up the dead which were in it; and death and Hell delivered up the dead which were in them." Those that have been so long buried that their dust is mingled with the soil, and has undergone a thousand transmutations, shall nevertheless be made to put in a personal appearance before the judgment-seat of Christ.

What an assize [court] will that be! You and I and all the myriad myriads of our race shall be gathered before the throne of the Son of God. Then, when all are gathered, the indictment will be read, and each one will be examined concerning things done in the body, according to that he hath done. Then the books shall be opened, and everything recorded there shall be read before the face of Heaven. Every sinner shall then hear the story of his life published to his everlasting shame. The good shall ask no concealment, and the evil shall find none. Angels and men shall then see the truth of things, and the saints shall judge the world. Then the great Judge himself shall give the decision: he shall pronounce sentence upon the wicked, and execute their punishment. No partiality shall there be seen; there shall be no private conferences to secure immunity for nobles, no hushing up of matters, that great men may escape contempt for their crimes. All men shall stand before the one great judgment-bar; evidence shall be given concerning them all, and a righteous sentence shall go forth from his mouth who knows not how to flatter the great.

This will be so, and it ought to be so: God should judge the world, because he is the universal ruler and sovereign. There has been a day for sinning, there ought to be a day for punishing; a long age of rebellion has been endured, and there must be a time when justice shall assert her supremacy. We have seen an age in which reformation has been commanded, in which mercy has been presented, in which expostulation and entreaty have been used, and there ought at last to come a day in which God shall judge both the quick and the dead, and measure out to each the final result of life. It ought to be so for the sake of the righteous. They have been slandered; they have been despised and ridiculed; worse than that, they have been imprisoned and beaten, and put to death times without number: the best have had the worst of it, and there ought to be a judgment to set these things right. Besides, the festering iniquities of each age cry out to God that he should deal with them. Shall such sin go unpunished? To what end is there a moral government at all, and how is its continuance to be secured, is there be not rewards and punishments and a day of account? For the display of his holiness, for the overwhelming of his adversaries, for the rewarding of those who have faithfully served him, there must be and shall be a day in which God will judge the world.

Why doth it not come at once? And when will it come? The precise date we cannot tell. Man nor angel knoweth that day, and it is idle and profane to guess at it, since even the Son of man, as such, knoweth not the time. It is sufficient for us that the Judgment Day will surely come; sufficient also to believe that it is postponed on purpose to give breathing time for mercy, and space for repentance. Why should the ungodly want to know when that day will come? What is that day to you? To you it shall be darkness, and not light. It shall be the day of your consuming as stubble fully dry: therefore bless the Lord that he delayeth his coming, and reckon that his longsuffering is for your salvation.

Moreover, the Lord keeps the scaffold standing till he hath built up the fabric of his church. Not yet are the elect all called out from among the guilty sons of men; not yet are all the redeemed with blood redeemed with power and brought forth out of the corruption of the age into the holiness in which they walk with God. Therefore the Lord waiteth for a while. But do not deceive yourselves. The great day of his wrath cometh on apace, and your days of reprieve are numbered. One day is with the Lord as a thousand years, and a thousand years as one day. Ye shall die, perhaps, before the appearing of the Son of man; but ye shall see his judgment-seat for all that, for ye shall rise again as surely as he rose. When the apostle addressed the Grecian sages at Athens he said,

> God now commandeth all men everywhere to repent, because he hath appointed a day, in the which he will judge the world in righteousness by that man whom he hath ordained; whereof he hath given assurance unto all men, in that he hath raised him from the dead.

See ye not, O ye impenitent ones, that a risen Savior is the sign of your doom. As God hath raised Jesus from the dead, so shall he raise your bodies, that in these you may come to judgment. Before the judgment-seat shall every man and woman in this house give an account of the things done in the body, whether they be good or whether they be evil. Thus saith the Lord.

II. Now I call your attention to the fact that *"God will judge the secrets of men."*

This will happen to all men, of every nation, of every age, of every rank, and of every character. The Judge will, of course, judge their outward acts, but these may be said to have gone before them to judgment: their secret acts are specially mentioned, because these will make judgment to be the more searching.

By "the secrets of men," the Scripture means those secret crimes which hide themselves away by their own infamy, which are too vile to be spoken of, which cause a shudder to go through a nation if they be but dragged, as they ought to be, into the daylight. Secret offenses shall be brought into judgment; the deeds of the night and of the closed room, the acts which require the finger to be laid upon the lip, and a conspiracy of silence to be sworn. Revolting and shameless sins which must never be mentioned lest the man who committed them should be excluded from his fellows as an outcast, abhorred even of other sinners—all these shall be revealed. All that you have done, any one of you, or are doing, if you are bearing the

Christian name and yet practicing secret sin, shall be laid bare before the universal gaze. If you sit here amongst the people of God, and yet where no eye sees you, if you are living in dishonesty, untruthfulness, or uncleanness, it shall all be known, and shame and confusion of face shall eternally cover you. Contempt shall be the inheritance to which you shall awake, when hypocrisy shall be no more possible. Be not deceived, God is not mocked; but he will bring the secrets of men into judgment.

Specially our text refers to the hidden motives of every action; for a man may do that which is right from a wrong motive, and so the deed may be evil in the sight of God, though it seem right in the sight of men. Oh, think what it will be to have your motives all brought to light, to have it proven that you were godly for the sake of gain, that you were generous out of ostentation, or zealous for love of praise, that you were careful in public to maintain a religious reputation, but that all the while everything was done for self, and self only! What a strong light will that be which God shall turn upon our lives, when the darkest chambers of human desire and motive shall be as manifest as public acts! What a revelation will that be which makes manifest all thoughts, and imaginings, and lustings, and desires! All angers, and envies, and prides, and rebellions of the heart—what a disclosure will these make!

All the sensual desires and imaginings of even the best-regulated, what a foulness will these appear! What a day will it be, when the secrets of men shall be set in the full blaze of noon!

God will also reveal secrets, that were secrets even to the sinners themselves, for there is sin in us which we have never seen, and iniquity in us which we have never yet discovered.

We have managed for our own comfort's sake to blind our eyes somewhat, and we take care to avert our gaze from things which it is inconvenient to see; but we shall be compelled to see all these evils in that day, when the Lord shall judge the secrets of men. I do not wonder that when a certain Rabbi read in the book of Ecclesiastes that God shall bring every work into judgment, with every secret thing, whether it be good, or whether it be evil, he wept. It is enough to make the best man tremble. Were it not for thee, O Jesus, whose precious blood hath cleansed us from all sin, where should we be! Were it not for thy righteousness, which shall cover those who believe in thee, who among us could endure the thought of that tremendous day? In thee, O Jesus, we are made righteous, and therefore we fear not the trial hour, but were it not for thee, our hearts would fail us for fear!

Now if you ask me why God should judge, especially the secrets of men—since this is not done in human courts, and cannot be, for secret things of this kind come not under cognizance of our short-sighted tribunals—I answer it is because there is really nothing secret from God. We make a difference between secret and public sins, but he doth not; for all things are naked and open to the eyes of him with whom we have to do. All deeds are done in the immediate presence of God, who is personally present everywhere. He knows and sees all things as one upon the spot, and every secret sin is but conceived to be secret through the deluded fantasy of our ignorance. God sees more of a secret sin than a man can see of that which is done before his face. "'Can any hide himself in secret places that I shall not see him?' saith the Lord."

The secrets of men will be judged because often the greatest of moral acts are done in secret. The brightest deeds that God delights in are those that are done by his servants when they have shut the door and are alone with him—when they have no motive but to please him; when they studiously avoid publicity, lest they should be turned aside by the praise of men; when the right hand knoweth not what the left hand doeth, and the loving, generous heart deviseth liberal things, and doeth it behind the screen, so that it should never be discovered how the deed was done. It were a pity that such deeds should be left out at the great audit. Thus, too, secret vices are also of the very blackest kind, and to exempt them were to let the worst of sinners go unpunished. Shall it be that these polluted beings shall escape because they have purchased silence with their wealth? I say solemnly, "God forbid." He does forbid it: what they have done in secret, shall be proclaimed upon the house-tops.

Besides, the secret things of men enter into the very essence of their actions. An action is, after all, good or bad very much according to its motive. It may seem good, but the motive may taint it; and so, if God did not judge the secret part of the action, he would not judge righteously. He will weigh our actions, and detect the design which led to them, and the spirit which prompted them.

Is it not certainly true that the secret thing is the best evidence of the man's condition? Many a man will not do in public that which would bring him shame; not because he is not black-hearted enough for it, but because he is too much of a coward. That which a man does when he thinks that he is entirely by himself is the best revelation of the man. That which thou wilt not do because it would be told of thee if thou didst ill, is a poor index of thy real character. That which thou wilt do because thou wilt be praised for doing well, is an equally faint test of thy heart. Such virtue is mere self-seeking, or mean-spirited subservience to thy fellow-man; but that which thou doest out of respect to no authority but thine own conscience and thy God; that which thou doest unobserved, without regard to what man will say concerning it—that it is which reveals thee, and discovers thy real soul. Hence God lays a special stress and emphasis here upon the fact that he will in that day judge "the secrets" of men by Jesus Christ.

Oh, friends, if it does not make you tremble to think of these things, it ought to do so. I feel the deep responsibility of preaching upon such matters, and I pray God of his infinite mercy to apply these truths to our hearts, that they may be forceful upon our lives. These truths ought to startle us, but I am afraid we hear them with small result; we have grown familiar with them, and they do not penetrate us as they should. We have to deal, brethren, with an omniscient God; with One who, once knowing, never forgets; with One to whom all things are always present; with One who will conceal nothing out of fear, or favor of any man's person; with One who will shortly bring the splendor of his omniscience and the impartiality of his justice to bear upon all human lives. God help us, where'er we rove and where'er we rest, to remember that each thought, word, and act of each moment lies in that fierce light which beats upon all things from the throng of God.

III. Another solemn revelation of our text lies in this fact, that *"God will judge the secrets of men by Jesus Christ."*

He that will sit upon the throng as the Vice-gerent [administrative deputy] of God, and as a Judge, acting for God, will be Jesus Christ. What a name for a Judge! The Savior-Anointed—Jesus Christ: he is to be the Judge of all mankind. Our Redeemer will be the Umpire of our destiny.

This will be, I doubt not, first for the display of his glory. What a difference there will be then between the babe of Bethlehem's manger, hunted by Herod, carried down by night into Egypt for shelter, and the King of kings and Lord of lords, before whom every knee must bow! What a difference between the weary man and full of woes, and he that shall then be girt with glory, sitting on a throne encircled with a rainbow! From the derision of men to the throne of universal judgment, what an ascent! I am unable to convey to you my own heart's sense of the contrast between the "despised and rejected of men," and the universally-acknowledged Lord, before whom Caesar and pontiffs shall bow into the dust. He who was judged at Pilate's bar, shall summon all to his bar. What a change from the shame and spitting, from the nails and the wounds, the mockery and the thirst, and the dying anguish, to the glory in which he shall come, whose eyes are as a flame of fire, and out of whose mouth there goeth a two-edged sword! He shall judge the nations, even he whom the nations abhorred. He shall break them in pieces like a potter's vessel, even those who cast him out as unworthy to live among them. Oh, how we ought to bow before him now as he reveals himself in his tender sympathy, and in his generous humiliation! Let us kiss the Son lest he be angry; let us yield to his grace, that we may not be crushed by his wrath. Ye sinners, bow before those pierced feet, which else will tread you like clusters in the wine-press. Look ye up to him with weeping, and confess your forgetfulness of him, and put your trust in him; lest he look down on you in indignation. Oh, remember that he will one day say, "But those mine enemies, which would not that I should reign over them, bring hither, and slay them before me." The holding of the judgment by the Lord

Jesus will greatly enhance his glory. It will finally settle one controversy which is still upheld by certain erroneous spirits: there will be no doubt about our Lord's deity in that day: there will be no question that this same Jesus who was crucified is both Lord and God. God himself shall judge, but he shall perform the judgment in the person of his Son Jesus Christ, truly man, but nevertheless most truly God. Being God, he is divinely qualified to judge the world in righteousness, and the people with his truth.

If you ask again, "Why is the Son of God chosen to be the final Judge?" I could give as a further answer that he receives this high office not only as a reward for all his pains, and as a manifestation of his glory, but also because men have been under his mediatorial sway, and he is their Governor and King. At the present moment we are all under the sway of the Prince Immanuel, God with us: we have been placed by an act of divine clemency, not under the immediate government of an offended God, but under the reconciling rule of the Prince of Peace. "All power is given unto him in Heaven and in earth." "The Father judgeth no man, but hath committed all judgment unto the Son: that all men should honor the Son, even as they honor the Father." We are commanded to preach unto the people, and "to testify that it is he which was ordained of God to be the judge of quick and dead." (Acts 10:42.) Jesus is our Lord and King, and it is meet that he should conclude his mediatorial sovereignty by rewarding his subjects according to their deeds.

But I have somewhat to say unto you which ought to reach your hearts, even if other thoughts have not done so. I think that God hath chosen Christ, the man Christ Jesus, to judge the world, that there may never be a cavil raised concerning that judgment. Men shall not be able to say—

> We were judged by a superior being who did not know our weaknesses and temptations, and therefore he judged us harshly, and without a generous consideration of our condition.

No, God shall judge the secrets of men by Jesus Christ, who was tempted in all points like as we are, yet without sin. He is our brother, bone of our bone and flesh of our flesh, partaker of our humanity, and therefore understands and knows what is in men. He has shown himself to be skillful in all the surgery of mercy throughout the ages, and at last he will be found equally skillful in dissecting motives and revealing the thoughts and intents of the heart. Nobody shall ever be able to look back on that august tribunal and say that he who sat upon it was too stern, because he knew nothing of human weakness. It will be the loving Christ, whose tears, and bloody sweat, and gaping wounds, attest his brotherhood with mankind; and it will be clear to all intelligences that however dread his sentences, he could not be unmerciful. God shall judge us by Jesus Christ, that the judgment may be indisputable.

But hearken well—for I speak with a great weight upon my soul—this judgment by Christ Jesus, puts beyond possibility all hope of any after-interposition. If the Savior condemns, and such a Savior, who can plead for us? The owner of the vineyard was about to cut down the barren tree, when the dresser of the vineyard pleaded, "Let it alone this year also"; but what can come of that tree when the vinedresser himself shall say to the master, "It must fall; I myself must cut it down"! If your Savior shall become your judge, you will be judged indeed. If *he* shall say, "Depart, ye cursed," who can call you back?

If he that bled to save men at last comes to this conclusion, that there is no more to be done, but they must be driven from his presence, then farewell hope. To the guilty, the judgment will indeed be a

> *Great day of dread, decision, and despair.*

An infinite horror shall seize upon their spirits as the words of the loving Christ shall freeze their very marrow, and fix them in the ice of eternal despair. There is, to my mind, a climax of solemnity in the fact that God shall judge the secrets of men by Jesus Christ.

Does not this also show how certain the sentence will be? For this Christ of God is too much in earnest to play with men. If he says, "Come, ye blessed," he will not fail to bring them to their inheritance. If he be driven to say, "Depart, ye cursed," he will see it done, and into the everlasting punishment they must go. Even when it cost him his life he did not draw back from doing the will of his Father, nor will he shrink in that day when he shall pronounce the sentence of doom. Oh, how evil must sin be, since it constrains the tender Savior to pronounce sentence of eternal woe! I am sure that many of us have been driven of late to an increased hatred of sin; our souls have recoiled within us because of the wickedness among which we dwell; it has made us feel as if we would fain borrow the Almighty's thunderbolts with which to smite iniquity. Such haste on our part may not be seemly, since it implies a complaint against divine long-suffering; but Christ's dealing with evil will be calm and dispassionate, and all the more crushing. Jesus, with his pierced hand, that bears the attestation of his supreme love to men, shall wave the impenitent away; and those fits which bade the weary rest in him shall solemnly say to the wicked, "depart, ye cursed, into everlasting fire prepared for the devil and his angels." To be trampled beneath the foot which was nailed to the cross will be to be crushed indeed: yet so it is— God shall judge the secrets of men by Jesus Christ.

It seems to me as if God, in this, intended to give a display of the unity of all his perfections. In this same man, Christ Jesus, the Son of God, you behold justice and love, mercy and righteousness, combined in equal measure. He turns to the right, and says, "come, ye blessed," with infinite suavity; and with the same lip, as he glances to the left, he says, "Depart, ye cursed." Men will then see at one glance how love and righteousness are one, and how they meet in equal splendor in the person of the Well-beloved, whom God has therefore chosen to be Judge of quick and dead.

IV. I have done when you have borne with me a minute or two upon my next point, which is this: and *all this is according to the gospel.*

That is to say, there is nothing in the gospel contrary to this solemn teaching. Men gather to us, to hear us preach of infinite mercy, and tell of the love that blots out sin; and our task is joyful when we are called to deliver such a message; but oh, sirs, remember that nothing in our message makes light of sin. The gospel offers you no opportunity of going on in sin, and escaping without punishment. Its own cry is, "Except ye repent, ye shall all likewise perish." Jesus has not come into the world to make sin less terrible. Nothing in the gospel excuses sin; nothing in it affords toleration for lust or anger, or dishonesty, or falsehood. The gospel is as truly a two-edged sword against sin, as ever the law can be. There is grace for the man who quits his sin, but there is tribulation and wrath upon every man that doeth evil. "If ye turn not, he will whet his sword; he hath bent his bow, and made it ready." The gospel is all tenderness to the repenting, but all terror to the obstinate offender. It has pardon for the very chief of sinners, and mercy for the vilest of the vile, if they will forsake their sins; but it is according to our gospel that he that goeth on in his iniquity, shall be cast into Hell, and he that believeth not shall be damned. With deep love to the souls of men, I bear witness to the truth that he who turns not with repentance and faith to Christ, shall go away into punishment as everlasting as the life of the righteous. This is according to our gospel: indeed, we had not needed such a gospel, if there had not been such a judgment. The background of the cross is the judgment-seat of Christ. We had not needed so great an atonement, so vast a sacrifice, if there had not been an exceeding sinfulness in sin, an exceeding justice in the judgment, and an exceeding terror in the sure rewards of transgression.

"According to my gospel," saith Paul; and he meant that the judgment is an essential part of the gospel creed. If I had to sum up the gospel I should have to tell you certain facts: Jesus, the Son of God, became man; he was born of the virgin Mary; lived a perfect life; was falsely accused of men, was crucified, dead, and buried; the third day he rose again from the dead; he ascended into Heaven and sitteth on the right hand of God; from whence he shall also come to judge the quick and the dead. This is one of the elementary truths of our gospel; we believe in the resurrection of the dead, the final judgment, and the life everlasting.

The judgment is according to our gospel, and in times of righteous indignation, its terrible significance seemeth a very gospel to the pure in heart. I mean this. I have read this and that concerning oppression, slavery, the treading down of the poor, and the shedding of blood, and I have rejoiced that there is a righteous Judge.

I have read of secret wickednesses among the rich men of this city, and I have said within myself, "Thank God, there will be a judgment day." Thousands of men have been hanged for much less crimes than those which now disgrace gentlemen whose names are on the lips of rank and beauty. Ah me, how heavy is our heart as we think of it! It has come like a gospel to us that the Lord will be revealed in flaming fire, taking vengeance on them that know not God, and that obey not the gospel of our Lord Jesus Christ. (2 Thessalonians 1:8.) The secret wickedness of London cannot go on forever. Even they that love men best, and most desire salvation for them, cannot but cry to God, "How long! How long! Great God, wilt thou forever endure this?" God hath appointed a day in which he will judge the world, and we sigh and cry until it shall end the reign of wickedness, and give rest to the oppressed.

Brethren, we must preach the coming of the Lord, and preach it somewhat more than we have done; because it is the driving power of the gospel. Too many have kept back these truths, and thus the bone has been taken out of the arm of the gospel. Its point has been broken; its edge has been blunted. The doctrine of judgment to come is the power by which men are to be aroused. There is another life; the Lord will come a second time; judgment will arrive; the wrath of God will he revealed. Where this is not preached, I am bold to say, the gospel is not preached. It is absolutely necessary to the preaching of the gospel of Christ that men be warned as to what will happen if they continue in their sins. Ho, ho, sir surgeon, you are too delicate to tell the man that he is ill! You hope to heal the sick without their knowing it. You therefore flatter them; and what happens? They laugh at you; they dance upon their own graves. At last they die! Your delicacy is cruelty; your flatteries are poisons; you are a murderer. Shall we keep men in a fool's paradise? Shall we lull them into soft slumbers from which they will awake in Hell? Are we to become helpers of their damnation by our smooth speeches? In the name of God we will not. It becomes every true minister of Christ to cry aloud and spare not, for God hath set a day in which he will "judge the secrets of men by Jesus Christ according to my gospel." As surely as Paul's gospel was true the judgment will come. Wherefore, flee to Jesus this day, O sinners. O ye saints, come hide yourselves again beneath the crimson canopy of the atoning sacrifice, that you may be now ready to welcome your descending Lord and escort him to his judgment-seat. O my hearers, may God bless you, for Jesus' sake. Amen.

The Two Appearings and the Discipline of Grace

Delivered on Lord's Day morning, April 4, 1886, at the Metropolitan Tabernacle, Newington. No. 1894.

For the grace of God that bringeth salvation hath appeared to all men, teaching us that, denying ungodliness and worldly lusts, we should live soberly, righteously, and godly, in this present world; looking for that blessed hope, and the glorious appearing of the great God and our Savior Jesus Christ; who gave himself for us, that he might redeem us from all iniquity, and purify unto himself a peculiar people, zealous of good works.—Titus 2:11–14

Upon reading this text, one sees at a glance that Paul believed in a divine Savior. He did not preach a Savior who was a mere man. He believed the Lord Jesus Christ to be truly man, but he also believed him to be God over all, and he therefore uses the striking words, "the glorious appearing of the great God and our Savior Jesus Christ." There is no appearing of God the Father; there is no such expression in Scripture; the appearing is the appearing of that second person of the blessed Trinity in unity who has already once appeared, and who will appear a second time without a sin, offering unto salvation in the latter days. Paul believed in Jesus as "the *great* God and our Savior." It was his high delight to extol the Lord who once was crucified in weakness. He calls him here, "the great God," thus specially dwelling upon his power, dominion, and glory; and this is the more remarkable because he immediately goes on to say, "who gave himself for us, that he might redeem us from all iniquity." He that gave himself, he that surrendered life itself upon the accursed tree, he that was stripped of all honor and glory and entered into the utmost depths of humiliation, was assuredly the great God, notwithstanding all. O brothers, if you take away the deity of Christ, what in the Gospel is left that is worth the preaching? None but the great God is equal to the work of being our Savior.

We learn also at first sight that Paul believed in a great redemption. "Who gave himself for us that he might redeem us from all iniquity." That word "redemption" sounds in my ears like a silver bell. We are ransomed, purchased back from slavery, and this at an immeasurable price; not merely by the obedience of Christ, nor the suffering of Christ, nor even the death of Christ, but by Christ's giving *himself* for us. All that there is in the great God and Savior was paid down that he might "redeem us from all iniquity." The splendor of the Gospel lies in the redeeming sacrifice of the Son of God, and we shall never fail to put this to the front in our preaching. It is the gem of all the Gospel gems. As the moon is among the stars, so is this great doctrine among all the lesser lights which God hath kindled to make glad the night of fallen man. Paul never hesitates; he has a divine Savior and a divine redemption, and he preaches these with unwavering confidence. Oh that all preachers were like him!

It is also clear that Paul looked upon the appearing of the Savior as a Redeemer from all iniquity, as a display of the grace of God. He says, "The grace of God that bringeth salvation hath appeared to all men." In the person of Christ, the grace of God is revealed, as when the sun ariseth and makes glad all lands. It is not a private vision of God to a favored prophet on the lone mountain's brow; but it is an open declaration of the grace of God to every creature under Heaven—a display of the grace of God to all eyes that are open to behold it. When the Lord Jesus Christ came to Bethlehem, and when he closed a perfect life by death upon Calvary, he manifested the grace of God more gloriously than has been done by creation or Providence. This is the clearest revelation of the everlasting mercy of the living God. In the Redeemer we behold the unveiling of the Father's face. What if I say the laying bare of the divine heart? To repeat the figure of the text, this is the dayspring from on high which hath visited us: the Sun which has arisen with healing in his wings. The grace of God hath shone forth conspicuously, and made itself visible to men of every rank in the person and work of the Lord Jesus. This was not given us because of any deservings on our part; it is a manifestation of free, rich, undeserved grace, and of that grace in its fullness. The grace of God has been made manifest to the entire universe in the appearing of Jesus Christ our Lord.

The grand object of the manifestation of divine grace in Christ Jesus is to deliver men from the dominion of evil. The world in Paul's day was sunk in immorality, debauchery, ungodliness, bloodshed, and cruelty of every kind. I have not time this morning to give you even an outline sketch of the Roman world when Paul wrote this letter to Titus. We are bad enough *now*; but the outward manners and customs of *that period* were simply horrible. The spread of the gospel has wrought a change for the better. In the apostle's days, the favorite spectacles for holiday entertainment were the butcheries of men; and such was the general depravity that vices which we hardly dare to mention were defended and gloried in. In the midnight of the world's history, our Lord appeared to put away sin. The Lord Jesus Christ, who is the manifestation of the divine grace to men, came into the world to put an end to the unutterable tyranny of evil. His work and teaching are meant to uplift mankind at large, and also to redeem his people from all iniquity, and to sanctify them to himself us his peculiar heritage.

Paul looks upon recovery from sin as being a wonderful proof of divine grace. He does not talk about a kind of grace that would leave men in sin, and yet save them from its punishment. No, his salvation is *salvation from sin*. He does not talk about a free grace which winks at iniquity, and makes nothing of transgression; but of a greater grace by far, which denounces the iniquity and condemns the transgression, and then delivers the victim of it from the habit which has brought him into bondage. He declares that the grace of God has shone upon the world in the work of Jesus, in order that the darkness of its sin and ignorance may disappear, and the brightness of holiness, and righteousness, and peace may rule the day. God send us to see these blessed results in every part of the world! God make us to see them in ourselves! May we ourselves feel that the grace of God has appeared to us individually! Our apostle would have Titus know that this grace was intended for all ranks of men, for the Cretians who were "always liars, evil beasts, slow bellies;" and even for the most despised bondslaves, who under the Roman empire were treated worse than dogs. To each one of us, whether rich or poor, prominent or obscure, the gospel has come, and its design is that we may be delivered by it from all ungodliness and worldly lusts.

This being the run of the text, I ask you to come closer to it, while I try to show how the apostle stimulates us to holiness, and urges us to overcome all evil. Firstly he describes *our position*; secondly, he describes *our instruction*; and, thirdly, he mentions *our encouragements*. May the good Spirit bless our meditations at this hour!

I. First of all, the apostle in this text describes *our position*.

The people of God stand between two appearances. In the eleventh verse he tells us that "The grace of God that bringeth salvation hath appeared to all men;" and then he says, in the thirteenth verse, "Looking for that blessed hope, and the glorious appearing of the great God and our Savior Jesus Christ." We live in an age which is an interval between two appearings of the Lord from Heaven. Believers in Jesus are shut off from the old economy by the first coming of our Lord. The times of

man's ignorance, God winked at, but now commandeth all men everywhere to repent. We are divided from the past by a wall of light, upon whose forefront we
read the words "Bethlehem, Gethsemane, Calvary." We date from the birth of the
Virgin's Son: we begin with *Anno Domini.* All the rest of time is before Christ, and is
marked off from the Christian era. Bethlehem's manger is our beginning. The chief
landmark in all time to us is the wondrous life of him who is the light of the world.
We look to the appearing of the grace of God in the form of the lowly One of Nazareth, for our trust is there. We confide in him who was made flesh and dwelt
among us, so that men beheld his glory, the glory as of the Only Begotten of the Father, full of grace and truth. The dense darkness of the heathen ages begins to be
broken when we reach the first appearing, and the dawn of a glorious day begins.

Brethren, we look forward to a second appearing. Our outlook for the
close of this present era is another appearing—an appearing of glory rather
than of grace. After our Master rose from the brow of Olivet, his disciples remained for a while in mute astonishment; but soon an angelic messenger reminded them of prophecy and promise by saying,

> Ye men of Galilee, why stand ye gazing up into Heaven? this same Jesus, which is
> taken up from you into Heaven, shall so come in like manner as ye have seen him go
> into Heaven.

We believe that our Lord in the fullness of time will descend from Heaven with a
shout, with the trump of the archangel, and the voice of God.

> *The Lord shall come! The earth shall quake;*
> *The mountains to their center shake;*
> *And, withering from the vault of night,*
> *The stars shall pale their feeble light.*

This is the terminus of the present age. We look from *Anno Domini,* in which he
came the first time, to that greater *Anno Domini,* or year of our Lord, in which he
shall come a second time, in all the splendor of his power, to reign in righteousness,
and break the evil powers as with a rod of iron.

See, then, where we are: we are compassed about, behind and before, with the
appearings of our Lord. Behind us is our trust; before us is our hope. Behind us is
the Son of God in humiliation; before us is the great God our Savior in his glory. To
use an ecclesiastical term, we stand between two Epiphanies: the first is the manifestation of the Son of God in human flesh, in dishonor and weakness; the second is
the manifestation of the same Son of God in all his power and glory. In what a position, then, do the saints stand! They have an era all to themselves which begins and
ends with the Lord's appearing.

Our position is further described in the text, if you look at it, as being *in this
present world,* or age. We are living in the age which lies between the two blazing
beacons of the divine appearings; and we are called to hasten from one to the

other. The sacramental host of God's elect is marching on, from the one appearing to the other, with hasty foot. We have everything to hope for in the last appearing, as we have everything to trust to in the first appearing; and we have now to wait with patient hope throughout that weary interval which intervenes. Paul calls it "this present world." This marks its fleeting nature. It is present, but it is scarcely future; for the Lord may come so soon, and thus end it all. It is present now, but it will not be present long. It is but a little time, and he that will come shall come, and will not tarry. Now it is this "present world:" oh, how present it is! How sadly it surrounds us! Yet by faith we count these present things to be unsubstantial as a dream; and we look to the things which are not seen, and not present, as being real and eternal. We pass through this world as men on pilgrimage. We traverse an enemy's country. Going from one manifestation to another, we are as birds migrating on the wing from one region to another: there is no rest for us by the way. We are to keep ourselves as loose as we can from this country through which we make our pilgrim-way; for we are strangers and foreigners, and here we have no continuing city. We hurry through this Vanity Fair: before us lies the Celestial City and the coming of the Lord who is the King thereof. As voyagers cross the Atlantic, and so pass from shore to shore, so do we speed over the waves of this ever-changing world to the glory-land of the bright appearing of our Lord and Savior Jesus Christ.

Already I have given to you, in this description of our position, the very best argument for a holy life. If it be so, my brethren, ye are not of the world even as Jesus is not of the world. If this be so—that before you blazes the supernatural splendor of the second advent, and behind you burns the everlasting light of the Redeemer's first appearing—what manner of people ought ye to be! If, indeed, you be but journeying through this present world, suffer not your hearts to be defiled with its sins; learn not the manner of speech of these aliens through whose country you are passing. Is it not written, "The people shall dwell alone, and shall not be reckoned among the nations?" "Come ye out from among them, and be ye separate, touch not the unclean thing," for the Lord hath said, "I will be a Father unto you, and ye shall be my sons and daughters." They that lived before the coming of Christ had responsibilities upon them, but not such as those which rest upon you who have seen the face of God in Jesus Christ, and who expect to see that face again. You live in light which renders their brightest know ledge a comparative darkness: walk as children of light. You stand between two mornings, between which there is no evening. The glory of the Lord has risen upon you once in the incarnation and atonement of your Lord: that light is shining more and more, and soon there will come the perfect day, which shall be ushered in by the second advent. The sun shall no more go down, but it shall unveil itself, and shed an indescribable splendor upon all hearts that look for it. "Put on therefore the armor of light." What a grand expression! Helmet of light, breastplate of light, shoes of light—everything of light. What a knight must he be who is clad, not in steel, but in light, light which shall flash confusion on his foes! There ought to be a holy light about you, O believer in Jesus, for there is the appearing of grace behind you, and the appearing of glory before you. Two manifestations of God shine upon you. Like a wall of fire the Lord's appearings are round about you: there ought to be a special glory of holiness in the midst. "Let your light so shine before men, that they may see your good works, and glorify your Father which is in Heaven." That is the position of the righteous according to my text, and it furnishes a loud call to holiness.

II. Secondly, I have to call your attention to *the instruction* which is given to us by the grace of God which has appeared unto all men.

Our translation runs thus: "The grace of God hath appeared to all men, teaching us that, denying ungodliness and worldly lusts, we should live soberly, righteously, and godly in this present world." A better translation would be, "The grace of God that bringeth salvation hath appeared to all men, disciplining us in order that we may deny ungodliness and worldly lusts." Those of you who know a little Greek will note that the word which in our version is rendered "teaching," is a scholastic term, and has to do with the education of children; not merely the teaching, but the training and bringing of them up. The grace of God has come to be a schoolmaster to us, to teach us, to train us, to prepare us for a more developed state. Christ has manifested in his own person that wonderful grace of God which is to deal with us as with sons, and to educate us unto holiness, and so to the full possession of our heavenly heritage. We are the many sons who are to be brought to glory by the discipline of grace.

So then, first of all, *grace has a discipline.* We generally think of law when we talk about schoolmasters and discipline; but grace itself has a discipline and a wonderful training power too. The manifestation of grace is preparing us for the manifestation of glory. What the law could not do, grace is doing. The free favor of God instills new principles, suggests new thoughts, and by inspiring us with gratitude, creates in us love to God and hatred of that which is opposed to God. Happy are they who go to school to the grace of God! This grace of God entering into us shows us what was evil even more clearly than the commandment does. We receive a vital, testing principle within, whereby we discern between good and evil. The grace of God provides us with instruction, but also with chastisement, as it is written, "As many as I love I rebuke and chasten." As soon as we come under the conscious enjoyment of the free grace of God, we find it to be a holy rule, a fatherly government, a heavenly training. We find, not self indulgence, much less licentiousness; but on the contrary, the grace of God both restrains and constrains us; it makes us free to holiness, and delivers us from the law of sin and death by "the law of the spirit of life in Christ Jesus."

Grace has its discipline, and *grace has its chosen disciples,* for you cannot help noticing that while the eleventh verse says that, "the grace of God that bringeth salvation hath appeared to all men," yet it is clear that this grace of God has not exercised its holy discipline upon all men, and therefore the text changes its "all men" into "us." Usually in Scripture when you get a generality, you soon find a particularity near it. The text hath it, "teaching *us* that, denying ungodliness and worldly lusts, *we* should live soberly, righteously, and godly, in this present world." Thus you see that grace has its own disciples. Are you a disciple of the grace of God? Did you ever come and submit yourself to it? Have you learned to spell that word "faith?" Have you childlike trust in Jesus? Have you learned to wash in the laver [bowl] of atonement? Have you learned those holy exercises which are taught by the grace of God? Can you say that your salvation is of grace? Do you know the meaning of that text, "By grace are ye saved through faith; and that not of yourselves: it is the gift of God?" If so, then you are his disciples, and the grace of God which has appeared so conspicuously has come to discipline you. As the disciples of grace, endeavor to adorn its doctrine. According to the previous verses, even a slave might do this. He might be an ornament to the grace of God. Let grace have such an effect upon your life and character that all may say, "See what grace can do! See how the grace of God produces holiness in believers!" All along I wish to be driving at the point which the apostle is aiming at: that we are to be holy—holy because grace exercises a purifying discipline, and because we are the disciples of that grace.

The discipline of grace, according to the apostle, has three results—denying, living, looking. You see the three words before you. The first is *"denying."* When a young man comes to college he usually has much to unlearn. If his education has been neglected, a sort of instinctive ignorance covers his mind with briars and brambles. If he has gone to some faulty school where the teaching is flimsy, his tutor has first of all to fetch out of him what he has been badly taught. The most difficult part of the training of young men is not to put the right thing into them, but to get the wrong thing out of them. A man proposes to teach a language in six months, and in the end a great thing is done if one of his pupils is able to forget all his nonsense in six years. When the Holy Spirit comes into the heart, he finds that we know so much already of what it were well to leave unknown; we are self-conceited, we are puffed up. We have learned lessons of worldly wisdom and carnal policy, and these we need to unlearn and deny. The Holy Spirit works this denying in us by the discipline of grace.

What have we to deny? *First, we have to deny ungodliness.* That is a lesson which many of you have great need to learn. Listen to working-men. "Oh," they say, "we have to work hard, we cannot think about God or religion." This is ungodliness! The grace of God teaches us to deny this; we come to loathe such atheism. Others are prospering in the world, and they cry,

> If you had as much business to look after as I have, you would have no time to think about your soul or another world. Trying to battle with the competition of the times leaves me no opportunity for prayer or Bible-reading; I have enough to do with my day-book and ledger.

This also is ungodliness! The grace of God leads us to deny this; we abhor such forgetfulness of God. A great work of the Holy Spirit is to make a man godly, to make him think of God, to make him feel that this present life is not all, but that there is a judgment to come, wherein he must give an account before God. God cannot be forgotten with impunity. If we treat him as if he were nothing, and leave him out of our calculations for life, we shall make a fatal mistake. O my hearer, there is a God, and as surely as you live, you are accountable to him. When the Spirit of God comes with the grace of the gospel, he removes our inveterate ungodliness, and causes us to deny it with joyful earnestness.

We next deny "worldly lusts:" that is, the lusts of the present world or age, which I described to you just now as coming in between the two appearings. This present age is as full of evil lusts as that in which Paul wrote concerning the Cretians. The lust of the eye, the lust of the flesh, and the pride of life are yet with us. Wherever the grace of God comes effectually, it makes the loose liver deny the desires of the flesh; it causes the man who lusted after gold to conquer his greediness; it brings the proud man away from his ambitions; it trains the idler to diligence, and it sobers the wanton mind which cared only for the frivolities of life. Not only do we leave these lusts, but we deny them. We have an abhorrence of those things wherein we formerly placed our delight. Our cry is, "What have I to do any more with idols?" To the worldling we say,

> these things may belong to you; but as for us, we cannot own them; sin shall no more have dominion over us. We are not of the world, and therefore its ways and fashions are none of ours.

The period in which we live shall have no paramount influence over us, for our truest life is with Christ in eternity; our conversation is in Heaven. The grace of God has made us deny the prevailing philosophies, glories, maxims, and fashions of this present world. In the best sense we are nonconformists. We desire to be crucified to the world and the world to us. This was a great thing for grace to do among the degraded sensualists of Paul's day, and it is not a less glorious achievement in these times.

But then, brethren, you cannot be complete with a merely negative religion; you must have something positive; and so the next word is living—that "we should live soberly, righteously, and godly, in this present world." Observe, brethren, that the Holy Ghost expects us to live in this present world, and therefore we are not to exclude ourselves from it. This age is the battle-field in which the soldier of Christ is to fight. Society is the place in which Christianity is to exhibit the graces of Christ. If it were possible for these good sisters to retire into a large house, and live secluded from the world, they would be shirking their duty rather than fulfilling it. If all the good men and true were to form a select colony, and do nothing else but pray and hear sermons, they would simply be refusing to serve God in his own appointed way. No, you have to live soberly, godly, righteously in this world, such as it is at present. It is of no use for you to scheme to escape from it. You are bound to breast this torrent, and buffet all its waves. If the grace of God is in you, that grace is meant to be displayed, not in a select and secluded retreat, but in this present world. You are to shine in the darkness like a light.

This life is described in a three-fold way. You are, first, to live *"soberly"*—that is, for yourself. "Soberly" in all your eating and your drinking, and in the indulgence of all bodily appetites—that goes without saying. Drunkards and gluttons, fornicators and adulterers, cannot inherit the kingdom of God. You are to live soberly in all your thinking, all your speaking, all your acting. There is to be sobriety in all your worldly pursuits. You are to have yourself well in hand: you are to be self-restrained. I know some brethren who are not often sober. I do not accuse them of being drunk with wine; but they are mentally intoxicated: they have no reason, no moderation, no judgment. They are all spur, and no rein. Right or wrong, they must have that which they have set their hearts upon. They never look round to take the full bearing of a matter: they never estimate calmly; but with closed eyes, they rush on like bulls. Alas for these unsober people! They are not to be depended on, they are everything by turns, and nothing long. The man who is disciplined by the grace of God becomes thoughtful, considerate, self-curtained; and he is no longer tossed about by passion, or swayed by prejudice. There is only one insobriety into which I pray we may fall; and truth to say, that is the truest sobriety. Of this the Scripture saith, "Be not drunk with wine, wherein is excess; but be filled with the Spirit." When the Spirit of God takes full possession of us, then we are borne along by his sacred energy, and are filled with a divine enthusiasm which needs no restraint. Under all other influences we must guard ourselves against yielding too completely, that thus we may live "soberly."

As to his fellow-men, the believer lives *"righteously."* I cannot understand that Christian who can do a dirty thing in business. Craft, cunning, overreaching, misrepresentation, and deceit are no instruments for the hand of godly men. I am told that my principles are too angelic for business life—that a man cannot be a match for his fellowmen in trade, if he is too Puritanic. Others are up to tricks, and he will be ruined if he cannot trick them in return. O my dear hearers, do not talk in this way. If you mean to go the way of the Devil, say so, and take the consequences; but if you profess to be servants of God, deny all partnership with unrighteousness. Dishonesty and falsehood are the opposites of godliness. A Christian man may be poor, but he must live righteously: he may lack sharpness, but he must not lack integrity. A Christian profession without uprightness is a lie. Grace must discipline us to righteous living.

Towards God, we are told in the text that we are to be *godly*. Every man who has the grace of God in him indeed and of a truth, will think much of God, and will seek first the kingdom of God and his righteousness. God will enter into all his calculations, God's presence will be his joy, God's strength will be his confidence, God's providence will be his inheritance, God's glory will be the chief end of his being, God's law the guide of his conversation. Now, if the grace of God, which has appeared so plainly to all men, has really come with its sacred discipline upon us, it is teaching us to live in this three-fold manner.

Once more, there is looking, as well as living. One work of the grace of God is to cause us to be "looking for that blessed hope of the glorious appearing of the great God and our Savior Jesus Christ." What is that "blessed hope?" Why, first, that when he comes we shall rise from the dead, if we have fallen asleep; and that, if we are alive and remain, we shall be changed at his appearing. Our hope is that we shall be approved of him and shall hear him say, "Well done, good and faithful servant." This hope is not of debt, but of grace: though our Lord will give us a reward, it will not be according to the law of works. We expect to be like Jesus when we shall see him as he is. When Jesus shines forth as the sun, "then shall the righteous shine forth as the sun in the kingdom of our Father." Our gain by godliness cannot be counted down into the palm of our hand. It lies in the glorious future; and yet to faith it is so near that at this moment I almost hear the chariot of the Coming One. The Lord cometh, and in the coming of the Lord lies the great hope of the believer, his great stimulus to overcome evil, his incentive to perfect holiness in the fear of the Lord. Oh to be found blameless in the day of the manifestation of our Lord! God grant us this! Do you not see, brethren, how the discipline of the doctrine of grace runs towards the separating of us from sin, and the making us to live unto God?

III. Lastly, and briefly, the text sets forth certain of *our encouragements*. I will only briefly hint at them.

In this great battle for right, and truth, and holiness, what could we do, my brethren and my sisters, if we were left alone? But our first encouragement is that *grace has come* to our rescue; for in the day when the Lord Jesus Christ appeared among men, he brought for us the grace of God to help us to overcome all iniquity. He that struggleth now against inbred sin has the Holy Spirit within him to help him. He that goes forth to fight against evil in other men by preaching the gospel has that same Holy Ghost going with the truth to make it like a fire and like a hammer. I would ground my weapons, and retreat from a fight so hopeless, were it not that the Lord of Hosts is with us, the God of Jacob is our refuge. The grace of God that bringeth salvation from sin hath flashed forth conspicuously like the lightning which is seen from one part of the heavens to the other, and our victory over darkness is insured. However hard the conflict with evil, it is not desperate. We may hope on and hope ever. A certain warrior was found in prayer, and when his king sneered, he answered that he was pleading with his majesty's august ally. I question whether God is the ally of anybody when he goes forth with gun and sword; but in using those weapons which are "not carnal, but mighty through God to the pulling down of strongholds," we may truly reckon upon our august ally. Speak the truth, man, for God speaks with you! Work for God, woman, for God works in you to will and to do of his own good pleasure. The appearance of the grace of God in the person of Christ is encouragement enough to those who are under the most difficult circumstances, and have to contend for righteousness against the deadliest odds. Grace has appeared; wherefore let us be of good courage!

A second encouragement is that another *appearing is coming.* He who bowed his head in weakness, and died in the moment of victory, is coming in all the glory of his endless life. Do not question it, the world is not going to darken into an eternal night: the morning cometh as well as the night, and though sin and corruption abound, and the love of many waxeth cold, these are but the tokens of his near advent who said that it would be so before his appearing. The right with the might, and the might with the right shall be: as surely as God lives, it shall be so. We are not fighting a losing battle. The Lord *must* triumph. Oh, if his suffering life and cruel death had been the only appearing, we might have feared; but it is not: it is but the first, and the prefatory part of his manifestation. He comes! He comes! None can hinder his coming! Every moment brings him nearer; nothing can delay his glory. When the hour shall strike he shall appear in the majesty of God to put an end to the dominion of sin, and bring in endless peace. Satan shall be bruised under our feet shortly; wherefore comfort one another with these words, and then prepare for further battle. Grind your swords, and be ready for close fighting! Trust in God, and keep your powder dry. Ever this [is] our war cry, "He must reign." We are looking for the appearing of the great God and Savior Jesus Christ.

Another encouragement is that *we are serving a glorious Master.* The Christ whom we follow is not a dead prophet like Mahomet. Truly we preach Christ crucified; but we also believe in Christ risen from the dead, in Christ gone up on high, in Christ soon to come a second time. He lives, and he lives as the great God and our Savior. If indeed ye are soldiers of such a Captain, throw fear to the winds. Can you be cowards when the Lord of hosts leads you? Dare you tremble when at your head is the Wonderful, the Counselor, the mighty God, the Everlasting Father, the Prince of Peace? The trumpet is already at the lip of the archangel; who will not play the man? The great drum which makes the universe to throb, summons you to action.

> Stand up, stand up for Jesus,
> Ye soldiers of the cross;
> Lift high his royal banner,
> It must not suffer loss.

His cross is the old cross still, and none can overthrow it. Hallelujah, hallelujah to the name of Jesus!

Then come the tender thoughts with which I finish, the memories of *what the Lord has done for us* to make us holy: "Who gave himself for us." Special redemption, redemption with a wondrous price—"who gave himself for us." Put away that trumpet and that drum; take down the harp and gently touch its sweetest strings. Tell how the Lord Jesus loved us, and gave himself for us. O sirs, if nothing else can touch our hearts, this must: "Ye are not your own, ye are bought with a price."

And he gave himself for us with these two objects: first, redemption, that he might redeem us from all iniquity; that he might break the bonds of sin asunder, and cast the cords of depravity far from us. He died—forget not that—died that your sins might die, died that every lust might be dragged into captivity at his chariot wheels. He gave himself for you that you might give yourselves for him.

Again [secondly], he died that he might purify us—purify us unto himself. How clean we must be if we are to be clean unto him. The holy Jesus will only commune with that which he has purified after the manner of his own nature; purified unto himself. He has purified us to be wholly his: no human hand may use the golden cup, no human incense may burn in the consecrated censer. We are purified unto himself, as the Hebrew would put it, to be his *segullah*, his peculiar possession. The translation "peculiar people" is unfortunate, because "peculiar" has come to mean odd, strange, singular. The passage really means that believers are Christ's own people, his choice and select portion. Saints are Christ's crown jewels, his box of diamonds; his very, very, very own. He carries his people as lambs in his bosom; he engraves their names on his heart. They are the inheritance to which he is the heir, and he values them more than all the universe beside. He would lose everything else sooner than lose one of them. He desires that you, who are being disciplined by his grace, should know that you are altogether his. You are Christ's men. You are each one to feel, "I do not belong to the world; I do not belong to myself; I belong only to Christ. I am set aside by him for himself only, and his I will be." The silver and the gold are his, and the cattle upon a thousand hills are his; but he makes small account of them: "The Lord's portion is his people."

The apostle finishes up by saying that we are to be a people "zealous of good works." Would to God that all Christian men and women were disciplined by divine grace till they became zealous for good works! In holiness, zeal is sobriety. We are not only to approve of good works, and speak for good works, but we are to be red-hot for them. We are to be on fire for everything that is right and true. We may not be content to be quiet and inoffensive, but we are to be zealous of good works. Oh that my Lord's grace would set us on fire in this way! There is plenty of fuel in the church, what is wanted is fire. A great many very respectable people are, in their sleepy way, doing as little as they can for any good cause. This will never do. We must wake up. Oh the quantity of ambulance work that Christ's soldiers have to do! One half of Christ's army has to carry the other half. Oh that our brethren could get off the sick-list! Oh that all of us were ardent, fervent, vigorous, zealous! Come, Holy Spirit, and quieten us! We may not go about to get this by our own efforts and energies, but God will work it by his grace. Grace given us in Christ is the fountain head of all holy impulse. O heavenly grace, come like a flood at this time and bear us right away!

Oh that those of you who have never felt the grace of God may be enabled to believe in the Lord Jesus Christ as to his first appearing! Then, trusting in his death upon the cross, you will learn to look for his second coming upon the throne, and you will rejoice therein. Unto his great name be glory forever and ever! Amen.

The Watchword for Today: "Stand Fast"

Delivered on Lord's Day morning, April 17, 1887, at the Metropolitan Tabernacle, Newington. No. 1959.

For our conversation is in Heaven, from whence also we look for the Savior, the Lord Jesus Christ: who shall change our vile body, that it may be fashioned like unto his glorious body, according to the working whereby he is able even to subdue all things unto himself. Therefore, my brethren, dearly beloved and longed for, my joy and crown, so stand fast in the Lord, my dearly beloved.—Philippians 3:20–21; 4:1

Every doctrine of the Word of God has its practical bearing. As each tree beareth seed after its kind, so doth every truth of God bring forth practical virtues. Hence you find the apostle Paul very full of "therefores"—his "therefores" being the conclusions drawn from certain statements of divine truth. I marvel that our excellent translators should have divided the argument from the conclusion by making a new chapter where there is least reason for it.

Last Lord's Day I spoke with you concerning the most sure and certain resurrection of our Lord Jesus: now there is a practical force in that truth, which constitutes part of what is meant by "the power of his resurrection." Since the Lord has risen, and will surely come a second time, and will raise the bodies of his people at his coming, there is something to wait for, and a grand reason for steadfastness while thus waiting. We are looking for the coming of our Lord and Savior Jesus Christ from Heaven, and that he shall "fashion anew the body of our humiliation, that it may be conformed to the body of his glory;" therefore let us stand fast in the position which will secure us this honor. Let us keep our posts until the coming of the great Captain shall release the sentinels. The glorious resurrection will abundantly repay us for all the toil and travail we may have to undergo in the battle for the Lord. The glory to be revealed even now casts a light upon our path, and causes sunshine within our hearts. The hope of this happiness makes us even now strong in the Lord, and in the power of his might.

Paul was deeply anxious that those in whom he had been the means of kindling the heavenly hope might be preserved faithful until the coming of Christ. He trembled lest any of them should seem to draw back, and prove traitors to their Lord. He dreaded lest he should lose what he hoped he had gained, by their turning aside from the faith. Hence he beseeches them to "stand fast." He expressed in the sixth verse of the first chapter his conviction that he who had begun a good work in them would perform it, but his intense love made him exhort them, saying, "Stand fast in the Lord, my dearly beloved." By such exhortations, final perseverance is promoted and secured.

Paul has fought bravely; and in the case of the Philippian converts he believes that he has secured the victory, and he fears lest it should yet be lost. He reminds me of the death of that British hero, Wolfe, who on the heights of Quebec received a mortal wound. It was just at the moment when the enemy fled, and when he knew that they were running, a smile was on his face, and he cried, "Hold me up. Let not my brave soldiers see me drop. The day is ours. Oh, do keep it!" His sole anxiety was to make the victory sure. Thus warriors die, and thus Paul lived. His very soul seems to cry, "We have won the day. Oh, do keep it!" O my beloved hearers, I believe that many of you are "in the Lord," but I entreat you to "stand fast in the Lord." In your case, also, the day is won; but oh, do keep it! There is the pith of all I have to say to you this morning: may God the Holy Spirit write it on your hearts! Having done all things well hitherto, I entreat you to obey the injunction of Jude, to "keep yourselves in the love of God," and to join with me in adoring him who alone is able to keep us from falling, and to present us faultless before his presence with exceeding great joy. Unto him be glory forever. Amen.

In leading out your thoughts I will keep to the following order:

First, it seems to me from the text that *the apostle perceived that these Philippian Christians were in their right place:* they were "in the Lord," and in such a position that he could safely bid them "stand fast" in it. Secondly, *he longed for them that they should keep their right place*—"Stand fast in the Lord, my dearly beloved"; and then, thirdly, *he urged the best motives for their keeping their place.* These motives are contained in the first two verses of our text, upon which we will enlarge further on.

I. Paul joyfully perceived that his *beloved converts were in their right place.*

It is a very important thing indeed that we should begin well. The start is not everything, but it is a great deal. It has been said by the old proverb, that "Well begun is half done"; and it is certainly so in the things of God. It is vitally important to enter in at the strait gate; to start on the heavenly journey from the right point. I have no doubt that many slips and falls and apostasies among professors are due to the fact that they were not right at first: the foundation was always upon the sand, and when the house came down at last, it was no more than might have been expected. A flaw in the foundation is pretty sure to be followed by a crack in the superstructure. Do see to it that you lay a good foundation. It is even better to have no repentance than a repentance which needs to be repented of: it is better to have no faith than a false faith: it is better to make no profession of religion than to make an untruthful one. God give us grace that we may not make a mistake in learning the alphabet of godliness, or else in all our learning we shall blunder on and increase in error. We should early learn the difference between grace and merit, between the purpose of God and the will of man, between trust in God and confidence in the flesh. If we do not start aright, the further we go, the further we shall be from our desired end, and the more thoroughly in the wrong shall we find ourselves. Yes, it is of prime importance that our new birth and our first love should be genuine beyond all question.

The only position, however, in which we can begin aright is to be "in the Lord." This is to begin as we may safely go on. This is the essential point. It is a very good thing for Christians to be in the church; but if you are in the church before you are in the Lord, you are out of place. It is a good thing to be engaged in holy work; but if you are in holy work before you are in the Lord, you will have no heart for it, neither will the Lord accept it. It is not essential that you should be in this church or in that church; but it is essential that you should be "in the Lord": it is not essential that you should be in the Sabbath-school, nor in the Working Meeting, nor in the Tract Society; but it is essential to the last degree that you should be in the Lord. The apostle rejoiced over those that were converted at Philippi because he knew that they were in the Lord. They were where he wished them to remain, therefore he said, "Stand fast in the Lord."

What is it to be "in the Lord"? Well, brethren, *we are in the Lord vitally and evidently when we fly to the Lord Jesus by repentance and faith,* and make him to be our refuge and hiding-place. Is it so with you? Have you fled out of self? Are you trusting in the Lord alone? Have you come to Calvary, and beheld your Savior? As the doves build their nests in the rock, have you thus made your home in Jesus? There is no shelter for a guilty soul but in His wounded side. Have you come there? Are you in him? Then keep there. You will never have a better refuge; in fact, there is no other. No other name is given under Heaven among men whereby we must be saved. I cannot tell you to stand fast in the Lord, unless you are there: hence my first enquiry is—Are you in Christ? Is he your only confidence? In his life, his death, and his resurrection, do you find the grounds of your hope? Is he himself all your salvation, and all your desire? If so, stand fast in him.

Next, these people, in addition to having fled to Christ for refuge, were now *in Christ as to their daily life*. They had heard him say, "Abide in me"; and therefore they remained in the daily enjoyment of him, in reliance upon him, in obedience to him, and in the earnest copying of his example. They were Christians, that is to say, persons upon whom was named the name of Christ. They were endeavoring to realize the power of his death and resurrection as a sanctifying influence, killing their sins and fostering their virtues. They were laboring to reproduce his image in themselves, that so they might bring glory to his name. Their lives were spent within the circle of their Savior's influence. Are you so, my dear friends? Then stand fast. You will never find a nobler example; you will never be saturated with a diviner spirit than that of Christ Jesus your Lord. Whether we eat or drink, or whatsoever we do, let us do all in the name of the Lord Jesus, and so live in him.

These Philippians had, moreover, realized that they were *in Christ by a real and vital union with him*. They had come to feel, not like separated individualities copying a model, but as members of a body made like to their head. By a living, loving, lasting union they were joined to Christ as their covenant head. They could say, "Who shall separate us from the love of God which is in Christ Jesus our Lord?" Do you know what it is to feel that the life which is in you, is first in Christ, and still flows from him, even as the life of the branch is mainly in the stem? "I live; yet not I, but Christ liveth in me." This is to be in Christ. Are you in him in this sense? Forgive my pressing the question. If you answer me in the affirmative, I shall then entreat you to "stand fast" in him. It is in him, and in him only, that spiritual life is to be sustained, even as only from him can it be received. To be engrafted into Christ is salvation; but to abide in Christ is the full enjoyment of it. True union to Christ is eternal life. Paul, therefore, rejoiced over these Philippians, because they were joined unto the Lord in one spirit.

This expression is very short, but very full. "In Christ." Does it not mean that we are in Christ as the birds are in the air which buoys them up, and enables them to fly? Are we not in Christ as the fish are in the sea? *Our Lord has become our element*—vital and all surrounding. In him we live, and move, and have our being. He is in us, and we are in him. We are filled with all the fullness of God, because in Christ doth all fullness dwell, and we dwell in him. Christ to us is all; he is in all; and he is all in all! Jesus to us is everything in everything. Without him we can *do* nothing, and we *are* nothing. Thus are we emphatically in him. If you have reached this point, "stand fast" in it. If you dwell in the secret place of the tabernacles of the Most high, abide under the shadow of the Almighty. Do you sit at his table, and eat of his dainties? Then prolong the visit, and think not of removal. Say in your soul—

> *Here would I find a settled rest,*
> *While others go and come;*
> *No more a stranger, or a guest,*
> *But like a child at home.*

Has Jesus brought you into his green pastures? Then lie down in them. Go no further, for you will never fare better. Stay with your Lord, however long the night, for only in him have you hope of morning.

You see, then, that these people were where they should be—in the Lord, and that this was the reason why the apostle took such delight in them. Kindly read the first verse of the fourth chapter, and see how he loves them, and joys over them. He heaps up titles of love! Some dip their morsel in vinegar, but Paul's words were saturated with honey. Here we not only have sweet words, but they mean something: his love was real and fervent. The very heart of Paul is written out large in this verse—"Therefore, my brethren, dearly beloved and longed for, my joy and crown, so stand fast in the Lord, my dearly beloved." Because they were in Christ, therefore first of all they were Paul's *brethren*. This was a new relationship, not earthly, but heavenly. What did this Jew from Tarsus know about the Philippians? Many of them were Gentiles. Time was when he would have called them dogs, and despised them as the uncircumcised; but now he says, "My brethren." That poor word has become very hackneyed. We talk of brethren without particularly much of brotherly love, but true brothers have a love for one another which is very unselfish and admirable, and so there is between real Christians a brotherhood which they will neither disown, nor dissemble, nor forget. It is said of our Lord, "For this cause he is not ashamed to call them brethren"; and surely they need never be ashamed to call one another brethren. Paul, at any rate, looks at the jailor, that jailor who had set his feet in the stocks, and he looks at the jailor's family, and at Lydia, and many others; in fact, at the whole company that he had gathered at Philippi, and he salutes them lovingly as "My brethren." Their names were written in the same family register because they were in Christ, and therefore had one Father in Heaven.

Next, the apostle calls them "my *dearly beloved*." The verse almost begins with this word, and it quite finishes with it. The repetition makes it mean, "My doubly dear ones." Such is the love which every true servant of Christ will have for those who have been begotten to the faith of Christ by his means. Oh, yes, if you are in Christ, his ministers must love you. How could there be a lack of affection in our hearts towards you, since we have been the means of bringing you to Jesus? Without cant or display we call you our "dearly beloved."

Then the apostle calls them his *"longed for,"* that is, his most desired ones. He first desired to see them converted; after that he desired to see them baptized; then he desired to see them exhibiting all the graces of Christians. When he saw holiness in them he desired to visit them and commune with them. Their constant kindness created in him a strong desire to speak with them face to face. He loved them, and desired their company, because they were in Christ. So he speaks of them as those for whom he longed. His delight was in thinking of them and in hoping to visit them.

Then he adds, "My joy and crown." Paul had been the means of their salvation, and when he thought of that blessed result he never regretted all that he had suffered: his persecutions among the Gentiles seemed light indeed since these priceless souls were his reward. Though he was nothing but a poor prisoner of Christ, yet he talks in right royal style: they are his crown. They were his *stephanos*, or crown given as a reward for his life-race. This among the Greeks was usually a wreath of flowers placed around the victor's brow. Paul's crown would never fade. He writes as he felt the amaranth around his temples: even now he looks upon the Philippians as his chaplet of honor: they were his joy and his crown; he anticipated, I do not doubt, that throughout eternity it would be a part of his Heaven to see them amid their blessedness, and to know that he helped to bring them to that felicity by leading them to Christ. O beloved, it is indeed our highest joy that we have not run in vain, neither labored in vain: you who have been snatched as "brands from the burning," and are now living to the praise of our Lord Jesus Christ—you are our prize, our crown, our joy.

These converts were all this to Paul simply because they were "in Christ." They had begun well, they were where they should be, and he, therefore, rejoiced in them.

II. But secondly, it was for this reason that *he longed that they should keep there*.

He entreated them to stand fast. "So stand fast in the Lord, my dearly beloved." The beginning of religion is not the whole of it. You must not suppose that the sum of godliness is contained within the experience of a day or two, or a week, or a few months, or even a few years. Precious are the feelings which attend conversion; but dream not that repentance, faith, and so forth, are for a season, and then all is done, and done with. I am afraid there are some who secretly say, "Everything is now complete; I have experienced the necessary change, I have been to see the elders and the pastor, and I have been baptized, and received into the church, and now all is right forever." That is a false view of your condition. In conversion you have started in the race, and you must ran to the end of the course. In your confession of Christ you have carried your tools into the vineyard, but the day's work now begins. Remember, "He that shall endure unto the end, the same shall be saved." Godliness is a lifelong business. The working out of the salvation which the Lord himself works in you is not a matter of certain hours, and of a limited period of life. Salvation is unfolded throughout all our sojourn here. We continue to repent and to believe, and even the process of our conversion continues as we are changed more and more into the image of our Lord. Final perseverance is the necessary evidence of genuine conversion.

In proportion as we rejoice over converts, we feel an intense bitterness when any disappoint us, and turn out to be merely temporary camp-followers. We sigh over the seed which sprang up so speedily, but which withers so soon because it has neither root nor depth of earth. We were ready to say—"Ring the bells of Heaven"; but the bells of Heaven did not ring, because these people talked about Christ, and said they were in Christ; but it was all a delusion. After a while, for one reason and another, they went back;

> they went out from us, but they were not of us; for if they had been of us, they would no doubt have continued with us: but they went out, that they might be made manifest that they were not all of us.

Our churches suffer most seriously from the great numbers who drop out of their ranks, and either go back to the world, or else must be pursuing a very secret and solitary path in their way to Heaven, for we hear no more of them. Our joy is turned to disappointment, our crown of laurel becomes a circle of faded leaves, and we are weary at the remembrance of it. With what earnestness, therefore, would we say to you who are beginning the race, "Continue in your course. We beseech you turn not aside, neither slacken your running, till you have won the prize!"

I heard an expression yesterday which pleased me much. I spoke about the difficulty of keeping on. "Yes," answered my friend, "and it is harder still to *keep on* keeping on." So it is. There is the pinch. I know lots of fellows who are wonders at the start. What a rush they make! But then there is no stay in them; they soon lose breath. The difference between the spurious and the real Christian lies in this *staying* power. The real Christian has a life within him which can never die—an incorruptible seed which liveth and abideth forever; but the spurious Christian begins after a fashion, but ends almost as soon as he begins. He is esteemed a saint; but turns out a hypocrite. He makes a fair show for a while, but soon he quits the way of holiness, and makes his own damnation sure. God save you, dear friends, from anything which looks like apostasy. Hence I would with all my might press upon you these two most weighty words: "Stand fast."

I will put the exhortation thus—"Stand fast *doctrinally*." In this age all the ships in the waters are pulling up their anchors: they are drifting with the tide; they are driven about with every wind. It is your wisdom to put down more anchors. I have taken the precaution to cast four anchors out of the stern, as well as to see that the great bower anchor is in its proper place. I will not budge an inch from the old doctrine for any man. Now that the cyclone is triumphant over many a bowing wall and tottering fence, those who are built upon the one foundation must prove its value by standing fast. We will hearken to no teaching but that of the Lord Jesus. If you see a truth to be in God's word, grasp it by your faith; and if it be unpopular, grapple it to you as with hooks of steel. If you are despised as a fool for holding it, hold it the more. Like an oak, take deeper root, because the winds would tear you from your place. Defy reproach and ridicule, and you have already vanquished it. Stand fast, like the British squares[1] in the olden times. When fierce assaults were made upon them, every man seemed transformed to rock. We might have wandered from the ranks a little in more peaceful times to look after the fascinating flowers which grow on every side of our march; but, now we know that the enemy surrounds us, we keep strictly to the line of march, and tolerate no roaming. The watchword of the host of God just now is—"Stand fast!" Hold you to the faith once delivered to the saints. Hold fast the form of sound words, and deviate not one jot or tittle therefrom. Doctrinally stand fast!

Practically, also, abide firm in the right, the true, the holy. This is of the utmost importance. The barriers are broken down; they would amalgamate church and world: yes, even church and stage. It is proposed to combine God and Devil in one service; Christ and Belial are to perform on one stage. Surely now is the time when the lion shall eat straw like the ox, and very dirty straw too. So they say; but I repeat to you this word, "Come out from among them, and be ye separate, and touch not the unclean thing." Write "holiness unto the Lord" not only on your altars, but upon the bells of the horses; let *everything* be done as before the living God. Do all things unto holiness and edification. Strive together to maintain the purity of the disciples of Christ; and take up your cross, and go without the camp bearing his reproach. If you have already stood apart in your decision for the Lord, continue to do so. Stand fast. In nothing moved by the laxity of the age, in nothing affected by the current of modern opinion—say to yourself, "I will do as Christ bids me to the utmost of my ability. I will follow the Lamb whithersoever he goeth." In these times of worldliness, impurity, self-indulgence, and error, it becomes the Christian to gather up his skirts and keep his feet and his garments clean from the pollution which lies all around him. We must be more Puritanic and precise than we have been. Oh, for grace to stand fast!

---

[1] British squares: "Squaring" was a tricky but effecitve infantry defense tactic against a cavalry charge, where the foot troops formed an outward-facing square to rain fire on the faster mounted troops from any direction. The highly trained British excelled at this manoeuver, and it was key to their victory over Napoleon at Waterloo in 1815, nearly 70 years before this sermon was preached.

Mind also that you stand fast *experimentally*. Pray that your inward experience may be a close adhesion to your Master. Do not go astray from his presence. Neither climb with those who dream of perfection in the flesh, nor grovel with those who doubt the possibility of present salvation. Take the Lord Jesus Christ to be your sole treasure, and let your heart be ever with him. Stand fast in faith in his atonement, in confidence in his divinity, in assurance of his Second Advent. I pine to know within my soul the power of his resurrection, and to have unbroken fellowship with him. In communion with the Father and the Son, let us stand fast. He shall fare well whose heart and soul, affections and understanding are wrapped up in Christ Jesus, and in none beside. Concerning your inward life, your secret prayer, your walk with God, here is the watchword of the day—"Stand fast."

To put it very plainly, "Stand fast *in the Lord,*" *without wishing for another trust.* Do not desire to have any hope but that which is in Christ. Do not entertain the proposition that you should unite another confidence to your confidence in the Lord. Have no hankering after any other fashion of faith except the faith of a sinner in his Savior. All hope but that which is set before us in the gospel, and brought to us by the Lord Jesus, is a poisoned delicacy, highly colored, but by no means to be so much as tasted by those who have been fed upon the bread of Heaven. What need we more than Jesus? What way of salvation do we seek but that of grace? What security but the precious blood? Stand fast; and wish for no other rock of salvation save the Lord Jesus.

Next, stand fast *without wavering in our trust.* Permit no doubt to worry you. Know that Jesus can save you, and, what is more, know that he has saved you. So commit yourself to his hands, that you are as sure of your salvation as of your existence. The blood of Jesus Christ this day cleanseth us from all sin; his righteousness covers us, and his life quickens us into newness of life. Tolerate no doubt, mistrust, suspicion, or misgiving. Believe in Christ up to the hilt. All for myself, I will yield to be lost forever if Jesus does not save me. I will have no other string to my bow, no second door of hope, or way of retreat. I could risk a thousand souls on my Lord's truth and feel no risk. Stand fast, without wishing for another trust, and without wavering in the trust you have.

Moreover, stand fast *without wandering into sin.* You are tempted this way and that way: stand fast. Inward passions rise; lusts of the flesh rebel, the devil hurls his fearful suggestions; the men of your own household tempt you: stand fast. Only so will you be preserved from the torrents of iniquity. Keep close to the example and spirit of your Master; and having done all, still stand.

As I have said, stand fast without wandering, so next I must say, stand fast *without wearying.* You are a little tired. Never mind, take a little rest and brush up again. "Oh," you say, "this toil is so monotonous." Do it better, and that will be a change. Your Savior endured his life and labor without this complaint, for zeal had eaten him up. "Alas!" you cry, "I cannot see results." Never mind; wait for results, even as the husbandman waiteth for the precious fruits of the earth. "Oh, sir, I plod along and make no progress." Never mind, you are a poor judge of your own success. Work on, for in due season you shall reap if you faint not. Practice perseverance. Remember that if you have the work of faith and the labor of love, you must complete the trio by adding the patience of hope. You cannot do without this last. "Be ye steadfast, unmovable, always abounding in the work of the Lord, forasmuch as ye know that your labor is not in vain in the Lord."

I am reminded of Sir Christopher Wren, when he cleared away old St. Paul's to make room for his splendid pile. He was compelled to use battering rams upon the massive walls. The workmen kept on battering and battering. An enormous force was brought to bear upon the walls for days and nights, but it did not appear to have made the least impression upon the ancient masonry. Yet the great architect knew what he was at: he bade them keep on incessantly, and the ram fell again and again upon the rocky wall, till at length the whole mass was disintegrating and coming apart; and then each stroke began to tell. At a blow it reeled, at another it quivered, at another it moved visibly, at another it fell over amid clouds of dust. These last strokes did the work. Do you think so? No, it was the combination of blows, the first as truly as the last. Keep on with the battering-ram. I hope to keep on until I die. And, mark you, I may die and I may not see the errors of the hour totter to their fall, but I shall be perfectly content to sleep in Christ, for I have a sure expectation that this work will succeed in the end. I shall be happy to have done my share of the work, even if I personally see little apparent result. Lord, let thy work appear unto thy servants, and we will be content that thy glory should be reserved for our children. Stand fast, my brethren, in incessant labors, for the end is sure.

And then, in addition to standing fast in that respect, stand fast *without warping*. Timber, when it is rather green, is apt to go this way or that. The spiritual weather is very bad just now for green wood: it is one day damp with superstition, and another day it is parched with skepticism. Rationalism and Ritualism are both at work. I pray that you may not warp.

Keep straight; keep to the truth, the whole truth, and nothing but the truth; for in the Master's name we bid you "Stand fast in the Lord."

Stand fast, for there is great need. Many walk of whom I have told you often, and now tell you even weeping, that they are the enemies of the cross of Christ.

Paul urged them to stand fast because, even in his own case, spiritual life was a struggle. Even Paul said, "Not as though I had already attained." He was pressing forward; he was straining his whole energy by the power of the Holy Ghost. He did not expect to be carried to Heaven on a featherbed; he was warring and agonizing. You, beloved, must do the same. What a grand example of perseverance did Paul set to us all! Nothing enticed him from his steadfastness. "None of these things move me," said he, "neither count I my life dear unto me." He has entered into his rest, because the Lord his God helped him to stand fast, even to the end. I wish I had power to put this more earnestly, but my very soul goes forth with it. "Stand fast in the Lord, my dearly beloved."

III. Thirdly, *the apostle urged the best motives for their standing fast.*

He says, "Stand fast *because of your citizenship.*" Read the twentieth verse: "For our citizenship is in Heaven." Now, if you are what you profess to be, if you are in Christ, you are citizens of the New Jerusalem. Men ought to behave themselves according to their citizenship, and not dishonor their city. When a man was a citizen of Athens, in the olden time, he felt it incumbent upon him to be brave. Xerxes said, "These Athenians are not ruled by kings: how will they fight?" "No," said one, "but every man respects the law, and each man is ready to die for his country." Xerxes soon had to know that the like obedience and respect of law ruled the Spartans, and that these, because they were of Sparta, were all brave as lions. He sends word to Leonidas and his little troop to give up their arms. "Come and take them," was the courageous reply. The Persian king had myriads of soldiers with him, while Leonidas had only three hundred Spartans at his side; yet they kept the pass, and it cost the eastern despot many thousands of men to force a passage. The sons of Sparta died rather than desert their post. Every citizen of Sparta felt that he must stand fast: it was not for such a man as he to yield. I like the spirit of Bayard, that "knight without fear and without reproach." He knew not what fear meant. In his last battle, his spine was broken, and he said to those around him, "Place me up against a tree, so that I may sit up and die with my face to the enemy." Yes, if our backs were broken, if we could no more bear the shield or use the sword, it would be incumbent upon us, as citizens of the New Jerusalem, to die with our faces towards the enemy. We must not yield, we dare not yield, if we are of the city of the great King. The martyrs cry to us to stand fast; the cloud of witnesses bending from their thrones above beseech us to stand fast; yea, all the hosts of the shining ones cry to us, "Stand fast." Stand fast for God, and the truth, and holiness, and let no man take you crown.

The next argument that Paul used was *their outlook.* "Our conversation is in Heaven; from whence also we look for the Savior, the Lord Jesus Christ." Brethren, Jesus is coming. He is even now on the way. You have heard our tidings till you scarcely credit us; but the word is true, and it will surely be fulfilled before long. The Lord is coming indeed. He promised to come to die, and he kept his word: he now promises to come to reign, and be you sure that he will keep his tryst with his people. He is coming. Ears of faith can hear the sound of his chariot wheels; every moment of time, every event of providence is bringing him nearer. Blessed are those servants who shall not be sleeping when he comes, nor wandering from their posts of duty; happy shall they be whom their Lord shall find faithfully watching, and standing fast in that great day!

To us, beloved, he is coming, not as Judge and Destroyer, but as *Savior*. We look for the Savior, the Lord Jesus Christ. Now, if we do look for him, let us "stand fast." There must be no going into sin, no forsaking the fellowship of the church, no leaving the truth, no trying to play fast and loose with godliness, no running with the hare and hunting with the hounds. Let us stand so fast in singleness of heart that, whenever Jesus comes, we shall be able to say, "Welcome, welcome, Son of God!"

Sometimes I wait through the weary years with great comfort. There was a ship some time ago outside a certain harbor. A heavy sea made the ship roll fearfully. A dense fog blotted out all buoys and lights. The captain never left the wheel. He could not tell his way into the harbor, and no pilot could get out to him for a long time. Eager passengers urged him to be courageous and make a dash for the harbor. He said "No; it is not my duty to run so great a risk. A pilot is required here, and I will wait for one if I wait a week." The truest courage is that which can bear to be charged with cowardice. To wait is much wiser than, when you cannot hear the foghorn and have no pilot, yet to steam on and wreck your vessel on the rocks. Our prudent captain waited his time, and at last he espied the pilot's boat coming to him over the boiling sea. When the pilot was at his work the captain's anxious waiting was over. The Church is like that vessel—she is pitched to and fro in the storm and the dark, and the pilot has not yet come. The weather is very threatening. All around, the darkness hang like a pall. But Jesus will come, walking on the water, before long; he will bring us safe to the desired haven. Let us wait with patience. Stand fast! Stand fast! For Jesus is coming, and in him is our sure hope.

Further, there was another motive. *There was an expectation.* "He shall change our vile body," or rather, "body of our humiliation." Only think of it, dear friends! No more headaches or heartaches, no more feebleness and fainting, no more inward tumor or consumption; but the Lord shall transfigure this body of our humiliation into the likeness of the body of his glory. Our frame is now made up of decaying substances, it is of the earth, earthy. "So to the dust return we must." This body groans, suffers, becomes diseased, and dies: blessed be God, it shall be wonderfully changed, and then there shall be no more death, neither sorrow nor crying, neither shall there be any more pain. The natural appetites of this body engender sad tendencies to sin, and in this respect it is a "vile body." It shall not always be so—the great change will deliver it from all that is gross and carnal. It shall be pure as the Lord's body! Whatever the body of Christ is now, our body is to be like it. We spoke of it last Sunday, you know, when we heard him say, "Handle me." We are to have a real, corporeal body as he had for substance and reality; and, like his body, it will be full of beauty, full of health and strength; it will enjoy peculiar immunities from evil, and special adaptations for good. That is what is going to happen to me and to you; therefore let us stand fast. Let us not willfully throw away our prospects of glory and immortality. What! Relinquish resurrection? Relinquish glory? Relinquish likeness to the risen Lord? O God, save us from such a terrible piece of apostasy! Save us from such immeasurable folly! Suffer us not to turn our backs in the day of battle, since that would be to turn our backs from the crown of life that fadeth not away.

Lastly, the apostle urges us to stand fast because of *our resources*. Somebody may ask, "How can this body of yours be transformed and transfigured until it becomes like the body of Christ?" I cannot tell you anything about the process; it will all be accomplished in the twinkling of an eye, at the last trump. But I can tell you by what power it will be accomplished. The Omnipotent Lord will lay bare his arm, and exercise his might, "according to the working whereby he is able even to subdue all things unto himself." O brethren, we may well stand fast, since we have infinite power at our backs. The Lord is with us with all his energy, even with his all-conquering strength, which shall yet subdue all his foes. Do not let us imagine that any enemy can be too strong for Christ's arm. If he is able to subdue all things unto himself, he can certainly bear us through all opposition. One glance of his eye may wither all opposers, or, better still, one word from his lips may turn them into friends. The army of the Lord is strong in reserves. These reserves have never yet been fully called out. We, who are in the field, are only a small squadron, holding the fort; but our Lord has at his back ten thousand times ten thousand who will carry war into the enemy's camp. When the Captain of our salvation comes to the front, he will bring his heavenly legions with him. Our business is to watch until he appears upon the scene, for when he comes, his infinite resources will be put in marching order. I like that speech of Wellington (who was so calm amid the roar of Waterloo), when an officer sent word, "Tell the Commander-in-Chief that he must move me, I cannot hold my position any longer, my numbers are so thinned." "Tell him," said the great general, "he *must* hold his place. Every Englishman today must die where he stands, or else win the victory." The officer read the command to stand, and he did stand till the trumpet sounded victory. And so it is now. My brethren, we must die where we are rather than yield to the enemy. If Jesus tarries, we must not desert our posts. Wellington knew that the heads of the Prussian columns would soon be visible, coming in to ensure the victory; and so by faith we can perceive the legions of our Lord approaching: in serried ranks his angels fly through the opening Heaven. The air is teeming with them. I hear their silver trumpets. Behold, he cometh with clouds! When he cometh he will abundantly recompense all who stood fast amid the rage of battle. Let us sing, "Hold the fort, for I am coming."

"He Cometh with Clouds"

1887, at the Metropolitan Tabernacle, Newington. No. 1989.

Behold, he cometh with clouds; and every eye shall see him, and they also which pierced him: and all kindreds of the earth shall wail because of him. Even so, Amen.—Revelation 1:7

In reading the chapter, we observed how the beloved John saluted the seven churches in Asia with, "Grace and peace be unto you." Blessed men scatter blessings. When the *benediction* of God rests on us, we pour out benedictions upon others.

From benediction, John's gracious heart rose into *adoration* of the great King of Saints. As our hymn puts it, "The holy to the holiest leads." They that are good at blessing men will be quick at blessing God.

It is a wonderful doxology which John has given us:

Unto him that loved us, and washed us from our sins in his own blood, and hath made us kings and priests unto God and his Father; to him be glory and dominion forever and ever. Amen.

I like the Revised Version for its alliteration in this case, although I cannot prefer it for other reasons. It runs thus: "Unto him that *loveth* us, and *loosed* us from our sins by his blood." Truly our Redeemer has loosed us from sin; but the mention of his blood suggests washing rather than loosing. We can keep the alliteration and yet retain the meaning of cleansing if we read the passage, "Unto him that loved us, and laved[1] us." *Loved* us, and *laved* us: carry those two words home with you: let them lie upon your tongue to sweeten your breath for prayer and praise. "Unto him that loved us, and laved us, be glory and dominion forever and ever."

Then John tells of the *dignity* which the Lord hath put upon us in making us kings and priests, and from this he ascribes royalty and dominion unto the Lord himself. John had been extolling the Great King, whom he calls, "The Prince of the kings of the earth." Such indeed he was, and is, and is to be. When John had touched upon that royalty which is natural to our divine Lord, and that dominion which has come to him by conquest, and by the gift of the Father, as the reward of all his travail, he then went on to note that he has "made us kings." Our Lord's royalty he diffuses among his redeemed. We praise him because he is in himself a king, and next, because he is a king-maker, the fountain of honor and majesty. He has not only enough of royalty for himself, but he hands a measure of his dignity to his people. He makes kings out of such common stuff as he finds in us poor sinners. Shall we not adore him for this? Shall we not cast our crowns at his feet? He gave our crowns to us—shall we not give them to him? "To him be glory and dominion forever and ever. Amen."

King by thy divine nature! King by filial right! King-maker, lifting up the beggar from the dunghill to set him among princes! King of kings by the unanimous love of all thy crowned ones! Thou art he whom thy brethren shall praise! Reign thou forever and ever! Unto thee be hosannas of welcome and hallelujahs of praise. Lord of the earth and Heaven, let all things that be, or ever shall be, render unto thee all glory in the highest degree. Brethren, do not your souls take fire as you think of the praises of Immanuel? Fain would I fill the universe with his praise. Oh for a thousand tongues to sing the glories of the Lord Jesus! If the Spirit who dictated the words of John has taken possession of our spirits, we shall find adoration to be our highest delight. Never are we so near to Heaven as when we are absorbed in the worship of Jesus, our Lord and God. Oh, that I could now adore him as I shall do when, delivered from this encumbering body, my soul shall behold him in the fullness of his glory!

It would seem from the chapter that the adoration of John was increased by his *expectation* of the Lord's second coming; for he cries, "Behold, he cometh with clouds." His adoration awoke his expectation, which all the while was lying in his soul as an element of that vehement heat of reverent love which he poured forth in his doxology. "Behold, he cometh," said he, and thus he revealed one source of his reverence. "Behold, he cometh," said he, and this exclamation was the result of his reverence. He adored until his faith realized [made real] his Lord, and became a second and nobler sight.

---

[1] Laved: washed or bathed.

I think, too, that his reverence was deepened and his adoration was rendered more fervent by his conviction of the speediness of his Lord's coming. "Behold, he cometh," or is coming: he means to assert that he is even now on his way. As workmen are moved to be more diligent in service when they hear their master's footfall, so, doubtless, saints are quickened in their devotion when they are conscious that he whom they worship is drawing near. He has gone away to the Father for a while, and so he has left us alone in this world; but he has said, "I will come again and receive you unto myself," and we are confident that he will keep his word. Sweet is the remembrance of that loving promise. That assurance is pouring its savor into John's heart while he is adoring; and it becomes inevitable, as well as most meet and proper, that his doxology should, at its close, introduce him to the Lord himself, and cause him to cry out, "Behold, he cometh." Having worshipped among the pure in heart, he sees the Lord: having adored the King, he sees him assume the judgment-seat, and appear in the clouds of Heaven. When once we enter upon heavenly things, we know not how far we can go, nor how high we can climb. John who began with blessing the churches now, beholds his Lord.

May the Holy Ghost help us reverently to think of the wondrous coming of our blessed Lord, when he shall appear to the delight of his people and the dismay of the ungodly!

There are three things in the text. They will seem common-places to some of you, and, indeed, they are the common-places of our divine faith, and yet nothing can be of greater importance. The first is, *our Lord Jesus comes*: "Behold he cometh with clouds." The second is, *our Lord Jesus Christ's coming will be seen of all*: "Every eye shall see him, and they also which pierced him." And, in the third place, *this coming will cause great sorrow*: "All kindreds of the earth shall wail because of him."

I. May the Holy Spirit help us while, in the first place, we remember that *our Lord Jesus Christ comes!*

This announcement is thought worthy of a note of admiration. As the Latins would say, there is an *"Ecce"* placed here—*"Behold*, he cometh." As in the old books, the printers put hands in the margin pointing to special passages—such is this "behold!" It is a *Nota Bene* calling upon us to note well what we are reading. Here is something which we are to *hold* and *behold*. We now hear a voice crying, "Come and see!" The Holy Spirit never uses superfluous words, nor redundant notes of exclamation: when he cries, "Behold!" it is because there is reason for deep and lasting attention. Will you turn away when he bids you pause and ponder, linger and look? Oh, you that have been beholding vanity, come and behold the fact that Jesus cometh. You that have been beholding this, and beholding that, and thinking of nothing worthy of your thoughts; forget these passing sights and spectacles, and for once behold a scene which has no parallel. It is not a monarch in her jubilee, but the King of kings in his glory. That same Jesus who went up from Olivet into Heaven, is coming again to earth in like manner as his disciples saw him go up into Heaven. Come and behold this great sight. If ever there was a thing in the world worth looking at, it is this. Behold and see if there was ever glory like unto his glory! Hearken to the midnight cry, "Behold, the bridegroom cometh!" It has practically to do with you. "Go ye forth to meet him." This voice is to *you*, O sons of men. Do not carelessly turn aside; for the Lord God himself demands your attention: he commands you to "Behold!" Will you be blind when God bids you behold? Will you shut your eyes when your Savior cries, "Behold"? When the finger of inspiration points the way, will not your eye follow where it directs you? "Behold, he cometh." O my hearers, look hither, I beseech you.

If we read the words of our text carefully, this "Behold" shows us first, that *this coming is to be vividly realized.* I think I see John. He is in the spirit; but on a sudden he seems startled into a keener and more solemn attention. His mind is more awake than usual, though he was ever a man of bright eyes that saw afar. We always liken him to the eagle for the height of his fight and the keenness of his vision; yet on a sudden, even he seems startled with a more astounding vision. He cries out, "Behold! Behold!" He has caught sight of his Lord. He says not, "He will come by-and-by," but, "I can see him; he is now coming." He has evidently realized the second advent. He has so conceived of the second coming of the Lord that it has become a matter of fact to him; a matter to be spoken of and even to be written down. "Behold, he cometh!" Have you and I ever realized the coming of Christ so fully as this? Perhaps we believe that he will come. I should hope that we all do *that.* If we believe that the Lord Jesus has come the first time, we believe also that he will come the second time; but are these equally assured truths to us? Peradventure we have vividly realized the first appearing: from Bethlehem to Golgotha, and from Calvary to Olivet we have traced the Lord, understanding that blessed cry, "Behold the Lamb of God, which taketh away the sin of the world!" Yes, the Word was made flesh and dwelt among us, and we beheld his glory, the glory as of the Only-begotten of the Father, full of grace and truth. But have we with equal firmness grasped the thought that he comes again, without a sin-offering unto salvation? Do we now say to each other, as we meet in happy fellowship, "Yes, our Lord cometh"? It should be to us not only a prophecy assuredly believed among us, but a scene pictured in our souls, and anticipated in our hearts. My imagination has often set forth that dread scene: but better still, my faith has realized it. I have heard the chariot-wheels of the Lord's approach, and I have endeavored to set my house in order for his reception. I have felt the shadow of that great cloud which shall attend him, damping the ardor of my worldliness. I hear even now in spirit the sound of the last trumpet, whose tremendous blast startles my soul to serious action, and puts force into my life. Would God that I lived more completely under the influence of that august event!

Brothers and sisters, to this realization I invite you. I wish that we could go together in this, until as we went out of the house we said to one another, "Behold, he cometh!" One said to his fellow, after the Lord had risen, "The Lord has risen indeed." I want you tonight to feel just as certain that *the Lord is coming indeed,* and I would have you say as much to one another. We are sure that he will come, and that he is on the way; but the benefit of a more vivid realization would be incalculable.

This coming is to be zealously proclaimed, for John does not merely calmly say, "He cometh," but he vigorously cries, "Behold, he cometh." Just as the herald of a king prefaces his message by a trumpet blast that calls attention, so John cries, "Behold!" As the old town-crier was wont to say, "O yes! O yes! O yes!" or to use some other striking formula by which he called upon men to note his announcement, so John stands in the midst of us, and cries, "Behold, he cometh!" He calls attention by that emphatic word "Behold!" It is no ordinary message that he brings, and he would not have us treat his word as a common-place saying. He throws his heart into the announcement. He proclaims it loudly, he proclaims it solemnly, and he proclaims it with authority: "Behold, he cometh."

Brethren, no truth ought to be more frequently proclaimed, next to the first coming of the Lord, than his second coming; and you cannot thoroughly set forth all the ends and bearings of the first advent if you forget the second. At the Lord's Supper, there is no discerning the Lord's body unless you discern his first coming; but there is no drinking into his cup to its fullness, unless you hear him say, "Until I come." You must look forward, as well as backward. So must it be with all our ministries; they must look to him on the cross *and* on the throne. We must vividly realize that he, who has once come, is coming yet again, or else our testimony will be marred, and one-sided. We shall make lame work of preaching and teaching if we leave out either advent.

And next, *it is to be unquestionably asserted.* "Behold, he cometh." It is not, "Perhaps, he will come"; nor, "Peradventure, he may yet appear." "Behold, he cometh" should be dogmatically asserted as an absolute certainty, which has been realized by the heart of the man who proclaims it. "Behold, he cometh." All the prophets say that he will come. From Enoch down to the last that spoke by inspiration, they declare, "The Lord cometh with ten thousands of his saints." You shall not find one who has spoken by the authority of God, who does not, either directly or by implication, assert the coming of the Son of man, when the multitudes born of woman shall be summoned to his bar, to receive the recompense of their deeds. All the promises are travailing with this prognostication, "Behold, he cometh." We have his own word for it, and this makes assurance doubly sure. He has told us that he will come again. He often assured his disciples that if he went away from them, he would come again to them; and he left us the Lord's Supper as a parting token to be observed until he comes. As often as we break bread we are reminded of the fact that, though it is a most blessed ordinance, yet it is a temporary one, and will cease to be celebrated when our absent Lord is once again present with us.

What, dear brethren, is there to hinder Christ from coming? When I have studied and thought over this word, "Behold, he cometh," yes, I have said to myself, "indeed he does; who shall hold him back?" His heart is with his church on earth. In the place where he fought the battle, he desires to celebrate the victory. His delights are with the sons of men. All his saints are waiting for the day of his appearing, and he is waiting also. The very earth in her sorrow and her groaning travaileth for his coming, which is to be her redemption. The creation is made subject to vanity for a little while; but when the Lord shall come again, the creation itself also shall be delivered from the bondage of corruption into the glorious liberty of the children of God. We might question whether he would come a second time if he had not already come the first time; but if he came to Bethlehem, be assured that his feet shall yet stand upon Olivet. If he came to die, doubt not that he will come to reign. If he came to be despised and rejected of men, why should we doubt that he will come to be admired in all them that believe? His sure coming is to be unquestionably asserted.

Dear friends, this fact that he will come again *is to be taught as demanding our immediate interest.* "Behold, he cometh with clouds." Behold, look at it; meditate on it. It is worth thinking of. It concerns yourself. Study it again and again. "He cometh." He will so soon be here that it is put in the present tense: "He cometh." That shaking of the earth; that blotting out of sun and moon; that fleeing of Heaven and earth before his face—all these are so nearly here that John describes them as accomplished. "Behold, he cometh."

There is this sense lying in the background—that *he is already on the way.* All that he is doing in providence and grace is a preparation for his coming. All the events of human history, all the great decisions of his august majesty whereby he ruleth all things—all these are tending towards the day of his appearing. Do not think that he delays his coming, and then, upon a sudden, he will rush hither in hot haste. He has arranged for it to take place as soon as wisdom allows. We know not what may make the present delay imperative; but the Lord knows, and that suffices. You grow uneasy because near two thousand years have passed since his ascension, and Jesus has not yet come; but you do not know what had to be arranged for, and how far the lapse of time was absolutely necessary for the Lord's designs. Those are no little matters which have filled up the great pause: the intervening centuries have teemed with wonders. A thousand things may have been necessary in Heaven itself ere the consummation of all things could be arrived at. When our Lord comes, it shall be seen that he came as quickly as he could, speaking after the manner of his infinite wisdom; for he cannot behave himself otherwise than wisely, perfectly, divinely. He cannot be moved by fear or passion so as to act hastily as you and I too often do. He dwells in the leisure of eternity, and in the serenity of omnipotence. He has not to measure out days, and months, and years, and to accomplish so much in such a space, or else leave his life-work undone; but according to the power of an endless life, he proceeds steadily on, and to him a thousand years are but as one day. Therefore be assured that the Lord is even now coming. He is making everything tend that way. All things are working towards that grand climax. At this moment, and every moment since he went away, the Lord Jesus has been coming back again. "Behold, he cometh!" He is on the way! He is nearer every hour!

And we are told that *his coming will be attended by a peculiar sign.* "Behold, he cometh *with clouds.*" We shall have no need to question whether it is the Son of man who has come, or whether he is indeed come.

This is to be no secret matter: his coming will be as manifest as yonder clouds. In the wilderness, the presence of Jehovah was known by a visible pillar of cloud by day, and an equally visible pillar of fire by night. That pillar of cloud was the sure token that the Lord was in his holy place, dwelling between the cherubim. Such is the token of the coming of the Lord Christ.

> *Every eye the cloud shall scan,*
> *Ensign of the Son of man.*

So it is written, "And then shall appear the sign of the Son of man in Heaven: and then shall all the tribes of the earth mourn, and they shall see the Son of man coming in the clouds of Heaven with power and great glory." I cannot quote at this time all those many passages of Scripture in which it is indicated that our Lord will come either sitting upon a cloud, or "with the clouds," or "with the clouds of Heaven"; but such expressions are abundant. Is it not to show that his coming will be majestic? He maketh the clouds his chariots. He cometh with hosts of attendants, and these of a nobler sort than earthly monarchs can summon to do them homage. With clouds of angels, cherubim and seraphim, and all the armies of Heaven, he comes. With all the forces of nature, thunder cloud and blackness of tempest, the Lord of all makes his triumphant entrance to judge the world. The clouds are the dust of his feet in that dread day of battle when he shall ease him of his adversaries, shaking them out of the earth with his thunder, and consuming them with the devouring flame of his lightning. All Heaven shall gather with its utmost pomp to the great appearing of the Lord, and all the terrible grandeur of nature shall then be seen at its full. Not as the Man of sorrows, despised and rejected of men, shall Jesus come, but as Jehovah came upon Sinai in the midst of thick clouds and a terrible darkness, so shall he come, whose coming shall be the final judgment.

The clouds are meant to set forth the *might,* as well as the majesty, of his coming. "Ascribe ye strength unto God: his excellency is over Israel, and his strength is in the clouds." This was the royal token given by Daniel the prophet in his seventh chapter, at the thirteenth verse, "I saw in the night visions, and, behold, one like the Son of man came with the clouds of Heaven." Not less than divine is the glory of the Son of God, who once had not where to lay his head. The sublimest objects in nature shall most fitly minister to the manifest glory of the returning King of men. "Behold, he cometh;" not with the swaddling-bands of his infancy, the weariness of his manhood, the shame of his death, but with all the glorious tapestry of heaven's high chambers. The hanging of the divine throne-room shall aid his state.

The clouds, also, denote *the terror of his coming to the ungodly.* His saints shall be caught up together with him in the clouds, to meet the Lord in the air; but to those that shall remain on earth, the clouds shall turn their blackness and horror of darkness. Then shall the impenitent behold this dread vision—the Son of man coming in the clouds of Heaven. The clouds shall fill them with dread, and the dread shall be abundantly justified, for those clouds are big with vengeance, and shall burst in judgment on their heads. His great white throne, though it be bright and lustrous with hope to his people, will, with its very brightness and whiteness of immaculate justice, strike dead the hopes of all those who trusted that they might live in sin and yet go unpunished. "Behold, he cometh. He cometh with clouds."

I am in happy circumstances tonight, because my subject requires no effort of imagination from me. To indulge fancy on such a theme would be a wretched profanation of so sublime a subject, which in its own simplicity should come home to all hearts. Think clearly for a moment, till the meaning becomes real to you. Jesus Christ is coming, coming in unwonted splendor. When he comes he will be enthroned far above the attacks of his enemies, the persecutions of the godless, and the sneers of skeptics. He is coming in the clouds of Heaven, and we shall be among the witnesses of his appearing. Let us dwell upon this truth.

II. Our second observation is this: *our Lord's coming will be seen of all.*

"Behold, he cometh with clouds, *and every eye shall see him, and they also which pierced him.*"

I gather from this expression, first, that *it will be a literal appearing, and an actual sight.* If the second advent was to be a spiritual manifestation, to be perceived by the minds of men, the phraseology would be, "Every mind shall perceive him." But it is not so: we read, "Every eye shall see him." Now—the mind can behold the spiritual, but the eye can only see that which is distinctly material and visible. The Lord Jesus Christ will not come spiritually, for in that sense he is always here, but he will come really and substantially, for every eye shall see him, even those unspiritual eyes which gazed on him with hate, and pierced him. Go not away and dream, and say to yourself, "Oh, there is some spiritual meaning about all this." Do not destroy the teaching of the Holy Ghost by the idea that there will be a spiritual manifestation of the Christ of God, but that a literal appearing is out of the question. That would be altering the record. The Lord Jesus shall come to earth a second time as literally as he has come a first time. The same Christ who ate a piece of a broiled fish and of a honeycomb after he had risen from the dead; the same who said, "Handle me, and see; for a spirit hath not flesh and bones, as ye see me have"—this same Jesus, with a material body, is to come in the clouds of Heaven. In the same manner as he went up, he shall come down. He shall be literally seen. The words cannot be honestly read in any other way.

"Every eye shall see him." Yes, I do literally expect to see my Lord Jesus with these eyes of mine, even as that saint expected who long ago fell asleep, believing that though the worms devoured his body, yet in his flesh he should see God, whom his eyes should see for himself, and not another. There will be a real resurrection of the body, though the moderns doubt it: such a resurrection that we shall see Jesus with our own eyes. We shall not find ourselves in a shadowy, dreamy land of floating fictions, where we may perceive, but cannot see. We shall not be airy nothings, mysterious, vague, impalpable; but we shall literally see our glorious Lord, whose appearing will be no phantom show, or shadow dance. Never day more real than the day of judgment; never sight more true than the Son of man upon the throne of his glory. Will you take this statement home, that you may feel the force of it? We are getting too far away from facts nowadays, and too much into the realm of myths and notions. "Every eye shall see him"—in this there shall be no delusion.

Note well that *he is to be seen of all kinds of living men:* every eye shall see him: the king and the peasant, the most learned and the most ignorant. Those that were blind before shall see when he appears. I remember a man born blind who loved our Lord most intensely, and he was wont to glory in this, that his eyes had been reserved for his Lord. Said he, "The first whom I shall ever see will be the Lord Jesus Christ. The first sight that greets my newly-opened eyes will be the Son of man in his glory." There is great comfort in this to all who are now unable to behold the sun. Since "every eye shall see him," you also shall see the King in his beauty. Small pleasure is this to eyes that are full of filthiness and pride: you care not for this sight, and yet you must see it, whether you please or do not please. You have hitherto shut your eyes to good things, but when Jesus comes, you *must* see him. All that dwell upon the face of the earth, if not at the same moment, yet with the same certainty, shall behold the once crucified Lord. They will not be able to hide themselves, nor to hide him from their eyes. They will dread the sight, but it will come upon them, even as the sun shines on the thief who delights in the darkness. They will be obliged to own in dismay that they behold the Son of man: they will be so overwhelmed with the sight that there will be no denying it.

He will be seen of those who have been long since dead. What a sight that will be for Judas, and for Pilate, and for Caiaphas and for Herod! What a sight it will be for those who, in their lifetime, said that there was no Savior, and no need of one; or that Jesus was a mere man, and that his blood was not a propitiation for sin! Those that scoffed and reviled him have long since died, but they shall all rise again, and rise to this heritage among the rest—that they shall see him whom they blasphemed sitting in the clouds of Heaven. Prisoners are troubled at the sight of the judge. The trumpet of assize brings no music to the ears of criminals. But thou must hear it, O impenitent sinner! Even in thy grave thou must hear the voice of the Son of God, and live, and come forth from the tomb, to receive the things done in thy body, whether they were good or bad. Death cannot hide thee, nor the vault conceal thee, nor rottenness and corruption deliver thee. Thou art bound to see in thy body the Lord who will judge both thee and thy fellows.

It is mentioned here that he will *especially be seen by those that pierced him*. In this is included all the company that nailed him to the tree, with those that took the spear and made the gash in his side; indeed, all that had a hand in his cruel crucifixion. It includes all of these, but it comprehends many more besides. "They also who pierced him" are by no means a few. Who have pierced him? Why those that once professed to love him, and have gone back to the world. Those that once ran well, "What did hinder them?" And now they use their tongues to speak against the Christ whom once they professed to love. They also have pierced him whose inconsistent lives have brought dishonor upon the sacred name of Jesus. They also have pierced him, who refused his love, stifled their consciences, and refused his rebukes. Alas, that so many of you should be piercing him now by your base neglect of his salvation! They that went every Sunday to hear of him, and that remained hearers only, destroying their own souls rather than yield to his infinite love: these pierced his tender heart. Dear hearers, I wish I could plead effectually with you tonight, so that you would not continue any longer among the number of those that pierced him. If you will look at Jesus now, and mourn for your sin, he will put your sin away; and then you will not be ashamed to see him in that day. Even though you did pierce him, you will be able to sing, "Unto him that loved us, and washed us from our sins in his own blood." But, remember, if you persevere in piercing him, and fighting against him, you will still have to see him in that day, to your terror and despair. He will be seen by you and by me, however ill we may behave. And what horror will that sight cost us!

I felt unfit to preach to you tonight; but last Lord's Day I said that I would preach tonight if I could possibly manage it. It seemed barely possible, but I could not do less than keep my word; and I also longed to be with you, for your sakes; for peradventure there may not remain many more occasions on which I shall be permitted to preach the gospel among you. I am often ill; who knows how soon I shall come to my end.[2] I would use all that remains to me of physical strength and providential opportunity. We never know how soon we may be cut off, and then we are gone forever from the opportunity of benefiting our fellow-men. It were a pity to be taken away with one opportunity of doing good unused. So would I earnestly plead with you under the shadow of this great truth: I would urge you to make ready, since we shall both behold the Lord in the day of his appearing. Yes, I shall stand in that great throng. You also will be there. How will you feel? You are not accustomed, perhaps, to attend a place of worship; but you will be there, and the spot will be very solemn to you. You may absent yourself from the assemblies of the saints, but you will not be able to absent yourself from the gathering of that day. You will be there, one in that great multitude; and you will see Jesus the Lord as truly as if you were the only person before him, and he will look upon you as certainly as if you were the only one that was summoned to his bar.

Will you kindly think of all this as I close this second head? Silently repeat to yourself the words, "Every eye shall see him, and they also that pierced him."

III. And now I must close with the third head, which is a painful one, but needs to be enlarged upon: *his coming will cause great sorrow.*

What does the text say about his coming? "All kindreds of the earth shall wail because of him."

"All kindreds of the earth." Then *this sorrow will be very general.* You thought, perhaps, that when Christ came, he would come to a glad world, welcoming him with song and music. You thought that there might be a few ungodly persons who would be destroyed with the breath of his mouth, but that the bulk of mankind would receive him with delight. See how different—"All kindreds of the earth," that is, all sorts of men that belong to the earth; all earth-born men, men out of all nations and kindreds and tongues, shall weep and wail, and gnash their teeth at his coming. O sirs, this is a sad outlook! We have no smooth things to prophesy. What think you of this?

And, next, *this sorrow will be very great.* They shall *"wail."* I cannot put into English the full meaning of that most expressive word. Sound it at length, and it conveys its own meaning. It is as when men wring their hands and burst out into a loud cry; or as when eastern women, in their anguish, rend their garments, and lift up their voices with the most mournful notes. All the kindreds of the earth shall wail: wail as a mother laments over her dead child; wail as a man might wail who found himself hopelessly imprisoned and doomed to die. Such will be the hopeless grief of all the kindreds of the earth at the sight of Christ in the clouds: if they remain impenitent, they shall not be able to be silent; they shall not be able to repress

---
[2] Spurgeon (1834-1894) preached this sermon in 1887.

or conceal their anguish, but they shall wail, or openly give vent to their horror. What a sound that will be which will go up before high Heaven when Jesus sits upon the cloud, and in the fullness of his power summons them to judgment! Then "they shall wail because of him."

Will your voice be heard in that wailing? Will your heart be breaking in that general dismay? How will you escape? If you are one of the kindreds of the earth, and remain impenitent, you will wail with the rest of them. Unless you now fly to Christ, and hide yourself in him, and so become one of the kindred of Heaven—one of his chosen and blood-washed ones—who shall praise his name for washing them from their sins—unless you do this, there will be wailing at the judgment-seat of Christ, and you will be in it.

Then it is quite clear that men will not be universally converted when Christ comes; because, if they were so, they would not wail. Then they would lift up the cry, "Welcome, welcome, Son of God!" The coming of Christ would be as the hymn puts it—

> *Hark, those bursts of acclamation!*
> *Hark, those loud triumphant chords!*
> *Jesus takes the highest station*
> *Oh, what joy the sight affords!*

These acclamations come from his people. But according to the text, the multitude of mankind will weep and wail, and therefore they will not be among his people. Do not, therefore, look for salvation to [appear on] some coming day, but believe in Jesus now, and find in him your Savior at once. If you joy in him now, you shall much more rejoice in him in that day, but if you will have cause to wail at his coming, it will be well to wail at once.

Note one more truth. It is quite certain that when Jesus comes in those latter days *men will not be expecting great things of him.* You know the talk they have nowadays about "a larger hope." Today they deceive the people with the idle dream of repentance and restoration after death, a fiction unsupported by the least tittle [character] of Scripture. If these kindreds of the earth expected that when Christ would come, they would all die out and cease to be, they would rejoice that thereby they escaped the wrath of God. Would not each unbeliever say, "It were a consummation devoutly to be wished"? If they thought that at his coming there would be a universal restoration and a general jail delivery of souls long shut up in prison, would they wail? If Jesus could be supposed to come to proclaim a general restoration, they would not wail, but shout for joy. Ah, no! It is because his coming, to the impenitent, is black with blank despair that they will wail because of him. If his first coming does not give you eternal life, his second coming will not. If you do not hide in his wounds when he comes as your Savior, there will be no hiding place for you when he comes as your Judge. They will weep and wail because, having rejected the Lord Jesus, they have turned their backs on the last possibility of hope.

Why do they wail *because of him?* Will it not be because they will see him in his glory, and they will recollect that they slighted and despised him? They will see him come to judge them, and they will remember that once he stood at their door with mercy in his hands and said, "Open to me," but they would not admit him. They refused his blood: they refused his righteousness: they trifled with his sacred name; and now they must give an account for this wickedness. They put him away in scorn, and now, when he comes, they find that they can trifle with him no longer. The days of child's-play and of foolish delay are over; and now they have solemnly to give in their life's account. See, the books are opened! They are covered with dismay as they remember their sins, and know that they are written down by a faithful pen. They must give an account; and unwashed and unforgiven, they cannot render that account without knowing that the sentence will be, "Depart, ye cursed." This is why they weep and wail because of him.

O souls, my natural love of ease makes me wish that I could preach pleasant things to you; but they are not in my commission. I need scarce wish, however, to preach a soft gospel, for so many are already doing it, to your cost. As I love your immortal souls, I dare not flatter you. As I shall have to answer for it in the last great day, I must tell you the truth.

> Ye sinners seek his face
> Whose wrath ye cannot bear.

Seek the mercy of God tonight. I have come here in pain to implore you to be reconciled to God. "Kiss the Son lest he be angry, and ye perish from the way, when his wrath is kindled but a little. Blessed are all they that put their trust in him."

But if you will not have my Lord Jesus, he comes all the same for that. He is on the road now, and when he comes, you will wail because of him. Oh that you would make him your friend, and then meet him with joy! Why will ye die? He gives life to all those who trust him. Believe, and live.

God save your souls tonight, and he shall have the glory. Amen.

Preparation for the Coming of the Lord

Delivered on Lord's Day morning, September 22, 1889, at the
Metropolitan Tabernacle, Newington. No. 2105.

And now, little children, abide in him; that, when he shall appear, we may have
confidence, and not be ashamed before him at his coming.—1 John 2:28

O ur first anxious desire is that our hearers would come to Christ. We lay ourselves out to lift him up, as Moses lifted up the serpent in the wilderness, and
to bid men look to him and live. There is no salvation except by faith in the Lord Jesus Christ. He said, "Look unto me, and be ye saved, all the ends of the earth: for I
am God, and there is none else."

When men have looked to Jesus, our next anxiety is that they may be in Christ,
the City of Refuge. We long to speak of them as "men in Christ Jesus." My beloved
hearers, you must be in living, loving, lasting union with the Son of God, or else
you are not in a state of salvation. That which begins with coming to Christ, as the
engrafted branch is bound to the vine, continues in your growing into him and receiving of his life. You must be in Christ as the stone is in the building, as the member is in the body.

When we have good hope that our hearers have come to Christ, and are "in
Christ," a further anxiety springs up in our hearts that they may "abide" in Christ.
Our longing is that, despite temptations to go away from him, they may always remain at his feet; that, notwithstanding the evil of their nature, they may never be-
tray their Master, but may faithfully hold to him. We would have them mindful of

that precept—"As ye have received Christ Jesus the Lord, so walk ye in him." Oh, that they may be rooted in him, and built up in him, and may always be in union with him! Then shall we present them to our Lord in the day of his appearing with exceeding great joy.

To this third anxiety of the minister of Christ I would give my mind this morning. John says, "Little children, abide in him." How sweetly those words must have flowed from the lips and the pen of such a venerable saint! Methinks he is in this the echo of the Lord Jesus; for in the fifteenth chapter of the gospel of John, the Lord Jesus said,

> Abide in me, and I in you. As the branch cannot bear fruit of itself, except it abide in the vine, no more can ye, except ye abide in me. If ye abide in me, and my words abide in you, ye shall ask what ye will, and it shall be done unto you.

That word, "abide," was a very favorite one with the Lord Jesus, and it became equally dear to that disciple whom Jesus loved. In our Authorized Version, the translators have interpreted it sometimes "remain," and sometimes "continue"; but it is not very wise of them to have so changed the rendering. It is one of the virtues of the Revised Version that it generally translates the same Greek word by the same English word. This may not be absolutely requisite, for a little variety may be tolerated; but it is eminently instructive, since it allows us to see in our own mother tongue where the Holy Spirit used the same word; and if the translation be correct in one case, we may naturally conclude it will not be incorrect in another. "Abide" is one of John's special words.

May the Lord help us to consider these blessed words! Better still, may he write them on our hearts, and may we fulfill their teaching!

First, notice *to what he urges them*—"abide in him"; secondly, *under what character he addresses them*—"little children"; and thirdly, *by what motive he exhorts them*—"that, when he shall appear, we may have confidence, and not be ashamed before him at his coming."

I. First, then, *observe to what he urges them*: "Abide in him."

By this he meant one thing; but that thing is so comprehensive that we may better understand it by viewing it from many sides.

He meant *fidelity to the truth taught by our Lord*. We are sure he meant this, because, a little previously, in the twenty-fourth verse, he had said, "If that which ye have heard from the beginning shall remain in you, ye also shall continue in the Son, and in the Father." Beloved, you have believed in the Lord Jesus Christ unto the salvation of your souls. You have trusted in him as the Son of God, the appointed Mediator, and the effectual sacrifice for your sin. Your hope has come from a belief in Christ as God has borne witness to him. Abide in the truth which you received from the beginning; for in your earliest days it wrought salvation in you. The foundation of your faith is not a changeable doctrine: you rest on a sure word of testimony. Truth is, in its very nature, fixed and unalterable. You know more about it than you did; but the thing itself is still the same, and must be the same. Take care that you abide in it. You will find it difficult to do so, for there is an element of changeableness about yourself: this you must overcome by grace. You will find many elements of seduction in the outside world. There are men whose business it is to shake the faith of others, and thereby to gain a repute for cleverness and depth of thought. Some seem to think it an ambition worthy of a Christian to be always questioning, or, as the apostle puts it, to be "ever learning, and never able to come to the knowledge of the truth." To throw doubt into minds which, by a gracious certainty, have been made blessed, is their chosen lifework. Therefore, you will be often led to try your foundation, and at times you will tremble as you cling to it. Hearken, then, to this word from the mouth of your Lord: "Abide in him." Keep you where you were as to the truth which you believe. That which has justified you, will sanctify you. That which has, in a measure, sanctified you, will yet perfect you. Make no change as to the eternal verities upon which you ground your hope. As a stone, you are built on the foundation; abide there. As a branch, you have been grafted into the stem; abide there. As a member, you are in the body; abide there; it is all over with you if you do not. Abide in that holy mould [soil] of doctrine into which you were at first delivered. Let no man deceive you with vain words, though there are many abroad in these days who "would deceive, if it were possible, the very elect." Abide in Jesus, by letting his words abide in you. Believe what you have found to be the means of your quickening. Believe it with a greater intensity and a greater practicalness; but "cast not away your confidence, which hath great recompense of reward."

Next, he means "abide in him" as to the *uniformity of your trust*. When you first enjoyed a hope, you rested upon Christ alone. I think I heard the first infant prattle of your faith when it said,

> *I'm a poor sinner and nothing at all,*
> *But Jesus Christ is my all in all.*

At the first, you had no experience upon which you could rely, you had no inward graces upon which you could depend: you rested wholly upon Christ and his finished work. You rested in no degree upon the works of the law, nor upon your own feelings, nor upon your own knowledge, nor upon your own resolves. Christ was all. Do you not remember how you used to tell others that the gospel precept was "Only believe?" You cried to them, "Trust in Jesus; get out of yourselves; find all your wants provided for in him." Now, beloved, you have experience; thank God for it. Now you have the graces of the Spirit; thank God for them. Now you know the things of God by the teaching of the Holy Spirit; be grateful for that knowledge. But do not now fly in the face of your Savior by putting your experience, or your graces, or your knowledge, where he and he alone must be. Depend today as simply as you depended then. If you have some idea that you are hastening towards perfection, take care that you do not indulge a vain conceit of yourself; but even if it be true, still mix not *your* perfection with *his* perfection, nor your advance in grace with the foundation which he has laid for you in his blood and righteousness. "Abide in him." He is that good ship into which you have entered, that he may bear you safe to the desired haven. Abide in the vessel: neither venture to walk on the water, like Peter, nor think to swim by your own strength; but "abide in him," and you shall weather every storm. Only as you keep to your first simple confidence in the perfect work of the Lord Jesus can you have peace and salvation; as it is written, "Thou wilt keep him in perfect peace, whose mind is stayed on thee; because he trusteth in thee."

Moreover, abide in the Lord Jesus Christ in making him the constant object of your life. As you live *by* Christ, so live *for* Christ. Ever since you trusted in Christ as dying for you, you have felt that if he died for you, then you died in him—that henceforth your life might be consecrated to him. You are not your own, but you are Christ's, and Christ's only. The first object of your being is to honor and serve him who loved you and gave himself for you. You have not followed after wealth, or honor, or self-pleasing, but you have followed Jesus: take heed that you "abide in him" by continuing to serve him.

> Love not the world, neither the things that are in the world. If any man love the world, the love of the Father is not in him. For all that is in the world, the lust of the flesh, and the lust of the eyes, and the pride of life, is not of the Father, but is of the world. And the world passeth away, and the lust thereof: but he that doeth the will of God abideth forever.

You may wisely continue where you are, for you have chosen the right pursuit, and you have entered upon the right road. That crown which glitters in your eye at the end of the race is worthy of all your running. You could not have a nobler motive power than the constraining love of Christ. To live for Christ is the highest style of living: continue in it more and more. If the Lord changes your circumstances, still live for Christ. If you go up, take Christ up with you: if you go down, Christ will go down with you. If you are in health, live for Christ earnestly; if you are bound to a sick bed, live for Christ patiently. Go about your business, and sing for Jesus; or if he bids you stay at home, and cough away your life, then sicken for Jesus; but let everything be for him. For you, "Excelsior" means higher consecration, more heavenly living.

Surely, we should also understand by "Abide in him," that we are to *persevere in our obedience to our Lord.* The next verse is, "If ye know that he is righteous, ye know that everyone that doeth righteousness is born of him." What your Lord bids you, continue to do. Call no man Master, but in all things submit your thoughts, your words, and your acts to the rule of the Lord Jesus. Obey him by whose obedience you are justified. Be precise and prompt in your execution of his commands. If others reckon you morbidly conscientious, heed not their opinion, but "Abide in him." The rule of the Master is always binding on all his disciples, and they depart from him in heart when they err from his rule. Reverence for the precept is as much included in our homage of Christ as credence of the doctrine. If you have been upright in your dealings, be upright; be accurate to the penny in every payment. If you have been loving and generous, continue loving and generous; for your Lord's law is love. If you have closely imitated the Lord Jesus, go on to copy him still more minutely. Seek no new model; pray the Holy Spirit to work you to the selfsame thing. To you, as a soldier, your Captain's word is law:

> *Yours is not to reason why,*
> *Yours but to dare and die.*

"Abide in him." I know you might be[come] rich by doing that un-Christly act; scorn to win wealth in such a way. I know you may involve yourself in persecution if you follow your Lord closely. Accept such persecution gladly, and rejoice in it, for his name's sake. I know that a great many would say that for charity's sake you had better make compromises, and keep in union with evil doctrine and worldly practice; but you know better. Be it yours to follow the Lamb whithersoever he goeth; for this is what his beloved apostle means when he says, "Abide in him."

But I have not completed the full description yet; I fear I am not able to do so, by reason of my shallow knowledge and forgetfulness. *Continue in spiritual union with your Lord.* All the life you have is life derived from him; seek no other. You are not a Christian except as Jesus is the Christ of God to you; you are not alive unto God, except as you are one with the risen Lord. You are not saved, except as he is your Savior; nor righteous, save as he is your Righteousness. You have not a single pulse of heavenly desire, nor a breath of divine life in you, but what was first given you from him, and is daily given to you by him. Abide in this vital union. Do not try to lead an independent life. "Abide in him," in complete dependence from day to day upon the life which is treasured up in him on your behalf.

Let your life "abide in him" in the sense of being directed by him. The head directs all the members. The order which lifts my hand, or spreads my palm, or closes my fist, or lowers my arm, comes from the brain, which is the headquarters of the soul. Abide in your Lord by implicitly owning [acknowledging] his headship. Let every regulation of your life come from him who is the head, and let it be obeyed as naturally as the desires of the mind coming from the brain are obeyed by every part of the body. There is no war between the hand and the foot, for they abide in the head, and so are ruled without force, and guided without violence. If the leg were to set up an independent authority over itself, instead of obeying the head, what strange walking we should see! Have you never met with afflicted people in whom the nerves have lost vigor, and the muscles seem to jerk at random, and throw out a leg or an arm without reason? Such movements are painful to see, and we know that such a man is diseased. Do not desire to be without law to Christ. Let that mind be in you which was also in Christ Jesus: in that respect "abide in him."

"Abide in him" as the element of your life. Let him encompass you as the air surrounds you on all sides. As a fish—whether it be the tiniest sprat or the hugest whale—abides in the sea, so do you abide in Christ. The fish does not seek the sky or the shore—it could not live out of the element of water; and even so, I beseech you, do not seek to live in the world and in its sins; for as a Christian you cannot live there: Christ is your life. There is room enough for you in the Lord Jesus Christ, for he is the infinite God. Go not out of him for anything. Seek not pleasure outside of Christ, nor treasure outside of Christ; for such pleasure or treasure would be ruinous. Have neither want, nor will, nor wish, beyond your Lord. Let him draw a line around you, and do you abide within that circle.

"Abide in him" in the sense of being *at home in him*. What a world of meaning I intend by that word "being at home in Christ"! and yet this is the sense of the word, "Abide in him." I was speaking yesterday to a friend who had bought a pleasant house, with a large garden; and he said to me,

> I now feel as if I had a *home*. I have lived in London for years, and I have changed from one house to another with as little regret as a man feels in changing an omnibus; but I have always longed for the home feeling which hung about my father's house in the country. Why, there we loved the cozy rooms, and the look-outs from the little windows, and the corner cupboards in the kitchen. As for the garden and the field, they yielded us constant delight, for there was that bush in the garden where the robin had built, and the tree with the blackbird's nest. We knew where the pike lay in the pool, and where the tortoise had buried itself for the winter, and where the first primroses would be found in the spring. There is a vast difference between a house and a home.

That is what John means with regard to Christ: we are not merely to call *on* him, but to abide *in* him. Do not go to Jesus one day and to the world another day: do not be a lodger with him, but abide in him. My friend spoke of changing from one omnibus to another, and I fear that some change from Christ to the world when the day changes from Sunday to Monday; but it should not be so. Say with Moses, "Lord, thou hast been our dwelling place in all generations." Thy cross is the roof-tree of the family of love; within the thorn-hedge of thy suffering love, our whole estate is shut in; thy name is named on our abiding-place. We are not to thee as tenants with a lease, but we have a freehold [ownership] in thee. We can truly say and sing—

> Here would I make a settled rest
> While others go and come:
> No more a stranger or a guest,
> But like a child at home.

Lord Jesus, I am at home nowhere but in thee; but in thee I abide. Wherever else I lodge, I have in due time to shift my quarters. Whatever else I have, I lose it, or leave it; but thou art the same, and thou changest not. What a comfort to have our Lord himself to be our chosen dwelling place in time and in eternity!

Now I think I have come nearer to the full sense of my text. "Abide in him" means, hold fast to him, live in him, let all your noblest powers be drawn forth in connection with him, as a man at home is all there. Feel at ease in fellowship with him. Say, "Return unto thy rest, o my soul; for the Lord hath dealt bountifully with thee."

Why does the apostle urge us to abide in Christ? Is there any likelihood of our going away? Yes; for in this very chapter he mentions apostates, who from disciples had degenerated into antichrists, of whom he says, "They went out from us, but they were not of us; for if they had been of us they would, no doubt, have continued with us." "Abide in him," then, and do not turn aside unto crooked ways, as many professors have done. The Savior once said to his apostles, "Will ye also go away?" and they answered him with that other question, "Lord, to whom shall we go?" I hope your heart is so conscious that he has the words of eternal life that you could not dream of going elsewhere.

"But surely it is implied in these warnings that saints do leave their Lord and perish?" I answer, "No." Carefully observe the provision which is made against that fatality—provision to enable us to carry out the precept of the text. Will you open your Testaments, and just look at the verse which immediately precedes my text. What do you see? "Ye shall abide in him. And now, little children, abide in him." There is a promise made to those who are in Christ that they shall "abide in him"; but that promise does not render the precept unnecessary; for the Lord dealeth with us as with reasonable beings, not as with stocks and stones; and he secures the fulfillment of his own promise that we shall abide in him, by impressing upon our hearts his sacred precept, whereby he bids us "abide in him." The force he uses to effect his purpose is instruction, heart-winning, and persuading. We abide in him, not by a physical law, as a mass of iron abides on the earth; but by a mental and spiritual law, by which the greatness of divine love and goodness holds us fast to the Lord Jesus. You have the guarantee that you shall abide in Christ in the covenant engagement, "I will put my fear in their hearts, that they shall not depart from me." What a blessed promise that is! You are to take care that you abide in Christ as much as if all depended upon yourself; and yet you can look to the promise of the covenant, and see that the real reason for your abiding in Christ lies in the operation of his unchanging love and grace.

Moreover, brethren, if you are in Christ Jesus, you have the Holy Ghost given you to enable you to abide in him. Read the twenty-seventh verse:

> But the anointing which ye have received of him abideth in you, and ye need not that any man teach you: but as the same anointing teacheth you of all things, and is truth, and is no lie, and even as it hath taught you, ye shall abide in him.

The Holy Ghost brings the truth home to your heart with savor and unction, endearing it to your inmost soul. The truth has so saturated you through the anointing, that you cannot give it up. Has not your Lord said, "The water that I shall give him shall be in him a well of water springing up unto everlasting life"? Thus, you see that what is commanded in one Scripture is promised and provided for in another. To his people, God's commandings are enablings. As he bids you abide in him, so by that very bidding, he causes you to abide in him to his praise and glory.

II. Secondly, notice *under what character John addresses these believers*. He says, "And now, *little children.*"

This indicates *the apostle's love to them*. John lived to [be] a great age; and the tradition is, that they used to carry him into the assembly, and, when he could do nothing else, he would lift his hand, and simply say, "Little children, love one another." Here, to show his tender concern for those to whom he wrote, he called them "little children." He could not wish them a greater blessing out of the depth of his heart's affection, than that they should faithfully abide in Christ.

Next, by this he suggests *their near and dear relation* to their Father in Heaven. You are the children of God; but as yet you are little ones—therefore do not leave your Father's house, nor run away from your elder brother's Love. Because you are little children, you are not of traveling years, therefore stay at home and abide in your Lord.

Does he not hint at *their feebleness?* Even if you were grown and strong, you would not be wise to gather all together and wander away into the far country; but as you are so young, so dependent, so feeble, it is essential that you abide in him. Shall a babe forsake its mother? What can you do apart from God? Is he not your life, your all?

Does not the apostle also gently hint at *their fickleness?* You are very changeable, like little babes. You are apt to be hot and cold in half an hour. You are this and that, and fifty other things, in the course of one revolving moon. But, little children as you are, be faithful to one point—abide in your Savior. Change not towards your Redeemer. Stretch out your hands and clasp him and cry,

> My Jesus, I love thee, I know thou art mine,
> For thee all the follies of sin, I resign.

Surrender yourself to him by an everlasting covenant, never to be cancelled. Be his forever and ever.

Did not this remind them of their *daily dependence* upon the Lord's care, as little children depend on their parents? Why, beloved, the Lord has to nurse you. He feeds you with the unadulterated milk of the Word; he comforts you as a mother doth her child; he carries you in his bosom, he bears you all your days. Your new life is as yet weak and struggling; do not carry it into the cold atmosphere of distance from Jesus. Little children, since you derive all from Jesus, abide in him. To go elsewhere will be to wander into a howling wilderness. The world is empty; only Christ has fullness. Away from Jesus, you will be as a child deserted by its mother, left to pine, and starve, and die; or as a little lamb on the hillside without a shepherd, tracked by the wolf, whose teeth will soon extract its heart's blood. Abide, O child, with thy mother! Abide, O lamb, with thy shepherd!

We may all come under John's description at this time. The beloved John speaketh unto us as unto little children, for we are none of us much more. We are not such wonderfully knowing people as certain of our neighbors; we are not such learned scientists and acute critics as they are; neither have we their marvelous moral consciousness, which is superior to inspiration itself; therefore we are bound by our very feebleness to venture less than they do. Let the men of the world choose what paths they will—we feel bound to abide in Christ because we know no other place of safety. They may push off into the sea of speculation; our smaller boats must hug the shore of certainty. To us, however, it is no small comfort that the Lord has revealed to babes the things which are hidden from the wise and prudent. Those who become as little children, enter into the kingdom of Heaven.

Cling to the Lord Jesus in your feebleness, in your fickleness, in your nothingness; and abidingly take him to be everything to you. "The conies [rabbits] are but a feeble folk, yet make they their houses in the rocks"; be you like them. Abide in the rifts of the Rock of Ages, and let nothing tempt you to quit your stronghold. You are no lion, able to fight your foes, and deliver yourself by main strength; you are only a little cony, and you will be wise to hide rather than fight. "Little children, abide in him."

III. I now come to my last point, which is most important, for it finds steam wherewith to drive the engine. Thirdly, we shall consider *by what motive John exhorts us to this pleasant and necessary duty of abiding in Christ.*

Kindly look at the text, for there is in it a little word to be noticed. The apostle exhorts us by *a motive in which he takes his share.* Let me read it: "Now, little children, abide in him; that, when he shall appear, *you* may have confidence." No, no. Look [again] at that little word: it runs thus, "that *we* may have confidence." The beloved John needed to have confidence at the appearing of the Lord, and confidence fetched from the same source as that to which he directed his little children. They must abide in Christ, that they might have confidence, and the dearest of the apostles must practice the same abiding. How wisely, and yet how sweetly, he puts himself upon our level in this matter!

Notice, further, that the motive is one *drawn from Jesus*. John does not drive believers with the lash of the law, but he draws them with the cords of love. I never like to see God's children whipped with rods gathered from the thorny sides of Sinai. We have not come to Mount Sinai, but to Mount Zion. When a man tries to pommel me to my duty by the law, I kick at the goad [whip] like a bullock [young ox] unaccustomed to the yoke; and rightly so, "For ye are not under the law, but under grace." The motive which sways a freeborn heir of Heaven is fetched from grace, and not from law; from Jesus, and not from Moses. Christ is our example, and our motive also, blessed be his name!

The motive is drawn from our Lord's expected advent. Notice how John puts it. He uses two words for the same thing: "When he shall appear," and, "at his coming." The second advent may be viewed in two lights. First, as the appearing of one who is here already, but is hidden; and next, as the coming of one who is absent. In the first sense, we know that our Lord Jesus Christ abides in his church; according to his word, "Lo, I am with you alway, even unto the end of the world." Yet, though spiritually present, he is unseen. Our Lord will, on a sudden, be "manifested," as the Revised Version has it. The spiritual and secret presence of Christ will become a visible and manifest presence in the day of his appearing.

The apostle also uses the term, "at his coming," or, "his presence." This is the same thing from another point of view. In a certain evident sense our Lord is absent: "He is not here, for he is risen." He has gone his way unto the Father. In that respect he will come a second time, "without a sin-offering, unto salvation." He who has gone from us will so come in like manner as he was seen to go up into Heaven. There is thus a difference of aspect between the second advent when it is described as "his appearing," and "his coming." John pleads the glorious manifestation of our Lord under both of these views as a reason for abiding in him.

As to our Lord's "appearing," he would have us abide in Christ, that we may have confidence when he appears. Confidence at his appearing is the high reward of constant abiding in Christ. The apostle keeps most prominent "the appearing" as an argument. A thousand things are to happen at our Lord's appearing; but John does not mention one of them. He does not hold it up as a thing to be desired that we may have confidence amid the wreck of matter and the crash of worlds, when the stars shall fall like autumn leaves, when the sun shall be turned into darkness, and the moon into blood; when the graves shall be opened, and the dead shall rise, or when the heavens, being on fire, shall be dissolved, and the elements shall melt with fervent heat; the earth also, and the works that are therein, shall be burned up. Those will be direful times, days of terror and dismay; but it is not of these that he speaks particularly; for he regards all these events as swallowed up in the one great fact of the glorious appearing of our Lord and Savior Jesus Christ.

His desire is that we may have confidence if he appear on a sudden. What does he mean by having confidence, when he shall appear? Why, this: that if you abide in him when you do not see him, you will be very bold should he suddenly reveal himself. Before he appears, you have dwelt in him, and he has dwelt in you; what fear could his appearing cause you? Faith has so realized him, that if suddenly he were to appear to the senses, it would be no surprise to you; and, assuredly, it would cause you joy rather than dismay. You would feel that you at last enjoyed what you had long expected, and saw, somewhat more closely, a friend with whom you had long been familiar. I trust, beloved, that some of us live in such a style that if, on a sudden, our Lord were to appear, it would cause no alarm to us. We have believed him to be present, though unseen, and it will not affect our conduct when he steps from behind the curtain, and stands in the open light. O Lord Jesus, if thou wert now to stand in our midst, we should remember that we had thy presence before, and lived in it, and now we should only be the more assured of that which we before knew by faith. We shall behold our Lord with confidence, freedom, assurance, and delight, feeling perfectly at home with him. The believer who abides in his Lord would be but little startled by his sudden appearing; he is serving his Lord now, and he would go on serving him; he loves him now, and he would go on loving him, only as he would have a clearer view of him, he would feel a more intense consecration to him.

The word translated "confidence" means freedom of speech. If our divine Lord were to appear in a moment, we should not lose our tongue through fear, but should welcome him with glad acclaim. To desert our Lord would rob us of that ease of mind which is betokened by free speech; but to cleave to him will secure us confidence. We now speak to him in secret, and he speaks again to us; we shall not cease to speak in tones of reverent love when he appears. I have preached concerning my Lord—while he is not seen—those truths which I shall not blush to own before his face. If my Lord and Master were, at this instant, to appear in his glory in this Tabernacle,[1] I dare with confidence hand in to him the volumes of my sermons, in proof that I have not departed from his truth, but have heartily continued in him. I ought to improve in many things, but I could not improve upon the gospel which I have preached among you. I am prepared to live by it, to die by it, or to meet my Lord upon it if he should this day appear. O my hearers, if you are in Christ, see to it that you so abide in him that, should he suddenly appear, you would behold him with confidence. If we abide in him, if he were to unveil his majestic face, we might be overcome with rapture, but our confidence in him would grow stronger, our freedom with him would be even more enlarged, and our joy in him would be made perfect. Has he not prayed for us, that we may be with him, and behold his glory; and can we be afraid of the answer to his loving prayer? If you

---

[1] Tabernacle: the Metropolitan Tabernacle, Spurgeon's church.

abide in Christ, the manifestation of Christ will be your manifestation, and that will be a matter of delight, and not of fear.

Beloved, if you do not abide in him, you will have no confidence. If I were to compromise the truth, and then my Lord were to appear, could I meet him with confidence? If, to preserve my reputation, or be thought liberal-minded, I played fast and loose with the gospel, how could I see my Lord's face with confidence? If any of you have failed to serve your Master; if you have preferred gain to godliness, and pleasure to holiness; if he were suddenly to shine forth in his glory, what confidence could you have in meeting him? A good man was asked, one day, "If the Lord were now to appear, how would you feel?" He replied. "My brother, I should not be afraid; but I think I should be ashamed." He meant that he was not afraid of condemnation, but he blushed to think how little he had served his Lord. In this case it was genuine humility. I pray you, get not only beyond being afraid, but may the Lord make you so to abide in him that you would not even be ashamed at his appearing!

The other point is, that you should "not be ashamed before him at his coming." That means, that having regarded him as being absent, you have not so lived that, if he should suddenly be present in person, you would be ashamed of your past life. What must it be to be driven with shame away from his presence into everlasting contempt! The text may have such a meaning. What have you been doing while he has been absent? This is a question for a servant to answer at his Lord's arrival. You are left in his house to take care of it while he is in the far-off country; and if you have been beating his servants, and eating and drinking with the drunken, you will be greatly ashamed when he returns. His coming will be in itself a judgment. "Who may abide the day of his coming? and who shall stand when he appeareth?" Blessed is that man who, with all his faults, has been so sanctified by grace that he will not be ashamed at his Lord's coming. Who is that man? It is the man who has learned to abide in Christ. What is the way to prepare for Christ's coming? By the study of the prophecies? Yes, if you are sufficiently instructed to be able to understand them. "To be prepared for the Lord's coming," some enthusiasts might say, "had I not better spend a month in retirement, and get out of this wicked world?" You may, if you like; and especially you will do so if you are lazy. But the one Scriptural prescription for preparing for his coming is this, "Abide in him." If you abide in the faith of him, holding his truth, following his example, and making him your dwelling-place, your Lord may come at any hour, and you will welcome him. The cloud, the great white throne, the blast of trumpets, the angelic attendants of the last assize, the trembling of creation, and the rolling up of the universe as a worn-out vesture, will have no alarms for you; for you will not be ashamed at his coming.

The date of that coming is concealed. When he shall come, no man can tell. Watch for him, and be always ready, that you may not be ashamed at his advent. Should a Christian man go into worldly assemblies and amusements? Would he not be ashamed should his Lord come and find him among the enemies of the cross? I dare not go where I should be ashamed to be found should my Lord come on a sudden. Should a Christian man ever be in a passion? Suppose his Lord should there and then come; would he not be ashamed at his coming? [Some]one here says of an offender, "I will never forgive her; she shall never darken my doors again." Would you not be ashamed if the Lord Jesus came, and found you unforgiving? Oh, that we may abide in him, and never be in such a state that his coming would be unwelcome to us! Beloved, so live from day to day in duty and in devotion, that your Lord's coming would be timely. Go about your daily business and abide in him, and then his coming will be a glorious delight to you.

I called to see one of our friends, and she was whitening the front steps of the house. She apologized very much, and said that she felt ashamed of being caught in such a position; but I assured her that I should like my Lord to come and find me, just as I found her, doing my daily work with all my heart. We are never in better trim for seeing our Master than when we are faithfully doing his work. There is no need for a pious smartening up; he that abides in Christ always wears garments of glory and beauty; he may go in with his Lord into the wedding, whenever the midnight cry is heard. Abide in him, and then none can make you ashamed. Who shall lay anything to your charge?

He will come—behold, he is coming even now. Hear ye not the sounding of his chariot wheels? He may arrive before yon sun goes down. "In such an hour as ye think not, the Son of man cometh." When the world is eating and drinking, marrying and giving in marriage, he will bring destruction upon the ungodly. Be ye so engaged, day by day, that you will not be taken at unawares. What will it be, to be caught up together with the saints in the clouds, to meet the Lord in the air! What will it be to see him come in the glory of the Father, and all his holy angels with him! What will it be to see him reign upon the earth, with his ancients gloriously! Can ye imagine the millennial splendor, the age of gold, the halcyon days of peace? As for the judgment of the world, know ye not that the saints shall judge angels? They shall appear as assessors with Christ, and the Lord shall bruise Satan under their feet. Glory awaits us, and nothing but glory, if we abide in Christ. Therefore, keep your garments unspotted, your loins girt [girded], your lamps trimmed, and your lights burning, and ye yourselves as men that look for your Lord—that, when he cometh, you may have confidence, and not shame. May the Holy Spirit, without whom this cannot be, be freely given to us this day, that we may abide in the Lord! And you who have never trusted in Christ for salvation, may you come to him, and then "abide in him" from this good hour! To his name be glory! Amen.

Watching for Christ's Coming

Delivered at the Metropolitan Tabernacle, Newington, on Lord's Day evening, April 7, 1889. Intended for reading on Lord's Day, April 2, 1893. No. 2302.

Blessed are those servants, whom the lord, when he cometh, shall find watching: verily I say unto you, that he shall gird himself, and make them to sit down to meat, and will come forth and serve them. And if he shall come in the second watch, or come in the third watch, and find them so, blessed are those servants.—Luke 12:37–38

I am about to speak of the Second Coming of Christ; and I felt thankful that my dear brother's prayer [before the sermon]—although we had not been in consultation with one another upon the matter—was in every way so suitable to the subject upon which I am to speak. He led us in prayer to think of our coming Lord; so that I trust you are on the margin of the subject now, and that you will not have to make any very great exertion of mind to plunge into mid-stream, and be carried away with the full current of thought concerning the Second Advent of the Savior. It is a very appropriate topic when we come to the Lord's table; for, as that prayer reminded us, the Lord's supper looks backward, and is a memorial of his agony; but it [also] looks forward and is an anticipation of his glory. Paul wrote to the church at Corinth, "For as often as ye eat this bread, and drink this cup, ye do shew the Lord's death till he come." By looking forward, in a right state of heart, to that Second Coming of Christ which is the joy of his Church, you will be also in a right state of heart for coming to the communion-table. May the Holy Ghost make it to be so!

The posture at the communion-table, as you know, according to our Lord's example, was not that of kneeling, but that of reclining. The easiest position which you can assume is the most fitting for the Lord's supper; and yet remember that the supper was no sooner finished, than "they sang a hymn," and when that hymn was concluded, they went out into the Mount of Olives, to the agonies of Gethsemane. It often seems to me as if now, after finding rest at the table by feeding upon Christ—whose real presence we have, not after a carnal sort, but after a spiritual sort—after that, we sing a hymn, as if we would go out to meet our Lord in his Second Coming, not going to the Mount of Olives to see him in a bloody sweat, but to hear that word of the angel, "This same Jesus, which is taken up from you into Heaven, shall so come in like manner as ye have seen him go into Heaven." I do not think we ought to feel at all surprised if we were to go out from the table of fellowship tonight, and meet our Lord at once; nay, we should be always waiting for his appearing, ever expecting him, not knowing at what hour the Master of the house shall come. The world does not expect him; it goes on with its eating and drinking, its marrying and giving in marriage; but his own family should expect him. When he will return from the wedding, I trust that he will not find the door shut against him, but that we shall be ready to open to our Lord immediately he knocketh. That is the object of the few words that I shall have to say tonight, to stir you up, and my own heart also, to be ever watching for Christ's Second Coming.

I. First, *the Lord will come.*

He that has come once, is to come again; he will come a second time. The Lord will come.

He will come again, for *he has promised to return.* We have his own word for it. That is our first reason for expecting him. Among the last of the words which he spoke to his servant John are these, "Surely I come quickly." You may read it, "I am coming quickly. I am even now upon the road. I am traveling as fast as wisdom allows. I am always coming, and coming quickly." Our Lord has promised to come, and to come in person. Some try to explain the Second Coming of Christ as though it meant the believer dying. You may, if you like, consider that Christ comes to his saints in death. In a certain sense, he does; but that sense will never bear out the full meaning of the teaching of the Second Advent with which the Scripture is full. No, "the Lord himself shall descend from Heaven with a shout, with the voice of the archangel, and with the trump of God." He who went up to Heaven will come down from Heaven, and stand in the latter day upon the earth. Every redeemed soul can say with Job, "Though after my skin, worms destroy this body, yet in my flesh shall I see God: whom I shall see for myself, and mine eyes shall behold, and not another." Christ will as certainly be here again in glory as he once was here in shame, for he has promised to return.

Moreover, *the great scheme of redemption requires Christ's return*. It is a part of that scheme that, as he came once with a sin-offering, he should come a second time *without* a sin-offering—that, as he came once to redeem, he should come a second time to claim the inheritance which he has so dearly bought. He came once, that his heel might be bruised; he comes again, to break the serpent's head, and, with a rod of iron, to dash his enemies in pieces, as potters' vessels. He came once, to wear the crown of thorns; he must come again, to wear the diadem of universal dominion. He comes to the marriage supper; he comes to gather his saints together; he comes to glorify them with himself on this same earth where once he and they were despised and rejected of men. Make you sure of this, that the whole drama of redemption cannot be perfected without this last act of the coming of the King. The complete history of Paradise Regained requires that the New Jerusalem should come down from God out of Heaven, prepared as a bride adorned for her husband; and it also requires that the heavenly Bridegroom should come riding forth on his white horse, conquering and to conquer, King of kings and Lord of lords, amidst the everlasting hallelujahs of saints and angels. It must be so. The man of Nazareth will come again. None shall spit in his face then; but every knee shall bow before him. The Crucified shall come again; and though the nail-prints will be visible, no nails shall then fasten his dear hands to the tree; but instead thereof, he shall grasp the scepter of universal sovereignty; and he shall reign forever and ever. Hallelujah!

When will he come? Ah, that is the question, the question of questions! *He will come in his own time.* He will come in due time. A brother minister, calling upon me, said, as we sat together, "I should like to ask you a lot of questions about the future."

"Oh, well!" I replied, "I cannot answer you, for I daresay I know no more about it than you do."

"But," said he, "what about the Lord's Second Advent? Will there not be the millennium first?"

I said, "I cannot tell whether there will be the millennium first; but this I know, the Scripture has left the whole matter, as far as I can see, with an intentional indistinctness, that we may be always expecting Christ to come, and that we may be watching for his coming at any hour and every hour. I think that the millennium will commence after his coming, and not before it. I cannot imagine the kingdom with the King absent. It seems to me to be an essential part of the millennial glory that the King shall then be revealed—at the same time, I am not going to lay down anything definite upon that point. He may not come for a thousand years; he may come tonight. The teaching of Scripture is, first of all, 'In such an hour as ye think not, the Son of man cometh.' It is clear that, if it were revealed that a thousand years must elapse before he would come, we might very well go to sleep for that time, for we should have no reason to expect that he would come, when Scripture told us he would not."

"Well," answered my friend, "but when Christ comes, that will be the general judgment, will it not?"

Then I quoted these texts, "The dead in Christ shall rise first."

"But the rest of the dead lived not again until the thousand years were finished. This is the first resurrection."

I said, "There is a resurrection from among the dead to which the Apostle Paul labored to attain. We shall all rise; but the righteous shall rise a thousand years before the ungodly. There is to be that interval of time between the one and the other; whether that is the millennial glory, or not, this deponent [witness] sayeth not, though he thinks it is. But this is the main point, the Lord shall come. We know not when we are to expect his coming; we are not to lay down, as absolutely fixed, any definite prediction or circumstance that would allow us to go to sleep until that prediction was fulfilled, or that circumstance was apparent."

"Will not the Jews be converted to Christ, and restored to their land?" enquired my friend.

I replied, "Yes, I think so. Surely they shall look on him whom they have pierced, and they shall mourn for him, as one mourneth for his only son; and God shall give them the kingdom and the glory, for they are his people, whom he has not forever cast away. The Jews, who are the natural olive branches, shall yet be grafted into their own olive tree again, and then shall be the fullness of the Gentiles."

"Will that be before Christ comes, or after?" asked my friend.

I answered, "I think it will be after he comes; but whether or no, I am not going to commit myself to any definite opinion on the subject."

To you, my dear friends, I say—read for yourselves, and search for yourselves; for still this stands first, and is the only thing that I will insist upon tonight, *the Lord will come*. He may come now; he may come tomorrow; he may come in the first watch of the night, or the second watch, or he may wait until the morning watch; but the one word that he gives to you all is, "Watch! Watch! Watch!"—that whenever he shall come, you may be ready to open to him, and to say, in the language of the hymn we sang just now—

> *Hallelujah!*
> *Welcome, welcome, Judge divine!*

So far [in our thought] I know that we are Scriptural, and therefore perfectly safe in our statements about the Lord's Second Advent.

Brethren, I would be earnest on this point, for *the notion of the delay of Christ's coming is always harmful,* however you arrive at it, whether it be by studying prophecy, or in any other way. If you come to be of the opinion of the servant mentioned in the forty-fifth verse, you are wrong:

> If that servant say in his heart, "My lord delayeth his coming"; and shall begin to beat the menservants and maidens, and to eat and drink, and to be drunken; the lord of that servant will come in a day when he looketh not for him, and at an hour when he is not aware, and will cut him in sunder, and will appoint him his portion with the unbelievers.

Do not, therefore, get the idea that the Lord delayeth his Coming, and that he will not or cannot come as yet. Far better would it be for you to stand on the tiptoe of expectation, and to be, rather, disappointed to think that he does not come. I do not wish you to be shaken in mind so as to act fanatically or foolishly, as certain people did in America, when they went out into the woods with ascension dresses on, so as to go straight up all of a sudden. Fall into none of those absurd ideas that have led people to leave a chair vacant at the table, and to put an empty plate, because the Lord might come and want it; and try to avoid all other superstitious nonsense. To stand star-gazing at the prophecies, with your mouth wide open, is just the wrong thing; far better will it be to go on working for your Lord, getting yourself and your service ready for his appearing, and cheering yourself all the while with this thought,

> While I am at work, my Master may come. Before I get weary, my Master may return. While others are mocking at me, my Master may appear; and whether they mock or applaud, is nothing to me. I live before the great Task-master's eye, and do my service knowing that he sees me, and expecting that, by-and-by, he will reveal himself to me, and then he will reveal me and my right intention to misrepresenting men.

That is the first point, brethren, *the Lord will come*. Settle that in your minds. He will come in his own time, and we are always to be looking for his appearing.

II. Now, secondly, *the Lord bids us watch for him.*

That is the marrow of the text: "Blessed are those servants, whom the lord, when he cometh, shall find watching."

Now, what is this watching? Not wishing to use my own words, I thought that I would call your attention to the context. The first essential part of this watching is that we are *not to be taken up with present things*. You remember that the twenty-second verse is about not taking thought what you shall eat, or what you shall drink; you are not to be absorbed in that. You who are Christians are not to live the fleshly, selfish life that asks, "What shall I eat and drink? How can I store up my goods? How can I get food and raiment here?" You are something more than dumb, driven cattle, that must think of hay and water. You have immortal spirits. Rise to the dignity of your immortality. Begin to think of the kingdom, the kingdom so soon to come, the kingdom which your Father has given you, and which, therefore, you must certainly inherit, the kingdom which Christ has prepared for you, and for which he is making you kings and priests unto God, that you may reign with him forever and ever. Oh, be not earthbound! Do not cast your anchor here in these troubled waters. Build not your nest on any of these trees; they are all marked for the axe, and are coming down; and your nest will come down, too, if you build it here. Set your affection on things above, up yonder—

> *Up where eternal ages roll,*
> *Where solid pleasures never die,*
> *And fruits eternal feast the soul;*

—there project your thoughts and your anxieties, and have a care about the world to come. Be not anxious about the things that pertain to this life. "Seek ye first the kingdom of God, and his righteousness; and all these things shall be added unto you."

Reading further down, in the thirty-fifth verse, you will notice that watching implies *keeping ourselves in a serviceable condition:* "Let your loins be girded about." You know how the Orientals wear flowing robes, which are always getting in their way. They cannot walk without being tripped up; so that, if a man has a piece of work on hand, he just tucks in his robe under his girdle, ties his girdle up tightly, and gets ready for his task, as we should say in English, turning the Oriental into the Western figure, "rolling up your shirtsleeves," and preparing for work. That is the way to wait for the Lord, ready for service, that, when he comes, he may never find you idle. I called to see a sister one morning; and when I called, she was cleaning the front steps with some whitening, and she said, "Oh, my dear pastor, I am sorry that you should call upon me just now! I would not have had you see me like this on any account."

I answered, "That is how I like to see you, busy at your work. I should not have liked to have come in, and caught you talking to your neighbor over the back palings [fence]. That would not have pleased me at all. May your Lord, when he comes, find you just so, doing your duty!" You see exactly what is meant; you are to be doing your duty; you are to be engaged about those vocations to which God has called you. You are to be doing it all out of love to Christ, and as service for him. Oh, that we might watch in that style, with our loins girded about! Work, and wait, and watch! Can you put those three things together? Work, and wait, and watch! This is what your Master asks of you.

And next, he would have us wait *with our lights burning.* If the Master comes home late, let us sit up late for him. It is not for us to go to bed till he comes home. Have the lights all trimmed; have his chamber well lit up; have the entrance-hall ready for his approach. When the King comes, have your torches flaming, that you may go out to meet the royal Bridegroom, and escort him to his home. If we are to watch for the Lord, as we ought, it must be with lamps burning. Are you making your light to shine among men? Do you think that your conduct and character are an example that will do your neighbors good, and are you trying to teach others the way of salvation? Some professors are like dark lanterns, or candles under a bushel. May we never be such! May we stand with our lamps trimmed, and our lights burning, and we ourselves like unto men that wait for their Lord; not walking in darkness, nor concealing our light, but letting it shine brightly! That is the way to watch for Christ, with your girdle tight about you because you are ready for work, and your lamp flaming out with brightness because you are anxious to illuminate the dark world in which you live.

To put it very plainly, I think that watching for the Coming of the Lord means *acting just as you would wish to be acting if he were to come.* I saw, in the Orphanage school-room, that little motto, "What would Jesus do?" That is a very splendid motto for our whole life, "What would Jesus do in such a case and in such a case?" Do just that. Another good motto is, "What would Jesus think of me if he were to come?" There are some places into which a Christian could not go, for he would not like his Master to find him there. There are some kinds of amusements into which a believer would never enter, for he would be ashamed for his Master to come and find him there. There are some conditions of angry temper, of pride, petulance, or spiritual sloth, in which you would not like to be, if you felt that the Master was coming. Suppose an angel's wing should brush your cheek just as you have spoken some unkind word, and a voice should say, "Your Master is coming"—you would tremble, I am sure, to meet him in such a condition. Oh, beloved, let us try every morning to get up as if that were the morning in which Christ would come; and when we go up to bed at night, may we lie down with this thought,

> Perhaps I shall be awakened by the ringing out of the silver trumpets heralding his Coming. Before the sun arises, I may be startled from my dreams by the greatest of all cries, "The Lord is come! The Lord is come!"

What a check, what an incentive, what a bridle, what a spur, such thoughts as these would be to us! Take this for the guide of your whole life. Act as if Jesus would come during the act in which you are engaged; and if you would not wish to be caught in that act by the Coming of the Lord, let it not be your act.

The second verse of our text speaks about the Master coming in the second watch, or in the third watch. *We are to act as those who keep the watches of the age for Christ.* Among the Romans, it was, as it is on board ship—there were certain watches. A Roman soldier, perhaps, stood on guard for three hours, and when he had been on the watch for three hours, there came another sentry who took his place, and the first man retired, and went back to the barracks, and the fresh sentinel stood in his place during his allotted time. Brethren, we have succeeded a long line of watchmen. Since the days of our Lord, when he sent out the chosen twelve to stand upon the citadel, and tell how the night waxed or waned, how have the watchers come and gone! Our God has changed the watchers, but he has kept the watch. He still sets watchmen on the walls of Zion, who cannot hold their peace day or night, but must watch for the Coming of their Master, watch against evil times, watch against error, and watch for the souls of men. At this time, some of us are called to be especially on the watch, and dare we sleep? After such a line of lynx-eyed watchmen, who counted not their lives dear unto them that they might hold their post, and watch against the foe, shall we be cravens, and be afraid; or shall we be sluggards, and go to our beds? By him that liveth, and was dead, and is alive for evermore, we pray that we may never be guilty of treason to his sacred name and truth; but may we watch on to the last moment, when there shall ring out the clarion cry, "Behold, the Bride-groom cometh; go ye out to meet him." People of the Tabernacle, you are set to watch tonight just as they did in the brave days of old! [George] Whitefield and [John] Wesley's men were watchers; and those before them, in the days of Luther and of Calvin, and backward even to the days of our Lord. They kept the watches of the night, and you must do the same, until—

> Upstarting at the midnight cry,
> "Behold your heavenly Bridegroom nigh,"

—you go forth to welcome your returning Lord.

We are to wait with one object in view, viz., *to open the door to him, and to welcome him:* "that when he cometh and knocketh, they may open unto him immediately." Perhaps you know what it is to go home to a loving, tender wife and children who are watching for you. You have been on a journey; you have been absent for some little time; you have written them letters which they have greatly valued; you have heard from them; but all that is nothing like your personal presence. They are looking out for you; and if, perchance, the boat should fail you, or the train be late, if you arrived at eleven or twelve o'clock at night, you would not expect to find the house all shut up, and nobody watching for you. No, you had told them that you would come, and you were quite sure that they would watch for you. I feel rebuked myself, sometimes, for not watching for my Master, when I know that, at this very time, my dogs are sitting against the door, waiting for me; and long before I reach home, there they will be, and at the first sound of the carriage-wheels, they will lift up their voices with delight because their master is coming home. Oh, if we loved our Lord as dogs love their masters, how we should catch the first sound of his Coming, and be waiting, always waiting, and never happy until at last we should see him! Pardon me for using a dog as a picture of what you ought to be; but when you have attained to a state above that, I will find another illustration to explain my meaning.

III. Now, lastly, *there is a reward for watchers.*

Their reward is this, "Blessed are those servants, whom the lord, when he cometh, shall find watching."

They have a present blessedness. It is a very blessed thing to be on the watch for Christ, it is a blessing to us now. How it detaches you from the world! You can be poor without murmuring; you can be rich without worldliness; you can be sick without sorrowing; you can be healthy without presumption. If you are always waiting for Christ's Coming, untold blessings are wrapped up in that glorious hope. "Every man that hath this hope in him, purifieth himself even as he is pure." Blessednesses are heaped up one upon another in that state of heart in which a man is always looking for his Lord.

But what will be the blessedness when Jesus does come? Well, a part of that blessedness will be *in future service.* You must not think that, when you have done working here, you Sunday-school teachers, and those of us who preach and teach, that the Master will say, "I have discharged you from my service. Go and sit on a heavenly mount, and sing yourselves away forever and ever." Not a bit of it. I am but learning how to preach now; I shall be able to preach by-and-by. You are only learning to teach now; you will be able to teach by-and-by. Yes, to angels, and principalities, and powers, you shall make known the manifold wisdom of God. I sometimes aspire to the thought of a congregation of angels and archangels, who shall sit and wonder, as I tell what God has done for me; and I shall be to them an everlasting monument of the grace of God to an unworthy wretch, upon whom he looked with infinite compassion, and saved with a wonderful salvation.

All those stars, those worlds of light, who knows how many of them are inhabited? I believe there are regions beyond our imagination to which every child of God shall become an everlasting illumination, a living example of the love of God in Christ Jesus. The people in those far distant lands could not see Calvary as this world has seen it; but they shall hear of it from the redeemed. Remember how the Lord will say, "Well done, thou good and faithful servant: thou hast been faithful over a few things, I will make thee ruler over many things." He is to keep on doing something, you see. Instead of having some little bit of a village to govern, he is to be made ruler over some great province. So it is in this passage. Read the forty-fourth verse: "Of a truth I say unto you, that he will make him ruler over all that he hath." That is, the man who has been a faithful and wise steward of God here, will be called of God to more eminent service hereafter. If he serve his Master well, when his Master comes, he will promote him to still higher service. Do you not know how it used to be in the Spartan army? Here is a man who has fought well, and been a splendid soldier. He is covered with wounds on his breast. The next time that there is a war, they say,

> Poor fellow, we will reward him! He shall lead the way in the first battle. He fought so well before, when he met one hundred with a little troop behind him; now he shall meet ten thousand with a larger troop.

"Oh!" say you, "that is giving him more work." That is God's way of rewarding his people, and a blessed thing it is for the industrious servant. His rest is in serving God with all his might. This shall be our heaven, not to go there to roost, but to be always on the wing; forever flying, and forever resting at the same time. "They do his commandments, hearkening unto the voice of his word." "His servants shall serve him: and they shall see his face." These two things blended together make a noble ambition for every Christian.

May the Lord keep you waiting, working, watching, that when he comes, you may have the blessedness of entering upon some larger, higher, nobler service than you could accomplish now, for which you are preparing by the lowlier and more arduous service of this world! God bless you, beloved, and if any of you do not know my Lord, and therefore do not look for his appearing, remember that he will come whether you look for him or not; and when he comes, you will have to stand at his bar. One of the events that will follow his Coming will be your being summoned before his judgment-seat, and how will you answer him then? How will you answer him if you have refused his love, and turned a deaf ear to the invitations of his mercy? If you have delayed, and delayed, and delayed, and delayed, how will you answer him? How will you answer him in that day? If you stand speechless, your silence will condemn you, and the King will say, "Bind him hand and foot, and take him away." God grant that we may believe in the Lord Jesus unto life eternal, and then wait for his appearing from Heaven, for his love's sake! Amen.

Sermons on the
Holy Spirit

The Comforter

Delivered on Sabbath evening, January 21, 1855, at New Park Street Chapel, Southwark. No. 5.

But the Comforter, which is the Holy Ghost, whom the Father will send in my name, he shall teach you all things, and bring all things to your remembrance, whatsoever I have said unto you.—John 14:26

Good old Simeon called Jesus the consolation of Israel; and so he was. Before his actual appearance, his name was the Day-Star—cheering the darkness, and prophetic of the rising sun. To him they looked with the same hope which cheers the nightly watcher, when, from the lonely castle-top, he sees the fairest of the stars, and hails her as the usher of the morn. When He was on earth, he must have been the consolation of all those who were privileged to be his companions. We can imagine how readily the disciples would run to Christ to tell him of their griefs, and how sweetly with that matchless intonation of his voice, he would speak to them and bid their fears be gone. Like children, they would consider him as their Father; and to him every want, every groan, every sorrow, every agony would at once be carried, and he, like a wise physician, had a balm for every wound; he had mingled a cordial for their every care; and readily did he dispense some mighty remedy to allay all the fever of their troubles. Oh! it must have been sweet to have lived with Christ. Surely sorrows then were but joys in masks because they gave an opportunity to go to Jesus to have them removed. Oh! would to God, some of us may say, that we could have lain our weary heads upon the bosom of Jesus, and that our birth had been in that happy era, when we might have heard his kind voice, and seen his kind look, when he said "Let the weary ones come unto me."

But now he was about to die. Great prophecies were to be fulfilled, and great purposes were to be answered; and therefore Jesus must go. It behooved him to suffer, that he might be made a propitiation for our sins. It behooved him to slumber in the dust awhile, that he might perfume the chamber of the grave, to make it

> No more a charnel house to fence
> The relics of lost innocence.

It behooved him to have a resurrection, that we, who shall one day be the dead in Christ, might [at the Second Coming] rise first, and in glorious bodies stand upon earth. And it behooved him that he should ascend up on high, that he might lead captivity captive; that he might chain the fiends of Hell; that he might lash them to his chariot wheels and drag them up high Heaven's hill, to make them feel a second overthrow from his right arm when he should dash them from the pinnacles of Heaven down to deeper depths beneath. "It is right I should go away from you," said Jesus, "for if I go not away, the Comforter will not come." Jesus must go. Weep ye disciples. Jesus must be gone. Mourn ye poor ones who are to be left without a Comforter. But hear how kindly Jesus speaks: "I will not leave you comfortless: I will pray the Father, and he shall send you another Comforter, who shall be with you, and shall dwell in you forever." He would not leave those few poor sheep alone in the wilderness; he would not desert his children and leave them fatherless. Albeit that he had a mighty mission which did fill his heart and hand; albeit that he had so much to perform that we might have thought that even *his* gigantic intellect would be overburdened. Albeit he had so much to suffer that we might suppose his whole soul to be concentrated upon the thought of the sufferings to be endured—yet it was not so; before he left, he gave soothing words of comfort; like the good Samaritan, he poured in oil and wine; and we see what he promised: "I will send you another Comforter—one who shall be just what I have been, yea even more; who shall console you in your sorrows, remove your doubts, comfort you in your afflictions, and stand as my vicar on earth, to do that which I would have done, had I tarried with you."

Before I discourse of the Holy Ghost as the Comforter, I must make one or two remarks on the different translations of the word rendered "Comforter." The Flemish translation, which you are aware is adopted by Roman Catholics, has left the word untranslated, and gives it "Paraclete." "But the Paraclete, which is the Holy Ghost, whom the Father will send in my name, he shall teach you all things." This is the original Greek word, and it has some other meanings besides "Comforter." Sometimes it means the monitor or instructor: "I will send you another monitor, another teacher." Frequently it means "advocate;" but the most common meaning of the word is that which we have here: "I will send you another *Comforter*." However, we cannot pass over those other two interpretations without saying something upon them.

"I will send you another *teacher*." Jesus Christ had been the official teacher for his saints whilst on earth. They called no man Rabbi except Christ. They sat at no men's feet to learn their doctrines; but they had them direct from the lips of him who "spake as never man spake." "And now," says he,

> . . . when I am gone, where shall you find the great infallible teacher? Shall I set you up a Pope at Rome, to whom you shall go, and who shall be your infallible oracle? Shall I give you the councils of the church to be held to decide all knotty points?

Christ said no such thing.

> I am the infallible paraclete or teacher, and when I am gone, I will send you another teacher, and he shall be the person who is to explain Scripture; he shall be the authoritative oracle of God, who shall make all dark things light, who shall unravel mysteries, who shall untwist all knots of revelation, and shall make you understand what you could not discover, had it not been for his influence.

And beloved, no man ever learns anything aright, unless he is taught of the Spirit. You may learn election [to salvation], and you may know it so that you shall be damned by it, if you are not taught of the Holy Ghost; for I have known some who have learned election to their soul's destruction; they have learned it, so that they said they were of the elect, whereas they had no marks, no evidences, and no work of the Holy Ghost in their souls. There is a way of learning truth in Satan's college, and holding it in licentiousness; but if so, it shall be to your souls as poison to your veins, and prove your everlasting ruin. No man can know Jesus Christ unless he is taught of God. There is no doctrine of the Bible which can be safely, thoroughly, and truly learned, except by the agency of the one authoritative teacher. Ah! tell me not of systems of divinity, tell me not of schemes of theology; tell me not of infallible commentators, or most learned and most arrogant doctors; but tell me of the Great Teacher, who shall instruct us, the sons of God, and shall make us wise to understand all things. He is *the* Teacher; it matters not what this or that man says; I rest on no man's boasting authority, nor will you. Ye are not to be carried away with the craftiness of men, nor sleight of words; this is the authoritative oracle, the Holy Ghost resting in the hearts of his children.

The other translation is *advocate*. Have you ever thought how the Holy Ghost can be said to be an advocate? You know Jesus Christ is called the wonderful, the counselor, and mighty God; but how can the Holy Ghost be said to be an advocate? I suppose it is thus: he is an advocate on earth to plead against the enemies of the cross. How was it that Paul could so ably plead before Felix and Agrippa?[1] How was it that the Apostles stood unawed before the magistrates and confessed their Lord? How has it come to pass that in all times God's ministers have been made fearless as lions, and their brows have been firmer than brass, their hearts sterner than steel, and their words like the language of God? Why, it is simply for this reason, that it was not the man who pleaded, but it was God the Holy Ghost pleading through him. Have you never seen an earnest minister, with hands uplifted and eyes dropping tears, pleading with the sons of men? Have you never admired that portrait from the hand of old John Bunyan? [It shows] a grave person with eyes uplifted to heaven, the best of books in his hand, the law of truth written on his lips, the world behind his back, standing as if he pleaded with men, and a crown of gold hanging over his head. Who gave that minister so blessed a manner and such goodly matter? Whence came his skill? Did he acquire it in the college? Did he learn it in the seminary? Ah! no; he learned it of the God of Jacob; he learned it of the Holy Ghost; for the Holy Ghost is the great counselor who teaches us how to advocate his cause aright.

But, besides this, the Holy Ghost is the advocate in men's hearts. Ah! I have known men reject a doctrine until the Holy Ghost began to illumine them. We who are the advocates of the truth are often very poor pleaders; we spoil our cause by the words we use; but it is a mercy that the brief is in the hand of a special pleader, who will advocate successfully and overcome the sinner's opposition. Did you ever know him fail once? Brethren, I speak to your souls—has not God in old times convinced you of sin? Did not the Holy Ghost come and prove that you were guilty, although no minister could ever get you out of your self-righteousness? Did he not advocate Christ's righteousness? Did he not stand and tell you that your works were filthy rags? And when you had well-nigh still refused to listen to his voice, did he not fetch Hell's drum and make it sound about your ears, bidding you look through the vista of future years and see the throne set, and the books open, and the sword brandished, and Hell burning, and fiends howling, and the damned shrieking forever? And did he not thus convince you of the judgment to come? He is a mighty advocate when he pleads in the soul of sin, of righteousness, and of the judgment to come. Blessed advocate! Plead in my heart, plead with my conscience. When I sin, make conscience bold to tell me of it; when I err, make conscience speak at once; and when I turn aside to crooked ways, then advocate the cause of righteousness, and bid me sit down in confusion, knowing my guiltiness in the sight of God.

But there is yet another sense in which the Holy Ghost advocates, and that is, he advocates our cause with Jesus Christ, with groanings that cannot be uttered. O my soul, thou art ready to burst within me! O my heart, thou art swelled with grief;

---

[1] Felix and Agrippa: rulers before whom Paul was able to witness about Jesus.

the hot tide of my emotion would well-nigh overflow the channels of my veins. I long to speak, but the very desire chains my tongue. I wish to pray, but the fervency of my feeling curbs my language. There is a groaning within that cannot be uttered. Do you know who can utter that groaning, who can understand it, and who can put it into heavenly language and utter it in a celestial tongue, so that Christ can hear it? Oh! yes; it is God the Holy Spirit; he advocates our cause with Christ, and then Christ advocates it with his Father. He is the advocate, who maketh intercession for us, with groanings that cannot be uttered.

Having thus explained the Spirit's office as teacher and advocate, we come now to the translation of our version—the *Comforter*; and here I shall have three divisions. First, the *comforter*; secondly, the *comfort*; and thirdly, the *comforted*.

I. First, then, the *Comforter*.

Briefly let me run over in my mind, and in your minds too, the characteristics of this glorious Comforter. Let me tell you some of the attributes of his comfort, so that you may understand how well adapted he is to your case.

And first, we will remark that God the Holy Ghost is a very *loving* Comforter. I am in distress and want consolation. Some passer-by hears of my sorrow, and he steps within, sits down and essays [attempts] to cheer me; he speaks soothing words—but he loves me not, he is a stranger, he knows me not at all, he has only come in to try his skill—and what is the consequence? His words run over me like oil upon a slab of marble—they are like the pattering rain upon the rock; they do not break my grief; it stands unmoved as adamant, because he has no love for me. But let someone who loves me dearly as his own life come and plead with me, then truly his words are music; they taste like honey; he knows the password of the doors of my heart, and my ear is attentive to every word, I catch the intonation of each syllable as it falls, for it is like the harmony of the harps of Heaven. Oh! there is a voice in love, it speaks a language which is its own—it is a idiom and an accent which none can mimic; wisdom cannot imitate it, oratory cannot attain unto it; it is love alone which can reach the mourning heart; love is the only handkerchief which can wipe the mourner's tears away. And is not the Holy Ghost a loving Comforter? Dost thou know, O saint, how much the Holy Spirit loves thee? Canst thou measure the love of the Spirit? Dost thou know how great is the affection of his soul towards thee? Go, measure Heaven with thy span; go, weigh the mountains in the scales; go, take the ocean's water, and tell [number] each drop; go count the sand upon the sea's wide shore, and when thou hast accomplished this, thou canst tell how much he loveth thee. He has loved thee long, he has loved thee well; he loved thee ever, and he still shall love thee. Surely he is the person to comfort thee, because he loves. Admit him, then, to your heart, O Christian, that he may comfort you in your distress.

But next he is a *faithful* Comforter. Love sometimes proves unfaithful. "Oh! sharper than a serpent's tooth"[2] is an unfaithful friend! Oh! far more bitter than the gall of bitterness, to have a friend to turn from me in my distress! Oh! woe of woes, to have one who loves me in my prosperity forsake me in the dark day of my trouble. Sad indeed—but such is not God's Spirit. He ever loves, and loves even to the end—a faithful Comforter. Child of God, you are in trouble. A little while ago you found him a sweet and loving Comforter; you obtained relief from him when others were but broken cisterns; he sheltered you in his bosom, and carried you in his arms. Oh, wherefore dost thou distrust him now? Away with thy fears! For he is a faithful Comforter. "Ah! but "thou sayest, "I fear I shall be sick and shall be deprived of his ordinances." Nevertheless, he shall visit thee on thy sick bed, and sit by thy side to give the consolation. "Ah! but I have distresses greater than you can conceive of, wave upon wave rolleth over me; deep calleth unto deep at the noise of the Eternal's waterspouts." Nevertheless, he will be faithful to his promise. "Ah! but I have sinned." So thou hast, but sin cannot sever thee from his love; he loves thee still. Think not, O poor downcast child of God, because the scars of thine old sins have marred thy beauty, that he loves thee less because of that blemish. Oh, no! He loved thee when he foreknew thy sin; he loved thee with the knowledge of what the aggregate of thy wickedness would be; and he does not love the less now. Come to him in all boldness of faith; tell him thou hast grieved him, and he will forget thy wandering, and will receive thee again; the kisses of his love shall be bestowed upon thee, and the arms of his grace shall embrace thee. He is faithful: trust him—he will never deceive you; trust him—he will never leave you.

Again, he is an *unwearied* Comforter. I have sometimes tried to comfort persons that have been tried. You now and then meet with the case of a nervous person. You ask, "What is your trouble?" You are told, and you essay, if possible, to remove it, but while you are preparing your artillery to batter the trouble, you find that it has shifted its quarters, and is occupying quite a different position. You change your argument and begin again; but lo, it is again gone, and you are bewildered. You feel like Hercules cutting off the ever-growing heads of the Hydra, and you give up your task in despair. You meet with persons whom it is impossible to comfort, reminding me of the man who locked himself up in fetters and threw the key away, so that nobody could unlock him. I have found some in the fetters of despair. "O, I am the man," say they, "that has seen affliction; pity me, pity me, O my friends;" and the more you try to comfort such people, the worse they get; and therefore, out of all heart [discouraged], we leave them to wander alone among the tombs of their former joys. But the Holy Ghost is never out of heart with those whom he wishes to comfort. He attempts to comfort us and we run away from the

---

[2] The full quote, from Shakespeare's "King Lear," is: "How sharper than a serpent's tooth it is; To have a thankless child!"

sweet cordial; he gives some sweet draught to cure us, and we will not drink it; he gives some wondrous potion to charm away all our troubles, and we put it away from us. Still he pursues us; and though we say that we will not be comforted, he says we *shall* be, and when he has said, he does it—he is not to be wearied by all our sins, not by all our murmurings.

And oh, how *wise* a Comforter is the Holy Ghost. Job had comforters, and I think he spoke the truth when he said, "Miserable comforters are ye all." But I dare say they esteemed themselves wise; and when the young man Elihu rose to speak, they thought he had a world of impudence. Were they not "grave and reverend seniors?" Did not they comprehend his grief and sorrow? If they could not comfort him, who could? But they did not find out the cause. They thought he was not really a child of God, that he was self-righteous; and they have him the wrong physic. It is a bad case when the doctor mistakes the disease and gives a wrong prescription, and so, perhaps, kills the patient. Sometimes, when we go and visit people, we mistake their disease— we want to comfort them on this point, whereas they do not require any such comfort at all, and they would be better left alone than spoiled by such unwise comforters as we are. But oh! How wise the Holy Spirit is! He takes the soul, lays it on the table, and dissects it in a moment; he finds out the root of the matter, he sees where the complaint is, and then he applies the knife where something is required to be taken away, or puts a plaster where the sore is; and he never mistakes. Oh! how wise, the blessed Holy Ghost! From every comforter, I turn and leave them all, for thou art he who alone givest the wisest consolation.

Then mark how *safe* a Comforter the Holy Ghost is. All comfort is not safe; mark that. There is a young man over there very melancholy. You know how he became so. He stepped into the house of God and heard a powerful preacher, and the word was blessed and convinced him of sin. When he went home, his father and the rest found there was something different about him, "Oh," they said, "John is mad; he is crazy," and what said his mother? "Send him into the country for a week, let him go to the ball or to the theater." John! Did you find any comfort there? "Ah no; they made me worse, for while I was there, I thought Hell might open and swallow me up." Did you find any relief in the gaieties of the world? "No," say you, "I thought it was [an] idle waste of time." Alas! this is miserable comfort, but it is the comfort of the worldling; and when a Christian gets into distress, how many will recommend him this remedy and the other. "Go and hear Mr. So-and-so preach; have a few friends at your house; read such-and-such a consoling volume;" and very likely it is the most unsafe advice in the world. The devil will sometimes come to men's souls as a false comforter, and he will say to the soul, "What need is there to make all this ado about repentance? You are no worse than other people," and he will try to make the soul believe that what is [actually] presumption is the real assurance of the Holy Ghost; thus he deceives many by false comfort. Ah, there have been many, like infants, destroyed by elixirs given to lull them to sleep; many have been ruined by the cry of "peace, peace," when there is no peace, hearing gentle things when they ought to be stirred to the quick. Cleopatra's asp was brought in a basket of flowers; and men's ruin often lurks in fair and sweet speeches. But the Holy Ghost's comfort is safe, and you may rest on it. Let him speak the word, and there is a reality about it; let him give the cup of consolation, and you may drink it to the bottom, for in its depths there are no dregs, nothing to intoxicate or ruin—it is all safe.

Moreover, the Holy Ghost is an *active* Comforter: he does not comfort by words, but by deeds. Some comfort by [saying,] "Be ye warmed and be ye filled"—giving nothing. But the Holy Ghost gives, he intercedes with Jesus; he gives us promises, he gives us grace, and so he comforts us. Mark again, he is always a *successful* Comforter; he never attempts what he cannot accomplish.

Then to close up, he is an *ever-present* Comforter, so that you never have to send for him. Your God is always near you, and when you need comfort in your distress, behold, the word is nigh thee, it is in thy mouth, and in thy heart; he is an ever-present help in time of trouble. I wish I had time to expand these thoughts; but I cannot.

II. The second thing is the *comfort*.

Now there are some persons who make a great mistake about the influence of the Holy Spirit. A foolish man who had [a] fancy to preach in a certain pulpit—though in truth he was quite incapable of the duty—called upon the minister, and assured him solemnly that it had been revealed to him by the Holy Ghost, that he was to preach in his pulpit. "Very well," said the minister, "I suppose I must not doubt your assertion, but as it has not been revealed to me that I am to let you preach, you must go your way until it is." I have heard many fanatical persons say the Holy Spirit revealed this and that to them. Now that is very generally revealed [eventually, to be] nonsense. The Holy Ghost does not reveal anything fresh now. He brings old things to our remembrance. "He shall teach you all things, and bring all things to your remembrance, whatsoever I have told you." The canon of revelation is closed; there is no more to be added. God does not give a fresh revelation, but he rivets the old one. When it has been forgotten, and laid in the dusty chamber of our memory, he fetches it out and cleans the picture, but does not paint a new one. There are no new doctrines, but the old ones are often revived. It is not, I say, by any new revelation that the Spirit comforts. He does so by telling us old things over again; he brings a fresh lamp to manifest the treasures hidden in Scripture; he unlocks the strong chests in which the truth had long lain, and he points to secret chambers filled with untold riches; but he coins no more, for enough is done. Believer! there is enough in the Bible for thee to live upon forever. If thou shouldst outnumber the years of Methusaleh, there would be no need for a fresh revelation; if thou shouldst live till Christ should come upon the earth, there would be no necessity for the addition of a single word; if thou shouldst go down as deep as Jonah, or even descend as David said he did, into the belly of Hell, still there would be enough in the Bible to comfort thee without a supplementary sentence. But Christ says, "He shall take of mine and shall show it unto you." Now let me just tell you briefly what it is the Holy Ghost tells us.

Ah! does he not whisper to the heart,

Saint, be of good cheer; there is one who died for thee; look to Calvary; behold his wounds; see the torrent gushing from his side; there is thy purchaser, and thou art secure. He loves thee with an everlasting love, and this chastisement is meant for thy good; each stroke is working thy healing; by the blueness of the wound, thy soul is made better. "Whom he loveth he chasteneth, and scourgeth every son whom he receiveth." Doubt not his grace, because of thy tribulation, but believe that he loveth thee as much in seasons of trouble as in times of happiness.

And then, moreover, he says, "What is all thy suffering compared with that of thy Lord's, or what, when weighed in the scales of Jesu's agonies, is all thy distress?" And especially at times does the Holy Ghost take back the veil of heaven, and lets the soul behold the glory of the upper world! Then it is that the saint can say, "Oh, thou art a Comforter to me!"

> Let cares like a wild deluge come,
> And storms of sorrow fall;
> May I but safely reach my home,
> My God, my heaven, my all.

Some of you could follow, were I to tell of manifestations of heaven. You too have left sun, moon, and stars, at your feet, while in your flight, outstripping the tardy lightning, you have seemed to enter the gates of pearl, and tread the golden streets, borne aloft on wings of the Spirit. But here we must not trust ourselves, lest, lost in reverie, we forget our theme.

III. And now thirdly, who are the *comforted* persons!

I like, you know, at the end of my sermon to cry out "Divide! Divide!" There are two parties here—some who are the comforted, and others who are the comfortless ones—some who have received the consolation of the Holy Ghost, and some who have not. Now let us try and sift you, and see which is the chaff; and which is the wheat; and may God grant that some of the chaff may this night be transformed into his wheat.

You may say, "How am I to know whether I am a recipient of the comfort of the Holy Ghost?" You may know it by one rule. If you have received one blessing from

God, you will receive all other blessings too. Let me explain myself. If I could come here as an auctioneer, and sell the gospel off in lots, I should dispose of it all. If I could say, "Here is justification through the blood of Christ, free, given away, gratis;" many a one would say, "I will have justification: give it me; I wish to be justified, I wish to be pardoned." Suppose I took sanctification, the giving up of all sin, a thorough change of heart, leaving off drunkenness and swearing. Many would say,

> I don't want *that*; I should like to go to Heaven, but I do not want that holiness; I should like to be saved at last, but I should like to have my drink still; I should like to enter glory, but then I must have an oath or two on the road.

Nay, but sinner, if thou hast one blessing, thou shalt have *all*. God will never divide the gospel. He will not give justification to that man, and sanctification to another; pardon to one and holiness to another. No, it all goes together. Whom he calls, them he justifies; whom he justifies, them he sanctifies; and whom he sanctifies, them he also glorifies. Oh; if I could lay down nothing but the *comforts* of the gospel, ye would fly to them as flies do to honey. When ye come to be ill, ye send for the clergyman. Ah! you all want your minister then to come and give you consoling words. But if he be an honest man, he will not give some of you a particle of consolation. He will not commence pouring oil, when the knife would be better. I want to make a man feel his sins before I dare tell him anything about Christ. I want to probe into his soul and make him feel that he is lost before I tell him anything about the purchased blessing. It is the ruin of many to tell them, "Now just believe on Christ, and that is all you have to do." If, instead of dying, they get better, they rise up whitewashed hypocrites—that is all. I have heard of a city missionary who kept a record of two thousand persons who were supposed to be on their death-bed, but recovered, and whom he should have put down as converted persons had they died, and how many do you think lived a Christian life afterwards, out of the two-thousand! Not two! Positively he could only find one who was found to live afterwards in the fear of God. Is it not horrible that when men and women come to die, they should cry, "Comfort, comfort?" and that hence their friends conclude that they are children of God, while, after all, they have no right to consolation, but are intruders upon the enclosed grounds of the blessed God. Oh God! May these people ever be kept from having comfort when they have no right to it! Have you the other blessings? Have you had conviction of sin? Have you ever felt your guilt before God? Have your souls been humbled at Jesus' feet? And have you been made to look to Calvary alone for your refuge? If not, you have no right to consolation. Do not take an atom of it. The Spirit is a Convincer before he is a Comforter; and you must have the other operations of the Holy Spirit before you can derive anything from this.

And now I have done. You have heard what this babbler hath said once more. What has it been? Something about the Comforter. But let me ask you, before you go—what do you know about the Comforter? Each one of you, before descending the steps of this chapel, let this solemn question thrill through your souls: "What do you know of the Comforter?" Oh! poor souls, if ye know not the Comforter, I will tell you what you shall know—you shall know the Judge! If ye know not the Comforter on earth, ye shall know the Condemner in the next world, who shall cry, "Depart, ye cursed, into everlasting fire in Hell." Well might [George] Whitfield call out, "O earth, earth, earth, hear the Word of the Lord!" If we were to live here forever, ye might slight the gospel; if ye had a lease of your lives, ye might despise the Comforter. But sirs, ye must die. Since last we met together, probably some have gone to their long last home; and ere we meet again in this sanctuary, some here will be amongst the glorified above, or amongst the damned below. Which will it be? Let your soul answer. If tonight you fell down dead in your pews, or where you are standing in the gallery, where would you be? In *Heaven* or in *Hell*?

Ah! deceive not yourselves; let conscience have its perfect work; and if, in the sight of God, you are obliged to say, "I tremble and fear lest my portion should be with unbelievers," listen one moment, and then I have done with thee. "He that believeth and is baptized shall be saved, and he that believeth not shall be damned." Weary sinner, hellish sinner, thou who art the Devil's castaway, reprobate, profligate, harlot, robber, thief, adulterer, fornicator, drunkard, swearer, Sabbath-breaker! I speak to thee as well as the rest. I exempt no man. God hath said there is no exemption here. "*Whosoever* believeth in the name of Jesus Christ shall be saved." Sin is no barrier: thy guilt is no obstacle. Whosoever—though he were as black as Satan, though he were filthy as a fiend—whosoever this night believes, shall have every sin forgiven, shall have every crime effaced, shall have every iniquity blotted out; shall be saved in the Lord Jesus Christ, and shall stand in Heaven safe and secure. That is the glorious gospel. God apply it home to your hearts, and give you faith in Jesus!

> *We have listened to the preacher—*
> *Truth by him has now been shown;*
> *But we want a greater teacher,*
> *From the everlasting throne:*
> Application *is the work of God alone.*

The Power of the Holy Ghost

Delivered on Sabbath morning, June 17, 1855, at New Park Street Chapel. No. 30.

The power of the Holy Ghost.—Romans 15:13

Power is the special and peculiar prerogative of God, and God alone. "Twice have I have heard this: that power belongeth unto God." God is God: and power belongeth to him. If he delegates a portion of it to his creatures, yet still it is *his* power. The sun, although he is "like a bridegroom coming out of his chamber, and rejoiceth as a strong man to run his race," yet has no power to perform his motions except as God directs him. The stars, although they travel in their orbits and none could stay them, yet have neither might nor force except that which God daily infuses into them. The tall archangel, near his throne, who outshines a comet in its blaze, though he is one of those who excel in strength and hearken to the voice of the commands of God, yet has no might except that which his Maker gives to him. As for Leviathan, who so maketh the sea to boil like a pot that one would think the deep were hoary [ancient]: as for Behemoth, who drinketh up Jordan at a draught, and boasteth that he can snuff up rivers; as for those majestic creatures that are found on earth, they owe their strength to him who fashioned their bones of steel and made their sinews of brass. And when we think of man, if he has might or power, it is so small and insignificant, that we can scarcely call it such; yea, when it is at its greatest—when he sways his scepter, when he commands hosts, when he rules nations—still the power belongeth unto God; and it is true, "Twice have I heard this, that power belongeth unto God." This exclusive prerogative of God is to be found in each of the three persons of the glorious Trinity. The Father hath power:

407

for by his word were the heavens made, and all the host of them, by his strength all things stand, and through him they fulfill their destiny. The Son hath power: for like his Father, he is the Creator of all things; "Without him was not anything made that was made," and "by him all things consist." And the Holy Spirit hath power. It is concerning the power of the Holy Ghost that I shall speak this morning; and may you have a practical exemplification of that attribute in your own hearts, when you shall feel that the influence of the Holy Ghost is being poured out upon me, so that I am speaking the words of the living God to your souls, and bestowed upon you when you are feeling the effects of it in your own spirits.

We shall look at the power of the Holy Ghost in three ways this morning. First, *the outward and visible displays of it*, second, *the inward and spiritual manifestations of it*, and third, *the future and expected works thereof*. The power of the Spirit will thus, I trust, be made clearly present to your souls.

First, then, we are to view the power of the Spirit in the *outward and visible displays of it*.

The power of the Spirit has not been dormant; it has exerted itself. Much has been done by the Spirit of God already; more than could have been accomplished by any being except the Infinite, Eternal, Almighty Jehovah, of whom the Holy Spirit is one person. There are four works which are the outward and manifest signs of the power of the Spirit: creation works; resurrection works; works of attestation or of witness; and works of grace. Of each of the works I shall speak very briefly.

1. First, the Spirit has manifested the omnipotence of his power in *creation works*; for though not very frequently in Scripture, yet sometimes creation is ascribed to the Holy Ghost, as well as to the Father and the Son. The creation of the heavens above us is said to be the work of God's Spirit. This you will see at once by referring to the sacred Scriptures, Job 26:13, "By his Spirit he hath garnished the heavens, his hand hath formed the crooked serpent." All the stars of heaven are said to have been placed aloft by the Spirit, and one particular constellation called the "crooked serpent" is specially pointed out as his handiwork. He looseth the bands of Orion; he bindeth the sweet influences of the Pleiades, and guides Aeturus with his sons. He made all those stars that shine in heaven. The heavens were garnished by his hands, and he formed the crooked serpent by his might. So also in those continued acts of creation which are still performed in the world; as the bringing forth of man and animals, their birth and generation. These are ascribed also to the Holy Ghost. If you look at the 104th Psalm, at the 29th verse, you will read,

> Thou hidest thy face, they are troubled: thou takest away their breath, they die, and return to their dust. Thou sendest forth thy Spirit, they are created and thou renewest the face of the earth.

So that the creation of every man is the work of the Spirit: and the creation of all life and all flesh—existence in this world is as much to be ascribed to the power of the Spirit as the first garnishing of the heavens, or the fashioning of the crooked serpent.

But if you will look in the 1st chapter of Genesis, you will there see more particularly set forth that peculiar operation of power upon the universe which was put forth by the Holy Spirit; you will then discover what was his special work. In the 2nd verse of the 1st chapter of Genesis, we read, "And the earth was without form, and void; and darkness was upon the face of the deep. And the Spirit of God moved upon the face of the waters." We know not how remote the period of the creation of this globe may be—certainly many millions of years before the time of Adam. Our planet has passed through various stages of existence, and different kinds of creatures have lived on its surface, all of which have been fashioned by God. But before that era came, wherein man should be its principal tenant and monarch, the Creator gave up the world to confusion. He allowed the inward fires to burst up from beneath and melt all the solid matter, so that all kinds of substances were commingled in one vast mass of disorder; the only name you could give to the world then was, that it was a chaotic mass of matter; what it should be, you could not guess or define. It was entirely without form, and void, and darkness was upon the face of the deep. The Spirit came, and stretching his broad wings, bade the darkness disperse, and as he moved over it, all the different portions of matter came into their places, and it was no longer "without form, and void"; but became round like its sister planets, and moved, singing the high praises of God—not discordantly as it had done before, but as one great note in the vast scale of creation.

Milton very beautifully describes this work of the Spirit in thus bringing order out of confusion, when the King of Glory, in his powerful Word and Spirit, came to create new worlds:

> On heavenly ground they stood; and from the shore
> They view'd the vast immeasurable abyss
> Outrageous as a sea, dark, wasteful, wild,
> Up from the bottom turn'd by furious winds
> And surging waves, as mountains, to assault
> Heaven's height, and with the center mix the pole.

> "Silence ye troubled waves, and thou deep, peace,"
> Said then the Omnific Word; "Your discord end."
> Then on the watery calm
> His brooding wings the Spirit of God outspread
> And vital virtue infused, and vital warmth
> Throughout the fluid mass.

This, you see then, is the power of the Spirit. Could we have seen that earth, all in confusion, we should have said, "Who can make a world out of this?" The answer would have been,

> The power of the Spirit can do it. By the simple spreading of his dove-like wings he can make all the things come together. Upon that there shall be order where there was nought but confusion.

Nor is this all the power of the Spirit. We have seen some of his works in creation.

But there was one particular instance of creation in which the Holy Spirit was more especially concerned, viz., the formation of the body of our Lord Jesus Christ. Though our Lord Jesus Christ was born of a woman and made in the likeness of sinful flesh, yet the power that begat him was entirely in God the Holy Spirit—as the Scriptures express it, "The power of the Highest shall overshadow thee." He was *begotten*, as the Apostles' Creed says, begotten of the Holy Ghost. "That holy thing which is born of thee shall be called the Son of the Highest." The corporeal frame of the Lord Jesus Christ was a masterpiece of the Holy Spirit. I suppose his body to have excelled all others in beauty; to have been like that of the first man, the very pattern of what the body is to be in Heaven, when it shall shine forth in all its glory. That fabric, in all its beauty and perfection, was modeled by the Spirit. In his book were all the members written when as yet there were none of them. He fashioned and formed him; and here again we have another instance of the creative energy of the Spirit.

2. A second manifestation of the Holy Spirit's power is to be found in the *resurrection of the Lord Jesus Christ*. If ye have ever studied this subject, ye have perhaps been rather perplexed to find that sometimes the resurrection of Christ is ascribed to himself. By his own power and Godhead he could not be held by the bond of death, but as he willingly gave up his life, he had power to take it again. In another portion of Scripture you find it ascribed to God the Father: "He raised him up from the dead;" "Him hath God the Father exalted." And many other passages of similar import. But, again, it is said in Scripture that Jesus Christ was raised by the Holy Spirit. Now all these things were true. He was raised by the Father because the Father said, "Loose the prisoner—let him go. Justice is satisfied. My law requires no more satisfaction—vengeance has had its due—let him go." Here he gave an official message which delivered Jesus from the grave. He was raised by his own majesty and power because he had a right to come out, and he felt he had, and therefore "burst the bonds of death: he could be no longer holden of them." But, he was raised by the Spirit as to that energy which his mortal frame received, by the which it rose again from the grave after having lain there for three days and nights. If you want proofs of this, you must open your Bibles again—1 Peter 3:18.

> For Christ also hath once suffered for sins, the just for the unjust, that he might bring us to God, being put to death in the flesh but quickened by the Spirit.

And a further proof you may find in Romans 8:11. (I love sometimes to be textual, for I believe the great fault of Christians is that they do not search the Scriptures enough, and I will make them search them when they are here if they do not do so anywhere else.)

> But if the Spirit of him that raised up Jesus from the dead dwell in you, he that raised up Christ from the dead shall also quicken your mortal bodies by his Spirit that dwelleth in you.

The resurrection of Christ, then, was effected by the agency of the Spirit, and here we have a noble illustration of his omnipotence. Could you have stepped, as angels did, into the grave of Jesus, and seen his sleeping body, you would have found it cold as any other corpse. Lift up the hand, it falls by the side. Look at the eye: it is glazed. And there is a death-thrust which must have annihilated life. See his hands; the blood distils not from them, they are cold and motionless. Can that body live? Can it start up? Yes; and be an illustration of the might of the Spirit. For when the power of the Spirit came on him, as it was when it fell upon the dry bones of the valley:

> He arose in the majesty of his divinity, and bright and shining, astonished the watchmen so that they fled away, yea, he arose no more to die, but to live forever, King of kings and Prince of the kings of the earth.

3. The third of the works of the Holy Spirit which have so wonderfully demonstrated his power, are *attestation works*. I mean by this, works of witnessing. When Jesus Christ went into the stream of baptism in the river Jordan, the Holy Spirit descended upon him like a dove, and proclaimed him God's beloved son. That was what I style an attestation work. And when afterwards Jesus Christ raised the dead, when he healed the leper, when he spoke to diseases and they fled apace, when demons rushed in thousands from those who were possessed of them, it was done by the power of the Spirit. The Spirit dwelt in Jesus without measure, and by that power all those miracles were worked. These were attestation works. And when Jesus Christ was gone, you will remember that master attestation of the Spirit when he came like a rushing mighty wind upon the assembled apostles, and cloven tongues sat upon them; and you will remember how he attested their ministry by giving them to speak with tongues as he gave them utterance; and how, also, miraculous deeds were wrought by them, how they taught, how Peter raised Dorcas how he breathed life into Eutycus, how great deeds were wrought by the apostles as well as their Master—so that "mighty signs and wonders were done by the Holy Ghost, and many believed thereby." Who will doubt the power of the Holy Spirit after that? Ah! those Socinians who deny the existence of the Holy Ghost and his absolute personality, what will

they do when we get them on creation, resurrection, and attestation? They must rush in the very teeth of Scripture. But mark! it is a stone upon which if any man fall he shall be bruised; but if it fall upon him, as it will do if he resists it, it shall grind him to powder. The Holy Spirit has power omnipotent, even the power of God.

4. Once more, if we want another outward and visible sign of the power of the Spirit, we may look at the *works of grace*. Behold a city where a sooth-sayer hath the power—who has given out himself to be some great one: a Philip enters it and preaches the Word of God—straightway a Simon Magus loses his power and himself seeks for the power of the Spirit to be given to him, fancying it might be purchased with money. See, in modern times, a country where the inhabitants live in miserable wigwams, feeding on rep-tiles and the meanest creatures; observe them bowing down before their idols and worshipping their false gods, and so plunged in superstition, so de-graded and debased, that it became a question whether they had souls or not; behold a Moffat go with the Word of God in his hand, hear him preach as the Spirit gives him utterance, and accompanies that Word with power. They cast aside their idols—they hate and abhor their former lusts; they build houses, wherein they dwell; they become clothed, and in their right mind. They break the bow, and cut the spear in sunder; the uncivilized become civi-lized; the savage becomes polite; he who knew nothing begins to read the Scriptures, thus out of the mouths of Hottentots,[1] God attests the power of his mighty Spirit.

Take a household in this city—and we could guide you to many such—the fa-ther is a drunkard; he has been the most desperate of characters; see him in his madness, and you might just as well meet an unchained tiger as meet such a man. He seems as if he could rend a man to pieces who should offend him. Mark his wife. She, too, has a spirit in her, and when he treats her ill she can resist him; many broils have been seen in that house, and often has the neighborhood been dis-turbed by the noise created there. As for the poor little children—see them in their rags and nakedness, poor untaught things. Untaught, did I say? They are taught and well taught in the devil's school, and are growing up to be the heirs of damnation.

But someone whom God has blessed by his Spirit is guided to the house. He may be but a humble city missionary perhaps, but he speaks to such a one: "O," says he, "come and listen to the voice of God." Whether it is by his own agency, or a minister's preaching, the Word, which is quick and powerful, cuts to the sinner's heart. The tears run down his cheeks—such as had never been seen before. He shakes and quivers. The strong man bows down—the

---

[1] Hottentots: black Africans. (Derogative.)

mighty man trembles—and those knees that never shook, begin to knock together. That heart which never quailed before, now begins to shake before the power of the Spirit. He sits down on a humble bench by the penitent; he lets his knees bend, whilst his lips utter a child's prayer, but, whilst a child's prayer, a prayer of a child of God. He becomes a changed character. Mark the reformation in his house! That wife of his becomes the decent matron. Those children are the credit of the house, and in due time they grow up like olive branches round his table, adorning his house like polished stones. Pass by the house—no noise or broils, but songs of Zion. See him—no drunken revelry; he has drained his last cup; and, now forswearing it, he comes to God and is his servant. Now, you will not hear at midnight the bacchanalian shout; but should there be a noise, it will be the sound of the solemn hymn of praise to God. And, now, is there not, such a thing as the power of the Spirit? Yes! and these must have witnessed it and seen it. I know a village, [that was] once, perhaps, the most profane in England—a village inundated by drunkenness and debauchery of the worst kind, where it was impossible almost for an honest traveler to stop in the public house without being annoyed by blasphemy; a place noted for incendiaries and robbers. One man, the ringleader of all, listened to the voice of God. That man's heart was broken. The whole gang came to hear the gospel preached, and they sat and seemed to reverence the preacher as if he were a God, and not a man. These men became changed and reformed; and everyone who knows the place affirms that such a change had never been wrought but by the power of the Holy Ghost.

Let the gospel be preached and the Spirit poured out, and you will see that it has such power to change the conscience, to ameliorate the conduct, to raise the debased, to chastise and to curb the wickedness of the race, that you must glory in it. I say, there is naught like the power of the Spirit. Only let that come, and, indeed, everything can be accomplished.

II. Now, for the second point, *the inward and spiritual power of the Holy Spirit.*

What I have already spoken of may be seen; what I am about to speak of must be *felt*, and no man will apprehend what I say with truth unless he has felt it. The other, even the infidel must confess; the other, the greatest blasphemer cannot deny if he speaks the truth; but this is what the one will laugh at as enthusiasm and what the other will say is but the invention of our fevered fancies. However, we have a more sure word of testimony than all that they may say. We have a witness within. We know it is the truth, and we are not afraid to speak of the inward spiritual power of the Holy Ghost. Let us notice two or three things wherein the inward and spiritual power of the Holy Ghost is very greatly to be seen and extolled.

1. First, in that the Holy Ghost has *a power over men's hearts*. Now, men's hearts are very hard to affect. If you want to get at them for any worldly object, you can do it. A cheating world can win man's heart, a little gold can win man's heart, a trump of fame and a little clamor of applause can win man's heart. But there is not a minister breathing that can win man's heart himself. He can win his ears and make them listen; he can win his eyes, and fix those eyes upon him; he can win the attention—but the heart is very slippery. Yes, the heart is a fish that troubles all gospel fishermen to hold. You may sometimes pull it almost all out of the water; but slimy as an eel, it slippeth between your fingers, and you have not captured it after all. Many a man has fancied that he has caught the heart, but has been disappointed. It would need a strong hunter to overtake the hart on the mountains. It is too fleet for human foot to approach. The Spirit alone has power over man's heart.

Do you ever try your power on a heart? If any man thinks that a minister can convert the soul, I wish he would try. Let him go and be a Sabbath-school teacher. He shall take his class, he shall have the best books that can be obtained, he shall have the best rules, he shall draw his lines of circumvallation [defense] about his spiritual Sebastopol [besieged city], he shall take the best boy in his class—and if he is not tired in a week, I shall be very much mistaken. Let him spend four or five Sabbaths in trying, but he will say, "The young fellow is incorrigible." Let him try another. And he will have to try another, and another, and another, before he will manage to convert one. He will soon find "It is not by might nor by power, but by my Spirit," saith the Lord. Can a minister convert? Can he touch the heart? David said, "Your hearts are as fat as grease." Ay, that is quite true; and we cannot get through so much grease at all. Our sword cannot get at the heart, it is encased in so much fatness, it is harder than a nether millstone. Many a good old Jerusalem blade has been blunted against the hard heart. Man, a piece of the true steel that God has put into the hands of his servants, has had the edge turned by being set up against the sinner's heart. We cannot reach the soul; but the Holy Spirit can. "My beloved can put in his hand by the hole in the door and my bowels will move for sin." He can give a sense of blood-bought pardon that shall dissolve a heart of stone. He can . . .

> Speak with that voice which wakes the dead,
> And bids the sinner rise:
> And makes the guilty conscience dread
> The death that never dies.

He can make Sinai's thunders audible; yea, and he can make the sweet whisperings of Calvary enter into the soul. He has power over the heart of man. And here is a glorious proof of the omnipotence of the Spirit that he has rule over the heart.

2. But if there is one thing more stubborn than the heart, it is *the will*. "My lord; Will-be-will," as Bunyan calls him in his *Holy War*, is a fellow who will not easily be bent. The will, especially in some men, is a very stubborn thing, and in all men, if the will is once stirred up to opposition, there is nothing can be done with them.

Freewill, somebody believes in. *Freewill,* many dream of. Freewill! Wherever is that to be found? Once there was free will in Paradise, and a terrible mess free will made there, for it all spoiled all Paradise and turned Adam out of the garden. Free will was once in Heaven, but it turned the glorious archangel out and a third part of the stars of Heaven fell into the abyss. I want nothing to do with free will, but I will try to see whether I have got a free will within. And I find I have. Very free will to evil, but very poor will to that which is good. Free will enough when I sin, but when I would do good, evil is present with me, and how to do that which I would, I find not. Yet some boast of free will. I wonder whether those who believe in it have any more power over persons wills than I have. I know I have not any. I find the old proverb very true, "One man can bring a horse to the water, but a hundred cannot make him drink." I find that I can bring you all to the water, and a great many more than can get into this chapel; but I cannot make you drink; and I don't think a hundred ministers could make you drink. I have read old Rowland Hill, and Whitfield, and several others to see what they did; but I cannot discover a plan of turning your wills. I cannot coax you; and you will not yield by any manner of means. I do not think any man has power over his fellow-creature's will, but the Spirit of God has. "I will make them willing in the day of my power." He maketh the unwilling sinner so willing that he is impetuous after the gospel; he who was obstinate, now hurries to the cross. He who laughed at Jesus, now hangs on his mercy; and he who would not believe, is now made by the Holy Spirit to do it, not only willingly, but eagerly; he is happy, is glad to do it, rejoices in the sound of Jesus' name, and delights to run in the way of God's commandments. The Holy Spirit has power over the will.

3. And yet there is one thing more which I think is *rather worse than the will.* You will guess what I mean. The will is somewhat worse than the heart to bend, but there is one thing that excels the will in its naughtiness, and that is the *imagination.* I hope that my will is managed by Divine Grace. But I am afraid my imagination is not at times. Those who have a fair share of imagination know what a difficult thing it is to control. You cannot restrain it. It will break the reins. You will never be able to manage it. The imagination will sometimes fly up to God with such a power that eagles' wings cannot match it. It sometimes has such might that it can almost see the King in his beauty, and the land which is very far off. With regard to myself, my imagination will sometimes take me over the gates of iron, across that infinite unknown, to the very gates of pearl, and discovers the blessed glorified.

But if it is potent one way, it is [also in] another; for my imagination has taken me down to the vilest kennels and sewers of earth. It has given me thoughts so dreadful that, while I could not avoid them, yet I was thoroughly horrified at them. These thoughts will come, and when I feel in the holiest frame, the most devoted to God, and the most earnest in prayer, it often happens that that is the very time when the plagues breaks out the worst. But I rejoice and think of one thing, that I can cry out when this imagination comes upon me. I know it is said in the book of Leviticus, when an act of evil was committed, if the maiden cried out against it, then her life was to be spared. So it is with the Christian. If he cries out there is hope. Can you chain your imagination? No; but the power of the Holy Ghost can. Ah, it shall do it, and it does do it at last; it does it, even on earth.

III. But the last thing was *the future and desired effects*—for, after all, though the Holy Spirit has done so much, he cannot say, "It is finished."

Jesus Christ could exclaim concerning his own labor—"It is finished." But the Holy Spirit cannot say that. He has more to do yet: and until the consummation of all things, when the Son himself becomes subject to the Father, it shall not be said by the Holy Spirit, "It is finished." What, then, has the Holy Spirit to do?

1. First, he has to *perfect us in holiness*. There are two kinds of perfection which a Christian needs—one is the perfection of justification in the person of Jesus; and the other is, the perfection of sanctification worked in him by the Holy Spirit. At present, corruption still rests even in the breasts of the regenerate. At present the heart is partially impure. At present there are still lusts and evil imaginations. But, Oh! my soul rejoices to know that the day is coming when God shall finish the work which he has begun; and he shall present my soul, not only perfect in Christ, but, perfect in the Spirit, without spot or blemish, or any such thing. And is it true that this poor depraved heart is to become as holy as that of God? And is it true that this poor spirit, which often cries, "O wretched man that I am, who shall deliver me from the body of this sin and death!" shall get rid of sin and death—I shall have no evil things to vex my ears, and no unholy thoughts to disturb my peace? Oh! happy hour! may it be hastened! Just before I die, sanctification will be finished; but not till that moment shall I ever claim perfection in myself. But at that moment when I depart, my spirit shall have its last baptism in the Holy Spirit's fire. It shall be put in the crucible for its last trying in the furnace; and then, free from all dross, and fine like a wedge of pure gold, it shall be presented at the feet of God without the least degree of dross or mixture. O glorious hour! O blessed moment! Methinks I long to die [even] if there were no Heaven, if I might but have that last purification, and come up from Jordan's stream most white from the washing. Oh! to be washed white, clean, pure, perfect! Not an angel more pure than I shall be—yea, not God himself more holy! And I shall be able to say, in a double sense, "Great God, I am clean—through Jesus's blood I am clean, through the Spirit's work, I am clean too!" Must we not extol the power of the Holy Ghost in thus making us fit to stand before our Father in Heaven?

2. Another great work of the Holy Spirit which is not accomplished is *the bringing on of the latter-day glory*. In a few more years—I know not when, I know not how—the Holy Spirit will be poured out in a far different style from the present. There are diversities of operations; and during the last few years it has been the case that the diversified operations have consisted in very little pouring out of the Spirit. Ministers have gone on in dull routine, continually preaching, preaching, preaching—and little good has been done. I do hope that perhaps a fresh era has dawned upon us, and that there is a better pouring out of the Spirit even now. For the hour is coming, and it may be even now is, when the Holy Ghost shall be poured out again in such a wonderful manner that many shall run to and fro, and knowledge shall be increased—the knowledge of the Lord shall cover the earth as the waters cover the surface of the great deep, when his kingdom shall come, and his will shall be done on earth even as it is in Heaven. We are not going to be dragging on forever like Pharoah, with the wheels off his chariot. My heart exults and my eyes flash with the thought that very likely I shall live to see the out-pouring of the Spirit when "the sons and the daughters of God again shall prophecy, and the young men shall see visions, and the old men shall dream dreams." Perhaps there shall be no miraculous gifts, for they will not be required; but yet there shall be such a miraculous amount of holiness, such an extraordinary fervor of prayer, such a real communion with God and so much vital religion, and such a spread of the doctrines of the cross, that everyone will see that verily the Spirit is poured out like water and the rains are descending from above. For that let us pray: let us continually labor for it, and seek it of God.

3. One more work of the Spirit which will especially manifest his power—*the general resurrection*. We have reason to believe from Scripture that the resurrection of the dead, whilst it will be effected by the voice of God and of his Word (the Son), shall also be brought about by the Spirit. That same power which raised Jesus Christ from the dead, shall also quicken your mortal bodies. The power of the resurrection is perhaps one of the finest proofs of the works of the Spirit. Ah! my friends, if this earth could but have its mantle torn away for a little while, if the green sod could be cut from it, and we could look about six feet deep into its bowels, what a world it would seem! What should we see? Bones, carcasses, rottenness, worms, corruption. And you would say, "Can these dry bones live? Can they start up?" "Yes! in a moment! in the twinkling of an eye, at the last trump, the dead shall be raised." He speaks: they are alive! See them scattered: bone comes to his bone! See them naked: flesh comes upon them! See them still lifeless: "Come from the four winds, O breath, and breathe upon these slain!" When the wind of the Holy Spirit comes, they live, and they stand upon their feet an exceeding great army.

I have thus attempted to speak of the power of the Spirit, and I trust I have shown it to you. We must now have a moment or two for practical inference. The

Spirit is very powerful, Christian! What do you infer from that fact? Why, that you never need distrust the power of God to carry you to Heaven. O how that sweet verse was laid to my soul yesterday:

> *His tried Almighty arm*
> *Is raised for your defense;*
> *Where is the power [that] can reach you there?*
> *Or what can pluck you thence?*

The power of the Holy Spirit is your bulwark, and all his omnipotence defends you. Can your enemies overcome omnipotence? Then they can conquer you. Can they wrestle with Diety, and hurl him to the ground? Then they might conquer you. For the power of the Spirit is *our* power; the power of the Spirit is *our* might.

Once again, Christians, if this is the power of the Spirit, *why should you doubt anything?* There is your son. There is that wife of yours, for whom you have supplicated so frequently: do not doubt the Spirit's power. "Though he tarry, wait for him." There is thy husband, O holy woman! and thou hast wrestled for his soul. And though he is ever so hardened and desperate a wretch, and treats thee ill, there is power in the Spirit. And, O ye who have come from barren churches with scarcely a leaf upon the tree: do not doubt the power of the Spirit to raise you up. For it shall be a "pasture for flocks, a den of wild asses," open, but deserted, until the Spirit is poured out from on high. And then the parched ground shall be made a pool, and the thirsty land springs of water, and in the habitations of dragons, where each lay shall be grass with reeds and rushes. And, O ye members of Park Street [Chapel], ye who remember what your God has done for you: especially never distrust the power of the Spirit. Ye have seen the wilderness blossom like Carmel, ye have seen the desert blossom like the rose; trust him for the future. Then go out and labor with this conviction, that the power of the Holy Ghost is able to do anything. Go to your Sunday-school; go to your tract distribution; go to your missionary enterprise, go to your preaching in your rooms, with the conviction that the power of the Spirit is our great help.

And now, lastly, to you sinners: what is there to be said to you about this power of the Spirit? Why, to me, there is some hope for some of you. I cannot save you: I cannot get at you. I make you cry sometimes—you wipe your eyes, and it is all over. But I know my Master can. That is my consolation. Chief of sinners, there is hope for thee! This power can save you as well as anybody else. It is able to break your heart, though it is an iron one; to make your eyes run with tears though they have been like rocks before. His power is able this morning, if he will, to change your heart, to turn the current of all your ideas, to make you at once a child of God, to justify you in Christ. There is power enough in the Holy Spirit. Ye are not straitened [in distress] in *Him,* but in your own bowels [strength]. He is able to bring sinners to Jesus: he is able to make you willing in the day of his power. Are you willing this morning? Has he gone so far as to make you desire his name, to make you wish for Jesus? Then, O sinner! whilst he draws you, say, "Draw me, I am wretched without thee." Follow him, follow him, and, while he leads, tread you in his footsteps, and rejoice that he has begun a good work in you, for there is an evidence that he will continue it even unto the end. And, O desponding one! put thy trust in the power of the Spirit. Rest on the blood of Jesus, and thy soul is safe, not only now, but throughout eternity. God bless you, my hearers. Amen.

The Holy Ghost, the Great Teacher

Delivered on Sabbath morning, November 18, 1855, at New Park Street Chapel, Southwark. No. 50.

Howbeit when he, the Spirit of truth, is come, he will guide you into all truth: for he shall not speak of himself; but whatsoever he shall hear, that shall he speak: and he will shew you things to come.—John 16:13

This generation hath gradually, and almost imperceptibly, become to a great extent a godless generation. One of the diseases of the present generation of mankind is their secret but deep-seated godlessness, by which they have so far departed from the knowledge of God. Science has discovered to us second causes; and hence, many have too much forgotten the first Great Cause, the Author of all: they have been able so far to pry into secrets, that the great axiom of the existence of a God has been too much neglected. Even among professing Christians, while there is a great amount of religion, there is too little godliness: there is much external formalism, but too little inward acknowledgment of God, too little living on God, living with God, and relying upon God. Hence arises the sad fact that when you enter many of our places of worship you will certainly hear the name of God mentioned; but except in the benediction, you would scarcely know there was a Trinity. In many places dedicated to Jehovah, the name of Jesus is too often kept in the background; the Holy Spirit is almost entirely neglected; and very little is said concerning his sacred influence. Even religious men have become to a large degree godless in this age. We sadly require more preaching regarding God; more preaching of those things which look not so much at the creature to be saved, as at God the Great One, to be extolled. My firm conviction is that, in proportion as we have more regard for the sacred godhead, the wondrous Trinity in Unity—shall we see a greater display of God's power, and a more glorious manifestation of his might in our churches. May God send us Christ-exalting, Spirit-loving ministry-men who shall proclaim God the Holy Ghost in all his offices, and shall extol God the Savior as the author and finisher of our faith, not neglecting that Great God, the Father of his people, who, before all worlds, elected us in Christ his Son, justified us through his righteousness, and will inevitably preserve us and gather us together in one, in the consummation of all things at the last great day.

Our text has regard to God the Holy Spirit; of him we shall speak and him only, if his sweet influence shall rest upon us.

The disciples had been instructed by Christ concerning certain elementary doctrines, but Jesus did not teach his disciples more than what we should call the "A-B-Cs" of religion. He gives his reasons for this in the 12th verse: "I have yet many things to say unto you, but you cannot bear them now." His disciples were not possessors of the Spirit. They had the Spirit so far as the work of conversion was concerned, but not as to the matters of bright illumination, profound instruction, prophecy, and inspiration. He says,

> I am now about to depart, and when I go from you I will send the Comforter unto you. Ye cannot bear these things now: howbeit, when he, the Spirit of truth is come, he will guide you into all truth.

The same promise that he made to his apostles, stands good to all his children; and in reviewing it, we shall take it as our portion and heritage, and shall not consider ourselves intruders upon the manor of the apostles, or upon their exclusive rights and prerogatives; for we conceive that Jesus says even to us, "When he, the Spirit of truth is come, he will guide you into all truth."

Dwelling exclusively upon our text, we have five things. First of all, here is *an attainment mentioned*—a knowledge of all truth; secondly, here is *a difficulty suggested*—which is, that we need guidance into all truth; thirdly, here is *a person provided*—"when he, the Spirit shall come, he shall guide you into all truth;" fourthly, here is *a manner hinted at*—"he shall guide you into all truth;" fifthly, here is *a sign given as to the working of the Spirit*—we may know whether he works, by his "guiding us into *all* truth"—into all of *one thing*; not *truths*, but *truth*.

I. Here is *an attainment mentioned,* which is a knowledge of all truth.

We know that some conceive doctrinal knowledge to be of very little importance, and of no practical use. We do not think so. We believe the science of Christ crucified and a judgment of the teachings of Scripture to be exceedingly valuable; we think it is right, that the Christian ministry should not only be arousing but instructing; not merely awakening, but enlightening: that it should appeal not only to the passions but to the understanding. We are far from thinking doctrinal knowledge to be of secondary importance; we believe it to be one of the first things in the Christian life, to know the truth, and then to practice it. We scarcely need this morning tell you how desirable it is for us to be well taught in things of the kingdom.

First of all, *nature itself,* (when it has been sanctified by grace,) *gives us a strong desire to know all truth.* The natural man separateth himself and intermeddleth with all knowledge. God has put an instinct in him by which he is rendered unsatisfied if he cannot probe mystery to its bottom; he can never be content until he can unriddle secrets. What we call curiosity is something given us of God impelling us to search into the knowledge of natural things; that curiosity, sanctified by the Spirit, is also brought to bear in matters of heavenly science and celestial wisdom. "Bless the Lord," said David, "O my soul, and *all that is within me* bless his holy name!" If there is a curiosity within us, it ought to be employed and developed in a search after truth. "All that is within me," sanctified by the Spirit, should be developed, And, verily, the Christian man feels an intense longing to bury his ignorance and receive wisdom. If he, when in his natural estate, panted for terrestrial knowledge, how much more ardent is the wish to unravel, if possible, the sacred mysteries of God's Word! A true Christian is always intently reading and searching the Scripture that he may be able to certify himself as to its main and cardinal truths. I do not think much of that man who does not wish to understand doctrines; I cannot conceive him to be in a right position when he thinks it is no matter whether he believes a lie or truth, whether he is heretic or orthodox, whether he received the Word of God as it is written, or as it is diluted and misconstrued by man. God's Word will ever be to a Christian a source of great anxiety; a sacred instinct within will lead him to pry into it; he will seek to understand it. Oh! there are some who forget this, men who purposely abstain from mentioning what are called high doctrines, because they think if they should mention high doctrines they would be dangerous; so they keep them back. Foolish men! They do not know anything of human nature; for if they did understand a grain's worth of humanity, they would know that the hiding of these things impels men to search them out. From the fact that they do not mention them, they drive men to places where these, and these only, are preached. They say, "If I preach election, and predestination, and these dark things, people will all go straight away, and become Antinomians."[1] I am not so sure if they were to be called Antinomians it would hurt them much; but hear me, oh, ye ministers that conceal these truths: that is the way to make them Antinomians, by silencing these doctrines. Curiosity is strong; if you tell them they

---

[1] Antinomians: A group opposed to or denying the fixed meaning or universal applicability of moral law. (*American Heritage Dictionary, 4th Edition,* 2000.)

must not pluck the truth, they will be sure to do it; but if you give it to them as you find it in God's Word, they will not seek to "wrest" it. Enlightened men *will* have the truth, and if they see election in Scripture, they will say, "*it is there,* and I will find it out. If I cannot get it in one place, I will get it in another." The true Christian has an inward longing and anxiety after it; he is hungry and thirsty after the word of righteousness, and he must and will feed on this bread of heaven, or at all hazards he will leave the husks which unsound divines would offer him.

Not only is this attainment to be desired because nature teaches us so, but a knowledge of all truth is *very essential for our comfort.* I do believe that many persons have been distressed half their lives from the fact that they had not clear views of truth. Many poor souls, for instance, under conviction, abide three or four times as long in sorrow of mind as they would require [need] to do if they had someone to instruct them in the great matter of justification. So there are believers who are often troubling themselves about falling away; but if they knew in their soul the great consolation that we are kept by the grace of God through faith unto salvation, they would be no more troubled about it. So have I found some distressed about the unpardonable sin—but if God instructs us in that doctrine, and shows us that no conscience that is really awakened ever can commit that sin, but that when it is committed, God gives us up to a seared conscience, so that we never fear or tremble afterwards—all that distress would be alleviated. Depend on this, the more you know of God's truth—all things else being equal—the more comfortable you will be as a Christian. Nothing can give a greater light on your path than a clear understanding of divine things. It is a mingle-mangled gospel too commonly preached, which causes the downcast faces of Christians. Give me the congregation whose faces are bright with joy, let their eyes glisten at the sound of the gospel, then will I believe that it is God's own words they are receiving. Instead thereof you will often see melancholy congregations whose visages are not much different from the bitter countenance of poor creatures swallowing medicine, because the word spoken terrifies them by its legality, instead of comforting them by its grace. We love a cheerful gospel, and we think "all the truth" will tend to comfort the Christian.

"Comfort again," says another, "always comfort." Ah, but there is another reason why we prize truth, because we believe that a true knowledge of all the truth *will keep us very much out of danger.* No doctrine is so calculated to preserve a man from sin as the doctrine of the grace of God. Those who have called it a licentious doctrine did not know anything at all about it. Poor ignorant things, they little knew that their own vile stuff was the most licentious doctrine under Heaven. If they knew the grace of God in truth, they would soon see that there was no preservative from lying like a knowledge that we are elect of God from the foundation of the world. There is nothing like a belief in my eternal perseverance, and the immutability of my Father's affection, which can keep me near to him from a motive of simple gratitude. Nothing makes a man so virtuous as belief of truth. A lying doctrine will soon beget a lying practice. A man cannot have an erroneous belief without by-and-bye having an erroneous life. I believe the one thing naturally begets the other. Keep near God's truth; keep near his word; keep the head right, and especially keep your heart right with regard to truth, and your feet will not go far astray.

Again, I hold also that this attainment to the knowledge of all truth is very desirable for *the usefulness which it will give us in the world at large*. We should not be selfish: we should always consider whether a thing will be beneficial to others. A knowledge of all truth will make us very serviceable in this world. We shall be skillful physicians who know how to take the poor distressed soul aside, to put the finger on his eye, and take the scale off for him, that heaven's light may comfort him. There will be no character, however perplexing may be its peculiar phase, but we shall be able to speak to it and comfort it. He who holds the truth, is usually the most useful man. As a good Presbyterian brother said to me the other day:

> I know God has blessed you exceedingly in gathering in souls, but it is an extraordinary fact that nearly all the men I know—with scarcely an exception—who have been made useful in gathering in souls, have held the great doctrines of the grace of God.

Almost every man whom God has blessed to the building up of the church in prosperity, and around whom the people have rallied, has been a man who has held firmly free grace from first to last, through the finished salvation of Christ. Do not you think you need have errors in your doctrine to make you useful. We have some who preach Calvinism all the first part of the sermon, and finish up with Arminianism, because they think that will make them useful. Useful nonsense! That is all it is. A man, if he cannot be useful with the truth, cannot be useful with an error. There is enough in the pure doctrine of God, without introducing heresies to preach to sinners. As far as I know, I never felt hampered or cramped in addressing the ungodly in my life. I can speak with as much fervency, and yet not in the same style as those who hold the contrary views of God's truth. Those who hold God's word, never need add something untrue in speaking to men. The sturdy truth of God touches every chord in every man's heart. If we can, by God's grace, put our hand inside man's heart, we want nothing but that whole truth to move him thoroughly, and to stir him up. There is nothing like the real truth and the whole truth, to make a man useful.

II. Now, again, here is a *difficulty suggested,* and that is—that we require a guide to conduct us into all truth.

The difficulty is that truth is not so easy to discover. There is no man born in this world by nature who has the truth in his heart. There is no creature that ever was fashioned, since the fall, who has a knowledge of truth innate and natural. It has been disputed by many philosophers whether there are such things as innate ideas at all; but [it] is of no use disputing as to whether there are any innate ideas of truth. There are none such. There are ideas of everything that is wrong and evil; but in us—that is, our flesh—there dwelleth no *good* thing: we are born in sin, and shapened in iniquity; in sin did our mother conceive us. There is nothing in us good, and no tendency to righteousness. Then, since we are not born with the truth, we have the task of searching for it. If we are to be blest by being eminently useful as Christian men, we must be well instructed in matters of revelation; but here is the difficulty—that we cannot follow without a guide the winding paths of truth. Why [is] this?

First, because of *the very great intricacy of truth itself.* Truth itself is no easy thing to discover. Those who fancy they know everything and constantly dogmatise with the spirit of "We are the men, and wisdom will die with us," of course see no difficulties whatever in the system they hold; but I believe, the most earnest student of Scripture will find things in the Bible which puzzle him; however earnestly he reads it, he will see some mysteries too deep for him to understand. He will cry out "Truth! I cannot find thee; I know not where thou art, thou art beyond me; I cannot fully view thee." Truth is a path so narrow that two can scarce walk together in it; we usually tread the narrow way in single file—two men can seldom walk arm in arm in the truth. We believe the same truth in the main, but we cannot walk together in the path, it is too narrow. The way of truth is very difficult. If you step an inch aside on the right you are in a dangerous error, and if you swerve a little to the left you are equally in the mire. On the one hand there is a huge precipice, and on the other a deep morass; and unless you keep to the true line, to the breadth of a hair, you will go astray. Truth is a narrow path indeed. It is a path the eagle's eye hath not seen, and a depth the diver hath not visited. It is like the veins of metal in a mine, it is often of excessive thinness, and moreover it runneth not in one continued layer. Lose it once, and you may dig for miles and not discover it again; the eye must watch perpetually the direction of the lode. Grains of truth are like the grains of gold in the rivers of Australia—they must be shaken by the hand of patience, and washed in the stream of honesty, or the fine gold will be mingled with sand. Truth is often mingled with error, and it is hard to distinguish it; but we bless God [that] it is said, "When the Spirit of truth is come, he will guide you into all truth."

Another reason why we need a guide is *the invidiousness of error*. It busily steals upon us, and, if I may so describe our position, we are often like we were on Thursday night in that tremendous fog. Most of us were feeling for ourselves, and wondering where on earth we were. We could scarcely see an inch before us. We came to a place where there were three turnings. We thought we knew the old spot. There was the lamp-post, and now we must take a sharp turn to the left; but not so. We ought to have gone a little to the right. We have been so often to the same place that we think we know every flag-stone—and there's our friend's shop over the way. It is dark, but we think we must be quite right, and all the while we are quite wrong, and find ourselves half-a-mile out of the way. So it is with matters of truth. We think, surely this is the right path; and the voice of the evil one whispers, "that is the way, walk ye in it." You do so, and you find to your great dismay, that instead of the path of truth, you have been walking in the paths of unrighteousness and erroneous doctrines. The way of life is a labyrinth; the grassiest paths and the most bewitching, are the farthest away from right; the most enticing, are those which are garnished with wrested truths. I believe there is not a counterfeit coin in the world so much like a genuine one as some errors are like the truth. One is base metal, the other is true gold; still, in externals they differ very little.

We also need a guide, because *we are so prone to go astray*. Why, if the path of Heaven were as straight as Bunyan pictures it, with no turning to the right hand or left—and no doubt it is—we are [still] so prone to go astray, that we should go to the right hand to the Mountains of Destruction, or to the left in the dark Wood of Desolation. David says, "I have gone astray like a lost sheep." That means very often: for if a sheep is put into a field twenty times, if it does not get out twenty-one times, it will be because it cannot; because the place is hurdled up, and it cannot find a hole in the hedge. If grace did not guide a man, he would go astray, though there were hand-posts all the way to Heaven. Let it be written, "*Miklat, Miklat,* the way to refuge." [Still] he would turn aside, and the avenger of blood would overtake him, if some guide did not, like the angels in Sodom, put his hand on his shoulders, and cry, "Escape, escape, for thy life! Look not behind thee; stay not in all the plain." These, then, are the reasons why we need a guide.

III. In the third place, here is *a person provided.*

This is none other than God, and this God is none other than a person. This person is "he, the Spirit," the "Spirit of truth"—not an influence or an emanation, but actually a person. "When the Spirit of truth is come, he shall guide you into all truth." Now, we wish you to look at this guide to consider how adapted he is to us.

In the first place, he is *infallible;* he knows everything and cannot lead us astray. If I pin my sleeve to another man's coat, he may lead me part of the way rightly, but by-and-bye he will go wrong himself, and I shall be led astray with him; but if I give myself to the Holy Ghost and ask his guidance, there is no fear of my wandering.

Again, we rejoice in this Spirit because he is *ever-present.* We fall into a difficulty sometimes; we say, "Oh, if I could take this to my minister, he would explain it; but I live so far off, and am not able to see him." That perplexes us, and we turn the text round and round and cannot make anything out of it. We look at the commentators. We take down pious Thomas Scott, and, as usual he says nothing about it if it be a dark passage. Then we go to holy Matthew Henry, and if it is an easy Scripture, he is sure to explain it; but if it is a text hard to be understood, it is likely enough, of course, left in his own gloom; and even Dr. Gill himself, the most consistent of commentators, when he comes to a hard passage, manifestly avoids it in some degree. But when we have no commentator or minister, we have still the Holy Spirit; and let me tell you a little secret: whenever you cannot understand a text, open your Bible, bend your knee, and pray over that text; and if it does not split into atoms and open itself, try again. If prayer does not explain it, it is one of the things God did not intend you to know, and you may be content to be ignorant of it. Prayer is the key that openeth the cabinets of mystery. Prayer and faith are sacred picklocks that can open secrets, and obtain great treasures. There is no college for holy education like that of the blessed Spirit, for he is an ever—present tutor, to whom we have only to bend the knee, and he is at our side, the great expositor of truth.

But there is one thing about the suitability of this guide which is remarkable. I do not know whether it has struck you—the Holy Spirit can "guide us *into* a truth." Now, man can guide us *to* a truth, but it is only the Holy Spirit who can "guide us *into* a truth." "When he, the Spirit of truth, shall come, he shall guide you *into*"—mark that word—"all truth." Now, for instance, it is a long while before you can lead some people to election; but when you have made them see its correctness, you have not led them "into" it. You may show them that it is plainly stated in Scripture, but they will turn away and hate it. You take them to another great truth, but they have been brought up in a different fashion, and though they cannot answer your arguments, they say, "The man is right, perhaps," and they whisper—but so low that conscience itself cannot hear—"but it is so contrary to my prejudices, that I cannot receive it." After you have led them *to* the truth, and they see it is true, how hard it is to lead them *into* it! There are many of my hearers who are brought *to* the truth of their depravity, but they are not brought *into* it, and made to feel it. Some of you are brought to know the truth that God keeps us from day to day; but you rarely get into it, so as to live in continual dependence upon God the Holy Ghost, and draw fresh supplies from him. The thing is, to get inside it. A Christian should do with truth as a snail does with his shell—live inside it, as well as carry it on his back, and bear it perpetually about with him. The Holy Ghost, it is said, shall lead us into all truth. You may be brought to a chamber where there is an abundance of gold and silver, but you will be no richer unless you effect an entrance. It is the Spirit's work to unbar the two leaved gates, and bring us into truth, so that we may get inside it, and, as dear old Rowland Hill said, "Not only hold the truth, but have the truth hold us."

IV. Fourthly, here is a *method suggested:* "He shall guide you into all truth."

Now I must have an illustration. I must compare truth to some cave or grotto that you have heard of, with wondrous stalactites hanging from the roof, and others starting from the floor; a cavern, glittering with spar and abounding in marvels. Before entering the cavern you inquire for a guide, who comes with his lighted flambeau. He conducts you down to a considerable depth, and you find yourself in the midst of the cave. He leads you through different chambers. Here he points to a little stream rushing from amid the rocks, and indicates its rise and progress; there he points to some peculiar rock and tells you its name; then takes you into a large natural hall, tells you how many persons once feasted in it; and so on. Truth is a grand series of caverns, it is our glory to have so great and wise a conductor. Imagine that we are coming to the darkness of it. He is a light shining in the midst of us to guide us; and by the light he shows us wondrous things. In three ways the Holy Ghost teaches us: by suggestion, direction, and illumination.

First, he guides us into all truth *by suggesting it.* There are thoughts that dwell in our minds that were not born there, but which were exotics brought from Heaven and put there by the Spirit. It is not a fancy that angels whisper into our ears, and that devils do the same: both good and evil spirits hold converse with men; and some of us have known it. We have had strange thoughts which were not the offspring of our souls, but which came from angelic visitants; and direct temptations and evil insinuations have we had which were not brewed in our own souls, but which came from the pestilential cauldron of Hell. So the Spirit doth speak in men's ears, sometimes in the darkness of the night. In ages gone by he spoke in dreams and visions, but now he speaketh by his Word. Have you not at times had unaccountably, in the middle of your business, a thought concerning God and heavenly things, and could not tell whence it came? Have you not been reading or studying the Scripture, but a text came across your mind, and you could not help it; though you even put it down, it was like cork in water, and would swim up again to the top of your mind. Well, that good thought was put there by the Spirit; he often guides his people into all truth by suggesting, just as the guide in the grotto does with his flambeau. He does not say a word, perhaps, but he walks into a passage himself, and you follow him: so the Spirit suggests a thought, and your heart follows it up. Well can I remember the manner in which I learned the doctrines of grace in a single instant. Born, as all of us are by nature, an Arminian, I still believed the old things I had heard continually from the pulpit, and did not see the grace of God. I remember sitting one day in the house of God and hearing a sermon as dry as possible, and as worthless as all such sermons are, when a thought struck my mind—"How came I to be converted?" "I prayed," thought I. Then I thought, "How came I to pray?" "I was induced to pray by reading the Scriptures." "How came I to read the Scriptures?" "Why—I did read them, and what led me to that?" And then, in a moment, I saw that God was at the bottom of all, and that he was the author of faith; and then the whole doctrine opened up to me, from which I have not departed.

But sometimes he leads us *by direction*. The guide points and says—"There, gentlemen, go along that particular path, that is the way." So the Spirit gives a direction and tendency to our thoughts; not suggesting a new one but letting a particular thought, when it starts, take such-and-such a direction; not so much putting a boat on the stream, as steering it when it is there. When our thoughts are considering sacred things, he leads us into a more excellent channel from that in which we started. Time after time have you commenced a meditation on a certain doctrine and, unaccountably, you were gradually led away into another, and you saw how one doctrine leaned on another, as is the case with the stones in the arch of a bridge, all hanging on the keystone of Jesus Christ crucified. You were brought to see these things, not by a new idea suggested, but by direction given to your thoughts.

But perhaps the best way in which the Holy Ghost leads us into all truth is by *illumination*. He illuminates the Bible. Now, have any of you an illuminated Bible at home? "No," says one, "I have a morocco Bible; I have a polyglot [multi-language] Bible; I have a marginal reference Bible." Ah! that is all very well, but have you an *illuminated* Bible? "Yes, I have a large family Bible with pictures in it." There is a picture of John the Baptist baptizing Christ by pouring water on his head, and many other nonsensical things; but that is not what I mean: have you an *illuminated* Bible? "Yes, I have a Bible with splendid engravings in it." Yes; I know you may have; but have you an *illuminated* Bible? "I don't understand what you mean by an illuminated Bible." Well, it is the Christian man who has an illuminated Bible. He does not buy it illuminated originally, but when he reads it . . .

> A glory gilds the sacred page,
> Majestic like the sun
> Which gives a light to every age,
> —It gives, but borrows none.

There is nothing like reading an illuminated Bible, beloved. You may read to all eternity, and never learn anything by it, unless it is illuminated by the Spirit; and then the words shine forth like stars. The book seems made of gold leaf; every single letter glitters like a diamond. Oh, it is a blessed thing to read an illuminated Bible lit up by the radiance of the Holy Ghost. Hast thou read the Bible and studied it, my brother, and yet have thine eyes been unenlightened? Go and say, "O Lord, gild the Bible for me. I want an expounded Bible. Illuminate it; shine upon it; for I cannot read it to profit, unless thou enlightenest me." Blind men may read the Bible with their fingers, but blind souls cannot. We want a light to read the Bible by, there is no reading it in the dark. Thus the Holy Spirit leads us into all truth, by suggesting ideas, by directing our thoughts, and by illuminating the Scriptures when we read them.

V. The last thing is *an evidence.*

The question arises, "How may I know whether I am enlightened by the Spirit's influence, and led into all truth?" First, you may know the Spirit's influence by its *unity*—he guides us into all *truth*: secondly, by its *universality*—he guides us into *all* truth.

First, if you are judging a minister, whether he has the Holy Ghost in him or not, you may know him in the first place, by *the constant unity of his testimony.* A man cannot be enlightened by the Holy Spirit, who preaches yea and nay. The Spirit never says one thing at one time and another thing at another time. There are indeed many good men who say both yea and nay, but still their contrary testimonies are not both from God the Spirit, for God the Spirit cannot witness to black and white, to a falsehood and truth. It has been always held as a first principle, that truth is one thing; but some persons say, "I find one thing in one part of the Bible and another thing in another, and though it contradicts itself I must believe it." All quite right, brother, if it did contradict itself; but the fault is not in the wood but in the carpenter. Many carpenters do not understand dovetailing—so there are many preachers who do not understand dovetailing. It is very nice work, and it is not easily learnt, it takes some apprenticeship to make all doctrines square together. Some preachers preach very good Calvinism for half-an-hour, and the next quarter-of-an-hour, Arminianism.[2] If they are Calvinists, let them stick to it; if they are Arminians, let them stick to it, let their preaching be all of a piece. Don't let them pile up things, only to kick them all down again; let us have one thing woven from the top throughout, and let us not rend it. How did Solomon know the true mother of the child? "Cut it in halves," said he. The woman who was not the mother did not care, so long as the other did not get the whole, and she consented. "Ah," said the true

---

2 Arminianism: a theology that rejects the Calvinist doctrines of predestination and election and believes that human free will is compatible with God's sovereignty. (*American Heritage Dictionary, 4th Edtion,* 2000.)

mother, "give her the living child. Let her have it, rather than cut it in halves." So the true child of God would say

> I give it up, let my opponent conquer; I do not want to have the truth cut in halves. I would rather be all wrong, than have the Word altered to my taste.

We do not want to have a divided Bible. No, we claim the whole living child, or none at all. We may rest assured of this, that until we get rid of our linsey-woolsey[3] doctrine, and cease to sow mingled seed, we shall not have a blessing. An enlightened mind cannot believe a gospel which denies itself; it must be one thing or the other. One thing cannot contradict another, and yet it and its opposite be equally true. You may know the Spirit's influence then, by the unity of its testimony.

And you may know it by its *universality*. The true child of God will not be led into *some* truth but into *all* truth. When first he starts, he will not know half the truth: he will believe it but not understand it; he will have the germ of it but not the sum total in all its breadth and length. There is nothing like learning by experience. A man cannot set up for a theologian in a week. Certain doctrines take years to develop themselves. Like the aloe that taketh a hundred years to be dressed, there be some truths that must lie long in the heart before they really come out and make themselves appear so that we can speak of them as that we do know; and testify of that which we have seen. The Spirit will gradually lead us into all truth. For instance if it be true that Jesus Christ is to reign upon the earth personally for a thousand years, as I am inclined to believe it is, if I be under the Spirit, that will be more and more opened to me, until I with confidence declare it. Some men begin very timidly. A man says, at first, "I know we are justified by faith, and have peace with God, but so many have cried out against eternal justification, that I am afraid of it." But he is gradually enlightened, and led to see that in the same hour when all his debts were paid, a full discharge was given; that in the moment when its sin was cancelled, every elect soul was justified in God's mind, though they were not; justified in their own minds till afterwards. The Spirit shall lead you into all truth.

Now, what are the practical inferences from this great doctrine? The first is with reference to the Christian who is afraid of his own ignorance. How many are there who are just enlightened and have tasted of heavenly things, who are afraid they are too ignorant to be saved! Beloved, God the Holy Spirit can teach anyone, however illiterate, however uninstructed. I have known some men who were almost idiots before conversion, but they afterwards had their faculties wonderfully developed. Some time ago there was a man who was so ignorant that he could not read, and he never spoke anything like grammar in his life, unless by mistake; and moreover, he was considered to be what the people in his neighborhood called "daft." But when he

---

[3] Linsey-woolsey: a coarse, blended fabric made of wool and cotton, or wool and linen.

was converted, the first thing he did was to pray. He stammered out a few words, and in a little time his powers of speaking began to develop themselves. Then he thought he would like to read the Scriptures, and after long, long months of labor, he learned to read; and what was the next thing? He thought he could preach; and he did preach a little in his own homely way, in his house. Then he thought "I must read a few more books." And so his mind expanded, until, I believe he is at the present day, a useful minister, settled in a country village, laboring for God. It needs but little intellect to be taught of God. If you feel your ignorance, do not despair. Go to the Spirit—the great Teacher—and ask his sacred influence, and it shall come to pass that he "shall guide you into all truth."

Another inference is this whenever any of our brethren do not understand the truth let us take a hint as to the best way of dealing with them. Do not let us controvert with them. I have heard many controversies, but never heard of any good from one of them. We have had controversies with certain men called Secularists, and very strong arguments have been brought against them; but I believe that the day of judgment shall declare that a very small amount of good was ever done by contending with these men. Better let them alone: where no fuel is, the fire goeth out; and he that debateth with them puts wood upon the fire. So with regard to Baptism. It is of no avail to quarrel with our Paedo-baptist[4] friends. If we simply pray for them that the God of truth may lead them to see the true doctrine, they will come to it far more easily than by discussions. Few men are taught by controversy, for

> A man convinced against his will,
> is of the same opinion still.

Pray for them that the Spirit of truth may lead them "into all truth." Do not be angry with your brother, but pray for him; cry, "Lord! open thou his eyes that he may behold wondrous things out of thy law."

Lastly, we speak to some of you who know nothing about the Spirit of truth, nor about the truth itself. It may be that some of you are saying, "We care not much which of you are right, we are happily indifferent to it." Ah! but, poor sinner, if thou knewest the gift of God, and who it was that spake the truth, thou wouldst not say, "I care not for it." If thou didst know how essential the truth is to thy salvation, thou wouldst not talk so. If thou didst know that the truth of God is—that thou art a worthless sinner, but if thou believest, then God from all eternity, apart from all thy merits, loved thee, and bought thee with the Redeemer's blood, and justified thee in the forum of Heaven, and will, by-and-by, justify thee in the forum of thy conscience through the Holy Ghost by faith; if thou didst know that there is

---

[4] Paedo-baptist: beliver in infant baptisim.

a Heaven for thee beyond the chance of a failure, a crown for thee, the lustre of which can never be dimmed—then thou wouldst say, "Indeed the truth is precious to my soul!" Why, my ungodly hearers, these men of error want to take away the truth, which alone can save you, the only gospel that can deliver you from Hell; they deny the great truths of free-grace, those fundamental doctrines which alone can snatch a sinner from Hell; and even though you do not feel interest in them now, I still would say, you ought to desire to see them promoted. May God give you to know the truth in your hearts! May the Spirit "guide you into all truth!" For if you do not know the truth here, recollect there will be a sorrowful learning of it in the dark chambers of the pit, where the only light shall be the flames of Hell! May you here know the truth! And the truth shall make you free: and if the Son shall make you free, you shall be free indeed, for he says, "I am the way, the truth, the life." Believe on Jesus, thou chief of sinners; trust his love and mercy, and thou art saved, for God the Spirit giveth faith and eternal life.

The Outpouring of the Holy Spirit

Delivered on Sabbath morning, June 20, 1858 at the Music Hall, Royal Surrey Gardens. No. 201.

While Peter yet spake these words, the Holy Ghost fell on all them which heard the Word.—Acts 10:44

The Bible is a book of the revelation of God. The God after whom the heathen blindly searched, and for whom reason gropes in darkness, is here plainly revealed to us in the pages of divine authorship, so that he who is willing to understand as much of Godhead as man can know, may here learn it if he be not willingly ignorant and willfully obstinate. The doctrine of the Trinity is specially taught in Holy Scripture. The word certainly does not occur, but the three divine persons of the One God are frequently and constantly mentioned, and Holy Scripture is exceedingly careful that we should all receive and believe that great truth of the Christian religion, that the Father is God, that the Son is God, that the Spirit is God, and yet there are not three Gods but one God: though they be each of them very God of very God, yet three in one and one in three is the Jehovah whom we worship. You will notice in the works of *creation* how carefully the Scriptures assure us that all the three divine persons took their share. "In the beginning Jehovah created the heavens and the earth;" and in another place we are told that God said "Let *us* make man"—not one person, but all three taking counsel with each other with regard to the making of mankind. We know that the Father hath laid the foundations and fixed those solid beams of light on which the blue arches of the sky are sustained; but we know with equal certainty that Jesus Christ, the eternal *Logos*, was with the Father in the beginning, and "without him was not anything made that was made:" moreover we have equal certainty that the Holy Spirit had a hand in Creation, for we are told that "the earth was without form and void, and darkness was upon the face of the earth; and the spirit of the Lord moved upon the face of the waters;" and brooding with his dove-like wing, he brought out of the egg of chaos this mighty thing, the fair round world. We have the like proof of the three persons in the Godhead in the matter of *salvation*. We know that God the Father gave his Son; we have abundant proof that God the Father chose his people from before the foundations of the world, that he did invent the plan of salvation, and hath always given his free, willing, and joyous consent to the salvation of his people. With regard to the share that the Son had in salvation, that is apparent enough to all. For us men and for our salvation he came down from Heaven; he was incarnate in a mortal body; he was crucified, dead, and buried; he descended into Hades; the third day he rose again from the dead; he ascended into Heaven; he sitteth at the right hand of God, where also he maketh intercession for us. As to the Holy Spirit, we have equally sure proof that the Spirit of God worketh in conversion; for everywhere we are said to be begotten of the Holy Spirit; continually it is declared, that unless a man be born again from above, he cannot see the kingdom of God; while all the virtues and the graces of Christianity are described as being the fruits of the Spirit, because the Holy Spirit doth from first to last work in us and carry out that which Jesus Christ hath beforehand worked for us in his great redemption, which also God the Father hath designed for us in his great predestinating scheme of salvation.

Now, it is to the work of the Holy Spirit that I shall this morning specially direct your attention; and I may as well mention the reason why I do so. It is this. We have received continually fresh confirmations of the good news from a far country, which has already made glad the hearts of many of God's people. In the United States of America there is certainly a great awakening. No sane man living there could think of denying it. There may be something of spurious excitement mixed up with it, but that good, lasting good, has been accomplished, no rational man can deny. Two hundred and fifty thousand persons—that is, a quarter of a million—profess to have been regenerated since December last; have made a profession of their faith; and have united themselves with different sections of God's church. The work still progresses, if anything, at a more rapid rate than before, and that which makes me believe the work to be genuine is just this—that the enemies of Christ's holy gospel are exceedingly wroth at it. When the devil roars at anything, you may rest assured there is some good in it. The devil is not like some dogs we know of; he never barks unless there is something to bark at. When Satan howls we may rest assured he is afraid his kingdom is in danger.

Now this great work in America has been manifestly caused by the outpouring of the Spirit, for no one minister has been a leader in it. All the ministers of the gospel have cooperated in it, but none of them have stood in the van[guard]. God himself has been the leader of his own hosts. It began with a desire for prayer. God's people began to pray; the prayer-meetings were better attended than before. It was then proposed to hold meetings at times that had never been set apart for prayer; these also were well attended; and now, in the city of Philadelphia, at the hour of noon, every day in the week, three thousand persons can always be seen assembled together for prayer in one place. Men of business, in the midst of their toil and labor, find an opportunity of running in there and offering a word of prayer, and then return to their occupations. And so, throughout all the States, prayer-meetings, larger or smaller in number, have been convened. And there has been real prayer. Sinners beyond all count have risen up in the prayer-meeting, and have requested the people of God to pray for them; thus making public to the world that they had a desire after Christ; they have been prayed for, and the church has seen that God verily doth hear and answer prayer. I find that the Unitarian ministers for a little while took no notice of it. Theodore Parker snarls and raves tremendously at it, but he is evidently in a maze; he does not understand the mystery, and acts with regard to it as swine are said to do with pearls. While the church was found asleep, and doing very little, the Socinian[1] could afford to stand in his pulpit and sneer at anything like evangelical religion, but now that there has been an awakening, he looks like a man that has just awakened out of sleep. He sees something; he does not know what it is. The power of religion is just that which will always puzzle the Unitarian, for he knows but little about that. At the form of religion he is not much amazed, for he can to an extent endorse that himself, but the supernaturalism of the gospel—the mystery—the miracle—the power—the demonstration of the Spirit that comes with the preaching, is what such men cannot comprehend, and they gaze and wonder, and then become filled with wrath, but still they have to confess there is something there they cannot understand, a mental phenomenon that is far beyond their philosophy—a thing which they cannot reach by all their science nor understand by all their reason.

Now, if we have the like effect produced in this land, the one thing we must seek is the outpouring of the Holy Spirit, and I thought, perhaps, this morning in preaching upon the work of the Holy Spirit, that text might be fulfilled—"Him that honoreth me I will honor." My sincere desire is to honor the Holy Spirit this morning, and if he will be pleased to honor his church in return, unto him shall be the glory forever.

"While Peter yet spake these words, the Holy Ghost fell on all them which heard the word." In the first place, I shall endeavor to describe *the method of the*

---

[1] Socinian: 16th century Unitarian sect that denied Jesus' divinity.

Spirit's operation, secondly, *the absolute necessity of the Holy Spirit's influence*, if we could see men converted, and then, in the third place, I shall suggest the ways and means by which under divine grace we may obtain a like falling down of the Spirit upon our churches.

I. In the first place, then, I will endeavor to explain *the method of the Holy Spirit's operations.*

But let me guard myself against being misunderstood. We can explain *what* the Spirit does, but *how* he does it, no man must pretend to know. The work of the Holy Spirit is the peculiar mystery of the Christian religion. Almost any other thing is plain, but this must remain an inscrutable secret into which it were wrong for us to attempt to pry. Who knoweth where the winds are begotten? Who knoweth, therefore, how the Spirit worketh, for he is like the wind?

> The wind bloweth where it listeth, and thou hearest the sound thereof but canst not tell whence it cometh, and whither it goeth: so is everyone that is born of the Spirit.

In Holy Scripture certain great secrets of nature are mentioned as being parallel with the secret working of the Spirit. The procreation of children is instanced as a parallel wonder, for we know not the mystery thereof; how much less, therefore, shall we expect to know that more secret and hidden mystery of the new birth and new creation of man in Christ Jesus. But let no man be staggered at this, for they are mysteries in nature: the wisest man will tell you there are depths in nature into which he cannot dive, and heights into which he cannot soar. He who pretends to have unraveled the knot of creation hath made a mistake, he may have cut the knot by his rough ignorance, and by his foolish conjectures, but the knot itself must remain beyond the power of man's unraveling, until God himself shall explain the secret. There are marvelous things, that, as yet, men have sought to know in vain. They may, perhaps, discover many of them, but how the Spirit works, no man can know. But now I wish to explain *what* the Holy Spirit does, although we cannot tell how he does it. I take it that the Holy Spirit's work in conversion is twofold. First it is an awakening of the powers that man already has, and secondly, it is an implantation of powers which he never had at all.

In the great work of the new birth, the Holy Spirit first of all *awakens the mental powers*; for be it remembered that the Holy Spirit never gives any man *new* mental powers. Take, for instance, reason—the Holy Spirit does not give men reason, for they have reason prior to their conversion. What the Holy Spirit does is to teach our reason, right reason—to set our reason in the right track, so that he can use it for the high purpose of discerning between good and evil; between the precious and vile. The Holy Spirit does not give man a will, for man has a will before; but he makes the will that was in bondage to Satan, free to the service of God. The Holy

Spirit gives no man the power to think, or the organ of belief—for man has power to believe or think, as far as the mental act is concerned; but he gives that belief which is already there, a tendency to believe the right thing, and he gives to the power of thought, the propensity to think in the right way, so that instead of thinking irregularly, we begin to think as God would have us think, and our mind desireth to walk in the steps of God's revealed truth. There may be here, this morning, a man of enlarged understanding in things political—but his understanding is darkened with regard to spiritual things—he sees no beauty in the person of Christ—he sees nothing desirable in the way of holiness—he chooses the evil and forsakes the good. Now the Holy Spirit will not give him a new understanding, but he will cleanse his old understanding so that he will discern between things that differ, and shall discover that it is but a poor thing to enjoy "the pleasures of sin for a season," and let go an "eternal weight of glory." There shall be a man here too who is desperately set against religion, and willeth not to come to God—and do what we will, we are not able to persuade him to change his mind and turn to God. The Holy Spirit will not make a new will in that man, but he will turn his old will, and instead of willing to do evil he will make him will to do right—he will make him will to be saved by Christ—he will make him "willing in the day of his power." Remember, there is no power in man so fallen but that the Holy Spirit can raise it up. However debased a man may be, in one instant, by the miraculous power of the Spirit, all his faculties may be cleansed and purged. Ill-judging reason may be made to judge rightly; stout, obstinate wills may be made to run willingly in the ways of God's commandments; evil and depraved affections may in an instant be turned to Christ, and old desires that are tainted with vice, may be replaced by heavenly aspirations.

The work of the Spirit on the mind is the re-modeling of it; the new forming of it. He doth not bring new material to the mind—it is in another part of the man that he puts up a new structure—but he puts the mind that had fallen out of order into its proper shape. He builds up pillars that had fallen down, and erects the palaces that had crumbled to the earth. This is the first work of the Holy Spirit upon the mind of man.

Besides this, the Holy Spirit gives to men *powers which they never had before*. According to Scripture, I believe man is constituted in a three-fold manner. He has a body; by the Holy Spirit that body is made the temple of the Lord. He has a mind; by the Holy Spirit that mind is made like an altar in the temple. But man by nature is nothing higher than that; he is mere body and soul. When the Spirit comes, he breathes into him a third higher principle which we call the spirit. The apostle describes man as man, "body, soul and spirit." Now if you search all the mental writers through, you will find they all declare there are only two parts—body and mind; and they are quite right, for they deal with unregenerate man; but in regenerate man there is a third principle as much superior to mere mind as mind is superior to dead animal matter. That third principle is that with which a man *prays*; it is that with which he lovingly believes; or rather it is that which compels the mind to perform these acts. It is that which, operating upon the mind, makes the same use of the mind as the mind does of the body. When, after desiring to walk, I make my legs move, it is my mind that compels them; and so my *spirit*, when I desire to pray, compels my mind to think the thought of prayer and compels my soul also, if I desire to praise, to think the thought of praise, and lift itself upward towards God. As the body without the soul is dead, so the soul without the spirit is dead, and one work of the spirit is to quicken the dead soul by breathing into it the firing Spirit. As it is written, "The first man, Adam, was made a living soul, but the second Adam was made a quickening *Spirit*"—and, "as we have borne the image of the earthly, so must we bear the image of the heavenly." That is, we must have in us, if we would be converted, the quickening spirit, which is put into us by God the Holy Ghost. I say again, the spirit has powers which the mind never has. It has the power of communion with Christ, which to a degree is a mental act, but it can no more be performed by man without the spirit, than the act of walking could be performed by man, if he were destitute of a soul to suggest the idea of walking. The spirit suggests the thoughts of communion which the mind obeys and carries out. Nay, there are times, I think, when the spirit leaves the mind altogether, times when we forget everything of earth and one almost ceases to think, to reason, to judge, to weigh, or to will. Our souls are like the chariots of Amminadib, drawn swiftly onwards without any powers of volition. We lean upon the breast of Jesus, and in rhapsody divine, and in ecstasy celestial, we enjoy the fruits of the land of the blessed, and pluck the clusters of Eschol before entering into the land of promise.

I think I have clearly put these two points before you. The work of the Spirit consists, first, in awakening powers already possessed by man, but which were asleep and out of order; and in the next place in putting into man powers which he had not before. And to make this simple to the humblest mind, let me suppose man to be something like a machine; all the wheels are out of order, the cogs do not strike upon each other, the wheels do not turn regularly, the rods will not act, the order is gone. Now, the first work of the Spirit is to put these wheels in the right place, to fit the wheels upon the axles, to put the right axle to the right wheel, then to put wheel to wheel, so that they may act upon each other. But that is not all his work. The next thing is to put fire and steam so that these things shall go to work. He does not put fresh wheels, he puts old wheels into order, and then he puts the motive power which is to move the whole. First he puts our mental powers into their proper order and condition, and then he puts a living quickening spirit, so that all these shall move according to the holy will and law of God.

But, mark you, this is not all the Holy Spirit does. For if he were to do this, and then leave us, none of us would get to Heaven. If any of you should be so near to Heaven that you could hear the angels singing over the walls—if you could almost see within the pearly gates, still, if the Holy Spirit did not help you the last step, you would never enter there. All the work is through his divine operation. Hence it is the Spirit who keeps the wheels in motion, and who tales away that defilement which, naturally engendered by our original sin, falls upon the machine and puts it out of order. He takes this away, and keeps the machine constantly going without injury, until at last he removes man from the place of defilement to the land of the blessed, a perfect creature, as perfect as he was when he came from the mold of his Maker.

And I must say, before I leave this point, that all the former part of what I have mentioned is done instantaneously. When a man is converted to God, it is done in a moment. Regeneration is an instantaneous work. Conversion to God, the fruit of regeneration, occupies all our life, but regeneration itself is effected in an instant. A man hates God; the Holy Spirit makes him love God. A man is opposed to Christ, he hates his gospel, does not understand it and will not receive it: the Holy Spirit comes, puts light into his darkened understanding, takes the chain from his bandaged will, gives liberty to his conscience, gives life to his dead soul, so that the voice of conscience is heard, and the man becomes a new creature in Christ Jesus. And all this is done, mark you, by the instantaneous supernatural influence of God the Holy Ghost working as he willeth among the sons of men.

II. Having thus dwelt upon the method of the Holy Spirit's work, I shall now turn to the second point, *the absolute necessity of the Spirit's work in order to conversion.*

In our text we are told that "while Peter spake these words, the Holy Ghost fell on all them which heard the word." Beloved, the Holy Ghost fell on Peter first, or else it would not have fallen on his hearers. There is a necessity that the preacher himself, if we are to have souls saved, should be under the influence of the Spirit. I have constantly made it my prayer that I might be guided by the Spirit even in the smallest and least important parts of the service; for you cannot tell but that the salvation of a soul may depend upon the reading of a hymn, or upon the selection of a chapter. Two persons have joined our church and made a profession of being converted simply through my reading a hymn—

Jesus, lover of my soul

They did not remember anything else in the hymn, but those words made such a deep impression upon their mind, that they could not help repeating them for days afterwards, and then the thought arose, "Do I love Jesus?" And then they considered what strange ingratitude it was that he should be the lover of their souls, and yet they should not love him. Now I believe the Holy Spirit led me to read that hymn. And many persons have been converted by some striking saying of the preacher. But why was it the preacher uttered that saying? Simply because he was led thereunto by the Holy Spirit. Rest assured, beloved, that when any part of the sermon is blessed to your heart, the minister said it because he was ordered to say it by his Master. I might preach today a sermon which I preached on Friday, and which was useful then, and there might be no good whatever come from it now, because it might not be the sermon which the Holy Ghost would have delivered today. But if with sincerity of heart I have sought God's guidance in selecting the topic, and he rests upon me in the preaching of the Word, there is no fear but that it shall be found adapted to your immediate wants. The Holy Spirit must rest upon your preachers. Let them have all the learning of the wisest men, and all the eloquence of such men as Desmosthenes and Cicero, still the Word cannot be blessed to you, unless first of all the Spirit of God hath guided the minister's mind in the selection of his subject, and in the discussion of it.

But if Peter himself were under the hand of the Spirit, that would fail unless the Spirit of God, then, did fall upon our hearers; and I shall endeavor now to show the absolute necessity of the Spirit's work in the conversion of men.

Let us remember what kind of thing the work is, and we shall see that other means are altogether out of the question. It is quite certain that men cannot be converted by physical means. The Church of Rome thought that she could convert men by means of armies; so she invaded countries, and threatened them with war and bloodshed unless they would repent and embrace her religion. However, it availed but little, and men were prepared to die rather than leave their faith. She therefore tried those beautiful things—stakes, racks, dungeons, axes, swords, fire; and by these things she hoped to convert men. You have heard of the man who tried to wind up his watch with a pick-axe. That man was extremely wise, compared with the man who thought to touch mind through matter. All the machines you like to invent cannot touch mind. Talk about tying angel's wings with green withes [reeds], or manacling the cherubim with iron chains, and then talk about meddling with the minds of men through physical means. Why, the things don't set; they cannot act. All the king's armies that ever were, and all the warriors clothed with mail, with all their ammunition, could never touch the mind of man. That is an impregnable castle which is not to be reached by physical agency.

Nor, again, can man be converted by moral argument. "Well," says one, "I think he may. Let a minister preach earnestly, and he may persuade men to be converted." Ah! beloved, it is for want of knowing better that you say so. Melancthon thought so, but you know what he said after he tried it—"Old Adam is too strong for young Melancthon." So will every preacher find it, if he thinks his arguments can ever convert man. Let me give you a parallel case. Where is the logic that can persuade an Ethiopian to change his skin? By what argument can you induce a leopard to renounce his spots? Even so may he that is accustomed to do evil, learn to do well. But if the Ethiopian's skin be changed it must be by a supernatural process, and if the leopard's spots be removed, he that made the leopard must do it. Even so is it with the heart of man. If sin were a thing *ab extra* and external, we could induce man to change it. For instance, you may induce a man to leave off drunkenness or swearing, because those things are not a part of his nature—he has added that vice to his original depravity. But the hidden evil at the heart is beyond all moralsuasion. I dare say a man might have enough argument to induce him to hang himself, but I am certain no argument will ever induce him to hang his sins, to hang his self-righteousness, and to come and humble himself at the foot of the cross; for the religion of Christ is so contrary to all the propensities of man, that it is like swimming against the stream to approach it, for the stream of man's will and man's desire is exactly the opposite of the religion of Jesus Christ. If you wanted a proof of that, at the lifting of my finger, there are thousands in this hall who would rise to prove it, for they would say,

> I have found it so, sir, in my experience; I hated religion as much as any men; I despised Christ, and his people, and I know not to this day how it is that I am what I am, unless it be the work of God.

I have seen the tears run down a man's cheeks when he has come to me in order to be united to the church of Christ, and he has said,

> Sir, I wonder how it is I am here today. If anyone had told me a year ago that I should think as I now think, and feel as I now feel, I should have called him a born fool for his pains. I used to say I never would be one of those canting Methodists, I liked to spend my Sunday in pleasure, and I did not see why I was to be cooping myself up in the house of God listening to a man talk. I pray, sire—no, not I! I said the best providence in all the world was a good strong pair of hands, and to take care of what you got. If any man talked to me about religion, why I would slam the door in his face, and pretty soon put him out; but the things that I loved then, I now hate, and the things that then I hated, now I love. I cannot do or say enough to show how total is the change that has been wrought in me. It must have been the work of God; it could not have been wrought by me, I feel assured; it must be someone greater than myself, who could thus turn my heart.

I think these two things are proofs that we want something more than nature, and since physical agency will not do, and mere moral suasion will never accomplish it, that there must be an absolute necessity for the Holy Spirit.

But again, if you will just think a minute what the work is, you will soon see that none but God can accomplish it. In the Holy Scripture, conversion is often spoken of as being a new creation. If you talk about creating yourselves, I should feel obliged if you would create a fly first. Create a gnat; create a grain of sand; and when you have created that, you may talk about creating a new heart. Both are alike impossible, for creation is the work of God. But still, if you could create a grain of dust, or create even a world, it would not be half the miracle, for you must first find a thing which has created itself. Could that be? Suppose you had no existence, how could you create yourself? Nothing cannot produce anything. Now, how can man re-create himself? A man cannot create himself into a new condition, when he has no being in that condition, but is, as yet, a thing that is not.

Then, again, the work of creation is said to be like the resurrection. "We are alive from the dead." Now, can the dead in the grave raise themselves? Let any minister who thinks he can convert souls, go and raise a corpse. Let him go and stand in one of the cemeteries, and bid the tombs open wide their mouths, and make room for those once buried there to awaken—and he will have to preach in vain. But if he could do it, that is not the miracle: it is for the dead to raise themselves, for an inanimate corpse to kindle in its own breast the spark of life anew. If the work be a resurrection, a creation, does it not strike you that it must be beyond the power of man? It must be wrought in him by no one less than God himself.

And there is yet one more consideration, and I shall have concluded this point. Beloved, even if man could save himself, I would have you recollect how averse he is to it. If we could make our hearers all willing, the battle would be accomplished. "Well," says one, "If I am willing to be saved, can I not be saved?" Assuredly you can, but the difficulty is, we cannot bring men to be willing. That shows, therefore, that there must be a constraint put upon their will. There must be an influence exerted upon them, which they have not in themselves, in order to make them willing in the day of God's power. And this is the glory of the Christian religion. The Christian religion has within its own bowels [insides] power to spread itself. We do not ask you to be willing first. We come and tell you the news, and we believe that the Spirit of God, working with us, will make you willing. If the progress of the Christian religion depended upon the voluntary assent of mankind, it would never go an inch further. But because the Christian religion has within an omnipotent influence, constraining men to believe it, it is therefore that it is, and must be, triumphant, "till like a sea of glory it spreads from shore to shore."

III. Now I shall conclude by bringing one or two thoughts forward, with regard to *what must be done at this time in order to bring down the Holy Spirit.*

It is quite certain, beloved, if the Holy Spirit willed to do it, that every man, woman, and child in this place might be converted now. If God, the Sovereign Judge of all, would be pleased now to send out his Spirit, every inhabitant of this million-peopled city might be brought at once to turn unto the living God. Without instrumentality, without the preacher, without books, without anything—God has it in his power to convert men. We have known persons about their business, not thinking about religion at all, who have had a thought injected into their heart, and that thought has been the prolific mother of a thousand meditations. and through these meditations they have been brought to Christ. Without the aid of the minister, the Holy Spirit has thus worked, and today he is not restrained. There may be some men, great in infidelity, staunch in opposition to the cross of Christ—but, without asking their consent, the Holy Spirit can pull down the strong man, and make the mighty man bow himself.

For when we talk of the Omnipotent God, there is nothing too great for him to do. But, beloved, God has been pleased to put great honor upon instrumentality; he could work without it if he pleased, but he does not do so. However, this is the first thought I want to give you; *if you would have the Holy Spirit exert himself in our midst, you must first of all look to him and not to instrumentality.* When Jesus Christ preached, there were very few converted under him, and the reason was, because the Holy Spirit was not abundantly poured forth. He had the Holy Spirit without measure himself, but on others the Holy Spirit was not as yet poured out. Jesus Christ said, "Greater works than these shall ye do, because I go to my Father, in order to send the Holy Spirit;" and recollect that those few who were converted under Christ's ministry, were not converted by him, but by the Holy Spirit that rested upon him at that time. Jesus of Nazareth was anointed of the Holy Spirit. Now then, if Jesus Christ, the great founder of our religion, needed to be anointed of the Holy Spirit, how much more our ministers? And if God would always make the distinction even between his own Son as an instrument, and the Holy Spirit as the agent, how much more ought we to be careful to do that between poor puny men and the Holy Spirit? Never let us hear you say again, "So many persons were converted by So-and so." They were not. If converted, they were not converted by man. Instrumentality is to be used, but the Spirit is to have the honor of it. Pay no more a superstitious reverence to man, think no more that God is tied to your plans, and to your agencies. Do not imagine that so many city missionaries [means] so much good will be done. Do not say, "So many preachers, so many sermons, so many souls saved." Do not say, "So many Bibles, so many tracts, so much good done." Not so: use these, but remember it is not in that proportion the blessing comes; it is: *"So much Holy Spirit, so many souls in-gathered."*

And now another thought. If we would have the Spirit, beloved, we must each of us try to honor him. There are some chapels into which, if you were to enter, you would never know there was a Holy Spirit. Mary Magdalene said of old, "They have taken away my Lord, and I know not where they have laid him," and the Christian might often say so, for there is nothing said about the Lord until they come to the end, and then there is just the benediction, or else you would not know that there were three persons in one God at all. Until our churches honor the Holy Spirit, we shall never see it abundantly manifested in our midst. Let the preacher always confess before he preaches that he relies upon the Holy Spirit. Let him burn his manuscript and depend upon the Holy Spirit. If the Spirit does not come to help him, let him be still and let the people go home and pray that the Spirit will help him next Sunday.

And do you also, in the use of all your agencies, always honor the Spirit? We often begin our religious meetings without prayer; it is all wrong. We must honor the Spirit; unless we put him first, he will never make crowns for us to wear. He will get victories, but he will have the honor of them, and if we do not give to him the honor, he will never give to us the privilege and success. And best of all, if you would have the Holy Spirit, let us meet together earnestly to pray for him. Remember, the Holy Spirit will not come to us as a church, unless we seek him. "For this thing will I be enquired of by the house of Israel to do it for them." We purpose during the coming week to hold meetings of special prayer, to supplicate for a revival of religion. On the Friday morning I opened the first prayer meeting at Trinity Chapel, Brixton; and, I think, at seven o'clock, we had as many as two hundred and fifty persons gathered together. It was a pleasant sight. During the hour, nine brethren prayed, one after the other; and I am sure there was the spirit of prayer there. Some persons present sent up their names, asking that we would offer special petitions for them; and I doubt not the prayers will be answered. At Park Street, on Monday morning, we shall have a prayer-meeting from eight to nine; then during the rest of the week there will be a prayer-meeting in the morning from seven to eight. On Monday evening we shall have the usual prayer-meeting at seven, when I hope there will be a large number attending. I find that my brother, Baptist Noel, has commenced morning and evening prayer-meetings, and they have done the same thing in Norwich and many provincial towns, where, without any pressure, the people are found willing to come.

I certainly did not expect to see so many as two hundred and fifty persons at an early hour in the morning meet together for prayer. I believe it was a good sign. The Lord hath put prayer into their hearts and therefore they were willing to come, "Prove me now here, saith the Lord of hosts, and see if I do not pour you out a blessing so that there shall not be room enough to receive it." Let us meet and pray, and if God doth not hear us, it will be the first time he has broken his promise. Come, let us go up to the sanctuary; let us meet together in the house of the Lord, and offer solemn supplication; and I say again, if the Lord doth not make bare his arm in the sight of all the people, it will be the reverse of all his previous actions, it will be the contrary of all his promises, and contradictory to himself. We have only to try him, and the result is certain. In dependence on his Spirit, if we only meet for prayer, the Lord shall bless us, and all the ends of the earth shall fear him. O Lord, lift up thyself because of thine enemies; pluck thy right hand out of thy bosom, O Lord our God, for Christ's sake, Amen.

The Holy Spirit Compared to the Wind

Preached at the Metropolitan Tabernacle, Newington. Published 1865. No. 630.

The wind bloweth where it listeth, and thou hearest the sound thereof, but canst not tell
whence it cometh, and whither it goeth: so is everyone that is born
of the Spirit.—John 3:8

At the present moment, I am not able to enter fully into the subject of the new birth. I am very weary, both in body and mind, and cannot attempt that great and mysterious theme. To everything there is a season and a time for every purpose under Heaven, and it is not the time to preach upon regeneration when the head is aching, nor to discourse upon the new nature when the mind is distracted. I selected my text with the intention of fixing upon one great illustration, which strikes me just now as being so suggestive, that with divine assistance, I may be able to work it out with profit to you, and ease to myself. I shall endeavor to bring before you the parallel which our Savior here draws, between the wind and the Holy Spirit. It is a remarkable fact, known I dare say to most of you, that both in the Hebrew and Greek languages the same word is used for spirit and for wind, so that our Savior as it were rode upon the wings of the wind, while he was instructing the seeking Rabbi in the deep things of God; he caught at the very name of the wind, as a means of fastening a spiritual truth upon the memory of the enquirer, hinting to us that language should be watched by the teacher, that he may find out suitable words, and employ those which will best assist the disciple to comprehend and to retain his teaching. "The wind," said he, "bloweth," and the very same word would have been employed if he had meant to say, "The Spirit bloweth where he listeth." There was intended, doubtless, to be a very close and intimate parallel between the Spirit of God and the wind, or otherwise the great ruler of providence, who invisibly controlled the confusion of Babel, would not have fashioned human language so that the same word should stand for both. Language, as well as nature, illustrates the wisdom of God.

It is only in *his* light that we see light: may the Holy Spirit be graciously pleased to reveal himself in his divine operations to all our waiting minds. We are taught in God's Word that the Holy Spirit comes upon the sons of men, and makes them new creatures. Until he enters them, they are "dead in trespasses and sins." They cannot discern the things of God, because divine truths are spiritual and spiritually discerned, and unrenewed men are carnal, and possess not the power to search out the deep things of God. The Spirit of God new-creates the children of God, and then in their new-born spirituality, they discover and come to understand spiritual things, but not before; and, therefore, my beloved hearers, unless you *possess* the Spirit, no metaphors, however simple, can reveal him to you. Let us not mention the name of the Holy Spirit without due honor. Forever blessed be thou, most glorious Spirit, co-equal and co-eternal with the Father and with the Son; let all the angels of God worship thee! Be thou had in honor, world without end!

I. We will consider *in what sense the Holy Ghost may be compared to the wind.*

The Spirit of God, to help the spiritually minded in their study of his character and nature condescends to compare himself to dew, fire, oil, water, and other suggestive types; and among the rest, our Savior uses the metaphor of wind. What was the first thought here but that of *mystery*? It was the objection on the score of mystery which our Lord was trying to remove from the mind of Nicodemus. Nicodemus in effect said,

> I cannot understand it; how can it be? A man born again when he is old, created over again, and that from an invisible agency from above? How can these things be?

Jesus at once directed his attention to the wind, which is none the less real and operative because of its mysterious origin and operation. You cannot tell whence the wind cometh: you know it blows from the north or from the west, but at what particular place does that wind start on its career? Where will it pause in its onward flight? You see that it is blowing to the east or to the west, but where is its halting-place? Whence came these particles of air which rush so rapidly past? Whither are they going? By what law are they guided in their course, and where will their journey end? The gale may be blowing due east here, but it may be driving west a hundred miles away. In one district the wind may be rushing from the north, and yet not far from it there may be a strong current from the south. Those who ascend in balloons tell us that they meet with cross currents; one wind blowing in this direction, and another layer of air moving towards an opposite quarter; how is this? If you have watched the skies, you must occasionally have noticed a stream of clouds hurrying to the right, while higher up, another company is sailing to the left. It is a question whether thunder and lightning may not be produced by the friction of two currents of air traveling in different directions; but why is it that this current takes it into its head to go this way, while another steers for quite another point? Will they meet across each other's path in regions far away? Are there whirlpools in the air as in the water? Are these eddies, currents, rivers of air, lakes of air? Is the whole atmosphere like the sea, only composed of less dense matter? If so, what is it that stirs up that great deep of air, and bids it howl in the hurricane, and then constrains it to subside into the calm?

The philosopher may scheme some conjecture to prove that the "trade winds" blow at certain intervals because of the sun crossing the equator at those periods, and that there must necessarily be a current of air going towards the equator because of the rarefaction; but he cannot tell you why the weathercock on yonder church steeple turned this morning from south-west to due east. He cannot tell me why it is that the sailor finds that his sails are at one time filled with wind, and in a few minutes they fall loosely about, so that he must steer upon another tack if he would make headway. The various motions of the air remain a mystery to all but the infinite Jehovah. My brethren, the like mystery is observed in the work of the Spirit of God. His person and work are not to be comprehended by the mind of man. He may be here tonight, but you cannot see him: he speaks to one heart, but others cannot hear his voice. He is not recognizable by the unrefined senses of the unregenerate. The spiritual man discerns him, feels him, hears him, and delights in him, but neither wit nor learning can lead a man into the secret. The believer is often bowed down with the weight of the Spirit's glory, or lifted up upon the wings of his majesty; but even he knows not how these feelings are wrought in him. The fire of holy life is at seasons gently fanned with the soft breath of divine comfort, or the deep sea of spiritual existence stirred with the mighty blast of the Spirit's rebuke; but still it is evermore a mystery how the eternal God comes into contact with the finite mind of his creature man, filling all heaven meanwhile, and yet dwelling in a human body as in a temple—occupying all space, and yet operating upon the will, the judgment, the mind of the poor insignificant creature called man. We may enquire, but who can answer us? We may search, but who shall lead us into the hidden things of the Most High? He brooded over chaos and produced order, but who shall tell us after what fashion he wrought? He overshadowed the Virgin and prepared a body for the Son of God, but into this secret who shall dare to pry? His is the anointing, sealing, comforting, and sanctifying of the saints, but how worketh he all these things? He maketh intercession for us according to the will of God, he dwelleth in us and leadeth us into all truth, but who among us can explain to his fellow the order of the divine working? Though veiled from human eye like the glory which shone between the cherubim, we believe in the Holy Ghost, and therefore see him; but if our faith needed sight to sustain it, we should never believe at all.

Mystery is far from being all which the Savior would teach by this simile. Surely he meant to show us that the operations of the Spirit are like the wind for *divinity*. Who can create a wind? The most ambitious of human princes would scarcely attempt to turn, much less to send forth the wind. These steeds of the storm know no bit nor bridle, neither will they come at any man's bidding. Let our senators do what they will, they will scarcely have the madness to legislate for winds. Old Boreas, as the heathens called him, is not to be bound with chains and welded on earthly anvil, or in vulcanian forge. "The wind bloweth where it listeth;" and it does so because God directeth it and suffereth it not to stay for man, nor to tarry for the sons of men. So with the Spirit of God. All the true operations of the Spirit are due in no sense whatever to man, but always to God and to his sovereign will. Revivalists may get up excitement with the best intentions, and may warm peoples' hearts till they begin to cry out, but all this ends in nothing unless it is divine work. Have I not said scores of times in this pulpit, "All that is of nature's spinning, must be unraveled?" Every particle which nature puts upon the foundation will turn out to be but "wood, hay, and stubble," and will be consumed. It is only "the gold, the silver, and the precious stones" of God's building that will stand the fiery test. "Ye must be born again from above," for human regenerations are a lie. Thou mayest blow with thy mouth and produce some trifling effects upon trifles as light as air; man in his zeal may set the windmills of silly minds in motion; but, truly, to stir men's hearts with substantial and eternal verities [truths], needs a celestial breeze, such as the Lord alone can send.

Did not our Lord also intend to hint at the *sovereignty* of the Spirit's work? For what other reason did he say, "The wind bloweth where it listeth?" There is an arbitrariness about the wind, it does just as it pleases, and the laws which regulate its changes are to man unknown. "Free as the wind," we say—"the wild winds." So is the mighty working of God. It is a very solemn thought, and one which should tend to make us humble before the Lord—that we are, as to the matter of salvation, entirely in his hand! If I have a moth in my hand tonight, I can bruise its wings, or I can crush it at my will, and by no attempts of its own can it escape from me. And every sinner is absolutely in the hand of God, and, let him recollect, he is in the hand of an angry God, too.[1] The only comfort is, that he is in the hand of a God who for Jesus' sake, delights to have mercy upon even the vilest of the vile.

Sinner, God can give thee the Holy Spirit if he wills; but if he should say, "Let him alone," thy fate is sealed; thy damnation is sure. It is a thought which some

---

[1] This is a reference to Jonathan Edwards' 1741 sermon, "Sinners in the Hand of an Angry God," one of the most famous "fire and brimstone" sermons ever preached.

would say is "enough to freeze all energy." Beloved, I would to God it would freeze the energy of the flesh, and make the flesh stick dead in the sense of power-lessness; for God never truly begins to show his might till we have seen an end of all human power. I tell thee, sinner, thou art as dead concerning spiritual things as the corpse that is laid in its coffin, nay, as the corpse that is rotting in its grave, and has become like Lazarus in the tomb, stinking and offensive. There is a voice that can call thee forth out of thy sepulcher, but if that voice come not, remember where thou art—justly damned, justly ruined, justly cut off forever from all hope. What sayest thou? Dost thou tremble at this? Dost thou cry, "O God! have pity upon me?" He will hear thy cry, sinner, for there never yet was a sincere cry that went up to Heaven, though it were never so feeble, but what it had an answer of peace. When one of the old saints lay dying, he could only say, "O Lord, I trust thee *languida fide*"—with a languid faith. It is poor work that, but, oh! it is safe work. You can only trust Christ with a feeble faith; if it is such a poor trembling faith that it does not grip him, but only touches the hem of his garment, it nevertheless saves you. If you can look at him, though it be only a great way off, yet it saves you. And, oh what a comfort this is, that you are still on pleading terms with him and in a place of hope. "Whosoever believeth is not condemned." But, oh, do not trifle with the day of grace, lest having frequently heard the warning, and hardened thy neck just as often, thou shouldest "suddenly be destroyed, and that without rem-edy;" for if he shut out, none can bid thee come in; if he do but put to the iron bar, thou art shut out in the darkness of obstinacy, obduracy, and despair forever, the victim of thine own delusions. Sinner, if God save thee; he shall have all the glory, for he hath a right to do as he will, for he says, "I will have mercy on whom I will have mercy, and I will have compassion on whom I will have compassion."

But still I think I have not yet brought out what is in the text. Do you not think that the text was intended to show the *varied methods* in which the Spirit of God works in the conversion and regeneration of men? "The wind bloweth where it listeth [pleases]." Now, observe the different *force* of the wind. This afternoon, the wind seemed as if it would tear up every tree, and doubtless, had they been in leaf, many of those noble princes of the forest must have stretched themselves prone upon the earth; but God takes care that in these times of boisterous gales there should be no leaf, and therefore the wind gets but little purchase with which to drag up a tree. But the wind does not always blow as it did this afternoon. On a summer's evening there is such a gentle zephyr that even the gnats who have been arranging a dance among themselves are not disturbed, but keep to their proper places. Yea, the aspen seems as if it could be quiet, though you know it keeps for-ever quivering. According to the old legend, it was the tree on which the Savior hung, and therefore trembles still as though through fear of the sin which came upon it. 'Tis but a legend. There are times when all is still and calm, when everything is quiet, and you can scarcely detect the wind at all. Now, just so it is with the Spirit of God. To some of us he came like a "rushing mighty wind." Oh, what tearings of soul there were then! My spirit was like a sea tossed up into tremendous waves; made, as Job says, "To boil like a pot," till one would think the deep were hoary[2]. Oh, how that wind came crashing through my soul, and every hope I had was bowed as the trees of the wood in the tempest. Read the story of John Bunyan's conversion: it was just the same. Turn to Martin Luther: you find his conversion of the same sort. So might I mention hundreds of biographies in which the Spirit of God came like a tornado sweeping everything before it, and the men could not but feel that God was in the whirlwind.

To others he comes so gently, they cannot tell when first the Spirit of God came. They recollect that night when mother prayed so with brothers and sisters, and when they could not sleep for hours, because the big tears stood in their eyes on account of sin. They recollect the Sunday-school and the teacher there. They remember that earnest minister. They cannot say exactly when they gave their hearts to God, and they cannot tell about any violent convictions. They are often comforted by that text, "One thing I know, whereas I was blind, now I see;" but they cannot get any farther: they sometimes wish they could. Well, they need not wish it, for the Spirit of God, as a sovereign, will always choose his own way of operation; and if it be but the wind of the Holy Spirit, recollect it is as saving in its gentleness as in its terror, and is as efficient to make us new creatures when it comes with the zephyr's breath as when it comes with the hurricane's force. Do not quarrel with God's way of saving you. If you are brought to the cross, be thankful for it: Christ will not mind how you got there. If you can say "He is all my salvation, and all my desire," you never came to that without the Spirit of God bringing you to it. Do not therefore think you came the wrong way, for that is impossible.

Again, the wind not only differs in force, but it differs in *direction*. We have been saying several times the wind is always shifting. Perhaps there never were two winds that did blow exactly in the same direction. I mean that if we had power to detect the minute points of the compass, there would be found some deviation in every current, although, of course, for all practical purposes, it blows from certain distinct points which the mariner marks out. Now, the Spirit of God comes from different directions. You know very well, dear friends, that sometimes the Spirit of God will blow with mighty force from one denomination of Christians; then on a sudden they seem to be left, and another body of Christians God will raise up, fill with himself, and qualify for usefulness. In the days of [Charles] Wesley and [George] Whitefield, there was very little of the divine Spirit anywhere, except among the Methodists. I am sure they have not a monopoly of him now, the divine Spirit blows also from other quarters. Sometimes he uses one man, sometimes another. We hear of a revival in the North of Ireland, by-and-by it is in the

---

[2] Hoary: grey or white, as with age; ancient.

South of Scotland. It comes just as God wills, for direction; and you know, too, dear friends, it comes through different instrumentalities in the same church. Sometimes the wind blows from this pulpit: God blesses me to your conversion. Another time it is from my good sister, Mrs. Bartlett's class; on a third occasion it is the Sunday-school; again, it may be another class, or the preaching of the young men, or from the individual exertion of private believers. God causes that wind to blow just which way he wills.

He works also through different texts of Scripture. *You* were converted and blessed under one text: it was quite another that was made useful to *me*. Some of you were brought to Christ by terrors, others of you by love, by sweet wooing words. The wind blows as God directs. Now, dear friends, whenever you take up a religious biography, do not sit down and say, "Now I will see whether I am just like this person." Nonsense! God never repeats himself. Men make steel pens—thousands of grosses of them—all alike, but I will be bound to say that in quills from the common, there are no two of them precisely the same. If you look, you will soon discover that they differ in a variety of ways.

Certain gardeners cut their trees into the shape of cheeses and a number of unnatural forms, but God's trees do not grow that way, they grow just anyhow—gnarl their roots and twist their branches. Great painters do not continually paint the same picture again, and again, and again, and my Divine Master never puts his pencil on the canvas to produce the same picture twice. Every Christian is a distinct work of grace on God's part, which has in it some originality, some portion distinct from all others. I do not believe in trying to make all history uniform. It is said that Richard III had a hump-back. Whether he really was deformed, or whether history gave him the hump-back, I cannot tell, but it is said, that all his courtiers thought it was the most beautiful hump-back that ever was seen, and they all began to grow hump-backs too; and I have known ministers who had some peculiar idiosyncrasy of experience which was nothing better than a spiritual hump-back; but their people all began to have hump-backs too—to think and talk all in the same way, and to have the same doubts and fears. Now that will not do. It is not the way in which the Most High acts with regard to the wind, and if he chooses to take all the points of the compass, and make use of them all, let us bless and glorify his name.

Are not the different winds *various in their qualities?* Few of us like an east wind. Most of us are very glad when the wind blows from the south. Vegetation seems to love much the southwest. A stiff north-easter is enough to make us perish; and long continuance of the north, may well freeze the whole earth; while from the west, the wind seems to come laden with health from the deep blue sea; and though sometimes too strong for the sick, yet it is never a bad time when the west wind blows. The ancients all had their different opinions about wind; some were dry, some were rainy, some affected this disease, some touched this part of men, some the other. Certain it is that God's Holy Spirit has different qualities. In the Canticles [Song of Solomon] he blows softly with the sweet breath of love turn on farther, and you get that same Spirit blowing fiercely with threatening and denunciation; sometimes you find him convincing the world "of sin, of righteousness, of judgment," that is the north wind; at other times opening up Christ to the sinner, and giving him joy and comfort; that is the south wind, that blows softly, and gives a balminess in which poor troubled hearts rejoice; and yet "all these worketh the self-same Spirit."

Indeed, my subject is all but endless, and therefore I must stay. But even in the matter of *duration,* you know how the wind will sometimes blow six weeks in this direction, and, again, continue in another direction. And the Spirit of God does not always work with us: he does as he pleases; he comes, and he goes. We may be in a happy hallowed frame at one time, and at another we may have to cry, "Come from the four winds, O breath!"

II. We will consider in the second place, *the parallel between the Holy Spirit and the effects of the wind.*

"Thou hearest the sound thereof." Ah, that we do! The wind sometimes wails as if you could hear the cry of mariners far out at sea, or the moanings of the widows that must weep for them. And, oh! the Spirit of God sets men wailing with an exceeding bitter cry for sin, as one that is in sorrow for his first-born, "Thou hearest the sound thereof." Oh, it is a blessed sound, that wailing! Angels rejoice over "one sinner that repenteth." Then comes the wind at another time with a triumphant sound, and if there be an Aeolian [wind] harp in the window, how it swells, sweeps, descends, then rises again, gives all the tones of music, and makes glad the air with its jubilant notes. So with the Holy Spirit; sometimes he gives us faith, makes us bold, full of assurance, confidence, joy and peace in believing. "Thou hearest the sound" of a full diapason [full harmonious sound] of the Holy Spirit's mighty melody within the soul of man, filling him with peace and joy, and rest, and love. Sometimes the wind comes, too, with another sound, as though it were contending. You heard it, perhaps, this afternoon. We who are a little in the country hear it more than you do: it is as though giants were struggling in the sky together. It seems as if two seas of air—both lashed to fury—met, and dashed against some unseen cliffs with terrible uproar. The Spirit of God comes into the soul sometimes, and makes great contention with the flesh. Oh, what a stern striving there is against unbelief, against lust, against pride, against every evil thing.

"Thou hearest the sound thereof." Thou that knowest what divine experience means, thou knowest when to go forth to fight thy sins. When thou canst hear "the sound of a going in the tops of the mulberry trees," then thou dost bestir thyself to smite thy sins. Sometimes the wind comes with a sweep as though it were going on forever. It came past, and dashed through the trees, sweeping away the rotten branches, then away across the Alps, dashing down an avalanche in its course, still onward; and as it flew, it bore away everything that was frail and weak, and on, on, on it sped its way to some unknown goal. And thus it is sometimes the Spirit of God will come right through us, as if he were bearing us away to that spiritual heritage which is our sure future destiny—bearing away coldness, barrenness, everything before it. We do not lament then that we do not pray, we do not believe that we cannot pray; but "I can do everything," is our joyful shout as we are carried on the wings of the wind. "Thou hearest the sound thereof." I hope you have heard it sometimes in all its powerful, overwhelming, mighty influence, till your soul has been blown away. "Thou hearest the sound thereof."

But then the wind does something more than make a sound; and so does the Holy Spirit. It *works* and produces manifest results. Just think what the wind is doing tonight. I cannot tell at what pitch it may be now. It is just possible that in some part of the ocean a vessel scuds along almost under bare poles; the mariners do their best to reef the sails: away she goes: now the mast is gone: they do their best to bear up, but they find that in the teeth of the gale they cannot stand; the ship dashes on the rocks, and she is wrecked.

And, oh! the Spirit of God is a *great wrecker* of false hopes and carnal confidences. I have seen the Spirit of God come to a sinner like a storm to a ship at sea. He had to take down the top-gallants of his pride, and then every thread of carnal confidence had to be reefed, and then his hope itself had to be cut away; and on, on, the vessel went, until she struck a rock, and down she went. The man from that time never dared trust in his merits, for he had seen his merits wrecked and broken in pieces by the wind.

The wind, too, recollect, is a *great leveler*. It always aims at everything that is high. If you are down low in the street, you escape its fury; but climb to the top of the Monument, or St. Paul's, and try whether you do not feel it. Get into the valley, it is all right. The lower branches of the trees are scarcely moved, but the top branches are rocked to and fro by it. It is a great leveler; so is the Holy Spirit. He never sees a man high but he brings him down. He makes every high thought bow before the majesty of his might; and if you have any high thought tonight, rest assured that when the Spirit of God comes, he will lay it low, even with the ground.

Now, do not let this make you fear the Holy Spirit. It is a blessed thing to be rocked so as to have our hopes tested, and it is a precious thing to have our carnal confidences shaken. And how blessedly the wind *purifies* the atmosphere! In the Swiss valleys there is a heaviness in the air which makes the inhabitants unhealthy. They take quinine, and you see them going about with big swellings in their necks. From Martigny to Bretagne [Switzerland], there is a great valley in which you will see hundreds of persons diseased. The reason is, that the air does not circulate. They are breathing the same air, or some of it, that their fathers breathed before them. There seems to be no ventilation between the two parts of the giant Alps, and the air never circulates; but if they have a great storm which sweeps through the valleys, it is a great blessing to the people. And so the Spirit of God comes and cleanses out our evil thoughts and vain imaginations, and though we do not like the hurricane, yet it brings spiritual health to our soul.

Again the wind is a great *trier of the nature of things.* Here comes a great rushing up the street: it sweeps over the heaps of rubbish lying in the road—away goes all the light chaff, paper, and other things which have no weight in them; they cannot stand the brunt of its whirling power; but see, the pieces of iron, the stones, and all weighty things are left unmoved. In the country you will often see the farmer severing the chaff from the wheat by throwing it up into a current of air, and the light husks all blow away, while the heavy wheat sinks on the heap, cleansed and purified.

So is the Holy Ghost the great testing power, and the result of his operations will be to show men what they are. Here is a hypocrite: he has passed muster hitherto, and reckons himself to be a true and genuine man, but there comes a blast from Heaven's mighty spirit, and he finds himself to be lighter than vanity: he has no weight in him, he is driven on and has no rest, can find no peace, he hurries from one refuge of lies to another. "There is no peace," saith my God, to the wicked. Thus also we try the doctrines of men, we bring the breath of inspiration to bear upon them: do they abide the test, or are they driven away? Can you hold that truth in the presence of God? Can you cling to it and find it stable in the hour of trial? Is it a nice pleasant speculation for a sunny day when all is calm and bright, or will it bear the rough rude blast of adversity, when God's Holy Spirit is purifying you with his healthful influence? True Christians and sound doctrines have ballast and weight in them: they are not moved nor driven away, but empty professors [of faith] and hollow dogmas are scattered like chaff before the wind when the Lord shall blow upon them with the breath of his Spirit. Examine yourselves therefore, try the doctrines and see if they be of God. "What is the chaff to the wheat?" saith the Lord. Have root in yourselves, then will you not wither in the hot blast, nor be driven away in the tempestuous day.

Is not the Spirit moreover like unto the wind in its *developing of character?* See the dust is lying all over the picture, you cannot see the fair features of the beauteous sketch beneath; blow off the dust, and the fine colors will be seen, and once more the skill of the painter will be admired. Have you never noticed some piece of fine mosaic, or perhaps some well cut engraving on metal, all hidden, and the fine lines filled up with dust? You have blown off the accumulation, and then you could admire the work. So does the Spirit of God. Men get all covered with dust in the hot dusty roadside of life till they are nearly the color of the earth itself; but they come to the hill-top of Calvary, and here they stand till the wind of Heaven has cleansed them from all the dust that has gathered around their garments. Oh, there is nothing like communion with the Spirit of God to counteract the earthly tendencies of a business life. There are some men that get covered with a yellow dust, till they are almost hidden by it; they can talk of nothing else but money. Gold, gold, gold, is getting to occupy nearly every thought. Now, I have no quarrel with money in its right place, but I do not like to see men *live* in it. I always try to drive away that mean and groveling spirit which lives for nothing else but to accumulate money, but I cannot always succeed. Now the Spirit of God will make a man see his folly and put his money into its right position, and place the graces of the Christian character where men can see them and glorify God in them. Never let your business character or professional skill dim and hide your Christianity. If you do, God's Spirit will come to brighten you up, and he will have no mercy on these, but will, in love to your soul, cleanse and give luster to God's work which is wrought in you.

I have also noticed how helpful the wind is to all who choose to avail themselves of it. In Lincolnshire, where the country is flat and below the level of the sea, they are obliged to drain the land by means of windmills, and hundreds of them may be seen pumping up the water so as to relieve the land of the excess of moisture. In many parts of the country, nearly all the wheat and corn is ground by means of the wind. If it was not then for the wind, the inhabitants would be put to great inconvenience. The Spirit of God is thus also a mighty helper to all who will avail themselves of his influences. You are inundated with sin, a flood of iniquity comes in; you can never bale out the torrent, but with the help of God's Spirit it can be done. He will so assist, that you shall see the flood gradually descending and your heart once more purified. You need ever to ask his help; fresh sin, like falling showers, will be poured into you by every passing day, and you will need a continuous power to cast it out; you may have it in God's Spirit; he will with ceaseless energy help you to combat against sin, and make you more than a conqueror. Or, on the other hand, if you need some power to break up and prepare for you your spiritual food, you will find no better help than what God's Spirit can give. In Eastern countries they grind corn by the hand, two sitting at a small stone mill; but it is a poor affair at best; so are our own vain attempts to prepare the bread of Heaven for ourselves. We shall only get a little, and that little, badly ground. Commentators are good in their way, but give me the teaching of the Holy Ghost. He makes the passage clear and gives me to eat of the finest of the wheat. How often we have found our utter inability to understand some part of divine truth; we asked some of God's people and they helped us a little, but after all, we were not satisfied till we took it to the throne of heavenly grace, and implored the teachings of the blessed Spirit; then how sweetly it was opened to us; we could eat of it spiritually. It was no longer husk and shell, hard to be understood; it was as bread to us, and we could eat to the full. Brethren, we must make more use of the wisdom which cometh from above, for the Spirit, like the wind, is open to us all, to employ for our own personal benefit.

I see also here a thought as to the co-operation of man and the Spirit in all Christian work. It has pleased God to make us coworkers with him, fellow laborers, both in the matter of our own salvation, and also in the effort to benefit others. Look for a moment at yon stately bark [ship]: she moves not because of her sails, but she would not reach the desired haven without them. It is the wind which propels her forward; but the wind would not act upon her as it does, unless she had the rigging all fixed, her masts standing, and her sails all bent, so as to catch the passing breeze. But now that human seamanship has done its best, see how she flies! She will soon reach her haven with such a favoring gale as that. You have only to stand still and see how the wind bears her on like a thing of life.

And so it is with the human heart. When the Spirit comes to the soul that is ready to receive such influences, then he helps you on to Christian grace and Christian work, and makes you bear up through all opposition, till you come to the port of peace, and can anchor safely there. Without him we can do nothing: without us, He will not work. We are to preach the gospel to every creature, and while one plants, and another waters, God adds the increase. We are to work out our own salvation, but he worketh in us to will and to do of his own good pleasure. We must go up to possess the goodly land with our own spear and sword; but the hornet goes before us to drive out the foe. Jericho shall be captured by a divine and miraculous interference, but even there, rams' horns shall find a work to do, and must be employed. The host of Midian shall be slain, but our cry is, "The sword of the Lord and of Gideon." We give God all the glory: nevertheless we use the means. The water of Jordan must be sought out, and used by all who desire a cleansing like Naaman the Syrian. A lump of figs must be used if other Hezekiahs are to be healed; but the Spirit is, after all, the great Cleanser and Healer of his people Israel. The lesson is clear to all: the wind turns mills that men make; fills sails that human hands have spread; and the Spirit blesses human effort, crowns with success our labors, establishes the work of our hands upon us, and teaches all through, that "the hand of the diligent maketh rich;" but "if a man will not work, neither shall he eat."

Another thought suggests itself to my mind in connection with the wind and human effort; it is this: how completely dependent men are upon the wind as to what it shall do for them. They are entirely at its mercy as to its time of blowing, its strength, and the direction it will take. I have already dwelt upon this thought of the sovereignty of the wind, but it comes up here in a more practical form. The steamer now can steer almost anywhere they please, and at all times it will proceed on its voyage; but the sailing-ship must tack according to the wind, and when becalmed must wait for the breeze to spring up. The water-mill and steam-mill can be worked night and day, but the mill that depends upon the wind must abide by the wind's times of blowing, and must turn round its sails so as to suit the direction of the current of air. In like manner we are compelled to wait the pleasure of the Spirit. There is no reservoir of water which we can turn on when we will, and work as we please. We should forget God far more than we do now if that were the case. The sailor who is depending on the wind anxiously looks up to the masthead to see how the breeze is shifting and turning round the vane; and he scans the heavens to see what weather he is likely to have. He would not need to care nearly so much as he does now that he is absolutely dependent on the wind, if he had steam-power, so as to sail in the very teeth of the storm if he so willed. God, then, keeps us looking up to Heaven by making us to be completely at his mercy as to the times and ways of giving us his helping-power. It is a blessed thing to wait on God, watching for his hand and in quiet contentment, leaving all to him. Brethren, let us do our part faithfully, spread every sail, make all as perfect as human skill and wisdom can direct, and then in patient continuance in well-doing, wait the Spirit's propitious gales, neither murmuring because he tarries, nor be taken unawares when he comes upon us in his sovereign pleasure to do that which seemeth good in his sight.

Now, tonight I have only given you some hints on this subject: you can work it out for yourselves. As you hear the wind, you may get more sermons out of it than I can give you just now. The thing is perfectly inexhaustible; and I think the business of the minister is not to say all that can be said about the subject. Somebody remarked concerning a certain minister, that he was a most unfair preacher, because he always exhausted the subject and left nothing for anybody else to say. That will never be said of me, and I would rather that it should not. A minister should suggest germs of thought, open up new ways, and present, if possible, the truth in such a method as to lead men to understand that the half is not told them.

And now, my dear hearer, whether you listen often to my voice, or have now stepped in for the first time, I would like to ring this in your ear, Dost thou know the Spirit of God? If ye have not the Spirit, ye are none of his. "Ye must be born again." "What, Lord—'*must?*' Dost thou not mean 'may?'" No, ye *must*. "Does it not mean, 'Ye can be?'" No, ye *must*. When a man says, "must," it all depends upon who he is. When God says, "*must,*" there it stands, and it cannot be questioned. There are the flames of Hell: would you escape from them? You must be born again. There are Heaven's glories sparkling in their own light: would you enjoy them? You must be born again. There is the peace and joy of a believer: would you have it? You must be born again. What, not a crumb from off the table without this? No, not one. Not a drop of water to cool your burning tongues except you are born again. This is the one condition that never moves. God never alters it, and never will. You must, *must,* MUST. Which shall it be? Shall your will stand, or God's will? O, let God's "must" ride right over you, and bow yourselves down, and say,

> Lord, I must, then I will; ah! and it has come to this—I must tonight. Give me Christ, or else I die. I have hold of the knocker of the door of thy mercy, and I must, I *will* get that door open. I will never let thee go except thou bless me. Thou sayest *must,* Lord, and I say *must* too.

"Ye must, ye must be born again." God fulfill the "must" in each of your cases, for Jesus Christ's sake. Amen.

The Withering Work of the Spirit

Delivered on Lord's Day morning, July 9, 1871, at the Metropolitan Tabernacle, Newington. No. 999.

The voice said, "Cry." And he said, "What shall I cry?" "All flesh is grass, and all the goodliness thereof is as the flower of the field: the grass withereth, the flower fadeth: because the Spirit of the Lord bloweth upon it: surely the people is grass. The grass withereth, the flower fadeth: but the word of our God shall stand forever."—Isaiah 40:6–8

Being born again, not of corruptible seed, but of incorruptible, by the word of God, which liveth and abideth forever. For all flesh is as grass, and all the glory of man as the flower of grass. The grass withereth, and the flower thereof falleth away: but the word of the Lord endureth forever. And this is the word which by the gospel is preached unto you.—1 Peter 1:23–25

The passage in Isaiah which I have just read in your hearing may be used as a very eloquent description of our mortality, and if a sermon should be preached from it upon the frailty of human nature, the brevity of life, and the certainty of death, no one could dispute the appropriateness of the text. Yet I venture to question whether such a discourse would strike the central teaching of the prophet. Something more than the decay of our material flesh is intended here; the carnal mind, the flesh in another sense, was intended by the Holy Ghost when he bade his messenger proclaim those

461

words. It does not seem to me that a mere expression of the mortality of our race was needed in this place, by the context; it would hardly keep pace with the sublime revelations which surround it, and would in some measure be a digression from the subject in hand. The notion that we are here [in this passage] simply and alone reminded of our mortality does not square with the New Testament exposition of it in Peter, which I have also placed before you as a text. There is another and more spiritual meaning here beside and beyond that which would be contained in the great and very obvious truth that all of us must die.

Look at the chapter in Isaiah with care. What is the subject of it? It is the divine consolation of Zion. Zion had been tossed to and fro with conflicts; she had been smarting under the result of sin. The Lord, to remove her sorrow, bids his prophets announce the coming of the long-expected Deliverer, the end and accomplishment of all her warfare, and the pardon of all her iniquity. There is no doubt that this is the theme of the prophecy; and further, there is no sort of question about the next point, that the prophet goes on to foretell the coming of John the Baptist as the harbinger of the Messiah. We have no difficulty in the explanation of the passage, "Prepare ye the way of the Lord, make straight in the desert a highway for our God;" for the New Testament again and again refers this to the Baptist and his ministry. The object of the coming of the Baptist and the mission of the Messiah, whom he heralded, was the manifestation of divine glory. Observe the fifth verse: "The glory of the Lord shall be revealed, and all flesh shall see it together: for the mouth of the Lord hath spoken it." Well, what next? Was it needful to mention man's mortality in this connection? We think not. But there is much more appropriateness in the succeeding verses, if we see their deeper meaning. Do they not mean this? *In order to make room for the display of the divine glory in Christ Jesus and his salvation, there would come a withering of all the glory wherein man boasts himself: the flesh should be seen in its true nature as corrupt and dying, and the grace of God alone should be exalted.* This would be seen under the ministry of John the Baptist first, and should be the preparatory work of the Holy Ghost in men's hearts, in all time, in order that the glory of the Lord should be revealed and human pride be forever confounded.

The Spirit blows upon the flesh, and that which seemed vigorous becomes weak, that which was fair to look upon is smitten with decay; the true nature of the flesh is thus discovered, its deceit is laid bare, its power is destroyed, and there is space for the dispensation of the ever-abiding word, and for the rule of the Great Shepherd, whose words are spirit and life.

There is a withering wrought by the Spirit which is the preparation for the sowing and implanting by which salvation is wrought.

The withering before the sowing was very marvelously fulfilled in the preaching of John the Baptist. Most appropriately he carried on his ministry in the desert, for a spiritual desert was all around him; he was the voice of one crying in the wilderness. It was not his work to plant, but to hew down. The fleshly religion of the Jews was then in its prime. Phariseeism stalked through the streets in all its pomp; men complacently rested in outward ceremonies only, and spiritual religion was at the lowest conceivable ebb. Here and there might be found a Simeon and an Anna, but for the most part men knew nothing of spiritual religion, but said in their hearts: "We have Abraham to our father," and this is enough. What a stir he [Jesus] made when he called the lordly Pharisees a generation of vipers! How he shook the nation with the declaration, "Now also the axe is laid unto the root of the trees"! Stern as Elias [Elijah], his work was to level the mountains, and lay low every lofty imagination. That word, "Repent," was as a scorching wind to the verdure of self-righteousness, a killing blast for the confidence of ceremonialism. His food and his dress called for fasting and mourning. The outward token of his ministry declared the death amid which he preached, as he buried in the waters of Jordan those who came to him. "Ye must die and be buried, even as he who is to come will save by death and burial." This was the meaning of the emblem which he set before the crowd. His typical act was as thorough in its teaching as were his words; and as if that were not enough, he warned them of a yet more searching and trying baptism with the Holy Ghost and with fire, and of the coming of one whose fan was in his hand, thoroughly to purge his floor. The Spirit in John blew as the rough north wind, searching and withering, and made him to be a destroyer of the vain gloryings of a fleshly religion, that the spiritual faith might be established.

When our Lord himself actually appeared, he came into a withered land, whose glories had all departed. Old Jesse's stem was bare, and our Lord was the branch which grew out of his root. The scepter had departed from Judah, and the lawgiver from between his feet, when Shiloh came. An alien sat on David's throne, and the Roman called the covenant-land his own. The lamp of prophecy burned but dimly, even if it had not utterly gone out. No Isaiah had arisen of late to console them, nor even a Jeremiah to lament their apostasy. The whole economy of Judaism was as a worn-out vesture; it had waxed old, and was ready to vanish away. The priesthood was disarranged. Luke tells us that Annas and Caiaphas were high priests that year—two in a year or at once, a strange setting aside of the laws of Moses. All the dispensation which gathered around the visible, or, as Paul calls it, the "worldly" sanctuary, was coming to a close; and when our Lord had finished his work, the veil of the temple was rent in twain, the sacrifices were abolished, the priesthood of Aaron was set aside, and carnal ordinances were abrogated, for the Spirit revealed spiritual things. When he came, who was made a priest, "not after the law of a carnal commandment, but after the power of an endless life," there was "a disannulling of the commandment going before for the weakness and unprofitableness thereof."

Such are the facts of history; but I am not about to dilate upon them: I am coming to your own personal histories—to the experience of every child of God. In every one of us it must be fulfilled, that all that is of the flesh in us, seeing it is but as grass, must be withered, and the comeliness thereof must be destroyed. The Spirit of God, like the wind, must pass over the field of our souls, and cause our beauty to be as a fading flower. He must so convince us of sin, and so reveal ourselves to ourselves, that we shall see that the flesh profiteth nothing; that our fallen nature is corruption itself, and that "they who are in the flesh cannot please God." There must be brought home to us the sentence of death upon our former legal and carnal life, that the incorruptible seed of the word of God, implanted by the Holy Ghost, may be in us, and abide in us forever.

The subject of this morning is the withering work of the Spirit upon the souls of men, and when we have spoken upon it, we shall conclude with a few words upon the implanting work, which always follows where this withering work has been performed.

I. Turning then to *the work of the Spirit in causing the goodliness of the flesh to fade,* let us, first, observe that the work of the Holy Spirit upon the soul of man in withering up that which is of the flesh, is *very unexpected.*

1. You will observe in our text that even the speaker himself, though doubtless one taught of God, when he was bidden to cry, said, *"What shall I cry?"* Even he did not know that, in order to the comforting of God's people, there must first be experienced a preliminary visitation. Many preachers of God's gospel have forgotten that the law is the schoolmaster to bring men to Christ. They have sown on the unbroken fallow ground and forgotten that the plough must break the clods. We have seen too much of trying to sew without the sharp needle of the Spirit's convincing power. Preachers have labored to make Christ precious to those who think themselves rich and increased in goods: and it has been labor in vain. It is our duty to preach Jesus Christ even to self-righteous sinners, but it is certain that Jesus Christ will never be accepted by them while they hold themselves in high esteem. Only the sick will welcome the physician. It is the work of the Spirit of God to convince men of sin, and until they are convinced of sin, they will never be led to seek the righteousness which is of God by Jesus Christ. I am persuaded, that wherever there is a real work of grace in any soul, it begins with a pulling down: the Holy Ghost does not build on the old foundation. Wood, hay, and stubble will not do for him to build upon. He will come as the fire, and cause a conflagration of all proud nature's Babels. He will break our bow and cut our spear in sunder, and burn our chariot in the fire. When every sandy foundation is gone, then, but not till then,

behold he will lay in our souls the great foundation stone, chosen of God, and precious. The awakened sinner, when he asks that God would have mercy upon him, is much astonished to find that, instead of enjoying a speedy peace, his soul is bowed down within him under a sense of divine wrath. Naturally enough he enquires:

> Is this the answer to my prayer? I prayed the Lord to deliver me from sin and self, and is this the way in which he deals with me? I said, "Hear me," and behold he wounds me with the wounds of a cruel one. I said, "Clothe me," and lo! He has torn off from me the few rags which covered me before, and my nakedness stares me in the face. I said, "Wash me," and behold he has plunged me in the ditch till mine own clothes do abhor me. Is this the way of grace?

Sinner, be not surprised: it is even so. Perceivest thou not the cause of it? How canst thou be healed while the proud flesh is in thy wound? It must come out. It is the only way to heal thee permanently: it would be folly to film over thy sore, or heal thy flesh, and leave the leprosy within thy bones. The great physician will cut with his sharp knife till the corrupt flesh be removed, for only thus can a sure healing work be wrought in thee. Dost thou not see that it is divinely wise that before thou art clothed, thou shouldst be stripped! What, wouldst thou have Christ's lustrous righteousness outside whiter than any fuller can make it, and thine own filthy rags concealed within? Nay, man; they must be put away; not a single thread of thine own must be left upon thee. It cannot be that God should cleanse thee until he has made thee see somewhat of thy defilement; for thou wouldst never value the precious blood which cleanses us from all sin if thou hadst not first of all been made to mourn that thou art altogether an unclean thing.

The convincing work of the Spirit, wherever it comes, is unexpected, and even to the child of God in whom this process has still to go on, it is often startling. We begin again to build that which the Spirit of God had destroyed. Having begun in the spirit, we act as if we would be made perfect in the flesh; and then when our mistaken upbuilding has to be leveled with the earth, we are almost as astonished as we were when first the scales fell from our eyes. In some such condition as this was Newton when he wrote:—

> *I asked the Lord that I might grow*
> *In faith and love and every grace,*
> *Might more of his salvation know,*
> *And seek more earnestly his face.*
>
> *Twas he who taught me thus to pray,*
> *And he, I trust, has answered prayer;*
> *But it has been in such a way*
> *As almost drove me to despair.*

> *I hop'd that in some favor'd hour,*
> *At once he'd answer my request,*
> *And by his love's constraining power*
> *Subdue my sins, and give me rest.*
>
> *Instead of this, he made me feel*
> *The hidden evils of my heart.*
> *And let the angry powers of hell*
> *Assault my soul in ev'ry part.*

Ah, marvel not, for thus the Lord is wont to answer his people. The voice which saith, "Comfort ye, comfort ye my people," achieves its purpose by first making them hear the cry, "All flesh is grass, and all the goodliness thereof is as the flower of the field."

2. Furthermore, this withering is *after the usual order of the divine operation*. If we consider well the way of God, we shall not be astonished that he beginneth with his people by terrible things in righteousness. Observe the method of creation. I will not venture upon any dogmatic theory of geology, but there seems to be every probability that this world has been fitted up and destroyed, refitted and then destroyed again, many times before the last arranging of it for the habitation of men. "In the beginning God created the Heaven and the earth;" then came a long interval, and at length, at the appointed time, during seven days, the Lord prepared the earth for the human race. Consider then the state of matters when the great architect began his work. What was there in the beginning? Originally, nothing. When he commanded the ordering of the earth how was it? "The earth was without form and void; and darkness was upon the face of the deep." There was no trace of another's plan to interfere with the great architect.

> With whom took he counsel, and who instructed him, and taught him in the path of judgment, and taught him knowledge, and showed to him the way of understanding?

He received no contribution of column or pillar towards the temple which he intended to build. The earth was, as the Hebrew puts it, *Tohu* and *Bohu*, disorder and confusion—in a word, chaos. So it is in the new creation. When the Lord new creates us, he borrows nothing from the old man, but makes all things new. He does not repair and add a new wing to the old house of our depraved nature, but he builds a new temple for his own praise. We are spiritually without form and empty, and darkness is upon the face of our heart, and his word comes to us, saying, "Light be," and there is light, and ere long, life and every precious thing.

To take another instance from the ways of God. When man has fallen, when did the Lord bring him the gospel? The first whisper of the gospel, as you know, was, "I will put enmity between thee and the woman, between thy seed and her seed. He shall bruise thy head." That whisper came to man shivering in the presence of his Maker, having nothing more to say by way of excuse; but standing guilty before the Lord. When did the Lord God clothe our parents? Not until first of all he had put the question, "Who told thee that thou wast naked?" Not until the fig-leaves had utterly failed did the Lord bring in the covering skin of the sacrifice, and wrap them in it. If you will pursue the meditation upon the acts of God with men, you will constantly see the same thing. God has given us a wonderful type of salvation in Noah's ark; but Noah was saved in that ark in connection with death; he himself, as it were, immured alive in a tomb, and all the world besides left to destruction. All other hope for Noah was gone, and then the ark rose upon the waters. Remember the redemption of the children of Israel out of Egypt: it occurred when they were in the saddest plight, and their cry went up to Heaven by reason of their bondage. When no arm brought salvation, then with a high hand and an outstretched arm, the Lord brought forth his people. Everywhere, before the salvation there comes the humbling of the creature, the overthrow of human hope. As in the backwoods of America, before there can be tillage, the planting of cities, the arts of civilization, and the transactions of commerce—the woodman's axe must hack and hew: the stately trees of centuries must fall: the roots must be burned, the odd reign of nature disturbed. The old must go before the new can come. Even thus the Lord takes away the first, that he may establish the second. The first Heaven and the first Earth must pass away, or there cannot be a new Heaven and a new Earth. Now, as it has been outwardly, we ought to expect that it would be the same within us, and when these witherings and fadings occur in our souls, we should only say "It is the Lord, let him do as seemeth him good."

3. *I would have you notice, thirdly, that we are taught in our text* how universal this process is in its range *over the hearts of all those upon whom the Spirit works.* The withering is a withering of what? Of *part* of the flesh and some portion of its tendencies? Nay, observe, "*All* flesh is grass; and *all* the goodliness thereof"—the very choice and pick of it—"is as the flower of the field," and what happens to the grass? Does any of it live? "The grass withereth," all of it. The flower, will not that abide? So fair a thing, has not that an immortality? No, it fades: it utterly falls away. So wherever the Spirit of God breathes on the soul of man, there is a withering of everything that is of the flesh, and it is seen that, to be carnally minded, is death. Of course, we all know and confess that where there is a work of grace, there must be a destruction of our delight in the pleasures of the flesh. When the Spirit of God breathes on us, that which was sweet becomes bitter; that which was bright becomes dim. A man cannot love sin and yet possess the life of God. If he takes pleasure in fleshly joys wherein he once delighted, he is still what he was: he minds the things of the flesh, and therefore he is after the flesh, and he shall die. The world and the lusts thereof are to the unregenerate as beautiful as the meadows in spring, when they are bedecked with flowers, but to the regenerate soul they are a wilderness, a salt land, and not inhabited. Of those very things wherein we once took delight we say,

"Vanity of vanities; all is vanity." We cry to be delivered from the poisonous joys of earth, we loathe them, and wonder that we could once riot in them. Beloved hearers, do you know what this kind of withering means? Have you seen the lusts of the flesh, and the pomps and the pleasures thereof all fade away before your eyes? It must be so, or the Spirit of God has not visited your soul.

But mark, wherever the Spirit of God comes, he destroys the goodliness and flower of the flesh; that is to say, our righteousness withers as our sinfulness. Before the Spirit comes, we think ourselves as good as the best. We say, "All these commandments have I kept from my youth up," and we superciliously ask, "What lack I yet?" Have we not been moral? Nay, have we not even been religious? We confess that we may have committed faults, but we think them very venial, and we venture, in our wicked pride, to imagine that, after all, we are not so vile as the word of God would lead us to think. Ah, my dear hearer, when the Spirit of God blows on the comeliness of thy flesh, its beauty will fade as a leaf, and thou wilt have quite another idea of thyself—thou wilt then find no language too severe in which to describe thy past character. Searching deep into thy motives, and investigating that which moved thee to thine actions, thou wilt see so much of evil, that thou wilt cry with the publican, "God be merciful to me, a sinner!"

Where the Holy Ghost has withered up in us our self-righteousness, he has not half completed his work; there is much more to be destroyed yet, and among the rest, away must go our boasted power of resolution. Most people conceive that they can turn to God whenever they resolve to do so. "I am a man of such strength of mind," says one, "that if I made up my mind to be religious, I should be without difficulty." "Ah," saith another volatile spirit, "I believe that one of these days I can correct the errors of the past, and commence a new life." Ah, dear hearers, the resolutions of the flesh are goodly flowers, but they must all fade. When visited by the Spirit of God, we find that even when the will is present with us, how to perform that which we would, we find not; yea, and we discover that our will is averse to all that is good, and that naturally we will not come unto Christ that we may have life. What poor frail things resolutions are when seen in the light of God's Spirit!

Still the man will say,

> I believe I have, after all, within myself an enlightened conscience and an intelligence that will guide me aright. The light of nature I will use, and I do not doubt that if I wander somewhat I shall find my way back again.

Ah, man! thy wisdom, which is the very flower of thy nature, what is it but folly, though thou knowest it not? Unconverted and unrenewed, thou art in God's sight no wiser than the wild ass's colt. I wish thou wert in thine own esteem humbled as a little child at Jesus' feet, and made to cry, "Teach thou me."

When the withering wind of the Spirit moves over the carnal mind, it reveals the death of the flesh in all respects, especially in the matter of power towards that which is good. We then learn that word of our Lord: "Without me ye can do nothing." When I was seeking the Lord, I not only *believed* that I could not pray without divine help, but I *felt* in my very soul that I could not. Then I could not even feel aright, or mourn as I would, or groan as I would. I longed to long more after Christ; but, alas! I could not even feel that I needed him as I ought to feel it. This heart was then as har,d as adamant, as dead, as those that rot in their graves. Oh, what would I at times have given for a tear! I wanted to repent, but could not; longed to believe, but could not; I felt bound, hampered, and paralyzed. This is a humbling revelation of God's Holy Spirit, but a needful one; for the faith of the flesh is not the faith of God's elect. The faith which justifies the soul is the gift of God and not of ourselves. That repentance which is the work of the flesh will need to be repented of. The flower of the flesh must wither; only the seed of the Spirit will produce fruit unto perfection. The heirs of Heaven are born not of blood, nor of the will of the flesh, nor of man, but of God. If the work in us be not the Spirit's working, but our own, it will droop and die when most we require its protection; and its end will be as the grass, which today is, and tomorrow is cast into the oven.

4. *You see, then, the universality of this withering work within us, but I beg you also to notice the* completeness *of it.* The grass, what does it do? Droop? Nay, wither. The flower of the field: what of that? Does it hang its head a little? No, according to Isaiah it fades; and according to Peter it falleth away. There is no reviving it with showers, it has come to its end. Even thus are the awakened led to see that in their flesh there dwelleth no good thing. What dying and withering work some of God's servants have had in their souls! Look at John Bunyan, as he describes himself in his *Grace Abounding!* For how many months and even years was the Spirit engaged in writing death upon all that was the old Bunyan, in order that he might become by grace a new man fitted to track the pilgrims along their heavenly way. We have not all endured the ordeal so long, but in every child of God there must be a death to sin, to the law, and to self, which must be fully accomplished ere he is perfected in Christ and taken to Heaven. Corruption cannot inherit incorruption; it is through the Spirit that we mortify the deeds of the body, and therefore live. But cannot the fleshly mind be improved? By no means; for "the carnal mind is enmity against God: for it is not subject to the law of God, neither indeed can be." Cannot you improve the old nature? No; "ye must be born again." Can it not be taught heavenly things? No. "The natural man receiveth not the things of the Spirit of God: for they are foolishness unto him: neither can he know them, because they are spiritually discerned." There is nothing to be done with the old nature but to let it be laid in the grave; it must be dead, and buried, and when it is so, then the incorruptible seed that liveth and abideth forever will develop gloriously, the fruit of the new birth will come to maturity, and grace shall be exalted in glory. The old nature never does improve: it is as earthly, and sensual, and devilish in the saint of eighty

years of age as it was when first he came to Christ; it is unimproved and unimprovable; towards God it is enmity itself: every imagination of the thoughts of the heart is evil, and that continually. The old nature called "the flesh lusteth against the Spirit, and the Spirit against the flesh: and these are contrary the one to the other," neither can there be peace between them.

5. Let us further notice that all this withering work in the soul is very painful. As you read these verses, do they not strike you as having a very funereal tone? "All flesh is grass, and all the goodliness thereof is as the flower of the field: the grass withereth, the flower fadeth." This is mournful work, but it must be done. I think those who experience much of it when they first come to Christ have great reason to be thankful. Their course in life will, in all probability, be much brighter and happier, for I have noticed that persons who are converted very easily, and come to Christ with but comparatively little knowledge of their own depravity, have to learn it afterwards, and they remain for a long time babes in Christ, and are perplexed with matters that would not have troubled them if they had experienced a deeper work at first. No, sir; if grace has begun to build in your soul and left any of the old walls of self-trust standing, they will have to come down sooner or later. You may congratulate yourself upon their remaining, but it is a false congratulation, your glorying is not good. I am sure of this, that Christ will never put a new piece upon an old garment, or new wine in old bottles: he knows the rent would be worse in the long run, and the bottles would burst. All that is of nature's spinning must be unraveled. The natural building must come down, lath and plaster, roof and foundation, and we must have a house not made with hands. It was a great mercy for our city of London that the great fire cleared away all the old buildings which were the lair of the plague—a far healthier city was then built; and it is a great mercy for a man when God sweeps right away all his own righteousness and strength, when he makes him feel that he is nothing and can be nothing, and drives him to confess that Christ must be all in all, and that his only strength lies in the eternal might of the ever-blessed Spirit.

Sometimes in a house of business, an old system has been going on for years, and it has caused much confusion, and allowed much dishonesty. You come in as a new manager, and you adopt an entirely new plan. Now, try if you can, and graft your method on to the old system. How it will worry you! Year after year you say to yourself, "I cannot work it: if I had swept the whole away and started afresh, clear from the beginning, it would not have given me one-tenth of the trouble." God does not intend to graft the system of grace upon corrupt nature, nor to make the new Adam grow out of the old Adam, but he intends to teach us this: "Ye are dead, and your life is hid with Christ in God." Salvation is not of the flesh but of the Lord alone; that which is born of the flesh is only flesh at the best; and only that which is born of the Spirit is spirit. It must be the Spirit's work altogether, or it is not what God will accept.

6. *Observe, brethren, that although this is painful,* it is inevitable. I have already entrenched upon this, and shown you how necessary it is that all of the old should be taken away; but let me further remark that it is inevitable that the old should go, because it is in itself corruptible. Why does the grass wither? Because it is a withering thing. "Its root is ever in its grave, and it must die." How could it spring out of the earth, and be immortal? It is no amaranth:[1] it blooms not in Paradise: it grows in a soil on which the curse has fallen. Every supposed good thing that grows out of your own self is, like yourself, mortal—and it must die. The seeds of corruption are in all the fruits of manhood's tree; let them be as fair to look upon as Eden's clusters, they must decay.

Moreover, it would never do, my brother, that there should be something of the flesh in our salvation and something of the Spirit; for if it were so, there would be a division of the honor. Hitherto the praises of God; beyond this, my own praises. If I were to win Heaven partly through what I had done, and partly through what Christ had done, and if the energy which sanctified me was in a measure my own, and in a measure divine, they that divide the work shall divide the reward, and the songs of Heaven while they would be partly to Jehovah must also be partly to the creature. But it shall not be. "Down, proud flesh! Down!" I say.

> Though thou cleanse and purge thyself as thou mayst, thou art to the core corrupt; though thou labor unto weariness, thou buildest wood that will be burned, and stubble that will be turned to ashes. Give up thine own self-confidence, and let the work be, and the merit be where the honor shall be, namely, with God alone.

It is inevitable, then, that there should be all this withering.

7. This last word is *by way of comfort* to any that are passing through the process we are describing, and I hope some of you are. It gives me great joy when I hear that you unconverted ones are very miserable, for the miseries which the Holy Spirit works are always the prelude to happiness. *It is the Spirit's work to wither.* I rejoice in our translation, "Because the Spirit of the Lord bloweth upon it." It is true the passage may be translated, "The wind of the Lord bloweth upon it." One word, as you know, is used in the Hebrew both for "wind" and "Spirit," and the same is true of the Greek; but let us retain the old translation here, for I conceive it to be the real meaning of the text. The Spirit of God it is that withers the flesh. It is not the devil that killed my self-righteousness. I might be afraid if it were: nor was it myself that humbled myself by a voluntary and needless self-degradation, but it was the Spirit of God. Better to be broken in pieces by the Spirit of God, than to be made whole by the flesh! What doth the Lord say? "I kill." But what next? "I make

---

[1] Amaranth: imaginary flower that never fades.

alive." He never makes any alive but those he kills. Blessed be the Holy Ghost when he kills me, when he drives the sword through the very bowels of my own merits and my self-confidence, for then he will make me alive. "I wound, and I heal." He never heals those whom he has not wounded. Then blessed be the hand that wounds; let it go on wounding; let it cut and tear; let it lay bare to me myself at my very worst, that I may be driven to self-despair, and may fall back upon the free mercy of God, and receive it as a poor, guilty, lost, helpless, undone sinner, who casts himself into the arms of sovereign grace, knowing that God must give all, and Christ must be all, and the Spirit must work all, and man must be as clay in the potter's hands, that the Lord may do with him as seemeth to him good. Rejoice, dear brother, how ever low you are brought, for if the Spirit humbles you, he means no evil, but he intends infinite good to your soul.

II. Now, let us close with a few sentences concerning *the implantation.*

According to Peter, although the flesh withers, and the flower thereof falls away, yet in the children of God there is an *un*withering something of another kind. "Being born again, not of corruptible seed, but of incorruptible, by the word of God, which liveth and abideth forever." "The word of the Lord endureth forever. And this is the word which by the gospel is preached unto you." Now, the gospel is of use to us because it is not of human origin. If it were of the flesh, all it could do for us would not land us beyond the flesh; but the gospel of Jesus Christ is super-human, divine, and spiritual. In its conception it was of God; its great gift, even the Savior, is a divine gift; and all its teachings are full of deity. If you, my hearer, believe a gospel which you have thought out for yourself, or a philosophical gospel which comes from the brain of man, it is of the flesh, and will wither, and you will die, and be lost through trusting in it. The only word that can bless you and be a seed in your soul must be the living and incorruptible word of the eternal Spirit. Now this is the incorruptible word, that "God was made flesh and dwelt among us;" that "God was in Christ, reconciling the world unto himself, not imputing their trespasses unto them." This is the incorruptible word, that "Whosoever believeth that Jesus is the Christ, is born of God." "He that believeth on him is not condemned: but he that believeth not is condemned already, because he hath not believed in the name of the only begotten Son of God." "God hath given to us eternal life, and this life is in his Son." Now, brethren, this is the seed; but before it can grow in your soul, it must be planted there by the Spirit. Do you receive it this morning? Then the Holy Spirit implants it in your soul. Do you leap up to it, and say, "I believe it! I grasp it! On the incarnate God I fix my hope; the substitutionary sacrifice, the complete atonement of Christ is all my confidence; I am reconciled to God by the blood of Jesus." Then you possess the living seed within your soul.

And what is the result of it? Why, then there comes, according to the text, a new life into us, as the result of the indwelling of the living word, and our being born again by it. A new life it is; it is not the old nature putting out its better parts; not the old Adam refining and purifying itself, and rising to something better. No; have we not said aforetime that the flesh withers and the flower thereof fades? It is an entirely new life. Ye are as much new creatures, at your regeneration, as if you had never existed, and had been for the first time created. "Old things are passed away; behold, all things are become new." The child of God is beyond and above other men. Other men do not possess the life which he has received. They are but duplex—body and soul have they. He is of triple nature—he is spirit, soul, and body. A fresh principle, a spark of the divine life has dropped into his soul; he is no longer a natural or carnal man, but he has become a spiritual man, understanding spiritual things and possessing a life far superior to anything that belongs to the rest of mankind. O that God, who has withered in the souls of any of you that which is of the flesh, may speedily grant you the new birth through the Word.

Now observe, to close, wherever this new life comes through the word, it is incorruptible, it lives and abides forever. To get the good seed out of a true believer's heart and to destroy the new nature in him, is a thing attempted by earth and hell, but never yet achieved. Pluck the sun out of the firmament, and you shall not even then be able to pluck grace out of a regenerate heart. It "liveth and abideth forever," saith the text; it neither can corrupt of itself nor be corrupted. "It sinneth not, because it is born of God." "I give unto them eternal life, and they shall never perish, neither shall any man pluck them out of my hand." "The water that I shall give him shall be in him a well of water springing up into everlasting life." You have a natural life—that will die, it is of the flesh. You have a spiritual life—of that it is written: "'Whosoever liveth and believeth in me shall never die." You have now within you the noblest and truest immortality: you must live as God liveth, in peace and joy, and happiness. But oh, remember, dear hearer, if you have not this, you "shall not see life." What then—shall you be annihilated? Ah! no, but "the wrath of the Lord is upon you." You shall exist, though you shall not live. Of life you shall know nothing, for that is the gift of God in Christ Jesus; but of an everlasting death, full of torment and anguish, you shall be the wretched heritor—"the wrath of God abideth on him." You shall be cast into "the lake of fire, which is the second death." You shall be one of those whose "worm dieth not, and whose fire is not quenched." May God, the ever-blessed Spirit, visit you! If he be now striving with you, O quench not his divine flame! Trifle not with any holy thought you have. If this morning you must confess that you are not born again, be humbled by it. Go and seek mercy of the Lord, entreat him to deal graciously with you, and save you. Many who have had nothing but moonlight have prized it, and ere long they have had sunlight. Above all, remember what the quickening seed is, and reverence it when you hear it preached, "for this is the word which by the gospel is preached unto you." Respect it, and receive it. Remember that the quickening seed is all wrapped up in this sentence: "Believe in the Lord Jesus Christ, and thou shalt be saved." "He that believeth and is baptised shall be saved; but he that believeth not shall be damned."

The Lord bless you, for Jesus' sake. Amen.

The Pentecostal Wind and Fire

Delivered on Lord's Day morning, September 18, 1881, at the Metropolitan
Tabernacle, Newington. No. 1619.

And suddenly there came a sound from Heaven as of a rushing mighty wind, and it filled
all the house where they were sitting. And there appeared unto them cloven tongues like
as of fire, and it sat upon each of them. And they were all filled with the Holy Ghost, and
began to speak with other tongues, as the Spirit gave them utterance.—Acts 2:2–4

From the descent of the Holy Ghost at the beginning we may learn something
concerning his operations at the present time. Remember at the outset that
whatever the Holy Spirit was at the first that he is now, for as God he remaineth
forever the same: whatsoever he then did he is able to do still, for his power is by no
means diminished. As saith the prophet Micah, "O thou that art named the house
of Jacob, is the spirit of the Lord straitened?" We should greatly grieve the Holy
Spirit if we supposed that his might was less today than in the beginning. Although
we may not expect, and need not desire, the miracles which came with the gift of
the Holy Spirit, so far as they were physical, yet we may both desire and expect that
which was intended and symbolized by them, and we may reckon to see the like
spiritual wonders performed among us at this day.

Pentecost, according to the belief of the Jews, was the time of the giving of the
law; and if, when the law was given, there was a marvelous display of power on Sinai, it was to be expected that, when the gospel was given—whose ministration is

475

far more glorious—there should be some special unveiling of the divine presence. If at the commencement of the gospel we behold the Holy Spirit working great signs and wonders, may we not expect a continuance—nay, if anything an increased display of his power, as the ages roll on? The law vanished away, but the gospel will never vanish; it shineth more and more to the perfect millennial day; therefore, I reckon that, with the sole exception of physical miracles, whatever was wrought by the Holy Ghost at the first, we may look to be wrought continually while the dispensation lasts. It ought not to be forgotten that Pentecost was the feast of first fruits; it was the time when the first ears of ripe corn were offered unto God. If, then, at the commencement of the gospel harvest we see so plainly the power of the Holy Spirit, may we not most properly expect infinitely more as the harvest advances, and most of all when the most numerous sheaves shall be ingathered? May we not conclude that if the Pentecost was thus marvelous, the actual harvest will be more wonderful still?

This morning my object is not to talk of the descent of the Holy Spirit as a piece of history, but to view it as a fact bearing upon us at this hour, even upon us who are called in these latter days to bear our testimony for the truth. The Father hath sent us the Comforter that he may dwell in us till the coming of the Lord. The Holy Ghost has never *returned,* for he came in accordance with the Savior's prayer, to abide with us forever. The gift of the Comforter was not temporary, and the display of his power was not to be once seen and [then] no more. The Holy Ghost is here, and we ought to expect his divine working among us: and if he does not so work, we should search ourselves to see what it is that hindereth, and whether there may not be somewhat in ourselves which vexes him, so that he restrains his sacred energy, and doth not work among us as he did aforetime. May God grant that the meditation of this morning may increase our faith in the Holy Ghost, and inflame our desires towards him, so that we may look to see him fulfilling his mission among men as at the beginning.

I. First, I shall call your attention to *the instructive symbols* of the Holy Spirit, which were made prominent at Pentecost.

They were two. There was a sound as of a rushing mighty wind, and there were cloven tongues as it were of fire.

Take the symbols separately. The first is *wind*—an emblem of Deity, and therefore a proper symbol of the Holy Spirit. Often under the Old Testament God revealed himself under the emblem of breath or wind: indeed, as most of you know, the Hebrew word for "wind" and "spirit" is the same. So, with the Greek word, when Christ talked to Nicodemus, it is not very easy for translators to tell us when he said "spirit" and when he said "wind;" indeed, some most correctly render the original all the way through by the word "wind," while others with much reason have also used the word "spirit" in their translation. The original word signified either the one or the other, or both. Wind is, of all material things, one of the most spiritual in appearance; it is invisible, ethereal, mysterious; hence, men have fixed upon it as being nearest akin to spirit. In Ezekiel's famous vision, when he saw the valley full of dry bones, we all know that the Spirit of God was intended by that vivifying wind, which came when the prophet prophesied, and blew upon the withered relics till they were quickened into life. "The Lord hath his way in the whirlwind," thus he displays himself when he works. "The Lord answered Job out of the whirlwind," thus he reveals himself when he teaches his servants.

Observe that this wind was, on the day of Pentecost, accompanied with a sound—a sound as of a rushing mighty wind; for albeit the Spirit of God can work in silence, yet in saving operations he frequently uses sound. I would be the last to depreciate meetings in which there is nothing but holy silence, for I could wish that we had more reverence for silence, and it is in stillness that the inner life is nourished; yet the Holy Ghost does not work for the advancement of the kingdom of God by silence alone, for faith cometh by hearing. There is a sound as of a rushing, mighty wind, when the word is sounded forth throughout whole nations by the publishing of the gospel. If the Lord had not given men ears or tongues, silent worship would have been not only appropriate but necessary, but inasmuch as we have ears, the Lord must have intended us to hear something, and as we have tongues, he must have meant us to speak. Some of us would be glad to be quiet, but where the gospel has free course, there is sure to be a measure of noise and stir. The sound came on this occasion, no doubt, to call the attention of the assembly to what was about to occur, to arouse them, and to fill them with awe! There is something indescribably solemn about the rush of a rising tempest; it bows the soul before the sublime mystery of divine power. What more fitting as an attendant upon divine working than the deeply solemn rush of a mighty wind?

With this awe-inspiring sound as of a mighty wind, there was clear indication of its coming from heaven. Ordinary winds blow from this or that quarter of the skies, but this descended from Heaven itself: it was distinctly like a down-draught from above. This sets forth the fact that the true Spirit, the Spirit of God, neither comes from this place nor that, neither can his power be controlled or directed by human authority, but his working is ever from above, from God himself. The work of the Holy Spirit is, so to speak, the breath of God, and his power is evermore in a special sense the immediate power of God. Coming downward, therefore, this mysterious wind passed into the chamber where the disciples were assembled, and filled the room. An ordinary rushing mighty wind would have been felt *outside* the room, and would probably have destroyed the house or injured the inmates, if it had been aimed at any one building; but this heavenly gust filled but did not destroy the room, it blessed but did not overthrow the waiting company.

The meaning of the symbol is that as breath, air, [or] wind is the very life of man, so is the Spirit of God, the life of the spiritual man. By him are we quickened at the first; by him are we kept alive afterwards; by him is the inner life nurtured, and increased, and perfected. The breath of the nostrils of the man of God is the Spirit of God.

This holy breath was not only intended to quicken them, but to invigorate them. What a blessing would a breeze be just now to us who sit in this heavy atmosphere! How gladly would we hail a gust from the breezy Down, or a gale from the open sea! If the winds of earth are so refreshing, what must a wind from Heaven be? That rushing mighty wind soon cleared away all earth-engendered damps and vapors; it aroused the disciples and left them braced up for the further work of the Lord. They took in great draughts of heavenly life; they felt animated, aroused, and bestirred. A sacred enthusiasm came upon them, because they were filled with the Holy Ghost; and, girt with that strength, they rose into a nobler form of life than they had known before.

No doubt this wind was intended to show the irresistible power of the Holy Ghost; for simple as the air is, and mobile and apparently feeble, yet set it in motion, and you feel that a thing of life is among you; make that motion more rapid, and who knows the power of the restless giant who has been awakened. See, it becomes a storm, a tempest, a hurricane, a tornado, a cyclone. Nothing can be more potent than the wind when it is thoroughly roused, and so, though the Spirit of God be despised among men, so much so that they do not even believe in his existence, yet let him work with the fullness of his power, and you will see what he can do. He comes softly, breathing like a gentle zephyr which fans the flowers, but does not dislodge the insect of most gauzy wing, and our hearts are comforted. He comes like a stirring breeze, and we are quickened to a livelier diligence: our sails are hoisted and we fly before the gale. He comes with yet greater strength, and we prostrate ourselves in the dust as we hear the thunder of his power, bringing down with a crash false confidences and refuges of lies! How the firm reliances of carnal men, which seemed to stand like rocks, are utterly cast down! How men's hopes, which appeared to be rooted like oaks, are torn up by the roots before the breath of the convincing Spirit! What can stand against him? Oh! that we did but see in these latter days something of that mighty rushing wind, which breaketh the cedars of Lebanon, and sweeps before it all things that would resist its power.

The second Pentecostal symbol was *fire*. Fire, again, is a frequent symbol of Deity. Abraham saw a burning lamp, and Moses beheld a burning bush. When Solomon had built his holy and beautiful house, its consecration lay in the fire of God descending upon the sacrifice to mark that the Lord was there; for when the Lord had dwelt aforetime in the Tabernacle, which was superseded by the Temple, he revealed himself in a pillar of cloud by day and a pillar of fire by night. "Our God is a consuming fire." Hence the symbol of fire is a fit emblem of God the Holy Spirit. Let us adore and worship him. Tongues of flame sitting on each man's head betoken a personal visitation to the mind and heart of each one of the chosen company. Not to consume them came the fires, for no one was injured by the flaming tongue; to men whom the Lord has prepared for his approach, there is no danger in his visitations. They see God, and their lives are preserved; they feel his fires, and are not consumed. This is the privilege of those alone who have been prepared and purified for such fellowship with God.

The intention of the symbol was to show them that the Holy Spirit would illuminate them, as fire gives light. "He shall lead you into all truth." Henceforth they were to be no more children untrained, but to be teachers in Israel, instructors of the nations whom they were to disciple unto Christ: hence the Spirit of light was upon them. But fire doth more than give light: it inflames; and the flames which sat upon each showed them that they were to be ablaze with love, intense with zeal, burning with self-sacrifice; and that they were to go forth among men to speak not with the chill tongue of deliberate logic, but with burning tongues of passionate pleading, persuading and entreating men to come unto Christ, that they might live. The fire signified inspiration. God was about to make them speak under a divine influence, to speak as the Spirit of God should give them utterance. Oh! blessed symbol, would God that all of us experienced its meaning to the full, and that the tongue of fire did sit upon every servant of the Lord. May a fire burn steadily within to destroy our sin, a holy sacrificial flame to make us whole burnt offerings unto God, a never-dying flame of zeal for God and devotion to the cross.

Note that the emblem was not only fire, but a *tongue of fire;* for God meant to have a speaking church: not a church that would fight with the sword (with that weapon we have nought to do) but a church that should have a sword proceeding *out of its mouth,* whose one weapon should be the proclamation of the gospel of Jesus Christ. I should think from what I know of some preachers, that when they had their Pentecost, the influence sat upon them in the form of tongues of flowers! But the apostolic Pentecost knew not flowers, but flames. What fine preaching we have nowadays! What new thoughts, and poetical turns! This is not the style of the Holy Ghost. Soft and gentle is the flow of smooth speech which tells of the dignity of man, the grandeur of the century, the toning down of all punishment for sin, and the probable restoration of all lost spirits, including the arch-fiend himself. This is the Satanic ministry, subtle as the serpent, bland as his seducing words to Eve.

The Holy Ghost calls us not to this mode of speech. Fire, intensity, zeal, passion: [have these] as much as you will; but as for aiming at effect by polished phrases and brilliant periods—these are fitter for those who would deceive men than for those who would tell them the message of the Most High. The style of the Holy Ghost is one which conveys the truth to the mind in the most forcible manner—it is plain but flaming, simple but consuming. The Holy Spirit has never written a cold period throughout the whole Bible, and never did he speak by a man a lifeless word, but evermore he gives and blesses the tongue of fire.

These, then, are the two symbols; and I should like you carefully to observe how the Holy Spirit teaches us by them.

When he came from the Father to his Son Jesus, it was as a dove. Let peace rest on that dear sufferer's soul through all his days of labor and through the passion which would close them. His anointing is that of peace: he needed no tongue of flame, for he was already all on fire with love.

When the Holy Spirit was bestowed by the Son of God upon his disciples, it was as breath—"He breathed on them and said, 'Receive the Holy Ghost.'" To have life more abundantly is a chief necessity of servants of the Lord Jesus, and therefore thus the Holy Ghost visits us.

Now that we have the Holy Spirit from Christ as our inner life and quickening, he also comes upon us with the intent to use us in blessing others, and this is the manner of his visitation—he comes as the wind, which wafts the words we speak, and as fire which, burns a way for the truth we utter. Our words are now full of life and flame; they are borne by the breath of the Spirit, and they fall like fire-flakes, and set the souls of men blazing with desire after God. If the Holy Spirit shall rest upon me or upon you, or upon any of us, to qualify us for service, it shall be after this fashion—not merely of life for ourselves, but of fiery energy in dealing with others. Come on us even now, O rushing mighty wind and tongue of fire, for the world hath great need. It lies stagnant in the malaria of sin and needs a healing wind; it is shrouded in dreadful night, and needs the flaming torch of truth. There is neither health nor light for it but from thee, O blessed Spirit; come, then, upon it through thy people.

Now put these two symbols together; only mind what you are at. Wind and fire together! I have kept them separate in my discourse hitherto; and you have seen power in each one; what are they together? Rushing mighty wind alone: how terrible! Who shall stand against it? See how the gallant ships dash together, and the monarchs of the forest bow their heads. And fire alone! Who shall stand against it when it devours its prey?

But set wind and fire to work in hearty union! Remember the old city of London. When first the flames began, it was utterly impossible to quench them, because the wind fanned the flame, and the buildings gave way before the fire-torrent. Set the prairie on fire. If a rain-shower falls, and the air is still, the grass may perhaps cease to burn, but let the wind encourage the flame, and see how the devourer sweeps along while the tall grass is licked up by tongues of fire. We have lately read of forests on fire. What a sight!

Hear how the mighty trees are crashing in the flame! What can stand against it! The fire setteth the mountains on a blaze. What a smoke blackens the skies; it grows dark at noon. As hill after hill offers up its sacrifice, the timid imagine that the great day of the Lord has come.

If we could see a spiritual conflagration of equal grandeur, it were a consummation devoutly to be wished. O God, send us the Holy Ghost in this fashion: give us both the breath of spiritual life and the fire of unconquerable zeal, till nation after nation shall yield to the sway of Jesus. O thou who art our God, answer us by fire, we pray thee. Answer us both by wind and fire, and then shall we see thee to be God indeed. The kingdom comes not, and the work is flagging. O that thou wouldest send the wind and the fire! Thou wilt do this when we are all of one accord, all believing, all expecting, all prepared by prayer. Lord, bring us to this waiting state.

II. Secondly, my brethren, follow me while I call your attention to *the immediate effects* of this descent of the Holy Spirit, for these symbols were not sent in vain.

There were two immediate effects: the first was *filling*, and the second was the *gift of utterance*. I call special attention to the first, namely, filling: "It filled all the house where they were sitting": and it did not merely fill the house, but the men—"They were all filled with the Holy Ghost." When they stood up to speak, even the ribald mockers in the crowd noticed this, for they said, "These men are full," and though they added "with new wine," yet they evidently detected a singular fullness about them. We are poor, empty things by nature, and useless while we remain so: we need to be filled with the Holy Ghost. Some people seem to believe in the Spirit of God giving utterance only, and they look upon instruction in divine things as of secondary importance. Dear, dear me, what trouble comes when we act upon that theory! How the empty vessels clatter, and rattle, and sound! Men in such case utter a wonderful amount of nothing, and even when that nothing is set on fire it does not come to much. I dread a revival of that sort, where the first thing and the last thing is everlasting talk. Those who set up for teachers ought to be themselves taught of the Lord; how can they communicate that which they have not received? Where the Spirit of God is truly at work, he first fills and then gives utterance: that is his way. Oh that you and I were at this moment filled with the Holy Ghost. "Full!" Then they were not cold, and dead, and empty of life as we sometimes are. "Full." Then there was no room for anything else in any one of them! They were too completely occupied by the heavenly power to have room for the desires of the flesh. Fear was banished, every minor motive was expelled: the Spirit of God, as it flooded their very being, drove out of them everything that was extraneous. They had many faults and many infirmities before, but that day, when they were filled with the Spirit of God, faults and infirmities were no more perceptible. They became different men from what they had ever been before: men full of God are the reverse of men full of self, The difference between an empty man and a full man is something very wonderful. Let a thirsty person have an empty vessel handed to him. There may be much noise in the handing, but what a mockery it is as it touches his lips. But fill it with refreshing water, and perhaps there may be all the more silence in the passing it, for a full cup needs careful handling; but oh, what a blessing when it reaches the man's lips! Out of a full vessel he may drink his fill. Out of a full church, the world shall receive salvation, but never out of an empty one. The first thing we want as a church is to be filled with the Holy Ghost: the gift of utterance will then come as a matter of course.

They ask me, "May the sisters speak anywhere? If not in the assembly, may they not speak in smaller meetings?" I answer, yes, if they are full of the Holy Ghost. Shall this brother or that be allowed to speak? Certainly, if he be filled, he may flow. May a layman preach? I know nothing about laymen except that I am no cleric myself; but let all speak who are full of the Holy Ghost. "Spring up, O well." If it be a fountain of living water, who would restrain it, who *could* restrain it? Let him overflow who is full, but mind he does not set up to pour out when there is nothing in him; for if he counts it his official duty to go pouring out, pouring out, pouring out, at unreasonable length, and yet nothing comes of it, I am sure he acts, not by the Holy Spirit, but according to his own vanity.

The next Pentecostal symbol was *utterance*. As soon as the Spirit of God filled them, they began to speak at once. It seems to me that they began to speak before the people had come together. They could not help it; the inner forces demanded expression, and they must speak. So when the Spirit of God really comes upon a man, he does not wait till he has gathered an audience of the size which he desires, but he seizes the next opportunity. He speaks to one person, he speaks to two, he speaks to three, to anybody: he must speak, for he is full, and must have vent.

When the Spirit of God fills a man, he speaks so as to be understood. The crowd spake different languages, and these Spirit-taught men spoke to them in the language of the country in which they were born. This is one of the signs of the Spirit's utterance. If my friend over yonder talks in a Latinized style to a company of costermongers [street venders], I will warrant you the Holy Ghost has nothing to do with him. If a learned brother fires over the heads of his congregation with a grand oration, he may trace his elocution, if he likes, to Cicero and Demosthenes, but do not let him ascribe it to the Holy Spirit, for that is not after His manner. The Spirit of God speaks so that his words may be understood, and if there be any obscurity, it lies in the language used by the Lord himself. The crowd not only understood, but they felt. There were lancets in this Pentecostal preaching, and the hearers "were pricked in the heart." The truth wounded men, and the slain of the Lord were many, for the wounds were in the most vital part. They could not make it out: they had heard speakers before, but this was quite a different thing. The men spake fire-flakes, and one hearer cried to his fellow, "What is this?" The preachers were speaking flame, and the fire dropped into the hearts of men till they were amazed and confounded.

Those are the two effects of the Holy Spirit: a fullness of the Spirit in the ministry and the church; and next, a fire ministry, and a church on fire, speaking so as to be felt and understood by those around. Causes produce effects like themselves, and this wind and fire ministry soon did its work. We read that this "was noised abroad." Of course it was, because there had been a noise as of a rushing mighty wind. Next to that we read that all the people came together, and were confounded. There was naturally a stir, for a great wind from Heaven was rushing. All were amazed and astonished, and while some enquired believingly, others began to mock. Of course they did: there was a fire burning, and fire is a dividing thing, and this fire began to separate between the precious and the vile, as it always will do when it comes into operation. We may expect at the beginning of a true revival to observe a movement among the people, a noise, and a stir. These things are not done in a corner. Cities will know of the presence of God, and crowds will be attracted by the event.

This was the immediate effect of the Pentecostal marvel, and I shall now ask you to follow me to my third point, which is this:

III. The Holy Spirit being thus at work, *what was the most prominent subject which these full men began to preach about, with words of fire?*

Suppose that the Holy Spirit should work mightily in the church, what would our ministers preach about? We should have a revival, should we not, of the old discussions about predestination and free agency? I do not think so: these are happily ended, for they tended towards bitterness, and for the most part the disputants were not equal to their task. We should hear a great deal about the pre-millennial and the post-millennial advent, should we not? I do not think so. I never saw much of the Spirit of God in discussions or dreamings upon times and seasons which are not clearly revealed. Should we not hear learned essays upon advanced theology? No, sir; when the devil inspires the church, we have modern theology; but when the Spirit of God is among us, that rubbish is shot out with loathing.

What did these men preach about? Their hearers said, "We do hear them speak in our own tongues the wonderful works of God." Their subject was the *wonderful works of God*. Oh, that this might be, to my dying day, my sole and only topic—"The wonderful works of God." For, first, they spoke of *redemption*, that wonderful work of God. Peter's sermon was a specimen of how they spoke of it. He told the people that Jesus was the Son of God, that they had crucified and slain him, but that he had come to redeem men, and that there was salvation through his precious blood. He preached redemption! Oh, how this land will echo again and again with "Redemption, redemption, redemption,

redemption by the precious blood," when the Holy Ghost is with us. This is fit fuel for the tongue of flame: this is something worthy to be wafted by the divine wind. "God was in Christ, reconciling the world unto himself, not imputing their trespasses unto them." "The blood of Jesus Christ his Son cleanseth us from all sin." This is one of the wonderful works of God of which we can never make too frequent mention.

They certainly spoke of the next wonderful work of God, namely, *regeneration*. There was no concealing of the work of the Holy Spirit in that primitive ministry. It was brought to the front. Peter said, "Ye shall receive the Holy Ghost." The preachers of Pentecost told of the Spirit's work by the Spirit's power: conversion, repentance, renewal, faith, holiness, and such things were freely spoken of and ascribed to their real author, the divine Spirit. If the Spirit of God shall give us once again a full and fiery ministry, we shall hear it clearly proclaimed, "Ye must be born again," and we shall see a people forthcoming which are born, not of blood, nor of the will of the flesh, but of the will of God, and by the energy which cometh from Heaven. A Holy Ghost ministry cannot be silent about the Holy Ghost and his sacred operations upon the heart.

And very plainly they spoke on a third wonderful work of God, namely, *remission of sin*. This was the point that Peter pushed home to them, that on repentance they should receive remission of sins. What a blessed message is this—pardon for crimes of deepest dye, a pardon bought with Jesus' blood, free pardon, full pardon, irreversible pardon given to the vilest of the vile when they ground their weapons of rebellion, and bow at the feet that once were nailed to the tree. If we would prove ourselves to be under divine influence, we must keep to the divine message of fatherly forgiveness to returning prodigals. What happier word can we deliver?

These are the doctrines which the Holy Ghost will revive in the midst of the land when he worketh mightily—redemption, regeneration, remission. If you would have the Spirit of God resting on your labors, dear brothers and sisters, keep these three things ever to the front, and make all men hear in their own tongue the wonderful works of God.

IV. I shall close by noticing, in the fourth place, what were the *glorious results* of all this.

Have patience with me, if you find the details somewhat long. The result of the Spirit coming as wind and fire—filling and giving utterance—was, first, in the hearers' *deep feeling*. There was never, perhaps, in the world such a feeling excited by the language of mortal man as that which was aroused in the crowds in Jerusalem on that day. You might have seen a group here, and a group there, all listening to the same story of the wondrous works of God, and all stirred and affected; for the heavenly wind and fire went with the preaching, and they could not help feeling its power. We are told that they were pricked in the heart. They had painful emotions, they felt wounds which killed their enmity. The word struck at the center of their being: it pierced the vital point. Alas, people come into our places of worship nowadays to hear the preacher, and their friends ask them on their return, "How did you like him?" Was that your errand, to see how you *liked* him? What practical benefit is there in such a mode of using the servants of God? Are we sent among you to give opportunities for criticism? Yet the mass of men seem to think that we are nothing better than fiddlers or play-actors, who come upon the stage to help you while away an hour. O my hearers, if we are true to our God, and true to you, ours is a more solemn business than most men dream. The object of all true preaching is the heart: we aim at divorcing the heart from sin, and wedding it to Christ. Our ministry has failed, and has not the divine seal set upon it, unless it makes men tremble, makes them sad, and then anon brings them to Christ, and causes them to rejoice. Sermons are to be heard in thousands, and yet how little comes of them all, because the heart is not aimed at, or else the archers miss the mark. Alas, our hearers do not present their hearts as our target, but leave them at home, and bring us only their ears, or their heads. Here we need the divine aid. Pray mightily that the Spirit of God may rest upon all who speak in God's name, for then they will create deep feeling in their hearers!

Then followed an *earnest enquiry.* "They were pricked in their heart, and they said to Peter and the rest of the apostles, 'Men and brethren, what shall we do?'" Emotion is of itself but a poor result unless it leads to practical action. To make men feel is well enough, but it must be a feeling which impels them to immediate movement, or at least to earnest enquiry as to what they shall do. O Spirit of God, if thou wilt rest on me, even me, men shall not hear and go their way and forget what they have heard! They will arise and seek the Father, and taste his love. If thou wouldst rest on all the brotherhood that publish thy word, men would not merely weep while they hear, and be affected while the discourse lasts, but they would go their way to ask, "What must we do to be saved?" This is what we need. We do not require new preachers, but we need anew anointing of the Spirit. We do not require novel forms of service, but we want the fire Spirit, the wind Spirit to work by us till everywhere men cry, "What must we do to be saved?"

Then came a *grand reception of the word.* We are told that they gladly received the word, and they received it in two senses: first, Peter bade them *repent*, and so they did. They were pricked to the heart from compunction on account of what they had done to Jesus, and they sorrowed after a godly sort, and quitted their sins. They also *believed* in him whom they had slain, and accepted him as their Savior there and then, without longer hesitancy. They trusted in him whom God had set forth to be a propitiation, and thus they fully received the word. Repentance and faith make up a complete reception of Christ and they bad both of these. Why should we not see this divine result today? We shall see it in proportion to our faith.

But what next? Why, they were *baptized* directly. Having repented and believed, the next step was to make confession of their faith; and they did not postpone that act for a single day; why should they? Willing hands were there, the whole company of the faithful were all glad to engage in the holy service, and that same day were they baptized into the name of the Father, and of the Son, and of the Holy Spirit. If the Holy Ghost were fully with us, we should never have to complain that many believers never confess their faith, for they would be eager to confess the Savior's name in his own appointed way. Backwardness to be baptized comes too often of fear of persecution, indecision, love of ease, pride, or disobedience; but all these vanish when the heavenly wind and fire are doing their sacred work. Sinful diffidence soon disappears, sinful shame of Jesus is no more seen, and hesitancy and delay are banished for ever when the Holy Spirit works with power.

Furthermore, there was not merely this immediate confession, but as a result of the Spirit of God, there was *great steadfastness*. "They continued steadfastly in the apostles' doctrine." We have had plenty of revivals of the human sort, and their results have been sadly disappointing. Under excitement, nominal converts have been multiplied: but where are they after a little testing? I am sadly compelled to own that, so far as I can observe, there has been much sown, and very little reaped that was worth reaping, from much of that which has been called revival. Our hopes were flattering as a dream; but the apparent result has vanished like a vision of the night. But where the Spirit of God is really at work, the converts stand: they are well rooted and grounded, and hence they are not carried about by every wind of doctrine, but they continue steadfast in the apostolic truth.

We see next that there was *abundant worship of God,* for they were steadfast not only in the doctrine, but in breaking of bread, and in prayer, and in fellowship. There was no difficulty in getting a prayer meeting then, no difficulty in maintaining daily communion then, no want of holy fellowship then; for the Spirit of God was among them, and the ordinances were precious in their eyes. "Oh," say some, "if we could get this minister or that evangelist, we should do well." Brothers, if you had the *Holy Spirit,* you would have everything else growing out of his presence, for all good things are summed up in him.

Next to this, there came *striking generosity*. Funds were not hard to raise: liberality overflowed its banks, for believers poured all that they had into the common fund. Then was it indeed seen to be true that the silver and the gold are the Lord's. When the Spirit of God operates powerfully, there is little need to issue telling appeals for widows and orphans, or to go down on your knees and plead for missionary fields which cannot be occupied for want of money. At this moment, our village churches can scarcely support their pastors at a starvation rate; but I believe that if the Spirit of God will visit all the churches, means will be forthcoming to keep all going right vigorously. If this does not happen, I tremble for our Nonconformist churches, for the means of their existence will be absent; both as to spiritual and temporal supplies, they will utterly fail. There will be no lack of money when there is no lack of grace. When the Spirit of God comes, those who have substance yield it to their Lord: those who have but little, grow rich by giving of that little, and those who are already rich become happy by consecrating what they have. There is no need to rattle the box when the rushing mighty wind is heard, and the fire is dissolving all hearts in love.

Then came *continual gladness.* "They did eat their meat with gladness." They were not merely glad at prayer-meetings and sermons, but glad at breakfast and at supper. Whatever they had to eat, they were for singing over it. Jerusalem was the happiest city that ever was when the Spirit of God was there. The disciples were singing from morning to night, and I have no doubt the outsiders asked, "What is it all about?" The temple was never so frequented as then; there was never such singing before; the very streets of Jerusalem, and the Hill of Zion, rang with the songs of the once despised Galileans.

They were full of gladness, and that gladness showed itself in praising God. I have no doubt they broke out now and then in the services with shouts of, "Glory! Hallelujah!" I should not wonder but what all propriety was scattered to the winds. They were so glad, so exhilarated, that they were ready to leap for joy. Of course we never say "Amen," or "Glory!" now. We have grown to be so frozenly proper that we never interrupt a service in any way, because, to tell the truth, we are not so particularly glad, we are not so specially full of praise, that we want to do anything of the sort. Alas, we have lost very much of the Spirit of God, and much of the joy and gladness which attend his presence, and so we have settled into a decorous apathy! We gather the pinks [flowers] of propriety instead of the palm branches of praise. God send us a season of glorious disorder. Oh, for a sweep of wind that will set the seas in motion, and make our ironclad brethren now lying so quietly at anchor to roll from stem to stern. As for us, who are as the little ships, we will fly before the gale if it will but speed us to our desired haven. Oh, for fire to fall again—fire which shall affect the most stolid! This is a sure remedy for indifference. When a flake of fire falls into a man's bosom, he knows it, and when the word of God comes home to a man's soul, he knows it too. Oh that such fire might first sit upon the disciples, and then fall on all [those] around!

For, to close, there was then a *daily increase* of the church—"The Lord added to the church daily such as should be saved." Conversion was going on perpetually; additions to the church were not events which happened once a year, but they were everyday matters, "so mightily grew the word of God and prevailed."

O Spirit of God, thou art ready to work with us today even as thou didst then! Stay [delay] not, we beseech thee, but work at once. Break down every barrier that hinders the incoming of thy might. Overturn, overturn, O sacred wind! Consume all obstacles, O heavenly fire, and give us now both hearts of flame and tongues of fire to preach thy reconciling word, for Jesus' sake. Amen.

The Indwelling and Outflowing of the Holy Spirit

Delivered on Lord's Day morning, May 28, 1882, at the Metropolitan
Tabernacle, Newington. No. 1662.

*He that believeth on me, as the scripture hath said, out of his belly shall flow rivers of
living water. (But this spake he of the Spirit, which they that believe on him should
receive: for the Holy Ghost was not yet given; because that Jesus was not yet
glorified.)—John 7:38–39*

*Nevertheless I tell you the truth; it is expedient for you that I go away: for if I go not
away, the Comforter will not come unto you; but if I depart, I will send him
unto you.—John 16:7*

It is essential, dear friends, that we should worship the living and true God. It will
be ill for us if it can be said, "Ye worship ye know not what." "Thou shalt worship the Lord thy God, and him only shalt thou serve." The heathen err from this command by multiplying gods, and making this and that image to be the object of their adoration. Their excess runs to gross superstition and idolatry. I fear that sometimes we who "profess and call ourselves Christians" err in exactly the opposite direction. Instead of worshipping *more* than God, I fear we worship *less* than God. This appears when we forget to pay due adoration to the Holy Spirit of God. The true God is triune: Father, Son, and Holy Spirit; and though there be but one

God, yet that one God has manifested himself to us in the trinity of his sacred persons. If then, I worship the Father and the Son, but forget or neglect to adore the Holy Spirit, I worship less than God. While the poor heathen, in his ignorance, goes far beyond and transgresses, I must take care lest I fall short and fail too. What a grievous thing it will be if we do not pay that loving homage and reverence to the Holy Spirit which is so justly his due. May it not be the fact that we enjoy less of his power and see less of his working in the world because the church of God has not been sufficiently mindful of him? It is a blessed thing to preach the work of Jesus Christ, but it is an evil thing to omit the work of the Holy Ghost; for the work of the Lord Jesus itself is no blessing to that man who does not know the work of the Holy Spirit. There is the ransom price, but it is only through the Spirit that we know the redemption: there is the precious blood, but it is as though the fountain had never been filled, unless the Spirit of God lead us with repenting faith to wash therein. The bandage is soft and the ointment is effectual, but the wound will never be healed till the Holy Spirit shall apply that which the great Physician has provided. Let us not therefore be found neglectful of the work of the divine Spirit, lest we incur guilt, and inflict upon ourselves serious damage.

You that are believers have the most forcible reasons to hold the Holy Ghost in the highest esteem; for what are you now without him? What were you, and what would you still have been, if it had not been for his gracious work upon you? He quickened you, else you had not been in the living family of God today. He gave you understanding that you might know the truth, else would you have been as ignorant as the carnal world is at this hour. It was he that awakened your conscience, convincing you of sin: it was he that gave you abhorrence of sin, and led you to repent: it was he that taught you to believe, and made you see that glorious Person who is to be believed, even Jesus, the Son of God. The Spirit has wrought in you your faith and love and hope, and every grace. There is not a jewel upon the neck of your soul which he did not place there.

> For every virtue we possess,
> And every victory won,
> And every thought of holiness,
> Are his alone.

What have we learned—if we have learned aright—except by the teaching of the Holy Ghost? What can we say either in prayer to God or in teaching to men that shall be acceptable, unless we receive the unction of the Holy One of Israel? Brethren, who is it that has comforted us in our distresses, directed us in our perplexities, strengthened us in our weaknesses, and helped our infirmities in ten thousand ways? Is it not the Comforter whom the Father hath sent in Jesus' name? Can I speak too highly of the riches of his grace toward us? Can I too much extol the love of the Spirit? I know I cannot, and you that know what he has wrought in you, delight to hear him highly spoken of and his work and offices set forth. We are bound by a thousand ties to seek his honor who has wrought in us our salvation. Let us never grieve him by our ingratitude, but let us endeavor to extol him. For my part, it shall be the labor of this morning to impress upon you the necessity for his work, and the superlative value of it.

Beloved brethren, notwithstanding all that the Spirit of God has already done in us, it is very possible that we have missed a large part of the blessing which he is willing to give, for he is able to "do exceeding abundantly above all that we ask or think." We have already come to Jesus, and we have drunk of the life-giving stream: our thirst is quenched, and we are made to live in him. Is this all? Now that we are living in him, and rejoicing to do so, have we come to the end of the matter? Assuredly not. We have reached as far as that first exhortation of the Master, "If any man thirst, let him come unto me and drink": but do you think that the generality of the church of God have ever advanced to the next, "He that believeth on me, as the Scripture hath said, out of his belly shall flow rivers of living water"? I think I am not going beyond the grievous truth if I say that only here and there will you find men and women who have believed up to that point. Their thirst is quenched, as I have said, and they live, and because Jesus lives, they shall live also; but health and vigor they have not—they have life, but they have not life more abundantly. They have little life with which to act upon others: they have no energy welling up and overflowing to go streaming out of them like rivers. They have not thought it possible, perhaps, or thinking it possible they have not imagined it possible to themselves; or believing it possible to themselves, they have not aspired to it, but they have stopped short of the fullest blessing. Their wading in to the sacred river has contented them, and they know nothing of "waters to swim in." Like the Israelites of old, they are slow to possess all the land of promise, but sit down when the war has hardly begun. Brothers, let us go in to get of God all that God will give us: let us set our heart upon this, that we mean to have by God's help all that the infinite goodness of God is ready to bestow. Let us not be satisfied with the sip that saves, but let us go on to the baptism which buries the flesh and raises us in the likeness of the risen Lord: even that baptism into the Holy Ghost and into fire which makes us spiritual and sets us all on flame with zeal for the glory of God and eagerness for usefulness by which that glory may be increased among the sons of men.

Thus I introduce you to my texts, and by their guidance we will enter upon the further consideration of the operations of the Holy Spirit, especially of those to which we would aspire.

I. We will commence with the remark that *the work of the Spirit is intimately connected with the work of Christ.*

It is a great pity when persons preach the Holy Spirit's work so as to obscure the work of Christ; and I have known some do that, for they have held up before the sinner's eye the inward experience of believers, instead of lifting up first and foremost the crucified Savior, to whom we must look and live. The gospel is not "Behold the Spirit of God" but "Behold the Lamb of God." It is an equal pity when Christ is so preached that the Holy Spirit is ignored; as if faith in Jesus prevented the necessity of the new birth, and *imputed* righteousness rendered *imparted* righteousness needless. Have I not often reminded you that in the third chapter of John—where Jesus taught Nicodemus the doctrine, "Except a man be born again of water and of the spirit, he cannot enter the kingdom of Heaven,"—we also read those blessed words,

> And as Moses lifted up the serpent in the wilderness, even so must the Son of man be lifted up: that whosoever believeth in him should not perish, but have eternal life. For God so loved the world, that he gave his only begotten Son, that whosoever believeth in him should not perish, but have everlasting life.

The necessity for regeneration by the Spirit is there put very clearly, and so is the free promise that those who trust in Jesus shall be saved. This is what we ought to do: we must take care to let both these truths stand out most distinctly—with equal prominence. They are intertwined with each other and are necessary, each to each: what God hath joined together, let no man put asunder.

They are so joined together that, first of all, *the Holy Spirit was not given until Jesus had been glorified.* Carefully note our first text; it is a very striking one: "This spake he out of the Spirit, which they that believe on him should receive, for the Holy Ghost was not yet." The word "given" is not in the original: it is inserted by the translators to help out the sense, and they were perhaps wise in making such an addition, but the words are more forcible by themselves. How strong the statement, "For the Holy Ghost was not yet." Of course, we none of us dream that the Holy Spirit was not yet existing, for he is eternal and self-existent, being most truly God, but he was not yet in fellowship with man to the full extent in which he now is, since Jesus Christ is glorified. The near and dear intercourse of God with man which is expressed by the indwelling of the Spirit could not take place till redeeming work was done and the Redeemer was exalted. As far as men were concerned, and the fullness of the blessing was concerned, indicated by the outflowing rivers of living water, the Spirit of God was not yet.

"Oh," say you, "but was not the Spirit of God in the church in the wilderness, and with the saints of God in all former ages?" I answer, "Certainly, but not in the manner in which the Spirit of God now resides in the church of Jesus Christ."

You read of the prophets, and of one and another gracious man, that the Spirit of God came upon them, seized them, moved them, spake by them; but he did not *dwell* in them. His operations upon men were a coming and a going: they were carried away by the Spirit of God, and came under his power, but the Spirit of God did not rest upon them or abide in them. Occasionally the sacred endowment of the Spirit of God came upon them, but they knew not "the communion of the Holy Ghost." As a French pastor very sweetly puts it,

> He appeared *unto* men; he did not incarnate himself *in* man. His action was intermittent: he went and came, like the dove which Noah sent forth from the ark, and which went to and fro, finding no rest; while in the new dispensation he *dwells*— he abides in the heart, as the dove, his emblem, which John the Baptist saw descending and alighting upon the head of Jesus. Affianced of the soul, the Spirit went off to see his betrothed, but was not yet one with her; the marriage was not consummated until the Pentecost, after the glorification of Jesus Christ.

You know how our Lord puts it, "He dwelleth with you, and shall be in you." That indwelling is another thing from being *with* us. The Holy Spirit was *with* the Apostles in the days when Jesus was with them; but he was not *in* them in the sense in which he filled them at and after the Day of Pentecost. The operations of the Spirit of God before our Lord's ascension were not according to the full measure of the gospel, but now the Spirit of God has been poured upon us from on high; now he has descended, and now he abides in the midst of the church, and now we enter into him and are baptized into the Holy Ghost, while he enters into us and makes our bodies to be his temples. Jesus said, "I will send you another Comforter, which shall abide with you forever;" not coming and going, but remaining in the midst of the church. This shows how intimately the gift of the Holy Ghost is connected with our Lord Jesus Christ, inasmuch as in the fullest sense of his indwelling the Holy Ghost could not be with us until Christ had been glorified. It has been well observed that our Lord sent out seventy evangelists to preach the gospel, even as he had aforetime sent out the twelve; and no doubt they preached with great zeal and produced much stir; but the Holy Ghost never took the trouble to preserve one of their sermons, or even the notes of one. I have not the slightest doubt that they were very crude and incomplete, showing more of human zeal than of divine unction, and hence they are forgotten; but no sooner had the Holy Spirit fallen than Peter's first sermon is recorded, and henceforth we have frequent notes of the utterances of apostles, deacons, and evangelists. There was an abiding fullness, and an overflowing of blessing, out of the souls of the saints after the Lord was glorified, which was not existing among men before that time.

Observe, too, that the Holy Spirit was given after the ascent of our divine Lord into his glory, partly *to make that ascent the more renowned*. When he ascended up on high, he led captivity captive and gave gifts to men. These gifts were men in whom the Holy Spirit dwelt, who preached the gospel unto the nations. The shedding of the Holy Spirit upon the assembled disciples on that memorable day was the glorification of the risen Christ upon the earth. I know not in what way the Father could have made the glory of Heaven so effectually to flow from the heights of the New Jerusalem and to come streaming down among the sons of men as by giving that chief of all gifts—the gift of the Holy Spirit, when the Lord had risen and gone into his glory. With emphasis, may I say of the Spirit at Pentecost, that he glorified Christ by descending at such a time. What grander celebration could there have been? Heaven rang with hosannas, and earth echoed the joy. The descending Spirit is the noblest testimony among men to the glory of the ascended Redeemer.

Was not the Spirit of God also sent at that time as *an evidence of our divine Master's acceptance?* Did not the Father thus say to the church, "My Son has finished the work, and has fully entered into his glory, therefore give I you of the Holy Spirit"? If you would know what a harvest is to come of the sowing of the bloody sweat and of the death wounds, see the first fruits. Behold how the Holy Spirit is given, himself to be the first fruits, the earnest of the glory which shall yet be revealed in us. I want no better attestation from God of the finished work of Jesus than this blazing, flaming seal of tongues of fire upon the heads of the disciples. He must have done his work, or such a boon as this would not have come from it.

Moreover, if you desire to see how the work of the Spirit comes to us in connection with the work of Christ, *recollect that it is the Spirit's work to bear witness of Jesus Christ.* He does not take of a thousand different matters and show them to us, but he shall take "of mine," saith Christ, "and he shall show them unto you." The Spirit of God is engaged in a service in which the Lord Jesus Christ is the beginning and the end. He comes to men that they may come to Jesus. Hence he comes to convince us of sin, that he may reveal the great sacrifice of sin: he comes to convince us of righteousness, that we may see the righteousness of Christ; and of judgment, that we may be prepared to meet him when he shall come to judge the quick and dead. Do not think that the Spirit of God has come or ever will come among us to teach us a new gospel, or something other than is written in the Scriptures. Men come to me with their fudges and fancies, and tell me that they were revealed to them by the Holy Spirit. I abhor their blasphemous impertinence, and refuse to listen to them for a minute. They tell me this and that absurdity, and then father it upon the Spirit of wisdom. It is enough to try our patience to hear their foolish ravings but to find the Holy Spirit charged with them is more than we can bear. We have tests and judgments by which to know whether they who claim to speak by the Holy Spirit do so or not: for the testimony of the Spirit is ever most honorable to our Lord Jesus Christ, and does not concern itself with the trifles of time and the follies of the flesh.

It is by the gospel of Jesus Christ that the Spirit of God works in the hearts of men. "Faith cometh by hearing, and hearing by the word of God": the Holy Spirit uses the hearing of the word of God for the conviction, conversion, consolation, and sanctification of men. His usual and ordinary method of operation is to fasten upon the mind the things of God, and to put life and force into the consideration of them. He revives in men's memories things that have long been forgotten, and he frequently makes these the means of affecting the heart and conscience. The men can hardly recollect hearing these truths, but still they were heard by them at some time or other. Saving truths are such matters as are contained in their substance in the word of God, and lie within the range of the teaching, or the person, or work, or offices of our Lord Jesus Christ. It is the Spirit's one business here below to reveal Christ to us and in us, and to that work he steadily adheres.

Moreover, *the Holy Spirit's work is to conform us to the likeness of Jesus Christ.* He is not working us to this or that human ideal, but he is working us into the likeness of Christ, that he may be the first-born among many brethren. Jesus Christ is that standard and model to which the Spirit of God by his sanctifying processes is bringing us till Christ be formed in us the hope of glory.

Evermore it is for the glory of Jesus that the Spirit of God works. He works not for the glory of a church or of a community: he works not for the honor of a man or for the distinction of a sect: his one great object is to glorify Christ. "He shall glorify me" is our Savior's declaration, and when he takes of the things of Christ and shows them unto us, we are led more and more to reverence and love and adore our blessed Lord Jesus Christ.

I will not detain you longer with this. You will see how the works of Jesus and of the Spirit are joined together indissolubly, so that we may neither set the work of Jesus before the work of the Spirit, nor the work of the Spirit before the work of Jesus, but we are glad to joy in both and to make much of them. As we delight in the Father's love and the grace of our Lord Jesus, so do we equally rejoice in the communion of the Holy Ghost, and these three agree in one.

II. We will now advance another step, and here we shall need our second text. *The operations of the Holy Spirit are of incomparable value.*

They are of such incomparable value that the very best thing we can think of was not thought to be so precious as these are. Our Lord himself says, "It is expedient for you that I go away: for if I go not away, the Comforter will not come unto you." Beloved friends, the presence of Jesus Christ was of inestimable value to his disciples, and yet it was not such an advantage to his servants as the indwelling of the Holy Spirit. Is not this a wonderful statement? Well might our Lord preface it by saying, "Now I tell you the truth," as if he felt that they would find it a hard saying, for a hard saying it is. Consider for a moment what Christ was to his disciples while he was here, and then see what must be the value of the Spirit's operations when it is expedient that they should lose all that blessing in order to receive the Spirit of God. Our Lord Jesus Christ was to them their teacher—they had learned everything from his lips. He was their leader—they had never to ask what to do, they had only to follow in his steps. He was their defender— whenever the Pharisees or Sadducees assailed them he was like a brazen wall to them. He was their comforter—in all times of grief they resorted to him, and his dear sympathetic heart poured out floods of comfort at once. What if I were to say that the Lord Jesus Christ was everything to them, their all in all? What a father is to his children, ay, what a mother is to her suckling, that was Jesus Christ to his disciples; and yet the Spirit of God's abiding in the church is better even than all this.

Now take another thought. What would you think if Jesus Christ were to come among us now as in the days of his flesh. I mean, not as he will come, but as he appeared at his first advent. What joy it would give you! Oh, the delights, the heavenly joys, to hear that Jesus Christ of Nazareth was on earth again, a man among men! Should we not clap our hands for joy? Our one question would be, "Master, where dwellest thou?" For we should all long to live just where he lived. We could then sympathize with the blacks when they flocked into Washington in large numbers to take up their residence there [after the Civil War]. Why, think you, did they come to live in that city? Because Massa Abraham Lincoln lived there, who had set them free, and they thought it would be glorious to live as near as possible to their great friend. If Jesus lived anywhere—it would not matter where, if it were in the desert or on the bleakest of mountains—there would be a rush to the place. How would the spot be crowded! What rents they would pay for the worst of tenements if Jesus was but in the neighborhood! But do you not see the difficulty? We could not all get near him in any literal or corporeal fashion. Now that the church is multiplied into millions of believers, some of the Lord's followers would never be able to see him, and the most could only hope to speak with him now and then. In the days of his flesh, the twelve might see him every day, and so might the little company of disciples, but the case is altered now that multitudes are trusting in his name.

If our Lord were at this time living in the United States, we should be much grieved to have an ocean between us and our leader. All the companies that could be formed would not be able to run enough boats to carry us over. If the Master personally came here to this little island, it would not hold all the vast company of the faithful who would flock to it. It is much better to have the Holy Spirit, because he is dwelling *with* us and *in* us. The difficulties of the bodily presence are too great, and so, though we would be thankful, like the apostles, if we had known Christ after the flesh, yet we do not marvel that they expressed little sorrow when they said that, after the flesh they knew even him no more. The Comforter had filled the void caused by his absence, and made them rejoice, because the Lord had gone unto his Father.

Are we not apt to think that if our Lord Jesus were here, it would give unspeakable strength to the church? Would not the enemy be convinced if they saw him? No, they would not. If they hear not Moses and the prophets, neither would they be converted, though one rose from the dead. Jesus rose, but they did not therefore believe. If our Lord had lingered here all this while, his personal presence would not have converted unbelievers, for nothing can do that but the power of the Holy Ghost.

"But," you say, "surely it would thrill the church with enthusiasm." Fancy the Lord himself standing on this platform this morning in the same garb as when he was upon earth. Oh, what rapturous worship! What burning zeal! What enthusiasm! We should go home in such a state of excitement as we never were in before. Yes, it is even so, but then the Lord is not going to carry on his kingdom by the force of mere mental excitement, not even by such enthusiasm as would follow the sight of his person. The work of the Holy Spirit is a truer work, a deeper work, a surer work, and will more effectually achieve the purposes of God than even would the enthusiasm to which we should be stirred by the bodily presence of our well-beloved Savior. The work is to be spiritual, and therefore the visible presence has departed. It is better that it should be so. We must walk by faith, and by faith alone—how could we do this if we could see the Lord with these mortal eyes? This is the dispensation of the unseen Spirit, in which we render glory to God by trusting in his word and relying upon the unseen energy. Now, faith works, and faith triumphs, though the world seeth not the foundation upon which faith is built, for the Spirit who works in us cannot be discerned by carnal minds—the world seeth him not, neither knoweth him.

Thus you see that the operations of the Holy Spirit must be inestimably precious. There is no calculating their value, since it is expedient that we lose the bodily presence of Christ rather than remain without the indwelling of the Spirit of God.

III. Now go back to my first text again, and follow me in the third head.

Those operations of the Spirit of God, of which I am afraid some Christians are almost ignorant, are of wondrous power. The text says, "He that believeth on me, out of the midst of him shall flow rivers of living water." *These operations are of marvellous power.* Brethren, do you understand my text? Do rivers of living water flow out of you?

Notice, first, that this is to be an inward work: the rivers of living water are to flow out of the midst of the man. The words are according to our version, "Out of his belly"—that is, from his heart and soul. The rivers do not flow out of his mouth: the promised power is not oratory. We have had plenty of words, floods of words; but this is *heart* work. The source of the rivers is found in the inner life. It is an inward work at its fountain head. It is not a work of talent, and ability, and show, and glitter, and glare: it is altogether an inward work. The life-flood is to come out of the man's inmost self, out of the bowels and essential being of the man. Homage is shown too generally to outward form and external observance, though these soon lose their interest and power. But when the Spirit of God rests within a man, it exercises a home rule [self-government] within him, and he gives great attention to what an old divine was wont to call "the home department." Alas, many neglect the realm within ,which is the chief province under our care. O my brother in Christ, if you would be useful, begin with yourself. It is out of your very soul that a blessing must come. It cannot come out of you if it is not in you: and it cannot be in you unless God the Holy Ghost places it there.

Next, *it is life-giving work*. Out of the heart of the man, out of the center of his life, are to flow rivers of living water; that is to say, he is instrumentally to communicate to others the divine life. When he speaks, when he prays, when he acts; he shall so speak and pray and act that there shall be going out of him an emanation [emission] which is full of the life of grace and godliness. He shall be a light by which others shall see. His life shall be the means of kindling life in other men's bosoms. "Out of his belly shall flow rivers of living water."

Note *the plenitude of it*. The figure would have been a surprising one if it had said, "Out of him shall flow a *river* of living water"; but it is not so: it says *rivers*. Have you ever stood by the side of a very abundant spring? We have some such not far from London. You see the water bubbling up from many little mouths. Observe the sand dancing as the water forces its way from the bottom; and there, just across the road, a mill is turned by the stream which has just been created by the spring, and when the waterwheel is turned you see a veritable river flowing forward to supply Father Thames [River]. Yet this is only one river; what would you think if you saw a spring yielding such supplies that a river flowed from it to the north, and a river to the south, a river to the east, and a river to the west? This is the figure before us: rivers of living water flowing out of the living man in all directions. "Ah," say you, "I have not reached to that." A point is gained when you know, confess, and deplore your failure. If you say, "I have all things and abound," I am afraid you will never reach the fullness of the blessing; but if you know something of your failure, the Lord will lead you further. It may be that the spirit of life which comes forth of you is but a trickling brooklet, or even a few tiny drops; then be sure to confess it, and you will be on the way to a fuller blessing. What a word is this! *Rivers of living water!!* Oh, that all professing Christians were such fountains.

See how *spontaneous* it is: "Out of the midst of him shall flow." No pumping is required; nothing is said about machinery and hydraulics; the man does not want exciting and stirring up, but, just as he is, influence of the best kind quietly flows away from him. Did you ever hear a great hubbub in the morning, a great outcry, a sounding of trumpets and drums, and did you ever ask, "What is it?" Did a voice reply, "The sun is about to rise, and he is making this noise that all may be aware of it"? No, he shines, but he has nothing to say about it; even so the genuine Christian just goes about flooding the world with blessing, and so far from claiming attention for himself, it may be that he himself is unconscious of what he is effecting. God so blesses him that his leaf does not wither, and whatsoever he doeth is prospering, for he is like a tree planted by the rivers of water that bringeth forth its fruit in its season: his verdure [greenery] and fruit are the natural outcome of his vigorous life. Oh, the blessed spontaneity of the work of grace when a man gets into the fullness of it, for then he seems to eat and drink and sleep eternal life, and he spreads a savor of salvation all round.

And this is to be perpetual—not like intermittent springs which burst forth and flow in torrents, and then cease—but it is to be an everyday outgushing. In summer and winter, by day and by night, wherever the man is, he shall be a blessing. As he breathes, he shall breathe benedictions; as he thinks, his mind shall be devising generous things; and when he acts, his acts shall be as though the hand of God were working by the hand of man.

I hope I hear many sighs rising up in the place! I hope I hear friends saying, "Oh, that I could get to that." I want you to attain the fullness of the favor. I pray that we may all get it; for, because Jesus Christ is glorified, therefore the Holy Spirit is given in this fashion, given more largely to those in the kingdom of Heaven than to all those holy men before the Lord's ascent to his glory. God gives no stinted blessing to celebrate the triumph of his Son: God giveth not the Spirit by measure [in limited amounts] unto him. On such an occasion, Heaven's grandest liberality was displayed. Christ is glorified in Heaven above, and God would have him glorified in the church below by vouchsafing a baptism of the Holy Ghost to each of us.

So I close by this, which I hope will be a very comforting and inspiriting reflection.

IV. *These operations of the Spirit of God are easily to be obtained by the Lord's children.*

Did you say you had not received them? They are to be had, they are to be had at once. First, they are to be had *by believing in Jesus.* "This spake he of the Spirit, which they that believe on him should receive." Do you not see that it is faith which gives us the first drink and causes us to live, and this second more abundant blessing, of being ourselves made fountains from which rivers flow, comes in the same way? Believe in Christ, for the blessing is to be obtained, not by the works of the law, nor by so much of fasting, and striving, and effort, but by belief in the Lord Jesus, for it. With him is the residue of the Spirit. He is prepared to give this to you, aye, to every one of you who believe on his name. He will not, of course, make all of you preachers; for who then would be hearers? If all were preachers, the other works of the church would be neglected; but he will give you this favor, that out of you there shall stream a divine influence all round you to bless your children, to bless your servants, to bless the workmen in the house where you are employed, and to bless the street you live in. In proportion, as God gives you opportunity these rivers of living water will flow in this channel and in that, and they will be pouring forth from you at all times, if you believe in Jesus for the full blessing, and can by faith receive it.

But there is another thing to be done as well, and that is *to pray;* and here I want to remind you of those blessed words of the Master,

> Everyone that asketh receiveth; and he that seeketh findeth; and to him that knocketh it shall be opened. If a son shall ask bread of any of you that is a father, will he give him a stone? Or if he ask a fish, will he for a fish give him a serpent? Or if he shall ask an egg, will he offer him a scorpion? If ye then, being evil, know how to give good gifts unto your children: how much more shall your heavenly Father give the Holy Spirit to them that ask him?

You see, there is a distinct promise to the children of God, that their heavenly Father will give them the Holy Spirit if they ask for his power; and that promise is made to be exceedingly strong by the instances joined to it. If there be a promise that God can break (which there is not), this is not the promise, for God has put it in the most forcible and binding way. I know not how to show you its wonderful force. Did you ever hear of a man who, when his child asked for bread, gave him a stone? Go to the worst part of London, and will you find a man of that kind? You shall, if you like, get among pirates and murderers, and when a little child cries, "Father, give me a bit of bread and meat," does the most wicked father fill his own little one's mouth with stones? Yet the Lord seems to say that this is what he would be doing if he were to deny us the Holy Spirit when we ask him for his necessary working: he would be like one that gave his children stones instead of bread. Do you think the Lord will ever bring himself down to that? But he says, *"How much more* shall your heavenly Father give the Holy Spirit to them that ask him?" He makes it a stronger case than that of an ordinary parent. The Lord must give us the Spirit when we ask him, for he has herein bound himself by no ordinary pledge. He has used a simile which would bring dishonor on his own name, and that of the very grossest kind, if he did not give the Holy Spirit to them that ask him.

Oh, then, let us ask him at once, with all our hearts. Am I not so happy as to have in this audience some who will immediately ask? I pray that some who have never received the Holy Spirit at all may now be led, while I am speaking, to pray, "Blessed Spirit, visit me; lead me to Jesus." But especially those of you that are the children of God—to you is this promise especially made. Ask God to make you all that the Spirit of God can make you, not only a satisfied believer who has drunk for himself, but a useful believer, who overflows the neighborhood with blessing. I see here a number of friends from the country who have come to spend their holiday in London. What a blessing it would be if they went back to their respective churches overflowing; for there are numbers of churches that need flooding; they are dry as a barn-floor, and little dew ever falls on them. Oh, that they might be flooded! What a wonderful thing a flood is! Go down to the river, look over the bridge, and see the barges and other craft lying in the mud. All the king's horses and all the king's men cannot tug them out to sea. There they lie, dead and motionless as the mud itself. What shall we do with them? What machinery can move them? Have we a great engineer among us who will devise a scheme for lifting these vessels and bearing them down to the river's month? No, it cannot be done. Wait till the tide comes in! What a change! Each vessel walks the water like a thing of life. What a difference between the low tide and the high tide. You cannot stir the boats when the water is gone; but when the tide is at the full, see how readily they move; a little child may push them with his hand. Oh, for a flood of grace. The Lord send to all our churches a great springtide! Then the indolent will be active enough, and those who were half dead will be full of energy. I know that in this particular dock, several vessels are lying that I should like to float, but I cannot stir them. They neither work for God nor come out to the prayer-meetings, nor give of their substance to spread the gospel. If the flood would come, you would see what they are capable of: they would be active, fervent, generous, abounding in every good word and work. So may it be! So may it be! May springs begin to flow in all our churches, and may all of you who hear me this day get your share of the streams! Oh, that the Lord may now fill you and then send you home bearing a flood of grace with you. It sounds oddly to speak of a man's carrying home a flood within him, and yet I hope it will be so, and that out of you shall flow rivers of living water. So may God grant, for Jesus' sake. Amen.

The Abiding of the Spirit
Is the Glory of the Church

Delivered on Lord's Day morning, September 5, 1886, at the Metropolitan Tabernacle, Newington. No. 1918.

"Yet now be strong, O Zerubbabel," saith the Lord; "and be strong, Joshua, son of Josedech, the high priest, and be strong, all ye people of the land," saith the Lord, "and work: for I am with you," saith the Lord of hosts: "according to the word that I covenanted with you when ye came out of Egypt, so my spirit remaineth among you: fear ye not."—Haggai 2:4–5

S atan is always doing his utmost to stay the work of God. He hindered these Jews from building the temple, and today he endeavors to hinder the people of God from spreading the gospel. A spiritual temple is to be built for the Most High, and if by any means the evil one can delay its uprising, he will stick at nothing: if he can take us off from working with faith and courage for the glory of God he will be sure to do it. He is very cunning, and knows how to change his argument and yet keep to his design: little cares he how he works, so long as he can hurt the cause of God. In the case of the Jewish people on their return from captivity, he sought to prevent the building of the temple by making them selfish and worldly, so that every man was eager to build his own house, and cared nothing for the house of the Lord. Each family pleaded its own urgent needs. In returning to a long-deserted and neglected land, much had to be done to make up for lost time; and to provide suitably for itself, every family needed all its exertions. They

503

carried this thrift and self-providing to a great extreme, and secured for themselves luxuries, while the foundations of the temple which had been laid years before remained as they were, or became still more thickly covered up with rubbish. The people could not be made to bestir themselves to build a house of God, for they answered to every exhortation, "The time is not come, the time that the Lord's house should be built." A more convenient season was always looming in the future, but it never came. Just now it was too hot, further on it was too cold; at one time the wet season was just setting in, and it was of no use to begin, and soon after the fair weather required that they should be in their own fields. Like some in our day, they saw to themselves first, and God's turn was very long in coming; hence the prophet cried, "Is it time for you, O ye, to dwell in your ceiled [roofed] houses, and this house lie waste?"

By the mouth of his servant Haggai, stern rebukes were uttered, and the whole people were aroused. We read in verse twelve of the first chapter,

> Then Zerubbabel the son of Shealtiel, and Joshua the son of Josedech, the high priest, with all the remnant of the people, obeyed the voice of the Lord their God, and the words of Haggai the prophet, as the Lord their God had sent him, and the people did fear before the Lord.

All hands were put to the work; course after course of stone began to rise; and then another stumbling-block was thrown in the way of the workers. The older folks remarked that this was a very small affair compared with the temple of Solomon, of which their fathers had told them; in fact, their rising building was nothing at all, and not worthy to be called a temple.

The prophet describes the feeling in the verse which precedes our text.

> Who is left among you that saw this house in her first glory? And how do ye see it now? Is it not in your eyes in comparison of it as nothing?

Feeling that their work would be very poor and insignificant, the people had little heart to go on. Being discouraged by the humiliating contrast, they began to be slack; and as they were quite willing to accept any excuse (and here was an excuse ready made for them) they would soon have been at a standstill had not the prophet met the wiles of the arch-enemy with another word from the Lord. Nothing so confounds the evil one as the voice of the Eternal. Our Lord himself defeated Satan by the word of the Lord; and the prophet Haggai did the same. The subtle craft of the enemy is defeated by the wisdom of the Most High, which reveals itself in plain words of honest statement. The Lord cuts the knots which bind his people, and sets them at liberty to do his will. He did this by assuring them that he was with them. Twice the voice was heard—*"I am with you, saith the Lord of hosts."* They were also assured that what they built was accepted, and that the Lord meant to fill the new house with glory; yea, he meant to light it up with a glory greater than that which honored the temple of Solomon. They were not spending their strength for nought, but were laboring with divine help and favor. Thus they were encouraged to put their shoulders to the work: the walls rose in due order, and God was glorified in the building up of his Zion.

The present times are, in many respects, similar to those of Haggai. History certainly repeats itself within the church of God as well as outside of it; and therefore the messages of God need to be repeated also. The words of some almost-forgotten prophet may be re-delivered by the watchman of the Lord in these present days, and be a timely word for the present emergency. We are not free from the worldliness which puts self first and God nowhere, else our various enterprises would be more abundantly supplied with the silver and the gold which are the Lord's, but which even professing Christians reserve for themselves. When this selfish greed is conquered, then comes in a timorous depression. Among those who have escaped from worldliness, there is apt to be too much despondency, and men labor feebly as for a cause which is doomed to failure. This last evil must be cured. I pray that our text may this morning came from the Lord's own mouth with all the fire which once blazed about it. May faint hearts be encouraged and drowsy spirits be aroused, as we hear the Lord say, *"My Spirit remaineth among you: fear ye not."*

I shall enter fully upon the subject, by the assistance of the Holy Spirit, by calling your attention to *discouragement forbidden.* Then I shall speak of *encouragement imparted,* and, having done so, I shall linger with this blessed text, which overflows with comfort, and shall speak, in the third place, of *encouragement further applied.* Oh that our Lord, who knows how to speak a word in season to him that is weary, may cheer the hearts of seekers by what shall be spoken under this last head of discourse!

I. To begin with, here is *discouragement forbidden.*

Discouragement comes readily enough to us poor mortals who are occupied in the work of God, seeing it is a work of faith, a work of difficulty, a work above our capacity, and a work much opposed.

Discouragement as very natural: it is a native of the soil of manhood. To believe is supernatural, faith is the work of the Spirit of God; to doubt is natural to fallen men; for we have within us an evil heart of unbelief. It is abominably wicked, I grant you; but still it is natural, because of the downward tendency of our depraved hearts. Discouragement towards good things is a weed that grows without sowing. To be faint-hearted and downcast happens to some of us when we are half drowned in this heavy atmosphere, and it also visits us on the wings of the east wind. It takes little to make some hands hang down: a word or a look will do it. I do not, therefore, excuse it; but the rather I condemn myself for having a nature prone to such evil.

Discouragement may come and does come to us, as it did to these people, from a consideration of the great things which God deserves at our hands, and the small things which we are able to render. When in Haggai's days the people thought of Jehovah, and of a temple for him, and then looked upon the narrow space which had been enclosed, and the common stones which had been laid for foundations, they were ashamed. Where were those hewn stones and costly stones which, of old, Solomon brought from afar? They said within themselves, "This house is unworthy of Jehovah: what do we by laboring thus?" Have you not felt the depressing weight of what is so surely true? Brethren, all that we do is little for our God; far too little for him that loved us and gave himself for us. For him that poured out his soul unto death on our behalf, the most splendid service, the most heroic self-denial, are all too little; and we feel it is so. Alabaster boxes of precious ointment are too mean a gift. It does not occur to our fervent spirit to imagine that there can be any waste when our best boxes are broken and the perfume is poured out lavishly for him. What we do fear is that our alabaster boxes are too few, and that our ointment is not precious enough. When we have done our utmost in declaring the glory of Jesus, we have felt that words are too poor and mean to set forth our adorable Lord.

When we have prayed for his kingdom, we have been disgusted with our own prayers; and all the efforts we have put forth in connection with any part of his service have seemed too few, too feeble for us to hope for acceptance. Thus have we been discouraged. The enemy has worked upon us by this means, yet he has made us argue very wrongly. Because we could not do much, we have half-resolved to do nothing! Because what we did was so poor, we were inclined to quit the work altogether! This is evidently absurd and wicked. The enemy can use humility for his purpose as well as pride. Whether he makes us think too much or too little of our work, it is all the same to him, so long as he can get us off from it.

It is significant that the man with one talent went and hid his Lord's money in the earth. He knew that it was but one, and for that reason he was the less afraid to bury it. Perhaps he argued that the interest on one talent could never come to much, and would never be noticed side by side with the result of five or ten talents; and he might as well bring nothing at all to his Lord as bring so little. Perhaps he might not have wrapped it up if it had not been so small that a napkin could cover it. The smallness of our gifts may be a temptation to us. We are consciously so weak and so insignificant, compared with the great God and his great cause, that we are discouraged, and think it vain to attempt anything.

Moreover, the enemy contrasts our work with that of others, and with that of those who have gone before us. We are doing so little as compared with other people, therefore let us give up. We cannot build like Solomon, therefore let us not build at all. Yet, brethren, there is a falsehood in all this, for, in truth, nothing is worthy of God. The great works of others, and even the amazing productions of Solomon, all fell short of His glory. What house could man build for God? What are cedar, and marble, and gold as compared with the glory of the Most High? Though the house was "exceeding magnifical," yet the Lord God had of old dwelt within curtains, and never was his worship more glorious than within the tent of badgers' skins; indeed, as soon as the great house was built, true religion declined. What of all human work can be worthy of the Lord? Our little labors do but share the insignificance of greater things, and therefore we ought not to withhold them: yet here is the temptation from which we must pray to be delivered.

The tendency to depreciate the present because of the glories of the past is also injurious. The old people looked back to the days of the former temple, even as we are apt to look upon the times of the great preachers of the past. What work was done in those past days! What Sabbaths were enjoyed then! What converts were added to the church! What days of refreshing were then vouchsafed! Everything has declined, decreased, degenerated! As for the former days, they beheld a race of giants, who are now succeeded by pigmies. We look at one of these great men, and cry,

> Why, man, he doth bestride the narrow world
> Like a Colossus; and we petty men
> Walk under his huge legs, and peep about
> To find ourselves dishonorable graves.

But, brethren, we must not allow this sense of littleness to hamper us; for God can bless our littleness, and use it for his glory. I notice that the great men of the past thought of themselves even as we think of ourselves. Certainly they were not more self-confident than we are. I find in the stories of the brave days of old, the same confessions and the same lamentations which we utter now. It is true that in spiritual strength we are not what our fathers were; I fear that Puritanic holiness and truthfulness of doctrine are dying out, while adherence to principle is far from common; but our fathers had also faults and follies to mourn over, and they did mourn over them most sincerely.

Instead of being discouraged because what we do is unworthy of God, and insignificant compared with what was done by others, let us gather up our strength to reform our errors, and reach to higher attainments. Let us throw our heart and soul into the work of the Lord, and yet do something more nearly in accordance with our highest ideal of what our God deserves of us. Let us excel our ancestors. Let us aspire to be even more godly, more conscientious, and more sound in the faith than they were, for the Spirit of God remaineth with us.

Brethren, it is clear that discouragement can be produced by these reasons, and yet they are a mere sample of a host of arguments which work in the same direction: hence *discouragement is very common*. Haggai was sent to speak to Zerubbabel, the governor, and to Joshua, the high priest, and to all the remnant of the people. The great man may become discouraged: he that leads the van [troops] has his fainting fits; even Elijah cries, "Let me die!" The consecrated servant of God, whose life is a priesthood, is apt to grow discouraged, too: standing at God's altar, he sometimes trembles for the ark of the Lord. The multitude of the people are all too apt to suffer from panic, and to flee at the sight of the enemy. How many are they who say, "The old truth cannot succeed: the cause of orthodoxy is desperate; we had better yield to the modern spirit!"

This faint-heartedness is so common that it has been the plague of Israel from her first day until now. They were discouraged at the Red Sea, at the mere rattling of Pharaoh's chariots; they were discouraged when they found no water; they were discouraged when they had eaten up the bread which they brought out of Egypt; they were discouraged when they heard of the giants, and of the cities walled to Heaven. I need not lengthen the wretched catalogue. What has not cowardice done? The fearful and unbelieving have brought terrible disasters upon our camps. Discouragement is the national epidemic of our Israel. "Being armed and carrying bows," we turn back in the day of battle. This is as common among Christians as consumption[1] among the inhabitants of this foggy island. Oh that God would save us all from distrust, and cause us to [a]quit ourselves like men!

Wherever discouragement comes in, it is dreadfully weakening. I am sure it is weakening, because the prophet was bidden to say three times to the governor, high priest, and people, "Be strong." This proves that they had become weak. Being discouraged, their hands hung down, and their knees were feeble. Faith girds us with omnipotence; but unbelief makes everything hang loose and limp about us. Distrust, and thou wilt fail in everything; believe, and according to thy faith so shall it be unto thee.

To lead a discouraged people to the Holy War is as difficult as [it was] for Xerxes' commanders to conduct the Persian troops to battle against the Greeks. The vassals of the great king were driven to the conflict by whips and sticks, for they were afraid to fight: do you wonder that they were defeated? A church that needs constant exhorting and compelling accomplishes nothing. The Greeks had no need of blows and threats, for each man was a lion, and courted the encounter, however great the odds against him. Each Spartan fought *con amore* [with zeal]; he was never more at home than when contending for the altars and the hearths of his country. We want Christian men of this same sort, who have faith in their principles, faith in the doctrines of grace, faith in God the Father, God the Son, and God the Holy Ghost, and who therefore contend earnestly for the faith in these days when piety is mocked at from the pulpit, and the gospel is sneered at by professional preachers. We need men who love the truth, to whom it is dear as their lives; men into whose hearts the old doctrine is burned by the hand of God's Spirit

---

[1]   Consumption: archaic term for pulmonary tuberculosis.

through a deep experience of its necessity and of its power. We need no more of those who will parrot what they are taught, but we want men who will speak what they know. Oh, for a troop of men like John Knox, heroes of the martyr and covenanter stock! Then would Jehovah of hosts have a people to serve him who would be strong in the Lord and in the power of his might.

Discouragement not only weakens men, but it *takes them off from the service of God.* It is significant that the prophet said to them, "'Be strong, all ye people of the land,' saith the Lord, 'and work.'" They had ceased to build: they had begun to talk and argue, but they had laid down the trowel. They were extremely wise in their observations, and criticisms, and prophecies; but the walls did not rise. One person knew exactly how big the former temple was; another declared that their present architect was not up to the mark, and that the structure was not built in a scientific manner: one objected to this, and another to that; but everybody was wiser than all the rest, and sneered at old-fashioned ways. It is always so when we are discouraged: we cease from the work of the Lord, and waste time in talk and nonsensical refinements. May the Lord take away discouragement from any of you who now suffer from it! I suppose some of you do feel it, for at times it creeps over my heart and makes me go with heaviness to my work.

I believe that God's truth will come to the front yet, but it hath many adversaries today. All sorts of unbeliefs are being hatched out from under the wings of "modern thought." The gospel seems to be regarded as a nose of wax, to be altered and shaped by every man who wishes to show his superior skill. Nor is it in doctrine alone, but in practice also, that the times are out of joint. Separateness from the world, and holy living, are to give place to gaiety and theater-going. To follow Christ fully has gone out of fashion with many of those from whom we once hoped better things. Yet are there some who waver not, some who are willing to be in the right, with two or three [others]. For my own part, even should I find none around me of the same mind, I shall not budge an inch from the old truth, nor sweat a hair for fear of its overthrow; but I shall abide confident that the eternal God, whose truth we know and hold, will vindicate himself ere long, and turn the wisdom of the world into babble, and its boasting into confusion. Blessed is the man who shall be able to stand fast by his God in these evil days. Let us not in any wise be discouraged. "Be strong; be strong; be strong," sounds as a threefold voice from the triune God. "Fear not" comes as a sweet cordial to the faint: therefore let no man's heart fail him. Thus much about the discouragement.

II. Secondly, here is *the encouragement imparted,* which is the grand part of our text.

"According to the word that I covenanted with you when ye came out of Egypt, so my spirit remaineth among you: fear ye not." God remembers his covenant and stands to his ancient promises. When the people came out of Egypt the Lord was with them by his Spirit: hence he spoke to them by Moses, and through Moses he guided, and judged, and taught them. He was with them also by his Spirit in inspiring Bezaleel and Aholiab as to the works of art which adorned the tabernacle. God always finds workmen for his work, and by his Spirit fits them for it. The Spirit of God rested upon the elders who were ordained to relieve Moses of his great burden. The Lord was also with his people in the fiery cloudy pillar which was conspicuous in the midst of the camp. His presence was their glory and their defense.

This is a type of the presence of the Spirit with the church. At the present day, if we hold the truth of God, if we live in obedience to his holy commands, if we are spiritually minded, if we cry unto God in believing prayer, if we have faith in his covenant and in his Son, the Holy Spirit abideth among us. The Holy Ghost descended upon the church at Pentecost, and he has never gone back again: there is no record of the Spirit's return to Heaven. He will abide with the true church evermore. This is our hope for the present struggle. The Spirit of God remaineth with us.

To what end, my brethren, is this Spirit with us? Let us think of this, that we may be encouraged at this time. The Spirit of God remaineth among you to aid and assist the ministry which he has already given. Oh, that the prayers of God's people would always go up for God's ministers, that they may speak with a divine power and influence which none shall be able to gainsay! We look too much for clever men; we seek out fluent and flowery speakers; we sigh for men cultured and trained in all the knowledge of the heathen: nay, but if we sought more for unction, for divine authority, and for that power which doth hedge about [surround] the man of God, how much wiser should we be! Oh, that all of us who profess to preach the gospel would learn to speak in entire dependence upon the direction of the Holy Spirit, not daring to utter our own words, but even trembling lest we should do so, and committing ourselves to that secret influence, without which nothing will be powerful upon the conscience or converting to the heart. Know ye not the difference between the power that cometh of human oratory, and that which cometh by the divine energy which speaks so to the heart that men cannot resist it? We have forgotten this too much. It were better to speak six words in the power of the Holy Ghost than to preach seventy years of sermons without the Spirit. He who rested on those who have gone to their reward in Heaven can rest this day upon our ministers and bless our evangelists, if we will but seek it of him. Let us cease to grieve the Spirit of God, and look to him for help to the faithful ministers who are yet spared to us.

This same Spirit who of old gave to his church eminent teachers can raise up other and more useful men. The other day, a brother from Wales told me of the great men he remembered: he said that he had never heard such a one as Christmas Evans,[2] who surpassed all men when he was in the hwyl. I asked him if he knew another Welsh minister who preached like Christmas Evans. "No," he said, "we have no such man in Wales in our days." So in England we have neither Wesley nor Whitefield, nor any of their order; yet, as with God is the residue of the Spirit, he can fetch out from some chimney-corner another Christmas Evans, or find in our Sunday-school another George Whitefield, who shall declare the gospel with the Holy Ghost sent down from Heaven. Let us never fear for the future, or despair for the present, since the Spirit of God remaineth with us. What if the growing error of the age should have silenced the last tongue that speaks out the old gospel? Let not faith be weakened. I hear the tramp of legions of soldiers of the cross. I hear the clarion voices of hosts of preachers. "The Lord give the word; great was the company of those that published it." Have faith in God through our Lord Jesus Christ! When he ascended on high he led captivity captive, and received gifts for men. He then gave apostles, teachers, preachers, and evangelists, and he can do the like again. Let us fall back upon the eternal God, and never be discouraged for an instant.

Nor is this all. The Holy Spirit being with us, *he can move the whole church to exercise its varied ministries.* This is one of the things we want very much—that every member of the church should recognize that he is ordained to service. Everyone in Christ, man or woman, hath some testimony to bear, some warning to give, some deed to do in the name of the holy child Jesus; and if the Spirit of God be poured out upon our young men and our maidens, each one will be aroused to energetic service. Both small and great will be in earnest, and the result upon the slumbering masses of our population will surprise us all. Sometimes we lament that the churches are so dull. There is an old proverb which says of So-and-so, that he was "as sound asleep as a church." I suppose there is nothing that can sleep so soundly as a church. But yet the Spirit of God still remaineth, and therefore churches go to be awakened. I mean that not only in part but as a whole, a church may be quickened. The dullest professor, the most slovenly believer, the most captious and useless member of a church, may yet be turned to good account. I see them like a stack of faggots, piled up, dead, and dry. Oh for the fire! We will have a blaze out of them yet.

Come, Holy Spirit, heavenly Dove, brood over the dark, disordered church as once thou didst over chaos, and order shall come out of confusion, and the darkness shall fly before the light. Only let the Spirit be with us, and we have all that is

---

[2]   Christmas Evans (1766-1838) was a Welsh Nonconformist divine born near the village of Llandyssul, Cardiganshire, on the 25th of December 1766. His father, a shoemaker, died early, and the boy grew up as an illiterate farm laborer. (Wikipedia.com)

wanted for victory. Give us his presence, and everything else will come in its due season for the profitable service of the entire church.

If the Spirit be with us, there will come multitudinous conversions. We cannot get at "the lapsed masses," as they are pedantically called. We cannot stir the crass infidelity of the present age: no, we cannot, but *He* can. All things are possible with God. If you walk down to our bridges [on the Thames River] at a certain hour of the day you will see barges and vessels lying in the mud; and all the king's horses and all the king's men cannot stir them. Wait until the tide comes in, and they will walk the water like things of life. The living flood accomplishes at once what no mortals can do. And so today our churches cannot stir. What shall we do? Oh, that the Holy Spirit would come with a flood-tide of his benign influences, as he will if we will but believe in him; as he must if we will but cry unto him; as he shall if we will cease to grieve him. Everything will be even as the saints desire when the Lord of saints is with us. The hope of the continuance and increase of the church lies in the remaining of the Spirit with us. The hope of the salvation of London lies in the wonder-working Spirit. Let us bow our heads and worship the omnipotent Spirit who deigns to work *in* us, *by* us, and *with* us.

Then, brethren, if this should happen—and I see not why it should not—then we may expect to see the Church put on her beautiful garments; then shall she begin to clear herself of the errors which now defile her; then shall she press to her bosom the truths which she now begins to forget; then will she go back to the pure fount of inspiration and drink from the Scriptures of truth; and then out of the midst of her shall flow no turbid streams, but rivers of living water. If the Holy Ghost will work among us, we shall rejoice in the Lord, and glory in the name of our God.

When once the Spirit of God putteth forth his might, all things else will be in accord with him. Notice that in the rest of the chapter—which I shall read now, not as relating to that temple at all, but to the church of God—there is great comfort given to us. If the Holy Spirit be once given, then we may expect providence to co-operate with the church of God. Read verse 6:

> Yet once, it is a little while, and I will shake Heaven and the earth, and the sea, and the dry land. I will shake all nations.

Great commotions will co-operate with the Holy Spirit. We may expect that God will work for his people in an extraordinary fashion if they will but be faithful to him. Empires will collapse, and times will change, for the truth's sake. Expect the unexpected, reckon upon that which is unlikely, if it be necessary for the growth of the kingdom. Of old the earth helped the woman when the dragon opened his mouth to drown her with the floods that he cast forth: unexpected help shall come to us when affairs are at their worst.

Specially do I look for a shaking among the hosts of unbelief. How often did the Lord of old rout his enemies without his Israel drawing sword! The watchword was, "Stand ye still, and see the salvation of the Lord." The adversaries of old fell out among themselves; and they will do so again. When Cadmus slew the dragon with his javelin, he was bidden to sow its teeth in the earth. When he did so, according to the classic fable, he saw rising out of the ground nodding plumes, and crested helmets, and broad shoulders of armed men. Up from the earth there sprang a host of warriors; but Cadmus needed not to fly; for the moment they found their feet, these children of the dragon fell upon each other till scarcely one was left. Error, like Saturn, devours its own children. Those that fight against the Lord of hosts are not agreed among themselves; they shall sheathe their swords in each other's bosoms.

I saw in the night vision the sea, the deep and broad sea of truth, flashing with its silver waves. Lo, a black horse came out of the darkness and went down to the deep, threatening to drink it dry. I saw him stand there drinking, and swelling as he drank. In his pride he trusted that he could snuff up Jordan at a draught. I stood by and saw him drink, and then plunge further into the sea, to drink still more. Again he plunged in with fury, and soon he lost his footing, and I saw him no more, for the deep had swallowed him that boasted that he would swallow it. Rest assured that every black horse of error that comes forth to swallow up the sea of divine truth shall be drowned therein. Wherefore be of good courage. God, who maketh the earth and the heavens to shake, shall cause each error to fall like an untimely fig.

And next, the Lord in this chapter promises his people that they shall have all the supplies they need for his work. They feared that they could not build his house, because of their poverty; but, saith the Lord of hosts, "The silver and the gold are mine." When the church of God believes in God, and goes forward bravely, she need not trouble as to supplies. Her God will provide for her. He that gives the Holy Ghost will give gold and silver according as they are needed; therefore let us be of good courage. If God is with us, why need we fear? One of our English kings once threatened the great city of London that if its councilors talked so independently, he would—yes—he would, indeed he would—take his court away from the city. The Lord Mayor on that occasion replied, that if his majesty would graciously leave the river Thames behind him, the citizens would try to get on without his court. If any say, "If you hold to these old-fashioned doctrines, you will lose the educated, the wealthy, the influential," we answer, "But if we do not lose the godly and the presence of the Holy Ghost, we are not in the least alarmed." If the Holy Ghost remaineth with us, there is a river, the streams whereof make glad the city of God. Brethren, my heart leaps within me as I cry, "The Lord of hosts is with us; the God of Jacob is our refuge." "Therefore will not we fear, though the earth be removed, and though the mountains be carried into the midst of the sea."

The best comfort of all remained: "The desire of all nations shall come." This was in a measure fulfilled when Jesus came into that latter house and caused all holy hearts to sing for gladness; but it was not wholly fulfilled in that way; for if you notice, in the ninth verse it is written, "The glory of this latter house shall be greater than of the former; and in this place will I give peace," which the Lord did not fully do to the second temple, since that was destroyed by the Romans. But there is another advent, when "the desire of all nations shall come" in power and glory; and this is our highest hope. Though truth may be driven back, and error may prevail, Jesus comes, and he is the great Lord and patron of truth: he shall judge the world in righteousness, and the people in equity. Here's our last resource; here are God's reserves. He whom we serve liveth and reigneth forever and ever; and he saith, "Behold, I come quickly; and my reward is with me, to give every man according as his work shall be." "Therefore, my beloved brethren, be ye steadfast, unmovable, always abounding in the work of the Lord, forasmuch as ye know that your labor is not in vain in the Lord."

III. I should have [been] done if it had not been that this text seemed to me to overflow so much, that it might not only refresh God's people, but give drink to thirsty sinners who are seeking the Lord. For a moment or two I give myself to *encouragement further applied.*

It is at the beginning of every gracious purpose that men have most fear, even as these people had who had newly begun to build. When first the Holy Spirit begins to strive with a man and to lead him to Jesus, he is apt to say—"I cannot; I dare not; it is impossible. How can I believe and live?"

Now I want to speak to some of you here who are willing to find Christ, and to encourage you by the truth that the Spirit lives to help you. I would even like to speak to those who are not anxious to be saved. I remember that Dr. Payson, an exceedingly earnest and useful man of God, once did a singular thing. He had been holding inquiry meetings with all sorts of people, and great numbers had been saved. At last, one Sunday he gave out that he should have a meeting on Monday night of those persons who did not desire to be saved; and, strange to say, some twenty persons came who did not wish to repent or believe. He spoke to them and said,

> I am sure that if a little film, thin as the web of the gossamer, were let down by God from Heaven to each one of you, you would not push it away from you. Although it were almost invisible, you would value even the slightest connection between you and Heaven. Now, your coming to meet me tonight is a little link with God. I want it to increase in strength till you are joined to the Lord forever.

He spoke to them most tenderly, and God blessed those people who did not desire to be saved, so that before the meeting was over, they were of another mind. The film had become a thicker thread, and it grew and grew until the Lord Christ held them by it forever. Dear friends, the fact of your being in the Tabernacle[3] this morning is like that filmy thread: do not put it away. Here is your comfort: the Holy Spirit still works with the preaching of the word.

Do I hear you say, "I cannot feel my need of Christ as I want to feel it?" The Spirit remaineth among us. He can make you feel more deeply the guilt of sin and your need of pardon.

"But I have heard so much about conviction and repentance; I do not seem to have either of them." Yet the Spirit remaineth with us, and that Spirit is able to work in you the deepest conviction and the truest repentance.

"O sir, I do not feel as if I could do anything:" but the Spirit remaineth with us, and all things that are needful for godliness, he can give. He can work in you to will and to do of his own good pleasure.

"But I want to believe in the Lord Jesus Christ unto eternal life." Who made you want to do that? Who but the Holy Spirit? Therefore he is still at work with you; and though as yet you do not understand what believing is (or else I am persuaded you would believe at once), the Spirit of God can instruct you in it. You are blind, but he can give you sight; you are paralyzed, but he can give you strength—the Spirit of God remaineth.

"Oh, but that doctrine of regeneration staggers me: you know, we must be born again." Yes, we are born again of the Spirit, and the Spirit remaineth still with us; he is still mighty to work that wondrous change, and to bring you out of the kingdom of Satan into the kingdom of God's dear Son. The Spirit remaineth with us, blessed be his name.

"Ah, dear sir," says one, "I want to conquer sin!" Who made you desire to conquer sin? Who, but the Spirit that remaineth with us? He will give you the sword of the Spirit and teach you how to use it, and he will give you both the will and the power to use it successfully. Through the Spirit's might, you can overcome every sin, even that which has dragged you down and disgraced you. The Spirit of God is still waiting to help you. When I think of the power of the Spirit of God, I look hopefully upon every sinner here this morning. I bless his name that he can work in you all that is pleasing in his sight. Some of you may be very careless, but he can make you thoughtful. Coming up to London to see the Exhibition, I hope you may yourselves become an exhibition of divine grace. You think not about things, but he can make you feel at this moment a sweet softness stealing over you, until you long to be alone and to get home to the old arm-chair and there seek the Lord. You can thus be led to salvation.

---

[3] Tabernacle: Metropolitan Tabernacle, Spurgeon's church.

I thought when I came in here that I should have a picked congregation; and so I have. You are one of them. Wherever you come from, I want you now to seek the Lord. He has brought you here, and he means to bless you. Yield yourselves to him while his sweet Spirit pleads with you. While the heavenly wind softly blows upon you, open wide every window. You have not felt that you wanted it, but that is the sure proof that you need it; for he who does not know his need of Christ, is most in need. Open wide your heart, that the Spirit may teach you your need; above all, breathe the prayer that he would help you this morning to look to the Lord Jesus Christ, for "there is life in a look at the Crucified One—there is life at this moment for you."

"Oh," you say, "if I were to begin I should not keep on." No; if *you* began, perhaps you would not; but if *he* begins with you he will keep on. The final perseverance of saints is the result of the final perseverance of the Holy Spirit; he perseveres to bless, and we persevere in receiving the blessing. If he begins, you have begun with a divine power that fainteth not neither is weary. I wish it might so happen that on this fifth day of the ninth month, not the prophet Haggai, but I, God's servant, may have spoken to you such a word as you shall never forget; and may the Lord add to the word, by the witness of the Holy Ghost, "From this day will I bless you!" Go away with that promise resting upon you. I would like to give a shake of the hand to every stranger here this morning, and say, "Brother, in the name of the Lord I wish you from this day a blessing." Amen and amen.

The Covenant Promise of the Spirit

Delivered on Lord's Day morning, April 10, 1891, at the Metropolitan Tabernacle, Newington. No. 2200.

And I will put my spirit within you.—Ezekiel 36:27

No preface is needed; and the largeness of our subject forbids our wasting time in beating about the bush. I shall try to do two things this morning: first, I would commend the text; and, secondly, I would in some measure expound the text.

I. First, as for *the commendation of the text*, the tongues of men and of angels might fail.

To call it a golden sentence would be much too commonplace: to liken it to a pearl of great price would be too poor a comparison. We cannot feel, much less speak, too much in praise of that great God who has put this clause into the covenant of his grace. In that covenant every sentence is more precious than Heaven and earth; and this line is not the least among his choice words of promise: "I will put my spirit within you."

I would begin by saying that *it is a gracious word*. It was spoken to a graceless people, to a people who had followed "their own way," and refused the way of God; a people who had already provoked something more than ordinary anger in the Judge of all the earth; for he himself said (verse 18), "I poured my fury upon them." These people, even under chastisement, caused the holy name of God to be profaned among the heathen whither they went. They had been highly favored, but they abused their privileges, and behaved worse than those who never knew the Lord. They sinned wantonly, willfully, wickedly, proudly and presumptuously; and by this they greatly provoked the Lord. Yet to them he made such a promise as this—"I will put my spirit within you." Surely, where sin abounded, grace did much more abound.

Clearly this is a word of grace, for the law saith nothing of this kind. Turn to the law of Moses, and see if there be any word spoken therein concerning the putting of the Spirit within men to cause them to walk in God's statutes. The law proclaims the statutes; but the gospel alone promises the spirit by which the statutes will be obeyed. The law commands and makes us know what God requires of us; but the gospel goes further, and inclines us to obey the will of the Lord, and enables us practically to walk in his ways. Under the dominion of grace, the Lord worketh in us to will and to do of his own good pleasure.

So great a boon as this could never come to any man by merit. A man might so act as to deserve a reward of a certain kind, in measure suited to his commendable action; but the Holy Spirit can never be the wage of human service: the idea verges upon blasphemy. Can any man deserve that Christ should die for him? Who would dream of such a thing? Can any man deserve that the Holy Ghost should dwell in him, and work holiness in him? The greatness of the blessing lifts it high above the range of merit, and we see that if the Holy Ghost be bestowed, it must be by an act of divine grace—grace infinite in bounty, exceeding all that we could have imagined. "Sovereign grace o'er sin abounding" is here seen in clearest light. "I will put my spirit within you" is a promise which drops with graces as the honeycomb with honey. Listen to the divine music which pours from this word of love. I hear the soft melody of grace, grace, grace, and nothing else but grace. Glory be to God, who gives to sinners the indwelling of his Spirit.

Note, next, that *it is a divine word*: "I will put my spirit within you." Who but the Lord could speak after this fashion? Can one man put the Spirit of God within another? Could all the church combined breathe the Spirit of God into a single sinner's heart? To put any good thing into the deceitful heart of man is a great achievement; but to put the Spirit of God into the heart, truly this is the finger of God. Nay, here I may say, the Lord has made bare his arm, and displayed the fullness of his mighty power. To put the Spirit of God into our nature is a work peculiar to the Godhead, and to do this within the nature of a free agent, such as man, is marvelous. Who but Jehovah, the God of Israel, can speak after this royal style, and, beyond all dispute, declare, "I will put my spirit within you." Men must always surround their resolves with conditions and uncertainties; but since omnipotence is at the back of every promise of God, he speaks like a king; yea, in a style which is only fit for the eternal God. He purposes and promises, and he as surely performs. Sure, then, is this sacred saying, "I will put my spirit within you." Sure, because divine. O sinner, if we poor creatures had the saving of you, we should break down in the attempt; but, behold, the Lord himself comes on the scene, and the work is done! All difficulties are removed by this one sentence, "I will put my spirit within you." We have wrought with our spirit, we have wept over you, and we have entreated you; but we have failed. Lo, there cometh one into the matter who will not fail, with whom nothing is impossible; and he begins his work by saying, "I will put my spirit within you." The word is of grace and of God; regard it, then as a pledge from God of grace.

To me there is much charm in further thought that *this is an individual and personal word*. The Lord means, "I will put my spirit within you": that is to say, within *you*, as individuals. "I will put my spirit within you" one by one. This must be so, since connection requires it. We read in verse 26, "A new heart also will I give you." Now, a new heart can only be given to one person. Each man needs a heart of his own, and each man must have a new heart for himself. "And a new spirit will I put within you." Within each one this must be done. "And I will take away the stony heart out of your flesh, and I will give you an heart of flesh"—these are all personal, individual operations of grace. God deals with men one by one in solemn matters of eternity, sin, and salvation. We are born one by one, and we die one by one: even so we must be born again one by one, and each one for himself must receive Spirit of God. Without this a man has nothing. He cannot be caused to walk in God's statutes except by the infusion of grace into him as an individual. I think I see among my hearers a lone man, or woman, who feels himself, or herself, to be all alone in world, and therefore hopeless. You can believe that God will do great things for a nation, but how shall the solitary be thought of? You are an odd person, one that could not be written down in any list; a peculiar sinner, with constitutional tendencies all your own. Thus saith God, "I will put my spirit within *you*"; within *your* heart—even *yours*. My dear hearers, you who have long been seeking salvation, but have not known power of Spirit—this is what you need. You have been striving in energy of flesh, but you have not understood where your true strength lieth. God saith to you, "Not by might, nor by power, but by my Spirit, saith the Lord"; and again, "I will put my spirit within you." Oh, that this word might be spoken of the Lord to that young man who is ready to despair; to that sorrowful woman who has been looking into herself for power to pray and believe! You are without strength or hope in and of yourself; but this meets your case in all points. "I will put my spirit within you"—within *you* as an individual. Enquire of the Lord for it. Lift up your heart in prayer to God, and ask him to pour upon you the Spirit of grace and of supplications. Plead with the Lord, saying, "Let thy good

Spirit lead me. Even me." Cry, "Pass me not, my gracious Father; but in me fulfill this wondrous word of thine, 'I will put my spirit within you.'"

Note, next, that *this is a separating word.* I do not know whether you will see this readily; but it must be so: this word separates a man from his fellows. Men by nature are of another spirit from that of God, and are under subjection to that evil spirit, the Prince of the power of the air. When the Lord comes to gather out his own, fetching them out from among the heathen, he effects separation by doing according to this word, "I will put my spirit within you." This done, the individual becomes a new man. Those who have the Spirit are not of the world, nor like the world; and soon have to come out from among the ungodly, and to be separate; for [the] difference of nature creates conflict. God's Spirit will not dwell with the evil spirit: you cannot have fellowship with Christ and with Belial; with the kingdom of Heaven and with this world. I wish that the people of God would again wake up to the truth that to gather out a people from among men is the great purpose of the present dispensation. It is still true, as James said at the Jerusalem Council, "Simeon hath declared how God at first did visit the Gentiles, to take out of them a people for his name." We are not to remain clinging to the old wreck with the expectation that we shall pump water out of her and get her safe into port. No; the cry is very different—"Take to the lifeboat! Take to the lifeboat!" You are to quit the wreck, and you are to carry away from the sinking mass that which God will save. You must be separate from the old wreck, lest it suck you down to sure destruction. Your only hope of doing good to the world is by yourselves being "not of the world," even as Christ was not of the world. For you to go down to the world's level will neither be good for it nor for you. That which happened in the days of Noah will be repeated; for when the sons of God entered into alliance with the daughters of men, and there was a league between the two races, the Lord could not endure the evil mixture, but drew up the sluices of the lower deep and swept the earth with a destroying flood. Surely, in that last day of destruction, when the world is overwhelmed with fire, it will be because the church of God shall have degenerated, and the distinctions between the righteous and the wicked shall have been broken down.

The Spirit of God, wherever he comes, doth speedily make and reveal the difference between Israel and Egypt; and in proportion as his active energy is felt, there will be an ever-widening gulf between those who are led of the Spirit and those who are under the dominion of the flesh. The possession of the Spirit will make you, my hearer, quite another sort of man from what you now are, and then you will be actuated by motives which the world will not appreciate; for the world knoweth us not, because it knew him not. Then you will act, and speak, and think, and feel in such a way, that this evil world will misunderstand and condemn you. Since the carnal mind knoweth not the things that are of God—for those things are spiritually discerned—it will not approve your objects and designs. Do not expect it to be your friend. The Spirit which makes you to be of the seed of the woman is not the spirit of the world. The seed of the serpent will hiss at you, and bruise your heel. Your Master said, "Because ye are not of the world, but I have chosen you out of the world; therefore the world hateth you." It is a separating word, this. Has it separated you? Has the Holy Spirit called you alone and blessed you? Do you differ from your old companions? Have you a life they do not understand? If not, may God in mercy put into you that most heavenly deposit, of which he speaks in our; text: "I will put my spirit within you"!

But now notice, that *it is a very uniting word*. It separates from the world, but it joins to God. Note how it runs: "I will put *my* Spirit within *you*." It is not merely *a* spirit, or *the* spirit, but *my* spirit. Now when God's own Spirit comes to reside within our mortal bodies, how near akin we are to the Most High! "Know ye not that your body is the temple of the Holy Ghost?" Does not this make a man sublime? Have you never stood in awe of your own selves, O ye believers? Have you enough regarded even this poor body, as being sanctified and dedicated, and elevated into a sacred condition, by being set apart to be the temple of the Holy Ghost? Thus are we brought into the closest union with God that we can well conceive of. Thus is the Lord our light and our life; while our spirit is subordinated to the divine Spirit. "I will put my spirit within you"—then God himself dwelleth in you. The Spirit of him that raised up Christ from the dead is in you. With Christ, in God your life is hid, and the Spirit seals you, anoints you, and abides in you. By the Spirit we have access to the Father; by the Spirit we perceive our adoption, and learn to cry, "Abba, Father"; by the Spirit we are made partakers of the divine nature, and have communion with the thrice holy Lord.

I cannot help adding here that *it is a very condescending word*—"I will put my spirit within you." Is it really so, that the Spirit of God who displays the power and energetic force of God, by whom God's Word is carried into effect—that the Spirit who of old moved upon the face of the waters, and brought order and life from chaos and death—can it be so that he will deign to sojourn in men? "God in our nature" is a very wonderful conception! God in the babe at Bethlehem, God in the carpenter of Nazareth, God in the "man of sorrows," God in the Crucified, God in him who was buried in the tomb—this is all marvelous. The incarnation is an infinite mystery of love; but we believe it. Yet, if it were possible to compare one illimitable wonder with another, I should say that God's dwelling in his people, and that repeated ten thousand times over, is more marvelous.

That the Holy Ghost should dwell in millions of redeemed men and women, is a miracle not surpassed by that of our Lord's espousal of human nature. For our Lord's body was perfectly pure, and the Godhead, while it dwells with his holy manhood, does at least dwell with a perfect and sinless nature; but the Holy Spirit bows himself to dwell in sinful men; to dwell in men who, after their conversion, still find the flesh warring against the spirit, and the spirit against the flesh; men who are not perfect, though they strive to be so, men who have to lament their shortcomings, and even to confess with shame a measure of unbelief. "I will put my spirit within you" means the abiding of the Holy Spirit in our imperfect nature.

Wonder of wonders! Yet is it as surely a fact as it is a wonder. Believers in the Lord Jesus Christ, you have the Spirit of God, for "if any man have not the Spirit of Christ, he is none of his." You could not bear the suspicion that you are not his; and therefore, as surely as you are Christ's, you have his Spirit abiding in you. The Savior has gone away on purpose that the Comforter might be given to dwell in you, and he does dwell in you. Is it not so? If it be so, admire this condescending God, and worship and praise his name. Sweetly submit to his rule in all things. Grieve not the Spirit of God. Watch carefully that nothing comes within you that may defile the temple of God. Let the faintest monition [warning] of the Holy Spirit be law to you. It was a holy mystery that the presence of the Lord was specially within the veil of the Tabernacle, and that the Lord God spake by Urim and Thummim to his people; it is an equally sacred marvel that now the Holy Ghost dwells in our spirits and abides within our nature and speaks to us whatsoever he hears of the Father. By divine impressions which the opened ear can apprehend, and the tender heart can receive, he speaketh still. God grant us to know his still small voice so as to listen to it with reverent humility and loving joy: then shall we know the meaning of these words, "I will put my spirit within you "

Nor have I yet done with commending my text, for I must not fail to remind you that *it is a very spiritual word*. "I will put my spirit within you" has nothing to do with our wearing a peculiar garb—that would be a matter of little worth. It has nothing to do with affectations of speech—those might readily become a deceptive peculiarity. Our text has nothing to do with outward rites and ceremonies; but goes much further and deeper. It is an instructive symbol when the Lord teaches us our death with Christ by burial in baptism: it is to our great profit that he ordains bread and wine to be tokens of our communion in the body and blood of his dear Son; but these are only outward things, and if they are unattended with the Holy Spirit, they fail of their design. There is something infinitely greater in this promise—"I will put my spirit within you." I cannot give you the whole force of the Hebrew, as to the words "within you," unless I paraphrase them a little, and read "I will put my spirit in the midst of you." The sacred deposit is put deep down in our life's secret place. God puts his Spirit not upon the surface of the man, but into the center of his being. The promise means—"I will put my spirit in your bowels, in your hearts, in the very soul of you." This is an intensely spiritual matter, without admixture [mingling] of anything material and visible. It is spiritual, you see, because it is the Spirit that is given; and he is given internally within our spirit. It is true the Spirit operates upon the external life, but it is through the secret and internal life, and of that inward operation our text speaks. This is what we so greatly require. Do you know what it is to attend a service and hear God's truth faithfully preached, and yet you are forced to say, "Somehow or other it did not enter into me; I did not feel the unction and taste the savor of it"? "I will put my spirit within you," is what you need. Do you not read your Bibles, and even pray, and do not both devotional exercises become too much external acts? "I will put my spirit *within* you" meets this evil. The good Spirit fires your heart; he penetrates your mind; he saturates your soul; he touches the secret and vital springs of your existence. Blessed Word! I love my text. I love it better than I can speak of it.

Observe once more that *this Word is a very effectual one.* "I will put my spirit within you, and cause you to walk in my statutes, and ye shall keep my judgments and do them." The Spirit is operative—first upon the inner life, in causing you to love the law of the Lord; and then it moves you openly to keep his statutes concerning himself, and his judgments between you and your fellow-men. Obedience, if a man should be flogged to it, would be of little worth; but obedience springing out of a life within, this is a priceless breastplate of jewels. If you have a lantern, you cannot make it shine by polishing the glass outside, you must put a candle within it: and this is what God does— he puts the light of the Spirit within us, and then our light shines. He puts his Spirit so deep down into the heart, that the whole nature feels it: it works upward, like a spring from the bottom of a well. It is, moreover, so deeply implanted that there is no removing it. If it were in the memory, you might forget it; if it were in the intellect, you might err in it; but "within you" it touches the whole man, and has dominion over you without fear of failure. When the very kernel of your nature is quickened into holiness, practical godliness is effectually secured. Blessed is he who knows by experience our Lord's words—"The water that I shall give him shall be in him a well of water springing up into everlasting life."

If I should fail in expounding the text, I hope I have so fully commended it to you, that you will turn it over and meditate upon it yourselves, and so get a home-born exposition of it. The key of the text is within its own self; for if the Lord gives you the Spirit, you will then understand his words—"I will put my spirit within you."

II. But now I must work upon *the exposition of the text.*

I trust the Holy Spirit will aid me therein. Let me show you how the good Spirit manifests the fact that he dwells in men. I have to be very brief on a theme that might require a great length of time; and can only mention a part of his ways and workings.

One of the first effects of the Spirit of God being put within us is *quickening.* We are dead by nature to all heavenly and spiritual things; but when the Spirit of God comes, then we begin to live. The man visited of the Spirit begins to feel; the terrors of God make him tremble, the love of Christ makes him weep. He begins to fear, and he begins to hope: a great deal of the first and a very little of the second, it may be. He learns spiritually to sorrow: he is grieved that he has sinned, and that he cannot cease from sinning. He begins to desire that which once he despised: he specially desires to find the way of pardon, and reconciliation with God. Ah, dear hearers! *I* cannot make you feel, *I* cannot make you sorrow for sin, *I* cannot make you desire eternal life; but it is all done as soon as this is fulfilled by the Lord, "I will put my spirit within you." The quickening Spirit brings life to the dead in trespasses and sins.

This life of the Spirit shows itself by causing the man to pray. The cry is the distinctive mark of the living child. He begins to cry, in broken accents, "God be merciful to me." At the same time that he pleads, he feels the soft relentings of repentance. He has a new mind towards sin, and he grieves that he should have grieved his God. With this comes faith; perhaps feeble and trembling, only a touch of the hem of the Savior's robe; but still Jesus is his only hope and his sole trust. To him he looks for pardon and salvation. He dares to believe that Christ can save even him. Then has life come into the soul, when trust in Jesus springs up in the heart.

Remember, dear friends, that as the Holy Spirit gives quickening at the first, so he must revive and strengthen it. Whenever you become dull and faint, cry for the Holy Spirit. Whenever you cannot feel in devotion as you wish to feel, and are unable to rise to any heights of communion with God, plead my text in faith, and beg the Lord to do as he hath said, namely, "I will put my spirit within you." Go to God with this covenant clause, even if you have to confess, "Lord, I am like a log, I am a helpless lump of weakness. Unless thou come and quicken me, I cannot live to thee." Plead importunately [naggingly] the promise, "I will put my spirit within you." All the life of the flesh will [en]gender corruption; all the energy that comes of mere excitement will die down into the black ashes of disappointment; the Holy Ghost alone is the life of the regenerated heart. Have you the Spirit? and if you have him within you, have you only a small measure of his life, and do you wish for more? Then go still where you went at first. There is only one river of the water of life: draw from its floods. You will be lively enough, and bright enough, and strong enough, and happy enough when the Holy Spirit is mighty within your soul.

When the Holy Spirit enters, after quickening, he gives *enlightening. We* cannot make men see the truth—they are so blind—but when the Lord puts his Spirit within them, their eyes are opened. At first they may see rather hazily; but still they do see. As the light increases, and the eye is strengthened, they see more and more clearly. What a mercy it is to see Christ—to look unto him—and so to be lightened! By the Spirit, souls see things in their reality: they see the actual truth of them, and perceive that they are facts. The Spirit of God illuminates every believer, so that he sees still more marvelous things out of God's law; but this never happens unless the Spirit opens his eyes. The apostle speaks of being brought "out of darkness into his marvelous light"; and it is a marvelous light, indeed, to come to the blind and dead. Marvelous because it reveals truth with clearness. It reveals marvelous things in a marvelous way. If hills and mountains, if rocks and stones were suddenly to be full of eyes, it would be a strange thing in the earth, but not more marvelous than for you and for me, by the illumination of the Holy Spirit, to see spiritual things. When you cannot make people see the truth, do not grow angry with them, but cry, "Lord, put thy Spirit within them." When you get into a puzzle over the Word of the Lord, do not give up in despair, but believingly cry, "Lord, put thy Spirit within me." Here lies the only true light of the soul. Depend upon it, all that you see by any light except the Spirit of God, you do not spiritually see. If you only see intellectually, or rationally, you do not see to salvation. Unless intellect and reason have received heavenly light, you may see, and yet not see; even as Israel of old. Indeed, your boasted clear sight may aggravate your ruin, like that of the Pharisees, of whom our Lord said, "But now ye say, 'We see', therefore your sin remaineth." O Lord, grant us the Spirit within, for our soul's illumination!

The Spirit also works *conviction*. Conviction is more forcible than illumination: it is the setting of a truth before the eye of the soul, so as to make it powerful upon the conscience. I speak to many here who know what conviction means; still I will explain it from my own experience. I knew what sin meant by my reading, and yet I never knew sin in its heinousness and horror, till I found myself bitten by it, as by a fiery serpent, and felt its poison boiling in my veins. When the Holy Ghost made sin to appear sin, then was I overwhelmed with the sight, and I would fain have fled from myself to escape the intolerable vision. A naked sin stripped of all excuse, and set in the light of truth, is a worse sight than to see the devil himself. When I saw sin as an offense against a just and holy God, committed by such a proud and yet insignificant creature as myself, then was I alarmed. Sirs, did you ever see and feel yourselves to be sinners? "Oh, yes," you say, "we are sinners." O sirs, do you mean it? Do you know what it means? Many of you are no more sinners in your own estimation than you are Hottentots.[1] The beggar who exhibits a sham sore knows not disease; if he did he would have enough of it without presences. To kneel down and say, "Lord, have mercy upon us miserable sinners," and then to get up and feel yourself a very decent sort of body, worthy of commendation, is to mock Almighty God. It is by no means a common thing to get hold of a real sinner, one who is truly so in his own esteem; and it is as pleasant as it is rare, for you can bring to the real sinner the real Savior, and he will welcome him. I do not wonder that Hart said:

> *A sinner is a saved thing,*
> *The Holy Ghost hath made him so.*

---

[1] Hottentots: black Africans (offensive).

The point of contact between a sinner and Christ is sin. The Lord Jesus gave himself for our sins; he never gave himself for our righteousnesses. He comes to heal the sick, and the point he looks to is our sickness. When a physician is called in, he has no patience with things apart from his calling. "Tut, tut!" he cries,

> I do not care about your furniture, nor the number of your cows, nor what income tax you pay, nor what politics you admire; I have come to see a sick man about his disease, and if you will not let me deal with it, I will be gone.

When a sinner's corruptions are loathsome to himself, when his guilt is foul in his own nostrils, when he fears the death that will come of it, then it is that he is really convinced by the Holy Spirit; and no one ever knows sin as his own personal ruin till the Holy Spirit shows it to him. Conviction as to the Lord Jesus comes in the same way. We do not know Christ as our Savior till the Holy Spirit is put within us. Our Lord says, "He shall receive of mine, and shall shew it unto you," and you never see the things of the Lord Jesus till the Holy Ghost shows them to you. To know Jesus Christ as your Savior, as one who died *for you* in particular, is a knowledge which only the Holy Spirit imparts. To apprehend present salvation, as your own personally, comes by your being convinced of it by the Spirit. Oh, to be convinced of righteousness, and convinced of acceptance in the Beloved! This conviction cometh only of him that hath called you, even of him of whom the Lord saith, "I will put my Spirit within you."

Furthermore, the Holy Spirit comes into us for *purification*. "I will put my spirit within you, and cause you to walk in my statutes, and ye shall keep my judgments, and do them." When the Spirit comes, he infuses a new life, and that new life is a fountain of holiness. The new nature cannot sin, because it is born of God, and "it is a living and incorruptible seed." This life produces good fruit, and good fruit only. The Holy Ghost is the life of holiness. At the same time, the coming of the Holy Ghost into the soul gives a mortal stab to the power of sin. The old man is not absolutely dead, but it is crucified with Christ. It is under sentence, and before the eye of the law it is dead; but as a man nailed to a cross may linger long, but yet he cannot live, so the power of evil dies hard, but die it must. Sin is an executed criminal: those nails which fasten it to the cross will hold it fast till no breath remains in it. God the Holy Ghost gives the power of sin its death wound. The old nature struggles in its dying agonies, but it is doomed, and die it must. But you never will overcome sin by your own power, nor by any energy short of that of the Holy Spirit. Resolves may bind it, as Samson was bound with cords; but sin will snap the cords asunder. The Holy Spirit lays the axe at the root of sin, and fall it must. The Holy Ghost within a man is "the Spirit of judgment, the Spirit of burning." Do you know him in that character? As the Spirit of judgment, the Holy Spirit pronounces sentence on sin, and it goes out with the brand of Cain upon it. He does more: he delivers sin over to burning. He executes the death penalty on that which he has judged. How many of our sins have we had to burn alive! And it has cost us no small pain to do it. Sin must be got out of us by fire, if no gentler means will serve; and the Spirit of God is a consuming fire. Truly, "our God is a consuming fire." They paraphrase it, "God, out of Christ, is a consuming fire"; but that is not Scripture. It is "*our* God," our covenant God, who is a consuming fire to refine us from sin. Has not the Lord said, "I will purely purge away all thy dross, and take away all thy sin"? This is what the Spirit does, and it is by no means easy work for the flesh, which would spare many a flattering sin if it could.

The Holy Spirit bedews the soul with purity till he saturates it. Oh, to have a heart saturated with holy influences till it shall be as Gideon's fleece, which held so much dew that Gideon could wring out a bowl full from it! Oh, that our whole nature were filled with the Spirit of God; that we were sanctified wholly—body, soul, and spirit! Sanctification is the result of the Holy Spirit being put within us.

Next, the Holy Ghost acts in the heart as the Spirit of *preservation*. Where he dwells, men do not go back unto perdition. He works in them a watchfulness against temptation day by day. He works in them to wrestle against sin. Rather than sin, a believer would die ten thousand deaths. He works [creates] in believers, union to Christ, which is the source and guarantee of acceptable fruitfulness. He creates in the saints those holy things which glorify God and bless the sons of men. All true fruit is the fruit of the Spirit. Every true prayer must be "praying in the Holy Ghost." He helpeth our infirmities in prayer. Even the hearing of the Word of the Lord is of the Spirit, for John says, "I was in the Spirit on the Lord's day, and heard behind me a great voice." Everything that comes of the man, or is kept alive in the man, is first infused and then sustained and perfected of the Spirit. "It is the spirit that quickeneth; the flesh profiteth nothing." We never go an inch towards Heaven in any other power than that of the Holy Ghost. We do not even stand fast and remain steadfast, except as we are upheld by the Holy Spirit. The vineyard which the Lord hath planted, he also preserves; as it is written, "I, the Lord, do keep it; I will water it every moment; lest any hurt it, I will keep it night and day." Did I hear that young man say, "I should like to become a Christian, but I fear I should not hold out. How am I to be preserved?" [This is] a very proper inquiry, for "He that endureth to the end, the same shall be saved." Temporary Christians are no Christians: only the believer who continues to believe will enter heaven. How, then, can we hold on in such a world as this? Here is the answer. "I will put my spirit within you." When a city has been captured in war, those who formerly possessed it seek to win it back again, but the king who captured it sends a garrison to live within the walls, and he says to the captain, "Take care of this city that I have conquered, and let not the enemy take it again." So the Holy Ghost is the garrison of God within our redeemed humanity, and he will keep us to the end. "May the peace of God, which passeth all understanding, keep your hearts and minds through Christ Jesus." For preservation, then, we look to the Holy Spirit.

Lest I weary you, I will be very brief upon the next point: the Holy Spirit within us is for *guidance*. The Holy Spirit is given to lead us into all truth. Truth is like a vast grotto, and the Holy Spirit brings torches and shows us all the splendor of the roof; and since the passages seem intricate, he knows the way, and he leads us into the deep things of God. He opens up to us one truth after another, by his light and by his guidance, and thus we are "taught of the Lord." He is also our practical guide to heaven, helping and directing us on the upward journey. I wish Christian people oftener inquired of the Holy Ghost as to guidance in their daily life. Know ye not that the Spirit of God dwelleth in you? You need not always be running to this friend and to that to get direction; wait upon the Lord in silence, sit still in quiet before the oracle of God. Use the judgment God has given you; but when that suffices not, resort to him whom Mr. Bunyan calls "the Lord High Secretary," who lives within, who is infinitely wise, and who can guide you by making you to "hear a voice behind you saying, 'This is the way, walk ye in it.'" The Holy Ghost will guide you in life, he will guide you in death, and he will guide you to glory. He will guard you from modern error and from ancient error too. He will guide you in a way that you know not; and through the darkness he will lead you in a way you have not seen. These things will he do unto you, and not forsake you.

Oh, this precious text! I seem to have before me a great cabinet full of jewels rich and rare. May God the Holy Ghost himself come and hand these out to you, and may you be adorned with them all the days of your life!

Last of all, "I will put my spirit within you," that is, by way of *consolation*, for his choice name is "The Comforter." Our God would not have his children unhappy, and therefore he himself, in the third Person of the blessed Trinity, has undertaken the office of Comforter. Why does your face such mournful colors wear? God can comfort you. You that are under the burden of sin; it is true no man can help you into peace, but the Holy Ghost can. O God, to every seeker here who has failed to find rest, grant thy Holy Spirit! Put thy Spirit within him, and he will rest in Jesus. And you, dear people of God, who are worried, remember that worry and the Holy Ghost are very contradictory one to another. "I will put my spirit within you" means that you shall become gentle, peaceful, resigned, and acquiescent in the divine will. Then you will have faith in God that all is well. That text with which I began my prayer this morning was brought home to my heart this week. Our dearly beloved friend Adolph Saphir passed away last Saturday, and his wife died three or four days before him. When my dear brother, Dr. Sinclair

Patteson, went to see him, the beloved Saphir said to him, "God is light, and in him is no darkness at all." Nobody would have quoted that passage but Saphir, the biblical student, the lover of the word, the lover of the God of Israel. "God is light, and in him is no darkness at all." His dear wife is gone, and he himself is ill; but "God is light, and in him is no darkness at all." This is a deep well of overflowing comfort, if you understand it well. God's providence is [his] light as well as his promise, and the Holy Spirit makes us know this. God's word and will and way are all light to his people, and in him is no darkness at all for them. God himself is purely and only light. What if there be darkness in me? There is no darkness in him, and his Spirit causes me to fly to him! What if there be darkness in my family? There is no darkness in my covenant God, and his Spirit makes me rest in him. What if there be darkness in my body by reason of my failing strength? There is no failing in him, and there is no darkness in him—his Spirit assures me of this. David says, "God my exceeding joy"—and such he is to us. "Yea, mine own God is he!" Can you say, "My God, my God"? Do you want anything more? Can you conceive of anything beyond your God? Omnipotent to work all forever! Infinite to give! Faithful to remember! He is all that is good. Light only—"in him is no darkness at all." I have all light, yea, all things, when I have my God. The Holy Spirit makes us apprehend this when he is put within us. Holy Comforter, abide with us, for then we enjoy the light of heaven. Then are we always peaceful and even joyful, for we walk in unclouded light. In him our happiness sometimes rises into great waves of delight, as if it leaped up to the glory. The Lord make this text your own:"I will put my Spirit within you." Amen.

Honey in the Mouth!

A sermon intended for reading on Lord's Day, July 19, 1891, at the conference of the Pastors' College Evangelical Association. No. 2213.

He shall glorify me: for he shall receive of mine, and shall shew it unto you. All things that the Father hath are mine: therefore said I, that he shall take of mine, and shall shew it unto you.—John 16:14–15

Beloved friends, here you have the Trinity, and there is no salvation apart from the Trinity. It must be the Father, the Son, and the Holy Ghost. "All things that the Father hath are mine," saith Christ, and the Father hath all things. They were always his; they are still his; they always will be his; and they cannot become ours till they change ownership, till Christ can say, "All things that the Father hath are mine"; for it is by virtue of the representative character of Christ, standing as the surety of the covenant, that the "all things" of the Father are passed over to the Son, that they might be passed over to us. "It pleased the Father that in him should all fullness dwell; and of his fullness have all we received." But yet we are so dull that, though the conduit-pipe is laid on to the great fountain, we cannot get at it. We are lame; we cannot reach thereto; and in comes the third Person of the divine unity, even the Holy Spirit, and he receives of the things of Christ, and then delivers them over to us. So we do actually receive, through Jesus Christ, by the Spirit, what is in the Father.

Ralph Erskine,[1] in his preface to a sermon upon the fifteenth verse [of this chapter of John], has a notable piece. He speaks of grace as honey—honey for the cheering of the saints, for the sweetening of their mouths and hearts; but he says that in the Father "the honey is in the flower, which is at such a distance from us that we could never extract it." In the Son,

> the honey is in the comb, prepared for us in our Immanuel, God-Man, Redeemer, the Word that was made flesh, saying, "All things that the Father hath are mine; and mine for your use and behoof [benefit]": it is in the comb. But then, next, we have honey in the mouth; the Spirit taking all things, and making application thereof, by showing them unto us, and making us to eat and drink with Christ, and share of these "all things"; yea, not only eat the honey, but the honeycomb with the honey; not only his benefits, but himself.

It is a very beautiful division of the subject. Honey in the flower in God, as in mystery; really there. There never will be any more honey than there is in the flower. There it is. But how shall you and I get at it? We have not wisdom to extract the sweetness. We are not as the bees that are able to find it out. It is bee-honey, but not man-honey. Yet you see in Christ it becomes the honey in the honeycomb, and hence he is sweet to our taste as honey dropping from the comb. Sometimes we are so faint that we cannot reach out a hand to grasp that honeycomb; and, alas! there was a time when our palates were so depraved that we preferred bitter things, and thought them sweet. But now the Holy Ghost has come, we have got the honey in the mouth, and the taste that enjoys it; yea, we have now so long enjoyed it, that the honey of grace has entered into our constitution, and we have become sweet unto God; his sweetness having been conveyed by this strange method unto us.

Beloved friends, I scarcely need say to you, do keep the existence of the Trinity prominent in your ministry. Remember, you cannot pray without the Trinity. If the full work of salvation requires a Trinity, so does that very breath by which we live. You cannot draw near to the Father except through the Son, and by the Holy Spirit. There is a trinity in nature undoubtedly. There certainly constantly turns up the need of a Trinity in the realm of grace; and when we get to Heaven we shall understand, perhaps, more fully what is meant by the Trinity in unity. But if that is a thing never to be understood, we shall at least apprehend it more lovingly; and we shall rejoice more completely as the three tones of our music shall rise up in perfect harmony unto Him who is one and indivisible, and yet is three, forever blessed, Father, Son, and Holy Ghost, one God.

Now, for the point which I am to open up to you this morning; though *I* cannot do it, but *he* must do it. We must sit here, and have the text acted out upon

---

[1] Ralph Erskine: Scottish clergyman, 1685-1752.

ourselves. "He shall glorify me. He shall take of mine, and shall shew it unto you." May it be so just now!

First, *what the Holy Spirit does*: "He shall take of mine, and shall shew it unto you." Secondly, *what the Holy Spirit aims at and really effects*: "He shall glorify me." And then, thirdly, *how in doing both these things he is the Comforter*. It is the Comforter that does this; and we shall find our richest, surest comfort in this work of the Holy Spirit, who shall take of the things of Christ, and show them unto us.

I. First, *what the Holy Spirit does.*

It is clear, beloved friends, that the Holy Spirit *deals with the things of Christ*. As our brother, Archibald Brown, said, when expounding the chapter just now, he [the Holy Spirit] does not aim at any originality. He deals with the things of Christ. All things that Christ had heard from his Father, he made known to us. He kept to them. And now the Spirit takes of the things of Christ, and of nothing else. Do not let us strain at anything new. The Holy Ghost could deal with anything in Heaven above, or in the earth beneath—the story of the ages past, the story of the ages to come, the inward secrets of the earth, the evolution of all things, if there be an evolution. He could do it all. Like the Master, he could handle any topic he chose; but he confines himself to the things of Christ, and therein finds unutterable liberty and boundless freedom.

Do you think, dear friend, that you can be wiser than the Holy Spirit? And if his choice must be a wise one, will yours be a wise one if you begin to take of the things of something or somebody else? You will have the Holy Spirit near you when you are receiving of the things of Christ; but, as the Holy Spirit is said never to receive anything else, when you are handling other things on the Sabbath-day, you will be handling them alone; and the pulpit is a dreary solitude, even in the midst of a crowd, if the Holy Ghost is not with you there. You may, if you please, excogitate [develop] a theology out of your own vast brain; but the Holy Ghost is not with you there. And, mark you! there are some of us that are resolved to tarry with the things of Christ, and keep on dealing with them as far as he enables us to do so; and we feel that we are in such blessed company with the divine Spirit, that we do not envy you that wider range of thought, if you prefer it.

The Holy Spirit still exists, and works, and teaches in the church; but we have a test by which to know whether what people claim to be revelation, is revelation or not: "He shall receive of mine." The Holy Ghost will never go farther than the cross and the coming of the Lord. He will go no farther than that which concerns Christ. "He shall receive of mine." When, therefore, anybody whispers in my ear that there has been revealed to him this or that, which I do not find in the teaching of Christ and his apostles, I tell him that we must be taught by the Holy Spirit. His one vocation is to deal with the things of Christ. If we do not remember this, we may be carried away by vagaries, as many have been. Those who will have to do with other things, let them; but as for us, we shall be satisfied to confine our thoughts and our teaching within these limitless limits: "He shall take of mine, and shall shew it unto you."

I like to think of the Holy Spirit handling such things. They seem so worthy of him. Now has he got among the hills. Now is his mighty mind among the infinities when he has to deal with Christ, for Christ is the Infinite veiled in the finite. Why, he seems something *more* than infinite when he gets into the finite; and the Christ of Bethlehem is less to be understood than the Christ of the Father's bosom. He seems, if it were possible, to have out-infinited the infinite, and the Spirit of God has themes here worthy of his vast nature.

When you have been the whole Sunday morning whittling away a text to the small end of nothing, what have you done? A king spent a day in trying to make a portrait on a cherry-stone—a king, who was ruling empires; and here is a minister, who professes to have been called of the Holy Ghost to the employ of taking of the things of Christ, who spent a whole morning with precious souls, who were dying while he spoke to them, in handling a theme, concerning which it did not signify the turn of a hair whether it was so or not. Oh, imitate the Holy Spirit! If you profess to have him dwelling in you, be moved by him. Let it be said of you in your measure, as of the Holy Ghost without measure, "He shall receive of mine, and shall shew it unto you."

But, next, what does the Holy Ghost do? Why, *he deals with feeble men*, yea, he dwells with us poor creatures. I can understand the Holy Ghost taking the things of Christ, and rejoicing therein; but the marvel is, that he should glorify Christ by coming and showing these things to us. And yet, brethren, it is among us that Christ is to get his glory. Our eyes must see him. An unseen Christ is little glorious; and the things of Christ unknown, the things of Christ untasted and unloved, seem to have lost their brilliance to a high degree. The Holy Spirit, therefore—feeling that to show a sinner the salvation of Christ glorifies him—spends his time, and has been spending these centuries, in taking of the things of Christ, and showing them to us. Ah! it is a great condescension on his part to show them to us; but it is a miracle, too. If it were reported that suddenly stones had life, and hills had eyes, and trees had ears, it would be a strange thing; but for us who were dead and blind and deaf in an awful sense—for the spiritual is more emphatic than the natural—for us to be so far gone, and for the Holy Ghost to be able to show the things of Christ to us, is to his honor. But he *does* do it. He comes from Heaven to dwell with us. Let us honor and bless his name.

I never could make up my mind which to admire most as an act of condescension; the incarnation of Christ, or the indwelling of the Holy Ghost. The incarnation of Christ is marvelous—that he should dwell in human nature; but, observe, the Holy Ghost dwells in human nature in its sinfulness; not in perfect human nature, but in imperfect human nature; and he continues to dwell, not in one body, which was fashioned strangely for himself, and was pure and without taint; but he dwells in *our* body. Know ye not that they are the temples of the Holy Ghost, which were defiled by nature, and in which a measure of defilement still remains, despite his indwelling? And this he has done these multitudes of years, not in one instance, nor in thousands of instances only, but in a number that no man can number. He continues still to come into contact with sinful humanity. Not to the angels, nor to the seraphim, nor to the cherubim, nor to the host who have washed their robes, and made them white in the blood of the Lamb, does he show the things of Christ; but he shall show them unto *us*.

I suppose that it means this, that *he takes of [all] the words of our Lord*—those which he spoke personally, *and* by his apostles. Let us never allow anybody to divide between the word of the apostles and the word of Christ. Our Savior has joined them together. "Neither pray I for these alone, but for them also which shall believe on me through their word." And if any begin rejecting the apostolic word, they will be outside the number for whom Christ prays; they shut themselves out by that very fact. I wish that they would solemnly recollect that the word of the apostles is the word of Christ. He tarried not long enough, after he had risen from the dead, to give us a further exposition of his mind and will; and he could not have given it before his death, because it would have been unsuitable. "I have yet many things to say unto you, but ye cannot bear them now." After the descent of the Holy Ghost, the disciples were prepared to receive that which Christ spoke by his servants Paul and Peter, and James and John. Certain doctrines which we are sometimes taunted about, as being not revealed by Christ, but by his apostles, were all revealed by Christ, everyone of them. They can all be found in his teaching; but they are very much in the parabolic [parable] form. It is after he has gone up into glory, and has prepared a people by his Spirit to understand the truth more fully, that he sends his apostles, and says, "Go forth, and open up to those whom I have chosen out of the world, the meaning of all I said." The meaning is all there, just as all the New Testament is in the Old; and sometimes I have thought that, instead of the Old being less inspired than the New, it is more inspired. Things are packed away more tightly in the Old Testament than in the New, if possible. There are worlds of meaning in one pregnant line in the Old Testament; and in Christ's words it is just so. He is the Old Testament to which the Epistles come in as a kind of New Testament; but they are all one and indivisible; they cannot be separated.

Well, now, the words of the Lord Jesus, and the words of his apostles, are to be *expounded* to us by the Holy Spirit. We shall never get at the center of their meaning apart from his teaching. We shall never get at their meaning at all, if we begin disputing about the words, saying, "Now, I cannot accept the words." If you will not have the shell, you will never have the chick. It is impossible. "The words are not inspired," they say. Here is a man in the witness-box, and he has sworn to speak the truth, and he says that he has done so; and now he is cross-examined, and he says, "Now, I have spoken the truth, but I do not stand by my words." The cross-examining lawyer has got hold of a certain statement of his. The witness says, "Oh, I do not swear to the words, you know." The question is asked, "What, then, do you swear to? There is nothing else. We do not know anything about your meaning. All that you have sworn to must be your words." But what the fellow means is this, that he is a liar; he is a perjurer. Well, I say no more than common-sense would suggest to you if you were sitting in a court. Now, if a man says, "I have spoken the truth, but still I do not swear to the words;" what is there left? If we have no inspiration in the words, we have got an impalpable inspiration that oozes away between your fingers, and leaves nothing behind.

Well, take the words, and never dispute over them. Still, into their soul-fullness of meaning you cannot come until the Holy Ghost shall lead you into them. They that wrote them for you did not fully understand what they wrote in many instances. There were some of them who enquired and searched diligently to know what manner of things those were, whereof the Holy Ghost had spoken to them, and of which he had made them speak. And you to whom the words come will have to do the same. You must go and say,

> Great Master, we thank thee for the Book with all our hearts; and we thank thee for putting the Book into words; but now, good Master, we will not cavil over the letter, as did the Jews and the rabbis and the scribes of old, and so miss thy meaning. Open wide the door of the words, that we may enter into the secret closet of the meaning; and teach us this, we pray thee. Thou hast the key. Lead us in.

Dear friends, whenever you want to understand a text of Scripture, try to read the original. Consult anybody who has studied what the original means; but remember that the quickest way into a text is praying in the Holy Ghost. Pray the chapter over. I do not hesitate to say that, if a chapter is read upon one's knees, looking up, at every word, to him that gave it, the meaning will come to you with infinitely more light than by any other method of studying it. "He shall glorify me: for he shall receive of mine, and shall shew it unto you." He shall re-deliver the Master's message to you in the fullness of its meaning.

But I do not think that is all that the text means. "He shall receive of mine." In the next verse the Lord goes on to say, "All things that the Father hath are mine." I do think that it means, therefore, *that the Holy Spirit will show us the things of Christ.* Here is a text for us—"The things of Christ." Christ speaks as if he had not any things just then which were specially his own, for he had not died then; he had not risen then; he was not pleading then as the great Intercessor in heaven: all that was to come. But still, he says,

> Even now all things that the Father hath are mine: all his attributes, all his glory, all his rest, all his happiness, all his blessedness. *All that* is mine, and the Holy Ghost shall show that to you.

But I might almost read my text in another light, for he *has* died, and risen, and gone on high, and lo, he cometh. His chariots are on the way. Now, there are certain things which the Father hath, and which Jesus Christ hath, which are truly the things of Christ, emphatically the things of Christ; and my prayer is, that you and I, preachers of the gospel, might have this text fulfilled in us: "He shall take of mine—my things—and shall show them unto you."

Suppose, dear brethren, that we are going to preach the word again, and the Holy Spirit shows to us our Master in his Godhead. Oh, how we will preach him as divine—how surely he can bless our congregation! How certainly he must be able to subdue all things unto himself, seeing that he is very God of very God! It is equally sweet to see him as man. Oh, to have the Spirit's view of Christ's manhood! Distinctly to recognize that he is bone of my bone, and flesh of my flesh, and that in his infinite tenderness he will compassionate me, and deal with my poor people, and with the troubled consciences that are round me; that I have still to go to them, and tell them of One who is touched with the feeling of their infirmities, having been tempted in all points like as they still are! Oh, my brothers, if we once—nay, if *every* time before we preach—we get a view of Christ in his divine and human natures, and come down fresh from that vision to speak about him, what glorious preaching it would be for our people!

It is a glorious thing to get a view of the offices of Christ by the Holy Spirit; but especially of his office as a Savior. I have often said to him,

> You must save my people. It is no business of mine. I never set up in that line [of work], or put over my door that I was a savior; but thou hast been apprenticed to this trade. Thou hast learned it by experience, and thou dost claim it as thine own honor. Thou art exalted on high to be a Prince and a Savior. Do thine own work, my Lord.

I took this text, and used it with sinners the other Sunday night, and I know that God blessed it when I said to them,

> May the Holy Ghost show you that Christ is a Savior! A physician does not expect you to make any apologies when you call upon him because you are ill, for he is a physician, and he wants you in order that he may prove his skill; so Christ is a Savior, and you need not apologize for going to him; because he cannot be a Savior if there is not somebody to be saved.

The fact is, Christ cannot get ahold of us anywhere except by our sin. The point of contact between the sick one and the physician is the disease. Our sin is the point of contact between us and Christ. Oh, that the Spirit of God would take of Christ's divine offices, especially that of a Savior, and show them unto us!

Did the Holy Ghost ever show to you these thing of Christ, namely, his covenant engagements? When he struck [shook] hands with the Father, it was that he would bring many sons unto glory; that of those whom the Father gave him, he would lose none, but that they should be saved; for he is under bonds to his Father to bring his elect home. When the sheep have to pass again under the hand of him that telleth them, they will go under the rod one by one, each one having the blood-mark; and he will never rest till the number in the heavenly fold shall tally with the number in the book. So I believe, and it has seemed delightful to me to have this shown to me when I have gone to preach. It is a dull, dreary, wet, foggy morning. There are only a few present. Yes; but they are picked people, whom God hath ordained to be there, and there will be the right number there. I shall preach, and there will be some saved. We do not go at a peradventure [uncertainty]; but, guided by the blessed Spirit of God, we go with a living certainty, knowing that God has a people that Christ is bound to bring home, and bring them home he will; and while he shall see of the travail of his soul, his Father shall delight in everyone of them. If you get a clear view of that, it will give you backbone and make you strong. "He shall take of mine, and shall show you my covenant engagements, and when you see them you shall be comforted."

But, beloved, the Holy Ghost favors you by taking what is peculiarly Christ's, namely, his love, and showing that to you. We have seen it, seen it sometimes more vividly than at other times. But if the full blaze of the Holy Spirit were to be concentrated upon the love of Christ, and our eyesight enlarged to its utmost capacity, it would be such a vision that Heaven could not excel it. We should sit with our Bible before us in our study, and feel, "Well now, here is a man, whether in the body or out of the body, I cannot tell. Such a man is caught up into the third heaven." Oh, to see the love of Christ in the light of the Holy Ghost! When it is so revealed to us, it is not merely the surface which we see, but the love of Christ itself. You know that you never saw anything yet, strictly speaking. You only see the appearance of the thing—the light reflected by it; that is all you see. But the Holy Ghost shows us the naked truth, the essence of the love of Christ; and what that essence is—that love without beginning, without change, without limit, without end; and that love set upon his people simply from motives within himself, and from no motive *ab extra*—what that must be, what tongue can tell? Oh, it is a ravishing sight!

I think that if there could be one sight more wonderful than the love of Christ, it would be the blood of Christ.

> *Much we talk of Jesu's blood,*
> *But how little's understood.*

It is the climax of God. I do not know of anything more divine. It seems to me as if all the eternal purposes worked up to the blood of the cross, and then worked from the blood of the cross towards the sublime consummation of all things. Oh, to think that he should become man! God has made spirit, pure spirit, embodied spirit; and then materialism; and somehow, as if he would take all up into one, the Godhead links himself with the material, and he wears dust about him even as we wear it; and taking it all up, he then goes, and, in that fashion, redeems his people from all the evil of their soul, their spirit, and their body, by the pouring out of a life which, while it was human, was so in connection with the divine, that we speak correctly of "the blood of God." Turn to the twentieth chapter of the Acts, and read how the apostle Paul puts it: "Feed the church of God, which he hath purchased with his own blood." I believe that Dr. [Isaac] Watts is not wrong when he says—"God that loved and died." It is an incorrect accuracy, a strictly absolute accuracy of incorrectness. So it must be ever when the finite talks of the Infinite. It was a wonderful sacrifice that could absolutely obliterate, annihilate, and extinguish sin, and all the traces that could possibly remain of it; for "He hath finished the transgression, made an end of sins, made reconciliation for iniquity, and brought in everlasting righteousness." Ah, dear friends! You have seen this, have you not? But you have to see more of it yet; and when we get to heaven, we shall then know what that blood means, and with what vigor shall we sing, "Unto him that loved us, and washed us from our sins in his own blood"! Will anybody be there to say, "Is not that the religion of the shambles?" as they blasphemously call it. Ah, my friends! They will find themselves where they will wish they *had* believed "the religion of the shambles"; and I think that it will burn like coals of juniper into the soul of any man that has ever dared to talk like that, that he did despite [contemptuous disregard] unto the blood of God, and so, by his own willful deeds, will be cast away forever.

May the Holy Spirit show unto you Gethsemane, and Gabbatha,[2] and Golgotha! and then, may it please him to give you a sight of what our Lord is now doing! Oh, how it would cheer you up at any time when you were depressed, only to see him standing and pleading for you! Do you not think that if your wife is ill, and your child is sick, and there is scant food in the cupboard; if you were to go out at the back door, and you saw him with the breastplate on, and all the stones glittering, and your name there, and him pleading for you, you would go in and say, "There, wife, it is all right. He is praying for us"? Oh, it would be a comfort if the Holy Ghost showed you a pleading Christ! And then, to think that he is reigning as well as pleading. He, is at the right hand of God, even the Father, who hath put all things under his feet. And he waits till the last enemy shall lie there. Now, you are not afraid, are you, of those who have been snubbing you and opposing you?

---

2 Gabbatha: The hall where Jesus was judged, John 18–19.

Remember, he hath said, "All power is given unto me in Heaven and in earth. Go ye therefore, and teach all nations; and lo, I am with you alway, even unto the end of the world."

Next, and best of all, may the Holy Spirit give you a clear view of his coming. This is our most brilliant hope: "Lo, he cometh!" The more the adversary waxes bold, and the less of faith there is, and when zeal seems almost extinct—these are the tokens of his coming. The Lord always said so; and that he would not come unless there was a falling away first; and so the darker the night grows, and the fiercer the storm becomes, the better will we remember that he of the lake of Galilee came to them upon the waves in the night when the storm was wildest. Oh, what will his enemies say when he comes? When they behold the nail-prints of the Glorified, and the Man with the thorn Crown—when they see him really come—they that have despised his word, and his ever-blessed blood, how will they flee before that face of injured love! And we, on the contrary, through his infinite mercy, will say, "This is what the Holy Ghost showed us; and now we behold it literally. We thank him for the foresights which he gave us of the beatific vision."

I have not done on the first head yet, because there is one point which I want you to recollect. When the Holy Ghost takes of the things of Christ, and shows them to us, he has a purpose in so doing. You will not laugh, I hope, when I remind you of what the little boys sometimes do at school with one another. I have seen a boy take out of his pocket an apple, and say to his schoolmate, "Do you see that apple?" "Yes," says the other. "Then, you may see me eat it," says he. But the Holy Ghost is no Tantalus, taking of the things of Christ, and holding them up to mock us. No: he says, "Do you see these things? If you can see them, you may have them." Did not Christ himself say, "Look unto me, and be ye saved, all the ends of the earth"? Looking gives you a claim; and if you can see him, he is yours. It is with you, with regard to the Spirit showing you things, as it was with Jacob. You know Jacob lay down, and went to sleep, and the Lord said to him, "The land whereon thou liest, to thee will I give it." Now, wherever you go, throughout the whole of Scripture, if you can find a place where you can lie down, that is yours. If you can sleep on a promise, that promise is yours. "Lift up now thine eyes," said God to Abraham, "and look from the place where thou art northward, and southward, and eastward, and westward: for all the land which thou seest, to thee will I give it." The Lord increase our holy vision of delighted faith; for there is nothing you see, but you may also enjoy; all that is in Christ, is there for you.

II. Now, secondly, *what the Holy Spirit aims at, and what he really accomplishes.* "He shall glorify me."

Ah, brothers! The Holy Ghost never comes to glorify *us*, or to glorify a denomination, or, I think, even to glorify a systematic arrangement of doctrines. He comes to glorify Christ. If we want to be in accord with him, we must preach in order to glorify Christ. May we never have this thought—"I will put that bit in; it will tell well. The friends will feel that oratory is not quite extinct, that Demosthenes lives again in this village." No, no. I should say, brother, though it is a very delightful piece, strike that out ruthlessly; because if you have had a thought of that kind about it, you had better not put yourself in the way of temptation by using it.

> Yes, that is a magnificent sentence! I do not know where I met with it, or whether it is my own. I am afraid that most of our friends will not understand it; but then it will give them an impression that they have a deep thinker in their pulpit.

Well then, it may be very admirable, and, further, it might be a very right thing to give them that precious piece; but if you have that thought about it, strike it out. Strike it out ruthlessly. Say,

> No, no, no! If it is not distinctly my aim to glorify Christ, I am not in accord with the aim of the Holy Ghost, and I cannot expect his help. We shall not be pulling the same way, and therefore I will have nothing of which I cannot say that I am saying it simply, sincerely, and only that I may glorify Christ.

How, then, does the Holy Spirit glorify Christ? It is very beautiful to think that he glorifies Christ *by showing Christ's things*. If you wanted to do honor to a man, you would perhaps take him a present to decorate his house. But here, if you want to glorify Christ, you must go and take the things *out* of Christ's house, "the things of Christ." Whenever we have to praise God, what do we do? We simply say what he is. "Thou art this, and thou art that." There is no other praise. We cannot fetch anything from elsewhere, and bring it to God; but the praises of God are simply the facts about himself. If you want to praise the Lord Jesus Christ, tell the people about him. Take of the things of Christ, and show them to the people, and you will glorify Christ. Alas! I know what you will do. You will weave words together, and you will form and fashion them, in a marvelous manner, till you have produced a charming piece of literature. When you have carefully done that, put it in the fire under the oven, and let it burn. Possibly you may help to bake some bread with it. Brethren, it is better for us to tell what Christ is, than to invent ten thousand fine words of praise in reference to him. "He shall glorify me, for he shall receive of mine, and shall shew it unto you."

Again, I think that the blessed Spirit glorifies Christ by showing us the things of Christ *as Christ's*. Oh, to be pardoned! Yes, it is a great thing; but to find that pardon in his wounds, that is a greater thing! Oh, to get peace! Yes, but to find that peace in the blood of his cross! Brethren, have the blood-mark very visibly on all your mercies. They are all marked with the blood of the cross; but sometimes we think so much of the sweetness of the bread, or of the coolness of the waters, that we forget whence these came, and how they came, and then they lack their choicest flavor. That it came from Christ is the best thing about the best thing that ever came from

Christ. That he saves me is, somehow, better than my being saved. It is a blessed thing to go to Heaven; but I do not know that it is not a better thing to be in Christ, and so, as the result of it, to get into heaven. It is himself, and that which comes of himself, that becomes best of all, because it comes of himself. So the Holy Ghost shall glorify Christ by making us see that these things of Christ are indeed of Christ, and completely of Christ, and still are in connection with Christ; and we only enjoy them because we are in connection with Christ.

Then it is said in the text, "He shall glorify me: for he shall take of mine, and shall shew it *unto you*?" Yes, it does glorify Christ for the Holy Spirit to show Christ to us. How often I have wished that men of great minds might be converted! I have wished that we could have a few Miltons, and such like men, to sing of the love of Christ; a few mighty men, who teach politics, and the like, to consecrate their talents to the preaching of the gospel. Why is it not so? Well, because the Holy Ghost does not seem to think that that would be the way to glorify Christ supremely; and he prefers, as a better way, to take us common-place sort of persons, and to take the things of Christ, and to show them to *us*. He does glorify Christ; and blessed be his name, that ever my bleary eyes should look upon his infinite loveliness; that ever such a wretch as I, who can understand everything but what I ought to understand, should be made to comprehend the heights and depths—and to know, with all saints, the love of Christ, that passeth knowledge. You see, in a school, that clever boy. Well, it is not much for the master to have made a scholar of him. But here is one who shines as a scholar, and his mother says that he was the greatest dolt in the family. All his schoolfellows say, "Why, he was our butt! He seemed to have no brains; but our master, somehow, got some brain into him, and made him know something which he appeared, at one time, incapable of knowing." Somehow, it does seem to be as if our very folly, and impotence, and spiritual death—if the Holy Ghost shows to us the things of Christ—will go towards the increase of that great glorifying of Christ at which the Holy Spirit aims.

Then, beloved brethren, since it is for the honor of Christ for his things to be shown to men, he will show them to us, *that we may go and show them to other people*. This we cannot do, except as he is with us to make the others to see; but he will be with us while we tell forth what he has taught us; and so the Holy Ghost will really be showing to others while he is showing to us. A secondary influence will flow from this service, for we shall be helped to *use the right means* to make others see the things of Christ.

III. Our time is almost gone; but in the third place I must just point out to you *how he is in both of these things our comforter.*

He is so, firstly, for this reason—that *there is no comfort in the world like a sight of Christ.* He shows to us the things of Christ. Oh, brethren, if you are poor, and if the

Holy Ghost shows you that Christ had not where to lay his head, what a sight for you! And if you are sick, and if the Holy Ghost shows you what sufferings Christ endured, what comfort comes to you! If you are made to see the things of Christ, each thing according to the condition which you are in, how speedily you are delivered out of your sorrow!

And then, if the Holy Ghost glorifies Christ, *that is the cure for every kind of sorrow*. He is the Comforter. I may have told you before, but I cannot help telling you again, that many years ago, after the terrible accident in the Surrey Gardens, I had to go away into the country, and keep quite still.[3] The very sight of the Bible made me cry. I could only keep alone in the garden; and I was heavy and sad, for people had been killed in the accident; and there I was, half dead myself; and I remember how I got back my comfort, and I preached on the Sabbath after I recovered. I had been walking round the garden, and I was standing under a tree. If it is there now, I should know it: And I remember these words: "Him hath God exalted with his right hand to be a Prince and a Savior." "Oh," I thought to myself, "I am only a common soldier. If I die in a ditch, I do not care. The king is honored. He wins the victory;" and I was like those French soldiers in the old times, who loved the emperor; and you know how, when they were dying, if he rode by, the wounded man would raise himself up on his elbow, and cry once more, *"Vive l'Empereur!"*—for the emperor was graven on his heart. And so, I am sure, it is with every one of you, my comrades, in this holy war. If our Lord and King is exalted, then let other things go which way they like: if he is exalted, never mind what becomes of us. We are a set of pigmies; it is all right if *he* is exalted. God's truth is safe, we are perfectly willing to be forgotten, derided, slandered, or anything else that men please. The cause is safe, and the King is on the throne. Hallelujah! Blessed be his name!

---

[3] "…On Sundays [the Surrey Music Hall] was used temporarily . . . for the religious services held by the late Mr. Spurgeon, on his first rush into popularity; and on the first occasion of holding these services—the evening of October 19, 1856—it was the scene of a serious and fatal accident, seven persons being killed by a false alarm of fire raised by some reckless and wanton jesters." From *Old And New London,* published 1897, as posted on the Internet at www.arthurlloyd.co.uk/Surreyhall.htm.

Indexes

Sermon Index by Key Scripture

Alphabetical Listing of Sermon Titles

Chronological Listing of Sermon Titles

Spurgeon's Sermons on Jesus and the Holy Spirit

The text of this book is set in Dante 11/13.5 and Delphin IA,
with Poetica® Ornaments.

Typeset in Corel Ventura Publisher.

Foreword by Patricia Klein.

Copyediting, interior design, and production by
Publication Resources, Inc., of Ipswich, MA.
www.pubresources.com